The Red Badge of Courage,
Maggie: A Girl of the Streets,
and Other Selected Writings

New Riverside Editions

General Editor for the American Volumes
Paul Lauter

STEPHEN CRANE, *The Red Badge of Courage, Maggie: A Girl of the
Streets, and Other Selected Writings*
Edited by Phyllis Frus and Stanley Corkin

RALPH WALDO EMERSON, *Selected Writings* and MARGARET FULLER,
Woman in the Nineteenth Century
Edited by John Carlos Rowe

OLAUDAH EQUIANO, MARY ROWLANDSON, AND OTHERS,
American Captivity Narratives
Edited by Gordon M. Sayre

HENRY DAVID THOREAU, *Walden and Civil Disobedience*
Edited by Paul Lauter

MARK TWAIN, *Adventures of Huckleberry Finn*
Edited by Susan K. Harris

EDITH WHARTON, *The Age of Innocence*
Edited by Carol J. Singley

Other Riverside Literature Titles

*Call and Response: The Riverside Anthology of the African American
Literary Tradition*
Edited by Patricia Liggins Hill et al.

The Riverside Anthology of Children's Literature, Sixth Edition
Edited by Judith Saltman

The Riverside Anthology of Literature, Third Edition
Edited by Douglas Hunt

The Riverside Anthology of Short Fiction: Convention and Innovation
Edited by Dean Baldwin

The Riverside Chaucer, Third Edition
Edited by Larry D. Benson

The Riverside Milton
Edited by Roy Flannagan

The Riverside Shakespeare, Second Edition
Edited by G. Blakemore Evans et al.

NEW RIVERSIDE EDITIONS

General Editor for the American Volumes
Paul Lauter, Trinity College

Stephen Crane

The Red Badge of Courage, Maggie: A Girl of the Streets, and Other Selected Writings

Complete Texts with Introduction
Historical Contexts • Critical Essays

edited by

Phyllis Frus
University of Michigan

Stanley Corkin
University of Cincinnati

HOUGHTON MIFFLIN COMP
Boston • *New York*

In memory of Roy Frus, and for Nelle Frus, Craig McCord,
Keren Schaffer, Joan Lichtman, Roxanne Corkin, Jesse Corkin

Senior Sponsoring Editor: Suzanne Phelps Weir
Associate Editor: Jennifer Roderick
Senior Project Editor: Kathryn Dinovo
Senior Cover Design Coordinator: Deborah Azerrad Savona
Manufacturing Manager: Florence Cadran
Senior Marketing Manager: Nancy Lyman
Associate Marketing Manager: Carla Gray

Cover design: Steven Cooley
Cover image: © Corbis/Bettmann

Credits appear on page 474, which constitutes a continuation of the copyright page.

Printed in the U.S.A.

Library of Congress Cataloging-in-Publication Data is available on file.

ISBN: 0-395-98074-7

123456789-QF-03 02 01 00 99

As part of Houghton Mifflin's ongoing
commitment to the environment, this text
has been printed on recycled paper.

Contents

America's literary heritage. Houghton Mifflin's New Riverside Series, initiated in the year 2000, is designed to uphold the Riverside reputation for excellence while offering a more inclusive range of authors. The Series also provides today's reader with books that contain, in addition to notable literary works, introductions by influential critics, as well as a variety of stimulating materials that bring alive the debates, the conversations, the social and cultural movements within which America's literary classics were formed.

Thus emerged the book you have in hand. Each volume of the New Riverside Editions will contain the basic elements that we think today's readers find interesting and useful: important literary works by significant authors, incisive introductions, and a variety of contextual materials to make the literary text fully engaging. These books will be useful in many kinds of classrooms, but they are also designed to offer the casual reader the enjoyment of a good read in a fresh and accessible format. Among the first group of New Riverside Editions are familiar titles, such as Henry David Thoreau's *Walden* and Mark Twain's *Adventures of Huckleberry Finn*. There are also works in fresh new combinations, such as the collection of early captivity narratives and the volume that pairs texts by Ralph Waldo Emerson and Margaret Fuller. And there are well-known works in distinctively interesting formats, such as the volume containing Edith Wharton's *The Age of Innocence* and the volume of writings by Stephen Crane. Future books will include classics as well as works drawing renewed attention.

The New Riverside Editions will provide discriminating readers with a wide range of important literary works, contextual materials that vividly illuminate those works, and the best of recent critical commentary and analysis. And because we have not confined our editors to a single monotonous format, we think our readers will find that each volume in this new series has a character appropriate to the literary work it presents.

We expect the New Riverside Editions to bring to the twenty-first century the same literary publishing distinction of its nineteenth- and twentieth-century predecessors.

About This Series

Paul Lauter

The Riverside name dates back well over a century. Readers of this book may have seen—indeed, may own—Riverside Editions of works by the best-known nineteenth-century American writers, such as Emerson, Thoreau, Lowell, Longfellow, and Hawthorne. Houghton Mifflin and its predecessor, Ticknor & Fields, were the primary publishers of the New England authors who constituted much of the undisputed canon of American literature until well into the twentieth century. The Riverside Editions of works by these writers, and of some later writers such as Amy Lowell, became benchmarks for distinguished and useful editions of standard American authors for home, library, and classroom.

In the 1950s and 1960s, the Riverside name was used for another series of texts, primarily for the college classroom, of well-known American and British literary works. These paperback volumes, edited by distinguished critics of that generation, were among the most widely used and appreciated of their day. They provided carefully edited texts in a handsome and readable format, with insightful critical introductions. They were books one kept beyond the exam, the class, or even the college experience.

In the last quarter century, however, ideas about the American literary canon have changed. Many scholars want to see a canon that reflects a broader American heritage, including significant literary works by previously marginalized writers, many of them women or men of color. These changes began to be institutionalized in curricula as well as in textbooks such as *The Heath Anthology of American Literature,* which Houghton Mifflin started publishing in 1998. The older Riverside series, excellent in its day, ran the risk of appearing outdated; the editors were long retired or deceased, and the authors were viewed by some as too exclusive.

Yet the name Riverside and the ideas behind it continued to have appeal. The name stood for distinction and worth in the publication of

Introduction

This volume presents Stephen Crane's major writings in the context of the late nineteenth century in the United States. While our primary focus is on the author, the links between his works and the world in which he wrote and published them and in which readers first encountered them are herein so well elaborated that this volume could also be used as an introduction to the period. The compilation is divided into four parts. In Part I, after a general essay introducing Crane and his times, we present a selection of texts by a range of prominent individuals who helped to define the era, such as Herbert Spencer, Andrew Carnegie, union leaders Terence Powderly and Samuel Gompers, W. E. B. Du Bois, Ida B. Wells-Barnett, and William Dean Howells. These pieces orient the reader to the social, economic, and literary currents of the time, including some of its formative debates. In the next three sections we provide groups of writings by Crane, following each group with a brief background essay and related pieces by his contemporaries, who presumably affected his thinking and the thinking of his readers. These contemporaries helped shape the local, regional, and national discussions that surrounded the production and reception of Crane's works. For example, in Part II, the Crane texts are *Maggie: A Girl of the Streets* and a few New York City sketches taken from his stint as a reporter there. The contextual materials include commentary by Crane's mother, Mary Helen Peck Crane, advocating temperance and deploring vice followed by discussions of urban poverty and reform efforts by noted journalist Jacob Riis; Chicago settlement house founder Jane Addams; and a former police commissioner of New York City, Theodore Roosevelt. Also included is a sketch by journalist, novelist, and magazine editor Theodore Dreiser. These contextual materials familiarize the reader both with the efforts that were being made to bring to public attention the then-hot topic of urban poverty and with the image in which reformers and antireformers cast the poor of the country's rapidly expanding cities.

Part III places *The Red Badge of Courage*—the novel without which Crane would have been relegated to the margins of the realist canon—and three of Crane's short stories about the Civil War in the context of other post–Civil War writings, the first of which are two accounts of the battle of Chancellorsville from *Battles and Leaders of the Civil War,* a series that ran in *Century* magazine from 1884 to 1887. In 1893, two years before he published *The Red Badge of Courage,* Crane pored over old copies of these issues in a competitive spirit, searching in vain for the emotion he assumed men must have felt in battle and, apparently, vowing he could do better. These accounts of Chancellorsville are followed by a selection from John William De Forest's recounting of a battle in *Miss Ravenel's Conversion from Secession to Loyalty,* a civil war novel with elements of realism—one of several such novels that Crane seems to have read. We conclude this section with Ambrose Bierce's short story "Killed at Resaca" and Mark Twain's account of his own abortive service with a group of Confederate irregulars in Missouri in 1861.

The period of Crane's life covered in Part IV might be subtitled "On the Way to the Spanish-American War and After." Part IV begins with "Stephen Crane's Own Story" and is followed by the featured short story of this section, "The Open Boat," Crane's tale of being shipwrecked off the coast of Jacksonville, Florida, in 1897. We also include two of his writings from Cuba, where he was a war correspondent, and two short stories that thematically develop his major concerns during this period, "The Upturned Face" and "The Monster." We have grouped these works by Crane with some of the major national voices of the day. We show Roosevelt and Henry Cabot Lodge advocating an American empire in the days just before Senator Albert Beveridge of Indiana declared that the twentieth century would be the American century.[1] We also include writings by prominent opponents of imperialism—Twain and José Martí—one for his own ethical reasons, one as a result of his hope for Cuban autonomy. This section also places Crane with other star journalists—Richard Harding Davis and Frank Norris—who were instrumental in providing a sense of the war to a vast number of readers in the United States. Indeed, writers like Crane,

---

[1] John Dos Passos opens *The 42nd Parallel,* the first novel of the *USA* trilogy, with a series of quotations from news stories. Among these "newsreels" is a quotation from Beveridge responding to the toast, "The Twentieth Century." He asserts, "The twentieth century will be American. American thought will dominate it. American progress will give it color and direction. American deeds will make it illustrious" (5).

Davis, and Norris grow in significance when we consider the Spanish-American War as a conflict that was partially brought into existence by the desire of newspaper editors and publishers to be able to report events so stirring that people felt compelled to buy their newspapers.

The criteria for selecting from Crane's writings were not simply literary, that is, work that has stood the test of time or works that literary critics have judged Crane's best by virtue of their style or aesthetic qualities. And close readings of Crane, critical essays that examine minute stylistic details of a text, are not reprinted herein. Indeed, there are no critical works reprinted in this volume, nor extensive or involved interpretations of the Crane writings. Instead, readers have the opportunity to peruse historical readings, to study materials that depict the cultural history on which Crane's work comments or from which it emerges. The goal is to help readers understand how talent interacts with institutional forces as well as with historical opportunities.

The period during which Crane lived (he was born in 1871 and died in the last year of the century, 1900) has been called the Gilded Age (after a satirical novel by Mark Twain), the age of the incorporation of America, and—in resonance with the time in which we write—the fin de siècle.[2] It is difficult to convey the conventionality of the literature of the period, but Sherwood Anderson provides a hint when, writing in the 1920s, a decade defined by Prohibition, he calls Crane's decade one of "literary prohibition" (xi). Besides the surge of historical romances and other swashbuckling tales, common genres were domestic and sentimental fiction, and there was a growing interest in slum tales. But the most revealing adjective applied to the writing is "genteel," for readers in the 1890s were, in the main, in thrall to traditions of Victorian propriety. In our day of permissiveness, when there seems to be nothing that cannot be said in print, on

---

[2] In calling his 1874 satire *The Gilded Age: A Tale of Today*, Twain and his collaborator Charles Dudley Warner were alluding to the Shakespearean lines,

> To gild refined gold, to paint the lily, . . .
> Is wasteful and ridiculous excess.

For "the age of incorporation," see Trachtenberg, *The Incorporation of America*. The 1890s have also been termed the Mauve Decade, after a group of artists, designers, and writers who were descendents of the aesthetes. Thomas Beer, author of the first Crane biography in 1923, wrote a study of the 1890s he called *The Mauve Decade* (1926). Another term for the decade is the "decadent nineties," and the publication in 1895 of Crane's second book, his first book of poetry, *The Black Riders and Other Lines*, with its avant-garde binding, cover art, and "cynical" and "enigmatic" poems, caused some critics to associate him with the English decadent poets (Weatherford 4, 11).

radio or television, in film, or on the Internet, it is extremely difficult to imagine the shock with which Crane's first readers greeted works like *Maggie* and "The Monster."

Possibly the most important label for the period in which Crane lived and wrote, however, is "post-Reconstruction America." This is the period following the abandonment of plans to rebuild the nation after the devastation caused by the Civil War, plans that would have meant full access to the rights of citizenship, education, and economic opportunity for all, specifically for African Americans. The author of *America in the Gilded Age,* Sean Cashman, calls the tragedy of American Reconstruction the most "harrowing" and "most controversial event" of that age (203–04). The failure of the federal government to win the hearts and minds of citizens with regard to black civil rights is only one reason—but a big one—for the dissension and turmoil of the age in which Crane grew up. Giving in to the desires of those who were afraid of African Americans becoming their equals and who were dismissive of their human rights resulted in both the ingraining and the ultimate spread of racist practices.

Our goal in this collection, then, is to help readers see the richness of approaching an author—in this volume, Stephen Crane—within the context of how the writer variously expresses, contradicts, and simply relates to the social, intellectual, and moral concerns and currents of his or her period. We have chosen materials from Crane's contemporaries that broaden and expand the reader's sense of the period and the author's place within it. Our choices highlight our desire to develop a complex of relationships between the texts and their world, between words on a page and actors in a material world.

Phyllis Frus
Stanley Corkin

A Note on the Texts

The only works of Stephen Crane selected for this volume about which there is some controversy are *Maggie: A Girl of the Streets* and *The Red Badge of Courage: An Episode of the American Civil War*. In both cases the editor has three choices: two from Crane's lifetime and one that is the result of modern textual editing conventions.[1] We have chosen what are now regarded as the standard versions because they are generally viewed by Crane scholars as closest to the author's intentions. The version of *Maggie* that Crane published privately early in 1893 under the pseudonym Johnston Smith clearly represents his intentions because he paid to have it printed even though every editor to whom he showed it regarded it as too scandalous to be acceptable to a genteel reading public. In 1896, wishing to bring out something by Crane to capitalize on the phenomenal success of *The Red Badge of Courage*, that novel's publisher, D. Appleton and Company, brought out an expurgated version of *Maggie*. Even with its language sanitized and Maggie's experience as a prostitute heavily disguised, it was a risky book to publish in that earlier time of "family values" sentimentalism. It did well, however, so no one looked at the self-published version until 1966, when Joseph Katz introduced a facsimile of the 1893 edition, arguing for its clear superiority in rendering the varieties of slum dialect and communicating the cruelty, the brutal reality, of Maggie's world. Katz says that Crane agreed to tone down the book's language out of a desire to give the novel wider exposure, and he shows that Crane recognized how drastically different the story became after more than 300 editorial changes (203–04).

  The Red Badge of Courage likewise has appeared in three different versions (besides the much-shortened newspaper version published in December 1894 by the Bacheller, Johnson, and Bacheller syndicate [a facsimile has been printed in book form]). The basic choice is between the manuscript version that Crane finished in April 1894, which S. S. McClure kept for an agonizing six months before Crane withdrew it to submit to Irving Bacheller, and the Appleton edition that made Crane famous in 1896.[2] When, on the advice of Ripley Hitchcock, to whom Crane had

---

[1] The MLA-approved scholarly edition of *Maggie*, vol. 1 of *The University of Virginia Edition of the Works of Stephen Crane* (1969), is a combination of the 1893 and 1896 editions and has been rejected by most Crane scholars. See Pizer, Rev.

[2] Once again, the Virginia edition (vol. 2 of *The Works of Stephen Crane*, 1975) is regarded as unsatisfactory because Bowers, the editor, second-guessed Crane's revisions for the Appleton edition. He ended up with an edition that incorporates some of Crane's changes but overrules others.

showed the newspaper clippings, Appleton agreed to publish the novel in February 1895, Crane revised it significantly, cutting Chapter 12 and making many substantive changes that reduced the irony the narrator directs at Henry Fleming and moderated Fleming's complaints about his role in the Union army.

The earlier version was overlooked until the early 1980s, when, encouraged by Herschel Parker, Henry Binder returned to the extant manuscripts: a partial draft Crane had apparently discarded and a nearly complete manuscript of 25 chapters. He resurrected the buried passages, producing a version he believed restored the fuller irony and increased Fleming's psychological complexity. Binder's edition is preferred by those who accept his argument that Crane had revised the version published by Appleton under pressure from the publisher in order to make the novel more acceptable to audiences.[3] Like most Crane critics, we are not convinced. The critiques collected in the 1986 Cambridge volume *New Essays on* The Red Badge of Courage rely on the Binder reconstruction, although they also give chapter citations to the Appleton text "upon which all other publishers currently rely," suggesting both the appeal of the Binder text and its failure to supplant the Appleton edition (Mitchell, *New Essays*, x). The text of *The Red Badge of Courage* reprinted here is therefore that of the first edition, published by Appleton in 1895.

The editions on which the other Crane texts are based are as follows: "Experiment in Misery," "The Men in the Storm," "Stephen Crane's Vivid Story of the Battle of San Juan," and "The Upturned Face" are reprinted from *The University of Virginia Edition of the Works of Stephen Crane,* ed. Fredson Bowers (Charlottesville, 1969–76). "A Mystery of Heroism" and "The Veteran" appeared in *The Little Regiment* (New York, 1896) and "An Episode of War" in *Last Words* (London 1902). "Stephen Crane's Own Story" is from the *New York Press* (7 Jan. 1897) and "The Open Boat" from *The Open Boat and Other Tales of Adventure* (New York, 1898). "Marines Signalling Under Fire at Guantanamo" is taken from *Wounds in the Rain* (London, 1900). "The Monster" is reprinted from *The Monster and Other Stories* (New York, 1899). Source notes in the text give information about first publication of the shorter Crane works and the background readings. In the texts of nineteenth-century works reprinted here, we have silently corrected typographical, spelling, and punctuation errors, and inconsistent rendering of dialect. We have also modernized archaic spellings and typographical conventions.

---

[3] For the various sides of the controversy, see Binder; Pizer, "The Red Badge"; Parker; and Colvert, "Crane, Hitchcock."

PART ONE

The Intellectual and Material World of Stephen Crane

THE HISTORICAL AND CULTURAL CONTEXTS OF STEPHEN CRANE

Phyllis Frus and Stanley Corkin, Volume Editors

Stephen Crane is notable not only for the extraordinary amount of writing and the amazing number of adventures he was able to cram into twenty-eight years but also for the way his work intersected with the major intellectual currents and debates of his day. This is not to say that he was an intellectual. In the words of biographer Christopher Benfey, for Crane, "Books were fine, but better to write them than read them" (51). The closest Crane comes to the intellectual persona is in his enigmatic poems, or "lines," as he called them. What does the reader encountering these lines in *War Is Kind* make of this exchange, for example?

> A man said to the universe:
> "Sir, I exist!"
> "However," replied the universe,
> "The fact has not created in me
> "A sense of obligation."
> (Crane, *Poems* 57)

Because Crane was fully immersed in the action of his times—war, urban migration, reform, empire building—and he wrote fiction and nonfiction about all of those topics, his work is an ideal prism through which to see and understand larger forces at work in history and the cultural movements to which they gave rise.

The connection between Crane's texts and his times can be approached through Crane's most famous book, the story of a young man's experience in a Civil War battle. Even though Crane was not born until six years after the war ended, in many ways *The Red Badge of Courage* is far more revealing, even intimate, than any account by a participant. At its publication, it was hailed as the best novel thus far produced about the Civil War. Although it is a historical novel and the setting is the Civil War, the work best expresses the climate of the country not during the war, but in the 1890s, with its economic recession, its frequent clashes between capital and labor, and its manifest examples of racial hatred—lynching, political repression, and social exclusion. Crane certainly had knowledge of such things just by being cognizant of the world in which he lived and wrote. Robert Shulman has examined the *New York Tribune* during the period when that newspaper published Crane's *Sullivan County Sketches*, discovering frequent headlines depicting racial violence and occasions

of African Americans physically resisting their white tormentors (4–5).
Further, Crane heard firsthand from his brother William about William's
futile efforts to save a black man from being lynched in his hometown of
Port Jervis in 1892 (L. H. Davis 217). Thus the historical context of *The
Red Badge of Courage* we have chosen to highlight is not the battles, nor
even the several varieties of modernist fiction that it led to, such as the
ironic antiwar novel, the story of disillusioned youth coming of age in a
mechanized world, or the minimalist fiction of Ernest Hemingway and
Willa Cather, stripped of plot and subplot and marked by understated
language. Rather, we emphasize that Crane produced the novel at a time
when an ideological adjustment was being made in popular attitudes toward the war. National reconciliation was becoming a priority, even if this
move to unity did not include one large group—African Americans, the
winning of whose human rights was one objective of the war.

One striking feature of Crane's output is its foreshadowing of modernity, for the 1890s, the decade of Crane's adult life, was a period when the
shape of the future crept clearly into view. He wrote about what was new
in this changing era and did so in a style that seemed to foresee the next
century. We can detect in his career and his output the results of important
innovations in mass communication, including the introduction of cinema
as a medium and as a mass entertainment, the reaction to romanticism
in the form of realist and naturalist fiction, and the growing role of the
adventurer-journalist as an on-the-scene observer and celebrity. This last
posture connects him not only to John Reed, Hemingway, and John Dos
Passos, but to later twentieth-century New Journalists like Norman Mailer
and Joan Didion. While reading Crane as a correspondent and participant
in the Spanish-American War we can almost imagine him wearing a bush
jacket and reporting from Vietnam.

Benfey says, "To his contemporaries Crane's short life had some of the
allure of pulp fiction . . . . If the lives of writers tend to be conspicuous for
their lack of outward event (one thinks of the quiet lives of [Nathaniel]
Hawthorne or [Emily] Dickinson or Wallace Stevens), Crane's life sometimes seems nothing but outward event—one wonders when he found
time to write" (4–5). But write he did: the University of Virginia's *The
Works of Stephen Crane* comes to ten volumes (1969–1975) and his output easily rivals those of writers who lived twice as long. Although some
of the best known of those writings—*Maggie, The Red Badge of Courage,*
"The Open Boat"—take pains to limit their explicit statements connecting the text to the world and Crane seems to have intended to transcend
the particular (the last thing he wanted to create was a documentary
record of his times), when we put his writing against the backdrop of his
times, the works are all the more interesting for the way in which they

change how we perceive the late nineteenth century. Approaching the works as elements of history alters the angle of vision we can ascribe to Crane, making him a more serious writer and showing his reaction to events to have depth and complexity.

Crane's response to his era, above all, was to commit to writing and to the life of the writer. To him, this did not mean being only a fiction writer; it meant taking on all manner of assignments as a journalist, signing contracts to serve as a correspondent for newspaper syndicates, and being an all-around freelance. The profession of letters had quite the novelty and allure in the 1890s. In this era before movie stars and sports heroes, famous writers occupied a prominent place in the imagination of the American public. At the turn of the century, Mark Twain personified the public man of letters as he strutted down New York's Fifth Avenue in his white suit—the Tom Wolfe of his day, though Twain likely attracted more stares. Crane did not write enough or live long enough to develop such a presence, but he certainly left his mark.

Born in 1871 Stephen was the last of fourteen children born to Jonathan Townley Crane, a Methodist minister and frequent author on social issues such as the dangers of popular amusements, and Mary Helen Peck Crane, an active participant in the Women's Christian Temperance Union (WCTU) and a lecturer, writer, and artist. Mrs. Crane was the daughter and niece of clergymen. Her father, the Reverend George Peck, was editor of the *Methodist Quarterly Review,* which frequently published her husband's essays, and her uncle, Jesse Peck, was a Methodist bishop and author of the tract "What Must I Do to Be Saved?"[1] Other writers in the family were Crane's sister Agnes and his brother Townley. Agnes, in her role as his surrogate mother (she was fifteen years older), encouraged Stephen. Townley, a successful journalist, gave Stephen his first writing job, hiring him to work in his summer news agency in Asbury Park, New Jersey, interviewing visitors and writing stories of meetings and parades for the *New York Tribune* and the Associated Press.[2]

Novelist Ralph Ellison believes that critics who overlook the influence of Crane's religious upbringing on his writing miss an important part of his motivation, particularly in view of the activism and zeal of both his parents. To Ellison, Crane's "dedication to art" was the equivalent of his ancestors' devotion to preaching, for he "was no less disciplined or deadly

---

[1] Published in 1858, this tract is echoed in Rebecca Harding Davis's 1861 reform-minded story of the effects of the industrial factory system on the poor, *Life in the Iron Mills* (1861), where the question is asked, "What must we do to be saved?"

[2] Wertheim, *Crane Encyclopedia,* is an excellent, succinct source of information on Crane's family as well as on the writer and his works.

serious" about his art than his parents were about their cause (61). Ellison detects a "desperate moral struggle" in Crane that belies his outwardly sensation-seeking life and career. Beyond Ellison's connecting the elder Cranes' religious zeal with Stephen's preternatural commitment to his writing, we can see Crane's engagement with the significant moral issues of his day as a further expression of his parents' religiosity.[3]

If this moral intensity is what drove Crane to be the consummate writer-as-artist, it did not show up in his early years. By all accounts Crane was a desultory student, attending, as did his older siblings, Claverack College in the Hudson Valley, north of New York City. By the time he got to Syracuse, New York, where he attended Syracuse University for two terms, he seems to have concluded that courses had little to offer, that it was more productive to spend his time reading, playing baseball, and exploring the city's night life. He was something of a history buff, however, and did show some interest in Professor Charles J. Little's class in ancient history. His college friend Frederic Lawrence recounted that Crane was extremely well versed in contemporary European history, knowing "the organization, the equipment, and methods of every important war force in Europe" (L. H. Davis 33–34). Stanley Wertheim notes that Crane was quite interested in the Civil War reminiscences of John B. Van Petten, one of his instructors at Claverack (349–50). This fascination with the oral recounting of battles was likely a holdover from his youth in Port Jervis, New York, a town that had provided the 124th New York regiment, a unit that fought at Chancellorsville, with many soldiers (Hungerford 214). This interest in history was also durable—in England during the last year of his life, Crane was planning a novel set in the American Revolutionary period, with his ancestor Stephen Crane (who had served in the First Continental Congress) and Henry Fleming's great-grandfather as characters (Wertheim 75).

Crane may have been, as William Dean Howells said, a writer who had "sprung into life fully armed," but this means only that we cannot trace his sources and the influences on his writing in any systematic way. Crane apparently had no apprenticeship period, very little formal education, and no mentors or advisers until after he published his first novel—*Maggie: A Girl of the Streets*—at age 21. We can point to only a few books we are certain he read. Cather believed that this deficiency in Crane's preparation was actually a virtue: "Perhaps it was because Stephen Crane had read so little, was so slightly acquainted with the masterpieces of fiction, that he felt no responsibility to be accurate or painstaking in accounting for things

---

[3] More evidence of their influence (and that of their religious belief) can be found in Crane's poetry. See Hoffman.

and people." This freed him to describe sparingly, a strategy which she, as advocate of an "unfurnished" style, admired extravagantly (70).

Although Crane was not the preface writer (or letter writer, for that matter) his older friend Henry James was, and so did not try to prepare readers for particular innovations, he did have theories about what he was doing. He wrote in one letter in 1894 that he had developed "all alone a little creed of art" and then learned it was similar to Howells's and Hamlin Garland's efforts to launch realism, or veritism. Crane had come to his version of realism as a reaction against popular romance, for in the same letter he says he has "renounced the clever school in literature," and his "Rudyard-Kipling style" (Wertheim and Sorrentino, *Correspondence* 173). Noting this reference, and the likelihood that Crane had read Kipling's *The Light That Failed* at an impressionable age (this novel was serialized in *Lippincott's Magazine* in 1891, when Crane was nineteen), James Colvert concludes that Crane adopted the artistic principles of Kipling's artist hero, Dick Heldar, and never really renounced them ("Origins" 178–79). These tenets assert the importance of absolute honesty, deem no subject unworthy of treatment by the artist, and hold that art is born out of need or privation. The implication of these beliefs is that the experiences one has are literary even before they are transformed by writing about them. Kiplingesque artists make of their bodies prisms through which to view the world. It follows, then, that one cannot write until one has seen everything, has come close to life in all its forms.

This attitude fits well with Crane's realist credo of faithfulness to nature and to writing so that ordinary people can comprehend the scenes evoked; indeed, it suggests one of the ways in which the realists elevated realistic treatment of the everyday world to art. This romantic emphasis on experience also contributes to his intellectual conception of his observer's role. In living like the out-of-work transients and the cadre of the permanent poor who waited in bread and soup lines and in his travels to war, Crane was acting very much in the spirit of the journalist, what Christopher Wilson calls a "social and political pathfinder" in the 1860s and 1870s: "The reporter became America's first public agent of exposure, the high priest of 'experience,' the expert on 'real life'—all key words emerging at the heart of American popular discourse" (17).

Newspapers fed the appetite for sentimental or sensationalized news stories by playing up the separation of audience from actors in the news. This correlates with polarities thrown into relief by the population shift to the cities, which others have noted: the contrast between spectacle and observer, such as a celebrity viewed by an anonymous individual in a crowd of onlookers; and the separation of production from consumption and of the prosperous from the poor, which resulted in new configurations of living and commercial space and the abutting of rich and poor neighbor-hoods. As Crane wrote in his second book of poetry, *War Is Kind,* the newspaper

> Spreads its curious opinion
> To a million merciful and sneering men,
> While families cuddle the joys of the fireside
> When spurred by tales of dire lone agony.
> (Crane, *Poems* 52)

Crane's way of dealing with these divisions in his reporting was to try to overcome the split between observer and the thing observed that is in-herent in the journalism of spectacle and sensation; he does this by draw-ing the reader into the space occupied by his persona or narrator. Then, wherever possible, he acknowledges his role in the production of perspec-tive, referring to the process of observation (frequently in painterly or impressionist terms) and paying inordinate attention to the look of things. Although Benfey overstates Crane's tendency to write first, experience later, clearly Crane's writing was deeply influenced by the cult of adventurer-reporters prominent in his culture.

In adopting this mode of adventure journalism, reporters tried to cap-ture the emotional response of people in dire circumstances, they sought out unusual experiences, and they were led to reproduce their sensations for vicarious identification by others. Colvert says that Crane may have sought "the final revelation of the mystery of existence in violent event and ultimate crisis" (Introduction). At any rate, Crane embraced his times and threw himself into their defining currents. Crane saw the action of Ameri-can life as taking place in its cities, so he moved to New York City in 1892, where he revised and self-published *Maggie: A Girl of the Streets* in 1893. (The subtitle indicated to Crane's contemporaries that Maggie was a pros-titute.) He would write about and live in New York intermittently until the end of 1896, sketching the street life of the most dynamic city in the United States, a city that in its extremes could stand for all of urban life. In Janu-ary 1895, just after the abbreviated version of *The Red Badge of Courage* appeared in newspapers in December 1894, Crane set out on a trip to the West and Mexico as a feature writer under contract to the Bacheller syn-dicate, which had serialized the novel. The trip lasted several months, and he gathered material not only for sketches and feature stories but for sev-eral fine short stories, including "The Blue Hotel." When he returned to New York, he had completed revisions of *The Red Badge of Courage.*

Crane wanted to experience everything. He saw that the world was in the process of a major political upheaval, so he became a war correspon-dent. He contracted to sail aboard the arms-carrier *Commodore* in late

1896 so that he could see firsthand the war between Cuban nationalists and Spanish imperialists. Since this conflict was taking place on an island only 90 miles from the U.S. mainland and was of considerable interest to national leaders who had imperialist designs, Crane made a heroic effort to get to Cuba and inadvertently became a hero of a different sort when the ship he had signed on as a crew member sank in January 1897. When that war didn't break out on demand (to rouse President McKinley and the Senate to action took another year, a suspicious explosion on the USS *Maine* while it was docked in Havana, and many jingoist editorials and stories of Spanish abuses), Crane arranged in April 1897 to report from Greece and Turkey during the Greco-Turkish war. This was another conflict with major historical ramifications, such as the decline of the once-great Ottoman empire and the remapping of the region. Finally, he got to Cuba and to the waters off Puerto Rico for that brief theater of the Spanish-American War in the summer of 1898.

It was, perhaps, already the age of the writer, and Crane helped make it so. His public career took off late in 1895, when *The Red Badge of Courage* "burst upon the American public with the effect of a Civil War projectile lain dormant beneath a city square for thirty years" (Ellison 64). Because of the expectation it aroused that he would simply mine the same vein over and over again to meet public demand, he came to call the novel "that accursed, damnable book" (L. H. Davis 333). Fame led to many satiric treatments and parodies of Crane's style, and soon Crane was being reported on as well as reporting. Fame even caused him difficulty in pursuing his work in New York as an investigative reporter. A notorious prostitute sued the city's police department for false arrest, and in testifying for her and writing about the experience in "Adventures of a Novelist," Crane aroused the ire of the police department (Theodore Roosevelt was then its chief commissioner) and was driven out of the city by the storm of negative publicity.[4] Stephen Crane is simply an individual phenomenon, however—a celebrity author around whom legends grew—until we put him back into his historical moment. Viewing the myriad of technological innovations and social changes that conspired to create the climate for adventurer journalists and celebrity novelists we can see Crane's career as less an anomaly, and more an outgrowth of his engagement with his times.

Mass literacy, developments in rail and water transportation, improvements in roads, the telephone, the telegraph—all enabled writers to

---

[4] For newspaper coverage of the incident, including Crane's "Adventures of a Novelist," see Stallman and Hagemann, eds., 217–63.

reach numbers of people as they never had before and to communicate information from remote places. Indeed, one of the key elements of modernity was the emergence of a truly mass media. In the late nineteenth century, Americans read newspapers and magazines in unprecedented numbers, as journals aggressively promoted their circulation in order to increase revenue with advertising, the means by which producers found a market for their newly available consumer goods. For readers of newspapers, to look at the marvels of the modern age depicted in advertising copy was to partake of modernity itself. The common use of photographs, which seemed to place the reader at the event, furthered this effect. The first photographs appeared in newspapers in 1880, soon altering the role of language in communicating an event, as prose could now embellish or augment visual information that caught the reader's eye first.

The medium of motion pictures, a prototype of which was displayed at the Columbian Exposition of 1893, also emerged in this period. It was a viable communications medium by the time Crane reported from Cuba in 1898. (One of the many short films shot by the Edison company that year captures 24 seconds of Spanish-American War correspondents rushing to send their dispatches from Key West, Florida; it is available on the Library of Congress American Memory Web page.)[5] The existence of newsreels, filmed reproductions of events, and even enactments that were clearly remote from the action in Cuba provided people in the United States with images of warfare that made it a kind of spectator sport in which most viewers had a clear rooting interest. With his writing, Crane helped create the new public sphere, and as a celebrity journalist, he participated in it.

Unlike Richard Harding Davis, who was also a star journalist and a popular novelist, Crane's stated desire was to produce texts that outlasted him, works that would appeal to an audience no longer acquainted with their explicit source materials—that is, to join the ranks of serious novelists. And it was his sense of himself as a serious writer that led to his developing a creed, which produced in his work a particular way of looking at the events of his time. Just as Ezra Pound enjoined writers to do some two decades after Crane's death, Crane wished to "make it new." And the

---

[5] The film, titled *War Correspondents,* is easily located on the topical index to the Spanish-American War at http://memory.loc.gov/ammem/sawhtml/satitles.html. The site also contains digitized versions of various other filmed scenes and reenactments. It is possible that Crane is one of the correspondents, as he was in Key West on April 28, the day the Edison Company filmed the scene; he filed a cable dispatch on that day, his first dispatch of the Cuban War, reporting on events of April 27. See Wertheim and Sorrentino, *Crane Log* 299. Apparently about 250 reporters were there, however (see L. H. Davis 246).

visual arts were clearly one of the primary influences on this new way of looking at events. Biographers have written of Crane's fascination with impressionist painting as he wrote *The Red Badge of Courage* and his later pieces and stories. He lived with a number of young artists and photographers in New York at the Art Students' League building in 1893, where he worked on the war novel, and he most certainly participated in artists' talk with these young men. His attempt to assimilate the impressionist aesthetic to his medium explicitly links him to later figures such as Ezra Pound, T. S. Eliot, Gertrude Stein, and Hemingway, among others. Indeed, James Nagel describes Crane's best-known novel as primarily "a record" of its protagonist's "progressive intensification of vision" (19). As Bernard Weisberger writes, Crane's style, particularly in *The Red Badge of Courage,* shows the influence of symbolist poetry, in which "certain sounds were identified with particular colors and the emotions which they evoked"; he notes that in the novel Crane "uses colors almost compulsively" (108– 09).[6] This picturesque quality of Crane's prose was noticed almost immediately. In 1896 novelist Harold Frederic's review of *The Red Badge of Courage* compared its effect "of photographic revelation" to that of Eadward Muybridge, a pioneer in the development of moving pictures as well as an esteemed photographer who documented animals (including humans) in motion (119).

   Crane's innovative prose style also connects him to developments in fictional realism, which was in some ways a response to the growing popularity and influence of photography, from the widespread use of the daguerreotype to the large numbers of exhibitions of photographs from the Civil War. Indeed, this connection at least partially accounts for Frederic's praise. As Howells realized in proselytizing for realism, because it was founded on being antiliterary it wouldn't do to wax eloquent about realism's specific techniques. Instead, Howells advised that the writer must not simply map life but should picture it. He also associated the goals of the realist writer with those of machines that invisibly captured truth, such as the spectroscope, the camera, and, especially, the apparatus for projecting moving pictures. Here is the awed response of George Parsons Lathrop (Nathaniel Hawthorne's son-in-law) to the kinetograph, an early version of the motion picture camera, in 1891: "Edison's machine . . . re-

---

[6] For an essay about the influence of paintings (by Winslow Homer) and photographs (Matthew Brady, Timothy O'Sullivan) on the composition of *The Red Badge of Courage,* see Gislason, *Imaging the Civil War,* on the University of Virginia Web site on Stephen Crane. For a selection of photographs in the collection of the Library of Congress see *Selected Civil War Photographs* on the American Memory Web page.

produces the movement and appearance of life with such truth of action that if colors could only be given at the same time, the illusion that one was looking at something really alive would be absolute" (Corkin 51).

Crane developed Howells's conception of realism by adding a more determinist philosophy. Crane was certainly influenced by Howells's credo, but in his efforts to expand the Howellsian definition of what fiction should be, he falls more easily into the naturalist category, a category that included contemporaries Frank Norris, Theodore Dreiser, Edith Wharton, and Upton Sinclair, among others. The naturalists derived their method from the French authors Honoré de Balzac and Émile Zola, who defined the surfaces of the world in the manner of the realists but employed an observational technique in order to show the inevitable laws of the universe. Writers working within this vein, Crane among them, conflated natural and social circumstances. Their theory of composition followed the efforts of Herbert Spencer to elaborate a single explanatory theory of all events. In such a universe, according to naturalists, one could either internalize the laws determining natural and social forces or be their victim.

We can see elements of this worldview throughout Crane's works, but perhaps most clearly in "The Open Boat," the story resulting from his first effort to get to Cuba in January 1897, when he was shipwrecked and spent 36 hours in a ten-foot dinghy with three other men before finally swimming to shore. In some readings, this story operates as a naturalist tour de force. The men in the dinghy are swamped by the power of the ocean and clearly at the mercy of nature. They must either swim with the current or be overwhelmed by the waves, and their survival may be more a matter of chance than of choice (Mitchell, "Naturalism" 535–36). Similarly, in *Maggie,* a ground-breaking character study that paints environment as more a character than Maggie herself, social circumstances become a force akin to the ocean. Some people, such as Maggie's suitor, Pete, accept these laws and survive or prosper with them; whereas for Maggie, to struggle against such a determined environment is to be crushed.

The juxtaposition of Crane's works and so-called nonliterary works of the era shows that the term *naturalism* is more than a marker of literary history. Assumptions about a world defined by naturalism inform virtually every selection in this volume. And as a broader cultural and historical definition, naturalism emerges as a means to create effects without necessarily elaborating on the causes. Naturalist texts thereby *naturalize* historical processes, that is, make them seem inevitable—including the process by which the realities of an era become universalized as such. Naturalism's historical context includes the mechanization of the workplace and a growing mass culture dominated by advertising, the purpose of which is creating the consumers that an advanced industrial society needs given its increased capacity to produce manufactured goods.

While Crane spoke to the realists, who were generally somewhat older, and the naturalists, who were his contemporaries, he also employed techniques that look ahead to modernist prose. This included not only emphasis on painterly effects in the manner of Hemingway and Stein, but also minimalism in the manner of a number of modernists, including, again, Hemingway and Stein and, in addition, Sherwood Anderson, Pound, and Cather. Cather herself sees the connection, saying about Crane's collection of reportage and short stories from the Spanish-American War, *Wounds in the Rain,* that he was wonderful at "'description' because he is the least describing," that is, he didn't try to "transfer tropical landscapes to paper." She quotes generously, as all admirers of Crane's painterly methods do, allowing the reader to appreciate the visual qualities of this story from the war: "The day wore down to the Cuban dusk. . . . The sun threw his last lance through the foliage. The steep mountain range on the right turned blue and as without detail as a curtain. The tiny ruby of light ahead meant that the ammunition guard were cooking their supper" (71). As Roger Angell wrote more recently, it may be more important to note what Crane left out of, rather than what he put into, a work like *The Red Badge of Courage* (87), for in this, as in his best work in general, Crane observes what would become the minimalist modernists' stock-in-trade—the thing left out, the importance of the thing not said.

Yet although his individual works typically reveal a minimalist aesthetic, Crane's career as a whole attests to his ethos of maximum production. According to biographer Linda Davis, in the years between publication of *The Red Badge of Courage* late in 1895 and his death in 1900 Crane "published five novels, two volumes of poetry, three big story collections, two books of war stories, and countless works of short fiction and reporting. And yet in three years he had earned just over $1,200 for his entire American output. . . . [and] just 20 pounds on English sales of his best-selling Civil War novel (332).[7] Most biographers and critics deplore the effect that the literary marketplace (as well as the Cranes' profligate spending habits) had on his talent. Yet his prolific output may ultimately be part of his legend. It certainly contributes to our sense of awe in encountering him, just as do descriptions of a fearless Crane, weakened by illness but braving bullets.

---

[7] A. J. Liebling wrote that Crane died "unwillingly, of the cause most common among American middle-class males—anxiety about money" (20).

Though Wertheim and Sorrentino lament the "embarrassing amount of uninspired journalism" Crane was forced by financial pressures to turn out, the writer himself seems to have believed that deprivation fostered creation. As he wrote of *The Red Badge of Courage* in 1896, "It was an effort born of pain, and I believe that this was beneficial to it as a piece of literature. It seems a pity that this should be so—that art should be a child of suffering; and yet such seems to be the case." Although Crane concedes this is not always true, he thinks that some writers would produce better work "if the conditions of their lives were harder," and he gives Bret Harte as an example (Wertheim and Sorrentino, *Correspondence* 230–31, 323).

Nevertheless, this guiding principle, if such it was, had serious consequences. Although Crane was apparently a sickly child and had frequent colds and coughs as an adult, we can surmise from accounts of his activities—camping, tramping the streets of New York, horseback riding on a scouting expedition in Cuba, and surviving many illnesses, including dysentery and malaria—that he had an amazingly strong constitution, which might have enabled him to survive if he had suffered less abuse of his body. His attempt to get to Cuba via Jacksonville, Florida, early in 1897 that ended with a shipwreck was the first in a series of ordeals caused by mishap or bad weather that he underwent during the next two years. Beginning with this abortive trip, Crane was in motion, moving to England with his companion Cora Taylor in 1897 (where they could live as a married couple, although she was unable to get a divorce to marry Stephen) and traveling with her to the Greco-Turkish War as a *Journal* and McClure-syndicated correspondent. (Cora became the first woman war correspondent by filing a few stories.) Returning from England in 1898 as soon as war was imminent, Crane tried to join the U.S. Navy to serve and, when he was rejected, covered it from Cuba and Puerto Rico for the *World* and, when fired, for the *Journal*. After this he slipped into Havana, where he went underground for a few months, perhaps with malaria; he resurfaced in New York and in the first days of 1899 returned to Cora in England, where they settled in an ancient English manor house for the last sixteen months of his life. This stay was broken only by short trips to Ireland (to gather atmosphere for a novel) and Switzerland (to place a niece in school there). He died in Germany, at a spa in the Black Forest, where Cora had taken him in desperate hope of a cure.

The struggle to survive the shipwreck, which resulted in "The Open Boat," apparently had very real physical consequences. Crane was one of two men who took turns rowing the tiny boat while getting drenched from waves breaking into the dinghy. He and the oiler exchanged places delicately, for, as the story's narrator says, "it is easier to steal eggs from under a hen than it was to change seats in the dinghy." Crane's family said he was never in good health after that (Cady 61). Yet he continued to behave recklessly, subjecting himself to bad weather and bad food, even to enemy fire in Cuba (R. H. Davis 125). He died of tuberculosis in 1900 at the age of twenty-eight, although there is some evidence that his case was curable or at least manageable (Liebling 20). Anyone doubting the lingering effects of the ordeal of the shipwreck on Crane's consciousness has only to learn of Cora's heart-wrenching description of Stephen's delirious ravings during his last illness, when she reported being driven to distraction by hearing him "try to change his place in the Open Boat" (Gilkes 257).

Perhaps there was something about the way that naturalist writers of this period fully engaged themselves in the world that resulted in their short lives. As Christopher Wilson points out, Crane was not the only popular naturalist writer who died young and, at least partially, from poor conditions while on assignment or seeing for himself wars and other newsworthy events. He mentions Jack London, Norris, and, later, Reed (194). The pressures of the marketplace on these writers ought not be underestimated, nor should their tremendous enthusiasm for being at the forefront of events. Unlike his champion Howells, who built his career on "house" positions such as editorships and regular columns, Crane was a freelance from adolescence to his death, and, as he told an editor, that is "hopeless work. Of all human lots for a person of sensibility that of an obscure freelance in literature or journalism is, I think, the most discouraging" (Wertheim and Sorrentino, *Correspondence* 232). Conceding that Crane's "improvidence" may have been a factor in his "agony," Cady nevertheless insists, "Whether pride or art or character caused it, Crane's suffering was real; and it produced important effects. It ruined his teeth, wracked his body, and doubtless presented him the tuberculosis which eventually killed him" (Cady 42).

In the materials of this section some of the major voices and issues of Crane's day are presented. Each of the figures excerpted was prolific and famous, and, in varying degrees, had an influence on Crane's method of writing, the subjects on which he wrote, and on his way of looking at the world. This is not to say that Crane was versed in the theories of all these individuals, for there is little direct evidence that he knew the work of any except Howells firsthand. But their ideas were in the air, part of the climate of ideas at this time.

The 1890s stand out as the decade during which the social changes that had marked the post–Civil War United States as dynamic and somewhat chaotic became all the more pronounced. As the quarter-century before had been marked by erratic economic cycles of boom and bust, the nineties featured an economic downturn that lasted most of the decade and was unprecedented in severity. Crane self-published *Maggie* in early 1893, almost squarely between the bloody Homestead strike of 1892 and the even more disruptive and violent Pullman strike of 1894. He had stories published in newspapers in July 1892 that featured front-page coverage of Homestead battles, virtual assurance that this upheaval was an unavoidable aspect of his world (Shulman 3–4). Thus we can view *Maggie* as the product of a sense of national crisis and upheaval at a time when there was a newly emerging awareness of the gap between the haves and have nots.

Though not explicitly characterized in *Maggie,* or in any of Crane's stories, the late nineteenth century featured a massive migration of people from the farm to the city. Industrial production drew agricultural workers and owners to these new centers of employment, as the shift to a national market for agricultural goods drove smaller farmers off the land. Farmers caught without sufficient capital to mechanize and to acquire larger tracts of land to compete in these new markets pushed for currency inflation in order to reduce the real cost of their existing debts as well as to create capital for further expansion. These individuals, whose livelihood was threatened by the emergence of agribusiness, formed the core of the Populist movement and adopted William Jennings Bryan as their voice in the presidential election of 1896. Bryan advocated replacing the gold standard for currency with silver, which would have inflated the number of dollars in circulation by a ratio of 16 to 1. It provides a revealing view of the 1890s to think of this proposal in contemporary terms, when a small glitch in any economic index results in the Federal Reserve either raising interest rates or threatening to do so, thereby reducing the amount of capital in circulation.

As they had since the 1870s, such economic disruptions created general social unrest. Masses of unemployed men roamed the land, the most notable being the group known as Coxey's Army. In 1894 Jacob Coxey led a group of marchers from his hometown of Massillon, Ohio, to demand a large public works program that would give work to the unemployed. He was arrested for his troubles, and the larger group was dispersed with clubs. In the nineties currency crises destabilized the dollar internationally, until the dollar had to be bolstered by private loans from J. P. Morgan. To most Americans, the world seemed to be in motion, though no one seemed to know quite where it was going or when it would reach its ultimate destination. Such dynamism provoked Crane's excitement and whetted his desire to place himself amidst the action. It also created the mood, if not the theme, of many works: the sense of an individual's anxiety as he or she waits for the culminating events of a great upheaval.

Intellectually, this period was an age infatuated with the potential that could be unleashed by the wonders of science. Expositions such as the Centennial in Philadelphia in 1876, the Columbian in Chicago in 1893, and the Pan American in Buffalo in 1901—not to mention numerous smaller events—celebrated the technological progress of the day. Indeed, a self-described man of an earlier age, Henry Adams, wrote of his visit to the Gallery of Machines at the Great Exposition of 1900 and of "having his historical neck broken by the sudden irruption of forces totally new" (382). Adams summed up well the general awe and sense of historical rupture that marked the age of Thomas Edison, Alexander Graham Bell, Orville and Wilbur Wright, and many other inventors, who also became celebrities and in some cases national icons.

It was almost inevitable that a kind of pseudoscience would emerge in the latter part of the nineteenth century to explain the chaos of the times. It was also a great period for theories of social life, as the rationalist impulse spawned all manner of social sciences. Intellectuals, armed only with their powers of observation and an excessive belief in the explanatory and creative powers of science, attempted to unlock a single explanation for the mysteries of the universe, beginning with the physical world, emanating to the social, then to the spiritual. Herbert Spencer was perhaps the most eminent and respected such figure. He believed that the universe was defined by a mechanistic and natural ordering of force. It was Spencer who coined the term "the survival of the fittest," reinterpreting Darwin's analyses of the natural world and applying them to the social. He argued that all matter was moving toward an ultimate state of perfection, and it was this natural movement that defined those who succeeded, prospered, and reproduced and those who failed and died off. Given this logic, Spencer argued that an individual should only pursue self-interest, as any attempt at social amelioration could endanger this process of selection and disrupt the movement toward a utopian end. In such a world, according to Spencer, competitive enterprises contain their own justice.

Though it is difficult to say how many Americans read the works of this Englishman who has been called the father of modern sociology, his ideas were certainly well known and often quoted by those who sought to explain why the underclass was beyond help and why avarice was a natural condition. Spencer's works were widely taught in the newly organized American research universities, and after they were published by Appleton in a popular edition in 1886, they rapidly became a fixture in American homes. His publications sold over 400,000 copies in the United

States alone. In the brief excerpt from *First Principles* that begins on page 29, Spencer's logic is apparent as he explains how energy derived from the environment creates energy in humans, which defines their social activities. Thus, humans as social creatures are overdetermined by their natural circumstances. Those who receive an abundance of natural energy rightfully dominate the world. No wonder Spencer is often noted as the theoretical progenitor of literary naturalism, for he provided writers with a theory that connected environment to character. This key thinker illuminates the naturalist dimension of Crane's writings, enabling a more complete understanding of his intellectual universe.

An intellectual disciple of Spencer was the business magnate Andrew Carnegie. Carnegie, born to a poor family in Scotland in 1835, rose to become the personal assistant to Thomas A. Scott when Scott was the superintendent of the Pennsylvania Railroad. With the capital gained through shrewd investments, Carnegie eventually became a major stockholder in the Iron Forge Company and, by the turn of the century, came to dominate the steel industry in the United States and then the world. As a public figure, Carnegie commanded the awe due an exemplar of the American Dream. He was frugal, morally certain, and eager to use his status to promote his social views. Carnegie was a prolific public speaker and writer who gained added stature as a result of his enormous philanthropic enterprises, which included libraries, universities, and museums.

In 1889 he published "The Gospel of Wealth" in *Century Magazine*. His essay endorses competitive enterprises and their results as "natural," condemning those who would disrupt increasing concentrations of wealth as "attacking the foundations upon which civilization itself rests." In such sentiments we can spy the influence of Spencer, and, indeed, Carnegie played a significant role in further popularizing the ideas of the English philosopher. But Carnegie also turns from his Spencerian explanations of the world as he calls upon those of great wealth to donate a significant portion of their estates—the amount in excess of what their heirs can productively use—to benefit the masses of humankind, "to help those who will help themselves." Such sentiments depart from pure Spencerian beliefs, though Carnegie attempts to reconcile these tenets with his disposition toward charity. Nevertheless, Carnegie strongly asserts the Spencerian logic of the universe, advancing it by speaking as a man who possesses great public stature, a prominence enhanced by his charitable donations.

Though the Spencerian concept of humans and society was well known and broadly discussed, it was not unanimously accepted. In order to see some of the terms of verbal and intellectual dispute of the day, we have included two prominent and divergent voices that argue for the right of laborers to organize, to be respected for their contributions to commerce and society, and to earn a living wage. The Knights of Labor were established in 1878 with the goal of creating, as noted in their constitution, "cooperative institutions productive and distributive." The Knights were formed in the aftermath of the great strike of 1877, when a 10 percent wage cut on the Baltimore and Ohio Railroad triggered a violent reaction in the small town of Martinsburg, Virginia, that radiated across the country, affecting workers in all industries and threatening to trigger a class war. The Knights attempted nothing less than to organize the working class as a whole—both the skilled and unskilled—into a formidable political force.

Terence Powderly became their leader in 1879. By the mid-1880s the organization had grown to more than 700,000 members and was instrumental in a number of successful strikes and in inspiring a growing militancy among workers. This seems to have been the pinnacle of the organization's power, however. Faced with the concerted and well-planned opposition of big business, the Knights' lack of an organizational structure and a plan for effecting their program made them susceptible to tactics that included termination of employment, lockouts, physical intimidation, and actual violence. Further, the economic downturn of the 1890s made workers even more susceptible to lockouts, as the increased pool of available employees made owners unafraid to balance their books by eliminating jobs and cutting salaries. The Knights gradually ebbed as a force in American labor and were defunct by the mid-1890s. When Powderly wrote his memoir, his group was already in decline. Yet we can hear Powderly answering Spencer and Carnegie by demonizing "the task-masters" and invoking the goal of collectivity to combat their God of individualism. Crane's notion of the collective—which in works like *The Red Badge of Courage* and "The Open Boat" is something closer to a community and is not a topic he probes or scrutinizes—suggests the predominant definitions of the day and hints at how an appeal like Powderly's may have been received by the general public.

After its founding in December 1886, the American Federation of Labor, headed by Samuel Gompers, was in direct competition with Powderly's Knights. Gompers offered a strategy of unionism that allowed for the basic structural distinctions between capital and labor and sought not to disturb them or redress them. Instead, Gompers focused on collective bargaining as his primary means for improving workers' wages and working conditions, and failing that, strikes. He neither developed nor supported a comprehensive political program and explicitly expressed his distrust of those who would attempt to adjudicate disagreements between workers and employers to further a political agenda. Gompers saw principled negotiation between interested parties as the key means for developing a necessary balance between capital and labor. In this excerpt we find him developing a response to the social Darwinists, though not rebutting their basic assertions as Powderly did. Gompers argues not for the redistribution of power or goods; rather, he seeks to sustain prosperity by calling for government spending to increase wages and employment (thus predicting modern Keynesian economics), and by providing workers with significant economic benefits.

Also part of Stephen Crane's world was the highly influential body of thought that resulted when social science became permeated by race theory. This racist pseudoscience appears as yet one more branch growing from the tree of Spencerian thought. The influential progenitors of this movement included, in England, Sir Francis Galton, who coined the term *eugenics* in his book *The Hereditary Genius* (1869) as he argued for the genetic fitness of the English upper class; and, in France, Count Arthur de Gobineau, whose book *Essays on the Inequality of the Races* (1855) argued for the racial distinction of the deposed French nobility as it concocted theories of racial purity and hierarchy. Both men had significant followings and helped spawn and further the cult of race that was prevalent in disciplines including sociology, anthropology, history, political science, and psychology. Indeed, pioneering figures within each of these areas of study in the United States entertained racist theories of environmental and genetic determinism. These included Herbert Baxter Adams in history, Edward A. Ross in sociology, G. Stanley Hall in psychology, John W. Burgess in political science, and William Z. Ripley in anthropology. Such a roster demonstrates how widespread and respectable these scientistic theories were.

To represent this general expression of racist thought an excerpt from Nathaniel Southgate Shaler's *Nature and Man in America* (1891) is included. Shaler was a natural scientist who assumed the chair of Louis Aggasiz at Harvard upon Aggasiz's death. He drew throngs of students to his geology lectures. He eventually became dean of the Lawrence School of Science at that university. Shaler's explanation of the connection between environment and group behavior determined that America as an environment, when acting upon the genetic type of the English, produced optimum group characteristics. On the other hand, that people of African descent had dwelled in America for more than 200 years, according to Shaler, resulted in no particular salutary effect. Shaler is a prime example of the manner in which pseudoscience was employed to concoct explanations that confirmed racial hierarchy and of the prevalence of such notions during the late nineteenth century.

In Henry Cabot Lodge's 1896 speech to the U.S. Senate, he used the arguments of respectable intellectuals, in this case employing the words of the French social psychologist Gustave Le Bon, to argue for the restriction or elimination of immigration by "Russians, Hungarians, Poles, Bohemians, Italians, Greeks, and even Asiatics." For Lodge, race was a matter of "mental, and above all, [a group's] moral characteristics." Lodge's bill to restrict immigration passed in the House of Representatives but failed in the Senate and was thus not enacted. Still, his call for a literacy test brings to mind the then-emerging system of apartheid in the American South, where a literacy test was employed as a device to steal the voting franchise from African Americans.

The most directly oppressive actions resulting from the scientism of race theory and its persistent use by respected academicians was the system of legal segregation known as "Jim Crow." For more than half a century, individuals who were defined as possessing some critical component of African blood were banned from all manner of public places where white people shopped, ate, were educated, and performed vital bodily functions (hospitals, toilets, drinking fountains). Such a system allowed the racist theories that proliferated never to be disrupted by personal encounter. Rather, people of color could be vilified, marginalized, and ultimately dehumanized. In response to such policies and rhetoric, a group of African American leaders spoke out often and powerfully, naming the racism that masqueraded as objective inquiry, and calling to task white leaders who failed to confront bigotry.

Perhaps paramount among these leaders as they coalesced at the turn of the century was W. E. B. Du Bois. Educated at Fisk University and Harvard, possessing a Ph.D. from the latter, and having also studied at the University of Berlin, Du Bois was perhaps the leading African American intellectual of the first half of the twentieth century. As a professor of sociology at Atlanta University from 1900 to 1910, he helped produce sixteen studies of African American life in a range of topics drawn from the many disciplinary areas of the social sciences. Many of these studies were seminal in their reorienting of common assumptions and assertions regarding people of color and were particularly effective in their being rooted in the very disciplinary discussions that were so dismissive of people of color. After 1910, Du Bois went on to even greater prominence as the editor of *The Crisis,* a journal sponsored by the NAACP, an organization that he helped found. *The Crisis* combined politics and aesthetics in a manner that expressed Du Bois's utter rejection of commonly constructed racial hierarchies and affirmed the specific powers of the cultured person of African descent.

In the piece included herein, collected in *The Souls of Black Folk* but first published in *The Atlantic* in 1897, Du Bois decried the historical condition and legacy of slavery. In response to the science of race, Du Bois offered the results of racism. This is not to say that race was a concept

Du Bois rejected. As a late-nineteenth-century intellectual, Du Bois was implicated in concepts of nation and biology that pervaded this period. The terms that organized concepts of groups and group identities were so pervasive that it is exceedingly difficult to find figures who did not accept them in some way. But it is instructive to note how Du Bois attempted to redefine this term without denying its potential power to justify discrimination. With this background in mind one should consider how such widespread beliefs in the connection between biology and culture may have influenced Crane's beliefs, as evidenced in any number of works.

Ida B. Wells-Barnett offered a more direct entreaty to human empathy as she put the Southern practice of lynching African Americans before a general audience. In agreement with Du Bois, she saw the period after emancipation as one marked by a steady effort to keep African Americans from becoming complete citizens, both by political wiles and through brute force. Once again, a catalog of historical acts was employed as a means of answering the sweeping assertions of the scientific racists.

Wells-Barnett directly challenged the oft-stated reason for lynching, the desire to defend white womanhood from the violations of men of African descent. By asserting the humanity of people of color while agreeing that rape is indeed inhuman, she dispelled the stereotype of the black rapist and condemned lynching as a horrible act in itself. She asked readers to rethink their racialized notions of the civilized and the uncivilized by seeing lynching outside of the bracketed vision produced by racial assumptions. But she also reached out to her white audience to assure them that she accepted African Americans' need of further education and socialization to undo the effects of slavery.

Selections from the critical writings of Howells are also included. From the end of the Civil War until around the turn of the century, Howells was the paramount figure in American letters—as novelist, critic, and essayist. He was an editor at some of the leading journals of the day, including the *Atlantic Monthly* from 1871 to 1881 and *Harper's* from 1886 to 1892, and a mover and a shaker in the marketplace for writers. He helped to publish authors ranging from Garland to Abraham Cahan to Charles Chesnutt. Though Howells was unable to help Crane find a publisher for the first version of *Maggie,* he did approve of the work and wrote a review of the edition published in 1896. He admired *The Red Badge of Courage* as well. Howells's career as a critic was largely spent asserting the power and defining the contours of the realist novel while denigrating the art and morality of popular romances. In the last decades of the nineteenth century, works such as *Ben Hur* (1880), *King Solomon's Mines* (1886), and *The Prisoner of Zenda* (1894) appeared on the bestseller list. Howells countered these costume epics by repeatedly asserting that the best art depicted life as it could be observed by the average person. He wrote of the goodness of "the real" and told of its powers to instill reason and proportion in its readers. Though Crane does not precisely fit the Howellsian definition of the realist author, he was clearly influenced by the older man. Because Howells's criticism is readily available, only one excerpt is included here—from his inaugural "Editor's Study" column for *Harper's* in 1887, in which he articulated his realist project and its desired effect. Howells wrote of his disdain for writers who find their inspiration in other writers and not in life itself. His famous example contrasts the ideal grasshopper with the real, arguing that while the ideal may be more picturesque, the real is more "simple, natural, and honest."

This section concludes with a brief excerpt from Garland's engaging portrait of Crane the writer. Garland's sense and description of him as "slim, boyish with sallow complexion and light hair" and later as "distressingly pale and thin" provides a picture of this intense young man and the physical decline that marked his last years (Benfrey 230). Crane emerges as one who so poured himself into his work that at the end there was nothing left.

Cather said something similar in 1900, describing his "eyes that seemed to be burning themselves out" (Benfey 121). She was recalling her meeting with him in the newspaper office in Lincoln, Nebraska, in February 1895, insisting that even then she saw the melancholy in his eyes. As she said, "Now that he is dead, it occurs to me that all his life was a preparation for sudden departure" (Wertheim and Sorrentino, *Correspondence* 40). In *The Green Hills of Africa,* someone asks Hemingway what happened to Stephen Crane. Responds Papa, with the knowledge of Thomas Beer's biography and the many legends that had grown up around this doomed young poet, "He died. He was dying from the start" (Benfey 230).

FROM *FIRST PRINCIPLES*

Herbert Spencer

. . . If the general law of transformation and equivalence holds of the forces we class as vital and mental, it must hold also of those which we class as social. Whatever takes place in a society is due to organic or inorganic

New York: Appleton, 1895.

agencies, or to a combination of the two—results either from the undirected physical forces around, from these physical forces as directed by men, or from the forces of the men themselves. No change can occur in its organization, its modes of activity, or the effects it produces on the face of the Earth, but what proceeds, mediately or immediately, from these. Let us consider first the correlation between the phenomena which societies display, and the vital phenomena.

Social power and life varies, other things equal, with the population. Though different races, differing widely in their fitness for combination, show us that the forces manifested in a society are not necessarily proportionate to the number of people; yet we see that under given conditions, the forces manifested are confined within the limits which the number of people imposes. A small society, no matter how superior the character of its members, cannot exhibit the same quantity of social action as a large one. The production and distribution of commodities must be on a comparatively small scale. A multitudinous press, a prolific literature, or a massive political agitation, is not possible. And there can be but a small total of results in the shape of art-products and scientific discoveries.

The correlation of the social with the physical forces through the intermediation of the vital ones, is, however, most clearly shown in the different amounts of activity displayed by the same society according as its members are supplied with different amounts of force from the external world. In the effects of good and bad harvests, we yearly see this relation illustrated. A greatly deficient yield of wheat is soon followed by a diminution of business. Factories are worked half-time, or close entirely; railway traffic falls; retailers find their sales much lessened; house-building is almost suspended; and if the scarcity rises to famine, a thinning of the population still more diminishes the industrial vivacity. Conversely, an unusually abundant harvest occurring under conditions not otherwise unfavourable, both excites the old producing and distributing agencies and sets up new ones. The surplus social energy finds vent in speculative enterprises. Capital seeking investment carries out inventions that have been lying unutilized. Labour is expended in opening new channels of communication. There is increased encouragement to those who furnish the luxuries of life and minister to the aesthetic faculties. There are more marriages, and a greater rate of increase in population. Thus the social organism grows larger, more complex, and more active.

When, as happens with most civilized nations, the whole of the materials for subsistence are not drawn from the area inhabited, but are partly imported, the people are still supported by certain harvests elsewhere grown at the expense of certain physical forces. Our own cotton-spinners and weavers supply the most conspicuous instance of a section in one nation living, in great part, on imported commodities, purchased by the labour they expend on other imported commodities. But though the social activities of Lancashire are due chiefly to materials not drawn from our own soil, they are none the less evolved from physical forces elsewhere stored up in fit forms and then brought here.

If we ask whence come these physical forces from which, through the intermediation of the vital forces, the social forces arise, the reply is of course as heretofore—the solar radiations. Based as the life of a society is on animal and vegetal products; and dependent as these animal and vegetal products are on the light and heat of the sun; it follows that the changes going on in societies are effects of forces having a common origin with those which produce all the other orders of changes that have been analyzed. Not only is the force expended by the horse harnessed to the plough, and by the labourer guiding it, derived from the same reservoir as is the force of the falling cataract and the roaring hurricane; but to this same reservoir are eventually traceable those subtler and more complex manifestations of force which humanity, as socially embodied, evolves. The assertion is a startling one, and by many will be thought ludicrous; but it is an unavoidable deduction which cannot here be passed over.

Of the physical forces that are directly transformed into social ones, the like is to be said. Currents of air and water, which before the use of steam were the only agencies brought in aid of muscular effort for the performance of industrial processes, are, as we have seen, generated by the heat of the sun. And the inanimate power that now, to so vast an extent, supplements human labour, is similarly derived. The late George Stephenson was one of the first to recognize the fact that the force impelling his locomotive, originally emanated from the sun. Step by step we go back— from the motion of the piston to the evaporation of the water; thence to the heat evolved during the oxidation of coal; thence to the assimilation of carbon by the plants of whose imbedded remains coal consists; thence to the carbonic acid from which their carbon was obtained; and thence to the rays of light that deoxidized this carbonic acid. Solar forces millions of years ago expended on the Earth's vegetation, and since locked up beneath its surface, now smelt the metals required for our machines, turn the lathes by which the machines are shaped, work them when put together, and distribute the fabrics they produce. And insofar as economy of labour makes possible the support of a larger population; gives a surplus of human power that would else be absorbed in manual occupations; and it facilitates the development of higher kinds of activity; it is clear that these social forces which are directly correlated with physical forces anciently derived from the sun, are only less important than those whose correlates are the vital forces recently derived from it.

Regarded as an induction, the doctrine set forth in this chapter will most likely be met by a demurrer. Many who admit that among physical phenomena at least, transformation of forces is now established, will probably say that inquiry has not yet gone far enough to enable us to predicate equivalence. And in respect of the forces classed as vital, mental, and social, the evidence assigned, however little to be explained away, they will consider by no means conclusive even of transformation, much less of equivalence.

To those who think thus, it must now however be pointed out, that the universal truth above illustrated under its various aspects, is a necessary corollary from the persistence of force. Setting out with the proposition that force can neither come into existence, nor cease to exist, the several foregoing general conclusions inevitably follow. Each manifestation of force can be interpreted only as the effect of some antecedent force: no matter whether it be an inorganic action, an animal movement, a thought, or a feeling. Either this must be conceded, or else it must be asserted that our successive states of consciousness are self-created. Either mental energies, as well as bodily ones, are quantitatively correlated to certain energies expended in their production, and to certain other energies which they initiate; or else nothing must become something and something must become nothing. The alternatives are, to deny the persistence of force, or to admit that every physical and psychial change is generated by certain antecedent forces, and that from given amounts of such forces neither more nor less of such physical and psychial changes can result. And since the persistence of force, being a datum of consciousness, cannot be denied, its unavoidable corollary must be accepted.

This corollary cannot indeed be made more certain by accumulating illustrations. The truth as arrived at deductively, cannot be inductively confirmed. For every one of such facts as those above detailed, is established only through the indirect assumption of that persistence of force, from which it really follows as a direct consequence. The most exact proof of correlation and equivalence which it is possible to reach by experimental inquiry, is that based on measurement of the forces expended and the forces produced. But, as was shown in the last chapter, any such process of measurement implies the use of some unit of force which is assumed to remain constant; and for this assumption there can be no warrant but that it is a corollary from the persistence of force. How then can any reasoning based on this corollary, prove the equally direct corollary that when a given quantity of force ceases to exist under one form, an equal quantity must come into existence under some other form or forms? Clearly the *a priori* truth expressed in this last corollary, cannot be more firmly established by any *a posteriori* proofs which the first corollary helps us to.

"What then," it may be asked, "is the use of these investigations by which transformation and equivalence of forces is sought to be established as an inductive truth? Surely it will not be alleged that they are useless. Yet if the correlation cannot be made more certain by them than it is already, does not their uselessness necessarily follow?" No. They are of value as disclosing the many particular implications which the general truth does not specify. They are of value as teaching us how much of one mode of force is the equivalent of so much of another mode. They are of value as determining under what conditions each metamorphosis occurs. And they are of value as leading us to inquire in what shape the remnant of force has escaped, when the apparent results are not equivalent to the cause.

"THE GOSPEL OF WEALTH"

Andrew Carnegie

The problem of our age is the proper administration of wealth, that the ties of brotherhood may still bind together the rich and poor in harmonious relationship. The conditions of human life have not only been changed, but revolutionized, within the past few hundred years. In former days there was little difference between the dwelling, dress, food, and environment of the chief and those of his retainers. The Indians are today where civilized man then was. When visiting the Sioux, I was led to the wigwam of the chief. It was like the others in external appearance, and even within the difference was trifling between it and those of the poorest of his braves. The contrast between the palace of the millionaire and the cottage of the laborer with us today measures the change which has come with civilization. This change, however, is not to be deplored, but welcomed as highly beneficial. It is well, nay, essential, for the progress of the race that the houses of some should be homes for all that is highest and best in literature and the arts, and for all the refinements of civilization, rather than that none should be so. Much better this great irregularity than universal squalor. Without wealth there can be no Mæcenas. The "good old

North American Review, June and Dec. 1889.

times" were not good old times. Neither master nor servant was as well situated then as today. A relapse to old conditions would be disastrous to both—not the least so to him who serves—and would sweep away civilization with it. But whether the change be for good or ill, it is upon us, beyond our power to alter, and, therefore, to be accepted and made the best of. It is a waste of time to criticize the inevitable.

It is easy to see how the change has come. One illustration will serve for almost every phase of the cause. In the manufacture of products we have the whole story. It applies to all combinations of human industry, as stimulated and enlarged by the inventions of this scientific age. Formerly, articles were manufactured at the domestic hearth, or in small shops which formed part of the household. The master and his apprentices worked side by side, the latter living with the master, and therefore subject to the same conditions. When these apprentices rose to be masters, there was little or no change in their mode of life, and they, in turn, educated succeeding apprentices in the same routine. There was, substantially, social equality, and even political equality, for those engaged in industrial pursuits had then little or no voice in the State.

The inevitable result of such a mode of manufacture was crude articles at high prices. Today the world obtains commodities of excellent quality at prices which even the preceding generation would have deemed incredible. In the commercial world similar causes have produced similar results, and the race is benefited thereby. The poor enjoy what the rich could not before afford. What were the luxuries have become the necessaries of life. The laborer has now more comforts than the farmer had a few generations ago. The farmer has more luxuries than the landlord had, and is more richly clad and better housed. The landlord has books and pictures rarer and appointments more artistic than the king could then obtain.

The price we pay for this salutary change is, no doubt, great. We assemble thousands of operatives in the factory, and in the mine, of whom the employer can know little or nothing, and to whom he is little better than a myth. All intercourse between them is at an end. Rigid castes are formed, and, as usual, mutual ignorance breeds mutual distrust. Each caste is without sympathy with the other, and ready to credit anything disparaging in regard to it. Under the law of competition, the employer of thousands is forced into the strictest economies, among which the rates paid to labor figure prominently, and often there is friction between the employer and the employed, between capital and labor, between rich and poor. Human society loses homogeneity.

The price which society pays for the law of competition, like the price it pays for cheap comforts and luxuries, is also great; but the advantages of this law are also greater still than its cost—for it is to this law that we owe our wonderful material development, which brings improved conditions in its train. But, whether the law be benign or not, we must say of it, as we say of the change in the conditions of men to which we have referred: It is here; we cannot evade it; no substitutes for it have been found; and while the law may be sometimes hard for the individual, it is best for the race, because it insures the survival of the fittest in every department. We accept and welcome, therefore, as conditions to which we must accommodate ourselves, great inequality of environment; the concentration of business, industrial and commercial, in the hands of a few; and the law of competition between these, as being not only beneficial, but essential to the future progress of the race. Having accepted these, it follows that there must be great scope for the exercise of special ability in the merchant and in the manufacturer who has to conduct affairs upon a great scale. That this talent for organization and management is rare among men is proved by the fact that it invariably secures enormous rewards for its possessor, no matter where or under what laws or conditions. The experienced in affairs always rate the MAN whose services can be obtained as a partner as not only the first consideration, but such as render the question of his capital scarcely worth considering: for able men soon create capital; in the hands of those without the special talent required, capital soon takes wings. Such men become interested in firms or corporations using millions; and, estimating only simple interest to be made upon the capital invested, it is inevitable that their income must exceed their expenditures and that they must, therefore, accumulate wealth. Nor is there any middle ground which such men can occupy, because the great manufacturing or commercial concern which does not earn at least interest upon its capital soon becomes bankrupt. It must either go forward or fall behind; to stand still is impossible. It is a condition essential to its successful operation that it should be thus far profitable, and even that, in addition to interest on capital, it should make profit. It is a law, as certain as any of the others named, that men possessed of this peculiar talent for affairs, under the free play of economic forces must, of necessity, soon be in receipt of more revenue than can be judiciously expended upon themselves; and this law is as beneficial for the race as the others.

Objections to the foundations upon which society is based are not in order, because the condition of the race is better with these than it has been with any other which has been tried. Of the effect of any new substitutes proposed we cannot be sure. The Socialist or Anarchist who seeks to overturn present conditions is to be regarded as attacking the foundation upon which civilization itself rests, for civilization took its start from the day when the capable, industrious workman said to his incompetent and lazy fellow, "If thou dost not sow, thou shalt not reap," and thus ended primitive Communism by separating the drones from the bees. One who studies this subject will soon be brought face to face with the conclusion that upon the sacredness of property civilization itself depends—the right of the laborer to his hundred dollars in the savings bank, and equally the legal right of the millionaire to his millions. Every man must be allowed "to sit under his own vine and fig tree, with none to make afraid," if human society is to advance, or even to remain so far advanced as it is. To those who propose to substitute Communism for this intense Individualism, the answer therefore is: The race has tried that. All progress from that barbarous day to the present time has resulted from its displacement. Not evil, but good, has come to the race from the accumulation of wealth by those who have had the ability and energy to produce it. But even if we admit for a moment that it might be better for the race to discard its present foundation, Individualism—that it is a nobler ideal that man should labor, not for himself alone, but in and for a brotherhood of his fellows, and share with them all in common, realizing Swedenborg's idea of heaven, where, as he says, the angels derive their happiness, not from laboring for self, but for each other—even admit all this, and a sufficient answer is, This is not evolution, but revolution. It necessitates the changing of human nature itself—a work of eons, even if it were good to change it, which we cannot know.

It is not practicable in our day or in our age. Even if desirable theoretically, it belongs to another and long-succeeding sociological stratum. Our duty is with what is practicable now—with the next step possible in our day and generation. It is criminal to waste our energies in endeavoring to uproot, when all we can profitably accomplish is to bend the universal tree of humanity a little in the direction most favorable to the production of good fruit under existing circumstances. We might as well urge the destruction of the highest existing type of man because he failed to reach our ideal as to favor the destruction of Individualism, Private Property, the Law of Accumulation of Wealth, and the Law of Competition; for these are the highest result of human experience, the soil in which society, so far, has produced the best fruit. Unequally or unjustly, perhaps, as these laws sometimes operate, and imperfect as they appear to the Idealist, they are, nevertheless, like the highest type of man, the best and most valuable of all that humanity has yet accomplished.

We start, then, with a condition of affairs under which the best interests of the race are promoted, but which inevitably gives wealth to the few. Thus far, accepting conditions as they exist, the situation can be surveyed and pronounced good. The question then arises—and if the foregoing be correct, it is the only question with which we have to deal—What is the proper mode of administering wealth after the laws upon which civilization is founded have thrown it into the hands of the few? And it is of this great question that I believe I offer the true solution. It will be understood that fortunes are here spoken of, not moderate sums saved by many years of effort, the returns from which are required for the comfortable maintenance and education of families. This is not wealth, but only competence, which it should be the aim of all to acquire, and which it is for the best interests of society should be acquired.

There are but three modes in which surplus wealth can be disposed of. It can be left to the families of the decedents; or it can be bequeathed for public purposes; or, finally, it can be administered by its possessors during their lives. Under the first and second modes most of the wealth of the world that has reached the few has hitherto been applied. Let us in turn consider each of these modes. The first is the most injudicious. In monarchical countries, the estates and the greatest portion of the wealth are left to the first son, that the vanity of the parent may be gratified by the thought that his name and title are to descend unimpaired to succeeding generations. The condition of this class in Europe today teaches the failure of such hopes or ambitions. The successors have become impoverished through their follies, or from the fall in the value of land. Even in Great Britain the strict law of entail has been found inadequate to maintain an hereditary class. Its soil is rapidly passing into the hands of the stranger. Under republican institutions the division of property among the children is much fairer; but the question which forces itself upon thoughtful men in all lands is, Why should men leave great fortunes to their children? If this is done from affection, is it not misguided affection? Observation teaches that, generally speaking, it is not well for the children that they should be so burdened. Neither is it well for the State. Beyond providing for the wife and daughters moderate sources of income, and very moderate allowances indeed, if any, for the sons, men may well hesitate; for it is no longer questionable that great sums bequeathed often work more for the injury than for the good of the recipients. Wise men will soon conclude that, for the best interests of the members of their families, and of the State, such bequests are an improper use of their means.

It is not suggested that men who have failed to educate their sons to earn a livelihood shall cast them adrift in poverty. If any man has seen fit to rear his sons with a view to their living idle lives, or, what is highly commendable, has instilled in them the sentiment that they are in a position to labor for public ends without reference to pecuniary considerations, then, of course, the duty of the parent is to see that such are provided for in moderation. There are instances of millionaires' sons unspoiled by wealth, who, being rich, still perform great services to the community. Such are the very salt of the earth, as valuable as, unfortunately, they are rare. It is not the exception, however, but the rule, that men must regard; and, looking at the usual result of enormous sums conferred upon legatees, the thoughtful man must shortly say, "I would as soon leave to my son a curse as the almighty dollar," and admit to himself that it is not the welfare of the children, but family pride, which inspires these legacies.

As to the second mode, that of leaving wealth at death for public uses, it may be said that this is only a means for the disposal of wealth, provided a man is content to wait until he is dead before he becomes of much good in the world. Knowledge of the results of legacies bequeathed is not calculated to inspire the brightest hopes of much posthumous good being accomplished by them. The cases are not few in which the real object sought by the testator is not attained, nor are they few in which his real wishes are thwarted. In many cases the bequests are so used as to become only monuments of his folly. It is well to remember that it requires the exercise of not less ability than that which acquires it, to use wealth so as to be really beneficial to the community. Besides this, it may fairly be said that no man is to be extolled for doing what he cannot help doing, nor is he to be thanked by the community to which he only leaves wealth at death. Men who leave vast sums in this way may fairly be thought men who would not have left it at all had they been able to take it with them. The memories of such cannot be held in grateful remembrance, for there is no grace in their gifts. It is not to be wondered at that such bequests seem so generally to lack the blessing.

The growing disposition to tax more and more heavily large estates left at death is a cheering indication of the growth of a salutary change in public opinion. The State of Pennsylvania now takes—subject to some exceptions—one tenth of the property left by its citizens. The budget presented in the British Parliament the other day proposes to increase the death duties; and, most significant of all, the new tax is to be a graduated one. Of all forms of taxation this seems the wisest. Men who continue hoarding great sums all their lives, the proper use of which for public ends would work good to the community from which it chiefly came, should be made to feel that the community, in the form of the State, cannot thus be deprived of its proper share. By taxing estates heavily at death the State marks its condemnation of the selfish millionaire's unworthy life.

It is desirable that nations should go much further in this direction. Indeed, it is difficult to set bounds to the share of a rich man's estate which should go at his death to the public at the agency of the State, and by all means such taxes should be graduated, beginning at nothing upon moderate sums to dependents, and increasing rapidly as the amounts swell, until of the millionaire's hoard, as of Shylock's, at least

The other half
Comes to the privy coffer of the State.

This policy would work powerfully to induce the rich man to attend to the administration of wealth during his life, which is the end that society should always have in view, as being by far the most fruitful for the people. Nor need it be feared that this policy would sap the root of enterprise and render men less anxious to accumulate, for, to the class whose ambition it is to leave great fortunes and to be talked about after their death, it will attract even more attention and, indeed, be a somewhat nobler ambition, to have enormous sums paid over to the State from their fortunes.

There remains, then, only one mode of using great fortunes; but in this we have the true antidote for the temporary unequal distribution of wealth, the reconciliation of the rich and the poor—a reign of harmony, another ideal, differing, indeed, from that of the Communist in requiring only the further evolution of existing conditions, not the total overthrow of our civilization. It is founded upon the present most intense Individualism, and the race is prepared to put it in practice by degrees whenever it pleases. Under its sway we shall have an ideal State, in which the surplus wealth of the few will become, in the best sense, the property of the many, because administered for the common good; and this wealth, passing through the hands of the few, can be made a much more potent force for the elevation of our race than if distributed in small sums to the people themselves. Even the poorest can be made to see this, and to agree that great sums gathered by some of their fellow citizens and spent for public purposes, from which the masses reap the principal benefit, are more valuable to them than if scattered among themselves in trifling amounts through the course of many years.

If we consider the results which flow from the Cooper Institute, for instance, to the best portion of the race in New York not possessed of means, and compare these with those which would have ensued for the good of the masses from an equal sum distributed by Mr. Cooper in his lifetime in the form of wages, which is the highest form of distribution, being for work done and not for charity, we can form some estimate of the possibilities for the improvement of the race which lie embedded in the present law of the accumulation of wealth. Much of this sum, if distributed in small quantities among the people, would have been wasted in the indulgence of appetite, some of it in excess, and it may be doubted whether even the part put to the best use, that of adding to the comforts of the home, would have yielded results for the race, as a race, at all comparable to those which are flowing and are to flow from the Cooper Institute from generation to generation. Let the advocate of violent or radical change ponder well this thought.

We might even go so far as to take another instance—that of Mr. Tilden's bequest of five millions of dollars for a free library in the city of New York; but in referring to this one cannot help saying involuntarily: How much better if Mr. Tilden had devoted the last years of his own life to the proper administration of this immense sum; in which case neither legal contest nor any other cause of delay could have interfered with his aims. But let us assume that Mr. Tilden's millions finally become the means of giving to this city a noble public library, where the treasures of the world contained in books will be open to all forever, without money and without price. Considering the good of that part of the race which congregates in and around Manhattan Island, would its permanent benefit have been better promoted had these millions been allowed to circulate in small sums through the hands of the masses? Even the most strenuous advocate of Communism must entertain a doubt upon this subject. Most of those who think will probably entertain no doubt whatever.

Poor and restricted are our opportunities in this life, narrow our horizon, our best work most imperfect; but rich men should be thankful for one inestimable boon. They have it in their power during their lives to busy themselves in organizing benefactions from which the masses of their fellows will derive lasting advantage, and thus dignify their own lives. The highest life is probably to be reached, not by such imitation of the life of Christ as Count Tolstoi gives us, but, while animated by Christ's spirit, by recognizing the changed conditions of this age, and adopting modes of expressing this spirit suitable to the changed conditions under which we live, still laboring for the good of our fellows, which was the essence of His life and teaching, but laboring in a different manner.

This, then, is held to be the duty of the man of wealth: To set an example of modest, unostentatious living, shunning display or extravagance; to provide moderately for the legitimate wants of those dependent upon him; and, after doing so, to consider all surplus revenues which come to him simply as trust funds, which he is called upon to administer, and strictly bound as a matter of duty to administer in the manner which, in his judgment, is best calculated to produce the most beneficial results for the community—the man of wealth thus becoming the mere trustee and agent for his poorer brethren, bringing to their service his superior wisdom, experience, and ability to administer, doing for them better than they would or could do for themselves. . . .

FROM *THIRTY YEARS OF LABOR: 1859 TO 1889*

Terence V. Powderly

"But let the free-winged angel Truth their guarded passes scale,
To teach that right is more than might, and justice more than mail."
—Whittier

"Day follows the darkest night; and when the time comes, the latest
fruits also ripen."
—Schiller

"We pray 'Thy kingdom come.' But not by prayer
Alone will it be built of breath in air.
In life thro' labor, must be brought to birth
The kingdom, as it is in heaven, on earth."
—Gerald Massey

The full extent of the good that has been done by the order of the Knights of Labor will never be known. It is not within the bounds of human possibility to detail the many acts that have gone to benefit the millions. One fact attests the value of the order: Its enemies have attacked it, belied its aims and purposes, and have opposed its advances as they never did those of any organization since the world began. Had the Knights of Labor been weak and unworthy of notice, this would not have been done. Had they not caused consternation among the enemies of human liberty, they would not have united to oppose the order. The various acts of State legislatures in the interest of the masses, the public opinion that has been created on the subject of labor, the education of philosophers, doctors, clergymen, scientists, and others on the industrial question, has not been in vain.

But the mission of the order is not yet complete. Having worked up a sentiment in favor of the measures advocated in its preamble, it still remains to put them into practical operation, and that duty rests with us to

Columbus, OH: Excelsior, 1889.

perform. The call has been sounded, the warning has been given, those who knew nothing of the danger which threatened us now realize its full importance. The great work is still ahead of us. We must look to the future for what we have been contending for in the past.

As it was in the beginning, so it is today with labor. It is still in the grasp of heartless wealth, that instrument which, if properly used and directed by advanced ideas, can be made the servant of industry. The volume of wealth is in the hands of task-masters, who use it to build up fortunes for those who already have enough for their own comfort, and too much for their country's good. Labor's ranks today contain more of keenly felt poverty than ever before when we consider the advancements which have been made in all that go to make the pathway of mankind smoother. Those who labor bend from morn till night as of old. They toil on and on as when "the sword was law"; but go among them and talk to them of the rights to which they were born, and not so many will stare in open-eyed wonder as would do so thirty years ago.

A revolution has taken place; others are to come. It need occasion no surprise if revolution after revolution shall arise in the days to come, gathering strength as they come and go, for when men have rights they will seek for them by the aid of that light which is held before their eyes. It is too close to the time when the evening gun of the nineteenth century shall sound in the ears of mankind to attempt to turn back the tide of education which is setting in.

Workingmen will find out, as certain as fate, what governments and nations owe to them; they will find out that which is of far greater importance: what they owe to themselves, and when the education shall have become more universal, he who speaks for humanity will not be called an agitator, a disturber, a breeder of discord, or a fanatic; he will be known as a saviour. For long ages men who arose here and there in the march of labor's hosts to point out to them the path which leads to that higher civilization, have been tied hand and foot by those for whom they plead; scourged as by scorpions by those whom they sought to serve, and at last were nailed to the cross of ingratitude between the two thieves—ignorance and wealth.

Poor struggling humanity! ever striving for something better, lifts its blood-shot eyes to heaven and gives forth, from the bottom of its tortured heart, the agonizing cry, "How long, O God, How long," will the idler, gambler, money-changer, and speculator gather what we sow? How long will profligacy rule in high places? How long will it be in the power of a few to hold the millions of dollars above the reach of the millions of men who need? How long will men, who have ceased to trust in the wisdom and goodness of God, be permitted to create trusts and combinations which bind to earth the aspirations, the hopes, and interests of the many of earth that the few may revel in wealth, the full sum of which they can not count during their earthly existence.

The fiat has gone forth that the toiler will not have to wait long for relief. Other eyes than his own are opened to his condition; other men are watching and other hands are assisting to build his castle of the future. His cause has been espoused by men who are with, but not of, him. Men of education, of thought, of ideas, of favorable condition in life; men who are to a great extent independent of monopoly or its influences, who have sufficient means of their own to enable them to live comfortably, are today ranged alongside of the laborer in his struggle for right.

The benefits of education and research are being conferred on the toiler by men who are the fortunate possessors of these advantages. In the eleven years of its existence under the General Assembly, men have entered the order of the Knights of Labor poor, ignorant, and friendless. They knew but little concerning their own condition, and nothing whatever about that of their neighbors. Through the instrumentality of the order these men have acquired an education; natural ability, which lay dormant within them, was stimulated, and they studied, struggled, and persevered until they passed the boundary line which separates the dependent from the independent workman. All over America are men who are either Knights of Labor, or who were such at one time, who have learned to know the wants of humanity through the teachings of the order.

The enemy of human liberty is stronger and better fortified than ever before, but it is standing face to face with a far more formidable adversary than entered the lists against it since Magna Charta was granted. Men who toil for a master dare not raise the voice in their own behalf, but other men dare to, and do, speak out from pulpit and forum, through magazine and daily press for the toiling one. The number of labor's advocates is growing greater day by day. They are becoming more aggressive, add their weight and influence to the education now winding its way among the hills and valleys of the labor world, and we have a mighty leviathan at work, against whose effort monopoly, trust, and combine will struggle in vain.

It is feared by some that before this labor agitation is at an end we will witness a revolution, not a peaceful one, doing its patient work among the masses, but a terrible, life-destroying revolution, which will cause cities and towns to weep tears of blood. There need be no fear of that if justice, immutable justice, is again seated on the bench now usurped by corporate power. What just man need fear a revolution? How much worse can a nation be with a bomb in every man's hand than to have every man's hand bound in chains? Who would not prefer a nation of men who would rather fight than be slaves, to a nation of creatures who would rather be slaves than fight?

Again, if every hope is taken from the laborer, if he is to continue on the down track until his home is a hovel, his hearthstone a grave, and his country a prison, what great debt will he owe to the nation that will cause him to keep the peace under such circumstances? Why should he care for the feelings of others when no one cares for him? Of what avail to tell him to respect the law when the law has permitted his fellow man to rob him of everything this earth holds dear? Of what avail to preach patience to the laborer while the ear-drum is receiving the sound of wailing distress from those whom God sent to gather within the circle of his protecting care? Of what avail to longer cry, "servants, obey your masters," when it is written in the full light of heaven's day that many of the masters are devils incarnate, whose only God is gold, and whose reward for labor is hell upon earth? The day must come when the Word of God, in all that that Word implies, must be preached among men again. The sound of the hammer which drove the nails through the quivering flesh of the God of the lowly, nineteen centuries ago, has not been heard in many a church for ages. The voice of agony has been drowned in the clink of the dollar until Murray Hill becomes the shrine before which many worship instead of Mount Calvary.

If the Sermon on the Mount were preached in many a church today, and the identity of the divine author concealed, fashionable pews would be emptied, the minister of God would be censured and warned never again to repeat the ravings of an utopiast. In the church where the minister is the only friend to the poor it shows that he has preached in vain not to have made more converts to the doctrine of Christ crucified.

But the world is changing. It is growing better, for men are searching for the truth. They have listened to the voice which arose above the din during the past few years in its plea for justice. When the Knights of Labor began their mission of education, all who advocated reform in land laws, in the regulation of transportation, in the issue of currency, were denounced as being insane or enemies to society. When the Knights of Labor began to direct the attention of the masses to the tendency of legislation, the various States were enacting tramp laws, conspiracy laws, and restrictive measures of all kinds.

Only the poor and lowly spoke for the lowly and the poor. Those who began the agitation for the practical operation of the principles of Knighthood, were sneeringly told that they "were seeking to bring the millennium," or that "mankind is not good enough to maintain such a state of society as would then exist." Others charged the advocates of Knighthood with being "visionaries and lunatics." No Knight of Labor ever advised his neighbor to "sell what thou hast and give to the poor," yet those who opposed the doctrines of Knighthood affected to be believers in and followers of the meek and lowly Jesus who gave that advice.

If what we are told of heaven is true, it is an abode of bliss; where love reigns supreme; where poverty, sin, death, and crime are unknown; where all things are enjoyed in common by all the inhabitants thereof.

Surely no Knight of Labor has ever presumed to ask that this earth should become better than such a heavenly place, and yet those who oppose us, who tell us that we are wrong, that we are asking for too much, kneel down to say to God: "Thy kingdom come; thy will be done on earth as it is in heaven." They cannot be right in both instances; they must be insincere in one or the other, and as their visible effort is directed against the fulfillment of the prayer which habit, not conviction, forces from their lips, we must believe that away down in their hearts they feel that Christ was wrong, or that he made an exception of them when he preached the Sermon on the Mount.

"Visionaries and lunatics" have striven for the happiness of humankind since the world began; their reward has been the cross and stake, but their words have lived in letters of everlasting light, to illumine the pathway of others who could not believe that prayers, teachings, sermons and precepts, should all advise a rule of action which directed men to heaven; while the actions of those who exercised unlimited power through the possession of wealth, tended to drive men to a hell of poverty and crime.

If prayers mean anything, those who say them should believe what they whisper when alone by the bedside or in the solitude of the closet. If prayers are right their teachings should be lived up to. No Knight of Labor asks for more than that. But, notwithstanding the opposition shown in the beginning, the work of Knighthood went on; the education in the principles of right and justice became general, and today we have "Single tax" men, "Nationalists," social reformers of every kind, advocating the measures which were first brought to the attention of the whole people by the Knights of Labor.

Had it not been for the work done by the order, it is more than likely that the pressure would have become so great, the turning of the screw of oppression so rapid, that those who would not listen to the voice of the poor would ere this have heard the roar which would have drowned the cry for mercy of him who had none for the laborer. It is far better to heed the voice of warning, while men can be reasoned with, than to wait until the workman becomes the brute, which the systems now crumbling to earth would have made of him. The historian of the future will record that the revolution inaugurated by the Knights of Labor, and carried forward by the force of thought and ideas, won more for the cause of human liberty than the revolutions which spilled the blood of humanity's advocates through all the centuries of time.

FROM *SEVENTY YEARS OF LIFE AND LABOR*
An Autobiography

Samuel Gompers

My Economic Philosophy

The first economic theory that came under my eyes was not calculated to make me think highly of economists. My mind intuitively rejected the iron law of wages, the immutable law of supply and demand, and similar so-called "natural laws." As a matter of fact, the laws had no connection with nature or economic forces, nor were they laws but merely theories which sought to justify existing practices. Everywhere those directing industries were seeking to bring about a control that served their purposes. Those who did not participate in determination of policies were treated as industrial spoils. As the control built up by the holders of capital rested upon strategic economic advantage, I saw no reason why it was not just as practical for employees to mobilize and control their economic power as a counter-move. The force of such economic organization would interpose a protecting barrier against arbitrary employers who failed to understand that those who supplied human labor for industries were human beings, and thus make possible the development of constructive methods. My unfailing support of voluntary principles reflects my aversion to any theory of economic fatalism.

My span of life includes a series of industrial periods marked by panics, business depression, and widespread unemployment followed by a period of recuperation leading gradually to a return of "prosperity," better wages, and general employment. The period of depression was often called a period of so-called overproduction, which was really a period of underconsumption for the people I knew, a period of hard times. In a country as big and as fertile as ours, with so many willing workers seeking the chance to give service, the periods of unemployment accompanying depression in the business cycle have seemed to me an unnecessary blot upon American institutions.

New York: Dutton, 1925.

During the fall and winter of 1893, there was widespread unemployment such as I had never seen before. When the session of the New York Legislature began the winter of 1893, I watched its deliberations carefully. Thomas C. Platt, president of the United States Express Company, was then a member of the Senate and controlled the Republican state party machine. When adjournment was approaching, there was no evidence of any constructive thought upon the unemployment problem. Even the appropriation bills carrying funds for public works were unpassed. Now I had no love for Platt and knew he had none for labor—but regardless of this, if Platt could do anything for the unemployed I was willing to use him as an instrumentality. I wrote him, asking that he consider the advisability of enacting legislation to appropriate money for public work, for I reminded him it would be bad policy to add to unemployment by failure to act upon the measure.

As I considered these facts, they seemed to me to indicate the necessity for a sustained policy of wage increases in order that consumption levels should be maintained commensurate with the increases in production levels, and that credit control should be based upon production needs rather than upon speculative gain.

Wage earners had to bear the consequences of the mismanagement and wrong-doings of others. In 1903 I noted indications of a recurring period of depression and in my report to the Boston Convention declared it the height of economic unwisdom to curtail the consuming power of the masses, because no industry or country could become great if founded upon poverty. Based upon my conception that wage rates can be used as a stabilizing force, I recommended that the working people should resist any attempt to reduce their wages or increase their hours of work.

When the business crisis came in 1907, I was prepared to make good use of my experiences. One of the functions of the annual meetings of the National Civic Federation is a dinner which is attended by important employers, big financiers, trade unionists, and many people well known nationally. The dinner furnished an extraordinarily advantageous stage from which to make a declaration for which I wanted national consideration. There were fully four hundred there talking conventionalities, men and women in evening clothes, the women gorgeous in gleaming jewels. Never have I felt more peculiarly alone. I was conscious that I was the spokesman of the "working class," and I didn't care how I startled or shocked the millionaires if I protected my fellows. I was ruthless in what I intended to do. The fire of the revolutionary was burning through me as I rose to make labor's reply to the careful, smug suggestions of retrenchment and wage reductions as the way out of the industrial stagnation. I fairly flung defiance at the buccaneers of industry as I declared, "Labor will not submit to any wage reductions."

The result of the 1907 experience convinced me that panics and business depression can be controlled, perhaps avoided, if we know contributing causes. I felt there must be certain fundamental principles of industrial order to which we could cling at such times. But I had to wait many years before I saw a comprehensive effort launched to study periods of depression and to determine principles of intelligent control. That came with the World War aftermath. Again labor opposed wage reductions and was fairly successful in holding normal increases. By this time management had begun to appreciate that maintaining wage levels means maintaining a stable purchasing demand and hence is a stabilizing force. Wage reductions by decreasing demand adds impetus to the trend toward business depression. On the other hand, gradual wage increases tend to absorb increases in production. It is my opinion based upon six decades of experience that the future will bring progressively high wage levels with gradual price decreases. When I contrast industrial conditions of the ten years following the War between the States and the conditions now, I am convinced that tendencies can be controlled in accord with principles developed through experience and study. As our knowledge widens, we shall be able to establish a stable industrial order in which organizations of wage earners will be an integral part.

My experience has extended over periods in economic development in which the whole nature and organization of industry have been transformed. Within my span of life have come inventions that have been revolutionizing in effect. Electricity both for lighting and power, the telephone, the wireless, the submarine cable, the radio, the transcontinental railroad, aeroplane, electric street cars, internal combustion engine, cold storage, are a few of the changes that I have seen come. Methods of work, methods and agencies of communication, and facilities for travel have brought society so close together that merging of economic interests and activities has been an inevitable result. The consolidation came so gradually that many did not see the trend of development until some of the new trusts were exercising their newly found and rapacious powers. American spirit rebelled against it as a new form of tyranny, and the trust problem became a foremost issue in public discussion. The reformers in state Legislatures and Congress began to discuss legislation to protect the people. Most of the politicians seemed to think that by making a law they could prohibit trusts.

From the first I mistrusted the proposal to take the trust problem into the political field. It seemed to me we could not safely trust policies of repression, and furthermore, the economic field was competent to deal with policies of regulation. Regardless of antitrust agitation, consolidation remained the trend. Quite contrary to the prevailing economic dogma that free competition was the necessary basis to industrial progress, the economies and efficiency of consolidation presaged tremendous strides.

When both in transportation and industrial organization there came pooling or merging of interests, the problem of financing the combines made the older financial game seem like child's play. Only central banks were competent to finance the large-scale undertakings, so the control of industry gravitated into the hands of Wall Street. The development seemed to me natural. The trust was a phase of the new industrial organization where groups replaced individual effort. Our problem was not to try to prevent a normal development but to find the principles and technique for utilizing group action and group production in furtherance of general welfare. It is a problem to whose solution the groups concerned should jointly contribute. The organization of management, finance, and producing workmen is the way to develop discipline and information within these groups. The next step, to my mind, is cooperation of all the groups with the pooling of information to determine control of the industry. The industry would thus become self-regulated and disciplined while checks interposed by organized consumers would deter nonsocial tendencies. As my contribution to this development, I have promoted the organization of workers and opposed attempts of politicians to bungle the economic development.

Organization was [the] response to economic forces, and therefore I did not believe that arbitrary limitations especially by law could prevail against it. When the Sherman Anti-Trust Law was proposed, I did not believe it would be effective in curbing trusts, but fearing that attempts would be made to use the law against collective action by wage earners, I went to several members of Congress and told them my fears. The bill originally introduced by Senator Sherman considered in the debates of 1890 was an antimonopoly bill intended to restore full and free competition. Senator Sherman did not share [the] apprehension, but in order to avoid confusion accepted a proposal made by Senator [James Z.] George which specifically excluded arrangements, agreements, and combinations between laborers made with a view of lessening the number of hours or increasing their wages. Similar exemptions were provided for persons engaged in horticultural or agricultural pursuits who were seeking to increase the prices of agricultural or horticultural products. The Sherman Anti-Monopoly proposal with the exemption proviso was referred back to the Committee on the Judiciary with instructions to report within twenty days. When the bill was reported at the end of that time, it had been changed from an antimonopoly to an anticombination bill. In view of this change, the Senators did not believe it necessary to include the labor exemption proviso. Events soon demonstrated that the law was to be applied to labor unions and that it was not effective in curbing trusts.

In addition to proscription of trusts, our government began to develop a system of state regulation of privately owned and operated enterprises— such as railways. To this effort I gave my hearty support and cooperation, but I have resisted unswervingly all proposals to inaugurate government ownership and operation for two reasons: first, because I believe our main dependence lay in individual initiative; and secondly, because I believe the economic field is essentially different from the political and the legal.

I reached this conclusion gradually after discarding proposals to which I temporarily subscribed. Some which I have discarded have not infrequently been suggested again by "progressives" who dub me "conservative" or even reactionary. My method of evolving my philosophy has been intuitive.

The principles of political freedom worked out in our Republic have been based upon political equality. If the rights of any individual are infringed, he has the right of counsel. But where political conditions touch a man's daily life once, economic conditions will affect it fifty times. To insure economic justice, therefore, I hold that the principle of the right of counsel maintains. By economic counsel, I mean an agent expert upon the matters in question selected with the approval of the individual. Thus the economic organization of the workers is basic. This economic organization, in addition to its defensive service, is free to develop constructive functions as soon as it is accepted by the management and its spokesmen admitted to conferences considering various problems in which their work is concerned. This procedure provides a way to utilize the experience and the information of workmen, which in turn can be collected and systematized only through organization. Ultimately perhaps, those things which concern all industry may be determined by a national economic body, truly representative, competent to make decisions and to secure compliance, or political regulation must develop a new technique and more competent personnel.

The methods and the agencies for progress in the economic world must be evolved out of economic experience and life. It is a serious mistake to confuse the two fields or to carry the problems of one into the other. Trade unions or voluntary associations of wage earners constitute one of the essential agencies for establishing procedure of control. The development of large-scale production, the increasing authority of science in determining processes, and the more recent investigations of management for the purpose of making it truly scientific, together with the marked tendency toward trade associations, are to me a most gratifying exemplification of my thought that discernment of the essential difference between the economic and the political clarifies the problem of progress.

Several times the plain question has been put to me by members of the Senate Committee on Judiciary: "Mr. Gompers, what can we do to allay the causes of strikes that bring discomfort and financial suffering to all alike?" I have had to answer, "Nothing." My answer has been interpreted as advocating a policy of drift. Quite the contrary to my real thought. Foremost in my mind is to tell the politicians to keep their hands off and thus to preserve voluntary institutions and opportunity for individual and group initiative and leave the way open to deal with problems as the experience and facts of industry shall indicate. I have, with equal emphasis, opposed submitting determination of industrial policies to courts. But it is difficult for lawyers to understand that the most important human justice comes through other agencies than the political.

Though frequently impatient with existing wrongs, I am not impatient with what sometimes seems the slow progress of the labor movement. My patience has rested upon realization of facts, not upon lack of idealism or sentiment. I realized that since the labor movement is a living, sentient thing, growth comes from life within. It can be aided, directed, but not forced. Just as a plant may be cultivated and pruned, cared for in every way, still it cannot be compelled to grow or flower, so the labor movement cannot be handled or computed as material quantities. I have worked a lifetime for the labor movement, and I feel that I know it as few others do. Out of that knowledge is born faith in its destiny and its high service.

FROM *NATURE AND MAN IN AMERICA*

Nathaniel Southgate Shaler

. . . Although the history of British settlements in torrid regions shows that the population of northern Europe is not suited to equatorial conditions, there is nothing in the experience of the race which would lead us to suppose that the measure of change undergone in passing from the parent country to the portion of the United States north of the region about the Mexican Gulf should produce any marked alteration in the racial qualities. It is a difficult matter to compare the condition of two bodies of people on opposite sides of the sea. We cannot trust to the impressions of travel, for no man can retain sufficiently accurate memories for such judgments. Here and there, however, we find certain data which serve as indices, and

New York: Scribner's, 1891.

perhaps afford a sufficient basis for an opinion on this point. The most important of these facts are those pertaining to longevity, as determined by the experience of life-insurance companies, those obtained by the measurements of soldiers and sailors, and the endurance which such men exhibit in their callings. The results of surgical operations serve also to indicate the vitality of the patient; and the success attained in games of a sort which demand a higher measure of mental and bodily vigor shows something concerning the essential qualities of the men. It would be desirable to add to this list the measurement derived from the intellectual accomplishment of the two countries, the success in various walks of a learned and imaginative work. Unfortunately, this last measurement cannot be justly applied, for the reason that intellectual accomplishment depends not so much on native ability as on peculiar circumstances of scholarly environment, on education, and on the competence of the social conditions to stimulate the mind to creative activities. Shakspeares or Bacons possibly may remain with their genius unknown even to themselves, unless there is the stimulating air to quicken the native spark into a flame.

Taking the conditions which I have mentioned in the order in which they are presented, we note in the first place the conviction on the part of our actuaries—the computers who determine the measure of insurance risk on human life—that the longevity of people in America is at least as great as in Europe; and this despite the fact that men's lives in this country are more seriously taxed than in the Old World. We are supposed to be dying of overwork; but the fact is that, witnessed by the duration of life in the case of men who have appeared on the records of insurance companies, there is no indication that the term allowed to man is growing less in this country than it is across the seas. On the contrary, the evidence seems to point to the conclusion that the American man lives longer than those of the same race in the Old World. . . .

. . . The foregoing considerations, as well as many other points which cannot be traced in this brief study concerning the effects of climatal and social conditions on the American man, have satisfied me—as I think they will satisfy any other unprejudiced inquirer—that our race is safe upon this continent; that we need to have no apprehensions concerning the effect of the existing conditions upon its development.

We may safely presume that the climate and other features of our continent, with perhaps the exception of the district about the Gulf of Mexico and the Arctic country, are on the whole as well fitted for the uses of northern Europeans as any part of the mother-country. We may reasonably conclude that it suits the whole Teutonic branch of the Aryan race.

As to the Latin peoples, the case is not so clear. The Canadian French are doubtless in the main descended from the people of northern France. It is likely that a large part of their blood is derived from the Northmen. There can be no question that, with certain limitations, this population has been thoroughly successful on American soil. The fact that they speak a foreign language and have been deprived of education, may account for their general failure to advance in the intellectual field. They are, however, people of vigorous minds and enduring bodies. They have developed a fecundity now unparalleled in France. They take naturally to laborious occupations, which is a proof of physical vigor. We may therefore consider the northern Frenchman as well fitted to the conditions of northern America. The Latin peoples about the Gulf of Mexico have not been equally successful. The upper class has maintained something of its pristine quality, but the peasant has not taken hold on the soil in a successful way. How much of this failure of the Spanish and French to attain a high development in the region about the Gulf of Mexico and the Caribbean is due to climate, and how much to the institution of slavery, or to their intermixture with the indigenous people, it is impossible to say.

There remains one important inquiry as to the effect of geographic conditions on the development of races from beyond the sea on the surface within the limits of North America—a question of the utmost importance to our political and social future. We have in this country a very large African population. Within the limits of the United States, the number of people of this blood probably exceeds that of any other stock, save that from the British Isles. As we have previously remarked, this race on the whole appears to have remained substantially unchanged by the conditions of the new field. Intellectual contact with the white has doubtless led to a certain development in the general status of the African, but except so far as his blood has been mingled with that of Aryan or Indian people, the bodily form, and in general the moral and mental characteristics, have remained substantially what they were on the parent continent of this people. There are two questions concerning this race which are of the utmost importance to the future of our nation—indeed, to that of all our own people in North America. The first concerns the natural fecundity of the population, their rate of increase from decade to decade;

and the second, the limitations which climate may put upon the extension of the folk.

The rate of increase of the negro has not yet been ascertained. During the conditions of slavery a satisfactory census was impossible. The slaves were subject to taxation, and the owners had a sinister interest in reducing the numbers which were given to the accounting officers. The census of 1870, the first taken after the overthrow of slavery, partly intentionally or by neglect, served to underestimate the total number of negroes. The next accounting, that of 1880, was careful, and doubtless gave us the first accurate knowledge as to the ratio of this element of our population to those of European blood. It will not be until we obtain returns of the census which has just been taken, that we shall know whether the negro is more or less prolific than the white. In case it should appear that in the extreme Southern States the negro increases in a greater ratio than the whites, the regions in which this increase is marked have a doubtful future before them; for unless the black population can be quickly lifted to a higher intellectual and moral plane than now characterizes it, those parts of the South will be apt to relapse into barbarism. The advance of the negro to a satisfactory grade in development still depends upon his remaining in close contact with the superior race. If he increases in numbers more rapidly than the whites, he is sure to create massive communities of his own stock, in which there can be no certainty as to the maintenance of our race motives.

As to the distribution of the African population in this country, though the evidence is not clear, it seems that the negro is not likely, in the immediate future at least, to extend for any considerable distance beyond the limits in which his race at present is fixed. There is now no distinct movement of the blacks toward the North. The scanty African population in the old non-slave-holding States has mainly accumulated in the cities, and would probably die out were it not for the occasional accessions it receives from the South. Unless the rate of increase of the negroes should be so great as to crowd them from the extreme Southern States, we may be pretty sure that this population will remain in good part limited to a small portion of our country—to a region which though not unfitted for the occupation of our race, is the most undesirable part of the country for its development.

Our review of the physiographic conditions which environ our race on this continent makes it tolerably plain that North America is well suited for the development of northern Europeans. We may dismiss the fear that our race is to deteriorate in this country. We may further put aside the notion that we are to be a massive, unvaried people, destitute of those differences which by their reaction bring about the advance of man. It is true that the continent is not divided into the separate areas which have constituted the cradle-lands of the Old World; but it is evident that the wide diversities in occupation will institute and maintain variations in the character of the people probably in time to be as great as those which in the more natural state of man depended on purely geographic conditions. At present, while the open structure of our social and economic life permits a rapid change in the occupations of men, the effect of industries dependent on physiographic conditions is not much felt; but with the increase and consolidation of our population, we may be sure that vocations will become more hereditary. Men will follow the occupations of the plough, the mine, or the mill from generation to generation, and so the communities will receive the individualized stamp which comes only through ancestral habit.

In the beginning mankind was dependent for culture and diffusion mainly upon geographic conditions. Each tribe was environed by rigid customs which fended off its neighbors. The movements were necessarily massive, for they were to result in displacements of preexisting peoples. Therefore the first stages of man's development resemble, as regards the conditions of increase and diffusion, those of his lower kindred in the ranks of life; the progress of intellectual capacity has given to certain races a large measure of control over their circumstances. Still, even in our own centuries, the implantation of our race in new lands already possessed by men has proved a task of exceeding difficulty. The would-be colonists of the sixteenth and seventeenth centuries, on the eastern coast of America, found something of the difficulty in gaining their foothold which stray plants or animals from one flora or fauna find when they are cast within a foreign field. Even in the present state of their development the most advanced races of men are limited by the climate, and can only dwell where the larger nature permits.

For all that we can foresee of the future, this dependence of man upon the conditions of his environment is of an insuperable nature. The good he wins he secures by obedience to the commands of his mother-earth. Looking back over the history of life upon the earth's surface, the physiographer is forced to the conclusion that its highest estate embodied in the moral and intellectual qualities of man has been, in the main, secured by the geographic variations which have slowly developed through the geological ages. Thus our continents and seas cannot be considered as physical accidents, in which and on which organic beings have found an ever-perilous resting-place, but as great engines operating in a determined way to secure the advance of life.

"THE RESTRICTION OF IMMIGRATION"

Henry Cabot Lodge

Mr. President: This bill is intended to amend the existing law so as to restrict still further immigration to the United States. Paupers, diseased persons, convicts, and contract laborers are now excluded. By this bill it is proposed to make a new class of excluded immigrants, and add to those which have just been named the totally ignorant. The bill is of the simplest kind. The first section excludes from the country all immigrants who cannot read and write either their own or some other language. The second section merely provides a simple test for determining whether the immigrant can read or write, and is added to the bill so as to define the duties of the immigrant inspectors, and to assure to all immigrants alike perfect justice and a fair test of their knowledge. . . .

During the present century, down to 1875, there have been three large migrations to this country in addition to the always steady stream from Great Britain; one came from Ireland about the middle of the century, and somewhat later one from Germany and one from Scandinavia, in which is included Sweden, Denmark, and Norway. The Irish, although of a different race stock originally, have been closely associated with the English-speaking people for nearly a thousand years. They speak the same language, and during that long period the two races have lived side by side, and to some extent intermarried. The Germans and Scandinavians are again people of the same race stock as the English who founded and built up the colonies. During this century, down to 1875, then, as in the two which preceded it, there had been scarcely any immigration to this country except from kindred or allied races, and no other which was sufficiently numerous to have produced any effect on the national characteristics, or to be taken into account here. Since 1875, however, there has been a great change. While the people who for two hundred and fifty years have been migrating to America have continued to furnish large numbers of immigrants to the United States, other races of totally different race origin, with whom the English-speaking people have never hitherto been assimilated or brought in contact, have suddenly begun to immigrate to the United States in large numbers. Russians, Hungarians, Poles, Bohemians, Italians, Greeks, and even Asiatics, whose immigration to America was almost unknown twenty years ago, have during the last twenty years poured

---

Speech in the U.S. Senate, 16 March 1896.

in in steadily increasing numbers, until now they nearly equal the immigration of those races kindred in blood or speech, or both, by whom the United States has hitherto been built up and the American people formed.

This momentous fact is the one which confronts us today, and if continued, it carries with it future consequences far deeper than any other event of our times. It involves, in a word, nothing less than the possibility of a great and perilous change in the very fabric of our race. . . .

That the peril is not imaginary or the offspring of race prejudice, I will prove by another disinterested witness, also a Frenchman. M. Paul Bourget, the distinguished novelist, visited this country a few years ago, and wrote a book containing his impressions of what he saw. He was not content, as many travelers are, to say that our cabs were high-priced, the streets of New York noisy, the cars hot, and then feel that he had disposed of the United States and the people thereof for time and for eternity. M. Bourget saw here a great country and a great people; in other words, a great fact in modern times. Our ways were not his ways, nor our thoughts his thoughts, and he probably liked his own country and his own ways much better; but he nonetheless studied us carefully and sympathetically. What most interested him was to see whether the socialistic movements, which now occupy the alarmed attention of Europe, were equally threatening here. His conclusion, which I will state in a few words, is of profound interest. He expected to find signs of a coming war of classes, and he went home believing that if any danger threatened the United States it was not from a war of classes, but a war of races.

Mr. President, more precious even than forms of government are the mental and moral qualities which make what we call our race. While those stand unimpaired all is safe. When those decline all is imperiled. They are exposed to but a single danger, and that is by changing the quality of our race and citizenship through the wholesale infusion of races whose traditions and inheritances, whose thoughts and whose beliefs are wholly alien to ours, and with whom we have never assimilated or even been associated in the past. The danger has begun. It is small as yet, comparatively speaking, but it is large enough to warn us to act while there is yet time and while it can be done easily and efficiently. There lies the peril at the portals of our land; there is pressing the tide of unrestricted immigration. The time has certainly come, if not to stop, at least to check, to sift, and to restrict those immigrants. In careless strength, with generous hand, we have kept our gates wide open to all the world. If we do not close them, we should at least place sentinels beside them to challenge those who would pass through. The gates which admit men to the United States and to citizenship in the great republic should no longer be left unguarded.

O Liberty, white Goddess! is it well
To leave the gates unguarded? On thy breast
Fold Sorrow's children, soothe the hurts of fate,
Lift the down-trodden, but with hand of steel
5   Stay those who to thy sacred portals come
To waste the gifts of freedom. Have a care
Lest from thy brow the clustered stars be torn
And trampled in the dust. For so of old
The thronging Goth and Vandal trampled Rome,
10 And where the temples of the Caesars stood
The lean wolf unmolested made her lair.*

"STRIVINGS OF THE NEGRO PEOPLE"

W. E. B. Du Bois

Between me and the other world there is ever an unasked question: unasked by some through feelings of delicacy; by others through the difficulty of rightly framing it. All, nevertheless, flutter 'round it. They approach me in a half-hesitant sort of way, eye me curiously or compassionately, and then, instead of saying directly, How does it feel to be a problem? they say, I know an excellent colored man in my town; or, I fought at Mechanicsville; or, Do not these Southern outrages make your blood boil? At these I smile, or am interested, or reduce the boiling to a simmer, as the occasion may require. To the real question, How does it feel to be a problem? I answer seldom a word.

And yet, being a problem is a strange experience—peculiar even for one who has never been anything else, save perhaps in babyhood and in Europe. It is in the early days of rollicking boyhood that the revelation first bursts upon one, all in a day, as it were. I remember well when the shadow swept across me. I was a little thing, away up in the hills of New England, where the dark Housatonic winds between Hoosac and Taghanic to the sea. In a wee wooden schoolhouse, something put it into the boys' and girls' heads to buy gorgeous visiting-cards—ten cents a package—and exchange. The exchange was merry, till one girl, a tall newcomer, refused my card—refused it peremptorily, with a glance. Then it dawned upon me

---

*Aldrich, *Unguarded Gates*. [Lodge's note.]
Atlantic Monthly, August 1897.

with a certain suddenness that I was different from the others; or like, may-hap, in heart and life and longing, but shut out from their world by a vast veil. I had thereafter no desire to tear down that veil, to creep through; I held all beyond it in common contempt, and lived above it in a region of blue sky and great wandering shadows. That sky was bluest when I could beat my mates at examination time, or beat them at a foot-race, or even beat their stringy heads. Alas, with the years all this fine contempt began to fade; for the world I longed for, and all its dazzling opportunities, were theirs, not mine. But they should not keep these prizes, I said; some, all, I would wrest from them. Just how I would do it I could never decide: by reading law, by healing the sick, by telling the wonderful tales that swam in my head—some way. With other black boys the strife was not so fiercely sunny: their youth shrunk into tasteless sycophancy, or into silent hatred of the pale world about them and mocking distrust of everything white; or wasted itself in a bitter cry. Why did God make me an outcast and a stranger in mine own house? The "shades of the prison-house" closed 'round about us all: walls straight and stubborn to the whitest, but relentlessly narrow, tall, and unscalable to sons of night who must plod darkly on in resignation, or beat unavailing palms against the stone, or steadily, half hopelessly watch the streak of blue above.

After the Egyptian and Indian, the Greek and Roman, the Teuton and Mongolian, the Negro is a sort of seventh son, born with a veil, and gifted with second sight in this American world—a world which yields him no self-consciousness, but only lets him see himself through the revelation of the other world. It is a peculiar sensation, this double consciousness, this sense of always looking at one's self through the eyes of others, of mea-suring one's soul by the tape of a world that looks on in amused contempt and pity. One ever feels his two-ness—an American, a Negro; two souls, two thoughts, two unreconciled strivings; two warring ideals in one dark body, whose dogged strength alone keeps it from being torn asunder. The history of the American Negro is the history of this strife—this longing to attain self-conscious manhood, to merge his double self into a better and truer self. In this merging he wishes neither of the older selves to be lost. He does not wish to Africanize America, for America has too much to teach the world and Africa; he does not wish to bleach his Negro blood in a flood of white Americanism, for he believes—foolishly, perhaps, but fer-vently—that Negro blood has yet a message for the world. He simply wishes to make it possible for a man to be both a Negro and an American without being cursed and spit upon by his fellows, without losing the op-portunity of self-development.

This is the end of his striving: to be a co-worker in the kingdom of culture, to escape both death and isolation, and to husband and use his best powers. These powers, of body and of mind, have in the past been so wasted and dispersed as to lose all effectiveness, and to seem like absence of all power, like weakness. The double-aimed struggle of the black artisan, on the one hand to escape white contempt for a nation of mere hewers of wood and drawers of water, and on the other hand to plough and nail and dig for a poverty-stricken horde, could only result in making him a poor craftsman, for he had but half a heart in either cause. By the poverty and ignorance of his people the Negro lawyer or doctor was pushed toward quackery and demagogism, and by the criticism of the other world toward an elaborate preparation that overfitted him for his lowly tasks. The would-be black savant was confronted by the paradox that the knowledge his people needed was a twice-told tale to his white neighbors, while the knowledge which would teach the white world was Greek to his own flesh and blood. The innate love of harmony and beauty that set the ruder souls of his people a-dancing, a-singing, and a-laughing raised but confusion and doubt in the soul of the black artist; for the beauty revealed to him was the soul-beauty of a race which his larger audience despised, and he could not articulate the message of another people.

This waste of double aims, this seeking to satisfy two unreconciled ideals, has wrought sad havoc with the courage and faith and deeds of eight thousand thousand people, has sent them often wooing false gods and invoking false means of salvation, and has even at times seemed destined to make them ashamed of themselves. In the days of bondage they thought to see in one divine event the end of all doubt and disappointment; eighteenth-century Rousseauism never worshiped freedom with half the unquestioning faith that the American Negro did for two centuries. To him slavery was, indeed, the sum of all villainies, the cause of all sorrow, the root of all prejudice; emancipation was the key to a promised land of sweeter beauty than ever stretched before the eyes of wearied Israelites. In his songs and exhortations swelled one refrain, liberty; in his tears and curses the god he implored had freedom in his right hand. At last it came— suddenly, fearfully, like a dream. With one wild carnival of blood and passion came the message in his own plaintive cadences:

> Shout, O children!
> Shout, you're free!
> The Lord has bought your liberty!

Years have passed away, ten, twenty, thirty. Thirty years of national life, thirty years of renewal and development, and yet the swarthy ghost of Banquo sits in its old place at the national feast. In vain does the nation cry to its vastest problem:

Take any shape but that, and my firm nerves
Shall never tremble!

The freedman has not yet found in freedom his promised land. Whatever of lesser good may have come in these years of change, the shadow of a deep disappointment rests upon the Negro people—a disappointment all the more bitter because the unattained ideal was unbounded save by the simple ignorance of a lowly folk.

The first decade was merely a prolongation of the vain search for freedom, the boom that seemed ever barely to elude their grasp—like a tantalizing will-o'-the-wisp, maddening and misleading the headless host. The holocaust of war, the terrors of the Ku Klux Klan, the lies of carpet-baggers, the disorganization of industry, and the contradictory advice of friends and foes left the bewildered serf with no new watchword beyond the old cry for freedom. As the decade closed, however, he began to grasp a new idea. The ideal of liberty demanded for its attainment powerful means, and these the Fifteenth Amendment gave him. The ballot, which before he had looked upon as a visible sign of freedom, he now regarded as the chief means of gaining and perfecting the liberty with which war had partially endowed him. And why not? Had not votes made war and emancipated millions? Had not votes enfranchised the freedmen? Was anything impossible to a power that had done all this? A million black men started with renewed zeal to vote themselves into the kingdom. The decade fled away— a decade containing, to the freedman's mind, nothing but suppressed votes, stuffed ballot-boxes, and election outrages that nullified his vaunted right of suffrage. And yet that decade from 1875 to 1885 held another powerful movement, the rise of another ideal to guide the unguided, another pillar of fire by night after a clouded day. It was the ideal of "book-learning"; the curiosity, born of compulsory ignorance, to know and test the power of the cabalistic letters of the white man, the longing to know. Mission and night schools began in the smoke of battle, ran the gauntlet of reconstruction, and at last developed into permanent foundations. Here at last seemed to have been discovered the mountain path to Canaan; longer than the highway of emancipation and law, steep and rugged, but straight, leading to heights high enough to overlook life.

Up the new path the advance guard toiled, slowly, heavily, doggedly; only those who have watched and guided the faltering feet, the misty minds, the dull understandings of the dark pupils of these schools know how faithfully, how piteously, this people strove to learn. It was weary work. The cold statistician wrote down the inches of progress here and there, noted also where here and there a foot had slipped or someone had fallen. To the tired climbers, the horizon was ever dark, the mists were often cold, the Canaan was always dim and far away. If, however, the vistas disclosed as yet no goal, no resting place, little but flattery and criticism, the journey at least gave leisure for reflection and self-examination; it changed the child of emancipation to the youth with dawning self-consciousness, self-realization, self-respect. In those sombre forests of his striving his own soul rose before him, and he saw himself—darkly as through a veil; and yet he saw in himself some faint revelation of his power, of his mission. He began to have a dim feeling that, to attain his place in the world, he must be himself, and not another. For the first time he sought to analyze the burden he bore upon his back, that dead-weight of social degradation partially masked behind a half-named Negro problem. He felt his poverty; without a cent, without a home, without land, tools, or savings, he had entered into competition with rich, landed, skilled neighbors. To be a poor man is hard, but to be a poor race in a land of dollars is the very bottom of hardships. He felt the weight of his ignorance—not simply of letters, but of life, of business, of the humanities; the accumulated sloth and shirking and awkwardness of decades and centuries shackled his hands and feet. Nor was his burden all poverty and ignorance. The red stain of bastardy, which two centuries of systematic legal defilement of Negro women had stamped upon his race, meant not only the loss of ancient African chastity, but also the hereditary weight of a mass of filth from white whoremongers and adulterers, threatening almost the obliteration of the Negro home.

A people thus handicapped ought not to be asked to race with the world, but rather allowed to give all its time and thought to its own social problems. But alas! while sociologists gleefully count his bastards and his prostitutes, the very soul of the toiling, sweating black man is darkened by the shadow of a vast despair. Men call the shadow prejudice, and learnedly explain it as the natural defense of culture against barbarism, learning against ignorance, purity against crime, the "higher" against the "lower" races. To which the Negro cries Amen! and swears that to so much of this strange prejudice as is founded on just homage to civilization, culture, righteousness, and progress he humbly bows and meekly does obeisance. But before that nameless prejudice that leaps beyond all this he stands helpless, dismayed, and well-nigh speechless; before that personal disrespect and mockery, the ridicule and systematic humiliation, the distortion of fact and wanton license of fancy, the cynical ignoring of the better and boisterous welcoming of the worse, the all-pervading desire to inculcate disdain for everything black, from Toussaint to the devil—before this there rises a sickening despair that would disarm and discourage any nation save that black host to whom "discouragement" is an unwritten word.

They still press on, they still nurse the dogged hope—not a hope of nauseating patronage, not a hope of reception into charmed social circles of stock-jobbers, pork-packers, and earl-hunters, but the hope of a higher synthesis of civilization and humanity, a true progress, with which the chorus

> Peace, good will to men,
> May make one music as before,
> But vaster.

Thus the second decade of the American Negro's freedom was a period of conflict, of inspiration and doubt, of faith and vain questionings, of Sturm and Drang. The ideals of physical freedom, of political power, of school training, as separate all-sufficient panaceas for social ills, became in the third decade dim and overcast. They were the vain dreams of credulous race childhood; not wrong, but incomplete and over-simple. The training of the schools we need today more than ever—the training of deft hands, quick eyes and ears, and the broader, deeper, higher culture of gifted minds. The power of the ballot we need in sheer self-defense, and as a guarantee of good faith. We may misuse it, but we can scarce do worse in this respect than our whilom masters. Freedom, too, the long-sought, we still seek—the freedom of life and limb, the freedom to work and think. Work, culture, and liberty—all these we need, not singly, but together; for today these ideals among the Negro people are gradually coalescing, and finding a higher meaning in the unifying ideal of race—the ideal of fostering the traits and talents of the Negro, not in opposition to, but in conformity with, the greater ideals of the American republic, in order that some day, on American soil, two world races may give each to each those characteristics which both so sadly lack. Already we come not altogether empty-handed: there is today no true American music but the sweet wild melodies of the Negro slave; the American fairy tales are Indian and African; we are the sole oasis of simple faith and reverence in a dusty desert of dollars and smartness. Will America be poorer if she replace her brutal, dyspeptic blundering with the light-hearted but determined Negro humility; or her coarse, cruel wit with loving, jovial good humor; or her Annie Rooney with "Steal Away"?

Merely a stern concrete test of the underlying principles of the great republic is the Negro problem, and the spiritual striving of the freedmen's sons is the travail of souls whose burden is almost beyond the measure of their strength, but who bear it in the name of a historic race, in the name of this land of their fathers' fathers, and in the name of human opportunity.

FROM *A RED RECORD*

Ida B. Wells-Barnett

The Case Stated

The student of American sociology will find the year 1894 marked by a pronounced awakening of the public conscience to a system of anarchy and outlawry which had grown during a series of ten years to be so common, that scenes of unusual brutality failed to have any visible effect upon the humane sentiments of the people of our land.

Beginning with the emancipation of the Negro, the inevitable result of unbridled power exercised for two and a half centuries, by the white man over the Negro, began to show itself in acts of conscienceless outlawry. During the slave regime, the Southern white man owned the Negro body and soul. It was to his interest to dwarf the soul and preserve the body. Vested with unlimited power over his slave, to subject him to any and all kinds of physical punishment, the white man was still restrained from such punishment as tended to injure the slave by abating his physical powers and thereby reducing his financial worth. While slaves were scourged mercilessly, and in countless cases inhumanly treated in other respects, still the white owner rarely permitted his anger to go so far as to take a life, which would entail upon him a loss of several hundred dollars. The slave was rarely killed, he was too valuable; it was easier and quite as effective, for discipline or revenge, to sell him "Down South."

But Emancipation came and the vested interests of the white man in the Negro's body were lost. The white man had no right to scourge the emancipated Negro, still less has he a right to kill him. But the Southern white people had been educated so long in that school of practice, in which might makes right, that they disdained to draw strict lines of action in dealing with the Negro. In slave times the Negro was kept subservient and submissive by the frequency and severity of the scourging, but, with freedom, a new system of intimidation came into vogue; the Negro was not only whipped and scourged; he was killed.

Not all nor nearly all of the murders done by white men, during the past thirty years in the South, have come to light, but the statistics as gathered and preserved by white men, and which have not been questioned, show that during these years more than ten thousand Negroes have been killed in cold blood, without the formality of judicial trial and legal execution. And yet, as evidence of the absolute impunity with which the white

Chicago: Donahue, 1895.

man dares to kill a Negro, the same record shows that during all these years, and for all these murders only three white men have been tried, convicted, and executed. As no white man has been lynched for the murder of colored people, these three executions are the only instances of the death penalty being visited upon white men for murdering Negroes.

Naturally enough the commission of these crimes began to tell upon the public conscience, and the Southern white man, as a tribute to the nineteenth century civilization, was in a manner compelled to give excuses for his barbarism. His excuses have adapted themselves to the emergency, and are aptly outlined by that greatest of all Negroes, Frederick Douglass, in an article of recent date, in which he shows that there have been three distinct eras of Southern barbarism, to account for which three distinct excuses have been made.

The first excuse given to the civilized world for the murder of unoffending Negroes was the necessity of the white man to repress and stamp out alleged "race riots." For years immediately succeeding the war there was an appalling slaughter of colored people, and the wires usually conveyed to northern people and the world the intelligence, first, that an insurrection was being planned by Negroes, which, a few hours later, would prove to have been vigorously resisted by white men, and controlled with a resulting loss of several killed and wounded. It was always a remarkable feature in these insurrections and riots that only Negroes were killed during the rioting, and that all the white men escaped unharmed.

From 1865 to 1872, hundreds of colored men and women were mercilessly murdered and the almost invariable reason assigned was that they met their death by being alleged participants in an insurrection or riot. But this story at last wore itself out. No insurrection ever materialized; no Negro rioter was ever apprehended and proven guilty, and no dynamite ever recorded the black man's protest against oppression and wrong. It was too much to ask thoughtful people to believe this transparent story, and the southern white people at last made up their minds that some other excuse must be had.

Then came the second excuse, which had its birth during the turbulent times of reconstruction. By an amendment to the Constitution the Negro was given the right of franchise, and, theoretically at least, his ballot became his invaluable emblem of citizenship. In a government "of the people, for the people, and by the people," the Negro's vote became an important factor in all matters of state and national politics. But this did not last long. The southern white man would not consider that the Negro had any right which a white man was bound to respect, and the idea of a republican form of government in the southern states grew into general contempt. It was maintained that "This is a white man's government," and regardless of numbers the white man should rule. "No Negro domination" became the new legend on the sanguinary banner of the sunny South, and under it rode the Ku Klux Klan, the Regulators, and the lawless mobs, which for any cause chose to murder one man or a dozen as suited their purpose best. It was a long, gory campaign; the blood chills and the heart almost loses faith in Christianity when one thinks of Yazoo, Hamburg, Edgefield, Copiah, and the countless massacres of defenseless Negroes, whose only crime was the attempt to exercise their right to vote.

But it was a bootless strife for colored people. The government which had made the Negro a citizen found itself unable to protect him. It gave him the right to vote, but denied him the protection which should have maintained that right. Scourged from his home; hunted through the swamps; hung by midnight raiders, and openly murdered in the light of day, the Negro clung to his right of franchise with a heroism which would have wrung admiration from the hearts of savages. He believed that in that small white ballot there was a subtle something which stood for manhood as well as citizenship, and thousands of brave black men went to their graves, exemplifying the one by dying for the other.

The white man's victory soon became complete by fraud, violence, intimidation and murder. The franchise vouchsafed to the Negro grew to be a "barren ideality," and regardless of numbers, the colored people found themselves voiceless in the councils of those whose duty it was to rule. With no longer the fear of "Negro Domination" before their eyes, the white man's second excuse became valueless. With the Southern governments all subverted and the Negro actually eliminated from all participation in state and national elections, there could be no longer an excuse for killing Negroes to prevent "Negro Domination."

Brutality still continued; Negroes were whipped, scourged, exiled, shot and hung whenever and wherever it pleased the white man so to treat them, and as the civilized world with increasing persistency held the white people of the South to account for its outlawry, the murderers invented the third excuse—that Negroes had to be killed to avenge their assaults upon women. There could be framed no possible excuse more harmful to the Negro and more unanswerable if true in its sufficiency for the white man.

Humanity abhors the assailant of womanhood, and this charge upon the Negro at once placed him beyond the pale of human sympathy. With such unanimity, earnestness and apparent candor was this charge made and reiterated that the world has accepted the story that the Negro is a monster which the Southern white man has painted him. And today, the Christian world feels, that while lynching is a crime, and lawlessness and anarchy the certain precursors of a nation's fall, it cannot by word or deed, extend sympathy or help to a race of outlaws, who might mistake their plea for justice and deem it an excuse for their continued wrongs.

The Negro has suffered much and is willing to suffer more. He recognizes that the wrongs of two centuries can not be righted in a day, and he tries to bear his burden with patience for today and be hopeful for tomorrow. But there comes a time when the veriest worm will turn, and the Negro feels today that after all the work he has done, all the sacrifices he has made, and all the suffering he has endured, if he did not, now, defend his name and manhood from this vile accusation, he would be unworthy even of the contempt of mankind. It is to this charge he now feels he must make answer.

If the Southern people in defense of their lawlessness, would tell the truth and admit that colored men and women are lynched for almost any offense, from murder to a misdemeanor, there would not now be the necessity for this defense. But when they intentionally, maliciously and constantly belie the record and bolster up these falsehoods by the words of legislators, preachers, governors and bishops, then the Negro must give to the world his side of the awful story.

A word as to the charge itself. In considering the third reason assigned by the Southern white people for the butchery of blacks, the question must be asked, what the white man means when he charges the black man with rape. Does he mean the crime which the statutes of the civilized states describe as such? Not by any means. With the Southern white man, any mésalliance existing between a white woman and a colored man is a sufficient foundation for the charge of rape. The Southern white man says that it is impossible for a voluntary alliance to exist between a white woman and a colored man, and therefore, the fact of an alliance is a proof of force. In numerous instances where colored men have been lynched on the charge of rape, it was positively known at the time of lynching, and indisputably proven after the victim's death, that the relationship sustained between the man and woman was voluntary and clandestine, and that in no court of law could even the charge of assault have been successfully maintained.

It was for the assertion of this fact, in the defense of her own race, that the writer hereof became an exile; her property destroyed and her return to her home forbidden under penalty of death, for writing the following editorial which was printed in her paper, the *Free Speech*, in Memphis, Tenn., May 21, 1892:

"Eight Negroes lynched since last issue of the *Free Speech* one at Little Rock, Ark., last Saturday morning where the citizens broke (?) into the penitentiary and got their man; three near Anniston, Ala., one near New Orleans; and three at Clarksville, Ga., the last three for killing a white man, and five on the same old racket—the new alarm about raping white women. The same programme of hanging, then shooting bullets into the lifeless bodies was carried out to the letter. Nobody in this section of the country believes the old threadbare lie that Negro men rape white women. If Southern white men are not careful, they will over-reach themselves and public sentiment will have a reaction; a conclusion will then be reached which will be very damaging to the moral reputation of their women."

But threats cannot suppress the truth, and while the Negro suffers the soul deformity, resultant from two and a half centuries of slavery, he is no more guilty of this vilest of all vile charges than the white man who would blacken his name.

During all the years of slavery, no such charge was ever made, not even during the dark days of the rebellion, when the white man, following the fortunes of war, went to do battle for the maintenance of slavery. While the master was away fighting to forge the fetters upon the slave, he left his wife and children with no protectors save the Negroes themselves. And yet during those years of trust and peril, no Negro proved recreant to his trust and no white man returned to a home that had been despoiled.

Likewise during the period of alleged "insurrection," and alarming "race riots," it never occurred to the white man, that his wife and children were in danger of assault. Nor in the Reconstruction era, when the hue and cry was against "Negro Domination," was there ever a thought that the domination would ever contaminate a fireside or strike to death the virtue of womanhood. It must appear strange indeed, to every thoughtful and candid man, that more than a quarter of a century elapsed before the Negro began to show signs of such infamous degeneration.

In his remarkable apology for lynching, Bishop Haygood, of Georgia, says: "No race, not the most savage, tolerates the rape of woman, but it may be said without reflection upon any other people that the Southern people are now and always have been most sensitive concerning the honor of their women — their mothers, wives, sisters and daughters." It is not the purpose of this defense to say one word against the white women of the South. Such need not be said, but it is their misfortune that the chivalrous white men of that section, in order to escape the deserved execration of the civilized world, should shield themselves by their cowardly and infamously false excuse, and call into question that very honor about which their distinguished priestly apologist claims they are most sensitive. To justify their own barbarism they assume a chivalry which they do not possess. True chivalry respects all womanhood, and no one who reads the record, as it is written in the faces of the million mulattoes in the South, will for a minute conceive that the southern white man had a very chivalrous regard for the honor due the women of his own race or respect for the womanhood which circumstances placed in his power. That chivalry which is "most sensitive concerning the honor of women" can hope for but little respect from the civilized world, when it confines itself entirely to the women who happen to be white. Virtue knows no color line, and the chivalry which depends upon complexion of skin and texture of hair can command no honest respect.

When emancipation came to the Negroes, there arose in the northern part of the United States an almost divine sentiment among the noblest, purest and best white women of the North, who felt called to a mission to educate and Christianize the millions of southern ex-slaves. From every nook and corner of the North, brave young white women answered that call and left their cultured homes, their happy associations and their lives of ease, and with heroic determination went to the South to carry light and truth to the benighted blacks. It was a heroism no less than that which calls for volunteers for India, Africa and the Isles of the sea. To educate their unfortunate charges; to teach them the Christian virtues and to inspire in them the moral sentiments manifest in their own lives, these young women braved dangers whose record reads more like fiction than fact. They became social outlaws in the South. The peculiar sensitiveness of the southern white men for women, never shed its protecting influence about them. No friendly word from their own race cheered them in their work; no hospitable doors gave them the companionship like that from which they had come. No chivalrous white man doffed his hat in honor or respect. They were "Nigger teachers"—unpardonable offenders in the social ethics of the South, and were insulted, persecuted and ostracised, not by Negroes, but by the white manhood which boasts of its chivalry toward women.

And yet these northern women worked on, year after year, unselfishly, with a heroism which amounted almost to martyrdom. Threading their way through dense forests, working in [the] schoolhouse, in the cabin and in the church, thrown at all times and in all places among the unfortunate and lowly Negroes, whom they had come to find and to serve, these northern women, thousands and thousands of them, have spent more than a quarter of a century in giving to the colored people their splendid lessons for home and heart and soul. Without protection, save that which innocence gives to every good woman, they went about their work, fearing no assault and suffering none. Their chivalrous protectors were hundreds of miles away in their northern homes, and yet they never feared any "great dark-faced mobs," they dared night or day to "go beyond their own roof trees." They never complained of assaults, and no mob was ever called into existence to avenge crimes against them. Before the world adjudges the Negro a moral monster, a vicious assailant of womanhood and a menace to the sacred precincts of home, the colored people ask the consideration of the silent record of gratitude, respect, protection and devotion of the millions of the race in the South, to the thousands of northern white women who have served as teachers and missionaries since the war.

The Negro may not have known what chivalry was, but he knew enough to preserve inviolate the womanhood of the South which was entrusted to his hands during the war. The finer sensibilities of his soul may have been crushed out by years of slavery, but his heart was full of gratitude to the white women of the North, who blessed his home and inspired his soul in all these years of freedom. Faithful to his trust in both of these instances, he should now have the impartial ear of the civilized world, when he dares to speak for himself as against the infamy wherewith he stands charged.

It is his regret, that, in his own defense, he must disclose to the world that degree of dehumanizing brutality which fixes upon America the blot of a national crime. Whatever faults and failings other nations may have in their dealings with their own subjects or with other people, no other civilized nation stands condemned before the world with a series of crimes so peculiarly national. It becomes a painful duty of the Negro to reproduce a record which shows that a large portion of the American people avow anarchy, condone murder and defy the contempt of civilization.

These pages are written in no spirit of vindictiveness, for all who give the subject consideration must concede that far too serious is the condition of that civilized government in which the spirit of unrestrained outlawry constantly increases in violence, and casts its blight over a continually growing area of territory. We plead not for the colored people alone, but for all victims of the terrible injustice which puts men and women to death without form of law. During the year 1894, there were 132 persons executed in the United States by due form of law, while in the same year, 197 persons were put to death by mobs who gave the victims no opportunity to make a lawful defense. No comment need be made upon a condition of public sentiment responsible for such alarming results. . . .

"THE EDITOR'S STUDY"

William Dean Howells

. . . The time is coming, we trust, when each new author, each new artist, will be considered, not in his proportion to any other author or artist, but in his relation to the human nature, known to us all, which it is his

Harper's New Monthly, December 1887.

privilege, his high duty, to interpret. "The true standard of the artist is in every man's power" already, as Burke says; Michelangelo's "light of the piazza," the glance of the common eye, is and always was the best light on a statue; Goethe's "boys and blackbirds" have in all ages been the real connoisseurs of berries; but hitherto the mass of common men have been afraid to apply their own simplicity, naturalness, and honesty to the appreciation of the beautiful. They have always cast about for the instruction of someone who professed to know better, and who browbeat wholesome common-sense into the self-distrust that ends in sophistication. They have fallen generally to the worst of this bad species, and have been "amused and misled" (how pretty that quaint old use of *amuse* is!) "by the false lights" of critical vanity and self-righteousness. They have been taught to compare what they see and what they read, not with the things that they have observed and known, but with the things that some other artist or writer has done. Especially if they have themselves the artistic impulse in any direction they are taught to form themselves, not upon life, but upon the masters who became masters only by forming themselves upon life. The seeds of death are planted in them, and they can produce only the still-born, the academic. They are not told to take their work into the public square and see if it seems true to the chance passer, but to test it by the work of the very men who refused and decried any other test of their own work. The young writer who attempts to report the phrase and carriage of everyday life, who tries to tell just how he has heard men talk and seen them look, is made to feel guilty of something low and unworthy by the stupid people who would like to have him show how Shakespeare's men talked and looked, of Scott's or Thackeray's, or Balzac's, or Hawthorne's, or Dickens's; he is instructed to idealize his personages, that is, to take the life-likeness out of them, and put the literary-likeness into them. He is approached in the spirit of the wretched pedantry into which learning, much or little, always decays when it withdraws itself and stands apart from experience in an attitude of imagined superiority, and which would say with the same confidence to the scientist: "I see that you are looking at a grasshopper there which you have found in the grass, and I suppose you intend to describe it. Now don't waste your time and sin against culture in *that* way. I've got a grasshopper here, which has been evolved at considerable pains and expense out of the grasshopper in general; in fact, it's a type. It's made up of wire and cardboard, very prettily painted in a conventional tint, and it's perfectly indestructible. It isn't very much like a real grasshopper, but it's a great deal nicer, and it's served to represent the notion of a grasshopper ever since man emerged from barbarism. You may say that it's artificial. Well, it *is* artificial; but then it's ideal too; and what you want to do is to cultivate the ideal. You'll find the books full of my kind of grasshopper, and scarcely a trace of yours in any of them. The thing that you are proposing to do is commonplace, but if you say that it isn't commonplace, for the very reason that it hasn't been done before, you'll have to admit that it's photographic."

As we said, we hope the time is coming when not only the artist, but the common, average man, who always "has the standard of the arts in his power," will have also the courage to apply it, and will reject the ideal grasshopper wherever he finds it, in science, in literature, in art, because it is not "simple, natural, and honest," because it is not like a real grasshopper. But we will own that we think the time is yet far off, and that the people who have been brought up on the ideal grasshopper, the heroic grasshopper, the impassioned grasshopper, the self-devoted, adventureful, good old romantic cardboard grasshopper, must die out before the simple, honest, and natural grasshopper can have a fair field.

"STEPHEN CRANE"

Hamlin Garland

In July of 1891, I gave a series of lectures at Avon-by-the Sea in a summer school managed by Mr. and Mrs. Alberti of New York. Among other of my addresses was one upon "The Local Novel," and I remember very distinctly the young reporter for the *Tribune* who came up to me after the lecture to ask for the loan of my notes.

He was slim, boyish, with sallow complexion, and light hair. His speech was singularly laconic. "My name is Crane," he said. "Stephen Crane," and later I was told that he had been a student in a school near by, but had left before graduating to become a newspaper writer in New York. As I recall it, his presence at Avon was due to the Albertis, who knew his family—anyhow, he was reporting for the assembly.

Although not particularly impressed with him in this short interview, the correctness of his report ["Howells Discussed at Avon-by-the-Sea," *New York Tribune*, 18 Aug. 1891] of my lecture next day surprised me. I recognized in it unusual precision of expression and set about establishing

---

From *Roadside Meetings*. New York: Macmillan, 1930.

a more intimate relationship. We met occasionally thereafter to "pass ball," and to discuss the science of pitching, the various theories which accounted for "inshoots" and "outdrops," for he, like myself, had served as a pitcher and gloried in being able to confound the laws of astronomy by making a sphere alter its course in mid-air.

In the middle of my second week he turned up at my boarding house in a very dejected mood. "Well, I've got the bounce," he said with a sour twist of his mouth. "The *Tribune* doesn't need me anymore."

Not taking him seriously, I laughingly said, "They're making a mistake."

"That's what I told them," he answered. "But you see I made a report of a labor parade the other day ["On the New Jersey Coast," *New York Tribune*, 21 Aug. 1892], which slipped in over the managing editor's fence. When he read it in print he sent for me, made a little speech, and let me out."

"I should like to see that report," I remarked.

Thereupon he took from his pocket a clipping from the *Tribune* and handed it to me. It was very short, but it was closely studied and quite merciless in its realism. It depicted that political parade of tailors, house painters, and other indoor workers exactly as they appeared—a pale-faced, weak-kneed, splay-footed lot, the slaves of a triumphant civilization, wearing their chains submissively, working in the dark for careless masters, voting for privilege, seemingly without the slightest comprehension of their own supine cowardice; but it was Crane's ironical comment, his corrosive and bitter reflection upon their servility, and especially their habit of marching with banners at the chariot wheels of their conquerors, which made his article so offensive to the party in power.

Handing the article back to him I asked, "What did you expect from your journal—a medal?"

He smiled again in bitter reflection. "I guess I didn't stop to consider that. I was so hot at the sight of those poor, misshapen fools shouting for monopoly that I gave no thought to its effect upon my own fortunes. I don't know that it would have made much difference if I had. I wanted to say those things anyway.". . .

The serial publication of *The Red Badge of Courage* brought him an admirer in the person of Ripley Hitchcock of Appleton's, who made him an offer for the book at "customary royalty." He accepted, glad of the chance. This helped him somewhat, but as royalties are only paid annually and as the book sold very slowly, he continued to suffer need.

At this point his affairs took a sudden turn upward. He became the figure I had hoped to see him become two years before. Some English critics wrote in highest praise of *The Red Badge*, and the book became a critical bone of contention between military objectors and literary enthusiasts. Crane was accepted as a man of genius. . . .

I saw Crane several times during his troubles with the New York police, and while I sympathized with him in his loyalty to a woman [Dora Clark] whom he considered had been unjustly accused of soliciting, his stubborn resolve to go on the stand in her defense was quixotic. Roosevelt discussed the case with me and said, "I tried to save Crane from press comment, but as he insisted on testifying, I could only let the law take its course."

The papers stated that Crane's rooms had been raided and that an opium layout had been discovered. Altogether it was a miserable time for him. The shady side of his bohemian life was turned to the light.

Meeting him in McClure's office one day, I said to him very earnestly, "Crane, why don't you cut loose from your associations here? Go to your brother's farm in Sullivan County and get back your tone. You don't look well. Settle down to the writing of a single big book up there, and take your time to do it."

Impulsively thrusting out his hand to me, he said, "I'll do it." Alas! He did not. He took a commission to go to Greece and report a war. On his return from Greece he went to Cuba. . . .

After the Cuban war, Crane married and went to England, where he lived till he was ordered into Germany for his health. I have only one letter from him while he was in England, and in that he told me nothing of himself. It was all about a new writer he had discovered, a certain Joseph Conrad. "Get his *Nigger of the Narcissus*," he wrote. "It is a crackerjack. Conrad knows your work. You should meet him when you come to England."

It was more than twenty years later when I met Conrad in Bishopsbourne and talked of *The Nigger* and of Crane. "A wealthy admirer turned over to the Cranes a great, half-ruined manor house not far from here," said Conrad, "and Stephen kept open house there. The place was so filled with his semi-bohemian associates in London that I seldom went there—I didn't enjoy his crowd, but I liked him and valued his work. I went over to see him when he was brought to Dover on his way to the Black Forest. He wore a beard and was greatly emaciated. The moment I looked into his eyes I knew that he was bound for a long voyage—and that I should not see him again. He died soon after in Bavaria."

PART TWO

Maggie's World

MAGGIE

A Girl of the Streets

A Story of New York

Stephen Crane

I

A very little boy stood upon a heap of gravel for the honor of Rum Alley. He was throwing stones at howling urchins from Devil's Row who were circling madly about the heap and pelting at him.

His infantile countenance was livid with fury. His small body was writhing in the delivery of great, crimson oaths.

"Run, Jimmie, run! Dey'll get yehs," screamed a retreating Rum Alley child.

"Naw," responded Jimmie with a valiant roar, "dese micks can't make me run."

Howls of renewed wrath went up from Devil's Row throats. Tattered gamins on the right made a furious assault on the gravel heap. On their small, convulsed faces there shone the grins of true assassins. As they charged, they threw stones and cursed in shrill chorus.

The little champion of Rum Alley stumbled precipitately down the other side. His coat had been torn to shreds in a scuffle, and his hat was gone. He had bruises on twenty parts of his body, and blood was dripping from a cut in his head. His wan features wore a look of a tiny, insane demon.

On the ground, children from Devil's Row closed in on their antagonist. He crooked his left arm defensively about his head and fought with cursing fury. The little boys ran to and fro, dodging, hurling stones and swearing in barbaric trebles.

From a window of an apartment house that upreared its form from amid squat, ignorant stables, there leaned a curious woman. Some laborers, unloading a scow at a dock at the river, paused for a moment and regarded the fight. The engineer of a passive tugboat hung lazily to a railing and watched. Over on the Island, a worm of yellow convicts came from the shadow of a gray ominous building and crawled slowly along the river's bank.

A stone had smashed into Jimmie's mouth. Blood was bubbling over his chin and down upon his ragged shirt. Tears made furrows on his dirt-stained cheeks. His thin legs had begun to tremble and turn weak, causing his small body to reel. His roaring curses of the first part of the fight had changed to a blasphemous chatter.

In the yells of the whirling mob of Devil's Row children there were notes of joy like songs of triumphant savagery. The little boys seemed to leer gloatingly at the blood upon the other child's face.

Down the avenue came boastfully sauntering a lad of sixteen years, although the chronic sneer of an ideal manhood already sat upon his lips. His hat was tipped with an air of challenge over his eye. Between his teeth, a cigar stump was tilted at the angle of defiance. He walked with a certain swing of the shoulders which appalled the timid. He glanced over into the vacant lot in which the little raving boys from Devil's Row seethed about the shrieking and tearful child from Rum Alley.

"Gee!" he murmured with interest. "A scrap. Gee!"

He strode over to the cursing circle, swinging his shoulders in a manner which denoted that he held victory in his fists. He approached at the back of one of the most deeply engaged of the Devil's Row children.

"Ah, what deh hell," he said, and smote the deeply-engaged one on the back of the head. The little boy fell to the ground and gave a hoarse, tremendous howl. He scrambled to his feet, and perceiving, evidently, the size of his assailant, ran quickly off, shouting alarms. The entire Devil's Row party followed him. They came to a stand a short distance away and yelled taunting oaths at the boy with the chronic sneer. The latter, momentarily, paid no attention to them.

"What deh hell, Jimmie?" he asked of the small champion.

Jimmie wiped his blood-wet features with his sleeve.

"Well, it was dis way, Pete, see! I was goin' teh lick dat Riley kid and dey all pitched on me."

Some Rum Alley children now came forward. The party stood for a moment exchanging vainglorious remarks with Devil's Row. A few stones were thrown at long distances, and words of challenge passed between small warriors. Then the Rum Alley contingent turned slowly in the direction of their home street. They began to give, each to each, distorted versions of the fight. Causes of retreat in particular cases were magnified. Blows dealt in the fight were enlarged to catapultian power, and stones thrown were alleged to have hurtled with infinite accuracy. Valor grew strong again, and the little boys began to swear with great spirit.

"Ah, we blokies kin lick deh hull damn Row," said a child, swaggering.

Little Jimmie was striving to stanch the flow of blood from his cut lips. Scowling, he turned upon the speaker.

"Ah, where deh hell was yeh when I was doin' all deh fightin'?" he demanded. "Youse kids makes me tired."

"Ah, go ahn," replied the other argumentatively.

Jimmie replied with heavy contempt. "Ah, youse can't fight, Blue Billie! I kin lick yeh wid one han'."

"Ah, go ahn," replied Billie again.

"Ah," said Jimmie threateningly.

"Ah," said the other in the same tone.

They struck at each other, clinched, and rolled over on the cobble stones.

"Smash 'im, Jimmie, kick deh damn guts out of 'im," yelled Pete, the lad with the chronic sneer, in tones of delight.

The small combatants pounded and kicked, scratched and tore. They began to weep and their curses struggled in their throats with sobs. The other little boys clasped their hands and wriggled their legs in excitement. They formed a bobbing circle about the pair.

A tiny spectator was suddenly agitated.

"Cheese it, Jimmie, cheese it! Here comes yer fader," he yelled.

The circle of little boys instantly parted. They drew away and waited in ecstatic awe for that which was about to happen. The two little boys fighting in the modes of four thousand years ago, did not hear the warning.

Up the avenue there plodded slowly a man with sullen eyes. He was carrying a dinner pail and smoking an apple-wood pipe.

As he neared the spot where the little boys strove, he regarded them listlessly. But suddenly he roared an oath and advanced upon the rolling fighters.

"Here, you Jim, git up, now, while I belt yer life out, you damned disorderly brat."

He began to kick into the chaotic mass on the ground. The boy Billie felt a heavy boot strike his head. He made a furious effort and disentangled himself from Jimmie. He tottered away, damning.

Jimmie arose painfully from the ground and confronting his father, began to curse him. His parent kicked him. "Come home, now," he cried, "an' stop yer jawin', er I'll lam the everlasting head off yehs."

They departed. The man paced placidly along with the apple-wood emblem of serenity between his teeth. The boy followed a dozen feet in the rear. He swore luridly, for he felt that it was degradation for one who aimed to be some vague soldier, or a man of blood with a sort of sublime license, to be taken home by a father.

II

Eventually they entered into a dark region where, from a careening building, a dozen gruesome doorways gave up loads of babies to the street and the gutter. A wind of early autumn raised yellow dust from cobbles and swirled it against a hundred windows. Long streamers of garments fluttered from fire-escapes. In all unhandy places there were buckets, brooms, rags and bottles. In the street infants played or fought with other infants or sat stupidly in the way of vehicles. Formidable women, with uncombed hair and disordered dress, gossiped while leaning on railings, or screamed in frantic quarrels. Withered persons, in curious postures of submission to something, sat smoking pipes in obscure corners. A thousand odors of cooking food came forth to the street. The building quivered and creaked from the weight of humanity stamping about in its bowels.

A small ragged girl dragged a red, bawling infant along the crowded ways. He was hanging back, baby-like, bracing his wrinkled, bare legs.

The little girl cried out: "Ah, Tommie, come ahn. Dere's Jimmie and fader. Don't be a-pullin' me back."

She jerked the baby's arm impatiently. He fell on his face, roaring. With a second jerk she pulled him to his feet, and they went on. With the obstinacy of his order, he protested against being dragged in a chosen direction. He made heroic endeavors to keep on his legs, denounce his sister and consume a bit of orange peeling which he chewed between the times of his infantile orations.

As the sullen-eyed man, followed by the blood-covered boy, drew near, the little girl burst into reproachful cries. "Ah, Jimmie, youse bin fightin' agin."

The urchin swelled disdainfully.

"Ah, what deh hell, Mag. See?"

The little girl upbraided him. "Youse allus fightin', Jimmie, an' yeh knows it puts mudder out when yehs come home half dead, an' it's like we'll all get a poundin'."

She began to weep. The babe threw back his head and roared at his prospects.

"Ah, what deh hell!" cried Jimmie. "Shut up er I'll smack yer mout'. See?"

As his sister continued her lamentations, he suddenly swore and struck her. The little girl reeled and, recovering herself, burst into tears and quaveringly cursed him. As she slowly retreated her brother advanced dealing her cuffs. The father heard and turned about.

"Stop that, Jim, d'yeh hear? Leave yer sister alone on the street. It's like I can never beat any sense into yer damned wooden head."

The urchin raised his voice in defiance to his parent and continued his attacks. The babe bawled tremendously, protesting with great violence. During his sister's hasty manoeuvres, he was dragged by the arm.

Finally the procession plunged into one of the gruesome doorways. They crawled up dark stairways and along cold, gloomy halls. At last the father pushed open a door and they entered a lighted room in which a large woman was rampant.

She stopped in a career from a seething stove to a pan-covered table. As the father and children filed in she peered at them.

"Eh, what? Been fightin' agin, by Gawd!" She threw herself upon Jimmie. The urchin tried to dart behind the others and in the scuffle the babe, Tommie, was knocked down. He protested with his usual vehemence, because they had bruised his tender shins against a table leg.

The mother's massive shoulders heaved with anger. Grasping the urchin by the neck and shoulder she shook him until he rattled. She dragged him to an unholy sink, and, soaking a rag in water, began to scrub his lacerated face with it. Jimmie screamed in pain and tried to twist his shoulders out of the clasp of the huge arms.

The babe sat on the floor watching the scene, his face in contortions like that of a woman at a tragedy. The father, with a newly-ladened pipe in his mouth, crouched on a backless chair near the stove. Jimmie's cries annoyed him. He turned about and bellowed at his wife:

"Let the damned kid alone for a minute, will yeh, Mary? Yer allus poundin' 'im. When I come nights I can't git no rest 'cause yer allus poundin' a kid. Let up, d'yeh hear? Don't be allus poundin' a kid."

The woman's operations on the urchin instantly increased in violence. At last she tossed him to a corner where he limply lay cursing and weeping.

The wife put her immense hands on her hips and with a chieftain-like stride approached her husband.

"Ho," she said, with a great grunt of contempt. "An' what in the devil are you stickin' your nose for?"

The babe crawled under the table and, turning, peered out cautiously. The ragged girl retreated and the urchin in the corner drew his legs carefully beneath him.

The man puffed his pipe calmly and put his great mudded boots on the back part of the stove.

"Go teh hell," he murmured, tranquilly.

The woman screamed and shook her fists before her husband's eyes. The rough yellow of her face and neck flared suddenly crimson. She began to howl.

He puffed imperturbably at his pipe for a time, but finally arose and began to look out at the window into the darkening chaos of back yards.

"You've been drinkin', Mary," he said. "You'd better let up on the bot', ol' woman, or you'll git done."

"You're a liar. I ain't had a drop," she roared in reply.

They had a lurid altercation, in which they damned each other's souls with frequence.

The babe was staring out from under the table, his small face working in his excitement.

The ragged girl went stealthily over to the corner where the urchin lay.

"Are yehs hurted much, Jimmie?" she whispered timidly.

"Not a damn bit! See?" growled the little boy.

"Will I wash deh blood?"

"Naw!"

"Will I—"

"When I catch dat Riley kid I'll break 'is face! Dat's right! See?"

He turned his face to the wall as if resolved to grimly bide his time.

In the quarrel between husband and wife, the woman was victor. The man grabbed his hat and rushed from the room, apparently determined upon a vengeful drunk. She followed to the door and thundered at him as he made his way down-stairs.

She returned and stirred up the room until her children were bobbing about like bubbles.

"Git outa deh way," she persistently bawled, waving feet with their dishevelled shoes near the heads of her children. She shrouded herself, puffing and snorting, in a cloud of steam at the stove, and eventually extracted a frying-pan full of potatoes that hissed.

She flourished it. "Come teh yer suppers, now," she cried with sudden exasperation. "Hurry up, now, er I'll help yeh!"

The children scrambled hastily. With prodigious clatter they arranged themselves at table. The babe sat with his feet dangling high from a precarious infant chair and gorged his small stomach. Jimmie forced, with feverish rapidity, the grease-enveloped pieces between his wounded lips. Maggie, with side glances of fear of interruption, ate like a small pursued tigress.

The mother sat blinking at them. She delivered reproaches, swallowed potatoes and drank from a yellow-brown bottle. After a time her mood changed and she wept as she carried little Tommie into another room and laid him to sleep with his fists doubled in an old quilt of faded red and green grandeur. Then she came and moaned by the stove. She rocked to and fro upon a chair, shedding tears and crooning miserably to the two children about their "poor mother" and "yer fader, damn 'is soul."

The little girl plodded between the table and the chair with a dish-pan on it. She tottered on her small legs beneath burdens of dishes.

Jimmie sat nursing his various wounds. He cast furtive glances at his mother. His practised eye perceived her gradually emerge from a muddled mist of sentiment until her brain burned in drunken heat. He sat breathless.

Maggie broke a plate.

The mother started to her feet as if propelled.

"Good Gawd," she howled. Her eyes glittered on her child with sudden hatred. The fervent red of her face turned almost to purple. The little boy ran to the halls, shrieking like a monk in an earthquake.

He floundered about in darkness until he found the stairs. He stumbled, panic-stricken, to the next floor. An old woman opened a door. A light behind her threw a flare on the urchin's quivering face.

"Eh, Gawd, child, what is it dis time? Is yer fader beatin' yer mudder, or yer mudder beatin' yer fader?"

III

Jimmie and the old woman listened long in the hall. Above the muffled roar of conversation, the dismal wailings of babies at night, the thumping of feet in unseen corridors and rooms, mingled with the sound of varied hoarse shoutings in the street and the rattling of wheels over cobbles, they heard the screams of the child and the roars of the mother die away to a feeble moaning and a subdued bass muttering.

The old woman was a gnarled and leathery personage who could don, at will, an expression of great virtue. She possessed a small music-box capable of one tune, and a collection of "God bless yehs" pitched in assorted keys of fervency. Each day she took a position upon the stones of Fifth Avenue, where she crooked her legs under her and crouched immovable and hideous, like an idol. She received daily a small sum in pennies. It was contributed, for the most part, by persons who did not make their homes in that vicinity.

Once, when a lady had dropped her purse on the sidewalk, the gnarled woman had grabbed it and smuggled it with great dexterity beneath her cloak. When she was arrested she had cursed the lady into a partial swoon, and with her aged limbs, twisted from rheumatism, had almost kicked the stomach out of a huge policeman whose conduct upon that occasion she referred to when she said: "The police, damn 'em."

"Eh, Jimmie, it's cursed shame," she said. "Go, now, like a dear an' buy me a can, an' if yer mudder raises 'ell all night yehs can sleep here."

Jimmie took a tendered tin-pail and seven pennies and departed. He passed into the side door of a saloon and went to the bar. Straining up on his toes he raised the pail and pennies as high as his arms would let him. He saw two hands thrust down and take them. Directly the same hands let down the filled pail and he left.

In front of the gruesome doorway he met a lurching figure. It was his father, swaying about on uncertain legs.

"Give me deh can. See?" said the man, threateningly.

"Ah, come off! I got dis can fer dat ol' woman an' it 'ud be dirt teh swipe it. See?" cried Jimmie.

The father wrenched the pail from the urchin. He grasped it in both hands and lifted it to his mouth. He glued his lips to the under edge and tilted his head. His hairy throat swelled until it seemed to grow near his chin. There was a tremendous gulping movement and the beer was gone.

The man caught his breath and laughed. He hit his son on the head with the empty pail. As it rolled clanging into the street, Jimmie began to scream and kicked repeatedly at his father's shins.

"Look at deh dirt what yeh done me," he yelled. "Deh ol' woman 'ill be raisin' hell."

He retreated to the middle of the street, but the man did not pursue. He staggered toward the door.

"I'll club hell outa yeh when I ketch yeh," he shouted, and disappeared.

During the evening he had been standing against a bar drinking whiskies and declaring to all comers, confidentially: "My home reg'lar livin' hell! Damndes' place! Reg'lar hell! Why do I come an' drin' whisk' here thish way? 'Cause home reg'lar livin' hell!"

Jimmie waited a long time in the street and then crept warily up through the building. He passed with great caution the door of the gnarled woman, and finally stopped outside his home and listened.

He could hear his mother moving heavily about among the furniture of the room. She was chanting in a mournful voice, occasionally interjecting bursts of volcanic wrath at the father, who, Jimmie judged, had sunk down on the floor or in a corner.

"Why deh blazes don' chere try teh keep Jim from fightin'? I'll break yer jaw," she suddenly bellowed.

The man mumbled with drunken indifference. "Ah, wha' deh hell. W'a's odds? Wha' makes kick?"

"Because he tears 'is clothes, yeh damn fool," cried the woman in supreme wrath.

The husband seemed to become aroused. "Go teh hell," he thundered fiercely in reply. There was a crash against the door and something broke into clattering fragments. Jimmie partially suppressed a howl and darted down the stairway. Below he paused and listened. He heard howls and curses, groans and shrieks, confusingly in chorus as if a battle were raging. With all was the crash of splintering furniture. The eyes of the urchin glared in fear that one of them would discover him.

Curious faces appeared in door-ways, and whispered comments passed to and fro. "Ol' Johnson's raisin' hell agin."

Jimmie stood until the noises ceased and the other inhabitants of the tenement had all yawned and shut their doors. Then he crawled upstairs with the caution of an invader of a panther den. Sounds of labored breathing came through the broken door-panels. He pushed the door open and entered, quaking.

A glow from the fire threw red hues over the bare floor, the cracked and soiled plastering, and the overturned and broken furniture.

In the middle of the floor lay his mother asleep. In one corner of the room his father's limp body hung across the seat of a chair.

The urchin stole forward. He began to shiver in dread of awakening his parents. His mother's great chest was heaving painfully. Jimmie paused and looked down at her. Her face was inflamed and swollen from drinking. Her yellow brows shaded eye-lids that had grown blue. Her tangled hair tossed in waves over her forehead. Her mouth was set in the same lines of vindictive hatred that it had, perhaps, borne during the fight. Her bare, red arms were thrown out above her head in positions of exhaustion, something, mayhap, like those of a sated villain.

The urchin bended over his mother. He was fearful lest she should open her eyes, and the dread within him was so strong, that he could not forbear to stare, but hung as if fascinated over the woman's grim face.

Suddenly her eyes opened. The urchin found himself looking straight into that expression, which, it would seem, had the power to change his blood to salt. He howled piercingly and fell backward.

The woman floundered for a moment, tossed her arms about her head as if in combat, and again began to snore.

Jimmie crawled back in the shadows and waited. A noise in the next room had followed his cry at the discovery that his mother was awake. He grovelled in the gloom, the eyes from out his drawn face riveted upon the intervening door.

He heard it creak, and then the sound of a small voice came to him. "Jimmie! Jimmie! Are yehs dere?" it whispered. The urchin started. The thin, white face of his sister looked at him from the door-way of the other room. She crept to him across the floor.

The father had not moved, but lay in the same death-like sleep. The mother writhed in uneasy slumber, her chest wheezing as if she were in the agonies of strangulation. Out at the window a florid moon was peering over dark roofs, and in the distance the waters of a river glimmered pallidly.

The small frame of the ragged girl was quivering. Her features were haggard from weeping, and her eyes gleamed from fear. She grasped the urchin's arm in her little trembling hands and they huddled in a corner.

The eyes of both were drawn, by some force, to stare at the woman's face, for they thought she need only to awake and all fiends would come from below.

They crouched until the ghost-mists of dawn appeared at the window, drawing close to the panes, and looking in at the prostrate, heaving body of the mother.

IV

The babe, Tommie, died. He went away in a white, insignificant coffin, his small waxen hand clutching a flower that the girl, Maggie, had stolen from an Italian.

She and Jimmie lived.

The inexperienced fibres of the boy's eyes were hardened at an early age. He became a young man of leather. He lived some red years without laboring. During that time his sneer became chronic. He studied human nature in the gutter, and found it no worse than he thought he had reason to believe it. He never conceived a respect for the world, because he had begun with no idols that it had smashed.

He clad his soul in armor by means of happening hilariously in at a mission church where a man composed his sermons of "yous." While they got warm at the stove, he told his hearers just where he calculated they stood with the Lord. Many of the sinners were impatient over the pictured depths of their degradation. They were waiting for soup-tickets.

A reader of words of wind-demons might have been able to see the portions of a dialogue pass to and fro between the exhorter and his hearers.

"You are damned," said the preacher. And the reader of sounds might have seen the reply go forth from the ragged people: "Where's our soup?"

Jimmie and a companion sat in a rear seat and commented upon the things that didn't concern them, with all the freedom of English gentlemen. When they grew thirsty and went out, their minds confused the speaker with Christ.

Momentarily, Jimmie was sullen with thoughts of a hopeless altitude where grew fruit. His companion said that if he should ever meet God he would ask for a million dollars and a bottle of beer.

Jimmie's occupation for a long time was to stand on street-corners and watch the world go by, dreaming blood-red dreams at the passing of pretty women. He menaced mankind at the intersections of streets.

On the corners he was in life and of life. The world was going on and he was there to perceive it.

He maintained a belligerent attitude toward all well-dressed men. To him fine raiment was allied to weakness, and all good coats covered faint hearts. He and his order were kings, to a certain extent, over the men of untarnished clothes, because these latter dreaded, perhaps, to be either killed or laughed at.

Above all things he despised obvious Christians and ciphers with the chrysanthemums of aristocracy in their button-holes. He considered himself above both of these classes. He was afraid of neither the devil nor the leader of society.

When he had a dollar in his pocket his satisfaction with existence was the greatest thing in the world. So, eventually, he felt obliged to work. His father died and his mother's years were divided up into periods of thirty days.

He became a truck driver. He was given the charge of a pains-taking pair of horses and a large rattling truck. He invaded the turmoil and tumble of the down-town streets and learned to breathe maledictory defiance at the police who occasionally used to climb up, drag him from his perch and beat him.

In the lower part of the city he daily involved himself in hideous tangles. If he and his team chanced to be in the rear he preserved a demeanor of serenity, crossing his legs and bursting forth into yells when foot-passengers took dangerous dives beneath the noses of his champing horses. He smoked his pipe calmly for he knew that his pay was marching on.

If in the front and the key-truck of chaos, he entered terrifically into the quarrel that was raging to and fro among the drivers on their high seats, and sometimes roared oaths and violently got himself arrested.

After a time his sneer grew so that it turned its glare upon all things. He became so sharp that he believed in nothing. To him the police were always actuated by malignant impulses and the rest of the world was composed, for the most part, of despicable creatures who were all trying to take advantage of him and with whom, in defense, he was obliged to quarrel on all possible occasions. He himself occupied a down-trodden position that had a private but distinct element of grandeur in its isolation.

The most complete cases of aggravated idiocy were, to his mind, rampant upon the front platforms of all the street cars. At first his tongue strove with these beings, but he eventually was superior. He became immured like an African cow. In him grew a majestic contempt for those strings of street cars that followed him like intent bugs.

He fell into the habit, when starting on a long journey, of fixing his eye on a high and distant object, commanding his horses to begin, and then going into a sort of a trance of observation. Multitudes of drivers might howl in his rear, and passengers might load him with opprobrium, he would not awaken until some blue policeman turned red and began to frenziedly tear bridles and beat the soft noses of the responsible horses.

When he paused to contemplate the attitude of the police toward himself and his fellows, he believed that they were the only men in the city who had no rights. When driving about, he felt that he was held liable by the police for anything that might occur in the streets, and was the common prey of all energetic officials. In revenge, he resolved never to move out of the way of anything, until formidable circumstances, or a much larger man than himself forced him to it.

Foot-passengers were mere pestering flies with an insane disregard for their legs and his convenience. He could not conceive their maniacal desires to cross the streets. Their madness smote him with eternal amazement. He was continually storming at them from his throne. He sat aloft and denounced their frantic leaps, plunges, dives and straddles.

When they would thrust at, or parry, the noses of his champing horses, making them swing their heads and move their feet, disturbing a solid dreamy repose, he swore at the men as fools, for he himself could perceive that Providence had caused it clearly to be written, that he and his team had the unalienable right to stand in the proper path of the sun chariot, and if they so minded, obstruct its mission or take a wheel off.

And, perhaps, if the god-driver had an ungovernable desire to step down, put up his flame-colored fists and manfully dispute the right of way, he would have probably been immediately opposed by a scowling mortal with two sets of very hard knuckles.

It is possible, perhaps, that this young man would have derided, in an axle-wide alley, the approach of a flying ferry boat. Yet he achieved a respect for a fire engine. As one charged toward his truck, he would drive fearfully upon a side-walk, threatening untold people with annihilation. When an engine would strike a mass of blocked trucks, splitting it into fragments, as a blow annihilates a cake of ice, Jimmie's team could usually be observed high and safe, with whole wheels, on the side-walk. The fearful coming of the engine could break up the most intricate muddle of heavy vehicles at which the police had been swearing for the half of an hour.

A fire engine was enshrined in his heart as an appalling thing that he loved with a distant dog-like devotion. They had been known to overturn street cars. Those leaping horses, striking sparks from the cobbles in their forward lunge, were creatures to be ineffably admired. The clang of the gong pierced his breast like a noise of remembered war.

When Jimmie was a little boy, he began to be arrested. Before he reached a great age, he had a fair record.

He developed too great a tendency to climb down from his truck and fight with other drivers. He had been in quite a number of miscellaneous fights, and in some general bar-room rows that had become known to the police. Once he had been arrested for assaulting a Chinaman. Two women in different parts of the city, and entirely unknown to each other, caused him considerable annoyance by breaking forth, simultaneously, at fateful intervals, into wailings about marriage and support and infants.

Nevertheless, he had, on a certain star-lit evening, said wonderingly and quite reverently: "Deh moon looks like hell, don't it?"

V

The girl, Maggie, blossomed in a mud puddle. She grew to be a most rare and wonderful production of a tenement district, a pretty girl.

None of the dirt of Rum Alley seemed to be in her veins. The philosophers up-stairs, down-stairs and on the same floor, puzzled over it.

When a child, playing and fighting with gamins in the street, dirt disguised her. Attired in tatters and grime, she went unseen.

There came a time, however, when the young men of the vicinity, said: "Dat Johnson goil is a puty good looker." About this period her brother remarked to her: "Mag, I'll tell yeh dis! See? Yeh've edder got teh go teh hell or go teh work!" Whereupon she went to work, having the feminine aversion of going to hell.

By a chance, she got a position in an establishment where they made collars and cuffs. She received a stool and a machine in a room where sat twenty girls of various shades of yellow discontent. She perched on the stool and treadled at her machine all day, turning out collars, the name of whose brand could be noted for its irrelevancy to anything in connection with collars. At night she returned home to her mother.

Jimmie grew large enough to take the vague position of head of the family. As incumbent of that office, he stumbled up-stairs late at night, as his father had done before him. He reeled about the room, swearing at his relations, or went to sleep on the floor.

The mother had gradually arisen to that degree of fame that she could bandy words with her acquaintances among the police-justices. Court-officials called her by her first name. When she appeared they pursued a course which had been theirs for months. They invariably grinned and cried out: "Hello, Mary, you here again?" Her grey head wagged in many a court. She always besieged the bench with voluble excuses, explanations, apologies and prayers. Her flaming face and rolling eyes were a sort of familiar sight on the island. She measured time by means of sprees, and was eternally swollen and dishevelled.

One day the young man, Pete, who as a lad had smitten the Devil's Row urchin in the back of the head and put to flight the antagonists of his friend, Jimmie, strutted upon the scene. He met Jimmie one day on the street, promised to take him to a boxing match in Williamsburg, and called for him in the evening.

Maggie observed Pete.

He sat on a table in the Johnson home and dangled his checked legs with an enticing nonchalance. His hair was curled down over his forehead in an oiled bang. His rather pugged nose seemed to revolt from contact with a bristling moustache of short, wire-like hairs. His blue double-breasted coat, edged with black braid, buttoned close to a red puff tie, and his patent-leather shoes looked like murder-fitted weapons.

His mannerisms stamped him as a man who had a correct sense of his personal superiority. There was valor and contempt for circum-stances in the glance of his eye. He waved his hands like a man of the world, who dismisses religion and philosophy, and says "Fudge." He had certainly seen everything and with each curl of his lip, he declared that it amounted to nothing. Maggie thought he must be a very elegant and graceful bartender.

He was telling tales to Jimmie.

Maggie watched him furtively, with half-closed eyes, lit with a vague interest.

"Hully gee! Dey makes me tired," he said. "Mos' e'ry day some farmer comes in an' tries teh run deh shop. See? But dey gits t'rowed right out! I jolt dem right out in deh street before dey knows where dey is! See?"

"Sure," said Jimmie.

"Dere was a mug come in deh place deh odder day wid an idear he wus goin' teh own deh place! Hully gee, he wus goin' teh own deh place! I see he had a still on an' I didn' wanna giv 'im no stuff, so I says: 'Git deh hell outa here an' don' make no trouble,' I says like dat! See? 'Git deh hell outa here an' don' make no trouble;' like dat. 'Git deh hell outa here,' I says. See?"

Jimmie nodded understandingly. Over his features played an eager desire to state the amount of his valor in a similar crisis, but the narrator proceeded.

"Well, deh blokie he says: 'T'hell wid it! I ain' lookin' for no scrap,' he says. See? 'But,' he says, 'I'm 'spectable cit'zen an' I wanna drink an' purtydamnsoon, too.' See? 'Deh hell,' I says. Like dat! 'Deh hell,' I says. See? 'Don' make no trouble,' I says. Like dat. 'Don' make no trouble.' See?

Den deh mug he squared off an' said he was fine as silk wid his dukes. See? An' he wanned a drink damnquick. Dat's what he said. See?"

"Sure," repeated Jimmie.

Pete continued. "Say, I jes' jumped deh bar an' deh way I plunked dat blokie was great. See? Dat's right! In deh jaw! See? Hully gee, he t'rowed a spittoon true deh front windee. Say, I taut I'd drop dead. But deh boss, he comes in after an' he says, 'Pete, yehs done jes' right! Yeh've gota keep order an' it's all right.' See? 'It's all right,' he says. Dat's what he said."

The two held a technical discussion.

"Dat bloke was a dandy," said Pete, in conclusion, "but he had'n' oughta made no trouble. Dat's what I says teh dem: 'Don' come in here an' make no trouble,' I says, like dat. 'Don' make no trouble.' See?"

As Jimmie and his friend exchanged tales descriptive of their prowess, Maggie leaned back in the shadow. Her eyes dwelt wonderingly and rather wistfully upon Pete's face. The broken furniture, grimy walls, and general disorder and dirt of her home of a sudden appeared before her and began to take a potential aspect. Pete's aristocratic person looked as if it might soil. She looked keenly at him, occasionally wondering if he was feeling contempt. But Pete seemed to be enveloped in reminiscence.

"Hully gee," said he, "dose mugs can't phase me. Dey knows I kin wipe up deh street wid any t'ree of dem."

When he said, "Ah, what deh hell," his voice was burdened with disdain for the inevitable and contempt for anything that fate might compel him to endure.

Maggie perceived that here was the beau ideal of a man. Her dim thoughts were often searching for far away lands where, as God says, the little hills sing together in the morning. Under the trees of her dreamgardens there had always walked a lover.

VI

Pete took note of Maggie.

"Say, Mag, I'm stuck on yer shape. It's outa sight," he said, parenthetically, with an affable grin.

As he became aware that she was listening closely, he grew still more eloquent in his descriptions of various happenings in his career. It appeared that he was invincible in fights.

"Why," he said, referring to a man with whom he had had a misunderstanding, "dat mug scrapped like a damn dago. Dat's right. He was dead easy. See? He tau't he was a scrapper. But he foun' out diff'ent! Hully gee."

He walked to and fro in the small room, which seemed then to grow even smaller and unfit to hold his dignity, the attribute of a supreme warrior. That swing of the shoulders that had frozen the timid when he was but a lad had increased with his growth and education at the ratio of ten to one. It, combined with the sneer upon his mouth, told mankind that there was nothing in space which could appall him. Maggie marvelled at him and surrounded him with greatness. She vaguely tried to calculate the altitude of the pinnacle from which he must have looked down upon her.

"I met a chump deh odder day way up in deh city," he said. "I was goin' teh see a frien' of mine. When I was a-crossin' deh street deh chump runned plump inteh me, an' den he turns aroun' an' says, 'Yer insolen' ruffin,' he says, like dat. 'Oh, gee,' I says, 'oh, gee, go teh hell and git off deh eart',' I says, like dat. See? 'Go teh hell an' git off deh eart',' like dat. Den deh blokie he got wild. He says I was a contempt'ble scoun'el, er someting like dat, an' he says I was doom' teh everlastin' pe'dition an' all like dat. 'Gee,' I says, 'gee! Deh hell I am,' I says. 'Deh hell I am,' like dat. An' den I slugged 'im. See?"

With Jimmie in his company, Pete departed in a sort of a blaze of glory from the Johnson home. Maggie, leaning from the window, watched him as he walked down the street.

Here was a formidable man who disdained the strength of a world full of fists. Here was one who had contempt for brass-clothed power; one whose knuckles could defiantly ring against the granite of law. He was a knight.

The two men went from under the glimmering street-lamp and passed into shadows.

Turning, Maggie contemplated the dark, dust-stained walls, and the scant and crude furniture of her home. A clock, in a splintered and battered oblong box of varnished wood, she suddenly regarded as an abomination. She noted that it ticked raspingly. The almost vanished flowers in the carpet-pattern, she conceived to be newly hideous. Some faint attempts she had made with blue ribbon, to freshen the appearance of a dingy curtain, she now saw to be piteous.

She wondered what Pete dined on.

She reflected upon the collar and cuff factory. It began to appear to her mind as a dreary place of endless grinding. Pete's elegant occupation brought him, no doubt, into contact with people who had money and manners. It was probable that he had a large acquaintance of pretty girls. He must have great sums of money to spend.

To her the earth was composed of hardships and insults. She felt instant admiration for a man who openly defied it. She thought that if the grim angel of death should clutch his heart, Pete would shrug his shoulders and say: "Oh, ev'ryt'ing goes."

She anticipated that he would come again shortly. She spent some of her week's pay in the purchase of flowered cretonne for a lambrequin. She made it with infinite care and hung it to the slightly-careening mantel, over the stove, in the kitchen. She studied it with painful anxiety from different points in the room. She wanted it to look well on Sunday night when, perhaps, Jimmie's friend would come. On Sunday night, however, Pete did not appear.

Afterward the girl looked at it with a sense of humiliation. She was now convinced that Pete was superior to admiration for lambrequins.

A few evenings later Pete entered with fascinating innovations in his apparel. As she had seen him twice and he had different suits on each time, Maggie had a dim impression that his wardrobe was prodigiously extensive.

"Say, Mag," he said, "put on yer bes' duds Friday night an' I'll take yehs teh deh show. See?"

He spent a few moments in flourishing his clothes and then vanished, without having glanced at the lambrequin.

Over the eternal collars and cuffs in the factory Maggie spent the most of three days in making imaginary sketches of Pete and his daily environment. She imagined some half dozen women in love with him and thought he must lean dangerously toward an indefinite one, whom she pictured with great charms of person, but with an altogether contemptible disposition.

She thought he must live in a blare of pleasure. He had friends, and people who were afraid of him.

She saw the golden glitter of the place where Pete was to take her. An entertainment of many hues and many melodies where she was afraid she might appear small and mouse-colored.

Her mother drank whiskey all Friday morning. With lurid face and tossing hair she cursed and destroyed furniture all Friday afternoon. When Maggie came home at half-past six her mother lay asleep amidst the wreck of chairs and a table. Fragments of various household utensils were scattered about the floor. She had vented some phase of drunken fury upon the lambrequin. It lay in a bedraggled heap in the corner.

"Hah," she snorted, sitting up suddenly, "where deh hell yeh been? Why deh hell don' yeh come home earlier? Been loafin' 'round deh streets. Yer gettin' teh be a reg'lar devil."

When Pete arrived Maggie, in a worn black dress, was waiting for him in the midst of a floor strewn with wreckage. The curtain at the window had been pulled by a heavy hand and hung by one tack, dangling to and fro in the draft through the cracks at the sash. The knots of blue ribbons appeared like violated flowers. The fire in the stove had gone out. The displaced lids and open doors showed heaps of sullen grey ashes. The remnants of a meal, ghastly, like dead flesh, lay in a corner. Maggie's red mother, stretched on the floor, blasphemed and gave her daughter a bad name.

VII

An orchestra of yellow silk women and bald-headed men on an elevated stage near the centre of a great green-hued hall, played a popular waltz. The place was crowded with people grouped about little tables. A battalion of waiters slid among the throng, carrying trays of beer glasses and making change from the inexhaustible vaults of their trousers pockets. Little boys, in the costumes of French chefs, paraded up and down the irregular aisles vending fancy cakes. There was a low rumble of conversation and a subdued clinking of glasses. Clouds of tobacco smoke rolled and wavered high in air about the dull gilt of the chandeliers.

The vast crowd had an air throughout of having just quitted labor. Men with calloused hands and attired in garments that showed the wear of an endless trudge for a living, smoked their pipes contentedly and spent five, ten, or perhaps fifteen cents for beer. There was a mere sprinkling of kid-gloved men who smoked cigars purchased elsewhere. The great body of the crowd was composed of people who showed that all day they strove with their hands. Quiet Germans, with maybe their wives and two or three children, sat listening to the music, with the expressions of happy cows. An occasional party of sailors from a war-ship, their faces pictures of sturdy health, spent the earlier hours of the evening at the small round tables. Very infrequent tipsy men, swollen with the value of their opinions, engaged their companions in earnest and confidential conversation. In the balcony, and here and there below, shone the impassive faces of women. The nationalities of the Bowery beamed upon the stage from all directions.

Pete aggressively walked up a side aisle and took seats with Maggie at a table beneath the balcony.

"Two beehs!"

Leaning back he regarded with eyes of superiority the scene before them. This attitude affected Maggie strongly. A man who could regard such a sight with indifference must be accustomed to very great things.

It was obvious that Pete had been to this place many times before, and was very familiar with it. A knowledge of this fact made Maggie feel little and new.

He was extremely gracious and attentive. He displayed the consideration of a cultured gentleman who knew what was due.

"Say, what deh hell? Bring deh lady a big glass! What deh hell use is dat pony?"

"Don't be fresh, now," said the waiter, with some warmth, as he departed.

"Ah, git off deh eart'," said Pete, after the other's retreating form.

Maggie perceived that Pete brought forth all his elegance and all his knowledge of high-class customs for her benefit. Her heart warmed as she reflected upon his condescension.

The orchestra of yellow silk women and bald-headed men gave vent to a few bars of anticipatory music and a girl, in a pink dress with short skirts, galloped upon the stage. She smiled upon the throng as if in acknowledgment of a warm welcome, and began to walk to and fro, making profuse gesticulations and singing, in brazen soprano tones, a song, the words of which were inaudible. When she broke into the swift rattling measures of a chorus some half-tipsy men near the stage joined in the rollicking refrain and glasses were pounded rhythmically upon the tables. People leaned forward to watch her and to try to catch the words of the song. When she vanished there were long rollings of applause.

Obedient to more anticipatory bars, she reappeared amidst the half-suppressed cheering of the tipsy men. The orchestra plunged into dance music and the laces of the dancer fluttered and flew in the glare of gas jets. She divulged the fact that she was attired in some half dozen skirts. It was patent that any one of them would have proved adequate for the purpose for which skirts are intended. An occasional man bent forward, intent upon the pink stockings. Maggie wondered at the splendor of the costume and lost herself in calculations of the cost of the silks and laces.

The dancer's smile of stereotyped enthusiasm was turned for ten minutes upon the faces of her audience. In the finale she fell into some of those grotesque attitudes which were at the time popular among the dancers in the theatres up-town, giving to the Bowery public the phantasies of the aristocratic theatre-going public, at reduced rates.

"Say, Pete," said Maggie, leaning forward, "dis is great."

"Sure," said Pete, with proper complacence.

A ventriloquist followed the dancer. He held two fantastic dolls on his knees. He made them sing mournful ditties and say funny things about geography and Ireland.

"Do dose little men talk?" asked Maggie.

"Naw," said Pete, "it's some damn fake. See?"

Two girls, on the bills as sisters, came forth and sang a duet that is heard occasionally at concerts given under church auspices. They supplemented it with a dance which of course can never be seen at concerts given under church auspices.

After the duettists had retired, a woman of debatable age sang a negro melody. The chorus necessitated some grotesque waddlings supposed to be an imitation of a plantation darkey, under the influence, probably, of music and the moon. The audience was just enthusiastic enough over it to have her return and sing a sorrowful lay, whose lines told of a mother's love and a sweetheart who waited and a young man who was lost at sea under the most harrowing circumstances. From the faces of a score or so in the crowd, the self-contained look faded. Many heads were bent forward with eagerness and sympathy. As the last distressing sentiment of the piece was brought forth, it was greeted by that kind of applause which rings as sincere.

As a final effort, the singer rendered some verses which described a vision of Britain being annihilated by America, and Ireland bursting her bonds. A carefully prepared crisis was reached in the last line of the last verse, where the singer threw out her arms and cried, "The star-spangled banner." Instantly a great cheer swelled from the throats of the assemblage of the masses. There was a heavy rumble of booted feet thumping the floor. Eyes gleamed with sudden fire, and calloused hands waved frantically in the air.

After a few moments' rest, the orchestra played crashingly, and a small fat man burst out upon the stage. He began to roar a song and stamp back and forth before the foot-lights, wildly waving a glossy silk hat and throwing leers, or smiles, broadcast. He made his face into fantastic grimaces until he looked like a pictured devil on a Japanese kite. The crowd laughed gleefully. His short, fat legs were never still a moment. He shouted and roared and bobbed his shock of red wig until the audience broke out in excited applause.

Pete did not pay much attention to the progress of events upon the stage. He was drinking beer and watching Maggie.

Her cheeks were blushing with excitement and her eyes were glistening. She drew deep breaths of pleasure. No thoughts of the atmosphere of the collar and cuff factory came to her.

When the orchestra crashed finally, they jostled their way to the sidewalk with the crowd. Pete took Maggie's arm and pushed a way for her, offering to fight with a man or two.

They reached Maggie's home at a late hour and stood for a moment in front of the gruesome doorway.

"Say, Mag," said Pete, "give us a kiss for takin' yeh teh deh show, will yer?"

Maggie laughed, as if startled, and drew away from him.

"Naw, Pete," she said, "dat wasn't in it."

"Ah, what deh hell?" urged Pete.

The girl retreated nervously.

"Ah, what deh hell?" repeated he.

Maggie darted into the hall, and up the stairs. She turned and smiled at him, then disappeared.

Pete walked slowly down the street. He had something of an astonished expression upon his features. He paused under a lamp-post and breathed a low breath of surprise.

"Gawd," he said, "I wonner if I've been played fer a duffer."

VIII

As thoughts of Pete came to Maggie's mind, she began to have an intense dislike for all of her dresses.

"What deh hell ails yeh? What makes yeh be allus fixin' and fussin'? Good Gawd," her mother would frequently roar at her.

She began to note, with more interest, the well-dressed women she met on the avenues. She envied elegance and soft palms. She craved those adornments of person which she saw every day on the street, conceiving them to be allies of vast importance to women.

Studying faces, she thought many of the women and girls she chanced to meet, smiled with serenity as though forever cherished and watched over by those they loved.

The air in the collar and cuff establishment strangled her. She knew she was gradually and surely shrivelling in the hot, stuffy room. The begrimed windows rattled incessantly from the passing of elevated trains. The place was filled with a whirl of noises and odors.

She wondered as she regarded some of the grizzled women in the room, mere mechanical contrivances sewing seams and grinding out, with heads bended over their work, tales of imagined or real girl-hood happiness, past drunks, the baby at home, and unpaid wages. She speculated how long her youth would endure. She began to see the bloom upon her cheeks as valuable.

She imagined herself, in an exasperating future, as a scrawny woman with an eternal grievance. Too, she thought Pete to be a very fastidious person concerning the appearance of women.

She felt she would love to see somebody entangle their fingers in the oily beard of the fat foreigner who owned the establishment. He was a detestable creature. He wore white socks with low shoes.

He sat all day delivering orations, in the depths of a cushioned chair. His pocket-book deprived them of the power of retort.

"What een hell do you sink I pie fife dolla a week for? Play? No, py damn!"

Maggie was anxious for a friend to whom she could talk about Pete. She would have liked to discuss his admirable mannerisms with a reliable mutual friend. At home, she found her mother often drunk and always raving.

It seems that the world had treated this woman very badly, and she took a deep revenge upon such portions of it as came within her reach. She broke furniture as if she were at last getting her rights. She swelled with virtuous indignation as she carried the lighter articles of household use, one by one under the shadows of the three gilt balls, where Hebrews chained them with chains of interest.

Jimmie came when he was obliged to by circumstances over which he had no control. His well-trained legs brought him staggering home and put him to bed some nights when he would rather have gone elsewhere.

Swaggering Pete loomed like a golden sun to Maggie. He took her to a dime museum where rows of meek freaks astonished her. She contemplated their deformities with awe and thought them a sort of chosen tribe.

Pete, raking his brains for amusement, discovered the Central Park Menagerie and the Museum of Arts. Sunday afternoons would sometimes find them at these places. Pete did not appear to be particularly interested in what he saw. He stood around looking heavy, while Maggie giggled in glee.

Once at the Menagerie he went into a trance of admiration before the spectacle of a very small monkey threatening to thrash a cageful because one of them had pulled his tail and he had not wheeled about quickly enough to discover who did it. Ever after Pete knew that monkey by sight and winked at him, trying to induce him to fight with other and larger monkeys.

At the Museum, Maggie said, "Dis is outa sight."

"Oh hell," said Pete, "wait till next summer an' I'll take yehs to a picnic."

While the girl wandered in the vaulted rooms, Pete occupied himself in returning stony stare for stony stare, the appalling scrutiny of the watchdogs of the treasures. Occasionally he would remark in loud tones: "Dat jay has got glass eyes," and sentences of the sort. When he tired of this amusement he would go to the mummies and moralize over them.

Usually he submitted with silent dignity to all which he had to go through, but, at times, he was goaded into comment.

"What deh hell," he demanded once. "Look at all dese little jugs! Hundred jugs in a row! Ten rows in a case an' 'bout a t'ousand cases! What deh blazes use is dem?"

Evenings during the week he took her to see plays in which the brain-clutching heroine was rescued from the palatial home of her guardian, who is cruelly after her bonds, by the hero with the beautiful sentiments. The latter spent most of his time out at soak in pale-green snow storms, busy with a nickel-plated revolver, rescuing aged strangers from villains.

Maggie lost herself in sympathy with the wanderers swooning in snow storms beneath happy-hued church windows. And a choir within singing "Joy to the World." To Maggie and the rest of the audience this was transcendental realism. Joy always within, and they, like the actor, inevitably without. Viewing it, they hugged themselves in ecstatic pity of their imagined or real condition.

The girl thought the arrogance and granite-heartedness of the magnate of the play was very accurately drawn. She echoed the maledictions that the occupants of the gallery showered on this individual when his lines compelled him to expose his extreme selfishness.

Shady persons in the audience revolted from the pictured villainy of the drama. With untiring zeal they hissed vice and applauded virtue. Unmistakably bad men evinced an apparently sincere admiration for virtue.

The loud gallery was overwhelmingly with the unfortunate and the oppressed. They encouraged the struggling hero with cries, and jeered the villain, hooting and calling attention to his whiskers. When anybody died in the pale-green snow storms, the gallery mourned. They sought out the painted misery and hugged it as akin.

In the hero's erratic march from poverty in the first act, to wealth and triumph in the final one, in which he forgives all the enemies that he has left, he was assisted by the gallery, which applauded his generous and noble sentiments and confounded the speeches of his opponents by making irrelevant but very sharp remarks. Those actors who were cursed with villainy parts were confronted at every turn by the gallery. If one of them rendered lines containing the most subtile distinctions between right and wrong, the gallery was immediately aware if the actor meant wickedness, and denounced him accordingly.

The last act was a triumph for the hero, poor and of the masses, the representative of the audience, over the villain and the rich man, his pockets stuffed with bonds, his heart packed with tyrannical purposes, imperturbable amid suffering.

Maggie always departed with raised spirits from the showing places of the melodrama. She rejoiced at the way in which the poor and virtuous eventually surmounted the wealthy and wicked. The theatre made her think. She wondered if the culture and refinement she had seen imitated, perhaps grotesquely, by the heroine on the stage, could be acquired by a girl who lived in a tenement house and worked in a shirt factory.

IX

A group of urchins were intent upon the side door of a saloon. Expectancy gleamed from their eyes. They were twisting their fingers in excitement.

"Here she comes," yelled one of them suddenly.

The group of urchins burst instantly asunder and its individual fragments were spread in a wide, respectable half-circle about the point of interest. The saloon door opened with a crash, and the figure of a woman appeared upon the threshold. Her grey hair fell in knotted masses about her shoulders. Her face was crimsoned and wet with perspiration. Her eyes had a rolling glare.

"Not a damn cent more of me money will yehs ever get, not a damn cent. I spent me money here fer t'ree years an' now yehs tells me yeh'll sell me no more stuff! T'hell wid yeh, Johnnie Murckre! 'Disturbance?' Disturbance be damned! T'hell wid yeh, Johnnie—"

The door received a kick of exasperation from within and the woman lurched heavily out on the sidewalk.

The gamins in the half-circle became violently agitated. They began to dance about and hoot and yell and jeer. Wide dirty grins spread over each face.

The woman made a furious dash at a particularly outrageous cluster of little boys. They laughed delightedly and scampered off a short distance, calling out over their shoulders to her. She stood tottering on the curbstone and thundered at them.

"Yeh devil's kids," she howled, shaking red fists. The little boys whooped in glee. As she started up the street they fell in behind and marched uproariously. Occasionally she wheeled about and made charges on them. They ran nimbly out of reach and taunted her.

In the frame of a gruesome doorway she stood for a moment cursing them. Her hair straggled, giving her crimson features a look of insanity. Her great fists quivered as she shook them madly in the air.

The urchins made terrific noises until she turned and disappeared. Then they filed quietly in the way they had come.

The woman floundered about in the lower hall of the tenement house and finally stumbled up the stairs. On an upper hall a door was opened and a collection of heads peered curiously out, watching her. With a wrathful snort the woman confronted the door, but it was slammed hastily in her face and the key was turned.

She stood for a few minutes, delivering a frenzied challenge at the panels.

"Come out in deh hall, Mary Murphy, damn yeh, if yehs want a row. Come ahn, yeh overgrown terrier, come ahn."

She began to kick the door with her great feet. She shrilly defied the universe to appear and do battle. Her cursing trebles brought heads from all doors save the one she threatened. Her eyes glared in every direction. The air was full of her tossing fists.

"Come ahn, deh hull damn gang of yehs, come ahn," she roared at the spectators. An oath or two, cat-calls, jeers and bits of facetious advice were given in reply. Missiles clattered about her feet.

"What deh hell's deh matter wid yeh?" said a voice in the gathered gloom, and Jimmie came forward. He carried a tin dinner-pail in his hand and under his arm a brown truckman's apron done in a bundle. "What deh hell's wrong?" he demanded.

"Come out, all of yehs, come out," his mother was howling. "Come ahn an' I'll stamp yer damn brains under me feet."

"Shet yer face, an' come home, yeh damned old fool," roared Jimmie at her. She strided up to him and twirled her fingers in his face. Her eyes were darting flames of unreasoning rage and her frame trembled with eagerness for a fight.

"T'hell wid yehs! An' who deh hell are yehs? I ain't givin' a snap of me fingers fer yehs," she bawled at him. She turned her huge back in tremendous disdain and climbed the stairs to the next floor.

Jimmie followed, cursing blackly. At the top of the flight he seized his mother's arm and started to drag her toward the door of their room.

"Come home, damn yeh," he gritted between his teeth.

"Take yer hands off me! Take yer hands off me," shrieked his mother.

She raised her arm and whirled her great fist at her son's face. Jimmie dodged his head and the blow struck him in the back of the neck. "Damn yeh," gritted he again. He threw out his left hand and writhed his fingers about her middle arm. The mother and the son began to sway and struggle like gladiators.

"Whoop!" said the Rum Alley tenement house. The hall filled with interested spectators.

"Hi, ol' lady, dat was a dandy!"

"T'ree to one on deh red!"

"Ah, stop yer damn scrappin'!"

The door of the Johnson home opened and Maggie looked out. Jimmie made a supreme cursing effort and hurled his mother into the room. He quickly followed and closed the door. The Rum Alley tenement swore disappointedly and retired.

The mother slowly gathered herself up from the floor. Her eyes glittered menacingly upon her children.

"Here, now," said Jimmie, "we've had enough of dis. Sit down, an' don' make no trouble."

He grasped her arm, and twisting it, forced her into a creaking chair.

"Keep yer hands off me," roared his mother again.

"Damn yer ol' hide," yelled Jimmie, madly. Maggie shrieked and ran into the other room. To her there came the sound of a storm of crashes and curses. There was a great final thump and Jimmie's voice cried: "Dere, damn yeh, stay still." Maggie opened the door now, and went warily out. "Oh, Jimmie."

He was leaning against the wall and swearing. Blood stood upon bruises on his knotty fore-arms where they had scraped against the floor or the walls in the scuffle. The mother lay screeching on the floor, the tears running down her furrowed face.

Maggie, standing in the middle of the room, gazed about her. The usual upheaval of the tables and chairs had taken place. Crockery was strewn broadcast in fragments. The stove had been disturbed on its legs, and now leaned idiotically to one side. A pail had been upset and water spread in all directions.

The door opened and Pete appeared. He shrugged his shoulders. "Oh, Gawd," he observed.

He walked over to Maggie and whispered in her ear. "Ah, what deh hell, Mag? Come ahn and we'll have a hell of a time."

The mother in the corner upreared her head and shook her tangled locks.

"Teh hell wid him and you," she said, glowering at her daughter in the gloom. Her eyes seemed to burn balefully. "Yeh've gone teh deh devil, Mag Johnson, yehs knows yehs have gone teh deh devil. Yer a disgrace teh yer people, damn yeh. An' now, git out an' go ahn wid dat doe-faced jude of yours. Go teh hell wid him, damn yeh, an' a good riddance. Go teh hell an' see how yeh likes it."

Maggie gazed long at her mother.

"Go teh hell now, an' see how yeh likes it. Git out. I won't have sech as yehs in me house! Get out, d'yeh hear! Damn yeh, git out!"

The girl began to tremble.

At this instant Pete came forward. "Oh, what deh hell, Mag, see," he whispered softly in her ear. "Dis all blows over. See? Deh ol' woman 'ill be all right in deh mornin'. Come ahn out wid me! We'll have a hell of a time."

The woman on the floor cursed. Jimmie was intent upon his bruised fore-arms. The girl cast a glance about the room filled with a chaotic mass of debris, and at the red, writhing body of her mother.

"Go teh hell an' good riddance."

She went.

X

Jimmie had an idea it wasn't common courtesy for a friend to come to one's home and ruin one's sister. But he was not sure how much Pete knew about the rules of politeness.

The following night he returned home from work at rather a late hour in the evening. In passing through the halls he came upon the gnarled and leathery old woman who possessed the music box. She was grinning in the dim light that drifted through dust-stained panes. She beckoned to him with a smudged fore-finger.

"Ah, Jimmie, what do yehs t'ink I got onto las' night. It was deh funnies' t'ing I ever saw," she cried, coming close to him and leering. She was trembling with eagerness to tell her tale. "I was by me door las' night when yer sister and her jude feller came in late, oh, very late. An' she, the dear, she was a-cryin' as if her heart would break, she was. It was deh funnies' t'ing I ever saw. An' right out here by me door she asked him did he love her, did he. An' she was a-cryin' as if her heart would break, poor t'ing. An' him, I could see by deh way what he said it dat she had been askin' orften, he says: 'Oh, hell, yes,' he says, says he, 'Oh, hell, yes.'"

Storm-clouds swept over Jimmie's face, but he turned from the leathery old woman and plodded on up stairs.

"Oh, hell, yes," called she after him. She laughed a laugh that was like a prophetic croak. "'Oh, hell, yes,' he says, says he, 'Oh, hell, yes.'"

There was no one in at home. The rooms showed that attempts had been made at tidying them. Parts of the wreckage of the day before had been repaired by an unskillful hand. A chair or two and the table, stood uncertainly upon legs. The floor had been newly swept. Too, the blue ribbons had been restored to the curtains, and the lambrequin, with its immense sheaves of yellow wheat and red roses of equal size, had been returned, in a worn and sorry state, to its position at the mantel. Maggie's jacket and hat were gone from the nail behind the door.

Jimmie walked to the window and began to look through the blurred glass. It occurred to him to vaguely wonder, for an instant, if some of the women of his acquaintance had brothers.

Suddenly, however, he began to swear.

"But he was me frien'! I brought 'im here! Dat's deh hell of it!"

He fumed about the room, his anger gradually rising to the furious pitch.

"I'll kill deh jay! Dat's what I'll do! I'll kill deh jay!"

He clutched his hat and sprang toward the door. But it opened and his mother's great form blocked the passage.

"What deh hell's deh matter wid yeh?" exclaimed she, coming into the rooms.

Jimmie gave vent to a sardonic curse and then laughed heavily.

"Well, Maggie's gone teh deh devil! Dat's what! See?"

"Eh?" said his mother.

"Maggie's gone teh deh devil! Are yehs deaf?" roared Jimmie, impatiently.

"Deh hell she has," murmured the mother, astounded.

Jimmie grunted, and then began to stare out at the window. His mother sat down in a chair, but a moment later sprang erect and delivered a maddened whirl of oaths. Her son turned to look at her as she reeled and swayed in the middle of the room, her fierce face convulsed with passion, her blotched arms raised high in imprecation.

"May Gawd curse her forever," she shrieked. "May she eat nothin' but stones and deh dirt in deh street. May she sleep in deh gutter an' never see deh sun shine agin. Deh damn—"

"Here, now," said her son. "Take a drop on yourself."

The mother raised lamenting eyes to the ceiling.

"She's deh devil's own chil', Jimmie," she whispered. "Ah, who would t'ink such a bad girl could grow up in our fambly, Jimmie, me son. Many deh hour I've spent in talk wid dat girl an' tol' her if she ever went on deh streets I'd see her damned. An' after all her bringin' up an' what I tol' her and talked wid her, she goes teh deh bad, like a duck teh water."

The tears rolled down her furrowed face. Her hands trembled.

"An' den when dat Sadie MacMallister next door to us was sent teh deh devil by dat feller what worked in deh soap-factory, didn't I tell our Mag dat if she—"

"Ah, dat's annuder story," interrupted the brother. "Of course, dat Sadie was nice an' all dat—but—see—it ain't dessame as if—well, Maggie was diff'ent—see—she was diff'ent."

He was trying to formulate a theory that he had always unconsciously held, that all sisters, excepting his own, could advisedly be ruined.

He suddenly broke out again. "I'll go t'ump deh hell outa deh mug what did her deh harm. I'll kill 'im! He t'inks he kin scrap, but when he gits me a-chasin' 'im he'll fin' out where he's wrong, deh damned duffer. I'll wipe up deh street wid 'im."

In a fury he plunged out of the doorway. As he vanished the mother raised her head and lifted both hands, entreating.

"May Gawd curse her forever," she cried.

In the darkness of the hallway Jimmie discerned a knot of women talking volubly. When he strode by they paid no attention to him.

"She allus was a bold thing," he heard one of them cry in an eager voice. "Dere wasn't a feller come teh deh house but she'd try teh mash 'im. My Annie says deh shameless t'ing tried teh ketch her feller, her own feller, what we useter know his fader."

"I could a' tol' yehs dis two years ago," said a woman, in a key of triumph. "Yessir, it was over two years ago dat I says teh my ol' man, I says, 'Dat Johnson girl ain't straight,' I says. 'Oh, hell,' he says. 'Oh, hell.' 'Dat's all right,' I says, 'but I know what I knows,' I says, 'an' it'ill come out later. You wait an' see,' I says, 'you see.'"

"Anybody what had eyes could see dat dere was somethin' wrong wid dat girl. I didn't like her actions."

On the street Jimmie met a friend. "What deh hell?" asked the latter. Jimmie explained. "An' I'll t'ump 'im till he can't stand."

"Oh, what deh hell," said the friend. "What's deh use! Yeh'll git pulled in! Everybody 'ill be onto it! An' ten plunks! Gee!"

Jimmie was determined. "He t'inks he kin scrap, but he'll fin' out diff'ent."

"Gee," remonstrated the friend. "What deh hell?"

XI

On a corner a glass-fronted building shed a yellow glare upon the pavements. The open mouth of a saloon called seductively to passengers to enter and annihilate sorrow or create rage.

The interior of the place was papered in olive and bronze tints of imitation leather. A shining bar of counterfeit massiveness extended down the side of the room. Behind it a great mahogany-appearing sideboard reached the ceiling. Upon its shelves rested pyramids of shimmering glasses that were never disturbed. Mirrors set in the face of the sideboard multiplied them. Lemons, oranges and paper napkins, arranged with mathematical precision, sat among the glasses. Many-hued decanters of liquor perched at regular intervals on the lower shelves. A nickel-plated cash register occupied a position in the exact center of the general effect. The elementary senses of it all seemed to be opulence and geometrical accuracy.

Across from the bar a smaller counter held a collection of plates upon which swarmed frayed fragments of crackers, slices of boiled ham, dishevelled bits of cheese, and pickles swimming in vinegar. An odor of grasping, begrimed hands and munching mouths pervaded.

Pete, in a white jacket, was behind the bar bending expectantly toward a quiet stranger. "A beeh," said the man. Pete drew a foam-topped glassful and set it dripping upon the bar.

At this moment the light bamboo doors at the entrance swung open and crashed against the siding. Jimmie and a companion entered. They swaggered unsteadily but belligerently toward the bar and looked at Pete with bleared and blinking eyes.

"Gin," said Jimmie.

"Gin," said the companion.

Pete slid a bottle and two glasses along the bar. He bended his head sideways as he assiduously polished away with a napkin at the gleaming wood. He had a look of watchfulness upon his features.

Jimmie and his companion kept their eyes upon the bartender and conversed loudly in tones of contempt.

"He's a dindy masher, ain't he, by Gawd?" laughed Jimmie.

"Oh, hell, yes," said the companion, sneering widely. "He's great, he is. Git onto deh mug on deh blokie. Dat's enough to make a feller turn hand-springs in 'is sleep."

The quiet stranger moved himself and his glass a trifle further away and maintained an attitude of oblivion.

"Gee! ain't he hot stuff!"

"Git onto his shape! Great Gawd!"

"Hey," cried Jimmie, in tones of command. Pete came along slowly, with a sullen dropping of the under lip.

"Well," he growled, "what's eatin' yehs?"

"Gin," said Jimmie.

"Gin," said the companion.

As Pete confronted them with the bottle and the glasses, they laughed in his face. Jimmie's companion, evidently overcome with merriment, pointed a grimy forefinger in Pete's direction.

"Say, Jimmie," demanded he, "what deh hell is dat behind deh bar?"

"Damned if I knows," replied Jimmie. They laughed loudly. Pete put down a bottle with a bang and turned a formidable face toward them. He disclosed his teeth and his shoulders heaved restlessly.

"You fellers can't guy me," he said. "Drink yer stuff an' git out an' don' make no trouble."

Instantly the laughter faded from the faces of the two men and expressions of offended dignity immediately came.

"Who deh hell has said anyt'ing teh you," cried they in the same breath.

The quiet stranger looked at the door calculatingly.

"Ah, come off," said Pete to the two men. "Don't pick me up for no jay. Drink yer rum an' git out an' don' make no trouble."

"Oh, deh hell," airily cried Jimmie.

"Oh, deh hell," airily repeated his companion.

"We goes when we git ready! See!" continued Jimmie.

"Well," said Pete in a threatening voice, "don' make no trouble."

Jimmie suddenly leaned forward with his head on one side. He snarled like a wild animal.

"Well, what if we does? See?" said he.

Dark blood flushed into Pete's face, and he shot a lurid glance at Jimmie.

"Well, den we'll see whose deh bes' man, you or me," he said.

The quiet stranger moved modestly toward the door.

Jimmie began to swell with valor.

"Don' pick me up fer no tenderfoot. When yeh tackles me yeh tackles one of deh bes' men in deh city. See? I'm a scrapper, I am. Ain't dat right, Billie?"

"Sure, Jimmie," responded his companion in tones of conviction.

"Oh, hell," said Pete, easily. "Go fall on yerself."

The two men again began to laugh.

"What deh hell is dat talkin'?" cried the companion.

"Damned if I knows," replied Jimmie with exaggerated contempt.

Pete made a furious gesture. "Git outa here now, an' don' make no trouble. See? Youse fellers er lookin' fer a scrap an' it's damn likely yeh'll fin' one if yeh keeps on shootin' off yer mout's. I know yehs! See? I kin lick better men dan yehs ever saw in yer lifes. Dat's right! See? Don' pick me up fer no stuff er yeh might be jolted out in deh street before yeh knows where yeh is. When I comes from behind dis bar, I t'rows yehs bote inteh deh street. See?"

"Oh, hell," cried the two men in chorus.

The glare of a panther came into Pete's eyes. "Dat's what I said! Unnerstan'?"

He came through a passage at the end of the bar and swelled down upon the two men. They stepped promptly forward and crowded close to him.

They bristled like three roosters. They moved their heads pugnaciously and kept their shoulders braced. The nervous muscles about each mouth twitched with a forced smile of mockery.

"Well, what deh hell yer goin' teh do?" gritted Jimmie.

Pete stepped warily back, waving his hands before him to keep the men from coming too near.

"Well, what deh hell yer goin' teh do?" repeated Jimmie's ally. They kept close to him, taunting and leering. They strove to make him attempt the initial blow.

"Keep back, now! Don' crowd me," ominously said Pete.

Again they chorused in contempt. "Oh, hell!"

In a small, tossing group, the three men edged for positions like frigates contemplating battle.

"Well, why deh hell don' yeh try teh t'row us out?" cried Jimmie and his ally with copious sneers.

The bravery of bull-dogs sat upon the faces of the men. Their clenched fists moved like eager weapons.

The allied two jostled the bartender's elbows, glaring at him with feverish eyes and forcing him toward the wall.

Suddenly Pete swore redly. The flash of action gleamed from his eyes. He threw back his arm and aimed a tremendous, lightning-like blow at Jimmie's face. His foot swung a step forward and the weight of his body was behind his fist. Jimmie ducked his head, Bowery-like, with the quickness of a cat. The fierce, answering blows of him and his ally crushed on Pete's bowed head.

The quiet stranger vanished.

The arms of the combatants whirled in the air like flails. The faces of the men, at first flushed to flame-colored anger, now began to fade to the pallor of warriors in the blood and heat of a battle. Their lips curled back and stretched tightly over the gums in ghoul-like grins. Through their white, gripped teeth struggled hoarse whisperings of oaths. Their eyes glittered with murderous fire.

Each head was huddled between its owner's shoulders, and arms were swinging with marvelous rapidity. Feet scraped to and fro with a loud scratching sound upon the sanded floor. Blows left crimson blotches upon pale skin. The curses of the first quarter-minute of the fight died away. The breaths of the fighters came wheezingly from their lips and the three chests were straining and heaving. Pete at intervals gave vent to low, labored hisses, that sounded like a desire to kill. Jimmie's ally gibbered at times like a wounded maniac. Jimmie was silent, fighting with the face of a sacrificial priest. The rage of fear shone in all their eyes and their blood-colored fists swirled.

At a tottering moment a blow from Pete's hand struck the ally and he crashed to the floor. He wriggled instantly to his feet and grasping the quiet stranger's beer glass from the bar, hurled it at Pete's head.

High on the wall it burst like a bomb, shivering fragments flying in all directions. Then missiles came to every man's hand. The place had heretofore appeared free of things to throw, but suddenly glass and bottles went singing through the air. They were thrown point blank at bobbing heads. The pyramid of shimmering glasses, that had never been disturbed, changed to cascades as heavy bottles were flung into them. Mirrors splintered to nothing.

The three frothing creatures on the floor buried themselves in a frenzy for blood. There followed in the wake of missiles and fists some unknown prayers, perhaps for death.

The quiet stranger had sprawled very pyrotechnically out on the side-walk. A laugh ran up and down the avenue for the half of a block.

"Dey've trowed a bloke inteh deh street."

People heard the sound of breaking glass and shuffling feet within the saloon and came running. A small group, bending down to look under the bamboo doors, watching the fall of glass, and three pairs of violent legs, changed in a moment to a crowd.

A policeman came charging down the side-walk and bounced through the doors into the saloon. The crowd bended and surged in absorbing anxiety to see.

Jimmie caught first sight of the on-coming interruption. On his feet he had the same regard for a policeman that, when on his truck, he had for a fire engine. He howled and ran for the side door.

The officer made a terrific advance, club in hand. One comprehensive sweep of the long night stick threw the ally to the floor and forced Pete to a corner. With his disengaged hand he made a furious effort at Jimmie's coat-tails. Then he regained his balance and paused.

"Well, well, you are a pair of pictures. What in hell yeh been up to?"

Jimmie, with his face drenched in blood, escaped up a side street, pursued a short distance by some of the more law-loving, or excited individuals of the crowd.

Later, from a corner safely dark, he saw the policeman, the ally and the bartender emerge from the saloon. Pete locked the doors and then followed up the avenue in the rear of the crowd-encompassed policeman and his charge.

On first thoughts Jimmie, with his heart throbbing at battle heat, started to go desperately to the rescue of his friend, but he halted.

"Ah, what deh hell?" he demanded of himself.

XII

In a hall of irregular shape sat Pete and Maggie drinking beer. A submissive orchestra dictated to by a spectacled man with frowsy hair and a dress suit, industriously followed the bobs of his head and the waves of his baton. A ballad singer, in a dress of flaming scarlet, sang in the inevitable voice of brass. When she vanished, men seated at the tables near the front applauded loudly, pounding the polished wood with their beer glasses. She returned attired in less gown, and sang again. She received another enthusiastic encore. She reappeared in still less gown and danced. The deafening rumble of glasses and clapping of hands that followed her exit indicated an overwhelming desire to have her come on for the fourth time, but the curiosity of the audience was not gratified.

Maggie was pale. From her eyes had been plucked all look of self-reliance. She leaned with a dependent air toward her companion. She was timid, as if fearing his anger or displeasure. She seemed to beseech tenderness of him.

Pete's air of distinguished valor had grown upon him until it threatened stupendous dimensions. He was infinitely gracious to the girl. It was apparent to her that his condescension was a marvel.

He could appear to strut even while sitting still and he showed that he was a lion of lordly characteristics by the air with which he spat.

With Maggie gazing at him wonderingly, he took pride in commanding the waiters who were, however, indifferent or deaf.

"Hi, you, git a russle on yehs! What deh hell yehs lookin' at? Two more beehs, d'yeh hear?"

He leaned back and critically regarded the person of a girl with a straw-colored wig who upon the stage was flinging her heels in somewhat awkward imitation of a well-known danseuse.

At times Maggie told Pete long confidential tales of her former home life, dwelling upon the escapades of the other members of the family and the difficulties she had to combat in order to obtain a degree of comfort. He responded in tones of philanthropy. He pressed her arm with an air of reassuring proprietorship.

"Dey was damn jays," he said, denouncing the mother and brother.

The sound of the music which, by the efforts of the frowsy-headed leader, drifted to her ears through the smoke-filled atmosphere, made the girl dream. She thought of her former Rum Alley environment and turned to regard Pete's strong protecting fists. She thought of the collar and cuff manufactory and the eternal moan of the proprietor: "What een hell do you sink I pie fife dolla a week for? Play? No, py damn." She contemplated Pete's man-subduing eyes and noted that wealth and prosperity was indicated by his clothes. She imagined a future, rose-tinted, because of its distance from all that she previously had experienced.

As to the present she perceived only vague reasons to be miserable. Her life was Pete's and she considered him worthy of the charge. She would be disturbed by no particular apprehensions, so long as Pete adored her as he now said he did. She did not feel like a bad woman. To her knowledge she had never seen any better.

At times men at other tables regarded the girl furtively. Pete, aware of it, nodded at her and grinned. He felt proud.

"Mag, yer a bloomin' good-looker," he remarked, studying her face through the haze. The men made Maggie fear, but she blushed at Pete's words as it became apparent to her that she was the apple of his eye.

Grey-headed men, wonderfully pathetic in their dissipation, stared at her through clouds. Smooth-cheeked boys, some of them with faces of stone and mouths of sin, not nearly so pathetic as the grey heads, tried to find the girl's eyes in the smoke wreaths. Maggie considered she was not what they thought her. She confined her glances to Pete and the stage.

The orchestra played negro melodies and a versatile drummer pounded, whacked, clattered and scratched on a dozen machines to make noise.

Those glances of the men, shot at Maggie from under half-closed lids, made her tremble. She thought them all to be worse men than Pete.

"Come, let's go," she said.

As they went out Maggie perceived two women seated at a table with some men. They were painted and their cheeks had lost their roundness. As she passed them the girl, with a shrinking movement, drew back her skirts.

XIII

Jimmie did not return home for a number of days after the fight with Pete in the saloon. When he did, he approached with extreme caution.

He found his mother raving. Maggie had not returned home. The parent continually wondered how her daughter could come to such a pass. She had never considered Maggie as a pearl dropped unstained into Rum Alley from Heaven, but she could not conceive how it was possible for her daughter to fall so low as to bring disgrace upon her family. She was terrific in denunciation of the girl's wickedness.

The fact that the neighbors talked of it, maddened her. When women came in, and in the course of their conversation casually asked, "Where's Maggie dese days?" the mother shook her fuzzy head at them and appalled

them with curses. Cunning hints inviting confidence she rebuffed with
violence.

"An' wid all deh bringin' up she had, how could she?" moaningly she
asked of her son. "Wid all deh talkin' wid her I did an' deh t'ings I tol' her
to remember? When a girl is bringed up deh way I bringed up Maggie, how
kin she go teh deh devil?"

Jimmie was transfixed by these questions. He could not conceive how
under the circumstances his mother's daughter and his sister could have
been so wicked.

His mother took a drink from a squdgy bottle that sat on the table.
She continued her lament.

"She had a bad heart, dat girl did, Jimmie. She was wicked teh deh
heart an' we never knowed it."

Jimmie nodded, admitting the fact.

"We lived in deh same house wid her an' I brought her up an' we never
knowed how bad she was."

Jimmie nodded again.

"Wid a home like dis an' a mudder like me, she went teh deh bad,"
cried the mother, raising her eyes.

One day, Jimmie came home, sat down in a chair and began to wriggle
about with a new and strange nervousness. At last he spoke shamefacedly.

"Well, look-a-here, dis t'ing queers us! See? We're queered! An'
maybe it 'ud be better if I—well, I t'ink I kin look 'er up an'—maybe it 'ud
be better if I fetched her home an'—"

The mother started from her chair and broke forth into a storm of
passionate anger.

"What! Let 'er come an' sleep under deh same roof wid her mudder
agin! Oh, yes, I will, won't I? Sure! Shame on yehs, Jimmie Johnson, fer
sayin' such a t'ing teh yer own mudder—teh yer own mudder! Little did I
t'ink when yehs was a babby playin' about me feet dat ye'd grow up teh
say sech a t'ing teh yer mudder—yer own mudder. I never taut—"

Sobs choked her and interrupted her reproaches.

"Dere ain't nottin' teh raise sech hell about," said Jimmie. "I on'y says
it 'ud be better if we keep dis t'ing dark, see? It queers us! See?"

His mother laughed a laugh that seemed to ring through the city and
be echoed and re-echoed by countless other laughs. "Oh, yes, I will, won't
I! Sure!"

"Well, yeh must take me fer a damn fool," said Jimmie, indignant at
his mother for mocking him. "I didn't say we'd make 'er inteh a little tin
angel, ner nottin', but deh way it is now she can queer us! Don' che see?"

"Aye, she'll git tired of deh life atter a while an' den she'll wanna be
a-comin' home, won' she, deh beast! I'll let 'er in den, won' I?"

"Well, I didn' mean none of dis prod'gal bus'ness anyway," explained Jimmie.

"It wasn't no prod'gal dauter, yeh damn fool," said the mother. "It was prod'gal son, anyhow."

"I know dat," said Jimmie.

For a time they sat in silence. The mother's eyes gloated on a scene her imagination could call before her. Her lips were set in a vindictive smile.

"Aye, she'll cry, won' she, an' carry on, an' tell how Pete, or some odder feller, beats 'er an' she'll say she's sorry an' all dat an' she ain't happy, she ain't, an' she wants to come home agin, she does."

With grim humor, the mother imitated the possible wailing notes of the daughter's voice.

"Den I'll take 'er in, won't I, deh beast. She kin cry 'er two eyes out on deh stones of deh street before I'll dirty deh place wid her. She abused an' ill-treated her own mudder—her own mudder what loved her an' she'll never git anodder chance dis side of hell."

Jimmie thought he had a great idea of women's frailty, but he could not understand why any of his kin should be victims.

"Damn her," he fervidly said.

Again he wondered vaguely if some of the women of his acquaintance had brothers. Nevertheless, his mind did not for an instant confuse himself with those brothers nor his sister with theirs. After the mother had, with great difficulty, suppressed the neighbors, she went among them and proclaimed her grief. "May Gawd forgive dat girl," was her continual cry. To attentive ears she recited the whole length and breadth of her woes.

"I bringed 'er up deh way a dauter oughta be bringed up an' dis is how she served me! She went teh deh devil deh first chance she got! May Gawd forgive her."

When arrested for drunkenness she used the story of her daughter's downfall with telling effect upon the police justices. Finally one of them said to her, peering down over his spectacles: "Mary, the records of this and other courts show that you are the mother of forty-two daughters who have been ruined. The case is unparalleled in the annals of this court, and this court thinks—"

The mother went through life shedding large tears of sorrow. Her red face was a picture of agony.

Of course Jimmie publicly damned his sister that he might appear on a higher social plane. But, arguing with himself, stumbling about in ways that he knew not, he, once, almost came to a conclusion that his sister would have been more firmly good had she better known why. However, he felt that he could not hold such a view. He threw it hastily aside.

XIV

In a hilarious hall there were twenty-eight tables and twenty-eight women and a crowd of smoking men. Valiant noise was made on a stage at the end of the hall by an orchestra composed of men who looked as if they had just happened in. Soiled waiters ran to and fro, swooping down like hawks on the unwary in the throng; clattering along the aisles with trays covered with glasses; stumbling over women's skirts and charging two prices for everything but beer, all with a swiftness that blurred the view of the co-coanut palms and dusty monstrosities painted upon the walls of the room. A bouncer, with an immense load of business upon his hands, plunged about in the crowd, dragging bashful strangers to prominent chairs, ordering waiters here and there and quarreling furiously with men who wanted to sing with the orchestra.

The usual smoke cloud was present, but so dense that heads and arms seemed entangled in it. The rumble of conversation was replaced by a roar. Plenteous oaths heaved through the air. The room rang with the shrill voices of women bubbling o'er with drink-laughter. The chief element in the music of the orchestra was speed. The musicians played in intent fury. A woman was singing and smiling upon the stage, but no one took notice of her. The rate at which the piano, cornet and violins were going, seemed to impart wildness to the half-drunken crowd. Beer glasses were emptied at a gulp and conversation became a rapid chatter. The smoke eddied and swirled like a shadowy river hurrying toward some unseen falls. Pete and Maggie entered the hall and took chairs at a table near the door. The woman who was seated there made an attempt to occupy Pete's attention and, failing, went away.

Three weeks had passed since the girl had left home. The air of spaniel-like dependence had been magnified and showed its direct effect in the peculiar off-handedness and ease of Pete's ways toward her.

She followed Pete's eyes with hers, anticipating with smiles gracious looks from him.

A woman of brilliance and audacity, accompanied by a mere boy, came into the place and took seats near them.

At once Pete sprang to his feet, his face beaming with glad surprise.

"By Gawd, there's Nellie," he cried.

He went over to the table and held out an eager hand to the woman.

"Why, hello, Pete, me boy, how are you," said she, giving him her fingers.

Maggie took instant note of the woman. She perceived that her black dress fitted her to perfection. Her linen collar and cuffs were spotless. Tan gloves were stretched over her well-shaped hands. A hat of a prevailing fashion perched jauntily upon her dark hair. She wore no jewelry and was painted with no apparent paint. She looked clear-eyed through the stares of the men.

"Sit down, and call your lady-friend over," she said cordially to Pete. At his beckoning Maggie came and sat between Pete and the mere boy.

"I thought yeh were gone away fer good," began Pete, at once. "When did yeh git back? How did dat Buff'lo bus'ness turn out?"

The woman shrugged her shoulders. "Well, he didn't have as many stamps as he tried to make out, so I shook him, that's all."

"Well, I'm glad teh see yehs back in deh city," said Pete, with awkward gallantry.

He and the woman entered into a long conversation, exchanging reminiscences of days together. Maggie sat still, unable to formulate an intelligent sentence upon the conversation and painfully aware of it.

She saw Pete's eyes sparkle as he gazed upon the handsome stranger. He listened smilingly to all she said. The woman was familiar with all his affairs, asked him about mutual friends, and knew the amount of his salary.

She paid no attention to Maggie, looking toward her once or twice and apparently seeing the wall beyond.

The mere boy was sulky. In the beginning he had welcomed with acclamations the additions.

"Let's all have a drink! What'll you take, Nell? And you, Miss what's-your-name. Have a drink, Mr. ——, you, I mean."

He had shown a sprightly desire to do the talking for the company and tell all about his family. In a loud voice he declaimed on various topics. He assumed a patronizing air toward Pete. As Maggie was silent, he paid no attention to her. He made a great show of lavishing wealth upon the woman of brilliance and audacity.

"Do keep still, Freddie! You gibber like an ape, dear," said the woman to him. She turned away and devoted her attention to Pete.

"We'll have many a good time together again, eh?"

"Sure, Nell," said Pete, enthusiastic at once.

"Say," whispered she, leaning forward, "let's go over to Billie's and have a heluva time."

"Well, it's dis way! See?" said Pete. "I got dis lady frien' here."

"Oh, t'hell with her," argued the woman.

Pete appeared disturbed.

"All right," said she, nodding her head at him. "All right for you! We'll see the next time you ask me to go anywheres with you."

Pete squirmed.

"Say," he said, beseechingly, "come wid me a minit an' I'll tell yer why."

The woman waved her hand.

"Oh, that's all right, you needn't explain, you know. You wouldn't come merely because you wouldn't come, that's all there is of it."

To Pete's visible distress she turned to the mere boy, bringing him speedily from a terrific rage. He had been debating whether it would be the part of a man to pick a quarrel with Pete, or would he be justified in striking him savagely with his beer glass without warning. But he recovered himself when the woman turned to renew her smilings. He beamed upon her with an expression that was somewhat tipsy and inexpressibly tender.

"Say, shake that Bowery jay," requested he, in a loud whisper.

"Freddie, you are so droll," she replied.

Pete reached forward and touched the woman on the arm.

"Come out a minit while I tells yeh why I can't go wid yer. Yer doin' me dirt, Nell! I never taut ye'd do me dirt, Nell. Come on, will yer?" He spoke in tones of injury.

"Why, I don't see why I should be interested in your explanations," said the woman, with a coldness that seemed to reduce Pete to a pulp.

His eyes pleaded with her. "Come out a minit while I tells yeh."

The woman nodded slightly at Maggie and the mere boy, "'Scuse me."

The mere boy interrupted his loving smile and turned a shrivelling glare upon Pete. His boyish countenance flushed and he spoke, in a whine, to the woman:

"Oh, I say, Nellie, this ain't a square deal, you know. You aren't goin' to leave me and go off with that duffer, are you? I should think—"

"Why, you dear boy, of course I'm not," cried the woman, affectionately. She bended over and whispered in his ear. He smiled again and settled in his chair as if resolved to wait patiently.

As the woman walked down between the rows of tables, Pete was at her shoulder talking earnestly, apparently in explanation. The woman waved her hands with studied airs of indifference. The doors swung behind them, leaving Maggie and the mere boy seated at the table.

Maggie was dazed. She could dimly perceive that something stupendous had happened. She wondered why Pete saw fit to remonstrate with the woman, pleading for forgiveness with his eyes. She thought she noted an air of submission about her leonine Pete. She was astounded.

The mere boy occupied himself with cock-tails and a cigar. He was tranquilly silent for half an hour. Then he bestirred himself and spoke.

"Well," he said, sighing, "I knew this was the way it would be." There was another stillness. The mere boy seemed to be musing.

"She was pulling m'leg. That's the whole amount of it," he said, suddenly. "It's a bloomin' shame the way that girl does. Why, I've spent over two dollars in drinks tonight. And she goes off with that plug-ugly who looks as if he had been hit in the face with a coin-die. I call it rocky treatment for a fellah like me. Here, waiter, bring me a cock-tail and make it damned strong."

Maggie made no reply. She was watching the doors. "It's a mean piece of business," complained the mere boy. He explained to her how amazing it was that anybody should treat him in such a manner. "But I'll get square with her, you bet. She won't get far ahead of yours truly, you know," he added, winking. "I'll tell her plainly that it was bloomin' mean business. And she won't come it over me with any of her 'now-Freddie-dears.' She thinks my name is Freddie, you know, but of course it ain't. I always tell these people some name like that, because if they got onto your right name they might use it sometime. Understand? Oh, they don't fool me much."

Maggie was paying no attention, being intent upon the doors. The mere boy relapsed into a period of gloom, during which he exterminated a number of cock-tails with a determined air, as if replying defiantly to fate. He occasionally broke forth into sentences composed of invectives joined together in a long string.

The girl was still staring at the doors. After a time the mere boy began to see cob-webs just in front of his nose. He spurred himself into being agreeable and insisted upon her having a charlotte-russe and a glass of beer.

"They's gone," he remarked, "they's gone." He looked at her through the smoke wreaths. "Shay, li'l girl, we mightish well make bes' of it. You ain't such bad lookin' girl, y'know. Not half-bad. Can't come up to Nell, though. No, can't do it! Well, I should shay not! Nell fine-lookin' girl! F—i—n—ine. You look damn bad longsider her, but by y'self ain't so bad. Have to do anyhow. Nell gone. On'y you left. Not half-bad, though."

Maggie stood up.

"I'm going home," she said.

The mere boy started.

"Eh? What? Home," he cried, struck with amazement. "I beg pardon, did hear say home?"

"I'm going home," she repeated.

"Great Gawd, what hava struck," demanded the mere boy of himself, stupefied.

In a semi-comatose state he conducted her on board an up-town car, ostentatiously paid her fare, leered kindly at her through the rear window and fell off the steps.

XV

A forlorn woman went along a lighted avenue. The street was filled with people desperately bound on missions. An endless crowd darted at the elevated station stairs and the horse cars were thronged with owners of bundles.

The pace of the forlorn woman was slow. She was apparently searching for some one. She loitered near the doors of saloons and watched men emerge from them. She scanned furtively the faces in the rushing stream of pedestrians. Hurrying men, bent on catching some boat or train, jostled her elbows, failing to notice her, their thoughts fixed on distant dinners.

The forlorn woman had a peculiar face. Her smile was no smile. But when in repose her features had a shadowy look that was like a sardonic grin, as if some one had sketched with cruel forefinger indelible lines about her mouth.

Jimmie came strolling up the avenue. The woman encountered him with an aggrieved air.

"Oh, Jimmie, I've been lookin' all over fer yehs—," she began.

Jimmie made an impatient gesture and quickened his pace.

"Ah, don't bodder me! Good Gawd!" he said, with the savageness of a man whose life is pestered.

The woman followed him along the sidewalk in somewhat the manner of a suppliant.

"But, Jimmie," she said, "yehs told me ye'd—"

Jimmie turned upon her fiercely as if resolved to make a last stand for comfort and peace.

"Say, fer Gawd's sake, Hattie, don' foller me from one end of deh city teh deh odder. Let up, will yehs! Give me a minute's res', can't yehs? Yehs makes me tired, allus taggin' me. See? Ain' yehs got no sense? Do yehs want people teh get onto me? Go chase yerself, fer Gawd's sake."

The woman stepped closer and laid her fingers on his arm. "But, look-a-here—"

Jimmie snarled. "Oh, go teh hell."

He darted into the front door of a convenient saloon and a moment later came out into the shadows that surrounded the side door. On the brilliantly lighted avenue he perceived the forlorn woman dodging about like a scout. Jimmie laughed with an air of relief and went away.

When he arrived home he found his mother clamoring. Maggie had returned. She stood shivering beneath the torrent of her mother's wrath.

"Well, I'm damned," said Jimmie in greeting.

His mother, tottering about the room, pointed a quivering fore-finger.

"Lookut her, Jimmie, lookut her. Dere's yer sister, boy. Dere's yer sister. Lookut her! Lookut her!"

She screamed in scoffing laughter.

The girl stood in the middle of the room. She edged about as if unable to find a place on the floor to put her feet.

"Ha, ha, ha," bellowed the mother. "Dere she stands! Ain' she purty? Lookut her! Ain' she sweet, deh beast? Lookut her! Ha, ha, lookut her!"

She lurched forward and put her red and seamed hands upon her daughter's face. She bent down and peered keenly up into the eyes of the girl.

"Oh, she's jes' dessame as she ever was, ain' she? She's her mudder's purty darlin' yit, ain' she? Lookut her, Jimmie! Come here, fer Gawd's sake, and lookut her."

The loud, tremendous sneering of the mother brought the denizens of the Rum Alley tenement to their doors. Women came in the hall-ways. Children scurried to and fro.

"What's up? Dat Johnson party on anudder tear?"

"Naw! Young Mag's come home!"

"Deh hell yeh say?"

Through the open door curious eyes stared in at Maggie. Children ventured into the room and ogled her, as if they formed the front row at a theatre. Women, without, bended toward each other and whispered, nodding their heads with airs of profound philosophy. A baby, overcome with curiosity concerning this object at which all were looking, sidled forward and touched her dress, cautiously, as if investigating a red-hot stove. Its mother's voice rang out like a warning trumpet. She rushed forward and grabbed her child, casting a terrible look of indignation at the girl.

Maggie's mother paced to and fro, addressing the doorful of eyes, expounding like a glib showman at a museum. Her voice rang through the building.

"Dere she stands," she cried, wheeling suddenly and pointing with dramatic finger. "Dere she stands! Lookut her! Ain' she a dindy? An' she was so good as to come home teh her mudder, she was! Ain' she a beaut'? Ain' she a dindy? Fer Gawd's sake!"

The jeering cries ended in another burst of shrill laughter.

The girl seemed to awaken. "Jimmie—"

He drew hastily back from her.

"Well, now, yer a hell of a t'ing, ain' yeh?" he said, his lips curling in scorn. Radiant virtue sat upon his brow and his repelling hands expressed horror of contamination.

Maggie turned and went.

The crowd at the door fell back precipitately. A baby falling down in front of the door, wrenched a scream like a wounded animal from its mother. Another woman sprang forward and picked it up, with a chivalrous air, as if rescuing a human being from an oncoming express train.

As the girl passed down through the hall, she went before open doors framing more eyes strangely microscopic, and sending broad beams of inquisitive light into the darkness of her path. On the second floor she met the gnarled old woman who possessed the music box.

"So," she cried, "'ere yehs are back again, are yehs? An' dey've kicked yehs out? Well, come in an' stay wid me teh-night. I ain' got no moral standin'."

From above came an unceasing babble of tongues, over all of which rang the mother's derisive laughter.

XVI

Pete did not consider that he had ruined Maggie. If he had thought that her soul could never smile again, he would have believed the mother and brother, who were pyrotechnic over the affair, to be responsible for it.

Besides, in his world, souls did not insist upon being able to smile. "What deh hell?"

He felt a trifle entangled. It distressed him. Revelations and scenes might bring upon him the wrath of the owner of the saloon, who insisted upon respectability of an advanced type.

"What deh hell do dey wanna raise such a smoke about it fer?" demanded he of himself, disgusted with the attitude of the family. He saw no necessity for anyone's losing their equilibrium merely because their sister or their daughter had stayed away from home.

Searching about in his mind for possible reasons for their conduct, he came upon the conclusion that Maggie's motives were correct, but that the two others wished to snare him. He felt pursued.

The woman of brilliance and audacity whom he had met in the hilarious hall showed a disposition to ridicule him.

"A little pale thing with no spirit," she said. "Did you note the expression of her eyes? There was something in them about pumpkin pie and virtue. That is a peculiar way the left corner of her mouth has of twitching, isn't it? Dear, dear, my cloud-compelling Pete, what are you coming to?"

Pete asserted at once that he never was very much interested in the girl. The woman interrupted him, laughing.

"Oh, it's not of the slightest consequence to me, my dear young man.

You needn't draw maps for my benefit. Why should I be concerned about it?"

But Pete continued with his explanations. If he was laughed at for his tastes in women, he felt obliged to say that they were only temporary or indifferent ones.

The morning after Maggie had departed from home, Pete stood behind the bar. He was immaculate in white jacket and apron and his hair was plastered over his brow with infinite correctness. No customers were in the place. Pete was twisting his napkined fist slowly in a beer glass, softly whistling to himself and occasionally holding the object of his attention between his eyes and a few weak beams of sunlight that had found their way over the thick screens and into the shaded room.

With lingering thoughts of the woman of brilliance and audacity, the bartender raised his head and stared through the varying cracks between the swaying bamboo doors. Suddenly the whistling pucker faded from his lips. He saw Maggie walking slowly past. He gave a great start, fearing for the previously-mentioned eminent respectability of the place.

He threw a swift, nervous glance about him, all at once feeling guilty. No one was in the room.

He went hastily over to the side door. Opening it and looking out, he perceived Maggie standing, as if undecided, on the corner. She was searching the place with her eyes.

As she turned her face toward him Pete beckoned to her hurriedly, intent upon returning with speed to a position behind the bar and to the atmosphere of respectability upon which the proprietor insisted.

Maggie came to him, the anxious look disappearing from her face and a smile wreathing her lips.

"Oh, Pete—," she began brightly.

The bartender made a violent gesture of impatience.

"Oh, my Gawd," cried he, vehemently. "What deh hell do yeh wanna hang aroun' here fer? Do yeh wanna git me inteh trouble?" he demanded with an air of injury.

Astonishment swept over the girl's features. "Why, Pete! yehs tol' me—"

Pete glanced profound irritation. His countenance reddened with the anger of a man whose respectability is being threatened.

"Say, yehs makes me tired. See? What deh hell deh yeh wanna tag aroun' atter me fer? Yeh'll git me inteh trouble wid deh ol' man an' dey'll be hell teh pay! If he sees a woman roun' here he'll go crazy an' I'll lose me job! See? Ain' yehs got no sense? Don' be allus bodderin' me. See? Yer brudder come in here an' raised hell an' deh ol' man hada put up fer it! An' now I'm done! See? I'm done."

The girl's eyes stared into his face. "Pete, don' yeh remem—"

"Oh, hell," interrupted Pete, anticipating.

The girl seemed to have a struggle with herself. She was apparently bewildered and could not find speech. Finally she asked in a low voice: "But where kin I go?"

The question exasperated Pete beyond the powers of endurance. It was a direct attempt to give him some responsibility in a matter that did not concern him. In his indignation he volunteered information.

"Oh, go teh hell," cried he. He slammed the door furiously and returned, with an air of relief, to his respectability.

Maggie went away.

She wandered aimlessly for several blocks. She stopped once and asked aloud a question of herself: "Who?"

A man who was passing near her shoulder, humorously took the questioning word as intended for him.

"Eh? What? Who? Nobody! I didn't say anything," he laughingly said, and continued his way.

Soon the girl discovered that if she walked with such apparent aimlessness, some men looked at her with calculating eyes. She quickened her step, frightened. As a protection, she adopted a demeanor of intentness as if going somewhere.

After a time she left rattling avenues and passed between rows of houses with sternness and stolidity stamped upon their features. She hung her head for she felt their eyes grimly upon her.

Suddenly she came upon a stout gentleman in a silk hat and a chaste black coat, whose decorous row of buttons reached from his chin to his knees. The girl had heard of the Grace of God and she decided to approach this man.

His beaming, chubby face was a picture of benevolence and kind-heartedness. His eyes shone good-will.

But as the girl timidly accosted him, he gave a convulsive movement and saved his respectability by a vigorous side-step. He did not risk it to save a soul. For how was he to know that there was a soul before him that needed saving?

XVII

Upon a wet evening, several months after the last chapter, two interminable rows of cars, pulled by slipping horses, jangled along a prominent side-street. A dozen cabs, with coat-enshrouded drivers, clattered to and fro. Electric lights, whirring softly, shed a blurred radiance. A flower dealer, his feet tapping impatiently, his nose and his wares glistening with rain-drops, stood behind an array of roses and chrysanthemums. Two or three theatres emptied a crowd upon the storm-swept pavements. Men pulled their hats over their eye-brows and raised their collars to their ears. Women shrugged impatient shoulders in their warm cloaks and stopped to arrange their skirts for a walk through the storm. People having been comparatively silent for two hours burst into a roar of conversation, their hearts still kindling from the glowings of the stage.

The pavements became tossing seas of umbrellas. Men stepped forth to hail cabs or cars, raising their fingers in varied forms of polite request or imperative demand. An endless procession wended toward elevated stations. An atmosphere of pleasure and prosperity seemed to hang over the throng, born, perhaps, of good clothes and of having just emerged from a place of forgetfulness.

In the mingled light and gloom of an adjacent park, a handful of wet wanderers, in attitudes of chronic dejection, was scattered among the benches.

A girl of the painted cohorts of the city went along the street. She threw changing glances at men who passed her, giving smiling invitations to men of rural or untaught pattern and usually seeming sedately unconscious of the men with a metropolitan seal upon their faces.

Crossing glittering avenues, she went into the throng emerging from the places of forgetfulness. She hurried forward through the crowd as if intent upon reaching a distant home, bending forward in her handsome cloak, daintily lifting her skirts and picking for her well-shod feet the dryer spots upon the pavements.

The restless doors of saloons, clashing to and fro, disclosed animated rows of men before bars and hurrying barkeepers.

A concert hall gave to the street faint sounds of swift, machine-like music, as if a group of phantom musicians were hastening.

A tall young man, smoking a cigarette with a sublime air, strolled near the girl. He had on evening dress, a moustache, a chrysanthemum, and a look of ennui, all of which he kept carefully under his eye. Seeing the girl walk on as if such a young man as he was not in existence, he looked back transfixed with interest. He stared glassily for a moment, but gave a slight convulsive start when he discerned that she was neither new, Parisian, nor theatrical. He wheeled about hastily and turned his stare into the air, like a sailor with a search-light.

A stout gentleman, with pompous and philanthropic whiskers, went stolidly by, the broad of his back sneering at the girl.

A belated man in business clothes, and in haste to catch a car, bounced against her shoulder. "Hi, there, Mary, I beg your pardon! Brace up, old girl." He grasped her arm to steady her, and then was away running down the middle of the street.

The girl walked on out of the realm of restaurants and saloons. She passed more glittering avenues and went into darker blocks than those where the crowd travelled.

A young man in light overcoat and derby hat received a glance shot keenly from the eyes of the girl. He stopped and looked at her, thrusting his hands in his pockets and making a mocking smile curl his lips. "Come, now, old lady," he said, "you don't mean to tell me that you sized me up for a farmer?"

A laboring man marched along with bundles under his arms. To her remarks, he replied: "It's a fine evenin', ain't it?"

She smiled squarely into the face of a boy who was hurrying by with his hands buried in his overcoat, his blonde locks bobbing on his youthful temples, and a cheery smile of unconcern upon his lips. He turned his head and smiled back at her, waving his hands.

"Not this eve—some other eve!"

A drunken man, reeling in her pathway, began to roar at her. "I ain' ga no money, dammit," he shouted, in a dismal voice. He lurched on up the street, wailing to himself, "Dammit, I ain' ga no money. Damn ba' luck. Ain' ga no more money."

The girl went into gloomy districts near the river, where the tall black factories shut in the street and only occasional broad beams of light fell across the pavements from saloons. In front of one of these places, from whence came the sound of a violin vigorously scraped, the patter of feet on boards and the ring of loud laughter, there stood a man with blotched features.

"Ah, there," said the girl.

"I've got a date," said the man.

Further on in the darkness she met a ragged being with shifting, blood-shot eyes and grimy hands. "Ah, what deh hell? T'ink I'm a millionaire?"

She went into the blackness of the final block. The shutters of the tall buildings were closed like grim lips. The structures seemed to have eyes that looked over her, beyond her, at other things. Afar off the lights of the avenues glittered as if from an impossible distance. Street car bells jingled with a sound of merriment.

When almost to the river the girl saw a great figure. On going forward she perceived it to be a huge fat man in torn and greasy garments. His grey hair straggled down over his forehead. His small, bleared eyes, sparkling from amidst great rolls of red fat, swept eagerly over the girl's upturned face. He laughed, his brown, disordered teeth gleaming under a grey, grizzled moustache from which beer-drops dripped. His whole body gently quivered and shook like that of a dead jelly fish. Chuckling and leering, he followed the girl of the crimson legions.

At their feet the river appeared a deathly black hue. Some hidden factory sent up a yellow glare, that lit for a moment the waters lapping oilily against timbers. The varied sounds of life, made joyous by distance and seeming unapproachableness, came faintly and died away to a silence.

XVIII

In a partitioned-off section of a saloon sat a man with a half-dozen women, gleefully laughing, hovering about him. The man had arrived at that stage of drunkenness where affection is felt for the universe.

"I'm good f'ler, girls," he said, convincingly. "I'm damn good f'ler. An'body treats me right, I allus trea's zem right! See?"

The women nodded their heads approvingly. "To be sure," they cried in hearty chorus. "You're the kind of a man we like, Pete. You're outa sight! What yeh goin' to buy this time, dear?"

"An'thing yehs wants, damn it," said the man in an abandonment of good will. His countenance shone with the true spirit of benevolence. He was in the proper mode of missionaries. He would have fraternized with obscure Hottentots. And above all, he was overwhelmed in tenderness for his friends, who were all illustrious.

"An'thing yehs wants, damn it," repeated he, waving his hands with beneficent recklessness. "I'm good f'ler, girls, an' if an'body treats me right I—here," called he through an open door to a waiter, "bring girls drinks, damn it. What 'ill yehs have, girls? An'thing yehs want, damn it!"

The waiter glanced in with the disgusted look of the man who serves intoxicants for the man who takes too much of them. He nodded his head shortly at the order from each individual, and went.

"Damn it," said the man, "we're havin' heluva time. I like you girls! Damn'd if I don't! Yer right sort! See?"

He spoke at length and with feeling, concerning the excellencies of his assembled friends.

"Don' try pull man's leg, but have a heluva time! Das right! Das way teh do! Now, if I sawght yehs tryin' work me fer drinks, wouldn' buy damn t'ing! But yer right sort, damn it! Yehs know how ter treat a f'ler, an' I stays by yehs 'til spen' las' cent! Das right! I'm good f'ler an' I knows when an'-body treats me right!"

Between the times of the arrival and departure of the waiter, the man discoursed to the women on the tender regard he felt for all living things. He laid stress upon the purity of his motives in all dealings with men in the world and spoke of the fervor of his friendship for those who were amiable. Tears welled slowly from his eyes. His voice quavered when he spoke to them.

Once when the waiter was about to depart with an empty tray, the man drew a coin from his pocket and held it forth.

"Here," said he, quite magnificently, "here's quar'."

The waiter kept his hands on his tray.

"I don' want yer money," he said.

The other put forth the coin with tearful insistence.

"Here, damn it," cried he, "tak't! Yer damn goo' f'ler an' I wan' yehs tak't!"

"Come, come, now," said the waiter, with the sullen air of a man who is forced into giving advice. "Put yer mon in yer pocket! Yer loaded an' yehs on'y makes a damn fool of yerself."

As the latter passed out of the door the man turned pathetically to the women.

"He don' know I'm damn goo' f'ler," cried he, dismally.

"Never you mind, Pete, dear," said a woman of brilliance and audacity, laying her hand with great affection upon his arm. "Never you mind, old boy! We'll stay by you, dear!"

"Das ri'," cried the man, his face lighting up at the soothing tones of the woman's voice.

"Das ri', I'm damn goo' f'ler an' w'en anyone trea's me ri', I treats zem ri'! Shee!"

"Sure!" cried the women. "And we're not goin' back on you, old man."

The man turned appealing eyes to the woman of brilliance and audacity. He felt that if he could be convicted of a contemptible action he would die.

"Shay, Nell, damn it, I allus trea's yehs shquare, didn' I? I allus been goo' f'ler wi' yehs, ain't I, Nell?"

"Sure you have, Pete," assented the woman. She delivered an oration to her companions. "Yessir, that's a fact. Pete's a square fellah, he is. He never goes back on a friend. He's the right kind an' we stay by him, don't we, girls?"

"Sure," they exclaimed. Looking lovingly at him they raised their glasses and drank his health.

"Girlsh," said the man, beseechingly, "I allus trea's yehs ri', didn' I? I'm goo' f'ler, ain' I, girlsh?"

"Sure," again they chorused.

"Well," said he finally, "le's have nozzer drink, zen."

"That's right," hailed a woman, "that's right. Yer no bloomin' jay! Yer spends yer money like a man. Dat's right."

The man pounded the table with his quivering fists.

"Yessir," he cried, with deep earnestness, as if someone disputed him. "I'm damn goo' f'ler, an' w'en anyone trea's me ri', I allus trea's—le's have nozzer drink."

He began to beat the wood with his glass.

"Shay," howled he, growing suddenly impatient. As the waiter did not then come, the man swelled with wrath.

"Shay," howled he again.

The waiter appeared at the door.

"Bringsh drinksh," said the man.

The waiter disappeared with the orders.

"Zat f'ler damn fool," cried the man. "He insul' me! I'm ge'man! Can' stan' be insul'! I'm goin' lickim when he comes!"

"No, no," cried the women, crowding about and trying to subdue him. "He's all right! He didn't mean anything! Let it go! He's a good fellah!"

"Din' he insul' me?" asked the man earnestly.

"No," said they. "Of course he didn't! He's all right!"

"Sure he didn' insul' me?" demanded the man, with deep anxiety in his voice.

"No, no! We know him! He's a good fellah. He didn't mean anything."

"Well, zen," said the man, resolutely, "I'm go' 'pol'gize!"

When the waiter came, the man struggled to the middle of the floor.

"Girlsh shed you insul' me! I shay damn lie! I 'pol'gize!"

"All right," said the waiter.

The man sat down. He felt a sleepy but strong desire to straighten things out and have a perfect understanding with everybody.

"Nell, I allus trea's yeh shquare, din' I? Yeh likes me, don' yehs, Nell? I'm goo' f'ler?"

"Sure," said the woman of brilliance and audacity.

"Yeh knows I'm stuck on yehs, don' yehs, Nell?"

"Sure," she repeated, carelessly.

Overwhelmed by a spasm of drunken adoration, he drew two or three bills from his pocket, and, with the trembling fingers of an offering priest, laid them on the table before the woman.

"Yehs knows, damn it, yehs kin have all got, 'cause I'm stuck on yehs, Nell, damn't, I—I'm stuck on yehs, Nell—buy drinksh—damn't—we're havin' heluva time—w'en anyone trea's me ri'—I—damn't, Nell—we're havin' heluva—time."

Shortly he went to sleep with his swollen face fallen forward on his chest.

The women drank and laughed, not heeding the slumbering man in the corner. Finally he lurched forward and fell groaning to the floor.

The women screamed in disgust and drew back their skirts.

"Come ahn," cried one, starting up angrily, "let's get out of here."

The woman of brilliance and audacity stayed behind, taking up the bills and stuffing them into a deep, irregularly-shaped pocket. A guttural snore from the recumbent man caused her to turn and look down at him. She laughed. "What a damn fool," she said, and went.

The smoke from the lamps settled heavily down in the little compartment, obscuring the way out. The smell of oil, stifling in its intensity, pervaded the air. The wine from an overturned glass dripped softly down upon the blotches on the man's neck.

XIX

In a room a woman sat at a table eating like a fat monk in a picture.

A soiled, unshaven man pushed open the door and entered.

"Well," said he, "Mag's dead."

"What?" said the woman, her mouth filled with bread.

"Mag's dead," repeated the man.

"Deh hell she is," said the woman. She continued her meal. When she finished her coffee she began to weep.

"I kin remember when her two feet was no bigger dan yer t'umb, and she weared worsted boots," moaned she.

"Well, whata dat?" said the man.

"I kin remember when she weared worsted boots," she cried.

The neighbors began to gather in the hall, staring in at the weeping woman as if watching the contortions of a dying dog. A dozen women entered and lamented with her. Under their busy hands the rooms took on that appalling appearance of neatness and order with which death is greeted.

Suddenly the door opened and a woman in a black gown rushed in with outstretched arms. "Ah, poor Mary," she cried, and tenderly embraced the moaning one.

"Ah, what ter'ble affliction is dis," continued she. Her vocabulary was derived from mission churches. "Me poor Mary, how I feel fer yehs! Ah, what a ter'ble affliction is a disobed'ent chil'."

Her good, motherly face was wet with tears. She trembled in eagerness to express her sympathy. The mourner sat with bowed head, rocking her body heavily to and fro, and crying out in a high, strained voice that sounded like a dirge on some forlorn pipe.

"I kin remember when she weared worsted boots an' her two feets was no bigger dan yer t'umb an' she weared worsted boots, Miss Smith," she cried, raising her streaming eyes.

"Ah, me poor Mary," sobbed the woman in black. With low, coddling cries, she sank on her knees by the mourner's chair, and put her arms about her. The other women began to groan in different keys.

"Yer poor misguided chil' is gone now, Mary, an' let us hope it's fer deh bes'. Yeh'll fergive her now, Mary, won't yehs, dear, all her disobed'ence? All her tankless behavior to her mudder an' all her badness? She's gone where her ter'ble sins will be judged."

The woman in black raised her face and paused. The inevitable sunlight came streaming in at the windows and shed a ghastly cheerfulness upon the faded hues of the room. Two or three of the spectators were sniffling, and one was loudly weeping. The mourner arose and staggered into the other room. In a moment she emerged with a pair of faded baby shoes held in the hollow of her hand.

"I kin remember when she used to wear dem," cried she. The women burst anew into cries as if they had all been stabbed. The mourner turned to the soiled and unshaven man.

"Jimmie, boy, go git yer sister! Go git yer sister an' we'll put deh boots on her feets!"

"Dey won't fit her now, yeh damn fool," said the man.

"Go git yer sister, Jimmie," shrieked the woman, confronting him fiercely.

The man swore sullenly. He went over to a corner and slowly began to put on his coat. He took his hat and went out, with a dragging, reluctant step.

The woman in black came forward and again besought the mourner.

"Yeh'll fergive her, Mary! Yeh'll fergive yer bad, bad, chil'! Her life was a curse an' her days were black an' yeh'll fergive yer bad girl? She's gone where her sins will be judged."

"She's gone where her sins will be judged," cried the other women, like a choir at a funeral.

"Deh Lord gives and deh Lord takes away," said the woman in black, raising her eyes to the sunbeams.

"Deh Lord gives and deh Lord takes away," responded the others.

"Yeh'll fergive her, Mary!" pleaded the woman in black. The mourner essayed to speak but her voice gave way. She shook her great shoulders frantically, in an agony of grief. Hot tears seemed to scald her quivering face. Finally her voice came and arose like a scream of pain.

"Oh, yes, I'll fergive her! I'll fergive her!"

"AN EXPERIMENT IN MISERY"

It was late at night, and a fine rain was swirling softly down, causing the pavements to glisten with hue of steel and blue and yellow in the rays of the innumerable lights. A youth was trudging slowly, without enthusiasm, with his hands buried deep in his trousers' pockets, toward the downtown places where beds can be hired for coppers. He was clothed in an aged and tattered suit, and his derby was a marvel of dust-covered crown and torn rim. He was going forth to eat as the wanderer may eat, and sleep as the homeless sleep. By the time he had reached City Hall Park he was so completely plastered with yells of "bum" and "hobo," and with various unholy epithets that small boys had applied to him at intervals, that he was in a state of the most profound dejection. The sifting rain saturated the old velvet collar of his overcoat, and as the wet cloth pressed against his neck, he felt that there no longer could be pleasure in life. He looked about him searching for an outcast of highest degree that the two might share miseries. But the lights threw a quivering glare over rows and circles of deserted benches that glistened damply, showing patches of wet sod behind them. It seemed that their usual freights had fled on this night to better things. There were only squads of well-dressed Brooklyn people who swarmed toward the Bridge.

New York Press, 12 April 1894.

[The following journalistic frame was deleted when the story was reprinted in *The Open Boat and Other Stories* (1898). Without it, the youth seems an actual participant in the life of the poor, whereas he is clearly performing an experiment. ED.]

Two men stood regarding a tramp.

"I wonder how he feels," said one, reflectively. "I suppose he is homeless, friendless, and has, at the most, only a few cents in his pocket. And if this is so, I wonder how he feels."

The other being the elder, spoke with an air of authoritative wisdom. "You can tell nothing of it unless you are in that condition yourself. It is idle to speculate about it from this distance."

"I suppose so," said the younger man, and then he added as from an inspiration: "I think I'll try it. Rags and tatters, you know, a couple of dimes, and hungry, too, if possible. Perhaps I could discover his point of view or something near it."

"Well, you might," said the other, and from those words begins this veracious narrative of an experiment in misery.

The youth went to the studio of an artist friend, who, from his store, rigged him out in an aged suit and a brown derby hat that had been made long years before. And then the youth went forth to try to eat as the tramp may eat, and sleep as the wanderers sleep. It was late at night, and a fine rain was swirling softly down, covering the pave-

The young man loitered about for a time and then went shuffling off down Park Row. In the sudden descent in style of the dress of the crowd he felt relief, and as if he were at last in his own country. He began to see tatters that matched his tatters. In Chatham Square there were aimless men strewn in front of saloons and lodging houses, standing sadly, patiently, reminding one vaguely of the attitudes of chickens in a storm. He aligned himself with these men, and turned slowly to occupy himself with the flowing life of the great street.

Through the mists of the cold and storming night, the cable cars went in silent procession, great affairs shining with red and brass, moving with formidable power, calm and irresistible, dangerful and gloomy, breaking silence only by the loud fierce cry of the gong. Two rivers of people swarmed along the side-walks, spattered with black mud, which made each shoe leave a scar-like impression. Overhead elevated trains with a shrill grinding of the wheels stopped at the station, which upon its leg-like pillars seemed to resemble some monstrous kind of crab squatting over the street. The quick fat puffings of the engines could be heard. Down an alley there were sombre curtains of purple and black, on which street lamps dully glittered like embroidered flowers.

A saloon stood with a voracious air on a corner. A sign leaning against the front of the doorpost announced: "Free hot soup tonight." The swing doors snapping to and fro like ravenous lips, made gratified smacks as the

---

ments with a bluish luster. He began a weary trudge toward the downtown places, where beds can be hired for coppers. By the time he had reached City Hall Park he was so completely plastered with yells of "bum" and "hobo," and with various unholy epithets that small boys had applied to him at intervals that he was in a state of profound dejection, and looked searchingly for an outcast of high degree that the two might share miseries. But the lights threw a quivering glare over rows and circles of deserted benches that glistened damply, showing patches of wet sod behind them. It seemed that their usual freights of sorry humanity had fled on this night to better things. There were only squads of well dressed Brooklyn people, who swarmed toward the Bridge.

HE FINDS HIS FIELD.

The young man loitered about for a time, and then went shuffling off down Park row. In the sudden descent in style of the dress of the crowd he felt relief. He began to see others whose tatters matched his tatters. In Chatham Square there were aimless men strewn in front of saloons and lodging houses. He aligned himself with these men, and turned slowly to occupy himself with the pageantry of the street.

The mists of the cold and damp night made an intensely blue haze, through which the gaslights in the windows of stores and saloons shone with a golden radiance. The street cars rumbled softly, as if going upon carpet stretched in the aisle made by the pillars of the elevated road. Two interminable processions of people went along the wet

saloon gorged itself with plump men, eating with astounding and endless appetite, smiling in some indescribable manner as the men came from all directions like sacrifices to a heathenish superstition.

Caught by the delectable sign, the young man allowed himself to be swallowed. A bartender placed a schooner of dark and portentous beer on the bar. Its monumental form upreared until the froth a-top was above the crown of the young man's brown derby.

"Soup over there, gents," said the bartender, affably. A little yellow man in rags and the youth grasped their schooners and went with speed toward a lunch counter, where a man with oily but imposing whiskers ladled genially from a kettle until he had furnished his two mendicants with a soup that was steaming hot and in which there were little floating suggestions of chicken. The young man, sipping his broth, felt the cordiality expressed by the warmth of the mixture, and he beamed at the man with oily but imposing whiskers, who was presiding like a priest behind an altar. "Have some more, gents?" he inquired of the two sorry figures before him. The little yellow man accepted with a swift gesture, but the youth shook his head and went out, following a man whose wondrous seediness promised that he would have a knowledge of cheap lodging houses.

On the side-walk he accosted the seedy man. "Say, do you know a cheap place t' sleep?"

The other hesitated for a time, gazing sideways. Finally he nodded in the direction of up the street. "I sleep up there," he said, "when I've got th' price."

"How much?"

"Ten cents."

The young man shook his head dolefully. "That's too rich for me."

At that moment there approached the two a reeling man in strange garments. His head was a fuddle of bushy hair and whiskers from which his eyes peered with a guilty slant. In a close scrutiny it was possible to dis-

---

pavements, spattered with black mud that made each shoe leave a scar-like impression. The high buildings lurked a-back, shrouded in shadows. Down a side street there were mystic curtains of purple and black, on which lamps dully glittered like embroidered flowers.

[CONCLUSION]

"Well," said the friend, "did you discover his point of view?"

"I don't know that I did," replied the young man; "but at any rate I think mine own has undergone a considerable alteration.

tinguish the cruel lines of a mouth, which looked as if its lips had just closed with satisfaction over some tender and piteous morsel. He appeared like an assassin steeped in crimes performed awkwardly.

But at this time his voice was tuned to the coaxing key of an affectionate puppy. He looked at the men with wheedling eyes and began to sing a little melody for charity.

"Say, gents, can't yeh give a poor feller a couple of cents t' git a bed. I got five an I gits anudder two I gits me a bed. Now, on th' square, gents, can't yeh jest gimme two cents t' git a bed. Now, yeh know how a re-specter'ble gentlem'n feels when he's down on his luck an' I—"

The seedy man, staring with imperturbable countenance at a train which clattered overhead, interrupted in an expressionless voice: "Ah, go t' h—!"

But the youth spoke to the prayerful assassin in tones of astonishment and inquiry. "Say, you must be crazy! Why don't yeh strike somebody that looks as if they had money?"

The assassin, tottering about on his uncertain legs, and at intervals brushing imaginary obstacles from before his nose, entered into a long explanation of the psychology of the situation. It was so profound that it was unintelligible.

When he had exhausted the subject the young man said to him: "Let's see th' five cents."

The assassin wore an expression of drunken woe at this sentence, filled with suspicion of him. With a deeply pained air he began to fumble in his clothing, his red hands trembling. Presently he announced in a voice of bitter grief, as if he had been betrayed: "There's on'y four."

"Four," said the young man thoughtfully. "Well, look-a-here, I'm a stranger here, an' if ye'll steer me to your cheap joint I'll find the other three."

The assassin's countenance became instantly radiant with joy. His whiskers quivered with the wealth of his alleged emotions. He seized the young man's hand in a transport of delight and friendliness.

"B'gawd," he cried, "if ye'll do that, b'gawd, I'd say yeh was a damned good feller, I would, an' I'd remember yeh all m' life, I would, b'gawd, an' if I ever got a chance I'd return th' compliment"—he spoke with drunken dignity—"b'gawd, I'd treat yeh white, I would, an' I'd allus remember yeh—"

The young man drew back, looking at the assassin coldly. "Oh, that's all right," he said. "You show me th' joint—that's all you've got t' do."

The assassin, gesticulating gratitude, led the young man along a dark street. Finally he stopped before a little dusty door. He raised his hand impressively. "Look-a-here," he said, and there was a thrill of deep and ancient wisdom upon his face, "I've brought yeh here, an' that's my part, ain't it? If th' place don't suit yeh, yeh needn't git mad at me, need yeh? There won't be no bad feelin', will there?"

"No," said the young man.

The assassin waved his arm tragically and led the march up the steep stairway. On the way the young man furnished the assassin with three pennies. At the top a man with benevolent spectacles looked at them through a hole in the board. He collected their money, wrote some names on a register, and speedily was leading the two men along a gloom-shrouded corridor.

Shortly after the beginning of this journey the young man felt his liver turn white, for from the dark and secret places of the building there suddenly came to his nostrils strange and unspeakable odors that assailed him like malignant diseases with wings. They seemed to be from human bodies closely packed in dens; the exhalations from a hundred pairs of reeking lips; the fumes from a thousand bygone debauches; the expression of a thousand present miseries.

A man, naked save for a little snuff-colored undershirt, was parading sleepily along the corridor. He rubbed his eyes, and, giving vent to a prodigious yawn, demanded to be told the time.

"Half past one."

The man yawned again. He opened a door, and for a moment his form was outlined against a black, opaque interior. To this door came the three men, and as it was again opened the unholy odors rushed out like released fiends, so that the young man was obliged to struggle as against an overpowering wind.

It was some time before the youth's eyes were good in the intense gloom within, but the man with benevolent spectacles led him skillfully, pausing but a moment to deposit the limp assassin upon a cot. He took the youth to a cot that lay tranquilly by the window, and, showing him a tall locker for clothes that stood near the head with the ominous air of a tombstone, left him.

The youth sat on his cot and peered about him. There was a gas jet in a distant part of the room that burned a small flickering orange-hued flame. It caused vast masses of tumbled shadows in all parts of the place, save where, immediately about it, there was a little gray haze. As the young man's eyes became used to the darkness he could see upon the cots that thickly littered the floor the forms of men sprawled out, lying in death-like silence or heaving and snoring with tremendous effort, like stabbed fish.

The youth locked his derby and his shoes in the mummy case near him and then lay down with his old and familiar coat around his shoulders. A blanket he handled gingerly, drawing it over part of the coat. The cot was leather covered and cold as melting snow. The youth was obliged to shiver for some time on this affair, which was like a slab. Presently, however, his chill gave him peace, and during this period of leisure from it he turned his head to stare at his friend, the assassin, whom he could dimly discern where he lay sprawled on a cot in the abandon of a man filled with drink. He was snoring with incredible vigor. His wet hair and beard dimly glistened and his inflamed nose shone with subdued luster like a red light in a fog.

Within reach of the youth's hand was one who lay with yellow breast and shoulders bare to the cold drafts. One arm hung over the side of the cot and the fingers lay full length upon the wet cement floor of the room. Beneath the inky brows could be seen the eyes of the man exposed by the partly opened lids. To the youth it seemed that he and this corpse-like being were exchanging a prolonged stare and that the other threatened with his eyes. He drew back, watching his neighbor from the shadows of his blanket edge. The man did not move once through the night, but lay in this stillness as of death, like a body stretched out, expectant of the surgeon's knife.

And all through the room could be seen the tawny hues of naked flesh, limbs thrust into the darkness, projecting beyond the cots; up-reared knees; arms hanging, long and thin, over the cot edges. For the most part they were statuesque, carven, dead. With the curious lockers standing all about like tombstones there was a strange effect of a graveyard, where bodies were merely flung.

Yet occasionally could be seen limbs wildly tossing in fantastic, nightmare gestures, accompanied by guttural cries, grunts, oaths. And there was one fellow off in a gloomy corner, who in his dreams was oppressed by some frightful calamity, for of a sudden he began to utter long wails that went almost like yells from a hound, echoing wailfully and weird through this chill place of tombstones, where men lay like the dead.

The sound, in its high piercing beginnings that dwindled to final melancholy moans, expressed a red and grim tragedy of the unfathomable possibilities of the man's dreams. But to the youth these were not merely the shrieks of a vision-pierced man. They were an utterance of the meaning of the room and its occupants. It was to him the protest of the wretch who feels the touch of the imperturbable granite wheels and who then cries with an impersonal eloquence, with a strength not from him, giving voice to the wail of a whole section, a class, a people. This, weaving into the young man's brain and mingling with his views of these vast and somber shadows that like mighty black fingers curled around the naked bodies, made the young man so that he did not sleep, but lay carving biographies for these men from his meager experience. At times the fellow in the corner howled in a writhing agony of his imaginations.

Finally a long lance point of gray light shot through the dusty panes of the window. Without, the young man could see roofs drearily white in the dawning. The point of light yellowed and grew brighter, until the golden rays of the morning sun came in bravely and strong. They touched with radiant color the form of a small, fat man, who snored in stuttering fashion. His round and shiny bald head glowed suddenly with the valor of a decoration. He sat up, blinked at the sun, swore fretfully and pulled his blanket over the ornamental splendors of his head.

The youth contentedly watched this rout of the shadows before the bright spears of the sun and presently he slumbered. When he awoke he heard the voice of the assassin raised in valiant curses. Putting up his head he perceived his comrade seated on the side of the cot engaged in scratching his neck with long finger nails that rasped like files.

"Hully Jee dis is a new breed. They've got can openers on their feet," he continued in a violent tirade.

The young man hastily unlocked his closet and took out his shoes and hat. As he sat on the side of the cot, lacing his shoes, he glanced about and saw that daylight had made the room comparatively commonplace and uninteresting. The men, whose faces seemed stolid, serene or absent, were engaged in dressing, while a great crackle of bantering conversation arose.

A few were parading in unconcerned nakedness. Here and there were men of brawn, whose skins shone clear and ruddy. They took splendid poses, standing massively, like chiefs. When they had dressed in their ungainly garments there was an extraordinary change. They then showed bumps and deficiencies of all kinds.

There were others who exhibited many deformities. Shoulders were slanting, humped, pulled this way and pulled that way. And notable among these latter men was the little fat man who had refused to allow his head to be glorified. His pudgy form, builded like a pear, bustled to and fro, while he swore in fishwife fashion. It appeared that some article of his apparel had vanished.

The young man, attired speedily, went to his friend, the assassin. At first the latter looked dazed at the sight of the youth. This face seemed to be appealing to him through the cloud wastes of his memory. He scratched his neck and reflected. At last he grinned, a broad smile gradually spreading until his countenance was a round illumination. "Hello, Willie," he cried, cheerily.

"Hello," said the young man. "Are yeh ready t' fly?"

"Sure." The assassin tied his shoe carefully with some twine and came ambling.

When he reached the street the young man experienced no sudden relief from unholy atmospheres. He had forgotten all about them, and had been breathing naturally and with no sensation of discomfort or distress.

He was thinking of these things as he walked along the street, when he was suddenly startled by feeling the assassin's hand, trembling with excitement, clutching his arm, and when the assassin spoke, his voice went into quavers from a supreme agitation.

"I'll be hully, bloomin' blowed, if there wasn't a feller with a nightshirt on up there in that joint!"

The youth was bewildered for a moment, but presently he turned to smile indulgently at the assassin's humor.

"Oh, you're a d— liar," he merely said.

Whereupon the assassin began to gesture extravagantly and take oath by strange gods. He frantically placed himself at the mercy of remarkable fates if his tale were not true. "Yes, he did! I cross m' heart thousan' times!" he protested, and at the time his eyes were large with amazement, his mouth wrinkled in unnatural glee. "Yessir! A nightshirt! A hully white nightshirt!"

"You lie!"

"Nosir! I hope ter die b'fore I kin git anudder ball if there wasn't a jay wid a hully, bloomin' white nightshirt!"

His face was filled with the infinite wonder of it. "A hully white nightshirt," he continually repeated.

The young man saw the dark entrance to a basement restaurant. There was a sign which read, "No mystery about our hash," and there were other age-stained and world-battered legends which told him that the place was within his means. He stopped before it and spoke to the assassin. "I guess I'll git somethin' t' eat."

At this the assassin, for some reason, appeared to be quite embarrassed. He gazed at the seductive front of the eating place for a moment. Then he started slowly up the street. "Well, goodby, Willie," he said, bravely.

For an instant the youth studied the departing figure. Then he called out, "Hol' on a minnet." As they came together he spoke in a certain fierce way, as if he feared that the other would think him to be weak. "Look-a-here, if yeh wanta git some breakfas' I'll lend yeh three cents t' do it with. But say, look-a-here, you've gota git out an' hustle. I ain't goin' t' support yeh, or I'll go broke b'fore night. I ain't no millionaire."

"I take me oath, Willie," said the assassin, earnestly, "th' on'y thing I really needs is a ball. Me t'roat feels like a fryin' pan. But as I can't git a ball, why, th' next bes' thing is breakfast, an' if yeh do that fer me, b'gawd, I'd say yeh was th' whitest lad I ever see."

They spent a few moments in dexterous exchanges of phrases, in which they each protested that the other was, as the assassin had originally said, a "respecter'ble gentlem'n." And they concluded with mutual assurances that they were the souls of intelligence and virtue. Then they went into the restaurant.

There was a long counter, dimly lighted from hidden sources. Two or three men in soiled white aprons rushed here and there.

The youth bought a bowl of coffee for two cents and a roll for one cent. The assassin purchased the same. The bowls were webbed with brown seams, and the tin spoons wore an air of having emerged from the first pyramid. Upon them were black, moss-like encrustations of age, and they were bent and scarred from the attacks of long forgotten teeth. But over their repast the wanderers waxed warm and mellow. The assassin grew affable as the hot mixture went soothingly down his parched throat, and the young man felt courage flow in his veins.

Memories began to throng in on the assassin, and he brought forth long tales, intricate, incoherent, delivered with a chattering swiftness as from an old woman. "—great job out'n Orange. Boss keep yeh hustlin', though, all time. I was there three days, and then I went an' ask 'im t' lend me a dollar. 'G-g-go ter the devil,' he ses, an' I lose me job.

—"South no good. Damn niggers work for twenty-five an' thirty cents a day. Run white man out. Good grub, though. Easy livin'.

—"Yas; useter work little in Toledo, raftin' logs. Make two or three dollars er day in the spring. Lived high. Cold as ice, though, in the winter—"

"I was raised in northern N'York. O-o-o-oh, yeh jest oughto live there. No beer ner whisky, though, way off in the woods. But all th' good hot grub yeh can eat. B'gawd, I hung around there long as I could till th' ol' man fired me. 'Git t'hell outa here, yeh wuthless skunk, git t'hell outa here an' go die,' he ses. 'You're a hell of a father,' I ses, 'you are,' an' I quit 'im."

As they were passing from the dim eating place they encountered an old man who was trying to steal forth with a tiny package of food, but a tall man with an indomitable mustache stood dragon fashion, barring the way of escape. They heard the old man raise a plaintive protest. "Ah, you always want to know what I take out, and you never see that I usually bring a package in here from my place of business."

As the wanderers trudged slowly along Park Row, the assassin began to expand and grow blithe. "B'gawd, we've been livin' like kings," he said, smacking appreciative lips.

"Look out or we'll have t' pay fer it t' night," said the youth, with gloomy warning.

But the assassin refused to turn his gaze toward the future. He went with a limping step, into which he injected a suggestion of lamb-like gambols. His mouth was wreathed in a red grin.

In the City Hall Park the two wanderers sat down in the little circle of benches sanctified by traditions of their class. They huddled in their old garments, slumbrously conscious of the march of the hours which for them had no meaning.

The people of the street hurrying hither and thither made a blend of black figures, changing, yet frieze-like. They walked in their good clothes as upon important missions, giving no gaze to the two wanderers seated upon the benches. They expressed to the young man his infinite distance from all that he valued. Social position, comfort, the pleasures of living, were unconquerable kingdoms. He felt a sudden awe.

And in the background a multitude of buildings, of pitiless hues and sternly high, were to him emblematic of a nation forcing its regal head into the clouds, throwing no downward glances; in the sublimity of its aspirations ignoring the wretches who may flounder at its feet. The roar of the city in his ear was to him the confusion of strange tongues, babbling heedlessly; it was the clink of coin, the voice of the city's hopes which were to him no hopes.

He confessed himself an outcast, and his eyes from under the lowered rim of his hat began to glance guiltily, wearing the criminal expression that comes with certain convictions.

"THE MEN IN THE STORM"

At about three o'clock of the February afternoon, the blizzard began to swirl great clouds of snow along the streets, sweeping it down from the roofs and up from the pavements until the faces of pedestrians tingled and burned as from a thousand needle-prickings. Those on the walks huddled their necks closely in the collars of their coats and went along stooping like a race of aged people. The drivers of vehicles hurried their horses furiously on their way. They were made more cruel by the exposure of their positions, aloft on high seats. The street cars, bound up-town, went slowly, the horses slipping and straining in the spongy brown mass that lay between the rails. The drivers, muffled to the eyes, stood erect and facing the wind, models of grim philosophy. Overhead the trains rumbled and roared, and the dark structure of the elevated railroad, stretching over the avenue, dripped little streams and drops of water upon the mud and snow beneath it.

All the clatter of the street was softened by the masses that lay upon the cobbles until, even to one who looked from a window, it became important music, a melody of life made necessary to the ear by the dreariness of the pitiless beat and sweep of the storm. Occasionally one could see black figures of men busily shovelling the white drifts from the walks. The sounds from their labor created new recollections of rural experiences which every man manages to have in a measure. Later, the immense windows of the shops became aglow with light, throwing great beams of orange and yellow upon the pavement. They were infinitely cheerful, yet in a way they accented the force and discomfort of the storm, and gave a meaning to the pace of the people and the vehicles, scores of pedestrians and drivers, wretched with cold faces, necks and feet, speeding for scores of unknown doors and entrances, scattering to an infinite variety of shelters, to places which the imagination made warm with the familiar colors of home.

There was an absolute expression of hot dinners in the pace of the people. If one dared to speculate upon the destination of those who came trooping, he lost himself in a maze of social calculations; he might fling a handful of sand and attempt to follow the flight of each particular grain. But as to the suggestion of hot dinners, he was in firm lines of thought, for it was upon every hurrying face. It is a matter of tradition; it is from the tales of childhood. It comes forth with every storm.

However, in a certain part of a dark West-side street, there was a collection of men to whom these things were as if they were not. In this street was located a charitable house where for five cents the homeless of the city could get a bed at night and, in the morning, coffee and bread.

During the afternoon of the storm, the whirling snows acted as drivers, as men with whips, and at half-past three, the walk before the closed doors of the house was covered with wanderers of the street, waiting. For some distance on either side of the place they could be seen lurking in doorways and behind projecting parts of buildings, gathering in close bunches in an effort to get warm. A covered wagon drawn up near the curb sheltered a dozen of them. Under the stairs that led to the elevated railway station, there were six or eight, their hands stuffed deep in their pockets, their shoulders stooped, jiggling their feet. Others always could be seen coming, a strange procession, some slouching along with the characteristic hopeless gait of professional strays, some coming with hesitating steps wearing the air of men to whom this sort of thing was new.

It was an afternoon of incredible length. The snow, blowing in twisting clouds, sought out the men in their meagre hiding-places and skillfully beat in among them, drenching their persons with showers of fine, stinging flakes. They crowded together, muttering, and fumbling in their pockets to get their red, inflamed wrists covered by the cloth.

Newcomers usually halted at one of the groups and addressed a question, perhaps much as a matter of form, "Is it open yet?"

Those who had been waiting inclined to take the questioner seriously and become contemptuous. "No; do yeh think we'd be standin' here?"

The gathering swelled in numbers steadily and persistently. One could always see them coming, trudging slowly through the storm.

Finally, the little snow plains in the street began to assume a leaden hue from the shadows of evening. The buildings upreared gloomily save where various windows became brilliant figures of light that made shimmers and splashes of yellow on the snow. A street lamp on the curb struggled to illuminate, but it was reduced to impotent blindness by the swift gusts of sleet crusting its panes.

In this half-darkness, the men began to come from their shelter places and mass in front of the doors of charity. They were of all types, but the nationalities were mostly American, German and Irish. Many were strong, healthy, clear-skinned fellows with that stamp of countenance which is not frequently seen upon seekers after charity. There were men of undoubted patience, industry and temperance, who in time of ill-fortune, do not habitually turn to rail at the state of society, snarling at the arrogance of the rich and bemoaning the cowardice of the poor, but who at these times are apt to wear a sudden and singular meekness, as if they saw the world's progress marching from them and were trying to perceive where they had failed, what they had lacked, to be thus vanquished in the race. Then there were others of the shifting, Bowery lodging-house element who were used to paying ten cents for a place to sleep, but who now came here because it was cheaper.

But they were all mixed in one mass so thoroughly that one could not have discerned the different elements but for the fact that the laboring men, for the most part, remained silent and impassive in the blizzard, their eyes fixed on the windows of the house, statues of patience.

The sidewalk soon became completely blocked by the bodies of the men. They pressed close to one another like sheep in a winter's gale, keeping one another warm by the heat of their bodies. The snow came down upon this compressed group of men until, directly from above, it might have appeared like a heap of snow-covered merchandise, if it were not for the fact that the crowd swayed gently with a unanimous, rhythmical motion. It was wonderful to see how the snow lay upon the heads and shoulders of these men, in little ridges an inch thick perhaps in places, the flakes steadily adding drop and drop, precisely as they fall upon the unresisting grass of the fields. The feet of the men were all wet and cold and the wish to warm them accounted for the slow, gentle, rhythmical motion. Occasionally some man whose ears or nose tingled acutely from the cold winds would wriggle down until his head was protected by the shoulders of his companions.

There was a continuous murmuring discussion as to the probability of the doors being speedily opened. They persistently lifted their eyes toward the windows. One could hear little combats of opinion.

"There's a light in th' winder!"

"Naw; it's a reflection f'm across th' way."

"Well, didn't I see 'em lite it?"

"You did?"

"I did!"

"Well, then, that settles it!"

As the time approached when they expected to be allowed to enter, the men crowded to the doors in an unspeakable crush, jamming and wedging in a way that it seemed would crack bones. They surged heavily against the building in a powerful wave of pushing shoulders. Once a rumor flitted among all the tossing heads.

"They can't open th' doors! Th' fellers er smack up ag'in 'em."

Then a dull roar of rage came from the men on the outskirts; but all the time they strained and pushed until it appeared to be impossible for those that they cried out against to do anything but be crushed to pulp.

"Ah, git away f'm th' door!"

"Git outa that!"

"Throw 'em out!"

"Kill 'em!"

"Say, fellers, now, what th' 'ell? Give 'em a chanct t' open th' door!"

"Yeh damned pigs, give 'em a chanct t' open th' door!"

Men in the outskirts of the crowd occasionally yelled when a boot-heel of one of the frantic trampling feet crushed their freezing extremities.

"Git off me feet, yeh clumsy tarrier!"

"Say, don't stand on me feet! Walk on th' ground!"

A man near the doors suddenly shouted: "O-o-oh! Le' me out—le' me out!" And another, a man of infinite valor, once twisted his head so as to half-face those who were pushing behind him. "Quit yer shovin', yeh—" and he delivered a volley of the most powerful and singular invectives straight into the faces of the men behind him. It was as if he was hammering the noses of them with curses of triple brass. His face, red with rage, could be seen; upon it, an expression of sublime disregard of consequences. But nobody cared to reply to his imprecations; it was too cold. Many of them snickered and all continued to push.

In occasional pauses of the crowd's movement the men had opportunity to make jokes; usually grim things, and no doubt very uncouth. Nevertheless, they are notable—one does not expect to find the quality of humor in a heap of old clothes under a snowdrift.

The winds seemed to grow fiercer as time wore on. Some of the gusts of snow that came down on the close collection of heads cut like knives and needles, and the men huddled, and swore, not like dark assassins, but in a sort of an American fashion, grimly and desperately, it is true, but yet with a wondrous under-effect, indefinable and mystic, as if there was some kind of humor in this catastrophe, in this situation in a night of snow-laden winds.

Once, the window of the huge dry-goods shop across the street furnished material for a few moments of forgetfulness. In the brilliantly-lighted space appeared the figure of a man. He was rather stout and very well clothed. His whiskers were fashioned charmingly after those of the Prince of Wales. He stood in an attitude of magnificent reflection. He slowly stroked his moustache with a certain grandeur of manner, and looked down at the snow-encrusted mob. From below, there was denoted a supreme complacence in him. It seemed that the sight operated inversely, and enabled him to more clearly regard his own environment, delightful relatively.

One of the mob chanced to turn his head and perceive the figure in the window. "Hello, lookit 'is whiskers," he said genially.

Many of the men turned then, and a shout went up. They called to him in all strange keys. They addressed him in every manner, from familiar and cordial greetings to carefully-worded advice concerning changes in his personal appearance. The man presently fled, and the mob chuckled ferociously like ogres who had just devoured something.

They turned then to serious business. Often they addressed the stolid front of the house.

"Oh, let us in fer Gawd's sake!"

"Let us in or we'll all drop dead!"

"Say, what's th' use o' keepin' all us poor Indians out in th' cold?"

And always some one was saying, "Keep off me feet."

The crushing of the crowd grew terrific toward the last. The men, in keen pain from the blasts, began almost to fight. With the pitiless whirl of snow upon them, the battle for shelter was going to the strong. It became known that the basement door at the foot of a little steep flight of stairs was the one to be opened, and they jostled and heaved in this direction like laboring fiends. One could hear them panting and groaning in their fierce exertion.

Usually some one in the front ranks was protesting to those in the rear: "O-o-ow! Oh, say, now, fellers, let up, will yeh? Do yeh wanta kill somebody?"

A policeman arrived and went into the midst of them, scolding and berating, occasionally threatening, but using no force but that of his hands and shoulders against these men who were only struggling to get in out of the storm. His decisive tones rang out sharply: "Stop that pushin' back there! Come, boys, don't push! Stop that! Here, you, quit yer shovin'! Cheese that!"

When the door below was opened, a thick stream of men forced a way down the stairs, which were of an extraordinary narrowness and seemed only wide enough for one at a time. Yet they somehow went down almost three abreast. It was a difficult and painful operation. The crowd was like a turbulent water forcing itself through one tiny outlet. The men in the rear, excited by the success of the others, made frantic exertions, for it seemed that this large band would more than fill the quarters and that many would be left upon the pavements. It would be disastrous to be of the last, and accordingly men with the snow biting their faces, writhed and twisted with their might. One expected that from the tremendous pressure, the narrow passage to the basement door would be so choked and clogged with human limbs and bodies that movement would be impossible. Once indeed the crowd was forced to stop, and a cry went along that a man had been injured at the foot of the stairs. But presently the slow movement began again, and the policeman fought at the top of the flight to ease the pressure on those who were going down.

A reddish light from a window fell upon the faces of the men when they, in turn, arrived at the last three steps and were about to enter. One could then note a change of expression that had come over their features. As they thus stood upon the threshold of their hopes, they looked suddenly content and complacent. The fire had passed from their eyes and the snarl had vanished from their lips. The very force of the crowd in the rear, which had previously vexed them, was regarded from another point of view, for it now made it inevitable that they should go through the little doors into the place that was cheery and warm with light.

The tossing crowd on the sidewalk grew smaller and smaller. The snow beat with merciless persistence upon the bowed heads of those who waited. The wind drove it up from the pavements in frantic forms of winding white, and it seethed in circles about the huddled forms, passing in, one by one, three by three, out of the storm.

URBAN LIFE AND REFORM
IN THE LATE NINETEENTH CENTURY

Phyllis Frus and Stanley Corkin, Volume Editors

Biographers and critics generally agree that by the time Stephen Crane moved to New York to work as a crime reporter in late 1891 he had begun to compose his first novella, the story of a girl of promise who succumbs to the brutal circumstances of her life in the slums of lower Manhattan. In *Maggie* Crane depicts the conditions of urban life in New York City and, perhaps more generally, in any American city, with the implicit moralism of reformers and the prose style of realism and naturalism. His Maggie is a flower who "blossomed in a mud puddle," an adolescent of promise and beauty who succumbs to the charms of Pete, a bartender. It is a seduction which brings about her ruin. As a reviewer of the 1893 novella wrote in the *Port Jervis Union,* Maggie "grows up under surroundings which repress all good impulses, stunt the moral growth, and render it inevitable that she should become what she eventually did, a creature of the streets" (Rev. of *Maggie* 143).

While living in Syracuse and attending Syracuse University sporadically during 1890 and 1891, Crane had shown an interest in the underside of that city, spending time investigating saloons and the areas that prostitutes frequented. Before that time, his interest in issues of alcohol and moral uplift had been more a matter of his upbringing than of experience. As a child Crane was inundated with the language of vice and redemption, which was a regular feature of late-nineteenth-century American life. His mother was president of the local chapter of the Women's Christian Temperance Union and a frequent lecturer on the debilitating effects of alcohol, and his father, a Methodist minister, was also outspoken about the immoral behavior of the day, including out-of-wedlock sexual activity and "popular amusements" such as "trashy novels" and billiards.[1] It is easy to

---

[1] One of J. T. Crane's books, *Popular Amusements* (1870), is available in digitized form on the Making of America Web site.

imagine how displeased both would have been by this work's graphic language and lack of a moral, had they lived to read it. After Richard Watson Gilder rejected *Maggie* for *Century* magazine, Crane soon came to understand how unacceptable his work would be for a mass audience and used a small inheritance to pay for a printing of 1,100 copies (what we would call vanity publishing). He used the pseudonym Johnston Smith to hide his identity from relatives he knew would be offended by the characters' profane and blasphemous oaths rendered in the dialect of the slums.

Crane sent copies to reformers and critics, and, although the publication earned him no fame and less money, it drew the attention of novelist Hamlin Garland and the dean of American letters, William Dean Howells, themselves in the midst of careers as realists. The reviewer for the *Port Jervis Union* seems to have adopted the description that Crane wrote on a number of copies for friends and reformers:[2] "It tries to show that environment is a tremendous thing in the world and frequently shapes lives regardless." The resounding success of *The Red Badge of Courage* led Appleton to issue a heavily revised version of *Maggie* in 1896, eliminating profanities and shortening scenes that emphasize Maggie's stint as a streetwalker. The revised novel is less explicit but retains the general flavor and confirms our sense that Maggie is inevitably a creature of her sordid circumstances.

Modern readers probably find naturalism—with its connotations of environmentally induced conditions and qualities—a more appropriate category in which to place *Maggie* than realism, but Crane's earliest readers were impressed by its unflinching honesty. For example, Garland, in an 1893 review, called it "pictorial, graphic, terrible in its directness" (38). And when Crane wanted to impress a woman he hoped to court (Lily Brandon Monroe), he told her he had written a book that had won superlatives from some "great men," including Garland, who said, "Egad, it has no style! Absolutely transparent! wonderful—wonderful" (Wertheim and Sorrentino, *Correspondence* 66). What makes the novella realistic is not Crane's ability to describe the particularities of the neighborhood— Rum Alley and Devil's Row in lower Manhattan—but the indirectness of his judgment. Crane's innovation was to substitute irony for the moralizing tendencies of pamphleteers and slum novelists whose main intent was reform. As Howells astutely pointed out, *Maggie* is a character study. And novelist Frank Norris, in a review of the 1896 edition, remarked on the

---

[2] Wertheim and Sorrentino have included two of these inscriptions in *Correspondence* 52–53.

novella's familiar character types—he called them "old acquaintances" from the literature of "mean streets" (151). As this comment by Norris suggests, when Crane began writing he knew relatively little about the characters as individuals but had a clear notion of the plot and of his heroine's inevitable downward slide. Though he did rewrite the novel extensively during the year before it was published in March 1893, when he was 21, he does not provide his characters with complex inner lives. This places the novella within the domain of naturalism, where individuals' fates are determined more by their experiences in the world than by their subjective acts of assimilating those experiences.

It is useful to compare Crane's work to other novels that fall within this deterministic philosophy, such as some by contemporaries, including Theodore Dreiser's *Sister Carrie* and Upton Sinclair's *The Jungle*. Each of these novels finds its central character trapped within a well-defined world that cannot be altered through his or her efforts. In comparing Crane's and Dreiser's depictions of New York, or Sinclair's elaboration of Chicago with Crane's of Manhattan, Crane's urban locale is to some extent as generic as his characters. One could draw a map of the New York neighborhoods that Dreiser's Carrie and Hurstwood move into and out of and of Hurstwood's journey to Brooklyn where he then drives a streetcar as a scab. Similarly, Sinclair's harrowing and precise descriptions of Packingtown in Chicago ask the reader to imagine the reality of his characters' lives. In contrast, Crane rarely elaborates on the specific geography of *Maggie*. Events take place in a typical music hall and a crowded tenement building, but upon entering the Bowery of the 1890s, it would be difficult to find, for example, the bar where Pete works. Crane's novel is also distinct from these others in its relative brevity, which stems from its minimal use of documentary detail. With its ironic understatement and rough approximation of street slang, this work looks forward to a minimalist form of modernist fiction. No wonder Ralph Ellison called *Maggie* one of the two "parents of the modern American novel"—the other being, of course, *Adventures of Huckleberry Finn* (65).

Although Crane does not render a specific social and political world in *Maggie,* readers should not assume that people and places quite similar to the characters and locales found in this novel did not exist in the urban centers of the United States in the 1890s. In this decade a million and a half people lived in New York, and of those a sizable number lived in poverty. As a result of the geometric increase in industrial production that took place in the United States after the Civil War, Americans who had lived in rural areas flocked to urban centers, so that by the turn of the century 40 percent of the nation's population lived in urban areas, whereas in 1850 scarcely 15 percent lived in cities of more than 2,500. In addition, this period saw immigration from abroad in unprecedented numbers. In the 1890s, New York was home to substantial numbers of newly arrived Jews, Italians, Chinese, Germans, and Irish. This stream of migration to New York created a city of density, squalor, and stunning disparities of wealth.

In the last decade of the nineteenth century New York had become something of a national symbol, coming to stand for both the bright future of American progress and fears that the nation was retreating from its foundational characteristics. Indeed, figures of this period ranging from Josiah Strong and Brook Adams to the authors grouped with Crane in this section entered into debate about the future of the nation in terms of its urban spaces. Other cities—such as Chicago, Boston, and Philadelphia— also featured in this discussion, but New York offered quintessential elements, probably because many of the nearly nine million immigrants entering the country in the last decades of the century came through this gateway. Alongside marvels of progress like skyscrapers and the newly built subway and elevated train systems, one could find, then play upon symbolically, extraordinary congestion, filth, and poverty along with vice and iniquity. In social and political terms New York, with its corrupt Tammany political machine and extremely low rate of property ownership, was evidence that the United States had not become a Jeffersonian utopia. It served as an index of what had gone wrong with the nation materially, morally, and racially. These were the impressions that Crane built upon, impressions that were confirmed by his years as a police reporter, during which he covered the streets of lower New York—the area where much of this crime and general unsavoriness was concentrated. Crane had worked as a reporter in Asbury Park, New Jersey, during the summer after his year in Syracuse, and in the fall of 1891 lived in his brother's home in Lake View, writing sketches of rural Sullivan County and making some forays into the city to observe life in slums. His first sketch of city life, "The Broken-Down Van," was published in July 1892. After he moved into a rooming house on Avenue A in the fall, his research into the alleys and beer gardens of lower Manhattan began in earnest. His roommate described Stephen's enthusiastic rendering of a "stone-fight" he had witnessed that soon became the opening scene in *Maggie*. And here Crane began the habit of slumming, going among the street people in old clothes with no money and begging for coins, even from a brother working on Beekman Street. He had previously warned his brother not to give him away if he asked for a nickel, but to simply give it to him (Wertheim and Sorrentino, *Crane Log* 81).

In the contextual materials that follow, the reader learns the source of Crane's knowledge and understanding of life in the slums of New York.

Some of it came from Jacob Riis, for Crane reported an illustrated lecture that celebrity journalist gave in Asbury Park in 1892. An immigrant from Denmark, Riis was a crime reporter with the *New York Tribune* until 1890, then a freelance journalist. His life's major work was to chronicle the conditions of New York's Lower East Side. His 1890 book, *How the Other Half Lives: Studies among the Tenements of New York,* became the documentary source for those interested in urban poverty and is generally counted as an early example of muckraking journalism.[3] (It began as stories printed in Richard Henry Dana's *Sun.*) This volume seems to have been instrumental in the development of Crane's curiosity about the great city.

Riis's mission, of course, was not simply to document the physical squalor of this region but to explain and advocate for its redress. As he wrote in the introduction to this, his first exposé, "What are you going to do about it? is the question of today." Riis decried the disease and social despair of the slums. But it is equally important to see him as a moral crusader. Like so many of his day, including Crane's parents, Riis saw alcohol as a major factor in the moral disruption of the city. He described the omnipresence of saloons in lower New York as an evil in itself, causing much of the squalor and disruption he witnessed. His broad assumptions regarding the role of temptation among the lower classes found their echo in Crane. Pete's station as a bartender provides him with disproportionate status, making his character inordinately attractive to this child of the Bowery, born to parents rendered unfit by their propensity to violence and drink. As Alan Trachtenberg remarks in his fascinating account of the mysteries of the city in *The Incorporation of America,* the role the press had taken on was to present the "other half" as comprising "the pathetic, disreputable drunkard and pauper . . . laced with appeals to 'charity,' and in Riis's writings, to middle-class worries over safety and security." In Trachtenberg's view, rather than concerning himself with bourgeois citizens' self-interest, Crane elevated the city's social mystery to spectacle (126).

Probably best known for her memoir of the settlement house she founded, *Life at Hull-House,* Jane Addams was also an astute analyst of economic and political impediments to progressive reform. Although

---

[3] Trachtenberg reports Riis's estimates in 1891 as follows: "nearly half the city's population lived in the 39,000 tenements packed in the lower end of the island, many without water or indoor toilets. Certain areas on the Lower East Side in the 1890s were calculated to be the densest regions of human habitation on earth" (128).

Addams made the poor of Chicago her lifelong concern, her analysis of the harmful effects of rampant industrialization on children fits New York or any other city as well. She was harshly critical of a factory-based economy which required even children and adolescents to work while making no "public provision for recreation." In *The Spirit of Youth and the City Streets,* Addams not only expressed indignation at the shameful neglect of amusements for the young, when their daily labor in factories and shops was so "monotonous and subdivided," but lamented the inevitable loss of capacity for beauty and joy in those who ought to feel it most strongly, particularly at a time when they ought to be engaged in the dance of courtship—if only there were opportunities beyond the dance halls and gambling dens. When Addams wrote that "even the most loutish tenement-house youth" was susceptible to beauty and to "delicate and tender" experiences, perhaps remembered dimly from childhood, she might have been referring to Maggie's coarsened brother Jimmie's remark "on a certain star-lit evening": "Deh moon looks like hell, don't it?"

In the fall of 1893, after Crane was well into work on *The Red Badge of Courage,* he returned to the city. Soon after, during the winter of 1894, he began his investigations into the lives of the poor in Manhattan. These experiences resulted in the two sketches reprinted in this section, in what his friend Corwin Knapp Linson called "the period of his tramp studies." The sketches were written while Crane was on assignment for the Bacheller and Johnson syndicate, apparently at Howells's and Garland's suggestion. Another friend, W. W. Carroll, reported going with him on these "dreary rounds" for three nights to cover the "bum lodging houses" of New York. They had about thirty cents each. Said Carroll, "His stories of these days and nights were strings of words that made one see flaring gas jets and dark interiors, where one could smell crude disinfectants— mingled with exhalations from many human bodies" (Wertheim and Sorrentino, *Crane Log* 97).

It was already a convention of news reporters to disguise themselves to go among the group they intended to study, as it later became for sociologists. For example, Winifred Sweet Black, who wrote under the name Annie Laurie, and Elizabeth Cochrane, who wrote under the name of Nellie Bly, undertook such experiments as falling down in the streets of San Francisco to test emergency medical care, taking menial jobs in order to investigate prostitution and poor working conditions for women, and pretending to be insane to get admitted to New York's asylum on Blackwell's Island (Bly's *Ten Days in a Madhouse,* published in 1887). (It is possible that Crane had read Bly's account of this searing experience. Ironically, rooms he lived in on Avenue A in 1893 overlooked Blackwell's

Island—now renamed Roosevelt Island—which also housed a tuberculosis sanitarium and a prison.) Rather than investigative reporters, however, these women were invariably labeled "sob sisters," and their reform impulses were regarded as stunts designed to raise circulation for their employers, Hearst and Pulitzer, respectively.

Though published in the *New York Press,* "Experiment in Misery" seems quite different from a typical article in a contemporary newspaper because of its highly descriptive language. Crane elevated his use of language in both sketches, apparently seeking to be more visually striking than the photographs that were a recent addition to newspapers in the United States. An artist's touch is also apparent, as Crane followed the contemporary example of the impressionist painters in emphasizing the effects of light in defamiliarizing objects. The opening sentence of "Experiment in Misery" is an example: "It was late at night, and a fine rain was swirling softly down, causing the pavements to glisten with hue of steel and blue and yellow in the rays of the innumerable lights." Such appeals to the reader's visual sense do appear in *Maggie,* but they are intensified in these later pieces.

The usual way to regard these sketches is as recorded by a morally neutral observer, who does not sentimentalize his characters or recommend solutions to the acutely depicted social ills; yet, the reader can detect some condescension creeping in along with the specificity. In "The Men in a Storm," the narrator compares the crowd of men queuing up to get into a charitable house for shelter during a blizzard to increasingly lifeless objects: The snowflakes fall on these men "precisely as they fall upon the unresisting grass of the fields"; he is surprised to find the men making small jokes, finding a sense of humor unlikely in "a heap of old clothes under a snowdrift." And when the door finally opens, the crowd squeezes in "like a turbulent water forcing itself through one tiny outlet." Dreiser's depiction of a similar situation in "The Bowery Mission" shows a more conventional journalist's style. Where Crane's language is playful, Dreiser's is more conventionally descriptive. Dreiser also personalizes his figures and sentimentalizes them in his own voice.

Crane's New York City journalism replicates a kind of top-down view of reform. Rather than social outrage, Crane expresses an abstract curiosity about the poor; ultimately he finds them less than human. He is surprised when he finds them bright or even with a sense of humor. Crane wrote in response to the curiosity of the public, in an era when such poverty was becoming a remarked-upon phenomenon and a kind of emblem of urban life. His sketches highlight the distinction between the writer and these objects who have no capacity to write themselves. Indeed, though

Crane's style of writing is distinctive, the objects he finds have little that defines them as singular human beings.

That Crane had trouble imagining the inner lives of the poor suggests a broad tendency of those from the middle and upper classes to judge and dismiss them. Such a view is readily available in an 1897 essay by Theodore Roosevelt, whose words are all the more intriguing for his association with the Progressive movement in national politics and for his more complete embracing of reform in the years after his presidency. Upon becoming president in 1901, Roosevelt almost immediately became the avatar of this movement. A native of New York who ran for mayor of that city in 1886, Roosevelt made his way onto the national stage as a publicity-seeking bureaucrat in the 1890s. Among the positions he held was the job of Commissioner of Police in New York City from 1895 to 1896. In that capacity he worked zealously to control the sale of alcohol in the city's slums and to reform the department's general corruption. Roosevelt had long regarded himself as a genetically fit heir to leadership, and his actions in positions of authority proceeded from this biological sense of entitlement. Roosevelt's arguments against socialists and for the perpetuation of the advantages of the wealthy had a distinct genetic element, as did his sympathy for immigration restriction. These sentiments fell well within the mainstream of the day, though they were more conservative than those he would profess as president. Still, as we see the future president spell out his arguments, we may wonder whether one of the subtexts of Crane's story is that his lower-class characters remain in poverty because they are genetically disposed to do so.[4]

Roosevelt and Crane knew each other, as Crane was still a police reporter in New York when Roosevelt came to work with its police force. Part of the commissioner's public relations strategy—designed to benefit both the force and himself—was to cozy up to police reporters. But Roosevelt's relationship with Crane soured abruptly when Crane wrote a story of police corruption in the case of Dora Clark, who had filed charges against an officer for wrongful arrest and harassment. Crane also testified on her behalf. The department aggressively went after the reporter in public, impugning his morals and accuracy. Thus, what had been an amicable relationship became the opposite. Said Roosevelt of Crane in 1902, years after

---

[4] Gerwin, Manolios, and Popodopoulos suggest using this novella to challenge students to understand how the various reformers of the Progressive movement viewed the poor, how the reformers' so-called facts relied on assumptions based on their position in the middle or upper class—in short, to see how the reform movement itself shaped public perceptions of the poor and how tractable the reformers viewed the problems of the poor to be.

the incident: "He was a man of bad character and he was simply consorting with loose women" (Wertheim, *Crane Encyclopedia* 298). Some even say that Crane left New York and began his voyage to Cuba aboard the *Commodore* as a result of the public humiliation this incident caused him.

"CHANGE OF BASE"

Mrs. M. H. Crane

The insidious wiles of the adversary of all good are made manifest by the strategy employed to switch human souls off the right track. In this beautiful place it is not the avowed skeptic, the open grog-shop, or the gambling hell that Christians are called upon to combat, but it is the growing taste for worldly amusements which keeps the young from the house of God, dissipating religious convictions, and makes the commands of God of no effect. In this category we may count card playing, dancing and theatre going. These frivolous amusements have little to recommend them. They are good as devices to "kill time," which means to waste the precious hours given us for holier uses. But says one, "young people must have innocent amusement." Just so, but cards have ever kept bad company. The young man, fearing death on board the ill fated *Columbus,* could not pray until he had parted company with the pack of cards in his pocket. Dancing and theatre going lead to late hours, unsafe companionship and a dissipation of mind which unfits one for the serious work of life.

In the little back room in the drug store our young men may be initiated into drinking habits, and take their places just as surely among the moderate drinkers ultimately to swell the great army one hundred thousand strong, who go to a drunkard's death every year, as in the open saloon. "No drunkard shall enter the kingdom of heaven."

The pool and billiard rooms, with their obscenity and profanity, are the training schools in which our boys may take the first steps in vice, and becoming infatuated with gaming, render themselves victims to a passion which is soul destroying, and from whose toils few ever escape. Surely Christians here need to remember that "eternal vigilance is the price of liberty."

Ocean Grove Record, 15 March 1884.

FROM *HOW THE OTHER HALF LIVES:*
Studies among the Tenements of New York

Jacob A. Riis

The Reign of Rum

Where God builds a church the devil builds next door—a saloon, is an old saying that has lost its point in New York. Either the devil was on the ground first, or he has been doing a good deal more in the way of building. I tried once to find out how the account stood, and counted to 111 Protestant churches, chapels, and places of worship of every kind, [and] below Fourteenth Street, 4,065 saloons. The worst half of the tenement population lives down there, and it has to this day the worst half of the saloons. Uptown the account stands a little better, but there are easily ten saloons to every church today. I am afraid, too, that the congregations are larger by a good deal; certainly the attendance is steadier and the contributions more liberal the week round, Sunday included. Turn and twist it as we may, over against every bulwark for decency and morality which society erects, the saloon projects its colossal shadow, omen of evil wherever it falls into the lives of the poor.

Nowhere is its mark so broad or so black. To their misery it sticketh closer than a brother, persuading them that within its doors only is refuge, relief. It has the best of the argument, too, for it is true, worse pity, that in many a tenement-house block the saloon is the one bright and cheery and humanly decent spot to be found. It is a sorry admission to make, that to bring the rest of the neighborhood up to the level of the saloon would be one way of squelching it; but it is so. Wherever the tenements thicken, it multiplies. Upon the direst poverty of their crowds it grows fat and prosperous, levying upon it a tax heavier than all the rest of its grievous burdens combined. It is not yet two years since the Excise Board made the rule that no three corners of any street-crossing, not already so occupied, should thenceforward be licensed for rum-selling. And the tardy prohibition was intended for the tenement districts. Nowhere else is there need of it. One may walk many miles through the homes of the poor searching vainly for an open reading-room, a cheerful coffee-house, a decent club that is not a cloak for the traffic in rum. The dramshop yawns at every step, the poor man's club, his forum and his haven of rest when weary and disgusted with the crowding, the quarrelling, and the wretchedness at home.

New York: Scribner's, 1890.

With the poison dealt out there he takes his politics, in quality not far apart. As the source, so the stream. The rumshop turns the political crank in New York. The natural yield is rum politics. Of what that means, successive Boards of Aldermen, composed in a measure, if not of a majority, of dive-keepers, have given New York a taste. The disgrace of the infamous "Boodle Board" will be remembered until some corruption even fouler crops out and throws it into the shade.

What relation the saloon bears to the crowds, let me illustrate by a comparison. Below Fourteenth Street were, when the Health Department took its first accurate census of the tenements a year and a half ago, 13,220 of the 39,390 buildings classed as such in the whole city. Of the eleven hundred thousand tenants, not quite half a million, embracing a host of more than sixty-three thousand children under five years of age, lived below that line. Below it, also, were 234 of the cheap lodging-houses accounted for by the police last year, with a total of four millions and a half of lodgers for the twelvemonth, 59 of the city's 110 pawnshops, and 4,065 of its 7,884 saloons. The four most densely peopled precincts, the Fourth, Sixth, Tenth, and Eleventh, supported together in round numbers twelve hundred saloons, and their returns showed twenty-seven percent of the whole number of arrests for the year. The Eleventh Precinct, that has the greatest and the poorest crowds of all—it is the Tenth Ward—and harbored one-third of the army of homeless lodgers and fourteen percent of all the prisoners of the year, kept 485 saloons going in 1889. It is not on record that one of them all failed for want of support. A number of them, on the contrary, had brought their owners wealth and prominence. From their bars these eminent citizens stepped proudly into the councils of the city and the State. The very floor of one of the bar-rooms, in a neighborhood that lately resounded with the cry for bread of starving workmen, is paved with silver dollars!

East Side poverty is not alone in thus rewarding the tyrants that sweeten its cup of bitterness with their treacherous poison. The Fourth Ward points with pride to the honorable record of the conductors of its "Tub of Blood," and a dozen bar-rooms with less startling titles; the West Side to the wealth and "social" standing of the owners of such resorts as the "Witches' Broth" and the "Plug Eat" in the region of Hell's Kitchen three-cent whiskey, names ominous of the concoctions brewed there and of their fatally generous measure. Another ward, that boasts some of the best residences and the bluest blood on Manhattan Island, honors with political leadership in the ruling party the proprietor of one of the most disreputable Black-and-Tan dives and dancing-hells to be found anywhere. Criminals and policemen alike do him homage. The list might be strung out to make texts for sermons with a stronger home flavor than many that are preached in our pulpits on Sunday. But I have not set out to write the political history of New York. Besides, the list would not be complete. Secret dives are skulking in the slums and out of them, that are not labelled respectable by a Board of Excise and support no "family entrance." Their business, like that of the stale-beer dives, is done through a side-door the week through. No one knows the number of unlicensed saloons in the city. Those who have made the matter a study estimate it at a thousand, more or less. The police make occasional schedules of a few and report them to headquarters. Perhaps there is a farce in the police court, and there the matter ends. Rum and "influence" are synonymous terms. The interests of the one rarely suffer for the want of attention from the other.

With the exception of these free lances that treat the law openly with contempt, the saloons all hang out a sign announcing in fat type that no beer or liquor is sold to children. In the down-town "morgues" that make the lowest degradation of tramp-humanity pan out a paying interest, as in the "reputable resorts" uptown where Inspector Byrnes's men spot their worthier quarry elbowing citizens whom the idea of associating with a burglar would give a shock they would not get over for a week, this sign is seen conspicuously displayed. Though apparently it means submission to a beneficent law, in reality the sign is a heartless, cruel joke. I doubt if one child in a thousand, who brings his growler to be filled at the average New York bar, is sent away empty-handed, if able to pay for what he wants. I once followed a little boy, who shivered in bare feet on a cold November night so that he seemed in danger of smashing his pitcher on the icy pavement, into a Mulberry Street saloon where just such a sign hung on the wall, and forbade the barkeeper to serve the boy. The man was as astonished at my interference as if I had told him to shut up his shop and go home, which in fact I might have done with as good a right, for it was after 1 A.M., the legal closing hour. He was mighty indignant too, and told me roughly to go away and mind my business, while he filled the pitcher. The law prohibiting the selling of beer to minors is about as much respected in the tenement-house districts as the ordinance against swearing. Newspaper readers will recall the story, told little more than a year ago, of a boy who after carrying beer a whole day for a shopful of men over on the East Side, where his father worked, crept into the cellar to sleep off the effects of his own share in the rioting. It was Saturday evening. Sunday his parents sought him high and low; but it was not until Monday morning, when the shop was opened, that he was found, killed and half-eaten by the rats that overran the place.

All the evil the saloon does in breeding poverty and in corrupting politics; all the suffering it brings into the lives of its thousands of innocent victims, the wives and children of drunkards it sends forth to curse the community; its fostering of crime and its shielding of criminals—it is all as nothing to this, its worst offence. In its affinity for the thief there is at least this compensation that, as it makes, it also unmakes him. It starts him on his career only to trip him up and betray him into the hands of the law, when the rum he exchanged for his honesty has stolen his brains as well. For the corruption of the child there is no restitution. None is possible. It saps the very vitals of society; undermines its strongest defences, and delivers them over to the enemy. Fostered and filled by the saloon, the "growler" looms up in the New York street boy's life, baffling the most persistent efforts to reclaim him. There is no escape from it; no hope for the boy, once its blighting grip is upon him. Thenceforward the logic of the slums, that the world which gave him poverty and ignorance for his portion "owes him a living," is his creed, and the career of the "tough" lies open before him, a beaten track to be blindly followed to a bad end in the wake of the growler.

FROM *THE SPIRIT OF YOUTH AND THE CITY STREETS*

Jane Addams

Youth in the City

Nothing is more certain than that each generation longs for a reassurance as to the value and charm of life, and is secretly afraid lest it lose its sense of the youth of the earth. This is doubtless one reason why it so passionately cherishes its poets and artists who have been able to explore for themselves and to reveal to others the perpetual springs of life's self-renewal.

And yet the average man cannot obtain this desired reassurance through literature, nor yet through glimpses of earth and sky. It can come to him only through the chance embodiment of joy and youth which life itself may throw in his way. It is doubtless true that for the mass of men the message is never so unchallenged and so invincible as when embodied in youth itself. One generation after another has depended upon its young to equip it with gaiety and enthusiasm, to persuade it that living is a pleasure, until men everywhere have anxiously provided channels through which this wine of life might flow, and be preserved for their delight. The classical city promoted play with careful solicitude, building the theater

New York: Macmillan, 1909.

and stadium as it built the market-place and the temple. The Greeks held their games so integral a part of religion and patriotism that they came to expect from their poets the highest utterances at the very moments when the sense of pleasure released the national life. In the medieval city the knights held their tourneys, the guilds their pageants, the people their dances, and the church made festival for its most cherished saints with gay street processions, and presented a drama in which no less a theme than the history of creation became a matter of thrilling interest. Only in the modern city have men concluded that it is no longer necessary for the municipality to provide for the insatiable desire for play. Insofar as they have acted upon this conclusion, they have entered upon a most difficult and dangerous experiment; and this at the very moment when the city has become distinctly industrial, and daily labor is continually more monotonous and subdivided. We forget how new the modern city is, and how short the span of time in which we have assumed that we can eliminate public provision for recreation.

A further difficulty lies in the fact that this industrialism has gathered together multitudes of eager young creatures from all quarters of the earth as a labor supply for the countless factories and workshops, upon which the present industrial city is based. Never before in civilization have such numbers of young girls been suddenly released from the protection of the home and permitted to walk unattended upon city streets and to work under alien roofs; for the first time they are being prized more for their labor power than for their innocence, their tender beauty, their ephemeral gaiety. Society cares more for the products they manufacture than for their immemorial ability to reaffirm the charm of existence. Never before have such numbers of young boys earned money independently of the family life, and felt themselves free to spend it as they choose in the midst of vice deliberately disguised as pleasure.

This stupid experiment of organizing work and failing to organize play has, of course, brought about a fine revenge. The love of pleasure will not be denied, and when it has turned into all sorts of malignant and vicious appetites, then we, the middle-aged, grow quite distracted and resort to all sorts of restrictive measures. We even try to dam up the sweet fountain itself because we are affrighted by these neglected streams; but almost worse than the restrictive measures is our apparent belief that the city itself has no obligation in the matter, an assumption upon which the modern city turns over to commercialism practically all the provisions for public recreation.

Quite as one set of men has organized the young people into industrial enterprises in order to profit from their toil, so another set of men and also of women, I am sorry to say, have entered the neglected field of recreation and have organized enterprises which make profit out of this invincible love of pleasure.

In every city arise so-called places—"gin-palaces," they are called in fiction; in Chicago we euphemistically say merely "places"—in which alcohol is dispensed, not to allay thrist, but, ostensibly to stimulate gaiety, it is sold really in order to empty pockets. Huge dance halls are opened to which hundreds of young people are attracted, many of whom stand wistfully outside a roped circle, for it requires five cents to procure within it for five minutes the sense of allurement and intoxication which is sold in lieu of innocent pleasure. These coarse and illicit merrymakings remind one of the unrestrained jollities of Restoration London, and they are indeed their direct descendants, properly commercialized, still confusing joy with lust, and gaiety with debauchery. Since the soldiers of Cromwell shut up the people's playhouses and destroyed their pleasure fields, the Anglo-Saxon city has turned over the provision for public recreation to the most evil-minded and the most unscrupulous members of the community. We see thousands of girls walking up and down the streets on a pleasant evening with no chance to catch a sight of pleasure even through a lighted window, save as those lurid places provide it. Apparently the modern city sees in these girls only two possibilities, both of them commercial: first, a chance to utilize by day their new and tender labor power in its factories and shops, and then another chance in the evening to extract from them their petty wages by pandering to their love of pleasure.

As these overworked girls stream along the street, the rest of us see only the self-conscious walk, the giggling speech, the preposterous clothing. And yet through the huge hat, with its wilderness of bedraggled feathers, the girl announces to the world that she is here. She demands attention to the fact of her existence, she states that she is ready to live, to take her place in the world. The most precious moment in human development is the young creature's assertion that he is unlike any other human being, and has an individual contribution to make to the world. The variation from the established type is at the root of all change, the only possible basis for progress, all that keeps life from growing unprofitably stale and repetitious.

Is it only the artists who really see these young creatures as they are—the artists who are themselves endowed with immortal youth? Is it our disregard of the artist's message which makes us so blind and so stupid, or are we so under the influence of our *Zeitgeist* that we can detect only commercial values in the young as well as in the old? It is as if our eyes were holden to the mystic beauty, the redemptive joy, the civic pride which these multitudes of young people might supply to our dingy towns.

The young creatures themselves piteously look all about them in order to find an adequate means of expression for their most precious message.

One day a serious young man came to Hull-House with his pretty young sister who, he explained, wanted to go somewhere every single evening, "although she could only give the flimsy excuse that the flat was too little and too stuffy to stay in." In the difficult role of elder brother, he had done his best, stating that he had taken her "to all the missions in the neighborhood, that she had had a chance to listen to some awful good sermons and to some elegant hymns, but that some way she did not seem to care for the society of the best Christian people." The little sister reddened painfully under this cruel indictment and could offer no word of excuse, but a curious thing happened to me. Perhaps it was the phrase "the best Christian people," perhaps it was the delicate color of her flushing cheeks and her swimming eyes, but certain it is, that instantly and vividly there appeared to my mind the delicately tinted piece of wall in a Roman catacomb where the early Christians, through a dozen devices of spring flowers, skipping lambs and a shepherd tenderly guiding the young, had indelibly written down that the Christian message is one of inexpressible joy. Who is responsible for forgetting this message delivered by the "best Christian people" two thousand years ago? Who is to blame that the lambs, the little ewe lambs, have been so caught upon the brambles?

But quite as the modern city wastes this most valuable moment in the life of the girl, and drives into all sorts of absurd and obscure expressions her love and yearning toward the world in which she forecasts her destiny, so it often drives the boy into gambling and drinking in order to find his adventure.

Of Lincoln's enlistment of two and a half million soldiers, a very large number were under twenty-one, some of them under eighteen, and still others were mere children under fifteen. Even in those stirring times when patriotism and high resolve were at the flood, no one responded as did "the boys," and the great soul who yearned over them, who refused to shoot the sentinels who slept the sleep of childhood, knew, as no one else knew, the precious glowing stuff of which his army was made. But what of the millions of boys who are now searching for adventurous action, longing to fulfil the same high purpose?

One of the most pathetic sights in the public dance halls in Chicago is the number of young men, obviously honest young fellows from the country, who stand about vainly hoping to make the acquaintance of some "nice girl." They look eagerly up and down the rows of girls, many of whom are drawn to the hall by the same keen desire for pleasure and social intercourse which the lonely young men themselves feel.

One Sunday night at twelve o'clock I had occasion to go into a large public dance hall. As I was standing by the rail looking for the girl I had come to find, a young man approached me and quite simply asked me to introduce him to some "nice girl," saying that he did not know any one there. On my replying that a public dance hall was not the best place in which to look for a nice girl, he said: "But I don't know any other place where there is a chance to meet any kind of a girl. I'm awfully lonesome since I came to Chicago." And then he added rather defiantly: "Some nice girls do come here! It's one of the best halls in town." He was voicing the "bitter loneliness" that many city men remember to have experienced, during the first years after they had "come up to town." Occasionally the right sort of man and girl meet each other in these dance halls and the romance with such a tawdry beginning ends happily and respectably. But, unfortunately, mingled with the respectable young men seeking to form the acquaintance of young women through the only channel which is available to them, are many young fellows of evil purpose, and among the girls who have left their lonely boarding houses or rigid homes for a "little fling" are likewise women who openly desire to make money from the young men whom they meet, and back of it all is the desire to profit by the sale of intoxicating and "doctored" drinks.

Perhaps never before have the pleasures of the young and mature become so definitely separated as in the modern city. The public dance halls filled with frivolous and irresponsible young people in a feverish search for pleasure, are but a sorry substitute for the old dances on the village green in which all of the older people of the village participated. Chaperonage was not then a social duty but natural and inevitable, and the whole courtship period was guarded by the conventions and restraint which were taken as a matter of course and had developed through years of publicity and simple propriety.

The only marvel is that the stupid attempt to put the fine old wine of traditional country life into the new bottles of the modern town does not lead to disaster oftener than it does, and that the wine so long remains pure and sparkling.

"THE BOWERY MISSION"

Theodore Dreiser

In the lower stretches of the Bowery, in New York, that street once famous for a tawdry sprightliness but now run to humdrum and commonplace, stands the Bowery Mission. It is really a pretentious affair of its

---

From *The Color of a Great City*. New York: Boni and Liveright, 1923.

kind, the most showy and successful of any religious effort directed toward reclaiming the bum, the sot, the crook, and the failure. As a matter of fact, the three former, and not always the latter, are not easily reclaimed by religion or anything else. It is only when the three former degenerate into the latter that the thought of religion seems at all enticing, and then only on the side that leans toward help for themselves. The Bowery Mission as an institution gathers its full quota of these failures, and its double row of stately old English benches, paid for by earnest Christians who have heard of it through much newspaper heralding of its services, are nightly filled and overflowing.

The spirit of this organization is peculiar. It really does not ask anything of its adherents or attendants, or whatever they might be called, except that they come in. No dues are collected, no services exacted. There is even a free lunchroom and an employment bureau run in connection with it, where the hungry can get a cup of coffee and a roll at midnight and the jobless can sometimes hear of something to their advantage during the day. The whole spirit of the place is one of helpfulness, though the task is of necessity dispiriting and in some of its aspects gruesome.

For these individuals who frequent this place of worship are surely, of all the flotsam of the city, the most helpless and woebegone. There is something about the type of soul which turns to religion *in extremis* which is not pleasing. It appears to turn to religion about as a drowning man turns to a raft. There is the taint of personal advantage about it and not a little of the cant and whine of one who would curry favor with life or the Lord. Granting this, yet here they are, and here they come, out of the Bowery and the side streets of the Bowery, that wonderful ganglia of lodging houses; and in this place, and I presume others of its stripe, listen to presumably inspiring sermons. In all fairness, the speakers seem to realize that they have a difficult task to perform in awakening these men to a consciousness of their condition. They know that there is, if not cant, at least mental and physical lethargy to overcome. These bodies are poisoned by their own inactivity and sense of defeat. When one looks at them collectively the idea instinctively forces itself forward: "What is there to save?"

And yet, shabby and depressing as are these facts, there is a collective, coherent charm and color about the effort itself which to one who views it entirely disinterestedly is not to be scoffed at. The hall itself, a long deep store turned to a semblance of Gothic beauty by a series of colored windows set in the store-front facing the Bowery, and by a gallery of high-backed benches of Gothic design at the back, and by mottoes and traceries in dark blue and gold which harmonize fittingly with the walnut stain of the woodwork, is inviting. Even the shabby greenish-brown and dusty gray coats of the audience blend well with the woodwork, and even the pale colorless faces of gray or ivory hue somehow add to what is unquestionably an artistic and ornamental effect.

The gospel of God the All-Forgiving is the only doctrine here thoroughly insisted upon. It is, in a way, a doctrine of inspiration. That it is really never too late to change, to come back and begin all over, is the basic idea. God, once appealed to, can do anything to restore the contrite heart to power and efficiency. Believe in God, believe that He really loves you, believe that He desires to make you all you should be, and you will be. Your fortunes will change. You will come into peace and decency and be respected once more. God will help you.

It is interesting to match the effect of this inspirational doctrine, driven home as it is by imaginative address, oratorical fire, and sometimes physical vehemence. The speakers, the ordinary religionists of an inspirational and moral turn, not infrequently possess real magnetism, the power to attract and sway their hearers. These dismal wanderers, living largely in doubt and despair, can actually be seen to take on a pseudo-courage as they listen. You can see them stir and shift, the idea that possibly something can be done for them if only they can get this belief into their minds, actually influencing their bodies. And now and then some one who has got a soft job, a place, through the ministrations of the mission workers or who has been pulled out of a state of absolute despair—or at least claims to have been—will arise and testify that such has been the case. His long wanderings in the dark will actually fascinate him by contrast and he will expatiate with shabby eloquence upon his present decency and comfort as contrasted with what he was. I remember one night hearing an old man tell what a curse he had been to a kind-hearted sister, and how he wanted but one thing, now that he was coming out of his dream of evil, and that was to let her see some day that he had really reformed. It was a pathetic wish, so little to hope for, but the wish was seemingly sincere and the speaker fairly recovered.

And they claim to recover a percentage, small though it is, to actual service and usefulness. The service may not be great, the usefulness not very important, but such as it is, there it is. And if one could but believe them, so dubious is all so-called reformation of this sort, there is something pleasing in the thought that out of the muck and waste of the slough of despond some of these might actually be brought to health and decency, a worthwhile living, say. Yet are they? Dirty, grimy, like flies immersed in glue, can they be—have they ever been—dragged to safety and set on their feet again, clean, hopeful, or even weakly so?

I remember listening one night to the story of the son of the man who founded the mission. It appears that the father was rich and the boy indulgently fostered, until at last he turned out to be a drunkard, rake and whatnot—all the nouns usually applied to those who do evil. His father had tried to retain a responsible position for him among his affairs but was finally compelled to cut him off. He ordered him out of his house, his business, had his will remade, cutting him off without a dollar, and declared vehemently and determinedly that he would never look upon him again.

The boy disappeared. Some five years later a thin, shabby, downhearted wastrel strolled into the mission and sat down, contenting himself with occupying a far corner and listening wearily to what was being said. After the services were over he came to the director in charge and confessed that he was the son of the man who had founded the mission, that he was actually at the end of his rope, hungry, and with no place to sleep—your prodigal son. The director, of course, at once took him in charge, gave him a meal and a bed, and set about considering whether anything could be done for him.

It appears that the youth, like his prototype of the parable, had actually had his fill of the husks, but in addition he was sick and dispirited and willing to die. The director encouraged him to hope. He was young yet. There was still a chance for him. He first gave him odd jobs about the mission, then secured him a place as waiter in a small restaurant, and finally, figuring out a notable idea, took him to the foreman of the father's own printing establishment and asked a place for him as a printer's devil. The character of the mission director was sufficient guarantee and the place was given, though no one knew who the rundown assistant really was. Finally, after over eleven months of service, the director went to the owner of the business and said: "Would you like to know where your boy is?"

"No," the father replied sharply, "I would not."

"If you knew he had reformed and had been working for at least a year and a half steadily in one place—wouldn't that make any difference?"

"Well," he replied, looking at him quizzically, "it might. Where is he?"

"Right here in your own establishment."

The old man got up. "What's he doing? Let me look at him."

The two traversed the halls of a great business establishment and finally came to the department where the youth was working. The father, eager but cautious, scanned the room and saw his son, himself unnoticed. He was sticking type, a green shade over his eyes.

For a moment the parent hesitated, then went over.

"Harry," he called.

The boy jumped.

"Father!" he cried.

It was described as a moment of intense emotion. The boy broke down and wept and the father shed tears over him. Finally he sobered himself and said: "Now you come with me. I guess you're all right enough to be my son again. You can set more type tomorrow." And he led him away.

Truth? Or Romance? I do not know.

The final answer to this form of service, however, is in the mission itself. Nightly you may see them rise and hear them testify. One night the speaker, pouring forth a fiery description of God's power, stopped in the midst of his address and said: "Is that you, Tommy Wilson, up there in the gallery?"

"Yes, sir."

"Tommy, I'm glad to see you. Won't you get up and sing 'My Lord and I'? I know there isn't any one here who wouldn't rather hear you sing than me preach any time. Will you?"

"Yes, sir."

Up in the gallery, three rows back, there arose a shabby little man, his dusty suit showing the well-worn marks of age. He was clean and docile, however, and seemed to be some one whom the mission had reclaimed in times past. In fact, the speaker made it clear that Tommy was a great card, for out of the gutter he had come to contribute a beautiful voice to the mission, a voice that was now missing because he had a job in a faraway part of the city.

Tommy sang. He put his hands in his coat pockets, stood perfectly erect, and with his head thrown back gave vent to such a sweet, clear melody that it moved every heart. It was not a strong voice, not showy, but pure and lovely, like a limpid stream. The song he sang was this:

> I have a Friend so precious,
>   So very dear to me;
> He loves me with such tender love,
>   He loves me faithfully.
> 5   I could not live apart from Him,
>   I love to feel Him nigh;
> And so we dwell together,
>   My Lord and I.
>
> Sometimes I'm faint and weary,
> 10 He knows that I am weak,
> And as He bids me lean on Him
>   His help I gladly seek;
> He leads me in the paths of light,
>   Beneath a sunny sky;
> 15 And so we walk together,
>   My Lord and I.

I tell Him all my sorrows,
  I tell Him all my joys,
I tell Him all that pleases me,
20   I tell Him what annoys;
He tells me what I ought to do,
  He tells me how to try;
And so we walk together,
  My Lord and I.

25 He knows how I'm longing
  Some weary soul to win,
And so He bids me go and speak
  The loving word for Him;
He bids me tell His wondrous love,
30   And why He came to die;
And so we work together
  My Lord and I.

As he sang I could not help thinking of this imaginatively personified Lord of the Universe in all His power and wisdom taking note of this singing, shabby ant—of the faith that it required to believe that He would. Then I thought of the vast forces that shift and turn in their mighty inscrutability. I thought of suns and planets that die, not knowing why they are born. Of the vast machinery, the vast chemistry, of things dark, ruthless, brutal, and then of love, and mercy and tenderness that is somehow present along with cruelty and savagery. And then I thought of this little, shabby reclaimed water-rat, this scraping of the mud crawled to the bank, who yet could stand there in his shabby coat and sing! What if, after all, as the Christian Scientists believe, the Lord was not distant from things but here, now, everywhere, divine goodness speaking in and through matter and man. What if evil and weakness and failure were dreams only, evil dreams, from which we wake to something different, better—Omnipotence, to essential unity with life and love? For a moment, so mysterious a thing is emotion and romance, the thought carried me with the singer, and I sang with him:

And so we walk together,
  My Lord and I.

But outside in the cold, hard street, with its trucks and cars, I knew the informing spirit is not quite like that, neither so kind nor helpful—at least not to all.

"HOW NOT TO HELP OUR POORER BROTHERS"

Theodore Roosevelt

There are plenty of ugly things about wealth and its possessors in the present age, and I suppose there have been in all ages. There are many rich people who so utterly lack patriotism, or show such sordid and selfish traits of character, or lead such mean and vacuous lives, that all right-minded men must look upon them with angry contempt; but, on the whole, the thrifty are apt to be better citizens than the thriftless; and the worst capitalist cannot harm laboring men as they are harmed by demagogues. As the people of a State grow more and more intelligent the State itself may be able to play a larger and larger part in the life of the community, while at the same time individual effort may be given freer and less restricted movement along certain lines; but it is utterly unsafe to give the State more than the minimum of power just so long as it contains masses of men who can be moved by the pleas and denunciations of the average Socialist leader of today. There may be better schemes of taxation than those at present employed; it may be wise to devise inheritance taxes, and to impose regulations on the kinds of business which can be carried on only under the special protection of the State; and where there is a real abuse by wealth it needs to be, and in this country generally has been, promptly done away with; but the first lesson to teach the poor man is that, as a whole, the wealth in the community is distinctly beneficial to him; that he is better off in the long run because other men are well off and that the surest way to destroy what measure of prosperity he may have is to paralyze industry and the well-being of those men who have achieved success.

I am not an empiricist; I would no more deny that sometimes human affairs can be much bettered by legislation than I would affirm that they can always be so bettered. I would no more make a fetish of unrestricted individualism than I would admit the power of the State offhand and radically to reconstruct society. It may become necessary to interfere even more than we have done with the right of private contract, and to shackle cunning as we have shackled force. All I insist upon is that we must be sure of our ground before trying to get any legislation at all, and that we must not expect too much from this legislation, nor refuse to better ourselves a little because we cannot accomplish everything at a jump. Above all, it is criminal to excite anger and discontent without proposing a remedy, or

Review of Reviews, 1897.

only proposing a false remedy. The worst foe of the poor man is the labor leader, whether philanthropist or politician, who tries to teach him that he is a victim of conspiracy and injustice, when in reality he is merely working out his fate with blood and sweat as the immense majority of men who are worthy of the name always have done and always will have to do.

The difference between what can and what cannot be done by law is well exemplified by our experience with the Negro problem. . . . The Negroes were formerly held in slavery. This was a wrong which legislation could remedy, and which could not be remedied except by legislation. Accordingly they were set free by law. This having been done, many of their friends believed that in some way, by additional legislation, we could at once put them on an intellectual, social, and business equality with the whites. The effort has failed completely. In large sections of the country the Negroes are not treated as they should be treated, and politically in particular the frauds upon them have been so gross and shameful as to awaken not merely indignation but bitter wrath; yet the best friends of the Negro admit that his hope lies, not in legislation, but in the constant working of those often unseen forces of the national life which are greater than all legislation.

It is but rarely that great advances in general social well-being can be made by the adoption of some far-reaching scheme, legislative or otherwise; normally they come only by gradual growth, and by incessant effort to do first one thing, then another, and then another. Quack remedies of the universal cure-all type are generally as noxious to the body politic as to the body corporal.

Often the head-in-the-air social reformers, because people of sane and wholesome minds will not favor their wild schemes, themselves decline to favor schemes for practical reform. For the last two years there has been an honest effort in New York to give the city good government, and to work intelligently for better social conditions, especially in the poorest quarters. We have cleaned the streets; we have broken the power of the ward boss and the saloon-keeper to work injustice; we have destroyed the most hideous of the tenement houses in which poor people are huddled like swine in a sty; we have made parks and playgrounds for the children in the crowded quarters; in every possible way we have striven to make life easier and healthier, and to give man and woman a chance to do their best work; while at the same time we have warred steadily against the pauper-producing, maudlin philanthropy of the free soup-kitchen and tramp lodging-house kind. In all this we have had practically no help from either the parlor socialists or the scarcely more noxious beer-room socialists who are always howling about the selfishness of the rich and their unwillingness to do anything for those who are less well off.

There are certain labor unions, certain bodies of organized labor—notably those admirable organizations which include the railway conductors, the locomotive engineers and the firemen—which to my mind embody almost the best hope that there is for healthy national growth in the future; but bitter experience has taught men who work for reform in New York that the average labor leader, the average demagogue who shouts for a depreciated currency, or for the overthrow of the rich, will not do anything to help those who honestly strive to make better our civic conditions. There are immense numbers of working-men to whom we can appeal with perfect confidence; but too often we find that a large proportion of the men who style themselves leaders of organized labor are influenced only by sullen short-sighted hatred of what they do not understand, and are deaf to all appeals, whether to their national or to their civic patriotism.

What I most grudge in all this is the fact that sincere and zealous men of high character and honest purpose . . . such as are to be found in all strata of our society, from the employer to the hardest-worked day laborer, go astray in their methods, and are thereby prevented from doing the full work for good they ought to. When a man goes on the wrong road himself he can do very little to guide others aright, even though these others are also on the wrong road. There are many wrongs to be righted; there are many measures of relief to be pushed; and it is a pity that when we are fighting what is bad and championing what is good, the men who ought to be our most effective allies should deprive themselves of usefulness by the wrong-headedness of their position. Rich men and poor men both do wrong on occasions, and whenever a specific instance of this can be pointed out all citizens alike should join in punishing the wrong-doer. Honesty and right-mindedness should be the tests; not wealth or poverty.

In our municipal administration here in New York we have acted with an equal hand toward wrong-doers of high and low degree. The Board of Health condemns the tenement-house property of the rich landowner, whether this landowner be priest or layman, banker or railroad president, lawyer or manager of a real estate business; and it pays no heed to the intercession of any politician, whether this politician be Catholic or Protestant, Jew or Gentile. At the same time the Police Department promptly suppresses, not only the criminal, but the rioter. In other words, we do strict justice. We feel we are defrauded of help to which we are entitled when men who ought to assist in any work to better the conditions of the people decline to aid us because their brains are turned by dreams only worthy of a European revolutionist.

Many working-men look with distrust upon laws which really would help them; laws for the intelligent restriction of immigration, for instance. I have no sympathy with mere dislike of immigrants; there are classes and even nationalities of them which stand at least on an equality with the citizens of native birth, as the last election showed. But in the interest of our working-men we must in the end keep out laborers who are ignorant, vicious, and with low standards of life and comfort just as we have shut out the Chinese.

Often labor leaders and the like denounce the present conditions of society, and especially of our political life, for shortcomings which they themselves have been instrumental in causing. In our cities the misgovernment is due, not to the misdeeds of the rich, but to the low standard of honesty and morality among citizens generally; and nothing helps the corrupt politician more than substituting either wealth or poverty for honesty as the standard by which to try a candidate. A few months ago a socialistic reformer in New York was denouncing the corruption caused by rich men because a certain judge was suspected of giving information in advance as to a decision in a case involving the interests of a great corporation. Now this judge had been elected some years previously, mainly because he was supposed to be a representative of the "poor man"; and the socialistic reformer himself, a year ago, was opposing the election of Mr. Beaman as judge because he was one of the firm of Evarts & Choate, who were friends of various millionaires and were counsel for various corporations. But if Mr. Beaman had been elected judge no human being, rich or poor, would have dared so much as hint at his doing anything improper.

Something can be done by good laws; more can be done by honest administration of the laws; but most of all can be done by frowning resolutely upon the preachers of vague discontent; and by upholding the true doctrine of self-reliance, self-help, and self-mastery. This doctrine sets forth many things. Among them is the fact that though a man can occasionally be helped when he stumbles, yet that it is useless to try to carry him when he will not or cannot walk; and worse than useless to try to bring down the work and reward of the thrifty and intelligent to the level of the capacity of the weak, the shiftless, and the idle. It further shows that the maudlin philanthropist and the maudlin sentimentalist are almost as noxious as the demagogue, and that it is even more necessary to temper mercy with justice than justice with mercy.

The worst lesson that can be taught a man is to rely upon others and to whine over his sufferings. If an American is to amount to anything he must rely upon himself, and not upon the State; he must take pride in his own work, instead of sitting idle to envy the luck of others; he must face life with resolute courage, win victory if he can, and accept defeat if he must, without seeking to place on his fellow men a responsibility which is not theirs.

PART THREE

Imagining the Civil War

THE RED BADGE OF COURAGE

An Episode of the American Civil War

Stephen Crane

I

The cold passed reluctantly from the earth, and the retiring fogs revealed an army stretched out on the hills, resting. As the landscape changed from brown to green, the army awakened, and began to tremble with eagerness at the noise of rumors. It cast its eyes upon the roads, which were growing from long troughs of liquid mud to proper thoroughfares. A river, amber-tinted in the shadow of its banks, purled at the army's feet; and at night, when the stream had become of a sorrowful blackness, one could see across it the red, eyelike gleam of hostile camp fires set in the low brows of distant hills.

Once a certain tall soldier developed virtues and went resolutely to wash a shirt. He came flying back from a brook waving his garment bannerlike. He was swelled with a tale he had heard from a reliable friend, who had heard it from a truthful cavalryman, who had heard it from his trustworthy brother, one of the orderlies at division headquarters. He adopted the important air of a herald in red and gold.

"We're goin' t' move t'morrah—sure," he said pompously to a group in the company street. "We're goin' 'way up the river, cut across, an' come around in behint 'em."

To his attentive audience he drew a loud and elaborate plan of a very brilliant campaign. When he had finished, the blue-clothed men scattered into small arguing groups between the rows of squat brown huts. A negro teamster who had been dancing upon a cracker box with the hilarious encouragement of two-score soldiers was deserted. He sat mournfully down. Smoke drifted lazily from a multitude of quaint chimneys.

"It's a lie! that's all it is—a thunderin' lie!" said another private loudly. His smooth face was flushed, and his hands were thrust sulkily into his trousers' pockets. He took the matter as an affront to him. "I don't believe the derned old army's ever going to move. We're set. I've got ready to move eight times in the last two weeks, and we ain't moved yet."

The tall soldier felt called upon to defend the truth of a rumor he himself had introduced. He and the loud one came near to fighting over it.

A corporal began to swear before the assemblage. He had just put a costly board floor in his house, he said. During the early spring he had refrained from adding extensively to the comfort of his environment because he had felt that the army might start on the march at any moment. Of late, however, he had been impressed that they were in a sort of eternal camp.

Many of the men engaged in a spirited debate. One outlined in a peculiarly lucid manner all the plans of the commanding general. He was opposed by men who advocated that there were other plans of campaign. They clamored at each other, numbers making futile bids for the popular attention. Meanwhile, the soldier who had fetched the rumor bustled about with much importance. He was continually assailed by questions.

"What's up, Jim?"

"Th' army's goin' t' move."

"Ah, what yeh talkin' about? How yeh know it is?"

"Well, yeh kin b'lieve me er not, jest as yeh like. I don't care a hang."

There was much food for thought in the manner in which he replied. He came near to convincing them by disdaining to produce proofs. They grew much excited over it.

There was a youthful private who listened with eager ears to the words of the tall soldier and to the varied comments of his comrades. After receiving a fill of discussions concerning marches and attacks, he went to his hut and crawled through an intricate hole that served it as a door. He wished to be alone with some new thoughts that had lately come to him.

He lay down on a wide bunk that stretched across the end of the room. In the other end, cracker boxes were made to serve as furniture. They were grouped about the fireplace. A picture from an illustrated weekly was upon the log walls, and three rifles were paralleled on pegs. Equipments hung on handy projections, and some tin dishes lay upon a small pile of firewood. A folded tent was serving as a roof. The sunlight, without, beating upon it, made it glow a light yellow shade. A small window shot an oblique square of whiter light upon the cluttered floor. The smoke from the fire at times neglected the clay chimney and wreathed into the room, and this flimsy chimney of clay and sticks made endless threats to set ablaze the whole establishment.

The youth was in a little trance of astonishment. So they were at last going to fight. On the morrow, perhaps, there would be a battle, and he would be in it. For a time he was obliged to labor to make himself believe. He could not accept with assurance an omen that he was about to mingle in one of those great affairs of the earth.

He had, of course, dreamed of battles all his life—of vague and bloody conflicts that had thrilled him with their sweep and fire. In visions he had seen himself in many struggles. He had imagined peoples secure in the shadow of his eagle-eyed prowess. But awake he had regarded battles as crimson blotches on the pages of the past. He had put them as things of the bygone with his thought-images of heavy crowns and high castles. There was a portion of the world's history which he had regarded as the time of wars, but it, he thought, had been long gone over the horizon and had disappeared forever.

From his home his youthful eyes had looked upon the war in his own country with distrust. It must be some sort of a play affair. He had long despaired of witnessing a Greeklike struggle. Such would be no more, he had said. Men were better, or more timid. Secular and religious education had effaced the throat-grappling instinct, or else firm finance held in check the passions.

He had burned several times to enlist. Tales of great movements shook the land. They might not be distinctly Homeric, but there seemed to be much glory in them. He had read of marches, sieges, conflicts, and he had longed to see it all. His busy mind had drawn for him large pictures extravagant in color, lurid with breathless deeds.

But his mother had discouraged him. She had affected to look with some contempt upon the quality of his war ardor and patriotism. She could calmly seat herself and with no apparent difficulty give him many hundreds of reasons why he was of vastly more importance on the farm than on the field of battle. She had had certain ways of expression that told him that her statements on the subject came from a deep conviction. Moreover, on her side, was his belief that her ethical motive in the argument was impregnable.

At last, however, he had made firm rebellion against this yellow light thrown upon the color of his ambitions. The newspapers, the gossip of the village, his own picturings, had aroused him to an uncheckable degree. They were in truth fighting finely down there. Almost every day the newspapers printed accounts of a decisive victory.

One night, as he lay in bed, the wind had carried to him the clangoring of the church bell as some enthusiast jerked the rope frantically to tell the twisted news of a great battle. This voice of the people rejoicing in the night had made him shiver in a prolonged ecstasy of excitement. Later, he had gone down to his mother's room and had spoken thus: "Ma, I'm going to enlist."

"Henry, don't you be a fool," his mother had replied. She had then covered her face with the quilt. There was an end to the matter for that night.

Nevertheless, the next morning he had gone to a town that was near his mother's farm and had enlisted in a company that was forming there. When he had returned home his mother was milking the brindle cow. Four others stood waiting. "Ma, I've enlisted," he had said to her diffidently. There was a short silence. "The Lord's will be done, Henry," she had finally replied, and had then continued to milk the brindle cow.

When he had stood in the doorway with his soldier's clothes on his back, and with the light of excitement and expectancy in his eyes almost defeating the glow of regret for the home bonds, he had seen two tears leaving their trails on his mother's scarred cheeks.

Still, she had disappointed him by saying nothing whatever about returning with his shield or on it. He had privately primed himself for a beautiful scene. He had prepared certain sentences which he thought could be used with touching effect. But her words destroyed his plans. She had doggedly peeled potatoes and addressed him as follows: "You watch out, Henry, an' take good care of yerself in this here fighting business—you watch out, an' take good care of yerself. Don't go a-thinkin' you can lick the hull rebel army at the start, because yeh can't. Yer jest one little feller amongst a hull lot of others, and yeh've got to keep quiet an' do what they tell yeh. I know how you are, Henry.

"I've knet yeh eight pair of socks, Henry, and I've put in all yer best shirts, because I want my boy to be jest as warm and comf'able as anybody in the army. Whenever they get holes in 'em, I want yeh to send 'em right-away back to me, so's I kin dern 'em.

"An' allus be careful an' choose yer comp'ny. There's lots of bad men in the army, Henry. The army makes 'em wild, and they like nothing better than the job of leading off a young feller like you, as ain't never been away from home much and has allus had a mother, an' a-learning 'em to drink and swear. Keep clear of them folks, Henry. I don't want yeh to ever do anything, Henry, that yeh would be 'shamed to let me know about. Jest think as if I was a-watching yeh. If yeh keep that in yer mind allus, I guess yeh'll come out about right.

"Yeh must allus remember yer father, too, child, an' remember he never drunk a drop of licker in his life, and seldom swore a cross oath.

"I don't know what else to tell yeh, Henry, excepting that yeh must never do no shirking, child, on my account. If so be a time comes when yeh have to be kilt or do a mean thing, why, Henry, don't think of anything 'cept what's right, because there's many a woman has to bear up 'ginst sech things these times, and the Lord 'll take keer of us all.

"Don't forgit about the socks and the shirts, child; and I've put a cup of blackberry jam with yer bundle, because I know yeh like it above all things. Good-by Henry. Watch out, and be a good boy."

He had, of course, been impatient under the ordeal of this speech. It had not been quite what he expected, and he had borne it with an air of irritation. He departed feeling vague relief.

Still, when he had looked back from the gate, he had seen his mother kneeling among the potato parings. Her brown face, upraised, was stained with tears, and her spare form was quivering. He bowed his head and went on, feeling suddenly ashamed of his purposes.

From his home he had gone to the seminary to bid adieu to many schoolmates. They had thronged about him with wonder and admiration. He had felt the gulf now between them and had swelled with calm pride. He and some of his fellows who had donned blue were quite overwhelmed with privileges for all of one afternoon, and it had been a very delicious thing. They had strutted.

A certain light-haired girl had made vivacious fun at his martial spirit, but there was another and darker girl whom he had gazed at steadfastly, and he thought she grew demure and sad at sight of his blue and brass. As he had walked down the path between the rows of oaks, he had turned his head and detected her at a window watching his departure. As he perceived her, she had immediately begun to stare up through the high tree branches at the sky. He had seen a good deal of flurry and haste in her movement as she changed her attitude. He often thought of it.

On the way to Washington his spirit had soared. The regiment was fed and caressed at station after station until the youth had believed that he must be a hero. There was a lavish expenditure of bread and cold meats, coffee, and pickles and cheese. As he basked in the smiles of the girls and was patted and complimented by the old men, he had felt growing within him the strength to do mighty deeds of arms.

After complicated journeyings with many pauses, there had come months of monotonous life in a camp. He had had the belief that real war was a series of death struggles with small time in between for sleep and meals; but since his regiment had come to the field the army had done little but sit still and try to keep warm.

He was brought then gradually back to his old ideas. Greeklike struggles would be no more. Men were better, or more timid. Secular and religious education had effaced the throat-grappling instinct, or else firm finance held in check the passions.

He had grown to regard himself merely as a part of a vast blue demonstration. His province was to look out, as far as he could, for his personal comfort. For recreation he could twiddle his thumbs and speculate on the thoughts which must agitate the minds of the generals. Also, he was drilled and drilled and reviewed, and drilled and drilled and reviewed.

The only foes he had seen were some pickets along the river bank. They were a sun-tanned, philosophical lot, who sometimes shot reflectively at the blue pickets. When reproached for this afterward, they usually expressed sorrow, and swore by their gods that the guns had exploded without their permission. The youth, on guard duty one night, conversed across the stream with one of them. He was a slightly ragged man, who spat skillfully between his shoes and possessed a great fund of bland and infantile assurance. The youth liked him personally.

"Yank," the other had informed him, "yer a right dum good feller." This sentiment, floating to him upon the still air, had made him temporarily regret war.

Various veterans had told him tales. Some talked of gray, bewhiskered hordes who were advancing with relentless curses and chewing tobacco with unspeakable valor; tremendous bodies of fierce soldiery who were sweeping along like the Huns. Others spoke of tattered and eternally hungry men who fired despondent powders. "They'll charge through hell's fire an' brimstone t' git a holt on a haversack, an' sech stomachs ain't a-lastin' long," he was told. From the stories, the youth imagined the red, live bones sticking out through slits in the faded uniforms.

Still, he could not put a whole faith in veterans' tales, for recruits were their prey. They talked much of smoke, fire, and blood, but he could not tell how much might be lies. They persistently yelled "Fresh fish!" at him, and were in no wise to be trusted.

However, he perceived now that it did not greatly matter what kind of soldiers he was going to fight, so long as they fought, which fact no one disputed. There was a more serious problem. He lay in his bunk pondering upon it. He tried to mathematically prove to himself that he would not run from a battle.

Previously he had never felt obliged to wrestle too seriously with this question. In his life he had taken certain things for granted, never challenging his belief in ultimate success, and bothering little about means and roads. But here he was confronted with a thing of moment. It had suddenly appeared to him that perhaps in a battle he might run. He was forced to admit that as far as war was concerned he knew nothing of himself.

A sufficient time before he would have allowed the problem to kick its heels at the outer portals of his mind, but now he felt compelled to give serious attention to it.

A little panic-fear grew in his mind. As his imagination went forward to a fight, he saw hideous possibilities. He contemplated the lurking menaces of the future, and failed in an effort to see himself standing stoutly in the midst of them. He recalled his visions of broken-bladed glory, but in the shadow of the impending tumult he suspected them to be impossible pictures.

He sprang from the bunk and began to pace nervously to and fro. "Good Lord, what's th' matter with me?" he said aloud.

He felt that in this crisis his laws of life were useless. Whatever he had learned of himself was here of no avail. He was an unknown quantity. He saw that he would again be obliged to experiment as he had in early youth. He must accumulate information of himself, and meanwhile he resolved to remain close upon his guard lest those qualities of which he knew nothing should everlastingly disgrace him. "Good Lord!" he repeated in dismay.

After a time the tall soldier slid dexterously through the hole. The loud private followed. They were wrangling.

"That's all right," said the tall soldier as he entered. He waved his hand expressively. "You can believe me or not, jest as you like. All you got to do is sit down and wait as quiet as you can. Then pretty soon you'll find out I was right."

His comrade grunted stubbornly. For a moment he seemed to be searching for a formidable reply. Finally he said: "Well, you don't know everything in the world, do you?"

"Didn't say I knew everything in the world," retorted the other sharply. He began to stow various articles snugly into his knapsack.

The youth, pausing in his nervous walk, looked down at the busy figure. "Going to be a battle, sure, is there, Jim?" he asked.

"Of course there is," replied the tall soldier. "Of course there is. You jest wait 'til tomorrow, and you'll see one of the biggest battles ever was. You jest wait."

"Thunder!" said the youth.

"Oh, you'll see fighting this time, my boy, what'll be regular out-and-out fighting," added the tall soldier, with the air of a man who is about to exhibit a battle for the benefit of his friends.

"Huh!" said the loud one from a corner.

"Well," remarked the youth, "like as not this story'll turn out jest like them others did."

"Not much it won't," replied the tall soldier, exasperated. "Not much it won't. Didn't the cavalry all start this morning?" He glared about him. No one denied his statement. "The cavalry started this morning," he continued. "They say there ain't hardly any cavalry left in camp. They're going to Richmond, or some place, while we fight all the Johnnies. It's some dodge like that. The regiment's got orders, too. A feller what seen 'em go to headquarters told me a little while ago. And they're raising blazes all over camp—anybody can see that."

"Shucks!" said the loud one.

The youth remained silent for a time. At last he spoke to the tall soldier. "Jim!"

"What?"

"How do you think the reg'ment 'll do?"

"Oh, they'll fight all right, I guess, after they once get into it," said the other with cold judgment. He made a fine use of the third person. "There's been heaps of fun poked at 'em because they're new, of course, and all that; but they'll fight all right, I guess."

"Think any of the boys 'll run?" persisted the youth.

"Oh, there may be a few of 'em run, but there's them kind in every regiment, 'specially when they first goes under fire," said the other in a tolerant way. "Of course it might happen that the hull kit-and-boodle might start and run, if some big fighting came first-off, and then again they might stay and fight like fun. But you can't bet on nothing. Of course they ain't never been under fire yet, and it ain't likely they'll lick the hull rebel army all-to-oncet the first time; but I think they'll fight better than some, if worse than others. That's the way I figger. They call the reg'ment 'Fresh fish' and everything; but the boys come of good stock, and most of 'em 'll fight like sin after they oncet git shootin'," he added, with a mighty emphasis on the last four words.

"Oh, you think you know—" began the loud soldier with scorn.

The other turned savagely upon him. They had a rapid altercation, in which they fastened upon each other various strange epithets.

The youth at last interrupted them. "Did you ever think you might run yourself, Jim?" he asked. On concluding the sentence he laughed as if he had meant to aim a joke. The loud soldier also giggled.

The tall private waved his hand. "Well," said he profoundly, "I've thought it might get too hot for Jim Conklin in some of them scrimmages, and if a whole lot of boys started and run, why, I s'pose I'd start and run. And if I once started to run, I'd run like the devil, and no mistake. But if everybody was a-standing and a-fighting, why, I'd stand and fight. Be jiminey, I would. I'll bet on it."

"Huh!" said the loud one.

The youth of this tale felt gratitude for these words of his comrade. He had feared that all of the untried men possessed great and correct confidence. He now was in a measure reassured.

II

The next morning the youth discovered that his tall comrade had been the fast-flying messenger of a mistake. There was much scoffing at the latter by those who had yesterday been firm adherents of his views, and there was even a little sneering by men who had never believed the rumor. The tall one fought with a man from Chatfield Corners and beat him severely.

The youth felt, however, that his problem was in no wise lifted from him. There was, on the contrary, an irritating prolongation. The tale had created in him a great concern for himself. Now, with the newborn question in his mind, he was compelled to sink back into his old place as part of a blue demonstration.

For days he made ceaseless calculations, but they were all wondrously unsatisfactory. He found that he could establish nothing. He finally concluded that the only way to prove himself was to go into the blaze, and then figuratively to watch his legs to discover their merits and faults. He reluctantly admitted that he could not sit still and with a mental slate and pencil derive an answer. To gain it, he must have blaze, blood, and danger, even as a chemist requires this, that, and the other. So he fretted for an opportunity.

Meanwhile he continually tried to measure himself by his comrades. The tall soldier, for one, gave him some assurance. This man's serene unconcern dealt him a measure of confidence, for he had known him since childhood, and from his intimate knowledge he did not see how he could be capable of anything that was beyond him, the youth. Still, he thought that his comrade might be mistaken about himself. Or, on the other hand, he might be a man heretofore doomed to peace and obscurity, but, in reality, made to shine in war.

The youth would have liked to have discovered another who suspected himself. A sympathetic comparison of mental notes would have been a joy to him.

He occasionally tried to fathom a comrade with seductive sentences. He looked about to find men in the proper mood. All attempts failed to bring forth any statement which looked in any way like a confession to those doubts which he privately acknowledged in himself. He was afraid to make an open declaration of his concern, because he dreaded to place some unscrupulous confidant upon the high plane of the unconfessed from which elevation he could be derided.

In regard to his companions his mind wavered between two opinions, according to his mood. Sometimes he inclined to believing them all heroes. In fact, he usually admitted in secret the superior development of the higher qualities in others. He could conceive of men going very insignificantly about the world bearing a load of courage unseen, and, although he had known many of his comrades through boyhood, he began to fear that his judgment of them had been blind. Then, in other moments, he flouted these theories, and assured himself that his fellows were all privately wondering and quaking.

His emotions made him feel strange in the presence of men who talked excitedly of a prospective battle as of a drama they were about to witness, with nothing but eagerness and curiosity apparent in their faces. It was often that he suspected them to be liars.

He did not pass such thoughts without severe condemnation of himself. He dinned reproaches at times. He was convicted by himself of many shameful crimes against the gods of traditions.

In his great anxiety his heart was continually clamoring at what he considered the intolerable slowness of the generals. They seemed content to perch tranquilly on the river bank, and leave him bowed down by the weight of a great problem. He wanted it settled forthwith. He could not long bear such a load, he said. Sometimes his anger at the commanders reached an acute stage, and he grumbled about the camp like a veteran.

One morning, however, he found himself in the ranks of his prepared regiment. The men were whispering speculations and recounting the old rumors. In the gloom before the break of the day their uniforms glowed a deep purple hue. From across the river the red eyes were still peering. In the eastern sky there was a yellow patch like a rug laid for the feet of the coming sun; and against it black and patternlike, loomed the gigantic figure of the colonel on a gigantic horse.

From off in the darkness came the trampling of feet. The youth could occasionally see dark shadows that moved like monsters. The regiment stood at rest for what seemed a long time. The youth grew impatient. It was unendurable the way these affairs were managed. He wondered how long they were to be kept waiting.

As he looked all about him and pondered upon the mystic gloom, he began to believe that at any moment the ominous distance might be aflare, and the rolling crashes of an engagement come to his ears. Staring once at the red eyes across the river, he conceived them to be growing larger, as the orbs of a row of dragons advancing. He turned toward the colonel and saw him lift his gigantic arm and calmly stroke his mustache.

At last he heard from along the road at the foot of the hill the clatter of a horse's galloping hoofs. It must be the coming of orders. He bent forward, scarce breathing. The exciting clickety-click, as it grew louder and louder, seemed to be beating upon his soul. Presently a horseman with jangling equipment drew rein before the colonel of the regiment. The two held a short, sharp-worded conversation. The men in the foremost ranks craned their necks.

As the horseman wheeled his animal and galloped away he turned to shout over his shoulder, "Don't forget that box of cigars!" The colonel mumbled in reply. The youth wondered what a box of cigars had to do with war.

A moment later the regiment went swinging off into the darkness. It was now like one of those moving monsters wending with many feet. The air was heavy, and cold with dew. A mass of wet grass, marched upon, rustled like silk.

There was an occasional flash and glimmer of steel from the backs of all these huge crawling reptiles. From the road came creakings and grumblings as some surly guns were dragged away.

The men stumbled along still muttering speculations. There was a subdued debate. Once a man fell down, and as he reached for his rifle a comrade, unseeing, trod upon his hand. He of the injured fingers swore bitterly and aloud. A low, tittering laugh went among his fellows.

Presently they passed into a roadway and marched forward with easy strides. A dark regiment moved before them, and from behind also came the tinkle of equipments on the bodies of marching men.

The rushing yellow of the developing day went on behind their backs. When the sunrays at last struck full and mellowingly upon the earth, the youth saw that the landscape was streaked with two long, thin, black columns which disappeared on the brow of a hill in front and rearward vanished in a wood. They were like two serpents crawling from the cavern of the night.

The river was not in view. The tall soldier burst into praises of what he thought to be his powers of perception.

Some of the tall one's companions cried with emphasis that they, too, had evolved the same thing, and they congratulated themselves upon it. But there were others who said that the tall one's plan was not the true one at all. They persisted with other theories. There was a vigorous discussion.

The youth took no part in them. As he walked along in careless line he was engaged with his own eternal debate. He could not hinder himself from dwelling upon it. He was despondent and sullen, and threw shifting glances about him. He looked ahead, often expecting to hear from the advance the rattle of firing.

But the long serpents crawled slowly from hill to hill without bluster of smoke. A dun-colored cloud of dust floated away to the right. The sky overhead was of a fairy blue.

The youth studied the faces of his companions, ever on the watch to detect kindred emotions. He suffered disappointment. Some ardor of the air which was causing the veteran commands to move with glee—almost with song—had infected the new regiment. The men began to speak of victory as of a thing they knew. Also, the tall soldier received his vindication. They were certainly going to come around in behind the enemy. They expressed commiseration for that part of the army which had been left upon the river bank, felicitating themselves upon being a part of a blasting host.

The youth, considering himself as separated from the others, was saddened by the blithe and merry speeches that went from rank to rank. The company wags all made their best endeavors. The regiment tramped to the tune of laughter.

The blatant soldier often convulsed whole files by his biting sarcasms aimed at the tall one.

And it was not long before all the men seemed to forget their mission. Whole brigades grinned in unison, and regiments laughed.

A rather fat soldier attempted to pilfer a horse from a dooryard. He planned to load his knapsack upon it. He was escaping with his prize when a young girl rushed from the house and grabbed the animal's mane. There followed a wrangle. The young girl, with pink cheeks and shining eyes, stood like a dauntless statue.

The observant regiment, standing at rest in the roadway, whooped at once, and entered whole-souled upon the side of the maiden. The men became so engrossed in this affair that they entirely ceased to remember their own large war. They jeered the piratical private, and called attention to various defects in his personal appearance; and they were wildly enthusiastic in support of the young girl.

To her, from some distance, came bold advice. "Hit him with a stick."

There were crows and catcalls showered upon him when he retreated without the horse. The regiment rejoiced at his downfall. Loud and vociferous congratulations were showered upon the maiden, who stood panting and regarding the troops with defiance.

At nightfall the column broke into regimental pieces, and the fragments went into the fields to camp. Tents sprang up like strange plants. Camp fires, like red, peculiar blossoms, dotted the night.

The youth kept from intercourse with his companions as much as circumstances would allow him. In the evening he wandered a few paces into the gloom. From this little distance the many fires, with the black forms of men passing to and fro before the crimson rays, made weird and satanic effects.

He lay down in the grass. The blades pressed tenderly against his cheek. The moon had been lighted and was hung in a treetop. The liquid stillness of the night enveloping him made him feel vast pity for himself. There was a caress in the soft winds; and the whole mood of the darkness, he thought, was one of sympathy for himself in his distress.

He wished, without reserve, that he was at home again making the endless rounds from the house to the barn, from the barn to the fields, from the fields to the barn, from the barn to the house. He remembered he had often cursed the brindle cow and her mates, and had sometimes flung milking stools. But, from his present point of view, there was a halo of happiness about each of their heads, and he would have sacrificed all the brass buttons on the continent to have been enabled to return to them. He told himself that he was not formed for a soldier. And he mused seriously upon the radical differences between himself and those men who were dodging implike around the fires.

As he mused thus he heard the rustle of grass, and, upon turning his head, discovered the loud soldier. He called out, "Oh, Wilson!"

The latter approached and looked down. "Why, hello, Henry; is it you? What you doing here?"

"Oh, thinking," said the youth.

The other sat down and carefully lighted his pipe. "You're getting blue my boy. You're looking thundering peeked. What the dickens is wrong with you?"

"Oh, nothing," said the youth.

The loud soldier launched then into the subject of the anticipated fight. "Oh, we've got 'em now!" As he spoke his boyish face was wreathed in a gleeful smile, and his voice had an exultant ring. "We've got 'em now. At last, by the eternal thunders, we'll lick 'em good!"

"If the truth was known," he added, more soberly, "*they've* licked *us* about every clip up to now; but this time—this time—we'll lick 'em good!"

"I thought you was objecting to this march a little while ago," said the youth coldly.

"Oh, it wasn't that," explained the other. "I don't mind marching, if there's going to be fighting at the end of it. What I hate is this getting moved here and moved there, with no good coming of it, as far as I can see, excepting sore feet and damned short rations."

"Well, Jim Conklin says we'll get aplenty of fighting this time."

"He's right for once, I guess, though I can't see how it come. This time we're in for a big battle, and we've got the best end of it, certain sure. Gee rod! How we will thump 'em!"

He arose and began to pace to and fro excitedly. The thrill of his enthusiasm made him walk with an elastic step. He was sprightly, vigorous, fiery in his belief in success. He looked into the future with clear, proud eye, and he swore with the air of an old soldier.

The youth watched him for a moment in silence. When he finally spoke his voice was as bitter as dregs. "Oh, you're going to do great things, I s'pose!"

The loud soldier blew a thoughtful cloud of smoke from his pipe. "Oh, I don't know," he remarked with dignity; "I don't know. I s'pose I'll do as well as the rest. I'm going to try like thunder." He evidently complimented himself upon the modesty of this statement.

"How do you know you won't run when the time comes?" asked the youth.

"Run?" said the loud one; "run?—of course not!" He laughed.

"Well," continued the youth, "lots of good-a-'nough men have thought they was going to do great things before the fight, but when the time come they skedaddled."

"Oh, that's all true, I s'pose," replied the other; "but I'm not going to skedaddle. The man that bets on my running will lose his money, that's all." He nodded confidently.

"Oh, shucks!" said the youth. "You ain't the bravest man in the world, are you?"

"No, I ain't," exclaimed the loud soldier indignantly; "and I didn't say I was the bravest man in the world, neither. I said I was going to do my share of fighting—that's what I said. And I am, too. Who are you, anyhow? You talk as if you thought you was Napoleon Bonaparte." He glared at the youth for a moment, and then strode away.

The youth called in a savage voice after his comrade: "Well, you needn't git mad about it!" But the other continued on his way and made no reply.

He felt alone in space when his injured comrade had disappeared. His failure to discover any mite of resemblance in their viewpoints made him more miserable than before. No one seemed to be wrestling with such a terrific personal problem. He was a mental outcast.

He went slowly to his tent and stretched himself on a blanket by the side of the snoring tall soldier. In the darkness he saw visions of a thousand-tongued fear that would babble at his back and cause him to flee, while others were going coolly about their country's business. He admitted that he would not be able to cope with this monster. He felt that every nerve in his body would be an ear to hear the voices, while other men would remain stolid and deaf.

And as he sweated with the pain of these thoughts, he could hear low, serene sentences. "I'll bid five." "Make it six." "Seven." "Seven goes."

He stared at the red, shivering reflection of a fire on the white wall of his tent until, exhausted and ill from the monotony of his suffering, he fell asleep.

III

When another night came the columns, changed to purple streaks, filed across two pontoon bridges. A glaring fire wine-tinted the waters of the river. Its rays, shining upon the moving masses of troops, brought forth here and there sudden gleams of silver or gold. Upon the other shore a dark and mysterious range of hills was curved against the sky. The insect voices of the night sang solemnly.

After this crossing the youth assured himself that at any moment they might be suddenly and fearfully assaulted from the caves of the lowering woods. He kept his eyes watchfully upon the darkness.

But his regiment went unmolested to a camping place, and its soldiers slept the brave sleep of wearied men. In the morning they were routed out with early energy, and hustled along a narrow road that led deep into the forest.

It was during this rapid march that the regiment lost many of the marks of a new command.

The men had begun to count the miles upon their fingers, and they grew tired. "Sore feet an' damned short rations, that's all," said the loud soldier. There were perspiration and grumblings. After a time they began to shed their knapsacks. Some tossed them unconcernedly down; others hid them carefully, asserting their plans to return for them at some convenient time. Men extricated themselves from thick shirts. Presently few carried anything but their necessary clothing, blankets, haversacks, canteens, and arms and ammunition. "You can now eat and shoot," said the tall soldier to the youth. "That's all you want to do."

There was sudden change from the ponderous infantry of theory to the light and speedy infantry of practice. The regiment, relieved of a burden, received a new impetus. But there was much loss of valuable knapsacks, and, on the whole, very good shirts.

But the regiment was not yet veteranlike in appearance. Veteran regiments in the army were likely to be very small aggregations of men. Once, when the command had first come to the field, some perambulating veterans, noting the length of their column, had accosted them thus: "Hey, fellers, what brigade is that?" And when the men had replied that they formed a regiment and not a brigade, the older soldiers had laughed, and said, "O Gawd!"

Also, there was too great a similarity in the hats. The hats of a regiment should properly represent the history of headgear for a period of years. And, moreover, there were no letters of faded gold speaking from the colors. They were new and beautiful, and the color bearer habitually oiled the pole.

Presently the army again sat down to think. The odor of the peaceful pines was in the men's nostrils. The sound of monotonous axe blows rang through the forest, and the insects, nodding upon their perches, crooned like old women. The youth returned to his theory of a blue demonstration.

One gray dawn, however, he was kicked in the leg by the tall soldier, and then, before he was entirely awake, he found himself running down a wood road in the midst of men who were panting from the first effects of speed. His canteen banged rythmically upon his thigh, and his haversack bobbed softly. His musket bounced a trifle from his shoulder at each stride and made his cap feel uncertain upon his head.

He could hear the men whisper jerky sentences: "Say—what's all this—about?" "What th' thunder—we—skedaddlin' this way fer?" "Billie—keep off m' feet. Yeh run—like a cow." And the loud soldier's shrill voice could be heard: "What th'devil they in sich a hurry for?"

The youth thought the damp fog of early morning moved from the rush of a great body of troops. From the distance came a sudden spattering of firing.

He was bewildered. As he ran with his comrades he strenuously tried to think, but all he knew was that if he fell down those coming behind would tread upon him. All his faculties seemed to be needed to guide him over and past obstructions. He felt carried along by a mob.

The sun spread disclosing rays, and, one by one, regiments burst into view like armed men just born of the earth. The youth perceived that the time had come. He was about to be measured. For a moment he felt in the face of his great trial like a babe, and the flesh over his heart seemed very thin. He seized time to look about him calculatingly.

But he instantly saw that it would be impossible for him to escape from the regiment. It enclosed him. And there were iron laws of tradition and law on four sides. He was in a moving box.

As he perceived this fact it occurred to him that he had never wished to come to the war. He had not enlisted of his free will. He had been dragged by the merciless government. And now they were taking him out to be slaughtered.

The regiment slid down a bank and wallowed across a little stream. The mournful current moved slowly on, and from the water, shaded black, some white bubble eyes looked at the men.

As they climbed the hill on the farther side artillery began to boom. Here the youth forgot many things as he felt a sudden impulse of curiosity. He scrambled up the bank with a speed that could not be exceeded by a bloodthirsty man.

He expected a battle scene.

There were some little fields girted and squeezed by a forest. Spread over the grass and in among the tree trunks, he could see knots and waving lines of skirmishers who were running hither and thither and firing at the landscape. A dark battle line lay upon a sun-struck clearing that gleamed orange color. A flag fluttered.

Other regiments floundered up the bank. The brigade was formed in line of battle, and after a pause started slowly through the woods in the rear of the receding skirmishers, who were continually melting into the scene to appear again farther on. They were always busy as bees, deeply absorbed in their little combats.

The youth tried to observe everything. He did not use care to avoid trees and branches, and his forgotten feet were constantly knocking against stones or getting entangled in briers. He was aware that these battalions with their commotions were woven red and startling into the gentle fabric of softened greens and browns. It looked to be a wrong place for a battle field.

The skirmishers in advance fascinated him. Their shots into thickets and at distant and prominent trees spoke to him of tragedies—hidden, mysterious, solemn.

Once the line encountered the body of a dead soldier. He lay upon his back staring at the sky. He was dressed in an awkward suit of yellowish brown. The youth could see that the soles of his shoes had been worn to the thinness of writing paper, and from a great rent in one the dead foot projected piteously. And it was as if fate had betrayed the soldier. In death it exposed to his enemies that poverty which in life he had perhaps concealed from his friends.

The ranks opened covertly to avoid the corpse. The invulnerable dead man forced a way for himself. The youth looked keenly at the ashen face. The wind raised the tawny beard. It moved as if a hand were stroking it. He vaguely desired to walk around and around the body and stare; the impulse of the living to try to read in dead eyes the answer to the Question.

During the march the ardor which the youth had acquired when out of view of the field rapidly faded to nothing. His curiosity was quite easily satisfied. If an intense scene had caught him with its wild swing as he came to the top of the bank, he might have gone roaring on. This advance upon Nature was too calm. He had opportunity to reflect. He had time in which to wonder about himself and to attempt to probe his sensations.

Absurd ideas took hold upon him. He thought that he did not relish the landscape. It threatened him. A coldness swept over his back, and it is true that his trousers felt to him that they were no fit for his legs at all.

A house standing placidly in distant fields had to him an ominous look. The shadows of the woods were formidable. He was certain that in this vista there lurked fierce-eyed hosts. The swift thought came to him that the generals did not know what they were about. It was all a trap. Suddenly those close forests would bristle with rifle barrels. Ironlike brigades would appear in the rear. They were all going to be sacrificed. The generals were stupids. The enemy would presently swallow the whole command. He glared about him, expecting to see the stealthy approach of his death.

He thought that he must break from the ranks and harangue his comrades. They must not all be killed like pigs; and he was sure it would come to pass unless they were informed of these dangers. The generals were idiots to send them marching into a regular pen. There was but one pair of eyes in the corps. He would step forth and make a speech. Shrill and passionate words came to his lips.

The line, broken into moving fragments by the ground, went calmly on through fields and woods. The youth looked at the men nearest him, and saw, for the most part, expressions of deep interest, as if they were investigating something that had fascinated them. One or two stepped with overvaliant airs as if they were already plunged into war. Others walked as upon thin ice. The greater part of the untested men appeared quiet and absorbed. They were going to look at war, the red animal—war, the blood-swollen god. And they were deeply engrossed in this march.

As he looked the youth gripped his outcry at his throat. He saw that even if the men were tottering with fear they would laugh at his warning. They would jeer him, and, if practicable, pelt him with missiles. Admitting that he might be wrong, a frenzied declamation of the kind would turn him into a worm.

He assumed, then, the demeanor of one who knows that he is doomed alone to unwritten responsibilities. He lagged, with tragic glances at the sky.

He was surprised presently by the young lieutenant of his company, who began heartily to beat him with a sword, calling out in a loud and insolent voice: "Come, young man, get up into ranks there. No skulking 'll do here." He mended his pace with suitable haste. And he hated the lieutenant, who had no appreciation of fine minds. He was a mere brute.

After a time the brigade was halted in the cathedral light of a forest. The busy skirmishers were still popping. Through the aisles of the wood could be seen the floating smoke from their rifles. Sometimes it went up in little balls, white and compact.

During this halt many men in the regiment began erecting tiny hills in front of them. They used stones, sticks, earth, and anything they thought might turn a bullet. Some built comparatively large ones, while others seemed content with little ones.

This procedure caused a discussion among the men. Some wished to fight like duelists, believing it to be correct to stand erect and be, from their feet to their foreheads, a mark. They said they scorned the devices of the cautious. But the others scoffed in reply, and pointed to the veterans on the flanks who were digging at the ground like terriers. In a short time there was quite a barricade along the regimental fronts. Directly, however, they were ordered to withdraw from that place.

This astounded the youth. He forgot his stewing over the advance movement. "Well, then, what did they march us out here for?" he demanded of the tall soldier. The latter with calm faith began a heavy explanation, although he had been compelled to leave a little protection of stones and dirt to which he had devoted much care and skill.

When the regiment was aligned in another position each man's regard for his safety caused another line of small entrenchments. They ate their noon meal behind a third one. They were moved from this one also. They were marched from place to place with apparent aimlessness.

The youth had been taught that a man became another thing in a battle. He saw his salvation in such a change. Hence this waiting was an ordeal to him. He was in a fever of impatience. He considered that there was denoted a lack of purpose on the part of the generals. He began to complain to the tall soldier. "I can't stand this much longer," he cried. "I don't see what good it does to make us wear out our legs for nothin'." He wished to return to camp, knowing that this affair was a blue demonstration; or else to go into a battle and discover that he had been a fool in his doubts, and was, in truth, a man of traditional courage. The strain of present circumstances he felt to be intolerable.

The philosophical tall soldier measured a sandwich of cracker and pork and swallowed it in a nonchalant manner. "Oh, I suppose we must go reconnoitering around the country jest to keep 'em from getting too close, or to develop 'em, or something."

"Huh!" cried the loud soldier.

"Well," cried the youth, still fidgeting, "I'd rather do anything 'most than go tramping 'round the country all day doing no good to nobody and jest tiring ourselves out."

"So would I," said the loud soldier. "It ain't right. I tell you if anybody with any sense was a-runnin' this army it—"

"Oh, shut up!" roared the tall private. "You little fool. You little damn' cuss. You ain't had that there coat and them pants on for six months, and yet you talk as if—"

"Well, I wanta do some fighting anyway," interrupted the other. "I didn't come here to walk. I could 'ave walked to home—'round an' 'round the barn, if I jest wanted to walk."

The tall one, red-faced, swallowed another sandwich as if taking poison in despair.

But gradually, as he chewed, his face became again quiet and contented. He could not rage in fierce argument in the presence of such sandwiches. During his meals he always wore an air of blissful contemplation of the food he had swallowed. His spirit seemed then to be communing with the viands.

He accepted new environment and circumstance with great coolness, eating from his haversack at every opportunity. On the march he went along with the stride of a hunter, objecting to neither gait nor distance. And he had not raised his voice when he had been ordered away from three little protective piles of earth and stone, each of which had been an engineering feat worthy of being made sacred to the name of his grandmother.

In the afternoon the regiment went out over the same ground it had taken in the morning. The landscape then ceased to threaten the youth. He had been close to it and become familiar with it.

When, however, they began to pass into a new region, his old fears of stupidity and incompetence reassailed him, but this time he doggedly let them babble. He was occupied with his problem, and in his desperation he concluded that the stupidity did not greatly matter.

Once he thought he had concluded that it would be better to get killed directly and end his troubles. Regarding death thus out of the corner of his eye, he conceived it to be nothing but rest, and he was filled with a momentary astonishment that he should have made an extraordinary commotion over the mere matter of getting killed. He would die; he would go to some place where he would be understood. It was useless to expect appreciation of his profound and fine senses from such men as the lieutenant. He must look to the grave for comprehension.

The skirmish fire increased to a long clattering sound. With it was mingled far-away cheering. A battery spoke.

Directly the youth would see the skirmishers running. They were pursued by the sound of musketry fire. After a time the hot, dangerous flashes of the rifles were visible. Smoke clouds went slowly and insolently across the fields like observant phantoms. The din became crescendo, like the roar of an oncoming train.

A brigade ahead of them and on the right went into action with a rending roar. It was as if it had exploded. And thereafter it lay stretched in the distance behind a long gray wall, that one was obliged to look twice at to make sure that it was smoke.

The youth, forgetting his neat plan of getting killed, gazed spellbound. His eyes grew wide and busy with the action of the scene. His mouth was a little ways open.

Of a sudden he felt a heavy and sad hand laid upon his shoulder. Awakening from his trance of observation he turned and beheld the loud soldier.

"It's my first and last battle, old boy," said the latter, with intense gloom. He was quite pale and his girlish lip was trembling.

"Eh?" murmured the youth in great astonishment.

"It's my first and last battle, old boy," continued the loud soldier. "Something tells me—"

"What?"

"I'm a gone coon this first time and—and I w-want you to take these here things—to—my—folks." He ended in a quavering sob of pity for himself. He handed the youth a little packet done up in a yellow envelope.

"Why, what the devil—" began the youth again.

But the other gave him a glance as from the depths of a tomb, and raised his limp hand in a prophetic manner and turned away.

IV

The brigade was halted in the fringe of a grove. The men crouched among the trees and pointed their restless guns out at the fields. They tried to look beyond the smoke.

Out of this haze they could see running men. Some shouted information and gestured as they hurried.

The men of the new regiment watched and listened eagerly, while their tongues ran on in gossip of the battle. They mouthed rumors that had flown like birds out of the unknown.

"They say Perry has been driven in with big loss."

"Yes, Carrott went t' th' hospital. He said he was sick. That smart lieutenant is commanding 'G' Company. Th' boys say they won't be under Carrott no more if they all have t' desert. They allus knew he was a—"

"Hannises' batt'ry is took."

"It ain't either. I saw Hannises' batt'ry off on th' left not more'n fifteen minutes ago."

"Well—"

"Th' general, he ses he is goin' t' take th' hull command of th' 304th when we go inteh action, an' then he ses we'll do sech fightin' as never another one reg'ment done."

"They say we're catchin' it over on th' left. They say th' enemy driv' our line inteh a devil of a swamp an' took Hannises' batt'ry."

"No sech thing. Hannises' batt'ry was 'long here 'bout a minute ago."

"That young Hasbrouck, he makes a good off'cer. He ain't afraid 'a nothin'."

"I met one of th' 148th Maine boys an' he ses his brigade fit th' hull rebel army fer four hours over on th' turnpike road an' killed about five thousand of 'em. He ses one more sech fight as that an' th' war 'll be over."

"Bill wasn't scared either. No, sir! It wasn't that. Bill ain't a-gittin' scared easy. He was jest mad, that's what he was. When that feller trod on his hand, he up an' sed that he was willin' t' give his hand t' his country, but he be dumbed if he was goin' t' have every dumb bushwhacker in th' kentry walkin' 'round on it. So he went t' th' hospital disregardless of th' fight. Three fingers was crunched. Th' dern doctor wanted t' amputate 'm, an' Bill, he raised a heluva row, I hear. He's a funny feller."

The din in front swelled to a tremendous chorus. The youth and his fellows were frozen to silence. They could see a flag that tossed in the smoke angrily. Near it were the blurred and agitated forms of troops. There came a turbulent stream of men across the fields. A battery changing position at a frantic gallop scattered the stragglers right and left.

A shell screaming like a storm banshee went over the huddled heads of the reserves. It landed in the grove, and exploding redly flung the brown earth. There was a little shower of pine needles.

Bullets began to whistle among the branches and nip at the trees. Twigs and leaves came sailing down. It was as if a thousand axes, wee and invisible, were being wielded. Many of the men were constantly dodging and ducking their heads.

The lieutenant of the youth's company was shot in the hand. He began to swear so wondrously that a nervous laugh went along the regimental line. The officer's profanity sounded conventional. It relieved the tightened senses of the new men. It was as if he had hit his fingers with a tack hammer at home.

He held the wounded member carefully away from his side so that the blood would not drip upon his trousers.

The captain of the company, tucking his sword under his arm, produced a handkerchief and began to bind with it the lieutenant's wound. And they disputed as to how the binding should be done.

The battle flag in the distance jerked about madly. It seemed to be struggling to free itself from an agony. The billowing smoke was filled with horizontal flashes.

Men running swiftly emerged from it. They grew in numbers until it was seen that the whole command was fleeing. The flag suddenly sank down as if dying. Its motion as it fell was a gesture of despair.

Wild yells came from behind the walls of smoke. A sketch in gray and red dissolved into a moblike body of men who galloped like wild horses.

The veteran regiments on the right and left of the 304th immediately began to jeer. With the passionate song of the bullets and the banshee shrieks of shells were mingled loud catcalls and bits of facetious advice concerning places of safety.

But the new regiment was breathless with horror. "Gawd! Saunders's got crushed!" whispered the man at the youth's elbow. They shrank back and crouched as if compelled to await a flood.

The youth shot a swift glance along the blue ranks of the regiment. The profiles were motionless, carven; and afterward he remembered that the color sergeant was standing with his legs apart, as if he expected to be pushed to the ground.

The following throng went whirling around the flank. Here and there were officers carried along on the stream like exasperated chips. They were striking about them with their swords and with their left fists, punching every head they could reach. They cursed like highwaymen.

A mounted officer displayed the furious anger of a spoiled child. He raged with his head, his arms, and his legs.

Another, the commander of the brigade, was galloping about bawling. His hat was gone and his clothes were awry. He resembled a man who had come from bed to go to a fire. The hoofs of his horse often threatened the heads of the running men, but they scampered with singular fortune. In this rush they were apparently all deaf and blind. They heeded not the largest and longest of the oaths that were thrown at them from all directions.

Frequently over this tumult could be heard the grim jokes of the critical veterans; but the retreating men apparently were not even conscious of the presence of an audience.

The battle reflection that shone for an instant in the faces on the mad current made the youth feel that forceful hands from heaven would not have been able to have held him in place if he could have got intelligent control of his legs.

There was an appalling imprint upon these faces. The struggle in the smoke had pictured an exaggeration of itself on the bleached cheeks and in the eyes wild with one desire.

The sight of this stampede exerted a floodlike force that seemed able to drag sticks and stones and men from the ground. They of the reserves had to hold on. They grew pale and firm, and red and quaking.

The youth achieved one little thought in the midst of this chaos. The composite monster which had caused the other troops to flee had not then appeared. He resolved to get a view of it, and then, he thought he might very likely run better than the best of them.

V

There were moments of waiting. The youth thought of the village street at home before the arrival of the circus parade on a day in the spring. He remembered how he had stood, a small, thrillful boy, prepared to follow the dingy lady upon the white horse, or the band in its faded chariot. He saw the yellow road, the lines of expectant people, and the sober houses. He particularly remembered an old fellow who used to sit upon a cracker box in front of the store and feign to despise such exhibitions. A thousand details of color and form surged in his mind. The old fellow upon the cracker box appeared in middle prominence.

Some one cried, "Here they come!"

There was rustling and muttering among the men. They displayed a feverish desire to have every possible cartridge ready to their hands. The boxes were pulled around into various positions, and adjusted with great care. It was as if seven hundred new bonnets were being tried on.

The tall soldier, having prepared his rifle, produced a red handkerchief of some kind. He was engaged in knitting it about his throat with exquisite attention to its position, when the cry was repeated up and down the line in a muffled roar of sound.

"Here they come! Here they come!" Gun locks clicked.

Across the smoke-infested fields came a brown swarm of running men who were giving shrill yells. They came on, stooping and swinging their rifles at all angles. A flag, tilted forward, sped near the front.

As he caught sight of them the youth was momentarily startled by a thought that perhaps his gun was not loaded. He stood trying to rally his faltering intellect so that he might recollect the moment when he had loaded, but he could not.

A hatless general pulled his dripping horse to a stand near the colonel of the 304th. He shook his fist in the other's face. "You've got to hold 'em back!" he shouted, savagely; "you've got to hold 'em back!"

In his agitation the colonel began to stammer. "A-all ri-right, General, all right, by Gawd! We-we'll do our—we-we'll d-d-do—do our best, General." The general made a passionate gesture and galloped away. The colonel, perchance to relieve his feelings, began to scold like a wet parrot. The youth, turning swiftly to make sure that the rear was unmolested, saw the commander regarding his men in a highly resentful manner, as if he regretted above everything his association with them.

The man at the youth's elbow was mumbling, as if to himself: "Oh, we're in for it now! oh, we're in for it now!"

The captain of the company had been pacing excitedly to and fro in the rear. He coaxed in schoolmistress fashion, as to a congregation of boys with primers. His talk was an endless repetition. "Reserve your fire, boys—don't shoot till I tell you—save your fire—wait till they get close up—don't be damned fools—"

Perspiration streamed down the youth's face, which was soiled like that of a weeping urchin. He frequently, with a nervous movement, wiped his eyes with his coat sleeve. His mouth was still a little ways open.

He got the one glance at the foe-swarming field in front of him, and instantly ceased to debate the question of his piece being loaded. Before he was ready to begin—before he had announced to himself that he was about to fight—he threw the obedient, well-balanced rifle into position and fired a first wild shot. Directly he was working at his weapon like an automatic affair.

He suddenly lost concern for himself, and forgot to look at a menacing fate. He became not a man but a member. He felt that something of which he was a part—a regiment, an army, a cause, or a country—was in a crisis. He was welded into a common personality which was dominated by a single desire. For some moments he could not flee, no more than a little finger can commit a revolution from a hand.

If he had thought the regiment was about to be annihilated perhaps he could have amputated himself from it. But its noise gave him assurance. The regiment was like a firework that, once ignited, proceeds superior to circumstances until its blazing vitality fades. It wheezed and banged with a mighty power. He pictured the ground before it as strewn with the discomfited.

There was a consciousness always of the presence of his comrades about him. He felt the subtle battle brotherhood more potent even than the cause for which they were fighting. It was a mysterious fraternity born of the smoke and danger of death.

He was at a task. He was like a carpenter who has made many boxes, making still another box, only there was furious haste in his movements. He, in his thought, was careering off in other places, even as the carpenter who as he works whistles and thinks of his friend or his enemy, his home or a saloon. And these jolted dreams were never perfect to him afterward, but remained a mass of blurred shapes.

Presently he began to feel the effects of the war atmosphere—a blistering sweat, a sensation that his eyeballs were about to crack like hot stones. A burning roar filled his ears.

Following this came a red rage. He developed the acute exasperation of a pestered animal, a well-meaning cow worried by dogs. He had a mad feeling against his rifle, which could only be used against one life at a time. He wished to rush forward and strangle with his fingers. He craved a power that would enable him to make a world-sweeping gesture and brush all back. His impotency appeared to him, and made his rage into that of a driven beast.

Buried in the smoke of many rifles his anger was directed not so much against the men who he knew were rushing toward him as against the swirling battle phantoms which were choking him, stuffing their smoke robes down his parched throat. He fought frantically for respite for his senses, for air, as a babe being smothered attacks the deadly blankets.

There was a blare of heated rage mingled with a certain expression of intentness on all faces. Many of the men were making low-toned noises with their mouths, and these subdued cheers, snarls, imprecations, prayers, made a wild, barbaric song that went as an undercurrent of sound, strange and chantlike with the resounding chords of the war march. The man at the youth's elbow was babbling. In it there was something soft and tender like the monologue of a babe. The tall soldier was swearing in a loud voice. From his lips came a black procession of curious oaths. Of a sudden another broke out in a querulous way like a man who has mislaid his hat. "Well, why don't they support us? Why don't they send supports? Do they think—"

The youth in his battle sleep heard this as one who dozes hears.

There was a singular absence of heroic poses. The men bending and surging in their haste and rage were in every impossible attitude. The steel ramrods clanked and clanged with incessant din as the men pounded them furiously into the hot rifle barrels. The flaps of the cartridge boxes were all unfastened, and bobbed idiotically with each movement. The rifles, once loaded, were jerked to the shoulder and fired without apparent aim into the smoke or at one of the blurred and shifting forms which, upon the field before the regiment, had been growing larger and larger like puppets under a magician's hand.

The officers, at their intervals, rearward, neglected to stand in picturesque attitudes. They were bobbing to and fro roaring directions and encouragements. The dimensions of their howls were extraordinary. They expended their lungs with prodigal wills. And often they nearly stood upon their heads in their anxiety to observe the enemy on the other side of the tumbling smoke.

The lieutenant of the youth's company had encountered a soldier who had fled screaming at the first volley of his comrades. Behind the lines these two were acting a little isolated scene. The man was blubbering and staring with sheeplike eyes at the lieutenant, who had seized him by the collar and was pommeling him. He drove him back into the ranks with many blows. The soldier went mechanically, dully, with his animal-like eyes upon the officer. Perhaps there was to him a divinity expressed in the voice of the other—stern, hard, with no reflection of fear in it. He tried to reload his gun, but his shaking hands prevented. The lieutenant was obliged to assist him.

The men dropped here and there like bundles. The captain of the youth's company had been killed in an early part of the action. His body lay stretched out in the position of a tired man resting, but upon his face there was an astonished and sorrowful look, as if he thought some friend had done him an ill turn. The babbling man was grazed by a shot that made the blood stream widely down his face. He clapped both hands to his head. "Oh!" he said, and ran. Another grunted suddenly as if he had been struck by a club in the stomach. He sat down and gazed ruefully. In his eyes there was mute, indefinite reproach. Farther up the line a man, standing behind a tree, had had his knee joint splintered by a ball. Immediately he had dropped his rifle and gripped the tree with both arms. And there he remained, clinging desperately and crying for assistance that he might withdraw his hold upon the tree.

At last an exultant yell went along the quivering line. The firing dwindled from an uproar to a last vindictive popping. As the smoke slowly eddied away, the youth saw that the charge had been repulsed. The enemy were scattered into reluctant groups. He saw a man climb to the top of the fence, straddle the rail, and fire a parting shot. The waves had receded, leaving bits of dark *débris* upon the ground.

Some in the regiment began to whoop frenziedly. Many were silent. Apparently they were trying to contemplate themselves.

After the fever had left his veins, the youth thought that at last he was going to suffocate. He became aware of the foul atmosphere in which he had been struggling. He was grimy and dripping like a laborer in a foundry. He grasped his canteen and took a long swallow of the warmed water.

A sentence with variations went up and down the line. "Well, we've helt 'em back. We've helt 'em back; derned if we haven't." The men said it blissfully, leering at each other with dirty smiles.

The youth turned to look behind him and off to the right and off to the left. He experienced the joy of a man who at last finds leisure in which to look about him.

Under foot there were a few ghastly forms motionless. They lay twisted in fantastic contortions. Arms were bent and heads were turned in incredible ways. It seemed that the dead men must have fallen from some great height to get into such positions. They looked to be dumped out upon the ground from the sky.

From a position in the rear of the grove a battery was throwing shells over it. The flash of the guns startled the youth at first. He thought they were aimed directly at him. Through the trees he watched the black figures of the gunners as they worked swiftly and intently. Their labor seemed a complicated thing. He wondered how they could remember its formula in the midst of confusion.

The guns squatted in a row like savage chiefs. They argued with abrupt violence. It was a grim pow-wow. Their busy servants ran hither and thither.

A small procession of wounded men were going drearily toward the rear. It was a flow of blood from the torn body of the brigade.

To the right and to the left were the dark lines of other troops. Far in front he thought he could see lighter masses protruding in points from the forest. They were suggestive of unnumbered thousands.

Once he saw a tiny battery go dashing along the line of the horizon. The tiny riders were beating the tiny horses.

From a sloping hill came the sound of cheerings and clashes. Smoke welled slowly through the leaves.

Batteries were speaking with thunderous oratorical effort. Here and there were flags, the red in the stripes dominating. They splashed bits of warm color upon the dark lines of troops.

The youth felt the old thrill at the sight of the emblem. They were like beautiful birds strangely undaunted in a storm.

As he listened to the din from the hillside, to a deep pulsating thunder that came from afar to the left, and to the lesser clamors which came from many directions, it occurred to him that they were fighting, too, over there, and over there, and over there. Heretofore he had supposed that all the battle was directly under his nose.

As he gazed around him the youth felt a flash of astonishment at the blue, pure sky and the sun gleaming on the trees and fields. It was surprising that Nature had gone tranquilly on with her golden process in the midst of so much devilment.

VI

The youth awakened slowly. He came gradually back to a position from which he could regard himself. For moments he had been scrutinizing his person in a dazed way as if he had never before seen himself. Then he picked up his cap from the ground. He wriggled in his jacket to make a more comfortable fit, and kneeling relaced his shoe. He thoughtfully mopped his reeking features.

So it was all over at last! The supreme trial had been passed. The red, formidable difficulties of war had been vanquished.

He went into an ecstasy of self-satisfaction. He had the most delightful sensations of his life. Standing as if apart from himself, he viewed that last scene. He perceived that the man who had fought thus was magnificent.

He felt that he was a fine fellow. He saw himself even with those ideals which he had considered as far beyond him. He smiled in deep gratification.

Upon his fellows he beamed tenderness and good will. "Gee! ain't it hot, hey?" he said affably to a man who was polishing his streaming face with his coat sleeves.

"You bet!" said the other, grinning sociably. "I never seen sech dum hotness." He sprawled out luxuriously on the ground. "Gee, yes! An' I hope we don't have no more fightin' till a week from Monday."

There were some handshakings and deep speeches with men whose features were familiar, but with whom the youth now felt the bonds of tied hearts. He helped a cursing comrade to bind up a wound of the shin.

But, of a sudden, cries of amazement broke out along the ranks of the new regiment. "Here they come ag'in! Here they come ag'in!" The man who had sprawled upon the ground started up and said, "Gosh!"

The youth turned quick eyes upon the field. He discerned forms begin to swell in masses out of a distant wood. He again saw the tilted flag speeding forward.

The shells, which had ceased to trouble the regiment for a time, came swirling again, and exploded in the grass or among the leaves of the trees. They looked to be strange war flowers bursting into fierce bloom.

The men groaned. The luster faded from their eyes. Their smudged countenances now expressed a profound dejection. They moved their stiffened bodies slowly, and watched in sullen mood the frantic approach of the enemy. The slaves toiling in the temple of this god began to feel rebellion at his harsh tasks.

They fretted and complained each to each. "Oh, say, this is too much of a good thing! Why can't somebody send us supports?"

"We ain't never goin' to stand this second banging. I didn't come here to fight the hull damn' rebel army."

There was one who raised a doleful cry. "I wish Bill Smithers had trod on my hand, insteader me treddin' on his'n." The sore joints of the regiment creaked as it painfully floundered into position to repulse.

The youth stared. Surely, he thought, this impossible thing was not about to happen. He waited as if he expected the enemy to suddenly stop, apologize, and retire bowing. It was all a mistake.

But the firing began somewhere on the regimental line and ripped along in both directions. The level sheets of flame developed great clouds of smoke that tumbled and tossed in the mild wind near the ground for a moment, and then rolled through the ranks as through a gate. The clouds were tinged an earth-like yellow in the sunrays and in the shadow were a sorry blue. The flag was sometimes eaten and lost in this mass of vapor, but more often it projected, sun-touched, resplendent.

Into the youth's eyes there came a look that one can see in the orbs of a jaded horse. His neck was quivering with nervous weakness and the muscles of his arms felt numb and bloodless. His hands, too, seemed large and awkward as if he was wearing invisible mittens. And there was a great uncertainty about his knee joints.

The words that comrades had uttered previous to the firing began to recur to him. "Oh, say, this is too much of a good thing! What do they take us for—why don't they send supports? I didn't come here to fight the hull damn' rebel army."

He began to exaggerate the endurance, the skill, and the valor of those who were coming. Himself reeling from exhaustion, he was astonished beyond measure at such persistency. They must be machines of steel. It was very gloomy struggling against such affairs, wound up perhaps to fight until sundown.

He slowly lifted his rifle and catching a glimpse of the thickspread field he blazed at a cantering cluster. He stopped then and began to peer as best as he could through the smoke. He caught changing views of the ground covered with men who were all running like pursued imps, and yelling.

To the youth it was an onslaught of redoubtable dragons. He became like the man who lost his legs at the approach of the red and green monster. He waited in a sort of a horrified, listening attitude. He seemed to shut his eyes and wait to be gobbled.

A man near him who up to this time had been working feverishly at his rifle suddenly stopped and ran with howls. A lad whose face had borne an expression of exalted courage, the majesty of he who dares give his life, was, at an instant, smitten abject. He blanched like one who has come to the edge of a cliff at midnight and is suddenly made aware. There was a revelation. He, too, threw down his gun and fled. There was no shame in his face. He ran like a rabbit.

Others began to scamper away through the smoke. The youth turned his head, shaken from his trance by this movement as if the regiment was leaving him behind. He saw the few fleeting forms.

He yelled then with fright and swung about. For a moment, in the great clamor, he was like a proverbial chicken. He lost his direction of safety. Destruction threatened him from all points.

Directly he began to speed toward the rear in great leaps. His rifle and cap were gone. His unbuttoned coat bulged in the wind. The flap of his cartridge box bobbed wildly, and his canteen, by its slender cord, swung out behind. On his face was all the horror of those things which he imagined.

The lieutenant sprang forward bawling. The youth saw his features wrathfully red, and saw him make a dab with his sword. His one thought of the incident was that the lieutenant was a peculiar creature to feel interested in such matters upon this occasion.

He ran like a blind man. Two or three times he fell down. Once he knocked his shoulder so heavily against a tree that he went headlong.

Since he had turned his back upon the fight his fears had been wondrously magnified. Death about to thrust him between the shoulder blades was far more dreadful than death about to smite him between the eyes. When he thought of it later, he conceived the impression that it is better to view the appalling than to be merely within hearing. The noises of the battle were like stones; he believed himself liable to be crushed.

As he ran on he mingled with others. He dimly saw men on his right and on his left, and he heard footsteps behind him. He thought that all the regiment was fleeing, pursued by these ominous crashes.

In his flight the sound of these following footsteps gave him his one meager relief. He felt vaguely that death must make a first choice of the men who were nearest; the initial morsels for the dragons would be then those who were following him. So he displayed the zeal of an insane sprinter in his purpose to keep them in the rear. There was a race.

As he, leading, went across a little field, he found himself in a region of shells. They hurtled over his head with long wild screams. As he listened he imagined them to have rows of cruel teeth that grinned at him. Once one lit before him and the livid lightning of the explosion effectually barred the way in his chosen direction. He groveled on the ground and then springing up went careering off through some bushes.

He experienced a thrill of amazement when he came within view of a battery in action. The men there seemed to be in conventional moods, altogether unaware of the impending annihilation. The battery was disputing with a distant antagonist and the gunners were wrapped in admiration of their shooting. They were continually bending in coaxing postures over the guns. They seemed to be patting them on the back and encouraging them with words. The guns, stolid and undaunted, spoke with dogged valor.

The precise gunners were coolly enthusiastic. They lifted their eyes every chance to the smoke-wreathed hillock from whence the hostile battery addressed them. The youth pitied them as he ran. Methodical idiots! Machine-like fools! The refined joy of planting shells in the midst of the other battery's formation would appear a little thing when the infantry came swooping out of the woods.

The face of a youthful rider, who was jerking his frantic horse with an abandon of temper he might display in a placid barnyard, was impressed deeply upon his mind. He knew that he looked upon a man who would presently be dead.

Too, he felt a pity for the guns, standing, six good comrades, in a bold row.

He saw a brigade going to the relief of its pestered fellows. He scrambled upon a wee hill and watched it sweeping finely, keeping formation in difficult places. The blue of the line was crusted with steel color, and the brilliant flags projected. Officers were shouting.

This sight also filled him with wonder. The brigade was hurrying briskly to be gulped into the infernal mouths of the war god. What manner of men were they, anyhow? Ah, it was some wondrous breed! Or else they didn't comprehend—the fools.

A furious order caused commotion in the artillery. An officer on a bounding horse made maniacal motions with his arms. The teams went swinging up from the rear, the guns were whirled about, and the battery scampered away. The cannon with their noses poked slantingly at the ground grunted and grumbled like stout men, brave but with objections to hurry.

The youth went on, moderating his pace since he had left the place of noises.

Later he came upon a general of division seated upon a horse that pricked its ears in an interested way at the battle. There was a great gleaming of yellow and patent leather about the saddle and bridle. The quiet man astride looked mouse-colored upon such a splendid charger.

A jingling staff was galloping hither and thither. Sometimes the general was surrounded by horsemen and at other times he was quite alone. He looked to be much harassed. He had the appearance of a business man whose market is swinging up and down.

The youth went slinking around this spot. He went as near as he dared trying to overhear words. Perhaps the general, unable to comprehend chaos, might call upon him for information. And he could tell him. He knew all concerning it. Of a surety the force was in a fix, and any fool could see that if they did not retreat while they had opportunity—why—

He felt that he would like to thrash the general, or at least approach and tell him in plain words exactly what he thought him to be. It was criminal to stay calmly in one spot and make no effort to stay destruction. He loitered in a fever of eagerness for the division commander to apply to him.

As he warily moved about, he heard the general call out irritably: "Tompkins, go over an' see Taylor, an' tell him not t' be in such an all-fired hurry; tell him t' halt his brigade in th' edge of th' woods; tell him t' detach a reg'ment—say I think th' center 'll break if we don't help it out some; tell him t' hurry up."

A slim youth on a fine chestnut horse caught these swift words from the mouth of his superior. He made his horse bound into a gallop almost from a walk in his haste to go upon his mission. There was a cloud of dust.

A moment later the youth saw the general bounce excitedly in his saddle.

"Yes, by heavens, they have!" The officer leaned forward. His face was aflame with excitement. "Yes, by heavens, they've held 'im! They've held 'im!"

He began to blithely roar at his staff: "We'll wallop 'im now. We'll wallop 'im now. We've got 'em sure." He turned suddenly upon an aide: "Here—you—Jones—quick—ride after Tompkins—see Taylor—tell him t' go in—everlastingly—like blazes—anything."

As another officer sped his horse after the first messenger, the general beamed upon the earth like a sun. In his eyes was a desire to chant a paean. He kept repeating, "They've held 'em, by heavens!"

His excitement made his horse plunge, and he merrily kicked and swore at it. He held a little carnival of joy on horseback.

VII

The youth cringed as if discovered in a crime. By heavens, they had won after all! The imbecile line had remained and become victors. He could hear cheering.

He lifted himself upon his toes and looked in the direction of the fight. A yellow fog lay wallowing on the treetops. From beneath it came the clatter of musketry. Hoarse cries told of an advance.

He turned away amazed and angry. He felt that he had been wronged.

He had fled, he told himself, because annihilation approached. He had done a good part in saving himself, who was a little piece of the army. He had considered the time, he said, to be one in which it was the duty of every little piece to rescue itself if possible. Later the officers could fit the little pieces together again, and make a battle front. If none of the little pieces were wise enough to save themselves from the flurry of death at such a time, why, then, where would be the army? It was all plain that he had proceeded according to very correct and commendable rules. His actions had been sagacious things. They had been full of strategy. They were the work of a master's legs.

Thoughts of his comrades came to him. The brittle blue line had withstood the blows and won. He grew bitter over it. It seemed that the blind ignorance and stupidity of those little pieces had betrayed him. He had been overturned and crushed by their lack of sense in holding the position, when intelligent deliberation would have convinced them that it was impossible. He, the enlightened man who looks afar in the dark, had fled because of his superior perceptions and knowledge. He felt a great anger against his comrades. He knew it could be proved that they had been fools.

He wondered what they would remark when later he appeared in camp. His mind heard howls of derision. Their destiny would not enable them to understand his sharper point of view.

He began to pity himself acutely. He was ill used. He was trodden beneath the feet of an iron injustice. He had proceeded with wisdom and from the most righteous motives under heaven's blue only to be frustrated by hateful circumstances.

A dull, animal-like rebellion against his fellows, war in the abstract, and fate grew within him. He shambled along with bowed head, his brain in a tumult of agony and despair. When he looked loweringly up, quivering at each sound, his eyes had the expression of those of a criminal who thinks his guilt and his punishment great, and knows that he can find no words.

He went from the fields into a thick wood, as if resolved to bury himself. He wished to get out of hearing of the cracking shots which were to him like voices.

The ground was cluttered with vines and bushes, and the trees grew close and spread out like bouquets. He was obliged to force his way with much noise. The creepers, catching against his legs, cried out harshly as their sprays were torn from the barks of trees. The swishing saplings tried to make known his presence to the world. He could not conciliate the forest. As he made his way, it was always calling out protestations. When he separated embraces of trees and vines the disturbed foliages waved their arms and turned their face leaves toward him. He dreaded lest these noisy motions and cries should bring men to look at him. So he went far, seeking dark and intricate places.

After a time the sound of musketry grew faint and the cannon boomed in the distance. The sun, suddenly apparent, blazed among the trees. The insects were making rhythmical noises. They seemed to be grinding their teeth in unison. A woodpecker stuck his impudent head around the side of a tree. A bird flew on lighthearted wing.

Off was the rumble of death. It seemed now that Nature had no ears.

This landscape gave him assurance. A fair field holding life. It was the religion of peace. It would die if its timid eyes were compelled to see blood. He conceived Nature to be a woman with a deep aversion to tragedy.

He threw a pine cone at a jovial squirrel, and he ran with chattering fear. High in a treetop he stopped, and, poking his head cautiously from behind a branch, looked down with an air of trepidation.

The youth felt triumphant at this exhibition. There was the law, he said. Nature had given him a sign. The squirrel, immediately upon recognizing danger, had taken to his legs without ado. He did not stand stolidly baring his furry belly to the missile, and die with an upward glance at the sympathetic heavens. On the contrary, he had fled as fast as his legs could carry him; and he was but an ordinary squirrel, too—doubtless no philosopher of his race. The youth wended, feeling that Nature was of his mind. She re-enforced his argument with proofs that lived where the sun shone.

Once he found himself almost into a swamp. He was obliged to walk upon bog tufts and watch his feet to keep from the oily mire. Pausing at one time to look about him he saw, out at some black water, a small animal pounce in and emerge directly with a gleaming fish.

The youth went again into the deep thickets. The brushed branches made a noise that drowned the sounds of cannon. He walked on, going from obscurity into promises of a greater obscurity.

At length he reached a place where the high, arching boughs made a chapel. He softly pushed the green doors aside and entered. Pine needles were a gentle brown carpet. There was a religious half light.

Near the threshold he stopped, horror-stricken at the sight of a thing.

He was being looked at by a dead man who was seated with his back against a columnlike tree. The corpse was dressed in a uniform that once had been blue, but was now faded to a melancholy shade of green. The eyes, staring at the youth, had changed to the dull hue to be seen on the side of a dead fish. The mouth was open. Its red had changed to an appalling yellow. Over the gray skin of the face ran little ants. One was trundling some sort of a bundle along the upper lip.

The youth gave a shriek as he confronted the thing. He was for moments turned to stone before it. He remained staring into the liquid-looking eyes. The dead man and the living man exchanged a long look. Then the youth cautiously put one hand behind him and brought it against a tree. Leaning upon this he retreated, step by step, with his face still toward the thing. He feared that if he turned his back the body might spring up and stealthily pursue him.

The branches, pushing against him, threatened to throw him over upon it. His unguided feet, too, caught aggravatingly in brambles; and with it all he received a subtle suggestion to touch the corpse. As he thought of his hand upon it he shuddered profoundly.

At last he burst the bonds which had fastened him to the spot and fled, unheeding the underbrush. He was pursued by the sight of the black ants swarming greedily upon the gray face and venturing horribly near to the eyes.

After a time he paused, and, breathless and panting, listened. He imagined some strange voice would come from the dead throat and squawk after him in horrible menaces.

The trees about the portals of the chapel moved soughingly in a soft wind. A sad silence was upon the little guarding edifice.

VIII

The trees began softly to sing a hymn of twilight. The sun sank until slanted bronze rays struck the forest. There was a lull in the noises of insects as if they had bowed their beaks and were making a devotional pause. There was silence save for the chanted chorus of the trees.

Then, upon this stillness, there suddenly broke a tremendous clangor of sounds. A crimson roar came from the distance.

The youth stopped. He was transfixed by this terrific medley of all noises. It was as if worlds were being rended. There was the ripping sound of musketry and the breaking crash of artillery.

His mind flew in all directions. He conceived the two armies to be at each other panther fashion. He listened for a time. Then he began to run in the direction of the battle. He saw that it was an ironical thing for him to be running thus toward that which he had been at such pains to avoid. But he said, in substance, to himself that if the earth and the moon were about to clash, many persons would doubtless plan to get upon the roofs to witness the collision.

As he ran, he became aware that the forest had stopped its music, as if at last becoming capable of hearing the foreign sounds. The trees hushed and stood motionless. Everything seemed to be listening to the crackle and clatter and ear-shaking thunder. The chorus pealed over the still earth.

It suddenly occurred to the youth that the fight in which he had been was, after all, but perfunctory popping. In the hearing of this present din he was doubtful if he had seen real battle scenes. This uproar explained a celestial battle; it was tumbling hordes a-struggle in the air.

Reflecting, he saw a sort of a humor in the point of view of himself and his fellows during the late encounter. They had taken themselves and the enemy very seriously and had imagined that they were deciding the war. Individuals must have supposed that they were cutting the letters of their names deep into everlasting tablets of brass, or enshrining their reputations forever in the hearts of their countrymen, while, as to fact, the affair would appear in printed reports under a meek and immaterial title. But he saw that it was good, else, he said, in battle every one would surely run save forlorn hopes and their ilk.

He went rapidly on. He wished to come to the edge of the forest that he might peer out.

As he hastened, there passed through his mind pictures of stupendous conflicts. His accumulated thought upon such subjects was used to form scenes. The noise was as the voice of an eloquent being, describing.

Sometimes the brambles formed chains and tried to hold him back. Trees, confronting him, stretched out their arms and forbade him to pass.

After its previous hostility this new resistance of the forest filled him with a fine bitterness. It seemed that Nature could not be quite ready to kill him.

But he obstinately took roundabout ways, and presently he was where he could see long gray walls of vapor where lay battle lines. The voices of cannon shook him. The musketry sounded in long irregular surges that played havoc with his ears. He stood regardant for a moment. His eyes had an awestruck expression. He gawked in the direction of the fight.

Presently he proceeded again on his forward way. The battle was like the grinding of an immense and terrible machine to him. Its complexities and powers, its grim processes, fascinated him. He must go close and see it produce corpses.

He came to a fence and clambered over it. On the far side, the ground was littered with clothes and guns. A newspaper, folded up, lay in the dirt. A dead soldier was stretched with his face hidden in his arm. Farther off there was a group of four or five corpses keeping mournful company. A hot sun had blazed upon the spot.

In this place the youth felt that he was an invader. This forgotten part of the battleground was owned by the dead men, and he hurried, in the vague apprehension that one of the swollen forms would rise and tell him to begone.

He came finally to a road from which he could see in the distance dark and agitated bodies of troops, smoke-fringed. In the lane was a blood-stained crowd streaming to the rear. The wounded men were cursing, groaning, and wailing. In the air, always, was a mighty swell of sound that it seemed could sway the earth. With the courageous words of the artillery and the spiteful sentences of the musketry mingled red cheers. And from this region of noises came the steady current of the maimed.

One of the wounded men had a shoeful of blood. He hopped like a schoolboy in a game. He was laughing hysterically.

One was swearing that he had been shot in the arm through the commanding general's mismanagement of the army. One was marching with an air imitative of some sublime drum major. Upon his features was an unholy mixture of merriment and agony. As he marched he sang a bit of doggerel in a high and quavering voice:

Sing a song 'a vic'try,
A pocketful 'a bullets,
Five an' twenty dead men
Baked in a—pie.

Parts of the procession limped and staggered to this tune.

Another had the gray seal of death already upon his face. His lips were curled in hard lines and his teeth were clenched. His hands were bloody

from where he had pressed them upon his wound. He seemed to be awaiting the moment when he should pitch headlong. He stalked like the specter
of a soldier, his eyes burning with the power of a stare into the unknown.

There were some who proceeded sullenly, full of anger at their wounds,
and ready to turn upon anything as an obscure cause.

An officer was carried along by two privates. He was peevish. "Don't
joggle so, Johnson, yeh fool," he cried. "Think m' leg is made of iron? If
yeh can't carry me decent, put me down an' let some one else do it."

He bellowed at the tottering crowd who blocked the quick march of his
bearers. "Say, make way there, can't yeh? Make way, dickens take it all."

They sulkily parted and went to the roadsides. As he was carried past
they made pert remarks to him. When he raged in reply and threatened
them, they told him to be damned.

The shoulder of one of the tramping bearers knocked heavily against
the spectral soldier who was staring into the unknown.

The youth joined this crowd and marched along with it. The torn bodies expressed the awful machinery in which the men had been entangled.

Orderlies and couriers occasionally broke through the throng in the
roadway, scattering wounded men right and left, galloping on, followed by
howls. The melancholy march was continually disturbed by messengers,
and sometimes by bustling batteries that came swinging and thumping
down upon them, the officers shouting orders to clear the way.

There was a tattered man, fouled with dust, blood and powder stain
from hair to shoes, who trudged quietly at the youth's side. He was listening with eagerness and much humility to the lurid descriptions of a
bearded sergeant. His lean features wore an expression of awe and admiration. He was like a listener in a country store to wondrous tales told
among the sugar barrels. He eyed the story-teller with unspeakable wonder. His mouth was agape in yokel fashion.

The sergeant, taking note of this, gave pause to his elaborate history
while he administered a sardonic comment. "Be keerful, honey, you'll be
a-ketchin' flies," he said.

The tattered man shrank back abashed.

After a time he began to sidle near to the youth, and in a different way
try to make him a friend. His voice was gentle as a girl's voice and his eyes
were pleading. The youth saw with surprise that the soldier had two
wounds, one in the head, bound with a blood-soaked rag, and the other in
the arm, making that member dangle like a broken bough.

After they had walked together for some time the tattered man mustered sufficient courage to speak. "Was pretty good fight, wasn't it?" he
timidly said. The youth, deep in thought, glanced up at the bloody and
grim figure with its lamblike eyes. "What?"

"Was pretty good fight, wa'n't it?"

"Yes," said the youth shortly. He quickened his pace.

But the other hobbled industriously after him. There was an air of apology in his manner, but he evidently thought that he needed only to talk for a time, and the youth would perceive that he was a good fellow.

"Was pretty good fight, wa'n't it?" he began in a small voice, and then he achieved the fortitude to continue. "Dern me if I ever see fellers fight so. Laws, how they did fight! I knowed th' boys 'd lick when they onct got square at it. Th' boys ain't had no fair chanct up t' now, but this time they showed what they was. I knowed it 'd turn out this way. Yeh can't lick them boys. No, sir! They're fighters, they be."

He breathed a deep breath of humble admiration. He had looked at the youth for encouragement several times. He received none, but gradually he seemed to get absorbed in his subject.

"I was talkin' 'cross pickets with a boy from Georgie, onct, an' that boy, he ses, 'Your fellers 'll all run like hell when they onct hearn a gun,' he ses. 'Mebbe they will,' I ses, 'but I don't b'lieve none of it,' I ses; 'an' b'jiminey,' I ses back t' 'um, 'mebbe your fellers 'll all run like hell when they onct hearn a gun,' I ses. He larfed. Well, they didn't run t'-day, did they, hey? No, sir! They fit, an fit, an fit."

His homely face was suffused with a light of love for the army which was to him all things beautiful and powerful.

After a time he turned to the youth. "Where yeh hit, ol' boy?" he asked in a brotherly tone.

The youth felt instant panic at this question, although at first its full import was not borne in upon him.

"What?" he asked.

"Where yeh hit?" repeated the tattered man.

"Why," began the youth, "I—I—that is—why—I—"

He turned away suddenly and slid through the crowd. His brow was heavily flushed, and his fingers were picking nervously at one of his buttons. He bent his head and fastened his eyes studiously upon the button as if it were a little problem.

The tattered man looked after him in astonishment.

IX

The youth fell back in the procession until the tattered soldier was not in sight. Then he started to walk on with the others.

But he was amid wounds. The mob of men was bleeding. Because of the tattered soldier's question he now felt that his shame could be viewed.

He was continually casting sidelong glances to see if the men were contemplating the letters of guilt he felt burned into his brow.

At times he regarded the wounded soldiers in an envious way. He conceived persons with torn bodies to be peculiarly happy. He wished that he, too, had a wound, a red badge of courage.

The spectral soldier was at his side like a stalking reproach. The man's eyes were still fixed in a stare into the unknown. His gray, appalling face had attracted attention in the crowd, and men, slowing to his dreary pace, were walking with him. They were discussing his plight, questioning him and giving him advice. In a dogged way he repelled them, signing to them to go on and leave him alone. The shadows of his face were deepening and his tight lips seemed holding in check the moan of great despair. There could be seen a certain stiffness in the movements of his body, as if he were taking infinite care not to arouse the passion of his wounds. As he went on, he seemed always looking for a place, like one who goes to choose a grave.

Something in the gesture of the man as he waved the bloody and pitying soldiers away made the youth start as if bitten. He yelled in horror. Tottering forward he laid a quivering hand upon the man's arm. As the latter slowly turned his waxlike features toward him the youth screamed:

"Gawd! Jim Conklin!"

The tall soldier made a little commonplace smile. "Hello, Henry," he said.

The youth swayed on his legs and glared strangely. He stuttered and stammered. "Oh, Jim—oh, Jim—oh, Jim—"

The tall soldier held out his gory hand. There was a curious red and black combination of new blood and old blood upon it. "Where yeh been, Henry?" he asked. He continued in a monotonous voice, "I thought mebbe yeh got keeled over. There's been thunder t' pay t'day. I was worryin' about it a good deal."

The youth still lamented. "Oh, Jim—oh, Jim—oh, Jim—"

"Yeh know," said the tall soldier, "I was out there." He made a careful gesture. "An', Lord, what a circus! An', b'jiminey, I got shot—I got shot. Yes, b'jiminey, I got shot." He reiterated this fact in a bewildered way, as if he did not know how it came about.

The youth put forth anxious arms to assist him, but the tall soldier went firmly on as if propelled. Since the youth's arrival as a guardian for his friend, the other wounded men had ceased to display much interest. They occupied themselves again in dragging their own tragedies toward the rear.

Suddenly, as the two friends marched on, the tall soldier seemed to be overcome by a terror. His face turned to a semblance of gray paste. He clutched the youth's arm and looked all about him, as if dreading to be overheard. Then he began to speak in a shaking whisper:

"I tell yeh what I'm 'fraid of, Henry—I'll tell yeh what I'm 'fraid of. I'm 'fraid I'll fall down—an' then yeh know—them damned artillery wagons—they like as not 'll run over me. That's what I'm 'fraid of—"

The youth cried out to him hysterically: "I'll take care of yeh, Jim! I'll take care of yeh! I swear t' Gawd I will!"

"Sure—will yeh, Henry?" the tall soldier beseeched.

"Yes—yes—I tell yeh—I'll take care of yeh, Jim!" protested the youth. He could not speak accurately because of the gulpings in his throat.

But the tall soldier continued to beg in a lowly way. He now hung babelike to the youth's arm. His eyes rolled in the wildness of his terror. "I was allus a good friend t' yeh, wa'n't I, Henry? I've allus been a pretty good feller, ain't I? An' it ain't much t' ask, is it? Jest t' pull me along outer th' road? I'd do it fer you, wouldn't I, Henry?"

He paused in piteous anxiety to await his friend's reply.

The youth had reached an anguish where the sobs scorched him. He strove to express his loyalty, but he could only make fantastic gestures.

However, the tall soldier seemed suddenly to forget all those fears. He became again the grim, stalking specter of a soldier. He went stonily forward. The youth wished his friend to lean upon him, but the other always shook his head and strangely protested. "No—no—no—leave me be— leave me be—"

His look was fixed upon the unknown. He moved with mysterious purpose, and all of the youth's offers he brushed aside. "No—no—leave me be—leave me be—"

The youth had to follow.

Presently the latter heard a voice talking softly near his shoulders. Turning he saw that it belonged to the tattered soldier. "Ye'd better take 'im outa th' road, pardner. There's a batt'ry comin' helitywhoop down th' road an' he'll git runned over. He's a goner anyhow in about five minutes—yeh kin see that. Ye'd better take 'im outa th' road. Where th' blazes does he git his stren'th from?"

"Lord knows!" cried the youth. He was shaking his hands helplessly.

He ran forward presently and grasped the tall soldier by the arm. "Jim! Jim!" he coaxed, "come with me."

The tall soldier weakly tried to wrench himself free. "Huh," he said vacantly. He stared at the youth for a moment. At last he spoke as if dimly comprehending. "Oh! Inteh th' fields? Oh!"

He started blindly through the grass.

The youth turned once to look at the lashing riders and jouncing guns of the battery. He was startled from this view by a shrill outcry from the tattered man.

"Gawd! He's runnin'!"

Turning his head swiftly, the youth saw his friend running in a staggering and stumbling way toward a little clump of bushes. His heart seemed to wrench itself almost free from his body at this sight. He made a noise of pain. He and the tattered man began a pursuit. There was a singular race.

When he overtook the tall soldier he began to plead with all the words he could find. "Jim—Jim—what are you doing—what makes you do this way—you'll hurt yerself."

The same purpose was in the tall soldier's face. He protested in a dulled way, keeping his eyes fastened on the mystic place of his intentions. "No—no—don't tech me—leave me be—leave me be—"

The youth, aghast and filled with wonder at the tall soldier, began quaveringly to question him. "Where yeh goin', Jim? What you thinking about? Where you going? Tell me, won't you, Jim?"

The tall soldier faced about as upon relentless pursuers. In his eyes there was a great appeal. "Leave me be, can't yeh? Leave me be fer a minnit."

The youth recoiled. "Why, Jim," he said, in a dazed way, "what's the matter with you?"

The tall soldier turned and, lurching dangerously, went on. The youth and the tattered soldier followed, sneaking as if whipped, feeling unable to face the stricken man if he should again confront them. They began to have thoughts of a solemn ceremony. There was something ritelike in these movements of the doomed soldier. And there was a resemblance in him to a devotee of a mad religion, blood-sucking, muscle-wrenching, bone-crushing. They were awed and afraid. They hung back lest he have at command a dreadful weapon.

At last, they saw him stop and stand motionless. Hastening up, they perceived that his face wore an expression telling that he had at last found the place for which he had struggled. His spare figure was erect; his bloody hands were quietly at his side. He was waiting with patience for something that he had come to meet. He was at the rendezvous. They paused and stood, expectant.

There was a silence.

Finally, the chest of the doomed soldier began to heave with a strained motion. It increased in violence until it was as if an animal was within and was kicking and tumbling furiously to be free.

This spectacle of gradual strangulation made the youth writhe, and once as his friend rolled his eyes, he saw something in them that made him sink wailing to the ground. He raised his voice in a last supreme call.

"Jim—Jim—Jim—"

The tall soldier opened his lips and spoke. He made a gesture. "Leave me be—don't tech me—leave me be—"

There was another silence while he waited.

Suddenly, his form stiffened and straightened. Then it was shaken by a prolonged ague. He stared into space. To the two watchers there was a curious and profound dignity in the firm lines of his awful face.

He was invaded by a creeping strangeness that slowly enveloped him. For a moment the tremor of his legs caused him to dance a sort of hideous hornpipe. His arms beat wildly about his head in expression of implike enthusiasm.

His tall figure stretched itself to its full height. There was a slight rending sound. Then it began to swing forward, slow and straight, in the manner of a falling tree. A swift muscular contortion made the left shoulder strike the ground first.

The body seemed to bounce a little way from the earth. "God!" said the tattered soldier.

The youth had watched, spellbound, this ceremony at the place of meeting. His face had been twisted into an expression of every agony he had imagined for his friend.

He now sprang to his feet and, going closer, gazed upon the pastelike face. The mouth was open and the teeth showed in a laugh.

As the flap of the blue jacket fell away from the body, he could see that the side looked as if it had been chewed by wolves.

The youth turned, with sudden, livid rage, toward the battlefield. He shook his fist. He seemed about to deliver a philippic.

"Hell—"

The red sun was pasted in the sky like a wafer.

X

The tattered man stood musing.

"Well, he was reg'lar jim-dandy fer nerve, wa'n't he," said he finally in a little awestruck voice. "A reg'lar jim-dandy." He thoughtfully poked one of the docile hands with his foot. "I wonner where he got 'is stren'th from? I never seen a man do like that before. It was a funny thing. Well, he was a reg'lar jim-dandy."

The youth desired to screech out his grief. He was stabbed, but his tongue lay dead in the tomb of his mouth. He threw himself again upon the ground and began to brood.

The tattered man stood musing.

"Look-a-here, pardner," he said, after a time. He regarded the corpse as he spoke. "He's up an' gone, ain' 'e, an' we might as well begin t' look out fer ol' number one. This here thing is all over. He's up an' gone, ain't 'e? An' he's all right here. Nobody won't bother 'im. An' I must say I ain't enjoying any great health m'self these days."

The youth, awakened by the tattered soldier's tone, looked quickly up. He saw that he was swinging uncertainly on his legs and that his face had turned to a shade of blue.

"Good Lord!" he cried, "you ain't goin' t'—not you, too."

The tattered man waved his hand. "Nary die," he said. "All I want is some pea soup an' a good bed. Some pea soup," he repeated dreamfully.

The youth arose from the ground. "I wonder where he came from. I left him over there." He pointed. "And now I find 'im here. And he was coming from over there, too." He indicated a new direction. They both turned toward the body as if to ask it a question.

"Well," at length spoke the tattered man, "there ain't no use in our stayin' here an' tryin' t' ask him anything."

The youth nodded an assent wearily. They both turned to gaze for a moment at the corpse.

The youth murmured something.

"Well, he was a jim-dandy, wa'n't 'e?" said the tattered man as if in response.

They turned their backs upon it and started away. For a time they stole softly, treading with their toes. It remained laughing there in the grass.

"I'm commencin' t' feel pretty bad," said the tattered man, suddenly breaking one of his little silences. "I'm commencin' t' feel pretty damn' bad."

The youth groaned. "O Lord!" He wondered if he was to be the tortured witness of another grim encounter.

But his companion waved his hand reassuringly. "Oh, I'm not goin' t' die yit! There too much dependin' on me fer me t' die yit. No, sir! Nary die; I *can't!* Ye'd oughta see th' swad a' chil'ren I've got, an' all like that."

The youth glancing at his companion could see by the shadow of a smile that he was making some kind of fun.

As they plodded on the tattered soldier continued to talk. "Besides, if I died, I wouldn't die th' way that feller did. That was th' funniest thing. I'd jest flop down, I would. I never seen a feller die th' way that feller did.

"Yeh know Tom Jamison, he lives next door t' me up home. He's a nice feller, he is, an' we was allus good friends. Smart, too. Smart as a steel trap. Well, when we was a-fightin' this afternoon, all-of-a-sudden he begin t' rip up an' cuss an' beller at me. 'Yer shot, yeh blamed infernal!'—he swear horrible—he ses t' me. I put up m' hand t' m' head an' when I looked at m' fingers, I seen, sure 'nough, I was shot. I give a holler an' be-gin t' run, but b'fore I could git away another one hit me in th' arm an' whirl' me clean 'round. I got skeared when they was all a-shootin' b'hind me an' I run t' beat all, but I cotch it pretty bad. I've an idee I'd a' been fightin' yit, if t'wasn't fer Tom Jamison."

Then he made a calm announcement: "There's two of 'em—little ones—but they're beginnin' t' have fun with me now. I don't b'lieve I kin walk much furder."

They went slowly on in silence. "Yeh look pretty peek-ed yerself," said the tattered man at last. "I bet yeh 've got a worser one than yeh think. Ye'd better take keer of yer hurt. It don't do t' let sech things go. It might be inside mostly, an' them plays thunder. Where is it located?" But he continued his harangue without waiting for a reply. "I see' a feller git hit plum in th' head when my reg'ment was a'standin' at ease onct. An' everybody yelled out to 'im: Hurt, John? Are yeh hurt much? 'No,' ses he. He looked kinder surprised, an' he went on tellin' 'em how he felt. He sed he didn't feel nothin'. But, by dad, th' first thing that feller knowed he was dead. Yes, he was dead—stone dead. So, yeh wanta watch out. Yeh might have some queer kind 'a hurt yerself. Yeh can't never tell. Where is your'n located?"

The youth had been wriggling since the introduction of this topic. He now gave a cry of exasperation and made a furious motion with his hand. "Oh, don't bother me!" he said. He was enraged against the tattered man, and could have strangled him. His companions seemed ever to play intol-erable parts. They were ever upraising the ghost of shame on the stick of their curiosity. He turned toward the tattered man as one at bay. "Now, don't bother me," he repeated with desperate menace.

"Well, Lord knows I don't wanta bother anybody," said the other. There was a little accent of despair in his voice as he replied, "Lord knows I've gota 'nough m' own t' tend to."

The youth, who had been holding a bitter debate with himself and casting glances of hatred and contempt at the tattered man, here spoke in a hard voice. "Good-by," he said.

The tattered man looked at him in gaping amazement. "Why—why, pardner, where yeh goin'?" he asked unsteadily. The youth looking at him, could see that he, too, like that other one, was beginning to act dumb and animal-like. His thoughts seemed to be floundering about in his head. "Now—now—look—a—here, you Tom Jamison—now—I won't have this—this here won't do. Where—where yeh goin'?"

The youth pointed vaguely. "Over there," he replied.

"Well, now look—a—here—now," said the tattered man, rambling on in idiot fashion. His head was hanging forward and his words were slurred. "This thing won't do, now, Tom Jamison. It won't do. I know yeh, yeh pig-headed devil. Yeh wanta go trompin' off with a bad hurt. It ain't right—now—Tom Jamison—it ain't. Yeh wanta leave me take keer of yeh, Tom Jamison. It ain't—right—it ain't—fer yeh t' go—trompin' off—with a bad hurt—it ain't—ain't—ain't right—it ain't."

In reply the youth climbed a fence and started away. He could hear the tattered man bleating plaintively.

Once he faced about angrily. "What?"

"Look—a—here, now, Tom Jamison—now—it ain't—"

The youth went on. Turning at a distance he saw the tattered man wandering about helplessly in the field.

He now thought that he wished he was dead. He believed that he envied those men whose bodies lay strewn over the grass of the fields and on the fallen leaves of the forest.

The simple questions of the tattered man had been knife thrusts to him. They asserted a society that probes pitilessly at secrets until all is apparent. His late companion's chance persistency made him feel that he could not keep his crime concealed in his bosom. It was sure to be brought plain by one of those arrows which cloud the air and are constantly pricking, discovering, proclaiming those things which are willed to be forever hidden. He admitted that he could not defend himself against this agency. It was not within the power of vigilance.

XI

He became aware that the furnace roar of the battle was growing louder. Great blown clouds had floated to the still heights of air before him. The noise, too, was approaching. The woods filtered men and the fields became dotted.

As he rounded a hillock, he perceived that the roadway was now a crying mass of wagons, teams, and men. From the heaving tangle issued exhortations, commands, imprecations. Fear was sweeping it all along. The cracking whips bit and horses plunged and tugged. The white-topped wagons strained and stumbled in their exertions like fat sheep.

The youth felt comforted in a measure by this sight. They were all retreating. Perhaps, then, he was not so bad after all. He seated himself and watched the terror-stricken wagons. They fled like soft, ungainly animals. All the roarers and lashers served to help him to magnify the dangers and horrors of the engagement that he might try to prove to himself that the thing with which men could charge him was in truth a symmetrical act.

There was an amount of pleasure to him in watching the wild march of this vindication.

Presently the calm head of a forward-going column of infantry appeared in the road. It came swiftly on. Avoiding the obstructions gave it the sinuous movement of a serpent. The men at the head butted mules with their musket stocks. They prodded teamsters indifferent to all howls. The men forced their way through parts of the dense mass by strength. The blunt head of the column pushed. The raving teamsters swore many strange oaths.

The commands to make way had the ring of a great importance in them. The men were going forward to the heart of the din. They were to confront the eager rush of the enemy. They felt the pride of their onward movement when the remainder of the army seemed trying to dribble down this road. They tumbled teams about with a fine feeling that it was no matter so long as their column got to the front in time. This importance made their faces grave and stern. And the backs of the officers were very rigid.

As the youth looked at them the black weight of his woe returned to him. He felt that he was regarding a procession of chosen beings. The separation was as great to him as if they had marched with weapons of flame and banners of sunlight. He could never be like them. He could have wept in his longings.

He searched about in his mind for an adequate malediction for the indefinite cause, the thing upon which men turn the words of final blame. It—whatever it was—was responsible for him, he said. There lay the fault.

The haste of the column to reach the battle seemed to the forlorn young man to be something much finer than stout fighting. Heroes, he thought, could find excuses in that long seething lane. They could retire with perfect self-respect and make excuses to the stars.

He wondered what those men had eaten that they could be in such haste to force their way to grim chances of death. As he watched, his envy grew until he thought that he wished to change lives with one of them. He would have liked to have used a tremendous force, he said, throw off himself and become a better. Swift pictures of himself, apart, yet in himself, came to him—a blue desperate figure leading lurid charges with one knee forward and a broken blade high—a blue, determined figure standing before a crimson and steel assault, getting calmly killed on a high place before the eyes of all. He thought of the magnificent pathos of his dead body.

These thoughts uplifted him. He felt the quiver of war desire. In his ears, he heard the ring of victory. He knew the frenzy of a rapid successful charge. The music of the trampling feet, the sharp voices, the clanking arms of the column near him made him soar on the red wings of war. For a few moments he was sublime.

He thought that he was about to start for the front. Indeed, he saw a picture of himself, dust-stained, haggard, panting, flying to the front at the proper moment to seize and throttle the dark, leering witch of calamity.

Then the difficulties of the thing began to drag at him. He hesitated, balancing awkwardly on one foot.

He had no rifle; he could not fight with his hands, said he resentfully to his plan. Well, rifles could be had for the picking. They were extraordinarily profuse.

Also, he continued, it would be a miracle if he found his regiment. Well, he could fight with any regiment.

He started forward slowly. He stepped as if he expected to tread upon some explosive thing. Doubts and he were struggling.

He would truly be a worm if any of his comrades should see him returning thus, the marks of his flight upon him. There was a reply that the intent fighters did not care for what happened rearward saving that no hostile bayonets appeared there. In the battle-blur his face would, in a way, be hidden, like the face of a cowled man.

But then he said that his tireless fate would bring forth, when the strife lulled for a moment, a man to ask of him an explanation. In imagination he felt the scrutiny of his companions as he painfully labored through some lies.

Eventually, his courage expended itself upon these objections. The debates drained him of his fire.

He was not cast down by this defeat of his plan, for, upon studying the affair carefully, he could not but admit that the objections were very formidable.

Furthermore, various ailments had begun to cry out. In their presence he could not persist in flying high with the wings of war; they rendered it almost impossible for him to see himself in a heroic light. He tumbled headlong.

He discovered that he had a scorching thirst. His face was so dry and grimy that he thought he could feel his skin crackle. Each bone of his body had an ache in it, and seemingly threatened to break with each movement. His feet were like two sores. Also, his body was calling for food. It was more powerful than a direct hunger. There was a dull, weightlike feeling in his stomach, and, when he tried to walk, his head swayed and he tottered. He could not see with distinctness. Small patches of green mist floated before his vision.

While he had been tossed by many emotions, he had not been aware of ailments. Now they beset him and made clamor. As he was at last compelled to pay attention to them, his capacity for self-hate was multiplied.

In despair, he declared that he was not like those others. He now conceded it to be impossible that he should ever become a hero. He was a craven loon. Those pictures of glory were piteous things. He groaned from his heart and went staggering off.

A certain mothlike quality within him kept him in the vicinity of the battle. He had a great desire to see, and to get news. He wished to know who was winning.

He told himself that, despite his unprecedented suffering, he had never lost his greed for a victory, yet, he said, in a half-apologetic manner to his conscience, he could not but know that a defeat for the army this time might mean many favorable things for him. The blows of the enemy would splinter regiments into fragments. Thus, many men of courage, he considered, would be obliged to desert the colors and scurry like chickens. He would appear as one of them. They would be sullen brothers in distress, and he could then easily believe he had not run any farther or faster than they. And if he himself could believe in his virtuous perfection, he conceived that there would be small trouble in convincing all others.

He said, as if in excuse for this hope, that previously the army had encountered great defeats and in a few months had shaken off all blood and tradition of them, emerging as bright and valiant as a new one; thrusting out of sight the memory of disaster, and appearing with the valor and confidence of unconquered legions. The shrilling voices of the people at home would pipe dismally for a time, but various generals were usually compelled to listen to these ditties. He of course felt no compunctions for proposing a general as a sacrifice. He could not tell who the chosen for the barbs might be, so he could center no direct sympathy upon him. The people were afar and he did not conceive public opinion to be accurate at long range. It was quite probable they would hit the wrong man who, after he had recovered from his amazement would perhaps spend the rest of his days in writing replies to the songs of his alleged failure. It would be very unfortunate, no doubt, but in this case a general was of no consequence to the youth.

In a defeat there would be a roundabout vindication of himself. He thought it would prove, in a manner, that he had fled early because of his superior powers of perception. A serious prophet upon predicting a flood should be the first man to climb a tree. This would demonstrate that he was indeed a seer.

A moral vindication was regarded by the youth as a very important thing. Without salve, he could not, he thought, wear the sore badge of his dishonor through life. With his heart continually assuring him that he was despicable, he could not exist without making it, through his actions, apparent to all men.

If the army had gone gloriously on he would be lost. If the din meant that now his army's flags were tilted forward he was a condemned wretch. He would be compelled to doom himself to isolation. If the men were advancing, their indifferent feet were trampling upon his chances for a successful life.

As these thoughts went rapidly through his mind, he turned upon them and tried to thrust them away. He denounced himself as a villain. He said that he was the most unutterably selfish man in existence. His mind pictured the soldiers who would place their defiant bodies before the spear of the yelling battle fiend, and as he saw their dripping corpses on an imagined field, he said that he was their murderer.

Again he thought that he wished he was dead. He believed that he envied a corpse. Thinking of the slain, he achieved a great contempt for some of them, as if they were guilty for thus becoming lifeless. They might have been killed by lucky chances, he said, before they had had opportunities to flee or before they had been really tested. Yet they would receive laurels from tradition. He cried out bitterly that their crowns were stolen and their robes of glorious memories were shams. However, he still said that it was a great pity he was not as they.

A defeat of the army had suggested itself to him as a means of escape from the consequences of his fall. He considered, now, however, that it was useless to think of such a possibility. His education had been that success for that mighty blue machine was certain; that it would make victories as a contrivance turns out buttons. He presently discarded all his speculations in the other direction. He returned to the creed of soldiers.

When he perceived again that it was not possible for the army to be defeated, he tried to bethink him of a fine tale which he could take back to his regiment, and with it turn the expected shafts of derision.

But, as he mortally feared these shafts, it became impossible for him to invent a tale he felt he could trust. He experimented with many schemes, but threw them aside one by one as flimsy. He was quick to see vulnerable places in them all.

Furthermore, he was much afraid that some arrow of scorn might lay him mentally low before he could raise his protecting tale.

He imagined the whole regiment saying: "Where's Henry Fleming? He run, didn't 'e? Oh, my!" He recalled various persons who would be quite sure to leave him no peace about it. They would doubtless question him with sneers, and laugh at his stammering hesitation. In the next engagement they would try to keep watch of him to discover when he would run.

Wherever he went in camp, he would encounter insolent and lingeringly cruel stares. As he imagined himself passing near a crowd of comrades, he could hear one say, "There he goes!"

Then, as if the heads were moved by one muscle, all the faces were turned toward him with wide, derisive grins. He seemed to hear some one make a humorous remark in a low tone. At it the others all crowed and cackled. He was a slang phrase.

XII

The column that had butted stoutly at the obstacles in the road-way was barely out of the youth's sight before he saw dark waves of men come sweeping out of the woods and down through the fields. He knew at once that the steel fibers had been washed from their hearts. They were bursting from their coats and their equipments as from entanglements. They charged down upon him like terrified buffaloes.

Behind them blue smoke curled and clouded above the treetops, and through the thickets he could sometimes see a distant pink glare. The voices of the cannon were clamoring in interminable chorus.

The youth was horrorstricken. He stared in agony and amazement. He forgot that he was engaged in combating the universe. He threw aside his mental pamphlets on the philosophy of the retreated and rules for the guidance of the damned.

The fight was lost. The dragons were coming with invincible strides. The army, helpless in the matted thickets and blinded by the overhanging night, was going to be swallowed. War, the red animal, war, the blood-swollen god, would have bloated fill.

Within him something bade to cry out. He had the impulse to make a rallying speech, to sing a battle hymn, but he could only get his tongue to call into the air: "Wh—why—what—what's th' matter?"

Soon he was in the midst of them. They were leaping and scampering all about him. Their blanched faces shone in the dusk. They seemed, for the most part, to be very burly men. The youth turned from one to another of them as they galloped along. His incoherent questions were lost. They were heedless of his appeals. They did not seem to see him.

They sometimes gabbled insanely. One huge man was asking of the sky: "Say, where de plank road? Where de plank road!" It was if he had lost a child. He wept in his pain and dismay.

Presently, men were running hither and thither in all ways. The artillery booming, forward, rearward, and on the flanks made jumble of ideas of direction. Landmarks had vanished into the gathered gloom. The youth began to imagine that he had got into the center of the tremendous quarrel, and he could perceive no way out of it. From the mouths of the fleeing men came a thousand wild questions, but no one made answers.

The youth, after rushing about and throwing interrogations at the heedless bands of retreating infantry, finally clutched a man by the arm. They swung around face to face.

"Why—why—" stammered the youth struggling with his balking tongue.

The man screamed: "Let go me! Let go me!" His face was livid and his eyes were rolling uncontrolled. He was heaving and panting. He still grasped his rifle, perhaps having forgotten to release his hold upon it. He tugged frantically, and the youth being compelled to lean forward was dragged several paces.

"Let go me! Let go me!"

"Why—why—" stuttered the youth.

"Well, then!" bawled the man in a lurid rage. He adroitly and fiercely swung his rifle. It crushed upon the youth's head. The man ran on.

The youth's fingers had turned to paste upon the other's arm. The energy was smitten from his muscles. He saw the flaming wings of lightning flash before his vision. There was a deafening rumble of thunder within his head.

Suddenly his legs seemed to die. He sank writhing to the ground. He tried to arise. In his efforts against the numbing pain he was like a man wrestling with a creature of the air.

There was a sinister struggle.

Sometimes he would achieve a position half erect, battle with the air for a moment, and then fall again, grabbing at the grass. His face was of a clammy pallor. Deep groans were wrenched from him.

At last, with a twisting movement, he got upon his hands and knees, and from thence, like a babe trying to walk, to his feet. Pressing his hands to his temples he went lurching over the grass.

He fought an intense battle with his body. His dulled senses wished him to swoon and he opposed them stubbornly, his mind portraying unknown dangers and mutilations if he should fall upon the field. He went tall soldier fashion. He imagined secluded spots where he could fall and be unmolested. To search for one he strove against the tide of his pain.

Once he put his hand to the top of his head and timidly touched the wound. The scratching pain of the contact made him draw a long breath through his clenched teeth. His fingers were dabbled with blood. He regarded them with a fixed stare.

Around him he could hear the grumble of jolted cannon as the scurrying horses were lashed toward the front. Once, a young officer on a besplashed charger nearly ran him down. He turned and watched the mass of guns, men, and horses sweeping in a wide curve toward a gap in a fence. The officer was making excited motions with a gauntleted hand. The guns followed the teams with an air of unwillingness, of being dragged by the heels.

Some officers of the scattered infantry were cursing and railing like fishwives. Their scolding voices could be heard above the din. Into the unspeakable jumble in the roadway rode a squadron of cavalry. The faded yellow of their facings shone bravely. There was a mighty altercation.

The artillery were assembling as if for a conference.

The blue haze of evening was upon the field. The lines of forest were long purple shadows. One cloud lay along the western sky partly smothering the red.

As the youth left the scene behind him, he heard the guns suddenly roar out. He imagined them shaking in black rage. They belched and howled like brass devils guarding a gate. The soft air was filled with the tremendous remonstrance. With it came the shattering peal of opposing infantry. Turning to look behind him, he could see sheets of orange light illumine the shadowy distance. There were subtle and sudden lightnings in the far air. At times he thought he could see heaving masses of men.

He hurried on in the dusk. The day had faded until he could barely distinguish place for his feet. The purple darkness was filled with men who lectured and jabbered. Sometimes he could see them gesticulating against the blue and somber sky. There seemed to be a great ruck of men and munitions spread about in the forest and in the fields.

The little narrow roadway now lay lifeless. There were overturned wagons like sun-dried boulders. The bed of the former torrent was choked with the bodies of horses and splintered parts of war machines.

It had come to pass that his wound pained him but little. He was afraid to move rapidly, however, for a dread of disturbing it. He held his head very still and took many precautions against stumbling. He was filled with anxiety, and his face was pinched and drawn in anticipation of the pain of any sudden mistake of his feet in the gloom.

His thoughts, as he walked, fixed intently upon his hurt. There was a cool, liquid feeling about it and he imagined blood moving slowly down under his hair. His head seemed swollen to a size that made him think his neck to be inadequate.

The new silence of his wound made much worriment. The little blistering voices of pain that had called out from his scalp were, he thought, definite in their expression of danger. By them he believed he could measure his plight. But when they remained ominously silent he became frightened and imagined terrible fingers that clutched into his brain.

Amid it he began to reflect upon various incidents and conditions of the past. He bethought him of certain meals his mother had cooked at home, in which those dishes of which he was particularly fond had occupied prominent positions. He saw the spread table. The pine walls of the kitchen were glowing in the warm light from the stove. Too, he remembered how he and his companions used to go from the schoolhouse to the bank of a shaded pool. He saw his clothes in disorderly array upon the grass of the bank. He felt the swash of the fragrant water upon his body. The leaves of the overhanging maple rustled with melody in the wind of youthful summer.

He was overcome presently by a dragging weariness. His head hung forward and his shoulders were stooped as if he were bearing a great bundle. His feet shuffled along the ground.

He held continuous arguments as to whether he should lie down and sleep at some near spot, or force himself on until he reached a certain haven. He often tried to dismiss the question, but his body persisted in rebellion and his senses nagged at him like pampered babies.

At last he heard a cheery voice near his shoulder: "Yeh seem t' be in a pretty bad way, boy?"

The youth did not look up, but he assented with thick tongue. "Uh!"

The owner of the cheery voice took him firmly by the arm. "Well," he said, with a round laugh, "I'm goin' your way. Th' hull gang is goin' your way. An' I guess I kin give yeh a lift." They began to walk like a drunken man and his friend.

As they went along, the man questioned the youth and assisted him with the replies like one manipulating the mind of a child. Sometimes he interjected anecdotes. "What reg'ment do yeh b'long teh? Eh? What's that? Th' 304th N'York? Why, what corps is that in? Oh, it is? Why, I thought they wasn't engaged t'-day—they're 'way over in th' center. Oh, they was, eh? Well, pretty nearly everybody got their share 'a fightin' t'-day. By dad, I give myself up fer dead any number 'a times. There was shootin' here an' shootin' there, an' hollerin' here an' hollerin' there, in th' damn' darkness, until I couldn't tell t' save m' soul which side I was on. Sometimes I thought I was sure 'nough from Ohier, an' other times I could a' swore I was from th' bitter end of Florida. It was th' most mixed up dern thing I ever see. An' these here hull woods is a reg'lar mess. It'll be a miracle if we find our reg'ments t'-night. Pretty soon, though, we'll meet a-plenty of guards an' provost-guards, an' one thing an' another. Ho! there they go with an off'cer, I guess. Look at his hand a-draggin'. He's got all th' war he wants, I bet. He won't be talkin' so big about his reputation an' all when they go t' sawin' off his leg. Poor feller! My brother's got whiskers jest like that. How did yeh git 'way over here, anyhow? Your reg'ment is a long way from here, ain't it? Well, I guess we can find it. Yeh know there was a boy killed in my comp'ny t'-day that I thought th' world an' all of.

Jack was a nice feller. By ginger, it hurt like thunder t' see ol' Jack jest git knocked flat. We was a-standin' purty peaceable for a spell, 'though there was men runnin' ev'ry way all 'round us, an' while we was a-standin' like that, 'long come a big fat feller. He began t' peck at Jack's elbow, an' he ses: 'Say, where's th' road t' th' river?' An' Jack, he never paid no attention, an' th' feller kept on a-peckin' at his elbow an' sayin': 'Say, where's th' road t' th' river?' Jack was a-lookin' ahead all th' time tryin' t' see th' Johnnies comin' through th' woods, an' he never paid no attention t' this big fat feller for a long time, but at last he turned 'round an' he ses: 'Ah, go t' hell an' find th' road t' th' river!' An' jest then a shot slapped him bang on th' side th' head. He was a sergeant, too. Them was his last words. Thunder, I wish we was sure a' findin' our reg'ments t'-night. It's goin' t' be long huntin'. But I guess we kin do it."

In the search which followed, the man of the cheery voice seemed to the youth to possess a wand of a magic kind. He threaded the mazes of the tangled forest with a strange fortune. In encounter with guards and patrols he displayed the keenness of a detective and the valor of a gamin. Obstacles fell before him and became of assistance. The youth, with his chin still on his breast, stood woodenly by while his companion beat ways and means out of sullen things.

The forest seemed a vast hive of men buzzing about in frantic circles, but the cheery man conducted the youth without mistakes, until at last he began to chuckle with glee and self-satisfaction. "Ah, there yeh are! See that fire?"

The youth nodded stupidly.

"Well, there's where your reg'ment is. An' now, good-by, ol' boy, good luck t' yeh."

A warm and strong hand clasped the youth's languid fingers for an instant, and then he heard a cheerful and audacious whistling as the man strode away. As he who had so befriended him was thus passing out of his life, it suddenly occurred to the youth that he had not once seen his face.

XIII

The youth went slowly toward the fire indicated by his departed friend. As he reeled, he bethought him of the welcome his comrades would give him. He had a conviction that he would soon feel in his sore heart the barbed missiles of ridicule. He had no strength to invent a tale; he would be a soft target.

He made vague plans to go off into the deeper darkness and hide, but they were all destroyed by the voices of exhaustion and pain from his body.

His ailments, clamoring, forced him to seek the place of food and rest, at whatever cost.

He swung unsteadily toward the fire. He could see the forms of men throwing black shadows in the red light, and as he went nearer it became known to him in some way that the ground was strewn with sleeping men.

Of a sudden he confronted a black and monstrous figure. A rifle barrel caught some glinting beams. "Halt! halt!" He was dismayed for a moment, but he presently thought that he recognized the nervous voice. As he stood tottering before the rifle barrel, he called out: "Why, hello, Wilson, you—you here?"

The rifle was lowered to a position of caution and the loud soldier came slowly forward. He peered into the youth's face. "That you, Henry?"

"Yes, it's—it's me."

"Well, well, ol' boy," said the other, "by ginger, I'm glad t' see yeh! I give yeh up fer a goner. I thought yeh was dead sure enough." There was husky emotion in his voice.

The youth found that now he could barely stand upon his feet. There was a sudden sinking of his forces. He thought he must hasten to produce his tale to protect him from the missiles already on the lips of his redoubtable comrades. So, staggering before the loud soldier, he began: "Yes, yes. I've—I've had an awful time. I've been all over. Way over on th' right. Ter'ble fightin' over there. I had an awful time. I got separated from the reg'ment. Over on th' right, I got shot. In th' head. I never see sech fightin'. Awful time. I don't see how I could a' got separated from th' reg'ment. I got shot, too."

His friend had stepped forward quickly. "What? Got shot? Why didn't yeh say so first? Poor ol' boy, we must—hol' on a minnit; what am I doin'? I'll call Simpson."

Another figure at that moment loomed in the gloom. They could see that it was the corporal. "Who yeh talkin' to, Wilson?" he demanded. His voice was anger-toned. "Who yeh talkin' to? Yeh th' derndest sentinel— why—hello, Henry, you here? Why, I thought you was dead four hours ago! Great Jerusalem, they keep turnin' up every ten minutes or so! We thought we'd lost forty-two men by straight count, but if they keep on a-comin' this way, we'll git th' comp'ny all back by mornin' yit. Where was yeh?"

"Over on th' right. I got separated"—began the youth with considerable glibness.

But his friend had interrupted hastily. "Yes, an' he got shot in th' head an' he's in a fix, an' we must see t' him right away." He rested his rifle in the hollow of his left arm and his right around the youth's shoulder.

"Gee, it must hurt like thunder!" he said.

The youth leaned heavily upon his friend. "Yes, it hurts—hurts a good deal," he replied. There was a faltering in his voice.

"Oh," said the corporal. He linked his arm in the youth's and drew him forward. "Come on, Henry. I'll take keer 'a yeh."

As they went on together the loud private called out after them: "Put 'im t' sleep in my blanket, Simpson. An'—hol' on a minnit—here's my canteen. It's full 'a coffee. Look at his head by th' fire an' see how it looks. Maybe it's a pretty bad un. When I git relieved in a couple 'a minnits, I'll be over an' see t' him."

The youth's senses were so deadened that his friend's voice sounded from afar and he could scarcely feel the pressure of the corporal's arm. He submitted passively to the latter's directing strength. His head was in the old manner hanging forward upon his breast. His knees wobbled.

The corporal led him into the glare of the fire. "Now, Henry," he said, "let's have look at yer ol' head."

The youth sat obediently and the corporal, laying aside his rifle, began to fumble in the bushy hair of his comrade. He was obliged to turn the other's head so that the full flush of the fire light would beam upon it. He puckered his mouth with a critical air. He drew back his lips and whistled through his teeth when his fingers came in contact with the splashed blood and the rare wound.

"Ah, here we are!" he said. He awkwardly made further investigations. "Jest as I thought," he added, presently. "Yeh've been grazed by a ball. It's raised a queer lump jest as if some feller had lammed yeh on th' head with a club. It stopped a-bleedin' long time ago. Th' most about it is that in th' mornin' yeh'll feel that a number ten hat wouldn't fit yeh. An' your head'll be all het up an' dry as burnt pork. An' yeh may get a lot 'a other sicknesses, too, by mornin'. Yeh can't never tell. Still, I don't much think so. It's jest a damn' good belt on th' head, an' nothin' more. Now, you jest sit here an' don't move, while I go rout out th' relief. Then I'll send Wilson t' take keer 'a yeh."

The corporal went away. The youth remained on the ground like a parcel. He stared with a vacant look into the fire.

After a time he aroused, for some part, and the things about him began to take form. He saw that the ground in the deep shadows was cluttered with men, sprawling in every conceivable posture. Glancing narrowly into the more distant darkness, he caught occasional glimpses of visages that loomed pallid and ghostly, lit with a phosphorescent glow. These faces expressed in their lines the deep stupor of the tired soldiers. They made them appear like men drunk with wine. This bit of forest might have appeared to an ethereal wanderer as a scene of the result of some frightful debauch.

On the other side of the fire the youth observed an officer asleep, seated bolt upright, with his back against a tree. There was something perilous in his position. Badgered by dreams, perhaps, he swayed with little bounces and starts, like an old, toddy-stricken grandfather in a chimney corner. Dust and stains were upon his face. His lower jaw hung down as if lacking strength to assume its normal position. He was the picture of an exhausted soldier after a feast of war.

He had evidently gone to sleep with his sword in his arms. These two had slumbered in an embrace, but the weapon had been allowed in time to fall unheeded to the ground. The brass-mounted hilt lay in contact with some parts of the fire.

Within the gleam of rose and orange light from the burning sticks were other soldiers, snoring and heaving, or lying deathlike in slumber. A few pairs of legs were stuck forth, rigid and straight. The shoes displayed the mud or dust of marches and bits of rounded trousers, protruding from the blankets, showed rents and tears from hurried pitchings through the dense brambles.

The fire cackled musically. From it swelled light smoke. Overhead the foliage moved softly. The leaves, with their faces turned toward the blaze, were colored shifting hues of silver, often edged with red. Far off to the right, through a window in the forest, could be seen a handful of stars lying, like glittering pebbles, on the black level of the night.

Occasionally, in this low-arched hall, a soldier would arouse and turn his body to a new position, the experience of his sleep having taught him of uneven and objectionable places upon the ground under him. Or, perhaps, he would lift himself to a sitting posture, blink at the fire for an unintelligent moment, throw a swift glance at his prostrate companion, and then cuddle down again with a grunt of sleepy content.

The youth sat in a forlorn heap until his friend, the loud young soldier, came, swinging two canteens by their light strings. "Well, now, Henry, ol' boy," said the latter, "we'll have yeh fixed up in jest about a minnit."

He had the bustling ways of an amateur nurse. He fussed around the fire and stirred the sticks to brilliant exertions. He made his patient drink largely from the canteen that contained the coffee. It was to the youth a delicious draught. He tilted his head afar back and held the canteen long to his lips. The cool mixture went caressingly down his blistered throat. Having finished, he sighed with comfortable delight.

The loud young soldier watched his comrade with an air of satisfaction. He later produced an extensive handkerchief from his pocket. He folded it into a manner of bandage and soused water from the other canteen upon the middle of it. This crude arrangement he bound over the youth's head, tying the ends in a queer knot at the back of the neck.

"There," he said, moving off and surveying his deed, "yeh look like th' devil, but I bet yeh feel better."

The youth contemplated his friend with grateful eyes. Upon his aching and swelling head the cold cloth was like a tender woman's hand.

"Yeh don't holler ner say nothin'," remarked his friend approvingly. "I know I'm a blacksmith at takin' keer 'a sick folks, an' yeh never squeaked. Yer a good un, Henry. Most 'a men would a' been in th' hospital long ago. A shot in th' head ain't foolin' business."

The youth made no reply, but began to fumble with the buttons of his jacket.

"Well, come, now," continued his friend, "come on. I must put yeh t' bed an' see that yeh git a good night's rest."

The other got carefully erect, and the loud young soldier led him among the sleeping forms lying in groups and rows. Presently he stooped and picked up his blankets. He spread the rubber one upon the ground and placed the woolen one about the youth's shoulders.

"There now," he said, "lie down an' git some sleep."

The youth, with his manner of doglike obedience, got carefully down like a crone stooping. He stretched out with a murmur of relief and comfort. The ground felt like the softest couch.

But of a sudden he ejaculated: "Hol' on a minnit! Where you goin' t' sleep?"

His friend waved his hand impatiently. "Right down there by yeh."

"Well, but hol' on a minnit," continued the youth. "What yeh goin' t' sleep in? I've got your—"

The loud young soldier snarled: "Shet up an' go on t' sleep. Don't be makin' a damn' fool 'a yerself," he said severely.

After the reproof the youth said no more. An exquisite drowsiness had spread through him. The warm comfort of the blanket enveloped him and made a gentle languor. His head fell forward on his crooked arm and his weighted lids went softly down over his eyes. Hearing a splatter of musketry from the distance, he wondered indifferently if those men sometimes slept. He gave a long sigh, snuggled down into his blanket, and in a moment was like his comrades.

XIV

When the youth awoke it seemed to him that he had been asleep for a thousand years, and he felt sure that he opened his eyes upon an unexpected world. Gray mists were slowly shifting before the first efforts of the sun rays. An impending splendor could be seen in the eastern sky. An icy dew had chilled his face, and immediately upon arousing he curled farther down into his blankets. He stared for a while at the leaves overhead, moving in a heraldic wind of the day.

The distance was splintering and blaring with the noise of fighting. There was in the sound an expression of a deadly persistency, as if it had not begun and was not to cease.

About him were the rows and groups of men that he had dimly seen the previous night. They were getting a last draught of sleep before the awakening. The gaunt, careworn features and dusty figures were made plain by this quaint light at the dawning, but it dressed the skin of the men in corpselike hues and made the tangled limbs appear pulseless and dead. The youth started up with a little cry when his eyes first swept over this motionless mass of men, thick-spread upon the ground, pallid, and in strange postures. His disordered mind interpreted the hall of the forest as a charnel place. He believed for an instant that he was in the house of the dead, and he did not dare to move lest these corpses start up, squalling and squawking. In a second, however, he achieved his proper mind. He swore a complicated oath at himself. He saw that this somber picture was not a fact of the present, but a mere prophecy.

He heard then the noise of a fire crackling briskly in the cold air, and, turning his head, he saw his friend pottering busily about a small blaze. A few other figures moved in the fog, and he heard the hard cracking of axe blows.

Suddenly there was a hollow rumble of drums. A distant bugle sang faintly. Similar sounds, varying in strength, came from near and far over the forest. The bugles called to each other like brazen gamecocks. The near thunder of the regimental drums rolled.

The body of men in the woods rustled. There was a general uplifting of heads. A murmuring of voices broke upon the air. In it there was much bass of grumbling oaths. Strange gods were addressed in condemnation of the early hours necessary to correct war. An officer's peremptory tenor rang out and quickened the stiffened movement of the men. The tangled limbs unraveled. The corpse-hued faces were hidden behind fists that twisted slowly in the eye sockets.

The youth sat up and gave vent to an enormous yawn. "Thunder!" he remarked petulantly. He rubbed his eyes, and then putting up his hand felt carefully of the bandage over his wound. His friend, perceiving him to be awake, came from the fire. "Well, Henry, ol' man, how do yeh feel this mornin'?" he demanded.

The youth yawned again. Then he puckered his mouth to a little pucker. His head, in truth, felt precisely like a melon, and there was an unpleasant sensation at his stomach.

"Oh, Lord, I feel pretty bad," he said.

"Thunder!" exclaimed the other. "I hoped ye'd feel all right this mornin'. Let's see th' bandage—I guess it's slipped." He began to tinker at the wound in rather a clumsy way until the youth exploded.

"Gosh-dern it!" he said in sharp irritation; "you're the hangdest man I ever saw! You wear muffs on your hands. Why in good thunderation can't you be more easy? I'd rather you'd stand off an' throw guns at it. Now, go slow, an' don't act as if you was nailing down carpet."

He glared with insolent command at his friend, but the latter answered soothingly. "Well, well, come now, an' git some grub," he said. "Then, maybe, yeh'll feel better."

At the fireside the loud young soldier watched over his comrade's wants with tenderness and care. He was very busy marshaling the little vagabonds of tin cups and pouring into them the streaming, iron colored mixture from a small and sooty tin pail. He had some fresh meat, which he roasted hurriedly upon a stick. He sat down then and contemplated the youth's appetite with glee.

The youth took note of a remarkable change in his comrade since those days of camp life upon the river bank. He seemed no more to be continually regarding the proportions of his personal prowess. He was not furious at small words that pricked his conceits. He was no more a loud young soldier. There was about him now a fine reliance. He showed a quiet belief in his purposes and his abilities. And this inward confidence evidently enabled him to be indifferent to little words of other men aimed at him.

The youth reflected. He had been used to regarding his comrade as a blatant child with an audacity grown from his inexperience, thoughtless, headstrong, jealous, and filled with a tinsel courage. A swaggering babe accustomed to strut in his own dooryard. The youth wondered where had been born these new eyes; when his comrade had made the great discovery that there were many men who would refuse to be subjected by him. Apparently, the other had now climbed a peak of wisdom from which he could perceive himself as a very wee thing. And the youth saw that ever after it would be easier to live in his friend's neighborhood.

His comrade balanced his ebony coffee cup on his knee. "Well, Henry," he said, "what d'yeh think th' chances are? D'yeh think we'll wallop 'em?"

The youth considered for a moment. "Day-b'fore-yestirday," he finally replied, with boldness, "you would 'a bet you'd lick the hull kit-an'-boodle all by yourself."

His friend looked a trifle amazed. "Would I?" he asked. He pondered. "Well, perhaps I would," he decided at last. He stared humbly at the fire.

The youth was quite disconcerted at this surprising reception of his remarks. "Oh, no, you wouldn't either," he said, hastily trying to retrace.

But the other made a deprecating gesture. "Oh, yeh needn't mind, Henry," he said. "I believe I was a pretty big fool in those days." He spoke as after a lapse of years.

There was a little pause.

"All th' officers say we've got th' rebs in a pretty tight box," said the friend, clearing his throat in a commonplace way. "They all seem t' think we've got 'em jest where we want 'em."

"I don't know about that," the youth replied. "What I seen over on th' right makes me think it was th' other way about. From where I was, it looked as if we was gettin' a good poundin' yestirday."

"D'yeh think so?" inquired the friend. "I thought we handled 'em pretty rough yestirday."

"Not a bit," said the youth. "Why, lord, man, you didn't see nothing of the fight. Why!" Then a sudden thought came to him. "Oh! Jim Conklin's dead."

His friend started. "What? Is he? Jim Conklin?"

The youth spoke slowly. "Yes. He's dead. Shot in th' side."

"Yeh don't say so. Jim Conklin . . . poor cuss!"

All about them were other small fires surrounded by men with their little black utensils. From one of these near came sudden sharp voices in a row. It appeared that two light-footed soldiers had been teasing a huge, bearded man, causing him to spill coffee upon his blue knees. The man had gone into a rage and had sworn comprehensively. Stung by his language, his tormentors had immediately bristled at him with a great show of resenting unjust oaths. Possibly there was going to be a fight.

The friend arose and went over to them, making pacific motions with his arms. "Oh, here, now, boys, what's th' use?" he said. "We'll be at th' rebs in less'n an hour. What's th' good fightin' 'mong ourselves?"

One of the light-footed soldiers turned upon him red-faced and violent. "Yeh needn't come around here with yer preachin'. I s'pose yeh don't approve a' fightin' since Charley Morgan licked yeh; but I don't see what business this here is 'a yours or anybody else."

"Well, it ain't," said the friend mildly. "Still I hate t' see—"

That was a tangled argument.

"Well, he—," said the two, indicating their opponent with accusative forefingers.

The huge soldier was quite purple with rage. He pointed at the two soldiers with his great hand, extended clawlike. "Well, they—"

But during this argumentative time the desire to deal blows seemed to pass, although they said much to each other. Finally the friend returned to his old seat. In a short while the three antagonists could be seen together in an amiable bunch.

"Jimmie Rogers ses I'll have t' fight him after th' battle t'-day," announced the friend as he again seated himself. "He ses he don't allow no interferin' in his business. I hate t' see th' boys fightin' 'mong themselves."

The youth laughed. "Yer changed a good bit. Yeh ain't at all like yeh was, I remember when you an' that Irish feller—" He stopped and laughed again.

"No, I didn't use t' be that way," said his friend thoughtfully. "That's true 'nough."

"Well, I didn't mean—" began the youth.

The friend made another deprecatory gesture. "Oh, yeh needn't mind, Henry."

There was another little pause.

"Th' reg'ment lost over half th' men yestirday," remarked the friend eventually. "I thought a course they was all dead, but, laws, they kep' a-comin' back last night until it seems, after all, we didn't lose but a few. They'd been scattered all over, wanderin' around in th' woods, fightin' with other reg'ments, an' everything. Jest like you done."

"So?" said the youth.

XV

The regiment was standing at order arms at the side of a lane, waiting for the command to march, when suddenly the youth remembered the little packet enwrapped in a faded yellow envelope which the loud young soldier with lugubrious words had entrusted to him. It made him start. He uttered an exclamation and turned toward his comrade.

"Wilson!"

"What?"

His friend, at his side in the ranks, was thoughtfully staring down the road. From some cause his expression was at that moment very meek. The youth, regarding him with sidelong glances, felt impelled to change his purpose. "Oh, nothing," he said.

His friend turned his head in some surprise, "Why, what was yeh goin' t' say?"

"Oh, nothing," repeated the youth.

He resolved not to deal the little blow. It was sufficient that the fact made him glad. It was not necessary to knock his friend on the head with the misguided packet.

He had been possessed of much fear of his friend, for he saw how easily questionings could make holes in his feelings. Lately, he had assured himself that the altered comrade would not tantalize him with a persistent curiosity, but he felt certain that during the first period of leisure his friend would ask him to relate his adventures of the previous day.

He now rejoiced in the possession of a small weapon with which he could prostrate his comrade at the first signs of a cross-examination. He was master. It would now be he who could laugh and shoot the shafts of derision.

The friend had, in a weak hour, spoken with sobs of his own death. He had delivered a melancholy oration previous to his funeral, and had doubtless, in the packet of letters, presented various keepsakes to relatives. But he had not died, and thus he had delivered himself into the hands of the youth.

The latter felt immensely superior to his friend, but he inclined to condescension. He adopted toward him an air of patronizing good humor.

His self-pride was now entirely restored. In the shade of its flourishing growth he stood with braced and self-confident legs, and since nothing could now be discovered he did not shrink from an encounter with the eyes of judges, and allowed no thoughts of his own to keep him from an attitude of manfulness. He had performed his mistakes in the dark, so he was still a man.

Indeed, when he remembered his fortunes of yesterday, and looked at them from a distance he began to see something fine there. He had license to be pompous and veteranlike.

His panting agonies of the past he put out of his sight.

In the present, he declared to himself that it was only the doomed and the damned who roared with sincerity at circumstance. Few but they ever did it. A man with a full stomach and the respect of his fellows had no business to scold about anything that he might think to be wrong in the ways of the universe, or even with the ways of society. Let the unfortunates rail; the others may play marbles.

He did not give a great deal of thought to those battles that lay directly before him. It was not essential that he should plan his ways in regard to them. He had been taught that many obligations of a life were easily avoided. The lessons of yesterday had been that retribution was a laggard and blind. With these facts before him he did not deem it necessary that he should become feverish over the possibilities of the ensuing twenty-four hours. He could leave much to chance. Besides, a faith in himself had secretly blossomed. There was a little flower of confidence growing within him. He was now a man of experience. He had been out among the dragons, he said, and he assured himself that they were not so hideous as he had imagined them. Also, they were inaccurate; they did not sting with precision. A stout heart often defied, and, defying, escaped.

And, furthermore, how could they kill him who was the chosen of gods and doomed to greatness?

He remembered how some of the men had run from the battle. As he recalled their terror-struck faces he felt a scorn for them. They had surely been more fleet and more wild than was absolutely necessary. They were weak mortals. As for himself, he had fled with discretion and dignity.

He was aroused from this reverie by his friend, who, having hitched about nervously and blinked at the trees for a time, suddenly coughed in an introductory way, and spoke.

"Fleming!"

"What?"

The friend put his hand up to his mouth and coughed again. He fidgeted in his jacket.

"Well," he gulped at last, "I guess yeh might as well give me back them letters." Dark, prickling blood had flushed into his cheeks and brow.

"All right, Wilson," said the youth. He loosened two buttons of his coat, thrust in his hand, and brought forth the packet. As he extended it to his friend the latter's face was turned from him.

He had been slow in the act of producing the packet because during it he had been trying to invent a remarkable comment on the affair. He could conjure nothing of sufficient point. He was compelled to allow his friend to escape unmolested with his packet. And for this he took unto himself considerable credit. It was a generous thing.

His friend at his side seemed suffering great shame. As he contemplated him, the youth felt his heart grow more strong and stout. He had never been compelled to blush in such manner for his acts; he was an individual of extraordinary virtues.

He reflected, with condescending pity: "Too bad! Too bad! The poor devil, it makes him feel tough!"

After this incident, and as he reviewed the battle pictures he had seen, he felt quite competent to return home and make the hearts of the people glow with stories of war. He could see himself in a room of warm tints telling tales to listeners. He could exhibit laurels. They were insignificant; still, in a district where laurels were infrequent, they might shine.

He saw his gaping audience picturing him as the central figure in blazing scenes. And he imagined the consternation and the ejaculations of his mother and the young lady at the seminary as they drank his recitals. Their vague feminine formula for beloved ones doing brave deeds on the field of battle without risk of life would be destroyed.

XVI

A sputtering of musketry was always to be heard. Later, the cannon had entered the dispute. In the fog-filled air their voices made a thudding sound. The reverberations were continued. This part of the world led a strange, battleful existence.

The youth's regiment was marched to relieve a command that had lain long in some damp trenches. The men took positions behind a curving line of rifle pits that had been turned up, like a large furrow, along the line of woods. Before them was a level stretch, peopled with short, deformed stumps. From the woods beyond came the dull popping of the skirmishers and pickets, firing in the fog. From the right came the noise of a terrific fracas.

The men cuddled behind the small embankment and sat in easy attitudes awaiting their turn. Many had their backs to the firing. The youth's friend lay down, buried his face in his arms, and almost instantly, it seemed, he was in a deep sleep.

The youth leaned his breast against the brown dirt and peered over at the woods and up and down the line. Curtains of trees interfered with his ways of vision. He could see the low line of trenches but for a short distance. A few idle flags were perched on the dirt hills. Behind them were rows of dark bodies with a few heads sticking curiously over the top.

Always the noise of skirmishers came from the woods on the front and left, and the din on the right had grown to frightful proportions. The guns were roaring without an instant's pause for breath. It seemed that the cannon had come from all parts and were engaged in a stupendous wrangle. It became impossible to make a sentence heard.

The youth wished to launch a joke—a quotation from newspapers. He desired to say, "All quiet on the Rappahannock," but the guns refused to permit even a comment upon their uproar. He never successfully concluded the sentence. But at last the guns stopped, and among the men in the rifle pits rumors again flew, like birds, but they were now for the most part black creatures who flapped their wings drearily near to the ground and refused to rise on any wings of hope. The men's faces grew doleful from the interpreting of omens. Tales of hesitation and uncertainty on the part of those high in place and responsibility came to their ears. Stories of disaster were borne into their minds with many proofs. This din of musketry on the right, growing like a released genie of sound, expressed and emphasized the army's plight.

The men were disheartened and began to mutter. They made gestures expressive of the sentence: "Ah, what more can we do?" And it could always be seen that they were bewildered by the alleged news and could not fully comprehend a defeat.

Before the gray mists had been totally obliterated by the sun rays, the regiment was marching in a spread column that was retiring carefully through the woods. The disordered, hurrying lines of the enemy could sometimes be seen down through the groves and little fields. They were yelling, shrill and exultant.

At this sight the youth forgot many personal matters and became greatly enraged. He exploded in loud sentences. "B'jiminey, we're generaled by a lot 'a lunkheads."

"More than one feller has said that t'day," observed a man.

His friend, recently aroused, was still very drowsy. He looked behind him until his mind took in the meaning of the movement. Then he sighed. "Oh, well, I s'pose we got licked," he remarked sadly.

The youth had a thought that it would not be handsome for him to freely condemn other men. He made an attempt to restrain himself, but the words upon his tongue were too bitter. He presently began a long and intricate denunciation of the commander of the forces.

"Mebbe, it wa'n't all his fault—not all together. He did th' best he knowed. It's our luck t' git licked often," said his friend in a weary tone. He was trudging along with stooped shoulders and shifting eyes like a man who has been caned and kicked.

"Well, don't we fight like the devil? Don't we do all that men can?" demanded the youth loudly.

He was secretly dumbfounded at this sentiment when it came from his lips. For a moment his face lost its valor and he looked guiltily about him. But no one questioned his right to deal in such words, and presently he recovered his air of courage. He went on to repeat a statement he had heard going from group to group at the camp that morning. "The brigadier said he never saw a new reg'ment fight the way we fought yestirday, didn't he? And we didn't do better than any another reg'ment, did we? Well, then, you can't say it's th' army's fault, can you?"

In his reply, the friend's voice was stern. "'A course not," he said. "No man dare say we don't fight like th' devil. No man will ever dare say it. Th' boys fight like hell-roosters. But still—still, we don't have no luck."

"Well, then, if we fight like the devil an' don't ever whip, it must be the general's fault," said the youth grandly and decisively. "And I don't see any sense in fighting and fighting and fighting, yet always losing through some derned old lunkhead of a general."

A sarcastic man who was tramping at the youth's side, then spoke lazily. "Mebbe yeh think yeh fit th' hull battle yestirday, Fleming," he remarked.

The speech pierced the youth. Inwardly he was reduced to an abject pulp by these chance words. His legs quaked privately. He cast a frightened glance at the sarcastic man.

"Why, no," he hastened to say in a conciliating voice, "I don't think I fought the whole battle yesterday."

But the other seemed innocent of any deeper meaning. Apparently, he had no information. It was merely his habit. "Oh!" he replied in the same tone of calm derision.

The youth, nevertheless, felt a threat. His mind shrank from going nearer to the danger, and thereafter he was silent. The significance of the sarcastic man's words took from him all loud moods that would make him appear prominent. He became suddenly a modest person.

There was low-toned talk among the troops. The officers were impatient and snappy, their countenances clouded with the tales of misfortune. The troops, sifting through the forest, were sullen. In the youth's company once a man's laugh rang out. A dozen soldiers turned their faces toward him and frowned with vague displeasure.

The noise of firing dogged their footsteps. Sometimes, it seemed to be driven a little way, but it always returned again with increased insolence. The men muttered and cursed, throwing black looks in its direction.

In a clear space the troops were at last halted. Regiments and brigades, broken and detached through their encounters with thickets, grew together again and lines were faced toward the pursuing bark of the enemy's infantry.

This noise, following like the yellings of eager, metallic hounds, increased to a loud and joyous burst, and then, as the sun went serenely up the sky, throwing illuminating rays into the gloomy thickets, it broke forth into prolonged pealings. The woods began to crackle as if afire.

"Whoop-a-dadee," said a man, "here we are! Everybody fightin'. Blood an' destruction."

"I was willin' t' bet they'd attack as soon as th' sun got fairly up," savagely asserted the lieutenant who commanded the youth's company. He jerked without mercy at his little mustache. He strode to and fro with dark dignity in the rear of his men, who were lying down behind whatever protection they had collected.

A battery had trundled into position in the rear and was thoughtfully shelling the distance. The regiment, unmolested as yet, awaited the moment when the gray shadows of the woods before them should be slashed by the lines of flame. There was much growling and swearing.

"Good Gawd," the youth grumbled, "we're always being chased around like rats! It makes me sick. Nobody seems to know where we go or why we go. We just get fired around from pillar to post and get licked here and get licked there, and nobody knows what it's done for. It makes a man feel like a damn' kitten in a bag. Now, I'd like to know what the eternal thunders we was marched into these woods for anyhow, unless it was to give the rebs a regular pot shot at us. We came in here and got our legs all tangled up in these cussed briers, and then we begin to fight-and the rebs had an easy time of it. Don't tell me it's just luck! I know better. It's this derned old—"

The friend seemed jaded, but he interrupted his comrade with a voice of calm confidence. "It'll turn out all right in th' end," he said.

"Oh, the devil it will! You always talk like a dog-hanged parson. Don't tell me! I know—"

At this time there was an interposition by the savage-minded lieutenant, who was obliged to vent some of his inward dissatisfaction upon his men. "You boys shut right up! There's no need 'a your wastin' your breath in long-winded arguments about this an' that an' th' other. You've been jawin' like a lot 'a old hens. All you've got t' do is to fight, an' you'll get plenty 'a that t' do in about ten minutes. Less talkin' an' more fightin' is what's best for our boys. I never saw sech gabbling jackasses."

He paused, ready to pounce upon any man who might have the temerity to reply. No words being said, he resumed his dignified pacing.

"There's too much chin music an' too little fightin' in this war, anyhow," he said to them, turning his head for a final remark.

The day had grown more white, until the sun shed his full radiance upon the thronged forest. A sort of a gust of battle came sweeping toward that part of the line where lay the youth's regiment. The front shifted a trifle to meet it squarely. There was a wait. In this part of the field there passed slowly the intense moments that precede the tempest.

A single rifle flashed in a thicket before the regiment. In an instant it was joined by many others. There was a mighty song of clashes and crashes that went sweeping through the woods. The guns in the rear, aroused and enraged by shells that had been thrown burr-like at them, suddenly involved themselves in a hideous altercation with another band of guns. The battle roar settled to a rolling thunder, which was a single, long explosion.

In the regiment there was a peculiar kind of hesitation denoted in the attitudes of the men. They were worn, exhausted, having slept but little and labored much. They rolled their eyes toward the advancing battle as they stood awaiting the shock. Some shrank and flinched. They stood as men tied to stakes.

XVII

This advance of the enemy had seemed to the youth like a ruthless hunting. He began to fume with rage and exasperation. He beat his foot upon the ground, and scowled with hate at the swirling smoke that was approaching like a phantom flood. There was a maddening quality in this seeming resolution of the foe to give him no rest, to give him no time to sit down and think. Yesterday he had fought and had fled rapidly. There had been many adventures. For today he felt that he had earned opportunities for contemplative repose. He could have enjoyed portraying to uninitiated listeners various scenes at which he had been a witness or ably discussing the processes of war with other proved men. Too it was important that he should have time for physical recuperation. He was sore and stiff from his experiences. He had received his fill of all exertions, and he wished to rest.

But those other men seemed never to grow weary; they were fighting with their old speed. He had a wild hate for the relentless foe. Yesterday, when he had imagined the universe to be against him, he had hated it, little gods and big gods; today he hated the army of the foe with the same great hatred. He was not going to be badgered of his life, like a kitten chased by boys, he said. It was not well to drive men into final corners; at those moments they could all develop teeth and claws.

He leaned and spoke into his friend's ear. He menaced the woods with a gesture. "If they keep on chasing us, by Gawd, they'd better watch out. Can't stand *too* much."

The friend twisted his head and made a calm reply. "If they keep on a-chasin' us they'll drive us all inteh th' river."

The youth cried out savagely at this statement. He crouched behind a little tree, with his eyes burning hatefully and his teeth set in a curlike snarl. The awkward bandage was still about his head, and upon it, over his wound, there was a spot of dry blood. His hair was wondrously tousled, and some straggling, moving locks hung over the cloth of the bandage down toward his forehead. His jacket and shirt were open at the throat, and exposed his young bronzed neck. There could be seen spasmodic gulpings at his throat.

His fingers twined nervously about his rifle. He wished that it was an engine of annihilating power. He felt that he and his companions were being taunted and derided from sincere convictions that they were poor and puny. His knowledge of his inability to take vengeance for it made his rage into a dark and stormy specter, that possessed him and made him dream of abominable cruelties. The tormentors were flies sucking insolently at his blood, and he thought that he would have given his life for a revenge of seeing their faces in pitiful plights.

The winds of battle had swept all about the regiment, until the one rifle, instantly followed by others, flashed in its front. A moment later the regiment roared forth its sudden and valiant retort. A dense wall of smoke settled slowly down. It was furiously slit and slashed by the knifelike fire from the rifles.

To the youth the fighters resembled animals tossed for a death struggle into a dark pit. There was a sensation that he and his fellows, at bay, were pushing back, always pushing fierce onslaughts of creatures who were slippery. Their beams of crimson seemed to get no purchase upon the bodies of their foes; the latter seemed to evade them with ease, and come through, between, around, and about with unopposed skill.

When, in a dream, it occurred to the youth that his rifle was an impotent stick, he lost sense of everything but his hate, his desire to smash into pulp the glittering smile of victory which he could feel upon the faces of his enemies.

The blue smoke-swallowed line curled and writhed like a snake stepped upon. It swung its ends to and fro in an agony of fear and rage.

The youth was not conscious that he was erect upon his feet. He did not know the direction of the ground. Indeed, once he even lost the habit of balance and fell heavily. He was up again immediately. One thought went through the chaos of his brain at the time. He wondered if he had fallen because he had been shot. But the suspicion flew away at once. He did not think more of it.

He had taken up a first position behind the little tree, with a direct determination to hold it against the world. He had not deemed it possible that his army could that day succeed, and from this he felt the ability to fight harder. But the throng had surged in all ways, until he lost directions and locations, save that he knew where lay the enemy.

The flames bit him, and the hot smoke broiled his skin. His rifle barrel grew so hot that ordinarily he could not have borne it upon his palms; but he kept on stuffing cartridges into it, and pounding them with his clanking, bending ramrod. If he aimed at some changing form through the smoke, he pulled his trigger with a fierce grunt, as if he were dealing a blow of the fist with all his strength.

When the enemy seemed falling back before him and his fellows, he went instantly forward, like a dog who, seeing his foes lagging, turns and insists upon being pursued. And when he was compelled to retire again, he did it slowly, sullenly, taking steps of wrathful despair.

Once he, in his intent hate, was almost alone, and was firing, when all those near him had ceased. He was so engrossed in his occupation that he was not aware of a lull.

He was recalled by a hoarse laugh and a sentence that came to his ears in a voice of contempt and amazement. "Yeh infernal fool, don't yeh know enough t' quit when there ain't anything t' shoot at? Good Gawd!"

He turned then and, pausing with his rifle thrown half into position, looked at the blue line of his comrades. During this moment of leisure they seemed all to be engaged in staring with astonishment at him. They had become spectators. Turning to the front again he saw, under the lifted smoke, a deserted ground.

He looked bewildered for a moment. Then there appeared upon the glazed vacancy of his eyes a diamond point of intelligence. "Oh," he said, comprehending.

He returned to his comrades and threw himself upon the ground. He sprawled like a man who had been thrashed. His flesh seemed strangely on fire, and the sounds of the battle continued in his ears. He groped blindly for his canteen.

The lieutenant was crowing. He seemed drunk with fighting. He called out to the youth: "By heavens, if I had ten thousand wild cats like you I could tear th' stomach outa this war in less'n a week!" He puffed out his chest with large dignity as he said it.

Some of the men muttered and looked at the youth in awestruck ways. It was plain that as he had gone on loading and firing and cursing without the proper intermission, they had found time to regard him. And they now looked upon him as a war devil.

The friend came staggering to him. There was some fright and dismay in his voice. "Are yeh all right, Fleming? Do yeh feel all right? There ain't nothin' th' matter with yeh, Henry, is there?"

"No," said the youth with difficulty. His throat seemed full of knobs and burrs.

These incidents made the youth ponder. It was revealed to him that he had been a barbarian, a beast. He had fought like a pagan who defends his religion. Regarding it, he saw that it was fine, wild, and, in some ways, easy. He had been a tremendous figure, no doubt. By this struggle he had overcome obstacles which he had admitted to be mountains. They had fallen like paper peaks, and he was now what he called a hero. And he had not been aware of the process. He had slept, and, awakening, found himself a knight.

He lay and basked in the occasional stares of his comrades. Their faces were varied in degrees of blackness from the burned powder. Some were utterly smudged. They were reeking with perspiration, and their breaths came hard and wheezing. And from these soiled expanses they peered at him.

"Hot work! Hot work!" cried the lieutenant deliriously. He walked up and down, restless and eager. Sometimes his voice could be heard in a wild, incomprehensible laugh.

When he had a particularly profound thought upon the science of war he always unconsciously addressed himself to the youth.

There was some grim rejoicing by the men. "By thunder, I bet this army'll never see another new reg'ment like us!"

"You bet!

"A dog, a woman, an' a walnut tree,
    Th' more yeh beat 'em, th' better they be!

That's like us."

"Lost a piler men, they did. If an ol' woman swep' up th' woods she'd git a dustpanful."

"Yes, an' if she'll come around ag'in in 'bout an hour she'll git a pile more."

The forest still bore its burden of clamor. From off under the trees came the rolling clatter of the musketry. Each distant thicket seemed a strange porcupine with quills of flame. A cloud of dark smoke, as from smoldering ruins, went up toward the sun now bright and gay in the blue, enameled sky.

XVIII

The ragged line had respite for some minutes, but during its pause the struggle in the forest became magnified until the trees seemed to quiver from the firing and the ground to shake from the rushing of the men. The voices of the cannon were mingled in a long and interminable row. It seemed difficult to live in such an atmosphere. The chests of the men strained for a bit of freshness, and their throats craved water.

There was one shot through the body, who raised a cry of bitter lamentation when came this lull. Perhaps he had been calling out during the fighting also, but at that time no one had heard him. But now the men turned at the woeful complaints of him upon the ground.

"Who is it? Who is it?"

"It's Jimmie Rogers. Jimmie Rogers."

When their eyes first encountered him there was a sudden halt, as if they feared to go near. He was thrashing about in the grass, twisting his shuddering body into many strange postures. He was screaming loudly. This instant's hesitation seemed to fill him with a tremendous, fantastic contempt, and he damned them in shrieked sentences.

The youth's friend had a geographical illusion concerning a stream, and he obtained permission to go for some water. Immediately canteens were showered upon him. "Fill mine, will yeh?" "Bring me some, too." "And me, too." He departed, laden. The youth went with his friend, feeling a desire to throw his heated body onto the stream and, soaking there, drink quarts.

They made a hurried search for the supposed stream, but did not find it. "No water here," said the youth. They turned without delay and began to retrace their steps.

From their position as they again faced toward the place of the fighting, they could of course comprehend a greater amount of the battle than when their visions had been blurred by the hurling smoke of the line. They could see dark stretches winding along the land, and on one cleared space there was a row of guns making gray clouds, which were filled with large flashes of orange-colored flame. Over some foliage they could see the roof of a house. One window, glowing a deep murder red, shone squarely through the leaves. From the edifice a tall leaning tower of smoke went far into the sky.

Looking over their own troops, they saw mixed masses slowly getting into regular form. The sunlight made twinkling points of the bright steel. To the rear there was a glimpse of a distant roadway as it curved over a slope. It was crowded with retreating infantry. From all the interwoven forest arose the smoke and bluster of the battle. The air was always occupied by a blaring.

Near where they stood shells were flip-flapping and hooting. Occasional bullets buzzed in the air and spanged into tree trunks. Wounded men and other stragglers were slinking through the woods.

Looking down an aisle of the grove, the youth and his companion saw a jangling general and his staff almost ride upon a wounded man who was crawling on his hands and knees. The general reined strongly at his charger's open and foamy mouth and guided it with dexterous horsemanship past the man. The latter scrambled in wild and torturing haste. His strength evidently failed as he reached a place of safety. One of his arms suddenly weakened, and he fell, sliding over upon his back. He lay stretched out, breathing gently.

A moment later the small, creaking cavalcade was directly in front of the two soldiers. Another officer, riding with the skillful abandon of a cowboy, galloped his horse to a position directly before the general. The two unnoticed foot soldiers made a little show of going on, but they lingered near in the desire to overhear the conversation. Perhaps, they thought, some great inner historical things would be said.

The general, whom the boys knew as the commander of their division, looked at the other officer and spoke coolly, as if he were criticising his clothes. "Th' enemy's formin' over there for another charge," he said. "It'll be directed against Whiterside, an' I fear they'll break through there unless we work like thunder t' stop them."

The other swore at his restive horse, and then cleared his throat. He made a gesture toward his cap. "It'll be hell t' pay stoppin' them," he said shortly.

"I presume so," remarked the general. Then he began to talk rapidly in a lower tone. He frequently illustrated his words with a pointing finger. The two infantrymen could hear nothing until finally he asked: "What troops can you spare?"

The officer who rode like a cowboy reflected for an instant. "Well," he said, "I had to order in th' 12th to help th' 76th, an' I haven't really got any. But there's th' 304th. They fight like a lot 'a mule drivers. I can spare them best of any."

The youth and his friend exchanged glances of astonishment.

The general spoke sharply. "Get 'em ready, then. I'll watch developments from here, an' send you word when t' start them. It'll happen in five minutes."

As the other officer tossed his fingers toward his cap and, wheeling his horse, started away, the general called out to him in a sober voice: "I don't believe many of your mule drivers will get back."

The other shouted something in reply. He smiled.

With scared faces, the youth and his companion hurried back to the line.

These happenings had occupied an incredibly short time, yet the youth felt that in them he had been made aged. New eyes were given to him. And the most startling thing was to learn suddenly that he was very insignificant. The officer spoke of the regiment as if he referred to a broom. Some part of the woods needed sweeping, perhaps, and he merely indicated a broom in a tone properly indifferent to its fate. It was war, no doubt, but it appeared strange.

As the two boys approached the line, the lieutenant perceived them and swelled with wrath. "Fleming—Wilson—how long does it take yeh to git water, anyhow—where yeh been to?"

But his oration ceased as he saw their eyes, which were large with great tales. "We're goin' t' charge—we're goin' t' charge!" cried the youth's friend, hastening with his news.

"Charge?" said the lieutenant. "Charge? Well, b'Gawd! Now; this is real fightin'." Over his soiled countenance there went a boastful smile. "Charge? Well, b'Gawd!"

A little group of soldiers surrounded the two youths. "Are we, sure 'nough? Well, I'll be derned! Charge? What fer? What at? Wilson, you're lyin'."

"I hope to die," said the youth's friend, pitching his tones to the key of angry remonstrance. "Sure as shooting, I tell you."

And the youth spoke in reinforcement. "Not by a blame sight, he ain't lyin'. We heard 'em talkin'."

They caught sight of two mounted figures a short distance from them. One was the colonel of the regiment and the other was the officer who had received orders from the commander of the division. They were gesticulating at each other. The soldier, pointing at them, interpreted the scene.

One man had a final objection: "How could yeh hear 'em talkin'?" But the men, for a large part, nodded, admitting that previously the two friends had spoken truth.

They settled back into reposeful attitudes with airs of having accepted the matter. And they mused upon it, with a hundred varieties of expression. It was an engrossing thing to think about. Many tightened their belts carefully and hitched at their trousers.

A moment later the officers began to bustle among the men, pushing them into a more compact mass and into a better alignment. They chased those that straggled and fumed at a few men who seemed to show by their attitudes that they had decided to remain at that spot. They were like critical shepherds struggling with sheep.

Presently, the regiment seemed to draw itself up and heave a deep breath. None of the men's faces were mirrors of large thoughts. The soldiers were bended and stooped like sprinters before a signal. Many pairs of glinting eyes peered from the grimy faces toward the curtains of the deeper woods. They seemed to be engaged in deep calculations of time and distance.

They were surrounded by the noises of the monstrous altercation between the two armies. The world was fully interested in other matters. Apparently, the regiment had its small affair to itself.

The youth, turning, shot a quick, inquiring glance at his friend. The latter returned to him the same manner of look. They were the only ones who possessed an inner knowledge. "Mule drivers— hell t' pay—don't believe many will get back." It was an ironical secret. Still, they saw no hesitation in each other's faces, and they nodded a mute and unprotesting assent when a shaggy man near them said in a meek voice: "We'll git swallowed."

XIX

The youth stared at the land in front of him. Its foliage now seemed to veil powers and horrors. He was unaware of the machinery of orders that started the charge, although from the corners of his eyes he saw an officer, who looked like a boy a-horseback, come galloping, waving his hat. Suddenly he felt a straining and heaving among the men. The line fell slowly forward like a toppling wall, and, with a convulsive gasp that was intended for a cheer, the regiment began its journey. The youth was pushed and jostled for a moment before he understood the movement at all, but directly he lunged ahead and began to run.

He fixed his eye upon a distant and prominent clump of trees where he had concluded the enemy were to be met, and he ran as toward a goal. He had believed throughout that it was a mere question of getting over an unpleasant matter as quickly as possible, and he ran desperately, as if pursued for a murder. His face was drawn hard and tight with the stress of his endeavor. His eyes were fixed in a lurid glare. And with his soiled and disordered dress, his red and inflamed features surmounted by the dingy rag with its spot of blood, his wildly swinging rifle and banging accouterments, he looked to be an insane soldier.

As the regiment swung from its position out into a cleared space the woods and thickets before it awakened. Yellow flames leaped toward it from many directions. The forest made a tremendous objection.

The line lurched straight for a moment. Then the right wing swung forward; it in turn was surpassed by the left. Afterward the center careered to the front until the regiment was a wedge-shaped mass, but an instant later the opposition of the bushes, trees, and uneven places on the ground split the command and scattered it into detached clusters.

The youth, light-footed, was unconsciously in advance. His eyes still kept note of the clump of trees. From all places near it the clannish yell of the enemy could be heard. The little flames of rifles leaped from it. The song of the bullets was in the air and shells snarled among the tree-tops. One tumbled directly into the middle of a hurrying group and exploded in crimson fury. There was an instant's spectacle of a man, almost over it, throwing up his hands to shield his eyes.

Other men, punched by bullets, fell in grotesque agonies. The regiment left a coherent trail of bodies.

They had passed into a clearer atmosphere. There was an effect like a revelation in the new appearance of the landscape. Some men working madly at a battery were plain to them, and the opposing infantry's lines were defined by the gray walls and fringes of smoke.

It seemed to the youth that he saw everything. Each blade of the green grass was bold and clear. He thought that he was aware of every change in the thin, transparent vapor that floated idly in sheets. The brown or gray trunks of the trees showed each roughness of their surfaces. And the men of the regiment, with their starting eyes and sweating faces, running madly, or falling, as if thrown headlong, to queer, heaped-up corpses—all were comprehended. His mind took a mechanical but firm impression, so that afterward everything was pictured and explained to him, save why he himself was there.

But there was a frenzy made from this furious rush. The men, pitching forward insanely, had burst into cheerings, moblike and barbaric, but tuned in strange keys that can arouse the dullard and the stoic. It made a mad enthusiasm that, it seemed, would be incapable of checking itself before granite and brass. There was the delirium that encounters despair and death, and is heedless and blind to the odds. It is a temporary but sublime absence of selfishness. And because it was of this order was the reason, perhaps, why the youth wondered, afterward, what reasons he could have had for being there.

Presently the straining pace ate up the energies of the men. As if by agreement, the leaders began to slacken their speed. The volleys directed against them had had a seeming windlike effect. The regiment snorted and blew. Among some stolid trees it began to falter and hesitate. The men, staring intently, began to wait for some of the distant walls of smoke to move and disclose to them the scene. Since much of their strength and their breath had vanished, they returned to caution. They were become men again.

The youth had a vague belief that he had run miles, and he thought, in a way, that he was now in some new and unknown land.

The moment the regiment ceased its advance the protesting splutter of musketry became a steadied roar. Long and accurate fringes of smoke spread out. From the top of a small hill came level belchings of yellow flame that caused an inhuman whistling in the air.

The men, halted, had opportunity to see some of their comrades dropping with moans and shrieks. A few lay under foot, still or wailing. And now for an instant the men stood, their rifles slack in their hands, and watched the regiment dwindle. They appeared dazed and stupid. This spectacle seemed to paralyze them, overcome them with fatal fascination.

They stared woodenly at the sights, and, lowering their eyes, looked from face to face. It was a strange pause, and a strange silence.

Then, above the sounds of the outside commotion, arose the roar of the lieutenant. He strode suddenly forth, his infantile features black with rage. "Come on, yeh fools!" he bellowed. "Come on! Yeh can't stay here. Yeh must come on." He said more, but much of it could not be understood.

He started rapidly forward, with his head turned toward the men, "Come on," he was shouting. The men stared with blank and yokel-like eyes at him. He was obliged to halt and retrace his steps. He stood then with his back to the enemy and delivered gigantic curses into the faces of the men. His body vibrated from the weight and force of his imprecations. And he could string oaths with the facility of a maiden who strings beads.

The friend of the youth aroused. Lurching suddenly forward and dropping to his knees, he fired an angry shot at the persistent woods. This action awakened the men. They huddled no more like sheep. They seemed suddenly to bethink them of their weapons, and at once commenced firing. Belabored by their officers, they began to move forward. The regiment, involved like a cart involved in mud and muddle, started unevenly with many jolts and jerks. The men stopped now every few paces to fire and load, and in this manner moved slowly on from trees to trees.

The flaming opposition in their front grew with their advance until it seemed that all forward ways were barred by the thin leaping tongues, and off to the right an ominous demonstration could sometimes be dimly discerned. The smoke lately generated was in confusing clouds that made it difficult for the regiment to proceed with intelligence. As he passed through each curling mass the youth wondered what would confront him on the farther side. The command went painfully forward until an open space interposed between them and the lurid lines. Here, crouching and cowering behind some trees, the men clung with desperation, as if threatened by a wave. They looked wild-eyed, and as if amazed at this furious disturbance they had stirred. In the storm there was an ironical expression of their importance. The faces of the men, too, showed a lack of a certain feeling of responsibility for being there. It was as if they had been driven. It was the dominant animal failing to remember in the supreme moments the forceful causes of various superficial qualities. The whole affair seemed incomprehensible to many of them.

As they halted thus the lieutenant again began to bellow profanely. Regardless of the vindictive threats of the bullets, he went about coaxing, berating, and bedamning. His lips, that were habitually in a soft and child-like curve, were now writhed into unholy contortions. He swore by all possible deities.

Once he grabbed the youth by the arm. "Come on, yeh lunkhead!" he roared. "Come on! We'll all git killed if we stay here. We've on'y got t' go across that lot. An' then"—the remainder of his idea disappeared in a blue haze of curses.

The youth stretched forth his arm. "Cross there?" His mouth was puckered in doubt and awe.

"Certainly. Jest 'cross th' lot! We can't stay here," screamed the lieutenant. He poked his face close to the youth and waved his bandaged hand. "Come on!" Presently he grappled with him as if for a wrestling bout. It was as if he planned to drag the youth by the ear on to the assault.

The private felt a sudden unspeakable indignation against his officer. He wrenched fiercely and shook him off.

"Come on yerself, then," he yelled. There was a bitter challenge in his voice.

They galloped together down the regimental front. The friend scrambled after them. In front of the colors the three men began to bawl: "Come on! come on!" They danced and gyrated like tortured savages.

The flag, obedient to these appeals, bended its glittering form and swept toward them. The men wavered in indecision for a moment, and then with a long, wailful cry the dilapidated regiment surged forward and began its new journey.

Over the field went the scurrying mass. It was a handful of men splattered into the faces of the enemy. Toward it instantly sprang the yellow tongues. A vast quantity of blue smoke hung before them. A mighty banging made ears valueless.

The youth ran like a madman to reach the woods before a bullet could discover him. He ducked his head low, like a football player. In his haste his eyes almost closed, and the scene was a wild blur. Pulsating saliva stood at the corners of his mouth.

Within him, as he hurled himself forward, was born a love, a despairing fondness for this flag which was near him. It was a creation of beauty and invulnerability. It was a goddess, radiant, that bended its form with an imperious gesture to him. It was a woman, red and white, hating and loving, that called him with the voice of his hopes. Because no harm could come to it he endowed it with power. He kept near, as if it could be a saver of lives, and an imploring cry went from his mind.

In the mad scramble he was aware that the color sergeant flinched suddenly, as if struck by a bludgeon. He faltered, and then became motionless, save for his quivering knees.

He made a spring and a clutch at the pole. At the same instant his friend grabbed it from the other side. They jerked at it, stout and furious, but the color sergeant was dead, and the corpse would not relinquish its trust. For a moment there was a grim encounter. The dead man, swinging with bended back, seemed to be obstinately tugging, in ludicrous and awful ways, for the possession of the flag.

It was past in an instant of time. They wrenched the flag furiously from the dead man, and, as they turned again, the corpse swayed forward with bowed head. One arm swung high, and the curved hand fell with heavy protest on the friend's unheeding shoulder.

XX

When the two youths turned with the flag they saw that much of the regiment had crumbled away, and the dejected remnant was coming back. The men, having hurled themselves in projectile fashion, had presently expended their forces. They slowly retreated, with their faces still toward the spluttering woods, and their hot rifles still replying to the din. Several officers were giving orders, their voices keyed to screams.

"Where in hell yeh goin'?" the lieutenant was asking in a sarcastic howl. And a red-bearded officer, whose voice of triple brass could plainly be heard, was commanding: "Shoot into 'em! Shoot into 'em, Gawd damn their souls!" There was a *mêlée* of screeches, in which the men were ordered to do conflicting and impossible things.

The youth and his friend had a small scuffle over the flag. "Give it t' me!" "No, let me keep it!" Each felt satisfied with the other's possession of it, but each felt bound to declare, by an offer to carry the emblem, his willingness to further risk himself. The youth roughly pushed his friend away.

The regiment fell back to the stolid trees. There it halted for a moment to blaze at some dark forms that had begun to steal upon its track. Presently it resumed its march again, curving among the tree trunks. By the time the depleted regiment had again reached the first open space they were receiving a fast and merciless fire. There seemed to be mobs all about them.

The greater part of the men, discouraged, their spirits worn by the turmoil, acted as if stunned. They accepted the pelting of the bullets with bowed and weary heads. It was of no purpose to strive against walls. It was of no use to batter themselves against granite. And from this consciousness that they had attempted to conquer an unconquerable thing there seemed to arise a feeling that they had been betrayed. They glowered with bent brows, but dangerously, upon some of the officers, more particularly upon the red-bearded one with the voice of triple brass.

However, the rear of the regiment was fringed with men, who continued to shoot irritably at the advancing foes. They seemed resolved to make every trouble. The youthful lieutenant was perhaps the last man in the disordered mass. His forgotten back was toward the enemy. He had been shot in the arm. It hung straight and rigid. Occasionally he would cease to remember it, and be about to emphasize an oath with a sweeping gesture. The multiplied pain caused him to swear with incredible power.

The youth went along with slipping, uncertain feet. He kept watchful eyes rearward. A scowl of mortification and rage was upon his face. He had thought of a fine revenge upon the officer who had referred to him and his fellows as mule drivers. But he saw that it could not come to pass. His dreams had collapsed when the mule drivers, dwindling rapidly, had wavered and hesitated on the little clearing, and then had recoiled. And now the retreat of the mule drivers was a march of shame to him.

A dagger-pointed gaze from without his blackened face was held toward the enemy, but his greater hatred was riveted upon the man, who, not knowing him, had called him a mule driver.

When he knew that he and his comrades had failed to do anything in successful ways that might bring the little pangs of a kind of remorse upon the officer, the youth allowed the rage of the baffled to possess him. This cold officer upon a monument, who dropped epithets unconcernedly down, would be finer as a dead man, he thought. So grievous did he think it that he could never possess the secret right to taunt truly in answer.

He had pictured red letters of curious revenge. "We *are* mule drivers, are we?" And now he was compelled to throw them away.

He presently wrapped his heart in the cloak of his pride and kept the flag erect. He harangued his fellows, pushing against their chests with his free hand. To those he knew well he made frantic appeals, beseeching them by name. Between him and the lieutenant, scolding and near to losing his mind with rage, there was felt a subtle fellowship and equality. They supported each other in all manner of hoarse, howling protests.

But the regiment was a machine run down. The two men babbled at a forceless thing. The soldiers who had heart to go slowly were continually shaken in their resolves by a knowledge that comrades were slipping with speed back to the lines. It was difficult to think of reputation when others were thinking of skins. Wounded men were left crying on this black journey.

The smoke fringes and flames blustered always. The youth, peering once through a sudden rift in a cloud, saw a brown mass of troops, interwoven and magnified until they appeared to be thousands. A fierce-hued flag flashed before his vision.

Immediately, as if the uplifting of the smoke had been prearranged, the discovered troops burst into a rasping yell, and a hundred flames jetted toward the retreating band. A rolling gray cloud again interposed as the regiment doggedly replied. The youth had to depend again upon his

misused ears, which were trembling and buzzing from the *mêlée* of musketry and yells.

The way seemed eternal. In the clouded haze men became panic-
stricken with the thought that the regiment had lost its path, and was proceeding in a perilous direction. Once the men who headed the wild procession turned and came pushing back against their comrades, screaming
that they were being fired upon from points which they had considered to
be toward their own lines. At this cry a hysterical fear and dismay beset the
troops. A soldier, who theretofore had been ambitious to make the regiment into a wise little band that would proceed calmly amid the huge-
appearing difficulties, suddenly sank down and buried his face in his arms
with an air of bowing to a doom. From another a shrill lamentation rang
out filled with profane allusions to a general. Men ran hither and thither,
seeking with their eyes roads of escape. With serene regularity, as if controlled by a schedule, bullets buffed into men.

The youth walked stolidly into the midst of the mob, and with his flag
in his hands took a stand as if he expected an attempt to push him to the
ground. He unconsciously assumed the attitude of the color bearer in the
fight of the preceding day. He passed over his brow a hand that trembled.
His breath did not come freely. He was choking during this small wait for
the crisis.

His friend came to him. "Well, Henry, I guess this is good-by—John."

"Oh, shut up, you damned fool!" replied the youth, and he would not
look at the other.

The officers labored like politicians to beat the mass into a proper
circle to face the menaces. The ground was uneven and torn. The men
curled into depressions and fitted themselves snugly behind whatever
would frustrate a bullet.

The youth noted with vague surprise that the lieutenant was standing
mutely with his legs far apart and his sword held in the manner of a cane.
The youth wondered what had happened to his vocal organs that he no
more cursed.

There was something curious in this little intent pause of the lieutenant.
He was like a babe which, having wept its fill, raises its eyes and fixes upon
a distant toy. He was engrossed in this contemplation, and the soft under
lip quivered from self-whispered words.

Some lazy and ignorant smoke curled slowly. The men, hiding from
the bullets, waited anxiously for it to lift and disclose the plight of the
regiment.

The silent ranks were suddenly thrilled by the eager voice of the youthful lieutenant bawling out: "Here they come! Right onto us, b'Gawd!" His
further words were lost in a roar of wicked thunder from the men's rifles.

The youth's eyes had instantly turned in the direction indicated by the awakened and agitated lieutenant, and he had seen the haze of treachery disclosing a body of soldiers of the enemy. They were so near that he could see their features. There was a recognition as he looked at the types of faces. Also he perceived with dim amazement that their uniforms were rather gay in effect, being light gray, accented with a brilliant-hued facing. Moreover, the clothes seemed new.

These troops had apparently been going forward with caution, their rifles held in readiness, when the youthful lieutenant had discovered them and their movement had been interrupted by the volley from the blue regiment. From the moment's glimpse, it was derived that they had been unaware of the proximity of their dark-suited foes or had mistaken the direction. Almost instantly they were shut utterly from the youth's sight by the smoke from the energetic rifles of his companions. He strained his vision to learn the accomplishment of the volley, but the smoke hung before him.

The two bodies of troops exchanged blows in the manner of a pair of boxers. The fast angry firings went back and forth. The men in blue were intent with the despair of their circumstances and they seized upon the revenge to be had at close range. Their thunder swelled loud and valiant. Their curving front bristled with flashes and the place resounded with the clangor of their ramrods. The youth ducked and dodged for a time and achieved a few unsatisfactory views of the enemy. There appeared to be many of them and they were replying swiftly. They seemed moving toward the blue regiment, step by step. He seated himself gloomily on the ground with his flag between his knees.

As he noted the vicious, wolflike temper of his comrades he had a sweet thought that if the enemy was about to swallow the regimental broom as a large prisoner, it could at least have the consolation of going down with bristles forward.

But the blows of the antagonist began to grow more weak. Fewer bullets ripped the air, and finally, when the men slackened to learn of the fight, they could see only dark, floating smoke. The regiment lay still and gazed. Presently some chance whim came to the pestering blur, and it began to coil heavily away. The men saw a ground vacant of fighters. It would have been an empty stage if it were not for a few corpses that lay thrown and twisted into fantastic shapes upon the sward.

At sight of this tableau, many of the men in blue sprang from behind their covers and made an ungainly dance of joy. Their eyes burned and a hoarse cheer of elation broke from their dry lips.

It had begun to seem to them that events were trying to prove that they were impotent. These little battles had evidently endeavored to demonstrate that the men could not fight well. When on the verge of submission to these opinions, the small duel had showed them that the proportions were not impossible, and by it they had revenged themselves upon their misgivings and upon the foe.

The impetus of enthusiasm was theirs again. They gazed about them with looks of uplifted pride, feeling new trust in the grim, always confident weapons in their hands. And they were men.

XXI

Presently they knew that no fighting threatened them. All ways seemed once more opened to them. The dusty blue lines of their friends were disclosed a short distance away. In the distance there were many colossal noises, but in all this part of the field there was a sudden stillness.

They perceived that they were free. The depleted band drew a long breath of relief and gathered itself into a bunch to complete its trip.

In this last length of journey the men began to show strange emotions. They hurried with nervous fear. Some who had been dark and unfaltering in the grimmest moments now could not conceal an anxiety that made them frantic. It was perhaps that they dreaded to be killed in insignificant ways after the times for proper military deaths had passed. Or, perhaps, they thought it would be too ironical to get killed at the portals of safety. With backward looks of perturbation, they hastened.

As they approached their own lines there was some sarcasm exhibited on the part of a gaunt and bronzed regiment that lay resting in the shade of the trees. Questions were wafted to them.

"Where th' hell yeh been?"

"What yeh comin' back fer?"

"Why didn't yeh stay there?"

"Was it warm out there, sonny?"

"Goin' home now, boys?"

One shouted in taunting mimicry: "Oh, mother, come quick an' look at th' sojers!"

There was no reply from the bruised and battered regiment, save that one man made broadcast challenges to fist fights and the red-bearded officer walked rather near and glared in great swashbuckler style at a tall captain in the other regiment. But the lieutenant suppressed the man who wished to fist fight, and the tall captain, flushing at the little fanfare of the red-bearded one, was obliged to look intently at some trees.

The youth's tender flesh was deeply stung by these remarks. From under his creased brows he glowered with hate at the mockers. He meditated upon a few revenges. Still, many in the regiment hung their heads in criminal fashion, so that it came to pass that the men trudged with sudden heaviness, as if they bore upon their bended shoulders the coffin of their honor. And the youthful lieutenant, recollecting himself, began to mutter softly in black curses.

They turned when they arrived at their old position to regard the ground over which they had charged.

The youth in this contemplation was smitten with a large astonishment. He discovered that the distances, as compared with the brilliant measurings of his mind, were trivial and ridiculous. The stolid trees, where much had taken place, seemed incredibly near. The time, too, now that he reflected, he saw to have been short. He wondered at the number of emotions and events that had been crowded into such little spaces. Elfin thoughts must have exaggerated and enlarged everything, he said.

It seemed, then, that there was bitter justice in the speeches of the gaunt and bronzed veterans. He veiled a glance of disdain at his fellows who strewed the ground, choking with dust, red from perspiration, misty-eyed, disheveled.

They were gulping at their canteens, fierce to wring every mite of water from them, and they polished at their swollen and watery features with coat sleeves and bunches of grass.

However, to the youth there was a considerable joy in musing upon his performances during the charge. He had had very little time previously in which to appreciate himself, so that there was now much satisfaction in quietly thinking of his actions. He recalled bits of color that in the flurry had stamped themselves unawares upon his engaged senses.

As the regiment lay heaving from its hot exertions the officer who had named them as mule drivers came galloping along the line. He had lost his cap. His tousled hair streamed wildly, and his face was dark with vexation and wrath. His temper was displayed with more clearness by the way in which he managed his horse. He jerked and wrenched savagely at his bridle, stopping the hard-breathing animal with a furious pull near the colonel of the regiment. He immediately exploded in reproaches which came unbidden to the ears of the men. They were suddenly alert, being always curious about black words between officers.

"Oh, thunder, MacChesnay, what an awful bull you made of this thing!" began the officer. He attempted low tones, but his indignation caused certain of the men to learn the sense of his words. "What an awful mess you made! Good Lord, man, you stopped about a hundred feet this side of a very pretty success! If your men had gone a hundred feet farther you would have made a great charge, but as it is—what a lot of mud diggers you've got anyway!"

The men, listening with bated breath, now turned their curious eyes upon the colonel. They had a ragamuffin interest in this affair.

The colonel was seen to straighten his form and put one hand forth in oratorical fashion. He wore an injured air; it was as if a deacon had been accused of stealing. The men were wiggling in an ecstasy of excitement.

But of a sudden the colonel's manner changed from that of a deacon to that of a Frenchman. He shrugged his shoulders. "Oh, well, general, we went as far as we could," he said calmly.

"As far as you could? Did you, b'Gawd?" snorted the other. "Well, that wasn't very far, was it?" he added, with a glance of cold contempt into the other's eyes. "Not very far, I think. You were intended to make a diversion in favor of Whiterside. How well you succeeded your own ears can now tell you." He wheeled his horse and rode stiffly away.

The colonel, bidden to hear the jarring noises of an engagement in the woods to the left, broke out in vague damnations.

The lieutenant, who had listened with an air of impotent rage to the interview, spoke suddenly in firm and undaunted tones. "I don't care what a man is—whether he is a general or what— if he says th' boys didn't put up a good fight out there he's a damned fool."

"Lieutenant," began the colonel, severely, "this is my own affair, and I'll trouble you—"

The lieutenant made an obedient gesture. "All right, colonel, all right," he said. He sat down with an air of being content with himself.

The news that the regiment had been reproached went along the line. For a time the men were bewildered by it. "Good thunder!" they ejaculated, staring at the vanishing form of the general. They conceived it to be a huge mistake.

Presently, however, they began to believe that in truth their efforts had been called light. The youth could see this conviction weigh upon the entire regiment until the men were like cuffed and cursed animals, but withal rebellious.

The friend, with a grievance in his eye, went to the youth. "I wonder what he does want," he said. "He must think we went out there an' played marbles! I never see sech a man!"

The youth developed a tranquil philosophy for these moments of irritation. "Oh, well," he rejoined, "he probably didn't see nothing of it at all and got mad as blazes, and concluded we were a lot of sheep, just because we didn't do what he wanted done. It's a pity old Grandpa Henderson got killed yesterday—he'd have known that we did our best and fought good. It's just our awful luck, that's what."

"I should say so," replied the friend. He seemed to be deeply wounded at an injustice. "I should say we did have awful luck! There's no fun in fightin' fer people when everything yeh do— no matter what—ain't done right. I have a notion t' stay behind next time an' let 'em take their ol' charge an' go t' th' devil with it."

The youth spoke soothingly to his comrade. "Well, we both did good. I'd like to see the fool what'd say we both didn't do as good as we could!"

"Of course we did," declared the friend stoutly. "An' I'd break th' feller's neck if he was as big as a church. But we're all right, anyhow, for I heard one feller say that we two fit th' best in th' reg'ment, an' they had a great argument 'bout it. Another feller, 'a course, he had t' up an' say it was a lie—he seen all what was goin' on an' he never seen us from th' beginnin' t' th' end. An' a lot more struck in an' ses it wasn't a lie—we did fight like thunder, an' they give us quite a send-off. But this is what I can't stand—these everlastin' ol' soldiers, titterin' an' laughin', an' then that general, he's crazy."

The youth exclaimed with sudden exasperation: "He's a lunkhead! He makes me mad. I wish he'd come along next time. We'd show 'im what—"

He ceased because several men had come hurrying up. Their faces expressed a bringing of great news.

"O Flem, yeh jest oughta heard!" cried one, eagerly.

"Heard what?" said the youth.

"Yeh jest oughta heard!" repeated the other, and he arranged himself to tell his tidings. The others made an excited circle. "Well, sir, th' colonel met your lieutenant right by us—it was damnedest thing I ever heard— an' he ses: 'Ahem! ahem!' he ses. 'Mr. Hasbrouck!' he ses, 'by th' way, who was that lad what carried th' flag?' he ses. There, Flemin', what d'yeh think 'a that? 'Who was th' lad what carried th' flag?' he ses, an' th' lieutenant, he speaks up right away: 'That's Flemin', an' he's a jimhickey,' he ses, right away. What? I say he did. 'A jimhickey,' he ses—those 'r his words. He did, too. I say he did. If you kin tell this story better than I kin, go ahead an' tell it. Well, then, keep yer mouth shet. Th' lieutenant, he ses: 'He's a jimhickey,' an' th' colonel, he ses: 'Ahem! ahem! he is, indeed, a very good man t' have, ahem! He kep' th' flag 'way t' th' front. I saw 'im. He's a good un,' ses th' colonel. 'You bet,' ses th' lieutenant, 'he an' a feller named Wilson was at th' head a' th' charge, an' howlin' like Indians all th' time,' he ses. 'Head a' th' charge all th' time,' he ses. 'A feller named Wilson,' he ses. There, Wilson, m'boy, put that in a letter an' send it hum t' yer mother, hay? 'A feller named Wilson,' he ses. An' th' colonel, he ses: 'Were they, indeed? Ahem! ahem! My sakes!' he ses. 'At the head a' th' reg'ment?' he ses. 'They were,' ses th' lieutenant. 'My sakes!' ses th' colonel. He ses: 'Well, well, well,' he ses, 'those two babies?' 'They were,' ses th' lieutenant.

'Well, well,' ses th' colonel, 'they deserve t' be major generals,' he ses. 'They deserve t' be major generals.'"

The youth and his friend had said: "Huh!" "Yer lyin', Thompson." "Oh, go t' blazes!" "He never sed it." "Oh, what a lie!" "Huh!" But despite these youthful scoffings and embarrassments, they knew that their faces were deeply flushing from thrills of pleasure. They exchanged a secret glance of joy and congratulation.

They speedily forgot many things. The past held no pictures of error and disappointment. They were very happy, and their hearts swelled with grateful affection for the colonel and the youthful lieutenant.

XXII

When the woods again began to pour forth the dark-hued masses of the enemy the youth felt serene self-confidence. He smiled briefly when he saw men dodge and duck at the long screechings of shells that were thrown in giant handfuls over them. He stood, erect and tranquil, watching the attack begin against a part of the line that made a blue curve along the side of an adjacent hill. His vision being unmolested by smoke from the rifles of his companions, he had opportunities to see parts of the hard fight. It was a relief to perceive at last from whence came some of these noises which had been roared into his ears.

Off a short way he saw two regiments fighting a little separate battle with two other regiments. It was in a cleared space, wearing a set-apart look. They were blazing as if upon a wager, giving and taking tremendous blows. The firings were incredibly fierce and rapid. These intent regiments apparently were oblivious of all larger purposes of war, and were slugging each other as if at a matched game.

In another direction he saw a magnificent brigade going with the evident intention of driving the enemy from a wood. They passed in out of sight and presently there was a most awe-inspiring racket in the wood. The noise was unspeakable. Having stirred this prodigious uproar, and, apparently, finding it too prodigious, the brigade, after a little time, came marching airily out again with its fine formation in nowise disturbed. There were no traces of speed in its movements. The brigade was jaunty and seemed to point a proud thumb at the yelling wood.

On a slope to the left there was a long row of guns, gruff and maddened, denouncing the enemy, who, down through the woods, were forming for another attack in the pitiless monotony of conflicts. The round red discharges from the guns made a crimson flare and a high, thick smoke.

Occasional glimpses could be caught of groups of the toiling artillerymen. In the rear of this row of guns stood a house, calm and white, amid bursting shells. A congregation of horses, tied to a long railing, were tugging frenziedly at their bridles. Men were running hither and thither.

The detached battle between the four regiments lasted for some time. There chanced to be no interference, and they settled their dispute by themselves. They struck savagely and powerfully at each other for a period of minutes, and then the lighter-hued regiments faltered and drew back, leaving the dark-blue lines shouting. The youth could see the two flags shaking with laughter amid the smoke remnants.

Presently there was a stillness, pregnant with meaning. The blue lines shifted and changed a trifle and stared expectantly at the silent woods and fields before them. The hush was solemn and churchlike, save for a distant battery that, evidently unable to remain quiet, sent a faint rolling thunder over the ground. It irritated, like the noises of unimpressed boys. The men imagined that it would prevent their perched ears from hearing the first words of the new battle.

Of a sudden the guns on the slope roared out a message of warning. A spluttering sound had begun in the woods. It swelled with amazing speed to a profound clamor that involved the earth in noises. The splitting crashes swept along the lines until an interminable roar was developed. To those in the midst of it it became a din fitted to the universe. It was the whirring and thumping of gigantic machinery, complications among the smaller stars. The youth's ears were filled up. They were incapable of hearing more.

On an incline over which a road wound he saw wild and desperate rushes of men perpetually backward and forward in riotous surges. These parts of the opposing armies were two long waves that pitched upon each other madly at dictated points. To and fro they swelled. Sometimes, one side by its yells and cheers would proclaim decisive blows, but a moment later the other side would be all yells and cheers. Once the youth saw a spray of light forms go in houndlike leaps toward the waving blue lines. There was much howling, and presently it went away with a vast mouthful of prisoners. Again, he saw a blue wave dash with such thunderous force against a gray obstruction that it seemed to clear the earth of it and leave nothing but trampled sod. And always in their swift and deadly rushes to and fro the men screamed and yelled like maniacs.

Particular pieces of fence or secure positions behind collections of trees were wrangled over, as gold thrones or pearl bedsteads. There were desperate lunges at these chosen spots seemingly every instant, and most of them were bandied like light toys between the contending forces. The youth could not tell from the battle flags flying like crimson foam in many directions which color of cloth was winning.

His emaciated regiment bustled forth with undiminished fierceness when its time came. When assaulted again by bullets, the men burst out in a barbaric cry of rage and pain. They bent their heads in aims of intent hatred behind the projected hammers of their guns. Their ramrods clanged loud with fury as their eager arms pounded the cartridges into the rifle barrels. The front of the regiment was a smoke-wall penetrated by the flashing points of yellow and red.

Wallowing in the fight, they were in an astonishingly short time resmudged. They surpassed in stain and dirt all their previous appearances. Moving to and fro with strained exertion, jabbering the while, they were, with their swaying bodies, black faces, and glowing eyes, like strange and ugly fiends jigging heavily in the smoke.

The lieutenant, returning from a tour after a bandage, produced from a hidden receptacle of his mind new and portentous oaths suited to the emergency. Strings of expletives he swung lashlike over the backs of his men, and it was evident that his previous efforts had in nowise impaired his resources.

The youth, still the bearer of the colors, did not feel his idleness. He was deeply absorbed as a spectator. The crash and swing of the great drama made him lean forward, intent-eyed, his face working in small contortions. Sometimes he prattled, words coming unconsciously from him in grotesque exclamations. He did not know that he breathed; that the flag hung silently over him, so absorbed was he.

A formidable line of the enemy came within dangerous range. They could be seen plainly—tall, gaunt men with excited faces running with long strides toward a wandering fence.

At sight of this danger the men suddenly ceased their cursing monotone. There was an instant of strained silence before they threw up their rifles and fired a plumping volley at the foes. There had been no order given; the men, upon recognizing the menace, had immediately let drive their flock of bullets without waiting for word of command.

But the enemy were quick to gain the protection of the wandering line of fence. They slid down behind it with remarkable celerity, and from this position they began briskly to slice up the blue men.

These latter braced their energies for a great struggle. Often, white clenched teeth shone from the dusky faces. Many heads surged to and fro, floating upon a pale sea of smoke. Those behind the fence frequently shouted and yelped in taunts and gibe-like cries, but the regiment maintained a stressed silence. Perhaps at this new assault the men recalled the fact that they had been named mud diggers, and it made their situation thrice bitter. They were breathlessly intent upon keeping the ground and thrusting away the rejoicing body of the enemy. They fought swiftly and with a despairing savageness denoted in their expressions.

The youth had resolved not to budge whatever should happen. Some arrows of scorn that had buried themselves in his heart had generated strange and unspeakable hatred. It was clear to him that his final and absolute revenge was to be achieved by his dead body lying, torn and gluttering upon the field. This was to be a poignant retaliation upon the officer who had said "mule drivers," and later "mud diggers," for in all the wild graspings of his mind for a unit responsible for his sufferings and commotions he always seized upon the man who had dubbed him wrongly. And it was his idea, vaguely formulated, that his corpse would be for those eyes a great and salt reproach.

The regiment bled extravagantly. Grunting bundles of blue began to drop. The orderly sergeant of the youth's company was shot through the cheeks. Its supports being injured, his jaw hung afar down, disclosing in the wide cavern of his mouth a pulsing mass of blood and teeth. And with it all he made attempts to cry out. In his endeavor there was a dreadful earnestness, as if he conceived that one great shriek would make him well.

The youth saw him presently go rearward. His strength seemed in nowise impaired. He ran swiftly, casting wild glances for succor.

Others fell down about the feet of their companions. Some of the wounded crawled out and away, but many lay still, their bodies twisted into impossible shapes.

The youth looked once for his friend. He saw a vehement young man, powder-smeared and frowzled, whom he knew to be him. The lieutenant, also, was unscathed in his position at the rear. He had continued to curse, but it was now with the air of a man who was using his last box of oaths.

For the fire of the regiment had begun to wane and drip. The robust voice, that had come strangely from the thin ranks, was growing rapidly weak.

XXIII

The colonel came running along back of the line. There were other officers following him. "We must charge'm!" they shouted. "We must charge'm!" they cried with resentful voices, as if anticipating a rebellion against this plan by the men.

The youth, upon hearing the shouts, began to study the distance between him and the enemy. He made vague calculations. He saw that to be firm soldiers they must go forward. It would be death to stay in the present place, and with all the circumstances to go backward would exalt too many others. Their hope was to push the galling foes away from the fence.

He expected that his companions, weary and stiffened, would have to be driven to this assault, but as he turned toward them he perceived with a certain surprise that they were giving quick and unqualified expressions of assent. There was an ominous, clanging overture to the charge when the shafts of the bayonets rattled upon the rifle barrels. At the yelled words of command the soldiers sprang forward in eager leaps. There was new and unexpected force in the movement of the regiment. A knowledge of its faded and jaded condition made the charge appear like a paroxysm, a display of the strength that comes before a final feebleness. The men scampered in insane fever of haste, racing as if to achieve a sudden success before an exhilarating fluid should leave them. It was a blind and despairing rush by the collection of men in dusty and tattered blue, over a green sward and under a sapphire sky, toward a fence, dimly outlined in smoke, from behind which spluttered the fierce rifles of enemies.

The youth kept the bright colors to the front. He was waving his free arm in furious circles, the while shrieking mad calls and appeals, urging on those that did not need to be urged, for it seemed that the mob of blue men hurling themselves on the dangerous group of rifles were again grown suddenly wild with an enthusiasm of unselfishness. From the many firings starting toward them, it looked as if they would merely succeed in making a great sprinkling of corpses on the grass between their former position and the fence. But they were in a state of frenzy, perhaps because of forgotten vanities, and it made an exhibition of sublime recklessness. There was no obvious questioning, nor figurings, nor diagrams. There were, apparently, no considered loopholes. It appeared that the swift wings of their desires would have shattered against the iron gates of the impossible.

He himself felt the daring spirit of a savage religion-mad. He was capable of profound sacrifices, a tremendous death. He had no time for dissections, but he knew that he thought of the bullets only as things that could prevent him from reaching the place of his endeavor. There were subtle flashings of joy within him that thus should be his mind.

He strained all his strength. His eyesight was shaken and dazzled by the tension of thought and muscle. He did not see anything excepting the mist of smoke gashed by the little knives of fire, but he knew that in it lay the aged fence of a vanished farmer protecting the snuggled bodies of the gray men.

As he ran a thought of the shock of contact gleamed in his mind. He expected a great concussion when the two bodies of troops crashed together. This became a part of his wild battle madness. He could feel the onward swing of the regiment about him and he conceived of a thunderous, crushing blow that would prostrate the resistance and spread consternation and amazement for miles. The flying regiment was going to have a catapultian effect. This dream made him run faster among his comrades, who were giving vent to hoarse and frantic cheers.

But presently he could see that many of the men in gray did not intend to abide the blow. The smoke, rolling, disclosed men who ran, their faces still turned. These grew to a crowd, who retired stubbornly. Individuals wheeled frequently to send a bullet at the blue wave.

But at one part of the line there was a grim and obdurate group that made no movement. They were settled firmly down behind posts and rails. A flag, ruffled and fierce, waved over them and their rifles dinned fiercely.

The blue whirl of men got very near, until it seemed that in truth there would be a close and frightful scuffle. There was an expressed disdain in the opposition of the little group, that changed the meaning of the cheers of the men in blue. They became yells of wrath, directed, personal. The cries of the two parties were now in sound an interchange of scathing insults.

They in blue showed their teeth; their eyes shone all white. They launched themselves as at the throats of those who stood resisting. The space between dwindled to an insignificant distance.

The youth had centered the gaze of his soul upon that other flag. Its possession would be high pride. It would express bloody minglings, near blows. He had a gigantic hatred for those who made great difficulties and complications. They caused it to be as a craved treasure of mythology, hung amid tasks and contrivances of danger.

He plunged like a mad horse at it. He was resolved it should not escape if wild blows and darings of blows could seize it. His own emblem, quivering and aflare, was winging toward the other. It seemed there would shortly be an encounter of strange beaks and claws, as of eagles.

The swirling body of blue men came to a sudden halt at close and disastrous range and roared a swift volley. The group in gray was split and broken by this fire, but its riddled body still fought. The men in blue yelled again and rushed in upon it.

The youth, in his leapings, saw, as through a mist, a picture of four or five men stretched upon the ground or writhing upon their knees with bowed heads as if they had been stricken by bolts from the sky. Tottering among them was the rival color bearer, whom the youth saw had been bitten vitally by the bullets of the last formidable volley. He perceived this man fighting a last struggle, the struggle of one whose legs are grasped by demons. It was a ghastly battle. Over his face was the bleach of death, but set upon it were the dark and hard lines of desperate purpose. With this terrible grin of resolution he hugged his precious flag to him and was stumbling and staggering in his design to go the way that led to safety for it. But his wounds always made it seem that his feet were retarded, held, and he fought a grim fight, as with invisible ghouls fastened greedily upon his limbs. Those in advance of the scampering blue men, howling cheers, leaped at the fence. The despair of the lost was in his eyes as he glanced back at them.

The youth's friend went over the obstruction in a tumbling heap and sprang at the flag as a panther at prey. He pulled at it and, wrenching it free, swung up its red brilliancy with a mad cry of exultation even as the color bearer, gasping, lurched over in a final throe and, stiffening convulsively, turned his dead face to the ground. There was much blood upon the grass blades.

At the place of success there began more wild clamorings of cheers. The men gesticulated and bellowed in an ecstasy. When they spoke it was as if they considered their listener to be a mile away. What hats and caps were left to them they often slung high in the air.

At one part of the line four men had been swooped upon, and they now sat as prisoners. Some blue men were about them in an eager and curious circle. The soldiers had trapped strange birds, and there was an examination. A flurry of fast questions was in the air.

One of the prisoners was nursing a superficial wound in the foot. He cuddled it, baby-wise, but he looked up from it often to curse with an astonishing utter abandon straight at the noses of his captors. He consigned them to red regions; he called upon the pestilential wrath of strange gods. And with it all he was singularly free from recognition of the finer points of the conduct of prisoners of war. It was as if a clumsy clod had trod upon his toe and he conceived it to be his privilege, his duty, to use deep, resentful oaths.

Another, who was a boy in years, took his plight with great calmness and apparent good nature. He conversed with the men in blue, studying their faces with his bright and keen eyes. They spoke of battles and conditions. There was an acute interest in all their faces during this exchange of viewpoints. It seemed a great satisfaction to hear voices from where all had been darkness and speculation.

The third captive sat with a morose countenance. He preserved a stoical and cold attitude. To all advances he made one reply without variation, "Ah, go t' hell!"

The last of the four was always silent and, for the most part, kept his face turned in unmolested directions. From the views the youth received he seemed to be in a state of absolute dejection. Shame was upon him, and with it profound regret that he was, perhaps, no more to be counted in the ranks of his fellows. The youth could detect no expression that would allow him to believe that the other was giving a thought to his narrowed future, the pictured dungeons, perhaps, and starvations and brutalities, liable to the imagination. All to be seen was shame for captivity and regret for the right to antagonize.

After the men had celebrated sufficiently they settled down behind the old rail fence, on the opposite side to the one from which their foes had been driven. A few shot perfunctorily at distant marks.

There was some long grass. The youth nestled in it and rested, making a convenient rail support the flag. His friend, jubilant and glorified, holding his treasure with vanity, came to him there. They sat side by side and congratulated each other.

XXIV

The roarings that had stretched in a long line of sound across the face of the forest began to grow intermittent and weaker. The stentorian speeches of the artillery continued in some distant encounter, but the crashes of the musketry had almost ceased. The youth and his friend of a sudden looked up, feeling a deadened form of distress at the waning of these noises, which had become a part of life. They could see changes going on among the troops. There were marchings this way and that way. A battery wheeled leisurely. On the crest of a small hill was the thick gleam of many departing muskets.

The youth arose. "Well, what now, I wonder?" he said. By his tone he seemed to be preparing to resent some new monstrosity in the way of dins and smashes. He shaded his eyes with his grimy hand and gazed over the field.

His friend also arose and stared. "I bet we're goin' t' git along out of this an' back over th' river," said he.

"Well, I swan!" said the youth.

They waited, watching. Within a little while the regiment received orders to retrace its way. The men got up grunting from the grass, regretting the soft repose. They jerked their stiffened legs, and stretched their arms over their heads. One man swore as he rubbed his eyes. They all groaned "O Lord!" They had as many objections to this change as they would have had to a proposal for a new battle.

They trampled slowly back over the field across which they had run in a mad scamper.

The regiment marched until it had joined its fellows. The reformed brigade, in column, aimed through a wood at the road. Directly they were in a mass of dust-covered troops, and were trudging along in a way parallel to the enemy's lines as these had been defined by the previous turmoil.

They passed within view of a stolid white house, and saw in front of it groups of their comrades lying in wait behind a neat breastwork. A row of guns were booming at a distant enemy. Shells thrown in reply were raising clouds of dust and splinters. Horsemen dashed along the line of entrenchments.

At this point of its march the division curved away from the field and went winding off in the direction of the river. When the significance of this movement had impressed itself upon the youth he turned his head and looked over his shoulder toward the trampled and *débris*-strewed ground. He breathed a breath of new satisfaction. He finally nudged his friend. "Well, it's all over," he said to him.

His friend gazed backward. "B'Gawd, it is," he assented. They mused.

For a time the youth was obliged to reflect in a puzzled and uncertain way. His mind was undergoing a subtle change. It took moments for it to cast off its battlefield ways and resume its accustomed course of thought. Gradually his brain emerged from the clogged clouds, and at last he was enable to more closely comprehend himself and circumstance.

He understood then that the existence of shot and countershot was in the past. He had dwelt in a land of strange, squalling upheavals and had come forth. He had been where there was red of blood and black of passion, and he was escaped. His first thoughts were given to rejoicings at this fact.

Later he began to study his deeds, his failures, and his achievements. Thus, fresh from scenes where many of his usual machines of reflection had been idle, from where he had proceeded sheeplike, he struggled to marshal all his acts.

At last they marched before him clearly. From this present viewpoint he was enabled to look upon them in spectator fashion and criticize them with some correctness, for his new condition had already defeated certain sympathies.

Regarding his procession of memory he felt gleeful and unregretting, for in it his public deeds were paraded in great and shining prominence. Those performances which had been witnessed by his fellows marched now in wide purple and gold, having various reflections. They went gayly with music. It was pleasure to watch these things. He spent delightful minutes viewing the gilded images of memory.

He saw that he was good. He recalled with a thrill of joy the respectful comments of his fellows upon his conduct.

Nevertheless, the ghost of his flight from the first engagement appeared to him and danced. There were small shoutings in his brain about these matters. For a moment he blushed, and the light of his soul flickered with shame.

A specter of reproach came to him. There loomed the dogging memory of the tattered soldier—he who, gored by bullets and faint for blood, had fretted concerning an imagined wound in another; he who had loaned his last of strength and intellect for the tall soldier; he who, blind with weariness and pain, had been deserted in the field.

For an instant a wretched chill of sweat was upon him at the thought that he might be detected in the thing. As he stood persistently before his vision, he gave vent to a cry of sharp irritation and agony.

His friend turned. "What's the matter, Henry?" he demanded. The youth's reply was an outburst of crimson oaths.

As he marched along the little branch-hung roadway among his prattling companions this vision of cruelty brooded over him. It clung near him always and darkened his view of these deeds in purple and gold. Whichever way his thoughts turned they were followed by the somber phantom of the desertion in the fields. He looked stealthily at his companions, feeling sure that they must discern in his face evidences of this pursuit. But they were plodding in ragged array, discussing with quick tongues the accomplishments of the late battle.

"Oh, if a man should come up an' ask me, I'd say we got a dum good lickin'."

"Lickin'—in yer eye! We ain't licked, sonny. We're going down here aways, swing aroun', and come in behint 'em."

"Oh, hush, with your comin' in behint 'em. I've seen all 'a that I wanta. Don't tell me about comin' in behint—"

"Bill Smithers, he ses he'd rather been in ten hundred battles than been in that heluva hospital. He ses they got shootin' in th' night-time, an' shells dropped plum among 'em in th' hospital. He ses sech hollerin' he never see."

"Hasbrouck? He's th' best off'cer in this here reg'ment. He's a whale."

"Didn't I tell yeh we'd come aroun' in behint 'em? Didn't I tell yeh so? We—"

"Oh, shet yer mouth!"

For a time this pursuing recollection of the tattered man took all elation from the youth's veins. He saw his vivid error, and he was afraid that it would stand before him all his life. He took no share in the chatter of his comrades, nor did he look at them or know them, save when he felt sudden suspicion that they were seeing his thoughts and scrutinizing each detail of the scene with the tattered soldier.

Yet gradually he mustered force to put the sin at a distance. And at last his eyes seemed to open to some new ways. He found that he could look back upon the brass and bombast of his earlier gospels and see them truly. He was gleeful when he discovered that he now despised them.

With the conviction came a store of assurance. He felt a quiet manhood, nonassertive but of sturdy and strong blood. He knew that he would no more quail before his guides wherever they should point. He had been to touch the great death, and found that, after all, it was but the great death. He was a man.

So it came to pass that as he trudged from the place of blood and wrath his soul changed. He came from hot plowshares to prospects of clover tranquilly, and it was as if hot plowshares were not. Scars faded as flowers.

It rained. The procession of weary soldiers became a bedraggled train, despondent and muttering, marching with churning effort in a trough of liquid brown mud under a low, wretched sky. Yet the youth smiled, for he saw that the world was a world for him, though many discovered it to be made of oaths and walking sticks. He had rid himself of the red sickness of battle. The sultry nightmare was in the past. He had been an animal blistered and sweating in the heat and pain of war. He turned now with a lover's thirst to images of tranquil skies, fresh meadows, cool brooks—an existence of soft and eternal peace.

Over the river a golden ray of sun came through the hosts of leaden rain clouds.

"A MYSTERY OF HEROISM"

The dark uniforms of the men were so coated with dust from the incessant wrestling of the two armies that the regiment almost seemed a part of the clay bank which shielded them from the shells. On the top of the hill a battery was arguing in tremendous roars with some other guns, and to the eye of the infantry the artillerymen, the guns, the caissons, the horses, were distinctly outlined upon the blue sky. When a piece was fired a red streak as round as a log flashed low in the heavens, like a monstrous bolt of lightning. The men of the battery wore white duck trousers, which somehow emphasized their legs; and when they ran and crowded in little groups at the bidding of the shouting officers, it was more impressive than usual to the infantry.

Fred Collins, of A Company, was saying: "Thunder! I wish I had a drink. Ain't there any water round here?" Then somebody yelled: "There goes th' bugler!"

As the eyes of half the regiment swept in one machinelike movement, there was an instant's picture of a horse in a great convulsive leap of a death wound and a rider leaning back with a crooked arm and spread fingers before his face. On the ground was the crimson terror of an exploding shell, with fibres of flame that seemed like lances. A glittering bugle swung clear of the rider's back as fell headlong the horse and the man. In the air was an odor as from a conflagration.

Sometimes they of the infantry looked down at a fair little meadow which spread at their feet. Its long green grass was rippling gently in a breeze. Beyond it was the grey form of a house half torn to pieces by shells and by the busy axes of soldiers who had pursued firewood. The line of an old fence was now dimly marked by long weeds and by an occasional post. A shell had blown the well-house to fragments. Little lines of grey smoke ribboning upward from some embers indicated the place where had stood the barn.

From beyond a curtain of green woods there came the sound of some stupendous scuffle, as if two animals of the size of islands were fighting. At a distance there were occasional appearances of swift-moving men, horses, batteries, flags, and with the crashing of infantry volleys were heard, often, wild and frenzied cheers. In the midst of it all Smith and Ferguson, two privates of A Company, were engaged in a heated discussion which involved the greatest questions of the national existence.

Syndicated by Bacheller on 1–2 Aug. 1895, with the subtitle, "A Detail of an American Battle."

The battery on the hill presently engaged in a frightful duel. The white legs of the gunners scampered this way and that way, and the officers redoubled their shouts. The guns, with their demeanors of stolidity and courage, were typical of something infinitely self-possessed in this clamor of death that swirled around the hill.

One of a "swing" team was suddenly smitten quivering to the ground, and his maddened brethren dragged his torn body in their struggle to escape from this turmoil and danger. A young soldier astride one of the leaders swore and fumed in his saddle and furiously jerked at the bridle. An officer screamed out an order so violently that his voice broke and ended the sentence in a falsetto shriek.

The leading company of the infantry regiment was somewhat exposed, and the colonel ordered it moved more fully under the shelter of the hill. There was the clank of steel against steel.

A lieutenant of the battery rode down and passed them, holding his right arm carefully in his left hand. And it was as if this arm was not at all a part of him, but belonged to another man. His sober and reflective charger went slowly. The officer's face was grimy and perspiring, and his uniform was tousled as if he had been in direct grapple with an enemy. He smiled grimly when the men stared at him. He turned his horse toward the meadow.

Collins, of A Company, said: "I wisht I had a drink. I bet there's water in that there ol' well yonder!"

"Yes; but how you goin' to git it?"

For the little meadow which intervened was now suffering a terrible onslaught of shells. Its green and beautiful calm had vanished utterly. Brown earth was being flung in monstrous handfuls. And there was a massacre of the young blades of grass. They were being torn, burned, obliterated. Some curious fortune of the battle had made this gentle little meadow the object of the red hate of the shells, and each one as it exploded seemed like an imprecation in the face of a maiden.

The wounded officer who was riding across this expanse said to himself: "Why, they couldn't shoot any harder if the whole army was massed here!"

A shell struck the gray ruins of the house, and as, after the roar, the shattered wall fell in fragments, there was a noise which resembled the flapping of shutters during a wild gale of winter. Indeed, the infantry paused in the shelter of the bank appeared as men standing upon a shore contemplating a madness of the sea. The angel of calamity had under its glance the battery upon the hill. Fewer white-legged men labored about the guns. A shell had smitten one of the pieces, and after the flare, the smoke, the dust, the wrath of this blow were gone, it was possible to see white legs stretched horizontally upon the ground. And at that interval to the rear where it is the business of battery horses to stand with their noses to the fight, awaiting the command to drag their guns out of the destruction, or into it, or wheresoever these incomprehensible humans demanded with whip and spur—in this line of passive and dumb spectators, whose fluttering hearts yet would not let them forget the iron laws of man's control of them—in this rank of brute-soldiers there had been relentless and hideous carnage. From the ruck of bleeding and prostrate horses, the men of the infantry could see one animal raising its stricken body with its forelegs and turning its nose with mystic and profound eloquence toward the sky.

Some comrades joked Collins about his thirst. "Well, if yeh want a drink so bad, why don't yeh go git it?"

"Well, I will in a minnet, if yeh don't shut up!"

A lieutenant of artillery floundered his horse straight down the hill with as little concern as if it were level ground. As he galloped past the colonel of the infantry, he threw up his hand in swift salute. "We've got to get out of that," he roared angrily. He was a black-bearded officer, and his eyes, which resembled beads, sparkled like those of an insane man. His jumping horse sped along the column of infantry.

The fat major, standing carelessly with his sword held horizontally behind him and with his legs far apart, looked after the receding horseman and laughed, "He wants to get back with orders pretty quick, or there'll be no batt'ry left," he observed.

The wise young captain of the second company hazarded to the lieutenant-colonel that the enemy's infantry would probably soon attack the hill, and the lieutenant-colonel snubbed him.

A private in one of the rear companies looked out over the meadow, and then turned to a companion and said, "Look there, Jim!" It was the wounded officer from the battery, who some time before had started to ride across the meadow, supporting his right arm carefully with his left hand. This man had encountered a shell, apparently, at a time when no one perceived him, and he could now be seen lying face downward with a stirruped foot stretched across the body of his dead horse. A leg of the charger extended slantingly upward, precisely as stiff as a stake. Around this motionless pair the shells still howled.

There was a quarrel in A Company. Collins was shaking his fist in the faces of some laughing comrades. "Dern yeh! I ain't afraid t' go. If yeh say much, I will go!"

"Of course, yeh will! You'll run through that there medder, won't yeh?"

Collins said, in a terrible voice: "You see now!" At this ominous threat his comrades broke into renewed jeers.

Collins gave them a dark scowl, and went to find his captain. The latter was conversing with the colonel of the regiment.

"Captain," said Collins, saluting and standing at attention—in those days all trousers bagged at the knees—"Captain, I want t' get permission to go git some water from that there well over yonder!"

The colonel and the captain swung about simultaneously and stared across the meadow. The captain laughed. "You must be pretty thirsty, Collins?"

"Yes, sir, I am."

"Well—ah," said the captain. After a moment, he asked, "Can't you wait?"

"No, sir."

The colonel was watching Collins's face. "Look here, my lad," he said, in a pious sort of voice—"Look here, my lad"—Collins was not a lad—"don't you think that's taking pretty big risks for a little drink of water?"

"I dunno," said Collins uncomfortably. Some of the resentment toward his companions, which perhaps had forced him into this affair, was beginning to fade. "I dunno wether 'tis."

The colonel and the captain contemplated him for a time.

"Well," said the captain finally.

"Well," said the colonel, "if you want to go, why, go."

Collins saluted. "Much obliged t'yeh."

As he moved away the colonel called after him. "Take some of the other boys' canteens with you, an' hurry back, now."

"Yes, sir, I will."

The colonel and the captain looked at each other then, for it had suddenly occurred that they could not for the life of them tell whether Collins wanted to go or whether he did not.

They turned to regard Collins, and as they perceived him surrounded by gesticulating comrades, the colonel said: "Well, by thunder! I guess he's going."

Collins appeared as a man dreaming. In the midst of the questions, the advice, the warnings, all the excited talk of his company mates, he maintained a curious silence.

They were very busy in preparing him for his ordeal. When they inspected him carefully, it was somewhat like the examination that grooms give a horse before a race; and they were amazed, staggered, by the whole affair. Their astonishment found vent in strange repetitions.

"Are yeh sure a-goin'?" they demanded again and again.

"Certainly I am," cried Collins at last, furiously.

He strode sullenly away from them. He was swinging five or six canteens by their cords. It seemed that his cap would not remain firmly on his head, and often he reached and pulled it down over his brow.

There was a general movement in the compact column. The long animal-like thing moved slightly. Its four hundred eyes were turned upon the figure of Collins.

"Well, sir, if that ain't th' derndest thing! I never thought Fred Collins had the blood in him for that kind of business."

"What's he goin' to do, anyhow?"

"He's goin' to that well there after water."

"We ain't dyin' of thirst, are we? That's foolishness."

"Well, somebody put him up to it, an' he's doin' it."

"Say, he must be a desperate cuss."

When Collins faced the meadow and walked away from the regiment, he was vaguely conscious that a chasm, the deep valley of all prides, was suddenly between him and his comrades. It was provisional, but the provision was that he return as a victor. He had blindly been led by quaint emotions, and laid himself under an obligation to walk squarely up to the face of death.

But he was not sure that he wished to make a retraction, even if he could do so without shame. As a matter of truth, he was sure of very little. He was mainly surprised.

It seemed to him supernaturally strange that he had allowed his mind to manœuvre his body into such a situation. He understood that it might be called dramatically great.

However, he had no full appreciation of anything, excepting that he was actually conscious of being dazed. He could feel his dulled mind groping after the form and color of this incident. He wondered why he did not feel some keen agony of fear cutting his sense like a knife. He wondered at this, because human expression had said loudly for centuries that men should feel afraid of certain things, and that all men who did not feel this fear were phenomena—heroes.

He was, then, a hero. He suffered that disappointment which we would all have if we discovered that we were ourselves capable of those deeds which we most admire in history and legend. This, then, was a hero. After all, heroes were not much.

No, it could not be true. He was not a hero. Heroes had no shames in their lives, and, as for him, he remembered borrowing fifteen dollars from a friend and promising to pay it back the next day, and then avoiding that friend for ten months. When, at home, his mother had aroused him for the early labor of his life on the farm, it had often been his fashion to be irritable, childish, diabolical; and his mother had died since he had come to the war.

He saw that, in this matter of the well, the canteens, the shells, he was an intruder in the land of fine deeds.

He was now about thirty paces from his comrades. The regiment had just turned its many faces toward him.

From the forest of terrific noises there suddenly emerged a little un-even line of men. They fired fiercely and rapidly at distant foliage on which appeared little puffs of white smoke. The spatter of skirmish firing was added to the thunder of the guns on the hill. The little line of men ran forward. A color-sergeant fell flat with his flag as if he had slipped on ice. There was hoarse cheering from this distant field.

Collins suddenly felt that two demon fingers were pressed into his ears. He could see nothing but flying arrows, flaming red. He lurched from the shock of this explosion, but he made a mad rush for the house, which he viewed as a man submerged to the neck in a boiling surf might view the shore. In the air little pieces of shell howled, and the earthquake explosions drove him insane with the menace of their roar. As he ran the canteens knocked together with a rhythmical tinkling.

As he neared the house, each detail of the scene became vivid to him. He was aware of some bricks of the vanished chimney lying on the sod. There was a door which hung by one hinge.

Rifle bullets called forth by the insistent skirmishers came from the far-off bank of foliage. They mingled with the shells and the pieces of shells until the air was torn in all directions by hootings, yells, howls. The sky was full of fiends who directed all their wild rage at his head.

When he came to the well, he flung himself face downward and peered into its darkness. There were furtive silver glintings some feet from the surface. He grabbled one of the canteens and, unfastening its cap, swung it down by the cord. The water flowed slowly in with an indolent gurgle.

And now, as he lay with his face turned away, he was suddenly smitten with the terror. It came upon his heart like the grasp of claws. All the power faded from his muscles. For an instant he was no more than a dead man.

The canteen filled with a maddening slowness, in the manner of all bottles. Presently he recovered his strength and addressed a screaming oath to it. He leaned over until it seemed as if he intended to try to push water into it with his hands. His eyes as he gazed down into the well shone like two pieces of metal, and in their expression was a great appeal and a great curse. The stupid water derided him.

There was the blaring thunder of a shell. Crimson light shone through the swift-boiling smoke, and made a pink reflection on part of the wall of the well. Collins jerked out his arm and canteen with the same motion that a man would use in withdrawing his head from a furnace.

He scrambled erect and glared and hesitated. On the ground near him lay the old well bucket, with a length of rusty chain. He lowered it swiftly into the well. The bucket struck the water and then, turning lazily over, sank. When, with hand reaching tremblingly over hand, he hauled it out, it knocked often against the walls of the well and spilled some of its contents.

In running with a filled bucket, a man can adopt but one kind of gait. So, through this terrible field over which screamed practical angels of death, Collins ran in the manner of a farmer chased out of a dairy by a bull.

His face went staring white with anticipating—anticipation of a blow that would whirl him around and down. He would fall as he had seen other men fall, the life knocked out of them so suddenly that their knees were no more quick to touch the ground than their heads. He saw the long blue line of the regiment, but his comrades were standing looking at him from the edge of an impossible star. He was aware of some deep wheelruts and hoofprints in the sod beneath his feet.

The artillery officer who had fallen in this meadow had been making groans in the teeth of the tempest of sound. These futile cries, wrenched from him by his agony, were heard only by shells, bullets. When wild-eyed Collins came running, this officer raised himself. His face contorted and blanched from pain, he was about to utter some great beseeching cry. But suddenly his face straightened, and he called: "Say, young man, give me a drink of water, will you?"

Collins had no room amid his emotions for surprise. He was mad from the threats of destruction.

"I can't!" he screamed, and in his reply was a full description of his quaking apprehension. His cap was gone and his hair was riotous. His clothes made it appear that he had been dragged over the ground by the heels. He ran on.

The officer's head sank down, and one elbow crooked. His foot in its brass-bound stirrup still stretched over the body of his horse, and the other leg was under the steed.

But Collins turned. He came dashing back. His face had now turned grey, and in his eyes was all terror. "Here it is! here it is!"

The officer was as a man gone in drink. His arm bent like a twig. His head drooped as if his neck were of willow. He was sinking to the ground, to lie face downward.

Collins grabbed him by the shoulder. "Here it is. Here's your drink. Turn over. Turn over, man, for God's sake!"

With Collins hauling at his shoulder, the officer twisted his body and fell with his face turned toward that region where lived the unspeakable noises of the swirling missiles. There was the faintest shadow of a smile on his lips as he looked at Collins. He gave a sigh, a little primitive breath like that from a child.

Collins tried to hold the bucket steadily, but his shaking hands caused the water to splash all over the face of the dying man. Then he jerked it away and ran on.

The regiment gave him a welcoming roar. The grimed faces were wrinkled in laughter.

His captain waved the bucket away. "Give it to the men!"

The two genial, skylarking young lieutenants were the first to gain possession of it. They played over it in their fashion.

When one tried to drink, the other teasingly knocked his elbow. "Don't Billie! You'll make me spill it," said the one. The other laughed.

Suddenly there was an oath, the thud of wood on the ground, and a swift murmur of astonishment among the ranks. The two lieutenants glared at each other. The bucket lay on the ground empty.

"THE VETERAN"

Out of the low window could be seen three hickory trees placed irregularly in a meadow that was resplendent in springtime green. Farther away, the old, dismal belfry of the village church loomed over the pines. A horse meditating in the shade of one of the hickories lazily swished his tail. The warm sunshine made an oblong of vivid yellow on the floor of the grocery.

"Could you see the whites of their eyes?" said the man who was seated on a soap box.

"Nothing of the kind," replied old Henry warmly. "Just a lot of flitting figures, and I let go at where they 'peared to be the thickest. Bang!"

"Mr. Fleming," said the grocer—his deferential voice expressed somehow the old man's exact social weight—"Mr. Fleming, you never was frightened much in them battles, was you?"

The veteran looked down and grinned. Observing his manner, the entire group tittered. "Well, I guess I was," he answered finally. "Pretty well scared, sometimes. Why, in my first battle I thought the sky was falling down. I thought the world was coming to an end. You bet I was scared."

Every one laughed. Perhaps it seemed strange and rather wonderful to them that a man should admit the thing, and in the tone of their laughter there was probably more admiration than if old Fleming had declared that he had always been a lion. Moreover, they knew that he had ranked as an orderly sergeant, and so their opinion of his heroism was fixed. None, to be sure, knew how an orderly sergeant ranked, but then it was understood to be somewhere just shy of a major general's stars. So, when old Henry admitted that he had been frightened, there was a laugh.

"The trouble was," said the old man, "I thought they were all shooting at me. Yes, sir, I thought every man in the other army was aiming at me in particular, and only me. And it seemed so darned unreasonable, you know. I wanted to explain to 'em what an almighty good fellow I was, because I thought then they might quit trying to hit me. But I couldn't explain, and they kept on being unreasonable—blim!—blam! bang! So I run!"

Two little triangles of wrinkles appeared at the corners of his eyes. Evidently he appreciated some comedy in this recital. Down near his feet, however, little Jim, his grandson, was visibly horror-stricken. His hands were clasped nervously, and his eyes were wide with astonishment at this terrible scandal, his most magnificent grandfather telling such a thing.

"That was at Chancellorsville. Of course, afterward I got kind of used to it. A man does. Lots of men, though, seem to feel all right from the start. I did, as soon as I 'got on to it,' as they say now; but at first I was pretty flustered. Now, there was young Jim Conklin, old Si Conklin's son—that used to keep the tannery—you none of you recollect him—well, he went into it from the start just as if he was born to it. But with me it was different. I had to get used to it."

When little Jim walked with his grandfather he was in the habit of skipping along on the stone pavement in front of the three stores and the hotel of the town and betting that he could avoid the cracks. But upon this day he walked soberly, with his hand gripping two of his grandfather's fingers. Sometimes he kicked abstractedly at dandelions that curved over the walk. Any one could see that he was much troubled.

"There's Sickles's colt over in the medder, Jimmie," said the old man. "Don't you wish you owned one like him?"

"Um," said the boy, with a strange lack of interest. He continued his reflections. Then finally he ventured: "Grandpa—now—was that true what you was telling those men?"

"What?" asked the grandfather. "What was I telling them?"

"Oh, about your running."

"Why, yes, that was true enough, Jimmie. It was my first fight, and there was an awful lot of noise, you know."

Jimmie seemed dazed that this idol, of its own will, should so totter. His stout boyish idealism was injured.

Presently the grandfather said: "Sickles's colt is going for a drink. Don't you wish you owned Sickles's colt, Jimmie?"

The boy merely answered: "He ain't as nice as our'n." He lapsed then into another moody silence.

One of the hired men, a Swede, desired to drive to the county seat for purposes of his own. The old man lent him a horse and an unwashed buggy. It appeared later that one of the purposes of the Swede was to get drunk.

After quelling some boisterous frolic of the farm hands and boys in the garret, the old man had that night gone peacefully to sleep, when he was aroused by clamoring at the kitchen door. He grabbed his trousers, and they waved out behind as he dashed forward. He could hear the voice of the Swede, screaming and blubbering. He pushed the wooden button, and, as the door flew open, the Swede, a maniac, stumbled inward, chattering, weeping, still screaming: "De barn fire! Fire! Fire! De barn fire! Fire! Fire! Fire!"

There was a swift and indescribable change in the old man. His face ceased instantly to be a face; it became a mask, a grey thing, with horror written about the mouth and eyes. He hoarsely shouted at the foot of the little rickety stairs, and immediately, it seemed, there came down an avalanche of men. No one knew that during this time the old lady had been standing in her night-clothes at the bedroom door, yelling: "What's th' matter? What's th' matter? What's th' matter?"

When they dashed toward the barn it presented to their eyes its usual appearance, solemn, rather mystic in the black night. The Swede's lantern was overturned at a point some yards in front of the barn doors. It contained a wild little conflagration of its own, and even in their excitement some of those who ran felt a gentle secondary vibration of the thrifty part of their minds at sight of this overturned lantern. Under ordinary circumstances it would have been a calamity.

But the cattle in the barn were trampling, trampling, trampling, and above this noise could be heard a humming like the song of innumerable bees. The old man hurled aside the great doors, and a yellow flame leaped out at one corner and sped and wavered frantically up the old grey wall. It was glad, terrible, this single flame, like the wild banner of deadly and triumphant foes.

The motley crowd from the garret had come with all the pails of the farm. They flung themselves upon the well. It was a leisurely old machine, long dwelling in indolence. It was in the habit of giving out water with a sort of reluctance. The men stormed at it, cursed it; but it continued to allow the buckets to be filled only after the wheezy windlass had howled many protests at the mad-handed men.

With his opened knife in his hand old Fleming himself had gone head-long into the barn, where the stifling smoke swirled with the air currents, and where could be heard in its fulness the terrible chorus of the flames, laden with tones of hate and death, a hymn of wonderful ferocity.

He flung a blanket over an old mare's head, cut the halter close to the manger, led the mare to the door, and fairly kicked her out to safety. He returned with the same blanket, and rescued one of the work horses. He took five horses out, and then came out himself, with his clothes bravely on fire. He had no whiskers, and very little hair on his head. They soused five pailfuls of water on him. His eldest son made a clean miss with the sixth pailful, because the old man had turned and was running down the decline and around to the basement of the barn, where were the stanchions of the cows. Some one noticed at the time that he ran very lamely, as if one of the frenzied horses had smashed his hip.

The cows, with their heads held in the heavy stanchions, had thrown themselves, strangled themselves, tangled themselves—done everything which the ingenuity of their exuberant fear could suggest to them.

Here, as at the well, the same thing happened to every man save one. Their hands went mad. They became incapable of everything save the power to rush into dangerous situations.

The old man released the cow nearest the door, and she, blind drunk with terror, crashed into the Swede. The Swede had been running to and fro, babbling. He carried an empty milk-pail, to which he clung with an unconscious fierce enthusiasm. He shrieked like one lost as he went under the cow's hoofs, and the milk-pail, rolling across the floor, made a flash of silver in the gloom.

Old Fleming took a fork, beat off the cow, and dragged the paralysed Swede to the open air. When they had rescued all the cows save one, which had so fastened herself that she could not be moved an inch, they returned to the front of the barn, and stood sadly, breathing like men who had reached the final point of human effort.

Many people had come running. Some one had even gone to the church, and now, from the distance, rang the tocsin note of the old bell. There was a long flare of crimson on the sky, which made remote people speculate as to the whereabouts of the fire.

The long flames sang their drumming chorus in voices of the heaviest bass. The wind whirled clouds of smoke and cinders into the faces of the spectators. The form of the old barn was outlined in black amid these masses of orange-hued flames.

And then came this Swede again, crying as one who is the weapon of the sinister fates. "De colts! De colts! You have forgot de colts!"

Old Fleming staggered. It was true: they had forgotten the two colts in the box stalls at the back of the barn. "Boys," he said, "I must try to get 'em out." They clamored about him then, afraid for him, afraid of what they should see. Then they talked wildly each to each. "Why, it's sure death!" "He would never get out!" "Why, it's suicide for a man to go in there!" Old Fleming stared absent-mindedly at the open doors. "The poor little things!" he said. He rushed into the barn.

When the roof fell in, a great funnel of smoke swarmed toward the sky, as if the old man's mighty spirit, released from its body—a little bottle—had swelled like the genie of fable. The smoke was tinted rose-hue from the flames, and perhaps the unutterable midnights of the universe will have no power to daunt the color of this soul.

"AN EPISODE OF WAR"

The lieutenant's rubber blanket lay on the ground, and upon it he had poured the company's supply of coffee. Corporals and other representatives of the grimy and hot-throated men who lined the breast-work had come for each squad's portion.

The lieutenant was frowning and serious at this task of division. His lips pursed as he drew with his sword various crevices in the heap, until brown squares of coffee, astoundingly equal in size, appeared on the blanket. He was on the verge of a great triumph in mathematics, and the corporals were thronging forward, each to reap a little square, when suddenly the lieutenant cried out and looked quickly at a man near him as if he suspected it was a case of personal assault. The others cried out also when they saw blood upon the lieutenant's sleeve.

He had winced like a man stung, swayed dangerously, and then straightened. The sound of his hoarse breathing was plainly audible. He looked sadly, mystically, over the breast-work at the green face of a wood, where now were many little puffs of white smoke. During this moment the men about him gazed statuelike and silent, astonished and awed by

The Gentlewoman, Dec. 1899.

this catastrophe which happened when catastrophes were not expected—
when they had leisure to observe it.

As the lieutenant stared at the wood, they too swung their heads, so
that for another instant all hands, still silent, contemplated the distant forest as if their minds were fixed upon the mystery of a bullet's journey.

The officer had, of course, been compelled to take his sword into his
left hand. He did not hold it by the hilt. He gripped it at the middle of the
blade, awkwardly. Turning his eyes from the hostile wood, he looked at
the sword as he held it there, and seemed puzzled as to what to do with it,
where to put it. In short, this weapon had of a sudden become a strange
thing to him. He looked at it in a kind of stupefaction, as if he had been
endowed with a trident, a sceptre, or a spade.

Finally he tried to sheathe it. To sheathe a sword held by the left hand,
at the middle of the blade, in a scabbard hung at the left hip, is a feat worthy of a sawdust ring. This wounded officer engaged in a desperate struggle
with the sword and the wobbling scabbard, and during the time of it he
breathed like a wrestler.

But at this instant the men, the spectators, awoke from their stonelike
poses and crowded forward sympathetically. The orderly sergeant took the
sword and tenderly placed it in the scabbard. At the time, he leaned nervously backward, and did not allow even his finger to brush the body of
the lieutenant. A wound gives strange dignity to him who bears it. Well
men shy from his new and terrible majesty. It is as if the wounded man's
hand is upon the curtain which hangs before the revelations of all existence—the meaning of ants, potentates, wars, cities, sunshine, snow, a
feather dropped from a bird's wing; and the power of it sheds radiance
upon a bloody form, and makes the other men understand sometimes that
they are little. His comrades look at him with large eyes thoughtfully.
Moreover, they fear vaguely that the weight of a finger upon him might
send him headlong, precipitate the tragedy, hurl him at once into the dim,
gray unknown. And so the orderly sergeant, while sheathing the sword,
leaned nervously backward.

There were others who proffered assistance. One timidly presented his
shoulder and asked the lieutenant if he cared to lean upon it, but the latter waved him away mournfully. He wore the look of one who knows he
is the victim of a terrible disease and understands his helplessness. He
again stared over the breast-work at the forest, and then, turning, went
slowly rearward. He held his right wrist tenderly in his left hand as if the
wounded arm was made of very brittle glass.

And the men in silence stared at the wood, then at the departing lieutenant; then at the wood, then at the lieutenant.

As the wounded officer passed from the line of battle, he was enabled to see many things which as a participant in the fight were unknown to him. He saw a general on a black horse gazing over the lines of blue infantry at the green woods which veiled his problems. An aide galloped furiously, dragged his horse suddenly to a halt, saluted, and presented a paper. It was, for a wonder, precisely like a historical painting.

To the rear of the general and his staff a group, composed of a bugler, two or three orderlies, and the bearer of the corps standard, all upon maniacal horses, were working like slaves to hold their ground, preserve their respectful interval, while the shells boomed in the air about them, and caused their chargers to make furious quivering leaps.

A battery, a tumultuous and shining mass, was swirling toward the right. The wild thud of hoofs, the cries of the riders shouting blame and praise, menace and encouragement, and, last, the roar of the wheels, the slant of the glistening guns, brought the lieutenant to an intent pause. The battery swept in curves that stirred the heart; it made halts as dramatic as the crash of a wave on the rocks, and when it fled onward this aggregation of wheels, levers, motors had a beautiful unity, as if it were a missile. The sound of it was a war-chorus that reached into the depths of man's emotion.

The lieutenant, still holding his arm as if it were of glass, stood watching this battery until all detail of it was lost, save the figures of the riders, which rose and fell and waved lashes over the black mass.

Later, he turned his eyes toward the battle, where the shooting sometimes crackled like bush fires, sometimes sputtered with exasperating irregularity, and sometimes reverberated like the thunder. He saw the smoke rolling upward and saw crowds of men who ran and cheered, or stood and blazed away at the inscrutable distance.

He came upon some stragglers, and they told him how to find the field hospital. They described its exact location. In fact, these men, no longer having part in the battle, knew more of it than others. They told the performance of every corps, every division, the opinion of every general. The lieutenant, carrying his wounded arm rearward, looked upon them with wonder.

At the roadside a brigade was making coffee and buzzing with talk like a girls' boarding school. Several officers came out to him and inquired concerning things of which he knew nothing. One, seeing his arm, began to scold. "Why, man, that's no way to do. You want to fix that thing." He appropriated the lieutenant and the lieutenant's wound. He cut the sleeve and laid bare the arm, every nerve of which softly fluttered under his touch. He bound his handkerchief over the wound, scolding away in the meantime. His tone allowed one to think that he was in the habit of being wounded every day. The lieutenant hung his head, feeling, in this presence, that he did not know how to be correctly wounded.

The low white tents of the hospital were grouped around an old schoolhouse. There was here a singular commotion. In the foreground two ambulances interlocked wheels in the deep mud. The drivers were tossing the blame of it back and forth, gesticulating and berating, while from the ambulances, both crammed with wounded, there came an occasional groan. An interminable crowd of bandaged men were coming and going. Great numbers sat under the trees nursing heads or arms or legs. There was a dispute of some kind raging on the steps of the schoolhouse. Sitting with his back against a tree a man with a face as gray as a new army blanket was serenely smoking a corncob pipe. The lieutenant wished to rush forward and inform him that he was dying.

A busy surgeon was passing near the lieutenant. "Good morning," he said, with a friendly smile. Then he caught sight of the lieutenant's arm, and his face at once changed. "Well, let's have a look at it." He seemed possessed suddenly of a great contempt for the lieutenant. This wound evidently placed the latter on a very low social plane. The doctor cried out impatiently: "What mutton-head tied it up that way anyhow?" The lieutenant answered, "Oh, a man."

When the wound was disclosed the doctor fingered it disdainfully. "Humph," he said. "You come along with me and I'll tend to you." His voice contained the same scorn as if he were saying: "You will have to go to jail."

The lieutenant had been very meek, but now his face flushed, and he looked into the doctor's eyes. "I guess I won't have it amputated," he said.

"Nonsense, man! Nonsense! Nonsense!" cried the doctor. "Come along, now. I won't amputate it. Come along. Don't be a baby."

"Let go of me," said the lieutenant, holding back wrathfully, his glance fixed upon the door of the old schoolhouse, as sinister to him as the portals of death.

And this is the story of how the lieutenant lost his arm. When he reached home, his sisters, his mother, his wife, sobbed for a long time at the sight of the flat sleeve. "Oh, well," he said, standing shamefaced amid these tears, "I don't suppose it matters so much as all that."

THE CIVIL WAR REMEMBERED

Phyllis Frus and Stanley Corkin, Volume Editors

Is it surprising that one of the United States' most canonical books is a novel set in the Civil War? Anyone who has seen grown men replaying the battles of that war on their laptop computers or read about whole families participating in laboriously staged battlefield reenactments knows the passion this bitter conflict arouses 135 years later. Indeed, consider the passions aroused by the initiatives to remove the emblem of the Confederate states from the state flags of Mississippi, Georgia, and South Carolina. The Civil War is studied as our greatest national tragedy and evoked nostalgically as the war of brother against brother. Even now, in 1999, it is the subject and title of a Broadway play, for which historian Eric Foner is a technical consultant. To the South, defeat in the war meant the loss of the Confederacy and the loss of a romanticized way of life—their mythic "lost cause," a term that was introduced as early as 1867 by Edward A. Pollard in his book by that name. Evidently it is not the reality of the war that forms the basis for this interest, even obsession. The myth-making activity of telling our nation's history has transformed four years of bloody battles—which produced mortality rates as high as 15 percent and casualty rates significantly higher—into a glorious pageant.

In this nostalgic version of the war's history, the failures of generals are redeemed by the bravery of individuals. Richard Slotkin, in *The Fatal Environment: The Myth of the Frontier in the Age of Industrialization, 1800–1890*, tells us,

> The Civil War had given Americans an extensive education in the capacity of individuals and societies to inflict and to suffer violence—and to justify that violence in terms of sacred mythology. The Protestant myth of blood atonement was perhaps the dominant metaphor through which Americans expressed the conviction that this colossal outburst of murder and destruction must lead to some benign and progressive transformation of society. (303)

Whether one had shown willingness to give one's life for the Union or the Confederacy, to have participated in this conflict earned one a mark of distinction.

Yet, as the narratives in this section reveal, soon after the war its putative justifications became increasingly difficult to recall. Even one of the war's primary goals and certainly, after the Emancipation Proclamation was signed on January 1, 1863, its central focus—to end the system of chattel slavery on which the South's economy was based—was gradually deemphasized. This cause ultimately became a footnote to the accepted version of U.S. history, as other reasons for the conflict were brought to the forefront, such as states' rights and the agrarian South's refusal to be governed by an industrialized North. Eventually, according to James Loewen, slavery as a primary cause of the war, arguably one of the principal issues dividing the country since its inception and to preserve which eleven Southern states seceded, was minimized. According to Loewen, this was still true as late as the 1960s in high school textbooks, the principal source of historical knowledge for generations of Americans (134–36).

The persistence of the mythic dimension of the Civil War is emphasized in order to raise the question of how *The Red Badge of Courage* fits into the elaboration of this myth, both in its production and its reception. The world Crane was born into was decidedly a postwar world and one marked by signs that the nation was failing to make good on the promise of the Emancipation Proclamation even as the war's meaning was assuming an increasingly defined shape in the national consciousness. By 1871, the year of Crane's birth, the Freedman's Bureau had been dead for some two years, and African Americans were in the process of being reduced to peonage under the sharecropping system. The legacy of slavery and the persistence of racism allowed little possibility for the "New Negro" to emerge. White veterans were adjusting to a social and economic world everywhere in transformation while preserving their memories of an exhausting war that distinguished them as featured players in the national drama—whatever the drama's master narrative. Stories and anecdotes of the war were readily available in novels, in magazines, and in the tales told by participants. And although recountings of battle and strife abounded, few defined the conflict as one to end slavery. Fewer still focused on the valiant efforts of African American soldiers.

The stream of narratives by participants was in full force by 1871, and young Stephen Crane could not have escaped the stories' effects as he was growing up. By the time he turned six, in 1877, the last federal troops had been removed from the South and the American system of apartheid was on the near horizon. As Ralph Ellison emphasizes, the failure of Reconstruction meant "the continuation of the Civil War by means other than arms"—that is, by "guerrilla politics" meant to achieve the South's goal. And these tactics succeeded to the extent that the North, "eager to lose any memory traces of those values for which it had gone to war," took the low moral ground by allowing the passage of Jim Crow laws and neglecting to safeguard the intended results of the Fourteenth and Fifteenth Amendments (67).

The guerrilla war to keep former slaves in slavelike conditions was many-faceted and began almost as soon as they were removed from slavery in 1863. This paradoxical situation came about because freedom and equality for African American men and women was the ultimate device employed by the federal government to bolster a flagging war effort; there was little commitment to achieving these ends. Slotkin explains how this happened, beginning with Lincoln's signing of the Emancipation Proclamation, which both reordered the national understanding of the reasons for the war and confirmed a battlefield strategy.

Relatively early in the war, Union generals came to understand that the Confederacy was so committed to defending its long-embattled way of life that it would yield only in the event of overwhelming defeat. As Slotkin, citing extensively military historian Russell Weigley, explains, "The successful strategists of Union victory built their policies on the understanding that the political and social stakes of the war were too fundamental to admit to compromise without military victory and that the battlefield triumph was, in the existing state of military technology and organization, less a matter of decisive battles than of steady commitment to a war of attrition" (303). The example par excellence of this commitment is Sherman's march to the sea: in late 1864 General William Tecumseh Sherman led his troops from Atlanta to the coast, leaving a path of burned and looted fields and homes in their wake, effectively ending the conflict. In order to persuade the North—leaders, soldiers, and a broad section of the citizenry—of the necessity of such a destructive campaign, a critical mass had to be convinced of the validity of their own cause. Defining its cause had always been problematic for the North, but, after 1863, emancipation became the unavoidable rationale for fighting to the finish. This explanation was especially controversial because of the pervasiveness of white racism in the North. Though Northern soldiers fought for their commanders, the cause for which they fought was now generally unacceptable, as the war's purpose had become that of freeing slaves and abolishing slavery. This only strengthened the South's resolution, and thus the necessity for the North to fight to the finish, as the idea of making African Americans their peers was outrageous to white Southerners.

Though the lack of support among Northerners for the goal of emancipation seems not to have had much of an effect on the Union generals' conduct of the war, it did have significant effects on soldiers and citizens in both the North and the South. Indeed, we can see the New York City draft riots of the summer of 1863 as resulting at least to a degree from a

lack of support for the now too visible cause of emancipation.[1] Slotkin says
that even those who supported the abolition of slavery and were central to
the execution of the war, including Generals McClellan and Sherman, had
significant reservations about the wisdom of emancipation (304).

As shown in the introductory materials compiled in Part I, particularly in the writings by Nathaniel Shaler, Ida Wells-Barnett, and W. E. B.
Du Bois, the persistence and even growth of extreme racist beliefs was a
fact of late-nineteenth-century American life. Thus, it is no wonder that
few in power made a significant effort to assist the former slaves in achieving full-citizen status or that few Americans defended African American
civil rights as Jim Crowism swept the nation in the last years of the century. Indeed, with this in mind, it becomes evident that the South's guerrilla tactics, in the form of vigilance squads, the knights of the Ku Klux
Klan, lynchings, and finally segregation enforced by intimidation and law,
were little resisted because of—among other social, political, and economic factors—widespread racism in both the North and the South.

Against this background, the lack of attention to the cause or intended effects of the war in *The Red Badge of Courage* might be attrib-
uted to an unspoken national agreement not to discuss the issue. Though
Crane's intentions for doing so cannot be known, the omission of cause
and intended effects and of references to specific battles and the generals
who conducted them—what Amy Kaplan calls the "illegibility of history" in the novel—has the effect of universalizing one young private's experience as an initiation into battle and into young adulthood, if not
maturity (78). The critical consensus was that *The Red Badge of Courage*
was refreshingly new because Crane created a psychologically real portrait of a young man undergoing a powerful experience; from such a point
of view, Henry Fleming transcends the circumstances of the Civil War
and stands in for every man who goes to war, no matter the cause.
"This is war from a new point of view," wrote Edward Marshall, "and
it seems more real than when seen with an eye only for large moments and

---

[1] When the federal government, unable to get enough volunteers to win the "war of attrition," instituted the draft, protests occurred in most northern states, with particular anger
aimed at the exemption that wealthy men could obtain by providing a substitute or paying $300. In New York City, a mob comprising many Irish immigrants, who resented the
fact that blacks had recently been used to replace striking Irish longshoremen, burned
down the draft building and raided an armory to steal rifles. This began three days of
looting, burning, and murder; victims were largely African Americans, including hundreds of black children in an orphanage that was burned. An estimated 1,000 deaths occurred. "Willing to fight for Uncle Sam," but not "for Uncle Sambo," said one Pennsylvania newspaper (*New York Draft Riots*).

general effects" (85–86). Furthermore, the story went against the tide of heroic accounts, of individual men or units standing their ground bravely. The *New York Times* said Crane's picture was "free from any suspicion of ideality, defying every accepted tradition of martial glory" (Rev. of *Red Badge* 88).

Although many of the novel's first readers found the record of one young Union soldier's initiation into battle utterly convincing (one veteran even claimed to have been with the author at Antietam [Stallman 181]), others did not. Apparently it depended on one's expectations of war narratives. One reviewer of a Chicago daily objected to the overwritten prose, saying it would make a "real soldier tired to follow him." This reviewer went on to say that Crane underplayed the "comradeship and spirit . . . of a great army and leads the reader to believe a regiment of American soldiers is made up of a thousand dull automatons with a great amount of coarseness . . ." (L. H. Davis 128). Others, who read it against the tide of Civil War reminiscences, memoirs, histories, and fiction that was cresting in the 1890s, admired the novel's realism, what H. L. Mencken called Crane's "honest endeavor to depict human life as men and women were actually living it in the world" (x). The two views probably persist today. Those who have made Michael Shaara's *The Killer Angels* (an account of Gettysburg) the most popular twentieth-century novel of the Civil War may miss the larger setting of the war and cultural specifics such as geographical names in *The Red Badge of Courage*.

But many, accustomed to Hemingway, find it easy to overlook the novel's almost complete lack of reference to the meaning and significance of the bloody conflict. And the latter group is probably not struck by the absence of overt interpretation of historical events, preferring the opportunity Crane presented to empathize with a young man who agonizes over his courage and who, after he has "skedaddled," runs an emotional gamut, from wishing he were dead to hoping that his side will lose so that his decision to run will be vindicated to praying for the chance to redeem himself. And because the subjective point of view of Henry Fleming is so vivid, the absence of the big picture is not important, perhaps not even noticed. Readers are on Henry's side because they feel with him. As Andrew Delbanco says, "Reading *The Red Badge* relieves us of our ideology and . . . replaces it with raw experience" (54). The verdict of Crane's contemporaries (it was a bestseller in England as well as in the United States) has been sustained by history. The novel has never been out of print, was canonized by the New Critics in the 1950s, and has been reconsidered by all manner of historicist critics. Furthermore, Crane began a subjectivist tradition of war that makes Hemingway, Mailer, and Vietnam novelist Tim O'Brien his literary heirs.

The critics who are part of American literature's turn to history in recent decades have laid the groundwork for a new understanding of how events and attitudes of the 1890s affected Crane's understanding of the Civil War and thus his particular way of representing it. Although these critics are not putting in the historical referents Crane left out, as Harold Hungerford did in 1963 in establishing the "factual framework" of the novel as the battle at Chancellorsville 100 years earlier, they are reading *The Red Badge of Courage* historically in some sense by locating signs of the later nineteenth century in Crane's narrative. For example, Robert Shulman finds among the "social, political, racial and economic realities" of Crane's day pervasive fear of anarchy and violence resulting from labor strife, reports of black men arming themselves in self-defense against rising numbers of lynchings and beatings, the use of militia and federal troops to put down worker uprisings, clashes between corporate thugs and strikers, in short, "acute industrial and racial warfare." He locates the influence of these fears in *The Red Badge of Courage* in the form of a "confused, fear-stricken protagonist," "imagery of war, fog, chaos and demons," an "unsettling irony," a "technique of blurring clear edges," and a "systematic undercutting of certainty" (1, 15). Daniel Shanahan emphasizes the "overwhelming transformation and retransformation" of the United States between 1880 and 1990 as an influence on the composition of the novel, particularly Crane's depiction of the war and the army itself as caught up in competition that mirrors the "grand competition" of industrial capitalism brought about by massive technological change (402–03).

These history-based essays are quite helpful to the reader who wants to know something of the currents of Crane's time. For the most part, however, when these critics go back to *The Red Badge of Courage* to locate how an awareness of the upheaval in his own time influences a reader's understanding of the novel, their analysis focuses on the formal features of the text or generalizes from them to assert a theme that collapses the time differential between the novel's setting and its composition.[2] Amy Kaplan's more extensive essay is an exception, for although she does make some general claims on the basis of Crane's rhetorical strategies, she anchors them in evidence from historiography and literature. Her primary argument is that the novel "reinterpret[s] the war through the cultural lenses

---

[2] For example, Shanahan concludes that at novel's end Fleming has become not only a man but "a man of his time. . . . Crane takes one aspect of his contemporary experience and uses it to develop a broader picture of the human condition" (408). And Shulman asserts that in *The Red Badge of Courage* Crane "successfully transform[s] into the universality of art the dominant imagery and much of the inner meaning of an exceptionally troubled era in American life" (17).

and political concerns of the late nineteenth century" ("Spectacle," 78). For example, from studying the *Battles and Leaders* series that was Crane's primary source as well as 1880s fiction of the Civil War, she concludes that veterans and writers increasingly began to distinguish between the war and the reasons it was fought. Whereas other critics have argued that Crane shredded conventions of traditional storytelling about the war in order to "achieve a more realistic representation, whether of detailed sensory perceptions or of internal subjective impressions," she sees his goal as presenting the reality of war as a "highly mediated spectacle," and thus shows Henry watching himself be a hero or a coward, imagining the cries and jeers of his regiment when he anticipates returning to it, and fantasizing the dead bodies he comes across as laughing at him (95, 100). Kaplan believes that in *The Red Badge of Courage*, Crane was responding both to newspaper and magazine coverage of the Civil War and to episodes of class conflict in the 1890s as spectacles of violence. She also sees him anticipating the way he would himself participate as a spectator-correspondent in imperial wars later in the decade. Kaplan quotes Crane making the explicit connection between this novel and his later experience in war. Said Crane, after he had seen war in Greece in 1897, "The Red Badge is all right" (102).

Crane's novel and the related short stories fall within a distinct tradition of writing about the Civil War that minimizes the larger cause and focuses on battlefield action and acts of individual bravery. This tradition can be traced back to the last days of the conflict. For example, in "First Time under Fire," published in 1864 and later collected in *A Volunteer's Adventures*, John William DeForest told of a looming battle in Louisiana in 1862. He apprised his readers of the difficulties of sleeping before battle, the propensity of troops under fire to use "extremity in language," and the advice of "never stop, and the enemy won't stay" as a strategy for victory (55, 65, 67). But there is no particular sense of what is arousing this effort. We do meet some African Americans who are not named as slaves or ex-slaves but who we assume are to be understood as newly freed men. They are depicted as responding to the troops "with acclamations of joy[,] 'God bless you massas.'" The narrator goes on to tell of the "tricks and robberies which were practiced upon them by our jokers and scapegraces. Nowhere in the South did I ever find or hear of one Negro who was hostile to us. But meanwhile they were not vindictive toward their masters." This somewhat neutral but clearly condescending treatment of African Americans in the slave states is not dismissive by intention but by habit.

Eventually, whatever conflicts are represented in these works, the resolution of disagreement becomes the primary object. The best explanation for this emphasis on resolution is to see it as a response to the enormous interclass conflict that was so pronounced in the nineties (which Shulman and Kaplan both show). Reconstructing the notion of a cohesive nation after such a divisive struggle relied on the elaboration of areas of agreement between the former rivals at the expense of those at the bottom of the hierarchy. Now all could agree to exclude African Americans from national life, support the expansionist voices calling for the United States to become an empire, and accept the view that a paternalist class should dominate national life. *The Red Badge of Courage* is one text among many contributing to this trend; that is, it illustrates the rhetorical tendency common during the 1880s and 1890s to characterize the war as a ritualized act of violence in which the combatants, for all their lumps and pains, shake hands at its conclusion and express their respect for the other side's efforts.

In addition, the novel anticipates later Civil War novels that further elaborate the casting aside of the differences of the war, such as Thomas Dixon's *The Clansman* (1905), in which former combatants can reconcile and even have their heirs marry, having reached agreement that the war was a great test but that its ultimate goal of emancipation was ill-conceived. This view also informs turn-of-the-century historiography. For example, John W. Burgess and William Dunning offered a racially based theory of reconstruction that became an academic staple in the first half of the century, lending support to the view that the war had served no good purpose, that it had only fostered folly among whites of both regions. Their view, that Reconstruction was the disruptive work of white Northern Republicans, who exacted further vengeance upon the South by visiting the entirely inappropriate—for genetic reasons—curse of "negro rule" upon the vanquished South, became a reigning academic—and then popular—view (Foner ix–xxvii). Even if we accept that Crane harbored no particular racial animosities, for him to have questioned whether the issue of the war was worth the slaughter that resulted would have been quite ordinary. The question Crane must have faced as he began to draft *The Red Badge of Courage* is, If the issues of the war were so deeply flawed, what did all those men fight and die for? No wonder the war in his representation becomes a matter of individual actions and ironic treatments of battlefield postures.

In *The Red Badge of Courage* Crane further extended the idea that dates from 1863 and is first noted in DeForest's account of 1864: the Civil War has no larger goal, and therefore bravery is reduced to individuals attempting to stay out of the way of bullets or fighting valiantly for some personal reason. The novel barely mentions the opposing forces in terms that can easily be linked to their representation of a distinct political position. The Confederacy is simply the enemy for the most part, while the Union

Army is the regiment, various troop numbers, and those who recognize Henry as one of them. This emphasis follows not only DeForest, but also Mark Twain, Ambrose Bierce, and others. Without any ostensible reason for engaging in battle, the soldiers of *The Red Badge of Courage* become strategic markers in an elaborate and dangerous game. In such a game the players' ability to control the moves they make is narrowly circumscribed. If they move in ways that generally reflect the desires of the master strategists, they run the distinct risk of being eliminated from the larger game, namely life itself. If they exercise the combination of will and instinct that causes them to flee—as Henry did—they so break their internalized code of conduct that their psyches bear a wound akin to that inflicted by a bullet. Indeed, Henry's torment is palpable as he attempts to rationalize his having fled the battle: "He shambled along with bowed head, his brain in a tumult of agony and despair. When he looked loweringly up, quivering at each sound, his eyes had the expression of those of a criminal who thinks his guilt and his punishment great and knows that he can find no words" (Chapter VII).

Because Henry has little ability to define his desires and act on them and no reason to fight, no cause or commitment, his actions take on the qualities of a performance or game. Like a marker in chess or checkers, Henry is moved and seeks to be on the board at the end of the game, and if he is, he will enhance his side's chances of victory. Others have commented on the way in which this novel can be seen as part of the emphasis on games and spectacle that was emerging in the United States during this period. These include Bill Brown, who notes Crane's remark that men "play to win" when they engage in war. Says Brown, "At the very least we are left facing the possibility that this famously realist account of the Civil War may depend for its reality effect on the conflation of war and sport" (2–3). Henry continually sees the battle from a distance as some organized sporting event. When he sees a battery in action, he is shocked at the men's "conventional moods": "The battery was disputing with a distant antagonist and the gunners were wrapped in admiration of their shooting. They were continually bending in coaxing postures over the guns. They seemed to be patting them on the back and encouraging them with words" (Chapter VI). At other times, "two bodies of troops exchanged blows in the manner of a pair of boxers" (Chapter XX). And in Chapter XXII, Fleming watches a series of fierce contests in which the same little hills or clumps of trees seem to be taken first by blue and then by gray figures. He even smiles to see "men dodge and duck at the long screechings of shells that were thrown in giant handfuls over them." He sees two regiments fighting apart from the rest. "They were blazing as if upon a wager, giving and taking tremendous blows. The firings were incredibly fierce and rapid. These intent regiments apparently were *oblivious of the larger purposes of war* and were slugging each other as if at a matched game" (italics added).

Such a presentation provides maximum distance from the Emancipation Proclamation and allows white Northerners to disinvest from the cause of African American equality. The abolition of slavery becomes the absent cause of conflict, as African Americans become invisible men and women. But with their presence reinserted this novel shows the way in which racial divisions have been historically employed to disrupt potential interclass alliances. That the working-class soldiers of the novel failed to consider their role in a larger initiative for racial justice is an indicator that race was employed in the United States as a hard fact separating individuals of similar economic interests. What a difference it would have made if these soldiers had seen themselves in their station in the military hierarchy as similar to slaves. Although Henry had enlisted, we can be sure that many in his regiment had been conscripted. When Henry runs, his fleeing is reminiscent of a slave escaping from similarly brutal and dangerous conditions.

> Since he had turned his back upon the fight his fears had been wondrously magnified. Death about to thrust him between the shoulder blades was far more dreadful than death about to smite him between the eyes. . . .
> . . . In his flight the sound of these following footsteps gave him his one meager relief. He felt vaguely that death must make a first choice of the men who were nearest; the initial morsels for the dragons would be then those who were following him. So he displayed the zeal of an insane sprinter in his purpose to keep them in the rear. There was a race. (Chapter VI)

The reader feels, as he does, that he has done something dishonorable and wrong. But to see Henry as impressed into his role and his choosing to run as an exercise of will brings the question of slavery and emancipation to the heart of the novel.

Such a reframing of Henry's plight may substantially alter our perspective when we pose the central question of the novel: is Henry a hero or a coward? Crane dwelled on individual acts in order to suggest that bravery is more a matter of individual qualities than actual outcome. But if the hierarchical relationships of the military are viewed as fundamental to the scenes of battle that Crane depicted, heroism becomes not a matter of summoning the greatness from within but of complying with the arbitrary and often ill-conceived demands of some vague superior. An officer's overheard slight (he calls Henry's regiment "mule drivers") spurring Henry into making his mark as a possible hero suggests how powerfully such men have entered Henry's mind. That Henry defends the flag of nation without knowing in particular what that flag is supposed to stand for shows that questions of volition (what Henry meant to do) should perhaps be viewed in the context of social position. If one performs as desired, the means of motivation matters little, and the result is that bravery is indistinguishable from stubborn resentment. Indeed, to act heroically may be to show one's utter compliance and lack of moral heroism.

The three short stories in this section have close connections to this novel. Two, "A Mystery of Heroism" and "An Episode of War," are set in the Civil War, and one, "The Veteran," takes up the character of Henry Fleming in the postwar world. This last story is also distinguished by its revelation of the name of the battle where Henry showed his reluctance to fight: Fleming says that when he ran, frightened from battle, "that was at Chancellorsville." (Of course, none of the participants in the battle knew the name of the battle while it was going on; thus, the proper name did not appear in the novel.) All three of these stories were written to capitalize on the success of *The Red Badge of Courage*. And all three focus on the very same matter as the novel: What defines bravery?

"A Mystery of Heroism" tells of an action that has the appearance of bravery, but somehow does not elevate itself appropriately. It is not a considered action but an impulse that propels a soldier to risk his life to retrieve water. Crane further complicates matters: no one really wants water and the bucket is empty when the soldier returns with it. All this leads the reader to ask about the nature of bravery, questioning whether any act can fit its dictionary definition. In this tale Crane also suggests another emerging current of his time—behavioral psychology as an explanation of why people do what they do. Indeed, as the soldier impulsively runs toward the well, he is acting out of one of William James's explanations of behavior as being caused by "the reflex effect of the exciting object."[3]

"An Episode of War" tells of a wound that ends with the amputation of a lieutenant's arm. Nothing is revealed of the engagement or even the war, nor any details of the officer's life. The character briefly expresses his fear of amputation, but this concern passes as he recognizes losing his arm as inevitable. Here Crane is ironically critiquing the glorious notion of war, a criticism that connects this story to Bierce's "Killed at Resaca" (1891) and Howells's Spanish-American War short story "Editha" (1905), in which a misguided heroine sends her fiancé off to his death in battle.

Because *The Red Badge of Courage* looks *back* on the Civil War, it would be, in some ways, anachronistic to include contemporary accounts

---

[3] For evidence that Crane knew something of James's theories, see Smith; this essay is summarized in relation to "A Mystery of Heroism" in Schaefer (277–78).

of the war in this section. The river of narratives about the Civil War that began to flow even before Grant and Lee met at the Appomattox Courthouse in 1865 has never stopped. The student can choose from memoirs, soldiers' autobiographies and letters, synthetic histories, military histories, biographies of participants, and historical novels. Indeed, Daniel Aaron has called the Civil War the most written about war in history (xiii). To provide a sense of the tradition from which *The Red Badge of Courage* emerged, the contextual materials herein are of a different sort. By approaching Crane's novel in relation to these other stories, readers can approximate the experience Crane's contemporaries had a century ago when they came across this intensely subjective rendering of what it may have been like to participate in the Civil War.

Soon after he began work on *The Red Badge of Courage* in 1893, Crane pored over the back issues of *Century* magazine that contained the series "Battles and Leaders of the Civil War." (The series filled four volumes when published in book form in 1887–88.) This series had been extremely popular when it appeared in that journal in 1884 and 1885 and was influential in developing Crane's conception of the war. Yet, even though these stories fascinated Crane, he was disappointed that he could not draw on accounts that told "how they *felt* in those scraps," for the men's emotions were missing; he found them "as emotionless as rocks" (Wertheim and Sorrentino, *Crane Log* 89). Or so he told his friend Corwin Knapp Linson, a painter and illustrator at whose apartment he read these issues. This "research" was likely prompted by an interest in the war planted by the stories of the many "middle-aged" veterans, "who were often as garrulous as they were ubiquitous" when Crane was growing up (Cady 119). Edwin Cady says that this oral tradition would certainly have been available to Crane in the person of his history teacher at Claverack, John V. Van Petten, who had served at several major battles, including those where panicked men had turned tail and run, much as Henry Fleming does in his first day of combat. Van Petten is also likely to have called his students' attention to a significant precursor of the realism of *The Red Badge of Courage*, DeForest's 1867 novel *Miss Ravenel's Conversion from Secession to Loyalty,* for Van Petten and DeForest had served together and DeForest mentions Van Petten several times in his memoirs (O'Donnell 578–80). Even if Crane did not read the novel he is likely to have read at least some of DeForest's five narratives of battles in Virginia published in *Harper's New Monthly Magazine* or *Galaxy* between 1864 and 1868. DeForest expanded and revised these journals and letters for publication as *A Volunteer's Adventures,* but that was not published until 1946.

DeForest was born in Connecticut in 1826 and was already a published author by the time of the Civil War. He enlisted after the Battle of

Bull Run and served for some six and a half years, rising to the rank of captain in the Twelfth Connecticut Regiment. *Miss Ravenel's Conversion* was championed by Howells, who called DeForest an advanced realist "before realism was known by name" (Howells 223). The contrast with Crane's interior, subjective view of the war through young Henry Fleming, however, could not be greater. DeForest's first-person narrator, who comments on his plot and characters, keeps the reader at a distance. The novel comes alive predominantly in the scenes of Captain Colburne's life in camp and in battle—which the narrator tells as though quoting from his letters. And indeed, these scenes of battle and of men's reactions are based on DeForest's own letters to his wife and on his journals, which he wrote soon after the events they depict.

DeForest's battle scenes are somewhat muted compared with those in *The Red Badge of Courage,* as a matter of the author's choice. DeForest told Howells in a letter that only Tolstoy in *War and Peace* told the whole truth about war and battle and that he didn't dare tell about how scary it is: "I actually did not dare state the extreme horror of battle, and the anguish with which the bravest soldiers struggle through it" (E. Wilson 684). Yet, though his war scenes seem to reduce our sense of their brutality, they were notable in the way in which they attempted to synthesize something of the soldier's point of view during battle. Edmund Wilson places DeForest's novel in a sequence that leads to Crane. The sequence includes Albion Tourgée's rendering of the battle of Bull Run in *Figs and Thistles* (1879), Ambrose Bierce's *Tales of Soldiers and Civilians* (1891), and Joseph Kirkland's *The Captain of Company K* (1891). Thus, before Crane's novel was published, a sequence of works that less effectively told of the brutality of war from a soldier's perspective had emerged (E. Wilson 685).

Ambrose Bierce's tale "Killed at Resaca," from the collection mentioned above, is also among the contextual materials in this section. Like DeForest, Bierce was a veteran who wrote from his own experiences. He served from 1861 to 1864 and in his position as a surveyor saw many famous and bloody battles. Though the story included here tells of a soldier's deeds from an external point of view, Bierce did at times experiment with a first person point of view, such as in "Chickamauga," named for a bloody battle at which the author served. Bierce was an experimental writer and an unconventional man. He produced a great range of types of writing, including an extended parody of turn-of-the-century life and mores, *The Devil's Dictionary* (published in part in 1906 under the title *The Cynic's Word Book*). "Killed at Resaca" fits well into the context of war stories concerned with actions in battle and the quality of bravery. Indeed, it is easy to see why Crane was so often compared to Bierce when *The Red*

Badge of Courage was reviewed. Yet Bierce hated the Crane novel and referred to him as "the Crane freak" (Wertheim 86). In 1913, at more than seventy years of age, he went to Mexico to meet the revolutionary Pancho Villa and was never heard from again.

Of the three veterans of the Civil War represented here, it is the most famous one who barely rates that name. In "The Private History of a Campaign that Failed" Twain tells of his brief tour with a group of Confederate irregulars in his native Missouri. By the time this piece was published in *Century* magazine in 1885, Twain was a famous humorist known for his public performances, his travel writing, and his fiction—especially for his notorious novel *Adventures of Huckleberry Finn,* published that year. This piece was commissioned for the "Battles and Leaders" series although—possibly beause of its antiwar stance—the *Century* editors did not include it in the four-volume book edition. Though published before Bierce's tale, "The Private History" makes a fitting conclusion to this section. In it Twain used war as a means of commenting on the uncomprehending callowness of his youth as well as on the shocking reality of seeing the consequences of this "game" of war. In its horror in response to death as well as in the immaturity of its point-of-view character, Twain's tale shares sentiments with Crane's novel. It also shares a certain lack of broad perspective, of a sense that the war is *for* anything. Indeed, this seems to be uniform among all these writers who depict the Civil War: there is little sense of the conflict regarding slavery that precipitated it.

FROM *BATTLES AND LEADERS OF THE CIVIL WAR* "WHEN STONEWALL JACKSON TURNED OUR RIGHT"

John L. Collins, 8th Pennsylvania Cavalry

On the afternoon of May 2d, 1863, the 8th Pennsylvania Cavalry were ordered to dismount, slack saddle-girths, and rest in the vicinity of General Hooker's headquarters at Chancellorsville. Some of the men fell asleep holding their horses, some began talking of the battle, while a knot of officers, who always improved such occasions in this way, sat down to

---

Vol. 3. New York: Century, 1888.

their favorite game of poker. Suddenly an order from headquarters made a complete change in the scene. At the word "Mount!" the sleepers as well as the talkers sprang to their saddles, the gamblers snatched up their stakes and their cards, and a regiment of cavalry took the place of a lounging crowd.

Passing to the left of the Chancellorsville House, we crossed our line of battle at the edge of a wood and came up with a reconnoitering party that had captured the 23d Georgia. We had heard that Lee was retreating, and supposed that this unfortunate regiment had been sacrificed to give the main body a chance to escape; but while we were commiserating the poor fellows, one of them defiantly said, "You may think you have done a big thing just now, but wait till Jackson gets round on your right."

We laughed at his harmless bravado, for we did not think he would betray Jackson's move had he known anything about it; but while we were yet trying to get through the thick wood the roar of musketry and artillery on our right confirmed his speech. We now came back at a gallop toward a point between the place where we were resting and the place where the battle was raging. As we rode into an elevated clearing, called Hazel Grove, the regiment (the 8th Pennsylvania) was brought into line. We surmised a disaster and nervously braced ourselves for the ordeal, not knowing whether we were to make an attack or wait there to receive one.

The roar of musketry was now heavier and nearer; the vast woods between us and Dowdall's tavern seemed to shake with it. There was no time to ask or to wonder what had happened, for the regiment was ordered off at a gallop. After riding about three hundred yards we turned into a narrow road that promised to take us into the midst of the enemy. Half a dozen horsemen in cadet gray—most likely a general's staff reconnoitering, as they did not ride in ranks—were in the road ahead of us, and turned and fled back to their lines.

The word "Charge!" was now passed from the leading squadron, and sabers flew into the air along our line; but none too soon, for we were already in the midst of the foe, and they were ready for us. The unfortunate squadron that led caught all the fire as we dashed along the narrow lane, and we who rode next it got only the smoke from the enemy's guns. We could reach nothing as yet, and could see nothing but fire and smoke, for their line of battle was safely posted behind a thicket that lined the left of the road, while their rifles were aimed through it.

It was a long lane and a hot lane to go through; but the lane had a turn, and we got to it at last when we reached the Plank road and struck Rodes's division right in the front. We struck it as a wave strikes a stately ship: the ship is staggered, maybe thrown on her beam ends, but the wave is dashed into spray, and the ship sails on as before.

Major Keenan, who led his battalion in the charge, the captain in command of the leading squadron, the adjutant, and a few score of their followers went down at this shock together. The detail sent over to recover their bodies after the battle said that the major had thirteen bullets in his body, the adjutant nine, and others fewer. It was reported by some who rode close upon the major that in falling he shouted, "To the right!" seeing that the impenetrable masses on his left could not be forced, and that there was no way out but over the thinner lines on the right. When turning at full speed, my horse was killed and I was pitched over his neck on the roadside. Here I parted company with the regiment. When I jumped to my feet I had time to take only one glance at my surroundings. My sole thought was to escape capture or death. On one side were the heavy lines of Confederate infantry doubled and bent by the charge, their officers trying to recover their alignment; on the other side the survivors of the leading squadrons were galloping in the Plank road, the others breaking over the Confederate skirmish lines as far back as I could see into the woods.

By instinct I turned toward the woods on the right of the Plank road as the best way out, and made a dash at the lines, which had just recovered from their surprise that a cavalry regiment should have ridden over them, and were firing after it. They were loading when I ran out between them, and when they began to fire I dropped down behind some trees that had been cut to make an abatis, or had been shot down by the cannon; when the volley was over I jumped up and ran as fast as before.

The Plank road, and the woods that bordered it, presented a scene of terror and confusion such as I had never seen before. Men and animals were dashing against one another in wild dismay before the line of fire that came crackling and crashing after them. The constantly approaching rattle of musketry, the crash of the shells through the trees, seemed to come from three sides upon the broken fragments of the Eleventh Corps that crowded each other on the road. The horses of the men of my regiment who had been shot, mingled with the pack-mules that carried the ammunition of the Eleventh Corps, tore like wild beasts through the woods. I tried in vain to catch one.

This employment of the mules for ammunition service was a device of General Hooker's, and this was the only field where they played their part. Each mule carried four or five boxes of spare ammunition, and being tied in couples, they seemed easier to catch than a horse. As a pair of them made for opposite sides of a tree, I ran toward them to get one, but before I could succeed a shell from the direction of the Plank road struck the tree, exploded the ammunition, and slaughtered the mules.

I now gave up hope of a mount, and seeing the Confederate lines coming near me, tried to save myself on foot. Once, when throwing myself down to escape the fury of the fire, I saw a member of my own regiment, whose horse also had been shot, hiding in a pine top that had been cut down by a shell. He had thrown his arms away that he might run the faster, and he begged me to do the same. This I refused to do, and I got in safely with my arms, while he was never seen again. I turned into the Plank road to join the very bad company that came pouring in by that route. More than half of the runaways had thrown their arms away, and all of them were talking a language that I did not understand, but, by their tones, evidently blaming some one for the disgrace and disaster that had befallen their corps. They appeared to share the prevailing confusion on that part of the field, where the front and the rear seemed reversed. Yet, as misery loves company, I cast my lot with them and continued my flight.

I doubt if any of us knew where we were going, further than that we were fleeing before the pursuing lines of the enemy. One of my own company, who was captured in the charge, afterward told me that in leaping an abatis, he was lifted from his saddle by a vine and remained suspended till made a prisoner.

In the very height of the flight, we came upon General Howard, who seemed to be the only man in his own command that was not running at that moment. He was in the middle of the road and mounted, his maimed arm embracing a stand of colors that some regiment had deserted, while with his sound arm he was gesticulating to the men to make a stand by their flag. With bared head he was pleading with his soldiers, literally weeping as he entreated the unheeding horde. Under different circumstances I should have considered it my duty to follow and find my command, and report for duty with it. But I could not go past the general. Maimed in his person and sublime in his patriotism, he seemed worthy to stand by, and out of pure compliment to his appearance I hooked up my saber and fell into the little line that gathered about him. As the front became clear, we fired a few shots at the advance line of the Confederates, but a fresh mass of fugitives in blue soon filled the road, and we had to stop firing. The general now ordered us to cover the whole line of retreat so as to let none pass, and the officers, inspired by his devotion, ran in front of their men, drew their swords, and attempted to stop them. As the number constantly increased, the pressure became greater upon the line that blocked the way; but this line was constantly reinforced by officers and others, and offered some resistance to the pressure. At last the seething, surging sea of humanity broke over the feeble barrier, and General Howard and his officers were carried away by main force with the tide. Pharaoh and his chariots could have held back the walls of the Red Sea as easily as those officers could resist this retreat. I started again on my race for life, this time alone, and toward the slopes of the Chancellorsville plateau, where it seemed to me probable that my regiment would re-form after the charge.

My course was right-oblique from the road, and I had not gone far before I saw lines that I knew were not retreating. Their flags were flying, and my heart took a bound as I beheld battery after battery galloping into position, and regiment after regiment wheeling into line behind them. A line of battle showed itself at last; the Third Corps had come up to stop the successful charge, and Jackson's men would find a difference between attacking the Third Corps in front and the Eleventh in the rear. Seeing the guns unlimber and load, I made my greatest effort at speed, but not caring for a few fugitives, the guns belched forth their fire before I could get in. However, I came safely through, and at last paused for a long breath. While congratulating myself upon my escape, I looked behind the line of battle, and there saw my own regiment drawn up for a charge, the line not so long as half an hour before by one-third, but still as shapely and resolute as ever. The horses were blown and nervous, and the men were, no doubt, a little depressed by the rough usage they had met with. A horse, that had followed the company riderless from the charge, was given to me, and my confidence and self-respect came back as I mounted him, for I was no longer a fugitive, but a soldier.

The fighting now began in earnest. The splendid divisions of Birney, Berry, and Whipple had to be met and vanquished before a farther advance could be made, and before Jackson could attain the great object of his march to our rear. The gathering darkness was favorable to the Confederates, for they could get near the guns before being seen; but it also added to the terror of the batteries, which were discharged double-shotted at the assailants, and lit up the heavens with fire that seemed supernatural. The dusky lines fell back into the woods in disorganized masses as often as they advanced, and the cheers of our troops rang out at each retreat. From the boldness and the frequency of the Confederate charges it was found necessary to move the infantry in front of the guns, lest the enemy should seize them before being discovered. The slope was so steep that a line of battle could be formed in front of the guns and a double skirmish line in front of that.

Our regiment now moved up to the guns, enabling us to see better the slopes and the woods when lit up by the flashes. Sometimes darkness and stillness would reign for a few minutes, and we would think the long day's fighting was over, but it would presently break out again. The stealthy rush from the woods could be heard first, then the sharp crack of the skirmisher's rifle, then a yell and a louder rushing of their lines met by the loud roll of the line of battle's fire. As the cheer of our men announced that the enemy's line was again in retreat, the blaze of forty or fifty cannons from the right to the left would light up the scene and carry death over the heads of our men into the woods beyond.

At last Jackson's men paused, for they had been marching and fighting since morning, and human nature could endure no more. But they were not allowed to hold the ground they had won; an advance was now ordered on our side, and it was made with a vigor that avenged the discomfiture of our comrades. Though it was now midnight the woods were lit up with the flame of the musketry as the combatants came face to face among the trees, and the battle began anew. The artillerists pushed on their guns by hand a hundred yards behind the infantry line, and shook the woods in their depths, as they had the hills to their foundations. At last, at 2 o'clock in the morning, we were told to sleep on our arms. But who could sleep while counting the dead of our commands? Comrades were gone; file-leaders and file-closers were gone; officers of every grade had perished. Stonewall Jackson himself had gone down in his greatest charge; and his men never again fought as on that day, nor came down on our flank with such fury.

FROM *BATTLES AND LEADERS OF THE CIVIL WAR* "HOOKER'S COMMENTS ON CHANCELLORSVILLE"

Samuel P. Bates

In October, 1876, I accompanied General Hooker to the battle-fields of Fredericksburg, Chancellorsville, and Antietam—fields on which he had borne conspicuous parts. It was the only occasion on which he visited them after the battles. He had previously placed in my hands his official papers and memoranda for the preparation of a history of the Battle of Chancellorsville, at the same time requesting me to make this journey with him, that I might have the advantage of a thorough knowledge of the field, and of his interpretation of the manner in which the battle was fought. At this period he was partly paralyzed from the injury received in the Chancellorsville battle, and he could move only with great difficulty by the aid of his valet.

After our arrival at Fredericksburg, General Hooker was the recipient of many courteous attentions from the leading citizens, and at night he was

Vol. 3. New York: Century, 1888.

serenaded, when a great crowd assembled in front of the hotel, to whose repeated cheers he made a brief response, in which he said that he had visited their city but once before, and although his reception now was not nearly so warm as on that former day, yet it was far more agreeable to him—a conceit which greatly pleased his hearers.

Our drive over the Fredericksburg field, which we visited on the way, was on one of the most perfect of autumnal days, and at every turn fresh reminiscences of that battle were suggested. As we approached the flagstaff of the National Cemetery, on the hill adjoining Marye's Heights, where more than fifteen thousand of the Union dead of Fredericksburg, Chancellorsville, the Wilderness, and Spotsylvania are buried, General Hooker said:

"I never think of this ground but with a shudder. The whole scene is indelibly fixed in my mind, as it appeared on that fatal day. Here on this ground were ranged the enemy's cannon, and the heights farther to his left were thickly planted with pieces; all the infantry he could use was disposed behind earthworks and stone walls. How this could have been selected as the point, above all others, for attack, and followed up until four whole divisions had been sacrificed, I cannot comprehend. As I stand here today, the impossibility of carrying this ground by direct assault is no more apparent than it was when I made my observation preparatory to ordering Humphreys's division forward. But it is evident that General Burnside never forgave me for counseling him on that occasion as I did, for on January 23d he drew up an order, known as General Orders, No. 8, of his series, dishonorably dismissing me from the service, together with three other prominent general officers, at the same time relieving five other officers from duty. I was grossly maligned by the press of that day, and it was generally believed by the people at the North that I had not faithfully supported General Burnside in this battle, and that I was aiming thereby to supplant him. If these brave men who are sleeping here beneath our feet could speak, they would bear testimony to my sincerity and fidelity to the cause we were battling for; and though I have suffered in silence, and my reputation has been grossly aspersed, I have rested in the firm belief that my conduct on that day would be justified by the American people." . . .

We were accompanied on our ride to the Chancellorsville field, some ten or twelve miles above Fredericksburg, by Major George E. Chancellor, a son of Melzi Chancellor, whose home at the time of the battle was at Dowdall's Tavern, where General Howard had his headquarters. On setting out, General Hooker suggested that we should take some lunch along with us, as, when he was there last there was very little to eat in all that region. Major Chancellor thought it unnecessary, and, in fact, we were feasted most sumptuously at his father's house.

Upon our arrival at the broad, open, rolling fields opposite Banks's Ford, some three or four miles up the stream, General Hooker exclaimed, waving his hand significantly: "Here, on this open ground, I intended to fight my battle. But the trouble was to get my army on it, as the banks of the stream are, as you see, rugged and precipitous, and the few fords were strongly fortified and guarded by the enemy. By making a powerful demonstration in front of and below the town of Fredericksburg with a part of my army, I was able, unobserved, to withdraw the remainder, and, marching nearly thirty miles up the stream, to cross the Rappahannock and the Rapidan unopposed, and in four days' time to arrive at Chancellorsville, within five miles of this coveted ground—and all this without General Lee having discovered that I had left my position in his front. So far, I regarded my movement as a great success. On the morning of the fifth day my army was astir, and was put in motion on three lines through the tangled forest (the Wilderness) which covers the whole country around Chancellorsville, and in three hours' time I would have been in position on these crests, and in possession of Banks's Ford, in short and easy communication with the other wing of my army. But at midnight General Lee had moved out with his whole army, and by sunrise was in firm possession of Banks's Ford, had thrown up this line of breastworks which you can still follow with the eye, and it was bristling with cannon from one end to the other. Before I had proceeded two miles the heads of my columns, while still upon the narrow roads in these interminable forests, where it was impossible to manoeuvre my forces, were met by Jackson with a full two-thirds of the entire Confederate army. I had no alternative but to turn back, as I had only a fragment of my command in hand, and take up the position about Chancellorsville which I had occupied during the night, as I was being rapidly outflanked upon my right, the enemy having open ground on which to operate.

"And here again my reputation has been attacked because I did not undertake to accomplish an impossibility, but turned back at this point; and every history of the war that has been written has soundly berated me because I did not fight here in the forest with my hands tied behind me, and allow my army to be sacrificed. I have always believed that impartial history would vindicate my conduct in this emergency."

Soon after leaving the open ground opposite Banks's Ford we entered the dense forest, or "Wilderness," which covers the entire Chancellorsville battle-ground—"a dense forest," says General Warren, "of not very large trees, but very difficult to get through; mainly of scrubby oak, what they call black-jack there, so that a man could hardly ride through it, and a man could not march through it very well with musket in hand, unless he trailed it."

Every important position was observed and commented upon by the man who on those fierce battle-days had wielded, on this very ground, an army of a hundred thousand men. On approaching the pine tree under which Generals Lee and Jackson had planned the mode of attack, General Hooker observed: "It was under that tree that the mischief was devised which came near ruining my army. My position at Chancellorsville was a good one for this monotonous country. I felt confident when I reached it that I had eighty chances in a hundred to win. To make sure that everything was firm and strong, very early on the 2d of May, the first day of the battle, I rode along the whole line, and personally examined every part, suggesting some changes and counseling extreme vigilance. Upon my return to headquarters I was informed that a continuous column of the enemy had been marching past my front since early in the morning, as of a corps with all its *impedimenta*. This put an entirely new phase upon the problem, and filled me with apprehension for the safety of my right wing, which was posted to meet a front attack from the south, but was in no condition for a flank attack from the west; for this marching of the enemy's corps, to my mind, meant a flank movement upon my right. I immediately dictated a dispatch to 'Generals Slocum and Howard,' the latter commanding the Eleventh Corps, which stood upon the extreme right, saying that I had good reason to believe that the enemy was moving to our right, and that they must be ready to meet an attack from the west. This was at 9:30 in the morning. In the course of two hours I got a dispatch from General Howard, saying that he could see a column of the enemy moving westward, and that he was taking the precautions necessary 'to resist an attack from the west.' I had previously put Williams's division of the Twelfth Corps on an interior line looking westward, and had it fortified, so that if Howard should give way, this interior line would be for safety, as it afterward proved my salvation.

"I sent Sickles to pierce this moving column of the enemy, and made preparations to flank the portion of Lee's army that was still upon my front, in the direction of Fredericksburg, and, sweeping down in reverse, to destroy it if possible. But a swamp intervened which had to be corduroyed, and a small stream had to be bridged, which consumed time; and though Sickles was successful in breaking in upon the enemy's column and making some captures, yet, before he was in position to make his decisive attack, Jackson, who had led his column by a long circuit, out of sight and hearing, through the dense forest, came in upon my right flank, and by one concentrated blow of his whole corps, some 25,000 men, had crushed and put to flight almost the entire corps of Howard; and it was with the utmost difficulty that I could lead up my reserves to the interior line of Williams, and bring Jackson's victorious forces to a halt. This failure of Howard to hold his ground cost us our position, and I was forced, in the presence of the enemy, to take up a new one. Upon investigation I found that Howard had failed properly to obey my instructions to prepare and meet the enemy from the west." . . .

When we arrived at the Chancellor House (which is all there is of Chancellorsville), where General Hooker had his headquarters, and where he received the hurt that came near proving mortal, General Hooker said, "I was standing on this step of the portico on the Sunday morning of the 3d of May, and was giving direction to the battle, which was now raging with great fury, the cannon-balls reaching me from both the east and the west, when a solid shot struck the pillar near me, splitting it in two, and throwing one-half longitudinally against me, striking my whole right side, which soon turned livid. For a few moments I was senseless, and the report spread that I had been killed. But I soon revived, and, to correct the misapprehension, I insisted on being lifted upon my horse, and rode back toward the white house, which subsequently became the center of my new position. Just before reaching it, the pain from my hurt became so intense that I was likely to fall, when I was assisted to dismount, and was laid upon a blanket spread out upon the ground, and was given some brandy. This revived me, and I was assisted to remount. Scarcely was I off the blanket when a solid shot, fired by the enemy at Hazel Grove, struck in the very center of that blanket, where I had a moment before been lying, and tore up the earth in a savage way." As he ended this recital General Hooker turned to Major Chancellor, who was standing by, and said, "Ah, Major! Your people were after me with a sharp stick on that day."

A short distance from the Chancellor House, in the direction of Dowdall's Tavern, our carriage was halted, and, dismounting, Major Chancellor led us a few paces out of the road, along a faint cart-path, when he said, "This is the place where Stonewall Jackson received the wounds that proved mortal." "I have always been struck," observed General Hooker, "with the last words of General Jackson, evincing how completely he was absorbed in the progress of the battle. In his delirium he was still upon the field, and he cried out, 'Order A. P. Hill to prepare for action—pass the infantry to the front rapidly—tell Major Hawks—' when he stopped with the sentence unfinished. After a little his brow relaxed, as if from relief, and he said, 'Let us cross over the river, and rest under the shade of the trees'—and these were his last words."

Arriving at Dowdall's Tavern, General Hooker pointed out the excellent position here afforded for Howard's corps to have made a stout defense. "Buschbeck's brigade of that corps," said he, "did wonders here, and held the whole impetuous onset of the enemy in check for an hour or more, which gave me opportunity to bring my reserves into position. The loss of this ground brought me into so cramped a condition that I was obliged to take up a new position, which I successfully accomplished. I now ordered Sedgwick, who commanded the Sixth Corps, the largest in my army, some 22,000 men, which had been left to demonstrate in front of Fredericksburg, to cross the river and move rapidly up to my left. The effect of so heavy a body of fresh troops coming in upon the enemy's flank I calculated would be decisive. But Sedgwick was dilatory in moving, which gave the enemy time to concentrate and stop him before he had moved over half the distance, and I consequently got no help from him."

I ventured to ask why he did not attack when he found that the enemy had weakened his forces in the immediate front and sent them away to meet Sedgwick. "That," said he, "would seem to have been the reasonable thing to do. But we were in this impenetrable thicket. All the roads and openings leading through it the enemy immediately fortified strongly, and planted thickly his artillery commanding all the avenues, so that with reduced numbers he could easily hold his lines, shutting me in, and it became utterly impossible to manoeuvre my forces. My army was not beaten. Only a part of it had been engaged. The First Corps, commanded by Reynolds, whom I regarded as the ablest officer under me, was fresh and ready and eager to be brought into action, as was my whole army. But I had been fully convinced of the futility of attacking fortified positions, and I was determined not to sacrifice my men needlessly, though it should be at the expense of my reputation as a fighting officer. We had already had enough grievous experience in that line. I made frequent demonstrations to induce the enemy to attack me, but he would not accept my challenge. Accordingly, when the eight days' rations with which my army started out were exhausted, I retired across the river. Before doing so I sent orders to General Sedgwick to hold his position near Banks's Ford, on the south side of the stream, and I would bring my whole army to his support; but the order failed to reach him until he had already recrossed the river. Could I have had my army on the open grounds at that point where I could have manoeuvred it properly, I felt assured that I could have gained a decisive victory. But this, my last chance, was frustrated."

FROM *MISS RAVENEL'S CONVERSION FROM SECESSION TO LOYALTY*

John William DeForest

At five o'clock on the morning of the 27th of May, Colburne was awakened by an order to fall in. Whether it signified an advance on our part, or a sally by the enemy, he did not know nor ask, but with a soldier's indifference proceeded to form his company, and, that done, ate his breakfast of raw pork and hard biscuit. He would have been glad to have Henry boil him a cup of coffee; but that idle freedman was "having a good time," probably sleeping, in some unknown refuge. For two hours the ranks sat on the ground, musket in hand; then Colburne saw the foremost line, a quarter of a mile in front, advance into the forest. One of Weitzel's aids now dashed up to Carter, and immediately his staff-officers galloped away to the different commanders of regiments. An admonishing murmur of "Fall in, men!"— "Attention men!" from the captains ran along the line of the Tenth, and the soldiers rose in their places to meet the grand, the awful possibility of battle. It was a long row of stern faces, bronzed with sunburn, sallow in many cases with malaria, grave with the serious emotions of the hour, but hardened by the habit of danger, and set as firm as flints toward the enemy. The old innocence of the peaceable New England farmer and mechanic had disappeared from these war-seared visages, and had been succeeded by an expression of hardened combativeness, not a little brutal, much like the look of a lazy bull-dog. Colburne smiled with pleasure and pride as he glanced along the line of his company, and noted this change in its physiognomy. For the purpose for which they were drawn up there they were better men than when he first knew them, and as good men as the sun ever shone upon.

At last the Lieutenant Colonel's voice rang out, "Battalion, forward. Guide right. March!"

To keep the ranks closed and aligned in any tolerable fighting shape while struggling through that mile of tangled forest and broken ground, was a task of terrible difficulty. Plunging through thickets, leaping over fallen trees, a continuous foliage overhead, and the fallen leaves of many seasons under foot, the air full of the damp, mouldering smell of virgin forest, the brigade moved forward with no sound but that of its own tramplings. It is peculiar of the American attack that it is almost always made in line, and always without music. The men expected to meet the enemy at every hillock, but they advanced rapidly, and laughed at each other's slippings

New York: Harper, 1867.

and tumbles. Every body was breathless with climbing over obstacles or running around them. The officers were beginning to swear at the broken ranks and unsteady pace. The Lieutenant Colonel, perceiving that the regiment was diverging from its comrades, and fearing the consequences of a gap in case the enemy should suddenly open fire, rode repeatedly up and down the line, yelling, "Guide right! Close up to the right!" Suddenly, to the amazement of every one, the brigade came upon bivouacs of Union regiments quietly engaged in distributing rations and preparing breakfast.

"What are you doing up here?" asked a Major of Colburne.

"We are going to attack. Don't you take part in it?"

"I suppose so. I don't know. We have received no orders."

Through this scene of tardiness, the result perhaps of one of those blunders which are known in military as well as in all other human operations, Weitzel's division steadily advanced, much wondering if it was to storm Port Hudson alone. The ground soon proved so difficult that the Tenth, unable to move in line of battle, filed into a faintly marked forest road and pushed forward by the flank in the ordinary column of march. The battle had already commenced, although Colburne could see nothing of it, and could hear nothing but a dull *pum-pum-pum* of cannon. He passed rude rifle-pits made of earth and large branches, which had been carried only a few minutes previous by the confused rush of the leading brigade. Away to the right, but not near enough to be heard above the roar of artillery, there was a wild, scattering musketry of broken lines, fighting and scrambling along as they best could over thicketed knolls, and through rugged gullies, on the track of the retiring Alabamians and Arkansans. It was the blindest and most perplexing forest labyrinth conceivable; it was impossible to tell whither you were going, or whether you would stumble on friends or enemies; the regiments were split into little squads from which all order had disappeared, but which nevertheless advanced.

The Tenth was still marching through the woods by the flank, unable to see either fortifications or enemy, when it came under the fire of artillery, and encountered the retiring stream of wounded. At this moment, and for two hours afterward, the uproar of heavy guns, bursting shells, falling trees and flying splinters was astonishing, stunning, horrible, doubled as it was by the sonorous echoes of the forest. Magnolias, oaks and beeches eighteen inches or two feet in diameter, were cut asunder with a deafening scream of shot and of splitting fibres, the tops falling after a pause of majestic deliberation, not sidewise, but stem downwards, like a descending parachute, and striking the earth with a dull shuddering thunder. They seemed to give up their life with a roar of animate anguish, as if they were savage beasts, or as if they were inhabited by Afreets and Demons.

The unusually horrible clamor and the many-sided nature of the danger had an evident effect on the soldiers, hardened as they were to scenes of ordinary battle. Grim faces turned in every direction with hasty stares of alarm, looking aloft and on every side, as well as to the front, for destruction. Pallid stragglers who had dropped out of the leading brigade drifted by the Tenth, dodging from trunk to trunk in an instinctive search for cover, although it was visible that the forest was no protection, but rather an additional peril. Every regiment has its two or three cowards, or perhaps its half-dozen, weakly-nerved creatures, whom nothing can make fight, and who never do fight. One abject hound, a corporal with his disgraced stripes upon his arm, came by with a ghastly backward glare of horror, his face colorless, his eyes projecting, and his chin shaking. Colburne cursed him for a poltroon, struck him with the flat of his sabre, and dragged him into the ranks of his own regiment; but the miserable creature was too thoroughly unmanned by the great horror of death to be moved to any show of resentment or even of courage by the indignity; he only gave an idiotic stare with outstretched neck toward the front, then turned with a nervous jerk, like that of a scared beast, and rushed rearward. Further on, six men were standing in single file behind a large beech, holding each other by the shoulders, when with a stunning crash the entire top of the tree flew off and came down among them butt foremost, sending out a cloud of dust and splinters. Colburne smiled grimly to see the paralyzed terror of their upward stare, and the frantic flight which barely saved them from being crushed jelly. A man who keeps the ranks hates a skulker, and wishes that he may be killed, the same as any other enemy.

"But in truth," says the Captain, in one of his letters, "the sights and sounds of this battle-reaped forest were enough to shake the firmest nerves. Never before had I been so tried as I was during that hour in this wilderness of death. It was not the slaughter which unmanned me, for our regiment did not lose very heavily; it was the stupendous clamor of the cannonade and of the crashing trees which seemed to overwhelm me by its mere physical power; and it made me unable to bear spectacles which I had witnessed in other engagements with perfect composure. When one of our men was borne by me with half his foot torn off by a round shot, the splintered bones projecting clean and white from the ragged raw flesh, I grew so sick that perhaps I might have fainted if a brother officer had not given me a sip of whiskey from his canteen. It was the only occasion in my fighting experience when I have had to resort to that support. I had scarcely recovered myself when I saw a broad flow of blood stream down the face of a color corporal who stood within arm's length of me. I thought he was surely a dead man; but it was only one of the wonderful escapes of battle. The bullet had skirted his cap where the fore-piece joins the cloth, forcing the edge of the leather through the skin, and making a clean cut to the bone from temple to temple. He went to the rear blinded and with a smart headache, but not seriously injured. That we were not slaughtered by the wholesale is wonderful, for we were closed up in a compact mass, and the shot came with stunning rapidity. A shell burst in the centre of my company, tearing one man's heel to the bone, but doing no other damage. The wounded man, a good soldier though as quiet and gentle as a bashful girl, touched his hat to me, showed his bleeding foot, and asked leave to go to the rear, which I of course granted. While he was speaking, another shell burst about six feet from the first, doing no harm at all, although so near to Van Zandt as to dazzle and deafen him."

Presently a section of Bainbridge's regular battery came up, winding slowly through the forest, the guns thumping over roots and fallen limbs, the men sitting superbly erect on their horses, and the color sergeant holding his battle-flag as proudly as a knight-errant ever bore his pennon. In a minute the two brass Napoleons opened with a sonorous *spang,* which drew a spontaneous cheer from the delighted infantry. The edge of the wood was now reached, and Colburne could see the enemy's position. In front of him lay a broad and curving valley, irregular in surface, and seamed in some places by rugged gorges, the whole made more difficult of passage by a multitude of felled trees, the leafless trunks and branches of which were tangled into an inextricable *chevaux de frise.* On the other side of this valley rose a bluff or table-land, partially covered with forest, but showing on its cleared spaces the tents and cabins of the Rebel encampments. Along the edge of the bluff, following its sinuosities, and at this distance looking like mere natural banks of yellow earth, ran the fortifications of Port Hudson. Colburne could see Paine's brigade of Weitzel's division descending into the valley, forcing its bloody way through a roaring cannonade and a continuous screech of musketry.

An order came to the commander of the Tenth to deploy two companies as skirmishers in the hollow in front of Bainbridge, and push to the left with the remainder of the regiment, throwing out other skirmishers and silencing the Rebel artillery. One of the two detached companies was Colburne's, and he took command of both as senior officer. At the moment that he filed his men out of the line a murmur ran through the regiment that the Lieutenant Colonel was killed or badly wounded. Then came an inquiry as to the whereabouts of the Major.

"By Jove! it wouldn't be a dangerous job to hunt for him," chuckled Van Zandt.

"Why? Where is he?" asked Colburne.

"I don't believe, by Jove! that I could say within a mile or two. I only know, by Jove! that he is *non est inventus.* I saw him a quarter of an hour ago charging for the rear with his usual impetuosity. I'll bet my everlasting salvation that he's in the safest spot within ten miles of this d—d unhealthy neighborhood."

The senior captain took command of the regiment, and led it to the left on a line parallel with the fortifications. Colburne descended with his little detachment, numbering about eighty muskets, into that Valley of the Shadow of Death, climbing over or creeping under the fallen trunks of the tangled labyrinth, and making straight for the bluff on which thundered and smoked the rebel stronghold. As his men advanced they deployed, spreading outward like the diverging blades of a fan until they covered a front of nearly a quarter of a mile. Every stump, every prostrate trunk, every knoll and gulley was a temporary breastwork, from behind which they poured a slow but fatal fire upon the rebel gunners, who could be plainly seen upon the hostile parapet working their pieces. The officers and sergeants moved up and down the line, each behind his own platoon or section, steadily urging it forward.

"Move on, men. Move on, men," Colburne repeated. "Don't expose yourselves. Use the covers; use the stumps. But keep moving on. Don't take root. Don't stop till we reach the ditch."

In spite of their intelligent prudence the men were falling under the incessant flight of bullets. A loud scream from a thicket a little to Colburne's right attracted his attention.

"Who is that?" he called.

"It is Allen!" replied a sergeant. "He is shot through the body. Shall I send him to the rear?"

"Not now, wait till we are relieved. Prop him up and leave him in the shade."

He had in his mind this passage of the Army Regulations: "Soldiers must not be permitted to leave the ranks to strip or rob the dead, nor even to assist the wounded, unless by express permission, which is only to be given after the action is decided. The highest interest and most pressing duty is to win the victory, by which only can a proper care of the wounded be ensured."

Turning to a soldier who had mounted a log and stood up at the full height of his six feet to survey the fortifications, Colburne shouted, "Jump down, you fool. You will get yourself hit for nothing."

"Captain, I can't see a chance for a shot," replied the fellow deliberately.

"Get down!" reiterated Colburne; but the man had waited too long already. Throwing up both hands he fell backward with an incoherent gurgle, pierced through the lungs by a rifle-ball. Then a little Irish soldier burst out swearing, and hastily pulled his trousers to glare at a bullet-hole through the calf of his leg, with a comical expression of mingled surprise, alarm and wrath. And so it went on: every few minutes there was an oath of rage or a shriek of pain; and each outcry marked the loss of a man. But all the while the line of skirmishers advanced.

The sickishness which troubled Colburne in the cannon-smitten forest had gone, and was succeeded by the fierce excitement of close battle, where the combatants grow angry and savage at sight of each other's faces. He was throbbing with elation and confidence, for he had cleaned off the gunners from the two pieces in his front. He felt as if he could take Port Hudson with his detachment alone. The contest was raging in a clamorous rattle of musketry on the right, where Paine's brigade, and four regiments of the Reserve Brigade, all broken into detachments by gullies, hillocks, thickets and fallen trees, were struggling to turn and force the fortifications. On his left other companies of the Tenth were slowly moving forward, deployed and firing as skirmishers. In his front the Rebel musketry gradually slackened, and only now and then could he see a broad-brimmed hat show above the earthworks and hear the hoarse whistle of a Minie-ball as it passed him. The garrison on this side was clearly both few in number and disheartened. It seemed to him likely, yes even certain, that Port Hudson would be carried by storm that morning. At the same time, half-mad as he was with the glorious intoxication of successful battle, he knew that it would be utter folly to push his unsupported detachment into the works, and that such a movement would probably end in slaughter or capture. Fifteen or twenty, he did not know precisely how many of his soldiers had been hit, and the survivors were getting short of cartridges.

"Steady, men!" he shouted. "Halt! Take cover and hold your position. Don't waste your powder. Fire slow and aim sure."

The orders were echoed from man to man along the extended, straggling line, and each one disappeared behind the nearest thicket, stump or fallen tree. Colburne had already sent three corporals to the regiment to recount his success and beg for more men; but neither had the messengers reappeared nor reinforcements arrived to support his proposed assault.

"Those fellows must have got themselves shot," he said to Van Zandt. "I'll go myself. Keep the line where it is, and save the cartridges."

Taking a single soldier with him, he hurried rearward by the clearest course that he could find through the prostrate forest, without minding the few bullets that whizzed by him. Suddenly he halted, powerless, as if struck by paralysis, conscious of a general nervous shock, and a sharp pain in his left arm. His first impulse—a very hurried impulse—was to take the arm with his right hand and twist it to see if the bone was broken. Next he looked about him for some shelter from the scorching and crazing sunshine. He espied a green bush, and almost immediately lost sight of it, for the shock made him faint although the pain was but momentary.

"Are you hurt, Captain?" asked the soldier.

"Take me to that bush," said Colburne, pointing—for he knew where the cover was, although he could not see it.

The soldier put an arm round his waist, led him to the bush, and laid him down.

"Shall I go for help, Captain?"

"No. Don't weaken the company. All right. No bones broken. Go on in a minute."

The man tied his handkerchief about the ragged and bloody hole in the coat-sleeve; then sat down and reloaded his musket, occasionally casting a glance at the pale face of the Captain. In two or three minutes Colburne's color came back, and he felt as well as ever. He rose carefully to his feet, looked about him as if to see where he was, and again set off for the regiment, followed by his silent companion. The bullets still whizzed about them, but did no harm. After a slow walk of ten minutes, during which Colburne once stopped to sling his arm in a handkerchief, he emerged from a winding gully to find himself within a few yards of Bainbridge's battery. Behind the guns was a colonel calmly sitting his horse and watching the battle.

"What is the matter?" asked the Colonel.

"A flesh wound," said Colburne. "Colonel, there is a noble chance ahead of you. Do you see that angle? My men are at the base of it, and some of them in the ditch. They have driven the artillerymen from the guns, and forced the infantry to lie low. For God's sake send in your regiment. We can certainly carry the place."

"The entire brigade that I command is engaged," replied the Colonel. "Don't you see them on the right of your position?"

"Is there no other force about here?" asked Colburne, sitting down as he felt the dizziness coming over him again.

"None that I know of. This is such an infernal country for movements that we are all dislocated. Nobody knows where anything is. But you had better go to the rear, Captain. You look used up."

Colburne was so tired, so weak with the loss of blood, so worn out by the heat of the sun, and the excitement of fighting that he could not help feeling discouraged at the thought of struggling back to the position of his company. He stretched himself under a tree to rest, and in ten minutes was fast asleep. When he awoke—he never knew how long afterward—he could not at first tell what he remembered from what he had dreamed, and only satisfied himself that he had been hit by looking at his bloody and bandaged arm. An artilleryman brought him to his full consciousness by shouting excitedly, "There, by God! they are trying a charge. The infantry are trying a charge."

Colburne rose up, saw a regiment struggling across the valley, and heard its long-drawn charging yell.

"I must go back," he exclaimed. "My men ought to go in and support those fellows." Turning to the soldier who attended him he added, "Run! Tell Van Zandt to forward."

The soldier ran, and Colburne after him. But he had not gone twenty paces before he fell straight forward on his face, without a word, and lay perfectly still.

"KILLED AT RESACA"

Ambrose Bierce

The best soldier of our staff was Lieutenant Herman Brayle, one of the two aides-de-camp. I don't remember where the general picked him up; from some Ohio regiment, I think; none of us had previously known him, and it would have been strange if we had, for no two of us came from the same State, nor even from adjoining States. The general seemed to think that a position on his staff was a distinction that should be so judiciously conferred as not to beget any sectional jealousies and imperil the integrity of that part of the country which was still an integer. He would not even choose officers from his own command, but by some jugglery at department headquarters obtained them from other brigades. Under such circumstances, a man's services had to be very distinguished indeed to be heard of by his family and the friends of his youth; and "the speaking trump of fame" was a trifle hoarse from loquacity, anyhow.

Lieutenant Brayle was more than six feet in height and of splendid proportions, with the light hair and gray-blue eyes which men so gifted usually find associated with a high order of courage. As he was commonly in full uniform, especially in action, when most officers are content to be less flamboyantly attired, he was a very striking and conspicuous figure. As to the rest, he had a gentleman's manners, a scholar's head, and a lion's heart. His age was about thirty.

We all soon came to like Brayle as much as we admired him, and it was with sincere concern that in the engagement at Stone's River—our first action after he joined us—we observed that he had one most objec-

From *Tales of Soldiers and Civilians*. San Francisco: Steele, 1891.

tionable and unsoldierly quality: he was vain of his courage. During all the vicissitudes and mutations of that hideous encounter, whether our troops were fighting in the open cotton fields, in the cedar thickets, or behind the railway embankment, he did not once take cover, except when sternly commanded to do so by the general, who usually had other things to think of than the lives of his staff officers—or those of his men, for that matter.

In every later engagement while Brayle was with us it was the same way. He would sit his horse like an equestrian statue, in a storm of bullets and grape, in the most exposed places—wherever, in fact, duty, requiring him to go, permitted him to remain—when, without trouble and with distinct advantage to his reputation for common sense, he might have been in such security as is possible on a battlefield in the brief intervals of personal inaction.

On foot, from necessity or in deference to his dismounted commander or associates, his conduct was the same. He would stand like a rock in the open when officers and men alike had taken to cover; while men older in service and years, higher in rank and of unquestionable intrepidity, were loyally preserving behind the crest of a hill lives infinitely precious to their country, this fellow would stand, equally idle, on the ridge, facing in the direction of the sharpest fire.

When battles are going on in open ground it frequently occurs that the opposing lines, confronting each other within a stone's throw for hours, hug the earth as closely as if they loved it. The line officers in their proper places flatten themselves no less, and the field officers, their horses all killed or sent to the rear, crouch beneath the infernal canopy of hissing lead and screaming iron without a thought of personal dignity.

In such circumstances the life of a staff officer of a brigade is distinctly "not a happy one," mainly because of its precarious tenure and the unnerving alternations of emotion to which he is exposed. From a position of that comparative security from which a civilian would ascribe his escape to a "miracle," he may be dispatched with an order to some commander of a prone regiment in the front line—a person for the moment inconspicuous and not always easy to find without a deal of search among men somewhat preoccupied, and in a din in which question and answer alike must be imparted in the sign language. It is customary in such cases to duck the head and scuttle away on a keen run, an object of lively interest to some thousands of admiring marksmen. In returning—well, it is not customary to return.

Brayle's practice was different. He would consign his horse to the care of an orderly—he loved his horse—and walk quietly away on his perilous errand with never a stoop of the back, his splendid figure, accentuated by his uniform, holding the eye with a strange fascination. We watched him with suspended breath, our hearts in our mouths. On one occasion of this kind, indeed, one of our number, an impetuous stammerer, was so possessed by his emotion that he shouted at me:

"I'll b-b-bet you t-two d-d-dollars they d-drop him b-b-before he g-gets to that d-d-ditch!"

I did not accept the brutal wager; I thought they would.

Let me do justice to a brave man's memory; in all these needless exposures of life there was no visible bravado nor subsequent narration. In the few instances when some of us had ventured to remonstrate, Brayle had smiled pleasantly and made some light reply, which, however, had not encouraged a further pursuit of the subject. Once he said:

"Captain, if ever I come to grief by forgetting your advice, I hope my last moments will be cheered by the sound of your beloved voice breathing into my ear the blessed words, 'I told you so.'"

We laughed at the captain—just why we could probably not have explained—and that afternoon when he was shot to rags from an ambuscade Brayle remained by the body for some time, adjusting the limbs with needless care—there in the middle of a road swept by gusts of grape and canister! It is easy to condemn this kind of thing, and not very difficult to refrain from imitation, but it is impossible not to respect, and Brayle was liked none the less for the weakness which had so heroic an expression. We wished he were not a fool, but he went on that way to the end, sometimes hard hit, but always returning to duty about as good as new.

Of course, it came at last; he who ignores the law of probabilities challenges an adversary that is seldom beaten. It was at Resaca, in Georgia, during the movement that resulted in the taking of Atlanta. In front of our brigade the enemy's line of earthworks ran through open fields along a slight crest. At each end of this open ground we were close up to him in the woods, but the clear ground we could not hope to occupy until night, when darkness would enable us to burrow like moles and throw up earth. At this point our line was a quarter-mile away in the edge of a wood. Roughly, we formed a semicircle, the enemy's fortified line being the chord of the arc.

"Lieutenant, go tell Colonel Ward to work up as close as he can get cover, and not to waste much ammunition in unnecessary firing. You may leave your horse."

When the general gave this direction we were in the fringe of the forest, near the right extremity of the arc. Colonel Ward was at the left. The suggestion to leave the horse obviously enough meant that Brayle was to take the longer line, through the woods and among the men. Indeed, the suggestion was needless; to go by the short route meant absolutely certain failure to deliver the message. Before anybody could interpose, Brayle had cantered lightly into the field and the enemy's works were in crackling conflagration.

"Stop that damned fool!" shouted the general.

A private of the escort, with more ambition than brains, spurred forward to obey, and within ten yards left himself and his horse dead on the field of honor.

Brayle was beyond recall, galloping easily along, parallel to the enemy and less than two hundred yards distant. He was a picture to see! His hat had been blown or shot from his head, and his long, blond hair rose and fell with the motion of his horse. He sat erect in the saddle, holding the reins lightly in his left hand, his right hanging carelessly at his side. An occasional glimpse of his handsome profile as he turned his head one way or the other proved that the interest which he took in what was going on was natural and without affectation.

The picture was intensely dramatic, but in no degree theatrical. Successive scores of rifles spat at him viciously as he came within range, and our own line in the edge of the timber broke out in visible and audible defense. No longer regardful of themselves or their orders, our fellows sprang to their feet, and swarming into the open sent broad sheets of bullets against the blazing crest of the offending works, which poured an answering fire into their unprotected groups with deadly effect. The artillery on both sides joined the battle, punctuating the rattle and roar with deep, earth-shaking explosions and tearing the air with storms of screaming grape, which from the enemy's side splintered the trees and spattered them with blood, and from ours defiled the smoke of his arms with banks and clouds of dust from his parapet.

My attention had been for a moment drawn to the general combat, but now, glancing down the unobscured avenue between these two thunderclouds, I saw Brayle, the cause of the carnage. Invisible now from either side, and equally doomed by friend and foe, he stood in the shot-swept space, motionless, his face toward the enemy. At some little distance lay his horse. I instantly saw what had stopped him.

As topographical engineer I had, early in the day, made a hasty examination of the ground, and now remembered that at that point was a deep and sinuous gully, crossing half the field from the enemy's line, its general course at right angles to it. From where we now were it was invisible, and Brayle had evidently not known about it. Clearly, it was impassable. Its salient angles would have afforded him absolute security if he had chosen to be satisfied with the miracle already wrought in his favor and leapt into it. He could not go forward, he would not turn back; he stood awaiting death. It did not keep him long waiting.

By some mysterious coincidence, almost instantaneously as he fell, the firing ceased, a few desultory shots at long intervals serving rather to accentuate than break the silence. It was as if both sides had suddenly repented of their profitless crime. Four stretcher-bearers of ours, following a sergeant with a white flag, soon afterward moved unmolested into the field, and made straight for Brayle's body. Several Confederate officers and men came out to meet them, and with uncovered heads assisted them to take up their sacred burden. As it was borne toward us we heard beyond the hostile works fifes and a muffled drum—a dirge. A generous enemy honored the fallen brave.

Amongst the dead man's effects was a soiled Russia-leather pocket-book. In the distribution of mementoes of our friend, which the general, as administrator, decreed, this fell to me.

A year after the close of the war, on my way to California, I opened and idly inspected it. Out of an overlooked compartment fell a letter without envelope or address. It was in a woman's handwriting, and began with words of endearment, but no name.

It had the following date line: "San Francisco, Cal., July 9, 1862." The signature was "Darling," in marks of quotation. Incidentally, in the body of the text, the writer's full name was given—Marian Mendenhall.

The letter showed evidence of cultivation and good breeding, but it was an ordinary love letter, if a love letter can be ordinary. There was not much in it, but there was something. It was this:

"Mr. Winters, whom I shall always hate for it, has been telling that at some battle in Virginia, where he got his hurt, you were seen crouching behind a tree. I think he wants to injure you in my regard, which he knows the story would do if I believed it. I could bear to hear of my soldier lover's death, but not of his cowardice."

These were the words which on that sunny afternoon, in a distant region, had slain a hundred men. Is woman weak?

One evening I called on Miss Mendenhall to return the letter to her. I intended, also, to tell her what she had done—but not that she did it. I found her in a handsome dwelling on Rincon Hill. She was beautiful, well bred—in a word, charming.

"You knew Lieutenant Herman Brayle," I said, rather abruptly. "You know, doubtless, that he fell in battle. Among his effects was found this letter from you. My errand here is to place it in your hands."

She mechanically took the letter, glanced through it with deepening color, and then, looking at me with a smile, said:

"It is very good of you, though I am sure it was hardly worth while." She started suddenly and changed color. "This stain," she said, "is it—surely it is not—"

"Madam," I said, "pardon me, but that is the blood of the truest and bravest heart that ever beat."

She hastily flung the letter on the blazing coals. "Uh! I cannot bear the sight of blood!" she said. "How did he die?"

I had involuntarily risen to rescue that scrap of paper, sacred even to me, and now stood partly behind her. As she asked the question she turned her face about and slightly upward. The light of the burning letter was reflected in her eyes and touched her cheek with a tinge of crimson like the stain upon its page. I had never seen anything so beautiful as this detestable creature.

"He was bitten by a snake," I replied.

"THE PRIVATE HISTORY OF A CAMPAIGN THAT FAILED"

Mark Twain

You have heard from a great many people who did something in the war; is it not fair and right that you listen a little moment to one who started out to do something in it, but didn't? Thousands entered the war, got just a taste of it, and then stepped out again, permanently. These, by their very numbers, are respectable, and are therefore entitled to a sort of voice—not a loud one, but a modest one; not a boastful one, but an apologetic one. They ought not to be allowed much space among better people—people who did something—I grant that; but they ought at least to be allowed to state why they didn't do anything, and also to explain the process by which they didn't do anything. Surely this kind of light must have a sort of value.

Out West there was a good deal of confusion in men's minds during the first months of the great trouble—a good deal of unsettledness, of leaning first this way, then that, then the other way. It was hard for us to get our bearings. I call to mind an instance of this. I was piloting on the Mississippi when the news came that South Carolina had gone out of the Union on the 20th of December, 1860. My pilot-mate was a New Yorker. He was strong for the Union; so was I. But he would not listen to me with any patience; my loyalty was smirched, to his eye, because my father had owned slaves. I said, in palliation of this dark fact, that I had heard my

Century Magazine, Dec. 1885.

father say, some years before he died, that slavery was a great wrong, and that he would free the solitary negro he then owned if he could think it right to give away the property of the family when he was so straitened in means. My mate retorted that a mere impulse was nothing—anybody could pretend to a good impulse; and went on decrying my Unionism and libeling my ancestry. A month later the secession atmosphere had considerably thickened on the Lower Mississippi, and I became a rebel; so did he. We were together in New Orleans, the 26th of January, when Louisiana went out of the Union. He did his full share of the rebel shouting, but was bitterly opposed to letting me do mine. He said that I came of bad stock—of a father who had been willing to set slaves free. In the following summer he was piloting a Federal gun-boat and shouting for the Union again, and I was in the Confederate army. I held his note for some borrowed money. He was one of the most upright men I ever knew; but he repudiated that note without hesitation, because I was a rebel, and the son of a man who owned slaves.

In that summer—of 1861—the first wash of the wave of war broke upon the shores of Missouri. Our State was invaded by the Union forces. They took possession of St. Louis, Jefferson Barracks, and some other points. The Governor, Claib Jackson, issued his proclamation calling out fifty thousand militia to repel the invader.

I was visiting in the small town where my boyhood had been spent—Hannibal, Marion County. Several of us got together in a secret place by night and formed ourselves into a military company. . . .

For a time, life was idly delicious, it was perfect: there was nothing to mar it. Then came some farmers with an alarm one day. They said it was rumored that the enemy were advancing in our direction, from over Hyde's prairie. The result was a sharp stir among us, and general consternation. It was a rude awakening from our pleasant trance. The rumor was but a rumor—nothing definite about it; so, in the confusion, we did not know which way to retreat. Lyman was for not retreating at all, in these uncertain circumstances; but he found that if he tried to maintain that attitude he would fare badly, for the command were in no humor to put up with insubordination. So he yielded the point and called a council of war—to consist of himself and the three other officers; but the privates made such a fuss about being left out, that we had to allow them to be present. I mean we had to allow them to remain, for they were already present, and doing the most of the talking too. The question was, which way to retreat; but all were so flurried that nobody seemed to have even a guess to offer. Except Lyman. He explained in a few calm words, that inasmuch as the enemy were approaching from over Hyde's prairie, our course was simple: all we had to do was not to retreat *toward* him; any other direction would answer our needs perfectly. Everybody saw in a moment how true this was, and how wise; so Lyman got a great many compliments. It was now decided that we should fall back on Mason's farm.

It was after dark by this time, and as we could not know how soon the enemy might arrive, it did not seem best to try to take the horses and things with us; so we only took the guns and ammunition, and started at once. The route was very rough and hilly and rocky, and presently the night grew very black and rain began to fall; so we had a troublesome time of it, struggling and stumbling along in the dark; and soon some person slipped and fell, and then the next person behind stumbled over him and fell, and so did the rest, one after the other; and then Bowers came with the keg of powder in his arms, whilst the command were all mixed together, arms and legs, on the muddy slope; and so he fell, of course, with the keg, and this started the whole detachment down the hill in a body, and they landed in the brook at the bottom in a pile, and each that was undermost pulling the hair and scratching and biting those that were on top of him; and those that were being scratched and bitten scratching and biting the rest in their turn, and all saying they would die before they would ever go to war again if they ever got out of this brook this time, and the invader might rot for all they cared, and the country along with him—and all such talk as that, which was dismal to hear and take part in, in such smothered, low voices, and such a grisly dark place and so wet, and the enemy may be coming any moment.

The keg of powder was lost, and the guns too; so the growling and complaining continued straight along whilst the brigade pawed around the pasty hillside and slopped around in the brook hunting for these things; consequently we lost considerable time at this; and then we heard a sound, and held our breath and listened, and it seemed to be the enemy coming, though it could have been a cow, for it had a cough like a cow; but we did not wait, but left a couple of guns behind and struck out for Mason's again as briskly as we could scramble along in the dark. But we got lost presently among the rugged little ravines, and wasted a deal of time finding the way again, so it was after nine when we reached Mason's stile at last; and then before we could open our mouths to give the countersign, several dogs came bounding over the fence, with great riot and noise, and each of them took a soldier by the slack of his trousers and began to back away with him. We could not shoot the dogs without endangering the persons they were attached to; so we had to look on, helpless, at what was perhaps the most mortifying spectacle of the civil war. There was light enough, and to spare, for the Masons had now run out on the porch with candles in their hands. The old man and his son came and undid the dogs without difficulty, all but Bowers's; but they couldn't undo his dog, they didn't know his combination; he was of the bull kind, and seemed to be set with a Yale time-lock; but they got him loose at last with some scalding water, of which Bowers got his share and returned thanks. Peterson Dunlap afterwards made up a fine name for this engagement, and also for the night march which preceded it, but both have long ago faded out of my memory.

We now went into the house, and they began to ask us a world of questions, whereby it presently came out that we did not know anything concerning who or what we were running from; so the old gentleman made himself very frank, and said we were a curious breed of soldiers, and guessed we could be depended on to end up the war in time, because no government could stand the expense of the shoe-leather we should cost it trying to follow us around. "Marion *Rangers!* good name, b'gosh!" said he. And wanted to know why we hadn't had a picket-guard at the place where the road entered the prairie, and why we hadn't sent out a scouting party to spy out the enemy and bring us an account of his strength, and so on, before jumping up and stampeding out of a strong position upon a mere vague rumor—and so on and so forth, till he made us all feel shabbier than the dogs had done, not half so enthusiastically welcome. So we went to bed shamed and low-spirited; except Stevens. Soon Stevens began to devise a garment for Bowers which could be made to automatically display his battle-scars to the grateful, or conceal them from the envious, according to his occasions; but Bowers was in no humor for this, so there was a fight, and when it was over Stevens had some battle-scars of his own to think about.

Then we got a little sleep. But after all we had gone through, our activities were not over for the night; for about two o'clock in the morning we heard a shout of warning from down the lane, accompanied by a chorus from all the dogs, and in a moment everybody was up and flying around to find out what the alarm was about. The alarmist was a horseman who gave notice that a detachment of Union soldiers was on its way from Hannibal with orders to capture and hang any bands like ours which it could find, and said we had no time to lose. Farmer Mason was in a flurry this time, himself. He hurried us out of the house with all haste, and sent one of his negroes with us to show us where to hide ourselves and our tell-tale guns among the ravines half a mile away. It was raining heavily.

We struck down the lane, then across some rocky pasture-land which offered good advantages for stumbling; consequently we were down in the mud most of the time, and every time a man went down he blackguarded the war, and the people that started it, and everybody connected with it, and gave himself the master dose of all for being so foolish as to go into it. At last we reached the wooded mouth of a ravine, and there we huddled ourselves under the streaming trees, and sent the negro back home. It was a dismal and heart-breaking time. We were like to be drowned with the rain, deafened with the howling wind and the booming thunder, and blinded by the lightning. It was indeed a wild night. The drenching we were getting was misery enough, but a deeper misery still was the reflection that the halter might end us before we were a day older. A death of this shameful sort had not occurred to us as being among the possibilities of war. It took the romance all out of the campaign, and turned our dreams of glory into a repulsive nightmare. As for doubting that so barbarous an order had been given, not one of us did that.

The long night wore itself out at last, and then the negro came to us with the news that the alarm had manifestly been a false one, and that breakfast would soon be ready. Straightway we were light-hearted again, and the world was bright, and life as full of hope and promise as ever— for we were young then. How long ago that was! Twenty-four years.

The mongrel child of philology named the night's refuge Camp Devastation, and no soul objected. The Masons gave us a Missouri country breakfast, in Missourian abundance, and we needed it: hot biscuits; hot "wheat bread" prettily criss-crossed in a lattice pattern on top; hot corn pone; fried chicken; bacon, coffee, eggs, milk, buttermilk, etc.—and the world may be confidently challenged to furnish the equal to such a breakfast, as it is cooked in the South.

We stayed several days at Mason's; and after all these years the memory of the dullness, the stillness and lifelessness of that slumberous farmhouse still oppresses my spirit as with a sense of the presence of death and mourning. There was nothing to do, nothing to think about; there was no interest in life. The male part of the household were away in the fields all day, the women were busy and out of our sight; there was no sound but the plaintive wailing of a spinning-wheel, forever moaning out from some distant room—the most lonesome sound in nature, a sound steeped and sodden with homesickness and the emptiness of life. The family went to bed about dark every night, and as we were not invited to intrude any new customs, we naturally followed theirs. Those nights were a hundred years long to youths accustomed to being up till twelve. We lay awake and miserable till that hour every time, and grew old and decrepit waiting through the still eternities for the clock-strikes. This was no place for town boys. So at last it was with something very like joy that we received news that the enemy were on our track again. With a new birth of the old warrior spirit, we sprang to our places in line of battle and fell back on Camp Ralls.

Captain Lyman had taken a hint from Mason's talk, and he now gave orders that our camp should be guarded against surprise by the posting of pickets. I was ordered to place a picket at the forks of the road in Hyde's prairie. Night shut down black and threatening. I told Sergeant Bowers to go out to that place and stay till midnight; and, just as I was expecting, he said he wouldn't do it. I tried to get others to go, but all refused. Some excused themselves on account of the weather; but the rest were frank enough to say they wouldn't go in any kind of weather. This kind of thing sounds odd now, and impossible, but there was no surprise in it at the time. On the contrary, it seemed a perfectly natural thing to do. There were scores of little camps scattered over Missouri where the same thing was happening. These camps were composed of young men who had been born and reared to a sturdy independence, and who did not know what it meant to be ordered around by Tom, Dick, and Harry, whom they had known familiarly all their lives, in the village or on the farm. It is quite within the probabilities that this same thing was happening all over the South. James Redpath recognized the justice of this assumption, and furnished the following instance in support of it. During a short stay in East Tennessee he was in a citizen colonel's tent one day, talking, when a big private appeared at the door, and without salute or other circumlocution said to the colonel:

"Say, Jim, I'm a-goin' home for a few days."

"What for?"

"Well, I hain't b'en there for a right smart while, and I'd like to see how things is comin' on."

"How long are you going to be gone?"

"'Bout two weeks."

"Well, don't be gone longer than that; and get back sooner if you can."

That was all, and the citizen officer resumed his conversation where the private had broken it off. This was in the first months of the war, of course. The camps in our part of Missouri were under Brigadier-General Thomas H. Harris. He was a townsman of ours, a first-rate fellow, and well liked; but we had all familiarly known him as the sole and modest-salaried operator in our telegraph office, where he had to send about one dispatch a week in ordinary times, and two when there was a rush of business; consequently, when he appeared in our midst one day, on the wing, and delivered a military command of some sort, in a large military fashion, nobody was surprised at the response which he got from the assembled soldiery:

"Oh, now, what'll you take to *don't*, Tom Harris!"

It was quite the natural thing. One might justly imagine that we were hopeless material for war. And so we seemed, in our ignorant state; but there were those among us who afterward learned the grim trade; learned to obey like machines; became valuable soldiers; fought all through the war, and came out at the end with excellent records. One of the very boys who refused to go out on picket duty that night, and called me an ass for thinking he would expose himself to danger in such a foolhardy way, had become distinguished for intrepidity before he was a year older.

I did secure my picket that night—not by authority, but by diplomacy. I got Bowers to go, by agreeing to exchange ranks with him for the time being, and go along and stand the watch with him as his subordinate. We stayed out there a couple of dreary hours in the pitchy darkness and the rain, with nothing to modify the dreariness but Bowers's monotonous growlings at the war and the weather; then we began to nod, and presently found it next to impossible to stay in the saddle; so we gave up the tedious job, and went back to the camp without waiting for the relief guard. We rode into camp without interruption or objection from anybody, and the enemy could have done the same, for there were no sentries. Everybody was asleep; at midnight there was nobody to send out another picket, so none was sent. We never tried to establish a watch at night again, as far as I remember, but we generally kept a picket out in the daytime.

In that camp the whole command slept on the corn in the big corn-crib; and there was usually a general row before morning, for the place was full of rats, and they would scramble over the boys' bodies and faces, annoying and irritating everybody; and now and then they would bite some one's toe, and the person who owned the toe would start up and magnify his English and begin to throw corn in the dark. The ears were half as heavy as bricks, and when they struck they hurt. The persons struck would respond, and inside of five minutes every man would be locked in a death-grip with his neighbor. There was a grievous deal of blood shed in the corn-crib, but this was all that was spilt while I was in the war. No, that is not quite true. But for one circumstance it would have been all. I will come to that now.

Our scares were frequent. Every few days rumors would come that the enemy were approaching. In these cases we always fell back on some other camp of ours; we never stayed where we were. But the rumors always turned out to be false; so at last even we began to grow indifferent to them. One night a negro was sent to our corn-crib with the same old warning: the enemy was hovering in our neighborhood. We all said let him hover. We resolved to stay still and be comfortable. It was a fine warlike resolution, and no doubt we all felt the stir of it in our veins—for a moment. We had been having a very jolly time, that was full of horse-play and school-boy hilarity; but that cooled down now, and presently the fast-waning of forced jokes and forced laughs died out altogether, and the company became silent. Silent and nervous. And soon uneasy—worried—apprehensive. We had said we would stay, and we were committed. We could have been persuaded to go, but there was nobody brave enough to suggest it.

An almost noiseless movement presently began in the dark, by a general but unvoiced impulse. When the movement was completed, each man knew that he was not the only person who had crept to the front wall and had his eye at a crack between the logs. No, we were all there; all there with our hearts in our throats, and staring out toward the sugar-troughs where the forest foot-path came through. It was late, and there was a deep woodsy stillness everywhere. There was a veiled moonlight, which was only just strong enough to enable us to mark the general shape of objects. Presently a muffled sound caught our ears, and we recognized it as the hoof-beats of a horse or horses. And right away a figure appeared in the forest path; it could have been made of smoke, its mass had so little sharpness of outline. It was a man on horseback; and it seemed to me that there were others behind him. I got hold of a gun in the dark, and pushed it through a crack between the logs, hardly knowing what I was doing, I was so dazed with fright. Somebody said "Fire!" I pulled the trigger. I seemed to see a hundred flashes and hear a hundred reports, then I saw the man fall down out of the saddle. My first feeling was of surprised gratification; my first impulse was an apprentice-sportsman's impulse to run and pick up his game. Somebody said, hardly audibly, "Good—we've got him!—wait for the rest." But the rest did not come. We waited—listened—still no more came. There was not a sound, not the whisper of a leaf; just perfect stillness; an uncanny kind of stillness, which was all the more uncanny on account of the damp, earthy, late-night smells now rising and pervading it. Then, wondering, we crept stealthily out, and approached the man. When we got to him the moon revealed him distinctly. He was lying on his back, with his arms abroad; his mouth was open and his chest heaving with long gasps, and his white shirt-front was all splashed with blood. The thought shot through me that I was a murderer; that I had killed a man—a man who had never done me any harm. That was the coldest sensation that ever went through my marrow. I was down by him in a moment, helplessly stroking his forehead; and I would have given anything then—my own life freely—to make him again what he had been five minutes before. And all the boys seemed to be feeling in the same way; they hung over him, full of pitying interest, and tried all they could to help him, and said all sorts of regretful things. They had forgotten all about the enemy; they thought only of this one forlorn unit of the foe. Once my imagination persuaded me that the dying man gave me a reproachful look out of his shadowy eyes, and it seemed to me that I could rather he had stabbed me than done that. He muttered and mumbled like a dreamer in his sleep, about his wife and his child; and I thought with a new despair, "This thing that I have done does not end with him; it falls upon *them* too, and they never did me any harm, any more than he."

In a little while the man was dead. He was killed in war; killed in fair and legitimate war; killed in battle, as you may say; and yet he was as sincerely mourned by the opposing force as if he had been their brother. The boys stood there a half hour sorrowing over him, and recalling the details of the tragedy, and wondering who he might be, and if he were a spy, and saying that if it were to do over again they would not hurt him unless he attacked them first. It soon came out that mine was not the only shot fired; there were five others—a division of the guilt which was a grateful relief to me, since it in some degree lightened and diminished the burden I was carrying. There were six shots fired at once; but I was not in my right mind at the time, and my heated imagination had magnified my one shot into a volley.

The man was not in uniform, and was not armed. He was a stranger in the country; that was all we ever found out about him. The thought of him got to preying upon me every night; I could not get rid of it. I could not drive it away, the taking of that unoffending life seemed such a wanton thing. And it seemed an epitome of war; that all war must be just that— the killing of strangers against whom you feel no personal animosity; strangers whom, in other circumstances, you would help if you found them in trouble, and who would help you if you needed it. My campaign was spoiled. It seemed to me that I was not rightly equipped for this awful business; that war was intended for men, and I for a child's nurse. I resolved to retire from this avocation of sham soldiership while I could save some remnant of my self-respect. These morbid thoughts clung to me against reason; for at bottom I did not believe I had touched that man. The law of probabilities decreed me guiltless of his blood; for in all my small experience with guns I had never hit anything I had tried to hit, and I knew I had done my best to hit him. Yet there was no solace in the thought. Against a diseased imagination, demonstration goes for nothing.

The rest of my war experience was of a piece with what I have already told of it. We kept monotonously falling back upon one camp or another, and eating up the country. I marvel now at the patience of the farmers and their families. They ought to have shot us; on the contrary, they were as hospitably kind and courteous to us as if we had deserved it. In one of these camps we found Ab Grimes, an Upper Mississippi pilot, who afterwards became famous as a dare-devil rebel spy, whose career bristled with desperate adventures. The look and style of his comrades suggested that they had not come into the war to play, and their deeds made good the conjecture later. They were fine horsemen and good revolver-shots; but their favorite arm was the lasso. Each had one at his pommel, and could snatch a man out of the saddle with it every time, on a full gallop, at any reasonable distance.

In another camp the chief was a fierce and profane old blacksmith of sixty, and he had furnished his twenty recruits with gigantic home-made bowie-knives, to be swung with the two hands, like the *machetes* of the Isthmus. It was a grisly spectacle to see that earnest band practicing their murderous cuts and slashes under the eye of that remorseless old fanatic.

The last camp which we fell back upon was in a hollow near the village of Florida, where I was born—in Monroe County. Here we were warned, one day, that a Union colonel was sweeping down on us with a whole regiment at his heels. This looked decidedly serious. Our boys went apart and consulted; then we went back and told the other companies present that the war was a disappointment to us and we were going to disband. They were getting ready, themselves, to fall back on some place or other, and were only waiting for General Tom Harris, who was expected to arrive at any moment; so they tried to persuade us to wait a little while, but the majority of us said no, we were accustomed to falling back, and didn't need any of Tom Harris's help; we could get along perfectly well without him—and save time too. So about half of our fifteen, including myself, mounted and left on the instant; the others yielded to persuasion and stayed—stayed through the war.

An hour later we met General Harris on the road, with two or three people in his company—his staff, probably, but we could not tell; none of them were in uniform; uniforms had not come into vogue among us yet. Harris ordered us back; but we told him there was a Union colonel coming with a whole regiment in his wake, and it looked as if there was going to be a disturbance; so we had concluded to go home. He raged a little, but it was of no use; our minds were made up. We had done our share; had killed one man, exterminated one army, such as it was; let him go and kill the rest, and that would end the war. I did not see that brisk young general again until last year; then he was wearing white hair and whiskers.

In time I came to know that Union colonel whose coming frightened me out of the war and crippled the Southern cause to that extent— General Grant. I came within a few hours of seeing him when he was as unknown as I was myself; at a time when anybody could have said, "Grant? Ulysses S. Grant? I do not remember hearing the name before." It seems difficult to realize that there was once a time when such a remark could be rationally made; but there *was,* and I was within a few miles of the place and the occasion too, though proceeding in the other direction.

The thoughtful will not throw this war-paper of mine lightly aside as being valueless. It has this value: it is a not unfair picture of what went on in many and many a militia camp in the first months of the rebellion, when the green recruits were without discipline, without the steadying and heartening influence of trained leaders; when all their circumstances were new and strange, and charged with exaggerated terrors, and before the invaluable experience of actual collision in the field had turned them from rabbits into soldiers. If this side of the picture of that early day has not before been put into history, then history has been to that degree incomplete, for it had and has its rightful place there. There was more Bull Run material scattered through the early camps of this country than exhibited itself at Bull Run. And yet it learned its trade presently, and helped to fight the great battles later. I could have become a soldier myself, if I had waited. I had got part of it learned; I knew more about retreating than the man that invented retreating.

PART FOUR

"The Open Boat" and Other Writings of the Spanish-American War

"STEPHEN CRANE'S OWN STORY"

He Tells How the Commodore *Was Wrecked and How He Escaped*
FEAR-CRAZED NEGRO NEARLY SWAMPS BOAT
Young Writer Compelled to Work in Stifling Atmosphere
of the Fire Room
BRAVERY OF CAPTAIN MURPHY AND HIGGINS
Tried to Tow Their Companions Who Were on the Raft—
Last Dash for the Shore Through the Surf

JACKSONVILLE, FLA., JAN 6 [1897]—It was the afternoon of New
Year's. The *Commodore* lay at her dock in Jacksonville and negro steve-
dores processioned steadily toward her with box after box of ammunition
and bundle after bundle of rifles. Her hatch, like the mouth of a monster,
engulfed them. It might have been the feeding time of some legendary creature of the sea. It was in broad daylight and the crowd of gleeful Cubans on
the pier did not forbear to sing the strange patriotic ballads of their island.

Everything was perfectly open. The *Commodore* was cleared with a
cargo of arms and munition for Cuba. There was none of that extreme
modesty about the proceeding which had marked previous departures of
the famous tug. She loaded up as placidly as if she were going to carry
oranges to New York, instead of Remingtons to Cuba. Down the river,
furthermore, the revenue cutter *Boutwell,* the old isosceles triangle that
protects United States interests in the St. John's, lay at anchor, with no sign
of excitement aboard her.

Exchanging Farewells

On the decks of the *Commodore* there were exchanges of farewells in two
languages. Many of the men who were to sail upon her had many intimates
in the old Southern town, and we who had left our friends in the remote
North received our first touch of melancholy on witnessing these strenuous and earnest goodbys.

It seems, however, that there was more difficulty at the custom house.
The officers of the ship and the Cuban leaders were detained there until a
mournful twilight settled upon the St. John's, and through a heavy fog the
lights of Jacksonville blinked dimly. Then at last the *Commodore* swung

---

New York Press, 7 Jan. 1897.

clear of the dock, amid a tumult of goodbys. As she turned her bow toward the distant sea the Cubans ashore cheered and cheered. In response the *Commodore* gave three long blasts of her whistle, which even to this time impressed me with their sadness. Somehow, they sounded as wails.

Then at last we began to feel like filibusters. I don't suppose that the most stolid brain could contrive to believe that there is not a mere trifle of danger in filibustering, and so as we watched the lights of Jacksonville swing past us and heard the regular thump, thump, thump of the engines we did considerable reflecting.

But I am sure that there were no hifalutin emotions visible upon any of the faces which confronted the speeding shore. In fact, from cook's boy to captain, we were all enveloped in a gentle satisfaction and cheerfulness. But less than two miles from Jacksonville, this atrocious fog caused the pilot to ram the bow of the *Commodore* hard upon the mud and in this ignominious position we were compelled to stay until daybreak.

Help from the *Boutwell*

It was to all of us more than a physical calamity. We were now no longer filibusters. We were men on a ship stuck in the mud. A certain mental somersault was made once more necessary.

But word had been sent to Jacksonville to the captain of the revenue cutter *Boutwell,* and Captain Kilgore turned out promptly and generously fired up his old triangle, and came at full speed to our assistance. She dragged us out of the mud, and again we headed for the mouth of the river. The revenue cutter pounded along a half mile astern of us, to make sure that we did not take on board at some place along the river men for the Cuban army.

This was the early morning of New Year's Day, and the fine golden southern sunlight fell upon the river. It flashed over the ancient *Boutwell,* until her white sides gleamed like pearl, and her rigging was spun into little threads of gold.

Cheers greeted the old *Commodore* from passing ship and from the shore. It was a cheerful, almost merry, beginning to our voyage. At Mayport, however, we changed our river pilot for a man who could take her to open sea, and again the *Commodore* was beached. The *Boutwell* was fussing around us in her venerable way, and, upon seeing our predicament, she came again to assist us, but this time, with engines reversed, the *Commodore* dragged herself away from the grip of the sand and again headed for the open sea.

The captain of the revenue cutter grew curious. He hailed the *Commodore:* "Are you fellows going to sea today?"

Captain Murphy of the *Commodore* called back: "Yes, sir."

And then as the whistle of the *Commodore* saluted him, Captain Kilgore doffed his cap and said: "Well, gentlemen, I hope you have a pleasant cruise," and this was our last word from shore.

When the *Commodore* came to enormous rollers that flee over the bar a certain light-heartedness departed from the ship's company.

Sleep Impossible

As darkness came upon the waters, the *Commodore* was a broad, flaming path of blue and silver phosphorescence, and as her stout bow lunged at the great black waves she threw flashing, roaring cascades to either side. And all that was to be heard was the rhythmical and mighty pounding of the engines. Being an inexperienced filibuster, the writer had undergone considerable mental excitement since the starting of the ship, and in consequence he had not yet been to sleep and so I went to the first mate's bunk to indulge myself in all the physical delights of holding one's-self in bed. Every time the ship lurched I expected to be fired through a bulkhead, and it was neither amusing nor instructive to see in the dim light a certain accursed valise aiming itself at the top of my stomach with every lurch of the vessel.

The Cook Is Hopeful

The cook was asleep on a bench in the galley. He is of a portly and noble exterior, and by means of a checker board he had himself wedged on this bench in such a manner the motion of the ship would be unable to dislodge him. He woke as I entered the galley and delivered himself of some dolorous sentiments: "God," he said in the course of his observations, "I don't feel right about this ship, somehow. It strikes me that something is going to happen to us. I don't know what it is, but the old ship is going to get it in the neck, I think."

"Well, how about the men on board of her?" said I. "Are any of us going to get out, prophet?"

"Yes," said the cook. "Sometimes I have these damned feelings come over me, and they are always right, and it seems to me, somehow, that you and I will both get out and meet again somewhere, down at Coney Island, perhaps, or some place like that."

One Man Has Enough

Finding it impossible to sleep, I went back to the pilot house. An old sea-man, Tom Smith, from Charleston, was then at the wheel. In the darkness I could not see Tom's face, except at those times when he leaned forward to scan the compass and the dim light from the box came upon his weather-beaten features.

"Well, Tom," said I, "how do you like filibustering?"

He said, "I think I am about through with it. I've been in a number of these expeditions and the pay is good, but I think if I ever get back safe this time I will cut it."

I sat down in the corner of the pilot house and almost went to sleep. In the meantime the captain came on duty and he was standing near me when the chief engineer rushed up the stairs and cried hurriedly to the captain that there was something wrong in the engine room. He and the captain departed swiftly.

I was drowsing there in my corner when the captain returned, and, going to the door of the little room directly back of the pilothouse, he cried to the Cuban leader:

"Say, can't you get those fellows to work? I can't talk their language and I can't get them started. Come on and get them going."

Helps in the Fireroom

The Cuban leader turned to me and said: "Go help in the fireroom. They are going to bail with buckets."

The engine room, by the way, represented a scene at this time taken from the middle kitchen of hades. In the first place, it was insufferably warm, and the lights burned faintly in a way to cause mystic and grue-some shadows. There was a quantity of soapish sea water swirling and sweeping and swishing among machinery that roared and banged and clattered and steamed, and, in the second place, it was a devil of a ways down below.

Here I first came to know a certain young oiler named Billy Higgins. He was sloshing around this inferno filling buckets with water and passing them to a chain of men that extended up the ship's side. Afterward we got orders to change our point of attack on water and to operate through a little door on the windward side of the ship that led into the engine room.

No Panic on Board

During this time there was much talk of pumps out of order and many other statements of a mechanical kind, which I did not altogether comprehend but understood to mean that there was a general and sudden ruin in the engine room.

There was no particular agitation at this time, and even later there was never a panic on board the *Commodore*. The party of men who worked with Higgins and me at this time were all Cubans, and we were under the direction of the Cuban leaders. Presently we were ordered again to the afterhold, and there was some hesitation about going into the abominable fireroom again, but Higgins dashed down the companionway with a bucket.

Lowering Boats

The heat and hard work in the fireroom affected me and I was obliged to come on deck again. Going forward, I heard as I went talk of lowering the boats. Near the corner of the galley the mate was talking with a man.

"Why don't you send up a rocket?" said this unknown man. And the mate replied: "What the hell do we want to send up a rocket for? The ship is all right."

Returning with a little rubber and cloth overcoat, I saw the first boat about to be lowered. A certain man was the first person in this first boat, and they were handing him a valise about as large as a hotel. I had not entirely recovered from astonishment and pleasure in witnessing this noble deed when I saw another valise go to him.

Human Hog Appears

This valise was not perhaps so large as a hotel, but it was a big valise anyhow. Afterward there went to him something which looked to me like an overcoat.

Seeing the chief engineer leaning out of his little window, I remarked to him:

"What do you think of that blank, blank, blank?"

"Oh, he's a bird," said the old chief.

It was now that was heard the order to get away the lifeboat, which was stowed on top of the deckhouse. The deckhouse was a mighty slippery place, and with each roll of the ship, the men there thought themselves likely to take headers into the deadly black sea.

Higgins was on top of the deckhouse, and, with the first mate and two colored stokers, we wrestled with that boat, which, I am willing to swear, weighed as much as a Broadway cable car. She might have been spiked to the deck. We could have pushed a little brick schoolhouse along a corduroy road as easily as we could have moved this boat. But the first mate got a tackle to her from a leeward davit, and on the deck below the captain corralled enough men to make an impression upon the boat.

We were ordered to cease hauling then, and in this lull the cook of the ship came to me and said: "What are you going to do?"

I told him of my plans, and he said:

"Well, by God, that's what I am going to do."

A Whistle of Despair

Now the whistle of the *Commodore* had been turned loose, and if there ever was a voice of despair and death, it was in the voice of this whistle. It had gained a new tone. It was as if its throat was already choked by the water, and this cry on the sea at night, with a wind blowing the spray over the ship, and the waves roaring over the bow, and swirling white along the decks, was to each of us probably a song of man's end.

It was now that the first mate showed a sign of losing his grip. To us who were trying in all stages of competence and experience to launch the lifeboat he raged in all terms of fiery satire and hammerlike abuse. But the boat moved at last and swung down toward the water.

Afterward, when I went aft, I saw the captain standing, with his arm in a sling, holding on to a stay with his one good hand and directing the launching of the boat. He gave me a five-gallon jug of water to hold, and asked me what I was going to do. I told him what I thought was about the proper thing and he told me then that the cook had the same idea, and ordered me to go forward and be ready to launch the ten-foot dinghy.

In the Ten-Foot Dinghy

I remember well that he turned then to swear at a colored stoker who was prowling around, done up in life preservers until he looked like a feather bed. I went forward with my five-gallon jug of water, and when the captain came we launched the dinghy, and they put me over the side to fend her off from the ship with an oar.

They handed me down the water jug, and then the cook came into the boat, and we sat there in the darkness, wondering why, by all our hopes of future happiness, the captain was so long in coming over to the side and ordering us away from the doomed ship.

The captain was waiting for the other boat to go. Finally he hailed in the darkness: "Are you all right, Mr. Graines?"

The first mate answered: "All right, sir."

"Shove off, then," cried the captain.

The captain was just about to swing over the rail when a dark form came forward and a voice said: "Captain, I go with you."

The captain answered: "Yes, Billy; get in."

Higgins Last to Leave Ship

It was Billy Higgins, the oiler. Billy dropped into the boat and a moment later the captain followed, bringing with him an end of about forty yards of lead line. The other end was attached to the rail of the ship.

As we swung back to leeward the captain said: "Boys, we will stay right near the ship till she goes down."

This cheerful information, of course, filled us all with glee. The line kept us headed properly into the wind, and as we rode over the monstrous waves we saw upon each rise the swaying lights of the dying *Commodore*.

When came the gray shade of dawn, the form of the *Commodore* grew slowly clear to us as our little ten-foot boat rose over each swell. She was floating with such an air of buoyancy that we laughed when we had time, and said, "What a gag it would be on those other fellows if she didn't sink at all."

But later we saw men aboard of her, and later still they began to hail us.

Helping Their Mates

I had forgot to mention that previously we had loosened the end of the lead line and dropped much further to leeward. The men on board were a mystery to us, of course, as we had seen all the boats leave the ship. We rowed back to the ship, but did not approach too near, because we were four men in a ten-foot boat, and we knew that the touch of a hand on our gunwale would assuredly swamp us.

The first mate cried out from the ship that the third boat had foundered alongside. He cried that they had made rafts, and wished us to tow them.

The captain said, "All right."

Their rafts were floating astern. "Jump in!" cried the captain, but there was a singular and most harrowing hesitation. There were five white men and two negroes. This scene in the gray light of morning impressed one as would a view into some place where ghosts move slowly. These seven men on the stern of the sinking *Commodore* were silent. Save the words of the mate to the captain there was no talk. Here was death, but here also was a most singular and indefinable kind of fortitude.

Four men, I remember, clambered over the railing and stood there watching the cold, steely sheen of the sweeping waves.

"Jump," cried the captain again.

The old chief engineer first obeyed the order. He landed on the outside raft and the captain told him how to grip the raft and he obeyed as promptly and as docilely as a scholar in riding school.

The Mate's Mad Plunge

A stoker followed him, and then the first mate threw his hands over his head and plunged into the sea. He had no life belt and for my part, even when he did this horrible thing, I somehow felt that I could see in the expression of his hands, and in the very toss of his head, as he leaped thus to death, that it was rage, rage, rage unspeakable that was in his heart at the time.

And then I saw Tom Smith, the man who was going to quit filibustering after this expedition, jump to a raft and turn his face toward us. On board the *Commodore* three men strode, still in silence and with their faces turned toward us. One man had his arms folded and was leaning against the deckhouse. His feet were crossed, so that the toe of his left foot pointed downward. There they stood gazing at us, and neither from the deck nor from the rafts was a voice raised. Still was there this silence.

Tried to Tow the Rafts

The colored stoker on the first raft threw us a line and we began to tow. Of course, we perfectly understood the absolute impossibility of any such thing; our dinghy was within six inches of the water's edge, there was an enormous sea running, and I knew that under the circumstances a tugboat would have no light task in moving these rafts.

But we tried it, and would have continued to try it indefinitely, but that something critical came to pass. I was at an oar and so faced the rafts. The cook controlled the line. Suddenly the boat began to go backward and then we saw this negro on the first raft pulling on the line hand over hand and drawing us to him.

He had turned into a demon. He was wild—wild as a tiger. He was crouched on this raft and ready to spring. Every muscle of him seemed to be turned into an elastic spring. His eyes were almost white. His face was the face of a lost man reaching upward, and we knew that the weight of his hand on our gunwale doomed us.

The *Commodore* Sinks

The cook let go of the line. We rowed around to see if we could not get a line from the chief engineer, and all this time, mind you, there were no shrieks, no groans, but silence, silence and silence, and then the *Commodore* sank.

She lurched to windward, then swung afar back, righted and dove into the sea, and the rafts were suddenly swallowed by this frightful maw of the ocean. And then by the men on the ten-foot dinghy were words said that were still not words—something far beyond words.

The lighthouse of Mosquito Inlet stuck up above the horizon like the point of a pin. We turned our dinghy toward the shore.

The history of life in an open boat for thirty hours would no doubt be instructive for the young, but none is to be told here and now. For my part I would prefer to tell the story at once, because from it would shine the splendid manhood of Captain Edward Murphy and of William Higgins, the oiler, but let it suffice at this time to say that when we were swamped in the surf and making the best of our way toward the shore the captain gave orders amid the wildness of the breakers as clearly as if he had been on the quarter deck of a battleship.

John Kitchell of Daytona came running down the beach, and as he ran the air was filled with clothes. If he had pulled a single lever and undressed, even as the fire horses harness, he could not seem to me to have stripped with more speed. He dashed into the water and grabbed the cook. Then he went after the captain, but the captain sent him to me, and then it was that he saw Billy Higgins lying with his forehead on sand that was clear of the water, and he was dead.

"THE OPEN BOAT"

*A Tale Intended to Be after the Fact: Being the Experience
of Four Men from the Sunk Steamer* Commodore

I

None of them knew the color of the sky. Their eyes glanced level, and were
fastened upon the waves that swept toward them. These waves were of
the hue of slate, save for the tops, which were of foaming white, and all of
the men knew the colors of the sea. The horizon narrowed and widened,
and dipped and rose, and at all times its edge was jagged with waves that
seemed thrust up in points like rocks.

Many a man ought to have a bathtub larger than the boat which here
rode upon the sea. These waves were most wrongfully and barbarously
abrupt and tall, and each froth-top was a problem in small-boat navigation.

The cook squatted in the bottom, and looked with both eyes at the
six inches of gunwale which separated him from the ocean. His sleeves
were rolled over his fat forearms, and the two flaps of his unbuttoned vest
dangled as he bent to bail out the boat. Often he said, "Gawd! that was
a narrow clip." As he remarked it he invariably gazed eastward over the
broken sea.

The oiler, steering with one of the two oars in the boat, sometimes
raised himself suddenly to keep clear of water that swirled in over the
stern. It was a thin little oar, and it seemed often ready to snap.

The correspondent, pulling at the other oar, watched the waves and
wondered why he was there.

The injured captain, lying in the bow, was at this time buried in that
profound dejection and indifference which comes, temporarily at least, to
even the bravest and most enduring when, willy-nilly, the firm fails, the
army loses, the ship goes down. The mind of the master of a vessel is rooted
deep in the timbers of her, though he command for a day or a decade; and
this captain had on him the stern impression of a scene in the grays of dawn
of seven turned faces, and later a stump of a topmast with a white ball on
it, that slashed to and fro at the waves, went low and lower, and down.
Thereafter there was something strange in his voice. Although steady, it
was deep with mourning, and of a quality beyond oration or tears.

"Keep 'er a little more south, Billie," said he.

Scribner's Magazine, June 1897.

"A little more south, sir," said the oiler in the stern.

A seat in this boat was not unlike a seat upon a bucking bronco, and, by the same token, a bronco is not much smaller. The craft pranced and reared and plunged like an animal. As each wave came, and she rose for it, she seemed like a horse making at a fence outrageously high. The manner of her scramble over these walls of water is a mystic thing, and, moreover, at the top of them were ordinarily these problems in white water, the foam racing down from the summit of each wave requiring a new leap, and a leap from the air. Then, after scornfully bumping a crest, she would slide and race and splash down a long incline, and arrive bobbing and nodding in front of the next menace.

A singular disadvantage of the sea lies in the fact that, after successfully surmounting one wave, you discover that there is another behind it just as important and just as nervously anxious to do something effective in the way of swamping boats. In a ten-foot dinghy one can get an idea of the resources of the sea in the line of waves that is not probable to the average experience, which is never at sea in a dinghy. As each slaty wall of water approached, it shut all else from the view of the men in the boat, and it was not difficult to imagine that this particular wave was the final outburst of the ocean; the last effort of the grim water. There was a terrible grace in the move of the waves, and they came in silence, save for the snarling of the crests.

In the wan light the faces of the men must have been gray. Their eyes must have glinted in strange ways as they gazed steadily astern. Viewed from a balcony, the whole thing would, doubtless, have been weirdly picturesque. But the men in the boat had no time to see it, and if they had had leisure, there were other things to occupy their minds. The sun swung steadily up the sky, and they knew it was broad day because the color of the sea changed from slate to emerald-green streaked with amber lights, and the foam was like tumbling snow. The process of the breaking day was unknown to them. They were aware only of this effect upon the color of the waves that rolled toward them.

In disjointed sentences the cook and the correspondent argued as to the difference between a life-saving station and a house of refuge. The cook had said: "There's a house of refuge just north of the Mosquito Inlet Light, and as soon as they see us they'll come off in their boat and pick us up."

"As soon as who see us?" said the correspondent.

"The crew," said the cook.

"Houses of refuge don't have crews," said the correspondent. "As I understand them, they are only places where clothes and grub are stored for the benefit of shipwrecked people. They don't carry crews."

"Oh, yes, they do," said the cook.

"No, they don't," said the correspondent.

"Well, we're not there yet, anyhow," said the oiler in the stern.

"Well," said the cook, "perhaps it's not a house of refuge that I'm thinking of as being near Mosquito Inlet Light; perhaps it's a life-saving station."

"We're not there yet," said the oiler in the stern.

II

As the boat bounced from the top of each wave the wind tore through the hair of the hatless men, and as the craft plopped her stern down again the spray slashed past them. The crest of each of these waves was a hill, from the top of which the men surveyed for a moment a broad, tumultuous expanse, shining and wind-riven. It was probably splendid, it was probably glorious, this play of the free sea, wild with lights of emerald and white and amber.

"Bully good thing it's an on-shore wind," said the cook. "If not, where would we be? Wouldn't have a show."

"That's right," said the correspondent.

The busy oiler nodded his assent.

Then the captain, in the bow, chuckled in a way that expressed humor, contempt, tragedy, all in one. "Do you think we've got much of a show now, boys?" said he.

Whereupon the three were silent, save for a trifle of hemming and hawing. To express any particular optimism at this time they felt to be childish and stupid, but they all doubtless possessed this sense of the situation in their minds. A young man thinks doggedly at such times. On the other hand, the ethics of their condition was decidedly against any open suggestion of hopelessness. So they were silent.

"Oh, well," said the captain, soothing his children, "we'll get ashore all right."

But there was that in his tone which made them think; so the oiler quoth, "Yes! if this wind holds."

The cook was bailing. "Yes! if we don't catch hell in the surf."

Canton-flannel gulls flew near and far. Sometimes they sat down on the sea, near patches of brown seaweed that rolled over the waves with a movement like carpets on a line in a gale. The birds sat comfortably in groups, and they were envied by some in the dinghy, for the wrath of the sea was no more to them than it was to a covey of prairie chickens a thousand miles inland. Often they came very close and stared at the men with black, bead-like eyes. At these times they were uncanny and sinister in their unblinking scrutiny, and the men hooted angrily at them, telling them to be gone. One came, and evidently decided to alight on the top of the captain's head. The bird flew parallel to the boat and did not circle, but made short sidelong jumps in the air in chicken fashion. His black eyes were wistfully fixed upon the captain's head. "Ugly brute," said the oiler to the bird. "You look as if you were made with a jackknife." The cook and the correspondent swore darkly at the creature. The captain naturally wished to knock it away with the end of the heavy painter, but he did not dare do it, because anything resembling an emphatic gesture would have capsized this freighted boat; and so, with his open hand, the captain gently and carefully waved the gull away. After it had been discouraged from the pursuit the captain breathed easier on account of his hair, and others breathed easier because the bird struck their minds at this time as being somehow gruesome and ominous.

In the meantime the oiler and the correspondent rowed; and also they rowed.

They sat together in the same seat, and each rowed an oar. Then the oiler took both oars; then the correspondent took both oars, then the oiler; then the correspondent.

They rowed and they rowed. The very ticklish part of the business was when the time came for the reclining one in the stern to take his turn at the oars. By the very last star of truth, it is easier to steal eggs from under a hen than it was to change seats in the dinghy. First the man in the stern slid his hand along the thwart and moved with care, as if he were of Sèvres. Then the man in the rowing-seat slid his hand along the other thwart. It was all done with the most extraordinary care. As the two sidled past each other, the whole party kept watchful eyes on the coming wave, and the captain cried: "Look out, now! Steady, there!"

The brown mats of seaweed that appeared from time to time were like islands, bits of earth. They were travelling, apparently, neither one way nor the other. They were, to all intents, stationary. They informed the men in the boat that it was making progress slowly toward the land.

The captain, rearing cautiously in the bow after the dinghy soared on a great swell, said that he had seen the lighthouse at Mosquito Inlet. Presently the cook remarked that he had seen it. The correspondent was at the oars then, and for some reason he too wished to look at the lighthouse; but his back was toward the far shore, and the waves were important, and for some time he could not seize an opportunity to turn his head. But at last there came a wave more gentle than the others, and when at the crest of it he swiftly scoured the western horizon.

"See it?" said the captain.

"No," said the correspondent, slowly; "I didn't see anything."

"Look again," said the captain. He pointed. "It's exactly in that direction."

At the top of another wave the correspondent did as he was bid, and this time his eyes chanced on a small, still thing on the edge of the swaying horizon. It was precisely like the point of a pin. It took an anxious eye to find a lighthouse so tiny.

"Think we'll make it, Captain?"

"If this wind holds and the boat don't swamp, we can't do much else," said the captain.

The little boat, lifted by each towering sea and splashed viciously by the crests, made progress that in the absence of seaweed was not apparent to those in her. She seemed just a wee thing wallowing, miraculously top up, at the mercy of five oceans. Occasionally a great spread of water, like white flames, swarmed into her.

"Bail her, cook," said the captain, serenely.

"All right, Captain," said the cheerful cook.

III

It would be difficult to describe the subtle brotherhood of men that was here established on the seas. No one said that it was so. No one mentioned it. But it dwelt in the boat, and each man felt it warm him. They were a captain, an oiler, a cook, and a correspondent, and they were friends— friends in a more curiously iron-bound degree than may be common. The hurt captain, lying against the water jar in the bow, spoke always in a low voice and calmly; but he could never command a more ready and swiftly obedient crew than the motley three of the dinghy. It was more than a mere recognition of what was best for the common safety. There was surely in it a quality that was personal and heartfelt. And after this devotion to the commander of the boat, there was this comradeship, that the correspondent, for instance, who had been taught to be cynical of men, knew even at the time was the best experience of his life. But no one said that it was so. No one mentioned it.

"I wish we had a sail," remarked the captain. "We might try my overcoat on the end of an oar, and give you two boys a chance to rest." So the cook and the correspondent held the mast, and spread wide the overcoat; the oiler steered; and the little boat made good way with her new rig. Sometimes the oiler had to scull sharply to keep a sea from breaking into the boat, but otherwise sailing was a success.

Meanwhile the lighthouse had been growing slowly larger. It had now almost assumed color, and appeared like a little gray shadow on the sky. The man at the oars could not be prevented from turning his head rather often to try for a glimpse of this little gray shadow.

At last, from the top of each wave, the men in the tossing boat could see land. Even as the lighthouse was an upright shadow on the sky, this land seemed but a long black shadow on the sea. It certainly was thinner than paper. "We must be about opposite New Smyrna," said the cook, who had coasted this shore often in schooners. "Captain, by the way, I believe they abandoned that life-saving station there about a year ago."

"Did they?" said the captain.

The wind slowly died away. The cook and the correspondent were not now obliged to slave in order to hold high the oar, but the waves continued their old impetuous swooping at the dinghy, and the little craft, no longer under way, struggled woundily over them. The oiler or the correspondent took the oars again.

Shipwrecks are *apropos* of nothing. If men could only train for them and have them occur when the men had reached pink condition, there would be less drowning at sea. Of the four in the dinghy none had slept any time worth mentioning for two days and two nights previous to embarking in the dinghy, and in the excitement of clambering about the deck of a foundering ship they had also forgotten to eat heartily.

For these reasons, and for others, neither the oiler nor the correspondent was fond of rowing at this time. The correspondent wondered ingenuously how in the name of all that was sane could there be people who thought it amusing to row a boat. It was not an amusement; it was a diabolical punishment, and even a genius of mental aberrations could never conclude that it was anything but a horror to the muscles and a crime against the back. He mentioned to the boat in general how the amusement of rowing struck him, and the weary-faced oiler smiled in full sympathy. Previously to the foundering, by the way, the oiler had worked double watch in the engine-room of the ship.

"Take her easy now, boys," said the captain. "Don't spend yourselves. If we have to run a surf you'll need all your strength, because we'll sure have to swim for it. Take your time."

Slowly the land arose from the sea. From a black line it became a line of black and a line of white—trees and sand. Finally the captain said that he could make out a house on the shore. "That's the house of refuge, sure," said the cook. "They'll see us before long, and come out after us."

The distant lighthouse reared high. "The keeper ought to be able to make us out now, if he's looking through a glass," said the captain. "He'll notify the life-saving people."

"None of those other boats could have got ashore to give word of the wreck," said the oiler, in a low voice, "else the life boat would be out hunting us."

Slowly and beautifully the land loomed out of the sea. The wind came again. It had veered from the northeast to the southeast. Finally a new sound struck the ears of the men in the boat. It was the low thunder of the surf on the shore. "We'll never be able to make the lighthouse now," said the captain. "Swing her head a little more north, Billie."

"A little more north, sir," said the oiler.

Whereupon the little boat turned her nose once more down the wind, and all but the oarsman watched the shore grow. Under the influence of this expansion doubt and direful apprehension were leaving the minds of the men. The management of the boat was still most absorbing, but it could not prevent a quiet cheerfulness. In an hour, perhaps, they would be ashore.

Their backbones had become thoroughly used to balancing in the boat, and they now rode this wild colt of a dinghy like circus men. The correspondent thought that he had been drenched to the skin, but happening to feel in the top of his coat, he found therein eight cigars. Four of them were soaked with sea water; four were perfectly scatheless. After a search, somebody produced three dry matches; thereupon the four waifs rode in their little boat and, with an assurance of an impending rescue shining in their eyes, puffed at the big cigars, and judged well and ill of all men. Everybody took a drink of water.

IV

"Cook," remarked the captain, "there don't seem to be any signs of life about your house of refuge."

"No," replied the cook. "Funny they don't see us!"

A broad stretch of lowly coast lay before the eyes of the men. It was of low dunes topped with dark vegetation. The roar of the surf was plain, and sometimes they could see the white lip of a wave as it spun up the beach. A tiny house was blocked out black upon the sky. Southward, the slim lighthouse lifted its little gray length.

Tide, wind, and waves were swinging the dinghy northward. "Funny they don't see us," said the men.

The surf's roar was here dulled, but its tone was nevertheless thunderous and mighty. As the boat swam over the great rollers the men sat listening to this roar. "We'll swamp sure," said everybody.

It is fair to say here that there was not a life-saving station within twenty miles in either direction; but the men did not know this fact, and in consequence they made dark and opprobrious remarks concerning the eyesight of the nation's life savers. Four scowling men sat in the dinghy and surpassed records in the invention of epithets.

"Funny they don't see us."

The light-heartedness of a former time had completely faded. To their sharpened minds it was easy to conjure pictures of all kinds of incompetency and blindness and, indeed, cowardice. There was the shore of the populous land, and it was bitter and bitter to them that from it came no sign.

"Well," said the captain, ultimately, "I suppose we'll have to make a try for ourselves. If we stay out here too long, we'll none of us have strength left to swim after the boat swamps."

And so the oiler, who was at the oars, turned the boat straight for the shore. There was a sudden tightening of muscles. There was some thinking.

"If we don't all get ashore," said the captain—"if we don't all get ashore, I suppose you fellows know where to send news of my finish?"

They then briefly exchanged some addresses and admonitions. As for the reflections of the men, there was a great deal of rage in them. Perchance they might be formulated thus: "If I am going to be drowned—if I am going to be drowned—if I am going to be drowned, why, in the name of the seven mad gods who rule the sea, was I allowed to come thus far and contemplate sand and trees? Was I brought here merely to have my nose dragged away as I was about to nibble the sacred cheese of life? It is preposterous! If this old ninny woman, Fate, cannot do better than this, she should be deprived of the management of men's fortunes. She is an old hen who knows not her intention. If she has decided to drown me, why did she not do it in the beginning and save me all this trouble? The whole affair is absurd. . . . But no; she cannot mean to drown me. She dare not drown me. She cannot drown me. Not after all this work!" Afterward the man might have had an impulse to shake his fist at the clouds. "Just you drown me, now, and then hear what I call you!"

The billows that came at this time were more formidable. They seemed always just about to break and roll over the little boat in a turmoil of foam. There was a preparatory and long growl in the speech of them. No mind unused to the sea would have concluded that the dinghy could ascend these sheer heights in time. The shore was still afar. The oiler was a wily surfman. "Boys," he said swiftly, "she won't live three minutes more, and we're too far out to swim. Shall I take her to sea again, Captain?"

"Yes; go ahead!" said the captain.

This oiler, by a series of quick miracles and fast and steady oarsman-
ship, turned the boat in the middle of the surf and took her safely to sea
again.

There was a considerable silence as the boat bumped over the furrowed sea to deeper water. Then somebody in gloom spoke: "Well, anyhow, they must have seen us from the shore by now."

The gulls went in slanting flight up the wind toward the gray, desolate
east. A squall, marked by dingy clouds and clouds brick-red, like smoke
from a burning building, appeared from the southeast.

"What do you think of those life-saving people? Ain't they peaches?"

"Funny they haven't seen us."

"Maybe they think we're out here for sport! Maybe they think we're
fishin'. Maybe they think we're damned fools."

It was a long afternoon. A changed tide tried to force them southward,
but wind and wave said northward. Far ahead, where coast-line, sea, and
sky formed their mighty angle, there were little dots which seemed to indicate a city on the shore.

"St. Augustine?"

The captain shook his head. "Too near Mosquito Inlet."

And the oiler rowed, and then the correspondent rowed; then the
oiler rowed. It was a weary business. The human back can become the
seat of more aches and pains than are registered in books for the composite anatomy of a regiment. It is a limited area, but it can become the
theater of innumerable muscular conflicts, tangles, wrenches, knots, and
other comforts.

"Did you ever like to row, Billie?" asked the correspondent.

"No," said the oiler; "hang it!"

When one exchanged the rowing-seat for a place in the bottom of
the boat, he suffered a bodily depression that caused him to be careless of
everything save an obligation to wiggle one finger. There was cold sea water swashing to and fro in the boat, and he lay in it. His head, pillowed on
a thwart, was within an inch of the swirl of a wave crest, and sometimes a
particularly obstreperous sea came inboard and drenched him once more.
But these matters did not annoy him. It is almost certain that if the boat
capsized he would have tumbled comfortably out upon the ocean as if he
felt sure that it was a great, soft mattress.

"Look! There's a man on the shore!"

"Where?"

"There! See 'im? See 'im?"

"Yes, sure! He's walking along."

"Now he's stopped. Look! He's facing us!"

"He's waving at us!"

"So he is! By thunder!"

"Ah, now we're all right! Now we're all right! There'll be a boat out here for us in half an hour."

"He's going on. He's running. He's going up to that house there."

The remote beach seemed lower than the sea, and it required a searching glance to discern the little black figure. The captain saw a floating stick, and they rowed to it. A bath towel was by some weird chance in the boat, and, tying this on the stick, the captain waved it. The oarsman did not dare turn his head, so he was obliged to ask questions.

"What's he doing now?"

"He's standing still again. He's looking, I think. . . . There he goes again—toward the house. . . . Now he's stopped again."

"Is he waving at us?"

"No, not now; he was, though."

"Look! There comes another man!"

"He's running."

"Look at him go, would you!"

"Why, he's on a bicycle. Now he's met the other man. They're both waving at us. Look!"

"There comes something up the beach."

"What the devil is that thing?"

"Why, it looks like a boat."

"Why, certainly, it's a boat."

"No; it's on wheels."

"Yes, so it is. Well, that must be the life boat. They drag them along shore on a wagon."

"That's the life boat, sure."

"No, by—it's—it's an omnibus."

"I tell you it's a life boat."

"It is not! It's an omnibus. I can see it plain. See? One of these big hotel omnibuses."

"By thunder, you're right. It's an omnibus, sure as fate. What do you suppose they are doing with an omnibus? Maybe they are going around collecting the life crew, hey?"

"That's it, likely. Look! There's a fellow waving a little black flag. He's standing on the steps of the omnibus. There come those other two fellows. Now they're all talking together. Look at the fellow with the flag. Maybe he ain't waving it!"

"That ain't a flag, is it? That's his coat. Why, certainly, that's his coat."

"So it is; it's his coat. He's taken it off and is waving it around his head. But would you look at him swing it!"

"Oh, say, there isn't any life-saving station there. That's just a winter-resort hotel omnibus that has brought over some of the boarders to see us drown."

"What's that idiot with the coat mean? What's he signalling, any-how?"

"It looks as if he were trying to tell us to go north. There must be a life-saving station up there."

"No; he thinks we're fishing. Just giving us a merry hand. See? Ah, there, Willie!"

"Well, I wish I could make something out of those signals. What do you suppose he means?"

"He don't mean anything; he's just playing."

"Well, if he'd just signal us to try the surf again, or to go to sea and wait, or go north, or south, or go to hell, there would be some reason in it. But look at him! He just stands there and keeps his coat revolving like a wheel. The ass!"

"There come more people."

"Now there's quite a mob. Look! Isn't that a boat?"

"Where? Oh, I see where you mean. No, that's no boat."

"That fellow is still waving his coat."

"He must think we like to see him do that. Why don't he quit it? It don't mean anything."

"I don't know. I think he is trying to make us go north. It must be that there's a life-saving station there somewhere."

"Say, he ain't tired yet. Look at 'im wave!"

"Wonder how long he can keep that up. He's been revolving his coat ever since he caught sight of us. He's an idiot. Why aren't they getting men to bring a boat out? A fishing boat—one of those big yawls—could come out here all right. Why don't he do something?"

"Oh, it's all right now."

"They'll have a boat out here for us in less than no time, now that they've seen us."

A faint yellow tone came into the sky over the low land. The shadows on the sea slowly deepened. The wind bore coldness with it, and the men began to shiver.

"Holy smoke!" said one, allowing his voice to express his impious mood, "if we keep on monkeying out here! If we've got to flounder out here all night!"

"Oh, we'll never have to stay here all night! Don't you worry. They've seen us now, and it won't be long before they'll come chasing out after us."

The shore grew dusky. The man waving a coat blended gradually into this gloom, and it swallowed in the same manner the omnibus and the group of people. The spray, when it dashed uproariously over the side, made the voyagers shrink and swear like men who were being branded.

"I'd like to catch the chump who waved the coat. I feel like soaking him one, just for luck."

"Why? What did he do?"

"Oh, nothing, but then he seemed so damned cheerful."

In the meantime the oiler rowed, and then the correspondent rowed, and then the oiler rowed. Gray-faced and bowed forward, they mechanically, turn by turn, plied the leaden oars. The form of the lighthouse had vanished from the southern horizon, but finally a pale star appeared, just lifting from the sea. The streaked saffron in the west passed before the all-merging darkness, and the sea to the east was black. The land had vanished, and was expressed only by the low and drear thunder of the surf.

"If I am going to be drowned—if I am going to be drowned—if I am going to be drowned, why, in the name of the seven mad gods who rule the sea, was I allowed to come thus far and contemplate sand and trees? Was I brought here merely to have my nose dragged away as I was about to nibble the sacred cheese of life?"

The patient captain, drooped over the water jar, was sometimes obliged to speak to the oarsman.

"Keep her head up! Keep her head up!"

"Keep her head up, sir." The voices were weary and low.

This was surely a quiet evening. All save the oarsman lay heavily and listlessly in the boat's bottom. As for him, his eyes were just capable of noting the tall black waves that swept forward in a most sinister silence, save for an occasional subdued growl of a crest.

The cook's head was on a thwart, and he looked without interest at the water under his nose. He was deep in other scenes. Finally he spoke. "Billie," he murmured dreamfully, "what kind of pie do you like best?"

V

"Pie!" said the oiler and the correspondent, agitatedly. "Don't talk about those things, blast you!"

"Well," said the cook, "I was just thinking about ham sandwiches, and—"

A night on the sea in an open boat is a long night. As darkness settled finally, the shine of the light, lifting from the sea in the south, changed to full gold. On the northern horizon a new light appeared, a small bluish gleam on the edge of the waters. These two lights were the furniture of the world. Otherwise there was nothing but waves.

Two men huddled in the stern, and distances were so magnificent in the dinghy that the rower was enabled to keep his feet partly warm by thrusting them under his companions. Their legs indeed extended far under the rowing-seat until they touched the feet of the captain forward. Sometimes, despite the efforts of the tired oarsman, a wave came piling into the boat, an icy wave of the night, and the chilling water soaked them anew. They would twist their bodies for a moment and groan, and sleep the dead sleep once more, while the water in the boat gurgled about them as the craft rocked.

The plan of the oiler and the correspondent was for one to row until he lost the ability, and then arouse the other from his seawater couch in the bottom of the boat.

The oiler plied the oars until his head drooped forward and the overpowering sleep blinded him; and he rowed yet afterward. Then he touched a man in the bottom of the boat, and called his name. "Will you spell me for a little while?" he said meekly.

"Sure, Billie," said the correspondent, awaking and dragging himself to a sitting position. They exchanged places carefully, and the oiler, cuddling down in the sea water at the cook's side, seemed to go to sleep instantly.

The particular violence of the sea had ceased. The waves came without snarling. The obligation of the man at the oars was to keep the boat headed so that the tilt of the rollers would not capsize her, and to preserve her from filling when the crests rushed past. The black waves were silent and hard to be seen in the darkness. Often one was almost upon the boat before the oarsman was aware.

In a low voice the correspondent addressed the captain. He was not sure that the captain was awake, although this iron man seemed to be always awake. "Captain, shall I keep her making for that light north, sir?"

The same steady voice answered him. "Yes. Keep it about two points off the port bow."

The cook had tied a life belt around himself in order to get even the warmth which this clumsy cork contrivance could donate, and he seemed almost stovelike when a rower, whose teeth invariably chattered wildly as soon as he ceased his labor, dropped down to sleep.

The correspondent, as he rowed, looked down at the two men sleeping underfoot. The cook's arm was around the oiler's shoulders, and, with their fragmentary clothing and haggard faces, they were the babes of the sea—a grotesque rendering of the old babes in the wood.

Later he must have grown stupid at his work, for suddenly there was a growling of water, and a crest came with a roar and a swash into the boat, and it was a wonder that it did not set the cook afloat in his life belt.

The correspondent plainly saw the soldier. He lay on the sand with his feet out straight and still. While his pale left hand was upon his chest in an attempt to thwart the going of his life, the blood came between his fingers. In the far Algerian distance, a city of low square forms was set against a sky that was faint with the last sunset hues. The correspondent, plying the oars and dreaming of the slow and slower movements of the lips of the soldier, was moved by a profound and perfectly impersonal comprehension. He was sorry for the soldier of the Legion who lay dying in Algiers.

The thing which had followed the boat and waited had evidently grown bored at the delay. There was no longer to be heard the slash of the cut water, and there was no longer the flame of the long trail. The light in the north still glimmered, but it was apparently no nearer to the boat. Sometimes the boom of the surf rang in the correspondent's ears, and he turned the craft seaward then and rowed harder. Southward, some one had evidently built a watch fire on the beach. It was too low and too far to be seen, but it made a shimmering, roseate reflection upon the bluff back of it, and this could be discerned from the boat. The wind came stronger, and sometimes a wave suddenly raged out like a mountain cat, and there was to be seen the sheen and sparkle of a broken crest.

The captain, in the bow, moved on his water jar and sat erect. "Pretty long night," he observed to the correspondent. He looked at the shore. "Those life-saving people take their time."

"Did you see that shark playing around?"

"Yes, I saw him. He was a big fellow, all right."

"Wish I had known you were awake."

Later the correspondent spoke into the bottom of the boat. "Billie!" There was a slow and gradual disentanglement. "Billie, will you spell me?"

"Sure," said the oiler.

As soon as the correspondent touched the cold, comfortable sea water in the bottom of the boat and had huddled close to the cook's life belt he was deep in sleep, despite the fact that his teeth played all the popular airs. This sleep was so good to him that it was but a moment before he heard a voice call his name in a tone that demonstrated the last stages of exhaustion. "Will you spell me?"

"Sure, Billie."

The light in the north had mysteriously vanished, but the correspondent took his course from the wide-awake captain.

Later in the night they took the boat farther out to sea, and the captain directed the cook to take one oar at the stern and keep the boat facing the seas. He was to call out if he should hear the thunder of the surf. This plan enabled the oiler and the correspondent to get respite together.

"We'll give those boys a chance to get into shape again," said the captain. They curled down and, after a few preliminary chatterings and trembles, slept once more the dead sleep. Neither knew they had bequeathed to the cook the company of another shark, or perhaps the same shark.

As the boat caroused on the waves, spray occasionally bumped over the side and gave them a fresh soaking, but this had no power to break their repose. The ominous slash of the wind and the water affected them as it would have affected mummies.

"Boys," said the cook, with the notes of every reluctance in his voice, "She's drifted in pretty close. I guess one of you had better take her to sea again." The correspondent, aroused, heard the crash of the toppled crests.

As he was rowing, the captain gave him some whiskey and water, and this steadied the chills out of him. "If I ever get ashore and anybody shows me even a photograph of an oar—"

At last there was a short conversation.

"Billie! . . . Billie, will you spell me?"

"Sure," said the oiler.

VII

When the correspondent again opened his eyes, the sea and the sky were each of the gray hue of the dawning. Later, carmine and gold was painted upon the waters. The morning appeared finally, in its splendor, with a sky of pure blue, and the sunlight flamed on the tips of the waves.

On the distant dunes were set many little black cottages, and a tall white windmill reared above them. No man, nor dog, nor bicycle appeared on the beach. The cottages might have formed a deserted village.

The voyagers scanned the shore. A conference was held in the boat. "Well," said the captain, "if no help is coming, we might better try a run through the surf right away. If we stay out here much longer we will be too weak to do anything for ourselves at all." The others silently acquiesced in this reasoning. The boat was headed for the beach. The correspondent wondered if none ever ascended the tall wind-tower, and if then they never looked seaward. This tower was a giant, standing with its back to the plight of the ants. It represented in a degree, to the correspondent, the serenity of Nature amid the struggles of the individual—Nature in the wind, and Nature in the vision of men. She did not seem cruel to him then, nor beneficent, nor treacherous, nor wise. But she was indifferent, flatly indifferent. It is, perhaps, plausible that a man in this situation, impressed with the unconcern of the universe, should see the innumerable flaws of his life and have them taste wickedly in his mind, and wish for another chance. A distinction between right and wrong seems absurdly clear to him, then, in this new ignorance of the grave-edge, and he understands that if he were given another opportunity he would mend his conduct and his words, and be better and brighter during an introduction or at a tea.

"Now, boys," said the captain, "she is going to swamp sure. All we can do is to work her in as far as possible, and then when she swamps, pile out and scramble for the beach. Keep cool now, and don't jump until she swamps sure."

The oiler took the oars. Over his shoulders he scanned the surf. "Captain," he said, "I think I'd better bring her about and keep her head-on to the seas, and back her in."

"All right, Billie," said the captain. "Back her in." The oiler swung the boat then, and, seated in the stern, the cook and the correspondent were obliged to look over their shoulders to contemplate the lonely and indifferent shore.

The monstrous inshore rollers heaved the boat high until the men were again enabled to see the white sheets of water scudding up the slanted beach. "We won't get in very close," said the captain. Each time a man could wrest his attention from the roller, he turned his glance toward the shore, and in the expression of the eyes during this contemplation there was a singular quality. The correspondent, observing the others, knew that they were not afraid, but the full meaning of their glances was shrouded.

As for himself, he was too tired to grapple fundamentally with the fact. He tried to coerce his mind into thinking of it, but the mind was dominated at this time by the muscles, and the muscles said they did not care. It merely occurred to him that if he should drown it would be a shame.

There were no hurried words, no pallor, no plain agitation. The men simply looked at the shore. "Now, remember to get well clear of the boat when you jump," said the captain.

Seaward the crest of a roller suddenly fell with a thunderous crash, and the long white comber came roaring down upon the boat.

"Steady now," said the captain. The men were silent. They turned their eyes from the shore to the comber and waited. The boat slid up the incline, leaped at the furious top, bounced over it, and swung down the long back of the wave. Some water had been shipped, and the cook bailed it out.

But the next crest crashed also. The tumbling, boiling flood of white water caught the boat and whirled it almost perpendicular. Water swarmed in from all sides. The correspondent had his hands on the gunwale at this time, and when the water entered at that place he swiftly withdrew his fingers, as if he objected to wetting them.

The little boat, drunken with this weight of water, reeled and snuggled deeper into the sea.

"Bail her out, cook! Bail her out!" said the captain.

"All right, Captain," said the cook.

"Now, boys, the next one will do for us sure," said the oiler. "Mind to jump clear of the boat."

The third wave moved forward, huge, furious, implacable. It fairly swallowed the dinghy, and almost simultaneously the men tumbled into the sea. A piece of life belt had lain in the bottom of the boat, and as the correspondent went overboard he held this to his chest with his left hand.

The January water was icy, and he reflected immediately that it was colder than he had expected to find it off the coast of Florida. This appeared to his dazed mind as a fact important enough to be noted at the time. The coldness of the water was sad; it was tragic. This fact was somehow mixed and confused with his opinion of his own situation so that it seemed almost a proper reason for tears. The water was cold.

When he came to the surface he was conscious of little but the noisy water. Afterward he saw his companions in the sea. The oiler was ahead in the race. He was swimming strongly and rapidly. Off to the correspondent's left, the cook's great white and corked back bulged out of the water; and in the rear the captain was hanging with one good hand to the keel of the overturned dinghy.

There is a certain immovable quality to a shore, and the correspondent wondered at it amid the confusion of the sea.

It seemed also very attractive; but the correspondent knew that it was a long journey, and he paddled leisurely. The piece of life preserver lay under him, and sometimes he whirled down the incline of a wave as if he were on a hand-sled.

But finally he arrived at a place in the sea where the travel was beset with difficulty. He did not pause swimming to inquire what manner of current had caught him, but there his progress ceased. The shore was set before him like a bit of scenery on a stage, and he looked at it, and understood with his eyes each detail of it.

As the cook passed, much farther to the left, the captain was calling to him, "Turn over on your back, cook! Turn over on your back and use the oar."

"All right, sir." The cook turned on his back, and, paddling with an oar, went ahead as if he were a canoe.

Presently the boat also passed to the left of the correspondent, with the captain clinging with one hand to the keel. He would have appeared like a man raising himself to look over a board fence if it were not for the extraordinary gymnastics of the boat. The correspondent marvelled that the captain could still hold to it.

They passed on nearer to shore—the oiler, the cook, the captain—and following them went the water jar, bouncing gaily over the seas.

The correspondent remained in the grip of this strange new enemy, a current. The shore, with its white slope of sand and its green bluff, topped with little silent cottages, was spread like a picture before him. It was very near to him then, but he was impressed as one who, in a gallery, looks at a scene from Brittany or Algiers.

He thought: "I am going to drown? Can it be possible? Can it be possible? Can it be possible?" Perhaps an individual must consider his own death to be the final phenomenon of Nature.

But later a wave perhaps whirled him out of this small deadly current, for he found suddenly that he could again make progress toward the shore. Later still he was aware that the captain, clinging with one hand to the keel of the dinghy, had his face turned away from the shore and toward him and was calling his name. "Come to the boat! Come to the boat!"

In his struggle to reach the captain and the boat, he reflected that when one gets properly wearied drowning must really be a comfortable arrangement—a cessation of hostilities accompanied by a large degree of relief; and he was glad of it, for the main thing in his mind for some moments had been horror of the temporary agony; he did not wish to be hurt.

Presently he saw a man running along the shore. He was undressing with most remarkable speed. Coat, trousers, shirt, everything flew magically off him.

"Come to the boat!" called the captain.

"All right, Captain." As the correspondent paddled, he saw the captain let himself down to bottom and leave the boat. Then the correspondent performed his one little marvel of the voyage. A large wave caught him and flung him with ease and supreme speed completely over the boat and far beyond it. It struck him even then as an event in gymnastics and a true miracle of the sea. An overturned boat in the surf is not a plaything to a swimming man.

The correspondent arrived in water that reached only to his waist, but his condition did not enable him to stand for more than a moment. Each wave knocked him into a heap, and the undertow pulled at him.

Then he saw the man who had been running and undressing, and undressing and running, come bounding into the water. He dragged ashore the cook, and then waded toward the captain; but the captain waved him away and sent him to the correspondent. He was naked—naked as a tree in winter; but a halo was about his head, and he shone like a saint. He gave a strong pull, and a long drag, and a bully heave at the correspondent's hand. The correspondent, schooled in the minor formulae, said, "Thanks, old man." But suddenly the man cried, "What's that?" He pointed a swift finger. The correspondent said, "Go."

In the shallows, face downward, lay the oiler. His forehead touched sand that was periodically, between each wave, clear of the sea.

The correspondent did not know all that transpired afterward. When he achieved safe ground he fell, striking the sand with each particular part of his body. It was as if he had dropped from a roof, but the thud was grateful to him.

It seems that instantly the beach was populated with men with blankets, clothes, and flasks, and women with coffee pots and all the remedies sacred to their minds. The welcome of the land to the men from the sea was warm and generous; but a still and dripping shape was carried slowly up the beach, and the land's welcome for it could only be the different and sinister hospitality of the grave.

When it came night, the white waves paced to and fro in the moonlight, and the wind brought the sound of the great sea's voice to the men on the shore, and they felt that they could then be interpreters.

"STEPHEN CRANE'S VIVID STORY OF THE BATTLE OF SAN JUAN"

IN FRONT OF SANTIAGO, JULY 4, VIA OLD POINT COMFORT, VA., JULY 13—The action at San Juan on July 1 was, particularly speaking, a soldiers' battle. It was like Inkerman, where the English fought half leaderless all day in a fog. Only the Cuban forest was worse than any fog.

No doubt when history begins to grind out her story we will find that many a thundering, fine, grand order was given for that day's work; but after all there will be no harm in contending that the fighting line, the men and their regimental officers, took the hill chiefly because they knew they could take it, some having no orders and others disobeying whatever orders they had.

In civil life the newspapers would have called it a grand, popular movement. It will never be forgotten as long as America has a military history.

A line of entrenched hills held by men armed with a weapon like the Mauser is not to be taken by a front attack of infantry unless the trenches

New York World, 14 July 1898.

have first been heavily shaken by artillery fire. Any theorist will say that it is impossible, and prove it to be impossible. But it was done, and we owe the success to the splendid gallantry of the American private soldier.

As near as one can learn headquarters expected little or no fighting on the 1st. Lawton's division was to go by the Caney road, chase the Spaniards out of that interesting village, and then, wheeling half to the left, march down to join the other divisions in some kind of attack on San Juan at daybreak on the 2d.

But somebody had been entirely misinformed as to the strength and disposition of the Spanish forces at Caney, and instead of taking Lawton six minutes to capture the town it took him nearly all day, as well it might.

The other divisions lying under fire, waiting for Lawton, grew annoyed at a delay which was, of course, not explained to them, and suddenly arose and took the formidable hills of San Juan. It was impatience suddenly exalted to one of the sublime passions.

Lawton was well out toward Caney soon after daybreak, and by 7 o'clock we could hear the boom of Capron's guns in support of the infantry. The remaining divisions—Kent's and Wheeler's—were trudging slowly along the muddy trail through the forest.

When the first gun was fired a grim murmur passed along the lean column. "They're off!" somebody said.

The marching was of necessity very slow and even then the narrow road was often blocked. The men, weighted with their packs, cartridge belts and rifles, forded many streams, climbed hills, slid down banks and forced their way through thickets.

Suddenly there was a roar of guns just ahead and a little to the left. This was Grimes's battery going into action on the hill which is called El Paso. Then, all in a moment, the quiet column moving forward was opposed by men carrying terrible burdens. Wounded Cubans were being carried to the rear. Most of them were horribly mangled.

The second brigade of dismounted American cavalry had been in support of the battery, its position being directly to the rear. Some Cubans had joined there. The Spanish shrapnel fired at the battery was often cut too long, and passing over burst amid the supports and the Cubans.

The loss of the battery, the cavalry and the Cubans from this fire was forty men in killed and wounded, the First regular cavalry probably suffering most grievously. Presently there was a lull in the artillery fire, and down through spaces in the trees we could see the infantry still plodding with its packs steadily toward the front.

The artillerymen were greatly excited. Some showed with glee fragments of Spanish shells which had come dangerously near their heads. They had gone through their ordeal and were talking over it lightly.

In the meantime Lawton's division, some three miles away, was making plenty of noise. Caney is just at the base of a high willow-green, crinkled mountain, and Lawton was making his way over little knolls which might be termed foothills. We could see the great white clouds of smoke from Capron's guns and hear their roar punctuating the incessant drumming of the infantry. It was plain even then that Lawton was having considerably more of a fete than anybody had supposed previously.

At about 2,500 yards in front of Grimes's position on El Paso arose the gentle green hills of San Juan, dotted not too plentifully with trees— hills that resembled the sloping orchards of Orange County in summer. Here and there were houses built evidently as summer villas, but now loopholed and barricaded. They had heavy roofs of red tiles and were shaped much like Japanese, or, better, Javanese houses. Here and there, too, along the crests of these curving hillocks were ashen streaks, the rifle-pits of the Spaniards.

At the principal position of the enemy were a flag, a redoubt, a blockhouse and some sort of pagoda, in the shade of which Spanish officers were wont to promenade during lulls and negligently gossip about the battle. There was one man in a summer-resort straw hat. He did a deal of sauntering in the coolest manner possible, walking out in the clear sunshine and gazing languidly in our direction. He seemed to be carrying a little cane.

At 11:25 our artillery reopened on the central blockhouse and entrenchments. The Spanish fire had been remarkably fine, but it was our turn now. Grimes had his ranges to a nicety. After the great "shout of the gun" came the broad, windy, diminishing noise of the flung shell; then a fainter boom and a cloud of red debris out of the blockhouse or up from the ground near the trenches.

The Spanish infantry in the trenches fired a little volley immediately after every one of the American shells. It puzzled many to decide at what they could be firing, but it was finally resolved that they were firing just to show us that they were still there and were not afraid.

It must have been about 2 o'clock when the enemy's battery again retorted.

The cruel thing about this artillery duel was that our battery had nothing but old-fashioned powder, and its position was always as clearly defined as if it had been the Chicago fire. There is no secrecy about a battery that uses that kind of powder. The great billowy white smoke can be seen for miles. On the other hand, the Spaniards were using the best smokeless. There is no use groaning over what was to be, but—!

However, fate elected that the Spanish shooting should be very bad. Only two-thirds of their shells exploded in this second affair. They all whistled high, and those that exploded raked the ground long since evacuated by the supports and the timbers. No one was hurt.

From El Paso to San Juan there is a broad expanse of dense forest, spotted infrequently with vividly green fields. It is traversed by a single narrow road which leads straight between the two positions, fording two little streams. Along this road had gone our infantry and also the military balloon. Why it was ever taken to such a position nobody knows, but there it was—huge, fat, yellow, quivering—being dragged straight into a zone of fire that would surely ruin it.

There were two officers in the car for the greater part of the way, and there surely were never two men who valued their lives less. But they both escaped unhurt, while the balloon sank down, torn to death by the bullets that were volleyed at it by the nervous Spaniards, who suspected dynamite. It was never brought out of the woods where it recklessly met its fate.

In these woods, unknown to some, including the Spaniards, was formulated the gorgeous plan of taking an impregnable position.

One saw a thin line of black figures moving across a field. They disappeared in the forest. The enemy was keeping up a terrific fire. Then suddenly somebody yelled: "By God, there go our boys up the hill!"

There is many a good American who would give an arm to get the thrill of patriotic insanity that coursed through us when we heard that yell.

Yes, they were going up the hill, up the hill. It was the best moment of anybody's life. An officer said to me afterward: "If we had been in that position and the Spaniards had come at us, we would have piled them up so high the last man couldn't have climbed over." But up went the regiments with no music save that ceaseless, fierce crashing of rifles.

The foreign attachés were shocked. "It is very gallant, but very foolish," said one sternly.

"Why, they can't take it, you know. Never in the world," cried another, much agitated. "It is slaughter, absolute slaughter."

The little Japanese shrugged his shoulders. He was one who said nothing.

The road from El Paso to San Juan was now a terrible road. It should have a tragic fame like the sunken road at Waterloo. Why we did not later hang some of the gentry who contributed from the trees to the terror of this road is not known.

The wounded were stringing back from the front, hundreds of them. Some walked unaided, an arm or a shoulder having been dressed at a field station. They stopped often enough to answer the universal hail "How is it going?" Others hobbled or clung to a friend's shoulders. Their slit trousers exposed red bandages. A few were shot horribly in the face and were led, bleeding and blind, by their mates.

And then there were the slow pacing stretcher-bearers with the dying or the insensible, the badly wounded, still figures with blood often drying brick color on their hot bandages.

Prostrate at the roadside were many others who had made their way thus far and were waiting for strength. Everywhere moved the sure-handed, invaluable Red Cross men.

Over this scene was a sort of haze of bullets. They were of two kinds. First, the Spanish lines were firing just a trifle high. Their bullets swept over our firing lines and poured into this devoted roadway, the single exit, even as it had been the single approach. The second fire was from guerillas concealed in the trees and in the thickets along the trail. They had come in under the very wings of our strong advance, taken good positions on either side of the road and were peppering our line of communication whenever they got a good target, no matter, apparently, what the target might be.

Red Cross men, wounded men, sick men, correspondents and attachés were all one to the guerilla. The move of sending an irregular force around the flanks of the enemy as he is making his front attack is so legitimate that some of us could not believe at first that the men hidden in the forest were really blazing away at the noncombatants or the wounded. Viewed simply as a bit of tactics, the scheme was admirable. But there is no doubt now that they intentionally fired at anybody they thought they could kill.

You can't mistake an ambulance driver when he is driving his ambulance. You can't mistake a wounded man when he is lying down and being bandaged. And when you see a field hospital you don't mistake it for a squadron of cavalry or a brigade of infantry.

After the guerillas had successfully rewounded some prostrate men in a hospital and killed an ambulance driver off his seat as he was taking his silent, suffering charges to the base, there were any number of humane and gentle-hearted men in the army who were extremely anxious to see any guerillas that were caught hanged to the trees in which they were found. Our greatest punishment, after all, is to feed them until they are in danger of bursting.

As we went along the road we suddenly heard a cry behind us. "Oh, come quick! Come quick!" We turned and saw a young soldier spinning around frantically and grabbing at his leg. Evidently he had been going to the stream to fill his canteen, but a guerilla had barred him from that drink. Two Red Cross men rushed for him.

At the last ford, in the shelter of the muddy bank, lay a dismal band, forty men on their backs with doctors working at them and bullets singing in flocks over their heads. They rolled their eyes quietly at us. There was no groaning. They exhibited that profound patience which has been the marvel of every one.

After the ford was passed the woods cleared. The road passed through lines of barbed wire. There were, in fact, barbed wire fences running in almost every direction.

The mule train, galloping like a troop of cavalry, dashed up with a reinforcement of ammunition, every mule on the jump, the cowboys swinging their whips. They were under a fairly strong fire, but up they went.

One does not expect gallantry in a pack train, but incidentally it may be said that this charge, led by the bell mare, was one of the sights of the day.

At a place where the road cut through the crest of the ridge Borrowe and some of his men were working over his dynamite gun. After the fifth discharge something had got jammed. There was never such devotion to an inanimate thing as these men give to their dynamite gun. They will quarrel for her, starve for her, lose sleep for her and fight for her to the last ditch.

In the army there has always been two opinions of the dynamite gun. Some have said it was a most terrific engine of destruction, while others have called it a toy. With the bullets winging their long flights not very high overhead, Borrowe and his crowd at sight of us began their little hymn of praise, the chief note of which was one of almost pathetic insistence. If they ever get that gun into action again, they will make her hum.

The discomfited Spaniards, recovering from their panic, opened from their second line a most furious fire. It was first directed against one part of our line and then against another, as if they were feeling for our weakest point, fumbling around after the throat of the army.

Somebody on the left caught it for a time and then suddenly the enemy apparently devoted their entire attention to the position occupied by the Rough Riders. Some shrapnel, with fuses cut too long, passed over and burst from 100 to 200 yards to the rear. They acted precisely like things with strings to them. When the string was jerked, bang! went the hurtling explosive. But the infantry fire was very heavy, albeit high.

The American reply was in measured volleys. Part of a regiment would remain on the firing line while the other companies rested near by under the brow of the hill. Parties were sent after the packs. The commands knew with what other organizations they were in touch on the two flanks. Otherwise they knew nothing, save that they were going to hold their ground. They said so.

From our line could be seen a long, gray Spanish entrenchment, from 400 to 1,000 yards away, according to what part of our line one measured from. From it floated no smoke and no men appeared there, but it was making a noise like a million champagne corks.

Back of their entrenchments, perhaps another thousand yards, was a long building of masonry tinted pink. It flew many Red Cross flags and near it were other smaller structures also flying Red Cross flags. In fact, the enemy's third line of defense seemed to be composed of hospitals.

The city itself slanted down toward the bay, just a glimpse of silver. In the clear, white sunshine the houses of the suburbs, the hospitals and the long gray trenches were so vivid that they seemed far closer than they were.

To the rear, over the ground that the army had taken, a breeze was gently stirring the long grass and ruffling the surface of a pool that lay in a sort of meadow. The army took its glory calmly. Having nothing else to do, the army sat down and looked tranquilly at the scenery. There was not that exuberance of enthusiasm which surrounds the vicinity of a candidate for the Assembly.

The army was dusty, dishevelled, its hair matted to its forehead with sweat, its shirts glued to its back with the same, and indescribably dirty, thirsty, hungry, and aweary from its bundles and its marches and its fights. It sat down on the conquered crest and felt satisfied.

"Well, hell! here we are."

News began to pass along the line. Lawton had taken Caney after a long fight and had lost heavily. The siege pieces were being unloaded at Siboney. Pando had succeeded in reinforcing Santiago that very morning with 8,400 men, 6,000 men, 4,500 men. Pando had not succeeded. And so on.

At dusk a comparative stillness settled upon the ridge. The shooting subsided to little nervous outbursts. In the trenches taken by our troops lay dead Spaniards.

The road to the rear increased its terrors in the darkness. The wounded men, stumbling along in the mud, a miasmic mist from the swampish ground filling their nostrils, heard often in the air the whiplash sound of a bullet that was meant for them by the lurking guerillas. A mile, two miles, two miles and a half to the rear, great populous hospitals had been formed.

The long lines of the hill began to entrench under cover of night, each regiment for itself, still, however, keeping in touch on the flanks. Each regiment dug in the ground that it had taken by its own valor. Some commands had two or three shovels, an axe or two, maybe a pick. Other regiments dug with their bayonets and shovelled out the dirt with their meat ration cans.

Darkness swallowed Santiago and the new entrenchments. The large tropic stars illumined the sky. On the safe side of the ridge our men had built some little red fires, no larger than hats, at which they cooked what food they possessed. There was no sound save to the rear, where throughout the night our pickets could be faintly heard exchanging shots with the guerillas.

On the very moment, it seemed, of the break of day, bang! the fight was on again. The firing broke out from one end of the prodigious V-shaped formation to the other. Our artillery took new advanced positions, but they were driven away by the swirling Mauser fire.

When the day was in full bloom Lawton's division, having marched all night, appeared in the road. The long, long column wound around the base of the ridge and disappeared among the woods and knolls on the right of Wheeler's line. The army was now concentrated in a splendid position.

It becomes necessary to speak of the men's opinion of the Cubans. To put it shortly, both officers and privates have the most lively contempt for the Cubans. They despise them. They came down here expecting to fight side by side with an ally, but this ally has done little but stay in the rear and eat army rations, manifesting an indifference to the cause of Cuban liberty which could not be exceeded by some one who had never heard of it.

In the great charge up the hills of San Juan the American soldiers who, for their part, sprinkled a thousand bodies in the grass, were not able to see a single Cuban assisting in what might easily turn out to be the decisive battle for Cuban freedom.

At Caney a company of Cubans came into action on the left flank of one of the American regiments just before the place was taken. Later they engaged a blockhouse at 2,000 yards and fired away all their ammunition. They sent back to the American commander for more, but they got only a snort of indignation.

As a matter of fact, the Cuban soldier, ignorant as only such isolation as has been his can make him, does not appreciate the ethics of the situation.

This great American army he views as he views the sky, the sea, the air; it is a natural and most happy phenomenon. He will go to sleep while this flood drowns the Spaniards.

The American soldier, however, thinks of himself often as a disinterested benefactor, and he would like the Cubans to play up to the ideal now and then. His attitude is mighty human. He does not really want to be thanked, and yet the total absence of anything like gratitude makes him furious. He is furious, too, because the Cubans apparently consider themselves under no obligation to take part in an engagement; because the Cubans will stay at the rear and collect haversacks, blankets, coats and shelter tents dropped by our troops.

The average Cuban here will not speak to an American unless to beg. He forgets his morning, afternoon or evening salutation unless he is reminded. If he takes a dislike to you he talks about you before your face, using a derisive undertone.

If he asks you a favor and you can't grant it his face grows sour in the expression of a man who has been deprived of an inalienable right. Then at all times he gibbers. Talk, talk, talk, talk. Heaven knows what it is all about; but certainly four Cubans can talk enough for four regiments.

The truth probably is that the food, raiment and security furnished by the Americans have completely demoralized the insurgents. When the force under Gomez came to Guantanamo to assist the marines they were a most efficient body of men. They guided the marines to the enemy and fought with them shoulder to shoulder, not very skillfully in the matter of shooting, but still with courage and determination.

After this action there ensued at Guantanamo a long peace. The Cubans built themselves a permanent camp and they began to eat, eat much, and to sleep long, day and night, until now, behold, there is no more useless body of men anywhere! A trifle less than half of them are on Dr. Edgar's sick list, and the others are practically insubordinate. So much food seems to act upon them like a drug.

Here with the army the demoralization has occurred on a big scale. It is dangerous, too, for the Cuban. If he stupidly, drowsily remains out of these fights, what weight is his voice to have later in the final adjustments? The officers and men of the army, if their feeling remains the same, will not be happy to see him have any at all. The situation needs a Gomez. It is more serious than these bestarred *machete* bearers know how to appreciate, and it is the worst thing for the cause of an independent Cuba that could possibly exist.

At San Juan the 2d of July was a smaller edition of the 1st. The men deepened their entrenchments, shot, slept and ate. On the 1st every man had been put into the fighting line. There was not a reserve as big as your hat. If the enemy broke through any part of the line there was nothing to stop them short of Siboney. On the 2d, however, some time after the arrival of Lawton, the Ninth Massachusetts and the Thirty-fourth Michigan came up.

Along the road from El Paso they had to pass some pretty grim sights. And there were some pretty grim odors, but the men were steady enough. "How far are they off?" they asked of a passing regular. "Oh, not far; but it's all right. We think they may run out of ammunition in the course of a week or ten days."

The volunteers laughed. But the pitiful thing about this advance was to see in the hands of the boys those terrible old rifles that smoke like brush fires and give the regimental line away to the enemy as plainly as an illuminated sign.

I remember that on the first day men of the Seventy-first who had lost their command would try to join one of the regular regiments, but the regulars would have none of them. "Get out of here with that d— gun!" the regulars would say. During the battle just one shot from a Springfield would call a volley, for the Spaniards then knew just where to shoot. It was very hard on the Seventy-first New York and the Second Massachusetts.

At Caney about two hundred prisoners were taken. Two big squads of them were soldiers of the regular Spanish infantry in the usual blue-and-white pajamas. The others were the rummiest-looking set of men one could possibly imagine. They were native-born Cubans, reconcentrados, traitors, guerillas of the kind that bushwhacked us so unmercifully. Some were doddering old men, shaking with the palsy of their many years. Some were slim, dirty, bad-eyed boys. They were all of a lower class than one could find in any United States jail.

At first they had all expected to be butchered. In fact, to encourage them to fight, their officers had told them that if they gave in they need expect no mercy from the dreadful Americans.

Our great, good, motherly old country has nothing in her heart but mercy, and nothing in her pockets but beef, hard-tack and coffee for all of them—lemon-colored refugee from Santiago, wild-eyed prisoner from the trenches, Spanish guerilla from out the thickets, half-naked insurgent from the mountains—all of them.

In the church at Caney lie fifty-two Spanish wounded, attended by our surgeons. For a temporary affair, inaugurated in a moment, it is as good a hospital as ever raised its flag after a day of blood, and our surgeons and our Red Cross assistants were giving the best of their trained intelligence to the cure of the hurts of these men even while, on the road from San Juan to El Paso, the guerillas were shooting at our wounded.

"MARINES SIGNALLING UNDER FIRE AT GUANTANAMO"

They were four Guantanamo marines, officially known for the time as signalmen, and it was their duty to lie in the trenches of Camp McCalla, that faced the water, and, by day, signal the *Marblehead* with a flag and, by night, signal the *Marblehead* with lanterns. It was my good fortune—at that time I considered it my bad fortune, indeed—to be with them on two of the nights when a wild storm of fighting was pealing about the hill; and, of all the actions of the war, none were so hard on the nerves, none

McClure's Magazine, Feb. 1899.

strained courage so near the panic point, as those swift nights in Camp McCalla. With a thousand rifles rattling; with the field-guns booming in your ears; with the diabolic Colt automatics clacking; with the roar of the *Marblehead* coming from the bay, and, last, with Mauser bullets sneering always in the air a few inches over one's head, and with this enduring from dusk to dawn, it is extremely doubtful if any one who was there will be able to forget it easily. The noise; the impenetrable darkness; the knowledge from the sound of the bullets that the enemy was on three sides of the camp; the infrequent bloody stumbling and death of some man with whom, perhaps, one had messed two hours previous; the weariness of the body, and the more terrible weariness of the mind, at the endlessness of the thing, made it wonderful that at least some of the men did not come out of it with their nerves hopelessly in shreds.

But, as this interesting ceremony proceeded in the darkness, it was necessary for the signal squad to coolly take and send messages. Captain McCalla always participated in the defence of the camp by raking the woods on two of its sides with the guns of the *Marblehead*. Moreover, he was the senior officer present, and he wanted to know what was happening. All night long the crews of the ships in the bay would stare sleeplessly into the blackness toward the roaring hill.

The signal squad had an old cracker-box placed on top of the trench. When not signalling they hid the lanterns in this box; but as soon as an order to send a message was received, it became necessary for one of the men to stand up and expose the lights. And then—oh, my eye—how the guerillas hidden in the gulf of night would turn loose at those yellow gleams!

Signalling in this way is done by letting one lantern remain stationary—on top of the cracker-box, in this case—and moving the other over to the left and right and so on in the regular gestures of the wig-wagging code. It is a very simple system of night communication, but one can see that it presents rare possibilities when used in front of an enemy who, a few hundred yards away, is overjoyed at sighting so definite a mark.

How, in the name of wonders, those four men at Camp McCalla were not riddled from head to foot and sent home more as repositories of Spanish ammunition than as marines is beyond all comprehension. To make a confession—when one of these men stood up to wave his lantern, I, lying in the trench, invariably rolled a little to the right or left, in order that, when he was shot, he would not fall on me. But the squad came off scathless, despite the best efforts of the most formidable corps in the Spanish army—the Escuadra de Guantanamo. That it was the most formidable corps in the Spanish army of occupation has been told me by many Spanish officers and also by General Menocal and other insurgent officers. General Menocal was Garcia's chief-of-staff when the latter was operating busily in Santiago province. The regiment was composed solely of *practicos,* or guides, who knew every shrub and tree on the ground over which they moved.

Whenever the adjutant, Lieutenant Draper, came plunging along through the darkness with an order—such as: "Ask the *Marblehead* to please shell the woods to the left"—my heart would come into my mouth, for I knew then that one of my pals was going to stand up behind the lanterns and have all Spain shoot at him.

The answer was always upon the instant:

"Yes, sir." Then the bullets began to snap, snap, snap, at his head while all the woods began to crackle like burning straw. I could lie near and watch the face of the signalman, illumed as it was by the yellow shine of lantern light, and the absence of excitement, fright, or any emotion at all on his countenance, was something to astonish all theories out of one's mind. The face was in every instance merely that of a man intent upon his business, the business of wig-wagging into the gulf of night where a light on the *Marblehead* was seen to move slowly.

These times on the hill resembled, in some days, those terrible scenes on the stage—scenes of intense gloom, blinding lightning, with a cloaked devil or assassin or other appropriate character muttering deeply amid the awful roll of the thunder-drums. It was theatric beyond words: one felt like a leaf in this booming chaos, this prolonged tragedy of the night. Amid it all one could see from time to time the yellow light on the face of a preoccupied signalman.

Possibly no man who was there ever before understood the true eloquence of the breaking of the day. We would lie staring into the east, fairly ravenous for the dawn. Utterly worn to rags, with our nerves standing on end like so many bristles, we lay and watched the east—the unspeakably obdurate and slow east. It was a wonder that the eyes of some of us did not turn to glass balls from the fixity of our gaze.

Then there would come into the sky a patch of faint blue light. It was like a piece of moonshine. Some would say it was the beginning of daybreak; others would declare it was nothing of the kind. Men would get very disgusted with each other in these low-toned arguments held in the trenches. For my part, this development in the eastern sky destroyed any of my ideas and theories concerning the dawning of the day; but then I had never before had occasion to give it such solemn attention.

This patch widened and whitened in about the speed of a man's accomplishment if he should be in the way of painting Madison Square Garden with a camel's hair brush. The guerillas always set out to whoop it up about this time, because they knew the occasion was approaching when it would be expedient for them to elope. I, at least, always grew furious with this wretched sunrise. I thought I could have walked around the world in the time required for the old thing to get up above the horizon.

One midnight, when an important message was to be sent to the *Marblehead,* Colonel Huntington came himself to the signal place with Adjutant Draper and Captain McCauley, the quartermaster. When the man stood up to signal, the colonel stood beside him. At sight of the lights, the Spaniards performed as usual. They drove enough bullets into that immediate vicinity to kill all the marines in the corps.

Lieutenant Draper was agitated for his chief. "Colonel, won't you step down, sir?"

"Why, I guess not," said the grey old veteran in his slow, sad, always-gentle way. "I am in no more danger than the man."

"But, sir—" began the adjutant.

"Oh, it's all right, Draper."

So the colonel and the private stood side to side and took the heavy fire without either moving a muscle.

Day was always obliged to come at last, punctuated by a final exchange of scattering shots. And the light shone on the marines, the dumb guns, the flag. Grimy yellow face looked into grimy yellow face, and grinned with weary satisfaction. Coffee!

Usually it was impossible for many of the men to sleep at once. It always took me, for instance, some hours to get my nerves combed down. But then it was great joy to lie in the trench with the four signalmen, and understand thoroughly that that night was fully over at last, and that, although the future might have in store other bad nights, one could never escape from the prison-house which we call the past.

At the wild little fight at Cusco there were some splendid exhibitions of wig-wagging under fire. Action began when an advanced detachment of marines under Lieutenant Lucas with the Cuban guides had reached the summit of a ridge overlooking a small valley where there was a house, a well, and a thicket of some kind of shrub with great broad, oily leaves. This thicket, which was perhaps an acre in extent, contained the guerillas. The valley was open to the sea. The distance from the top of the ridge to the thicket was barely two hundred yards.

The *Dolphin* had sailed up the coast in line with the marine advance, ready with her guns to assist in any action. Captain Elliott, who commanded the two hundred marines in this fight, suddenly called out for a signalman. He wanted a man to tell the *Dolphin* to open fire on the house and the thicket. It was a blazing, bitter hot day on top of the ridge with its shrivelled chaparral and its straight, tall cactus plants. The sky was bare and blue, and hurt like brass. In two minutes the prostrate marines were red and sweating like so many hull-buried stokers in the tropics.

Captain Elliott called out:

"Where's a signalman? Who's a signalman here?"

A red-headed "mick"—I think his name was Clancy—at any rate, it will do to call him Clancy—twisted his head from where he lay on his stomach pumping his Lee, and, saluting, said that he was a signalman.

There was no regulation flag with the expedition, so Clancy was obliged to tie his blue polka-dot neckerchief on the end of his rifle. It did not make a very good flag. At first Clancy moved a ways down the safe side of the ridge and wig-wagged there very busily. But what with the flag being so poor for the purpose, and the background of ridge being so dark, those on the *Dolphin* did not see it. So Clancy had to return to the top of the ridge and outline himself and his flag against the sky.

The usual thing happened. As soon as the Spaniards caught sight of this silhouette, they let go like mad at it. To make things more comfortable for Clancy, the situation demanded that he face the sea and turn his back to the Spanish bullets. This was a hard game, mark you—to stand with the small of your back to volley firing. Clancy thought so. Everybody thought so. We all cleared out of his neighbourhood. If he wanted sole possession of any particular spot on that hill, he could have it for all we would interfere with him.

It cannot be denied that Clancy was in a hurry. I watched him. He was so occupied with the bullets that snarled close to his ears that he was obliged to repeat the letters of his message softly to himself. It seemed an intolerable time before the *Dolphin* answered the little signal. Meanwhile, we gazed at him, marvelling every second that he had not yet pitched headlong. He swore at times.

Finally the *Dolphin* replied to his frantic gesticulation, and he delivered his message. As his part of the transaction was quite finished— whoop!—he dropped like a brick into the firing line and began to shoot; began to get "hunky" with all those people who had been plugging at him. The blue polka-dot neckerchief still fluttered from the barrel of his rifle. I am quite certain that he let it remain there until the end of the fight.

The shells of the *Dolphin* began to plough up the thicket, kicking the bushes, stones, and soil into the air as if somebody was blasting there.

Meanwhile, this force of two hundred marines and fifty Cubans and the force of—probably—six companies of Spanish guerillas were making such an awful din that the distant Camp McCalla was all alive with excitement. Colonel Huntington sent out strong parties to critical points

on the road to facilitate, if necessary, a safe retreat, and also sent forty
men under Lieutenant Magill to come up on the left flank of the two companies in action under Captain Elliott. Lieutenant Magill and his men
had crowned a hill which covered entirely the flank of the fighting companies, but when the *Dolphin* opened fire, it happened that Magill was in
the line of the shots. It became necessary to stop the *Dolphin* at once. Captain Elliott was not near Clancy at this time, and he called hurriedly for another signalman.

Sergeant Quick arose, and announced that he was a signalman. He
produced from somewhere a blue polka-dot neckerchief as large as a quilt.
He tied it on a long, crooked stick. Then he went to the top of the ridge,
and turning his back to the Spanish fire, began to signal to the *Dolphin*.
Again we gave a man sole possession of a particular part of the ridge. We
didn't want it. He could have it and welcome. If the young sergeant had
had the smallpox, the cholera, and the yellow fever, we could not have slid
out with more celerity.

As men have said often, it seemed as if there was in this war a God of
Battles who held His mighty hand before the Americans. As I looked at
Sergeant Quick wig-wagging there against the sky, I would not have given
a tin tobacco-tag for his life. Escape for him seemed impossible. It seemed
absurd to hope that he would not be hit; I only hoped that he would be hit
just a little, little, in the arm, the shoulder, or the leg.

I watched his face, and it was as grave and serene as that of a man
writing in his own library. He was the very embodiment of tranquillity in
occupation. He stood there amid the animal-like babble of the Cubans, the
crack of rifles, and the whistling snarl of the bullets, and wig-wagged whatever he had to wig-wag without heeding anything but his business. There
was not a single trace of nervousness or haste.

To say the least, a fight at close range is absorbing as a spectacle. No
man wants to take his eyes from it until that time comes when he makes
up his mind to run away. To deliberately stand up and turn your back to a
battle is in itself hard work. To deliberately stand up and turn your back
to a battle and hear immediate evidences of the boundless enthusiasm with
which a large company of the enemy shoot at you from an adjacent thicket
is, to my mind at least, a very great feat. One need not dwell upon the detail of keeping the mind carefully upon a slow spelling of an important
code message.

I saw Quick betray only one sign of emotion. As he swung his clumsy
flag to and fro, an end of it once caught on a cactus pillar, and he looked
sharply over his shoulder to see what had it. He gave the flag an impatient
jerk. He looked annoyed.

"THE MONSTER"

I

Little Jim was, for the time, engine Number 36, and he was making the run between Syracuse and Rochester. He was fourteen minutes behind time, and the throttle was wide open. In consequence, when he swung around the curve at the flower-bed, a wheel of his cart destroyed a peony. Number 36 slowed down at once and looked guiltily at his father, who was mowing the lawn. The doctor had his back to this accident, and he continued to pace slowly to and fro, pushing the mower.

Jim dropped the tongue of the cart. He looked at his father and at the broken flower. Finally he went to the peony and tried to stand it on its pins, resuscitated, but the spine of it was hurt, and it would only hang limply from his hand. Jim could do no reparation. He looked again toward his father.

He went on to the lawn, very slowly, and kicking wretchedly at the turf. Presently his father came along with the whirring machine, while the sweet, new grass blades spun from the knives. In a low voice, Jim said, "Pa!"

The doctor was shaving this lawn as if it were a priest's chin. All during the season he had worked at it in the coolness and peace of the evenings after supper. Even in the shadow of the cherry trees the grass was strong and healthy. Jim raised his voice a trifle. "Pa!"

The doctor paused, and with the howl of the machine no longer occupying the sense, one could hear the robins in the cherry trees arranging their affairs. Jim's hands were behind his back, and sometimes his fingers clasped and unclasped. Again he said, "Pa!" The child's fresh and rosy lip was lowered.

The doctor stared down at his son, thrusting his head forward and frowning attentively. "What is it, Jimmie?"

"Pa!" repeated the child at length. Then he raised his finger and pointed at the flower-bed. "There!"

"What?" said the doctor, frowning more. "What is it, Jim?"

After a period of silence, during which the child may have undergone a severe mental tumult, he raised his finger and repeated his former word— "There!" The father had respected this silence with perfect courtesy. Afterwards his glance carefully followed the direction indicated by the child's finger, but he could see nothing which explained to him. "I don't understand what you mean, Jimmie," he said.

Harper's Magazine, Aug. 1898.

It seemed that the importance of the whole thing had taken away the boy's vocabulary. He could only reiterate, "There!"

The doctor mused upon the situation, but he could make nothing of it. At last he said, "Come, show me."

Together they crossed the lawn toward the flower-bed. At some yards from the broken peony Jimmie began to lag. "There!" The word came almost breathlessly.

"Where?" said the doctor.

Jimmie kicked at the grass. "There!" he replied.

The doctor was obliged to go forward alone. After some trouble he found the subject of the incident, the broken flower. Turning then, he saw the child lurking at the rear and scanning his countenance.

The father reflected. After a time he said, "Jimmie, come here." With an infinite modesty of demeanor the child came forward. "Jimmie, how did this happen?"

The child answered, "Now—I was playin' train—and—now—I runned over it."

"You were doing what?"

"I was playin' train."

The father reflected again. "Well, Jimmie," he said, slowly, "I guess you had better not play train any more today. Do you think you had better?"

"No, sir," said Jimmie.

During the delivery of the judgment the child had not faced his father, and afterwards he went away, with his head lowered, shuffling his feet.

II

It was apparent from Jimmie's manner that he felt some kind of desire to efface himself. He went down to the stable. Henry Johnson, the negro who cared for the doctor's horses, was sponging the buggy. He grinned fraternally when he saw Jimmie coming. These two were pals. In regard to almost everything in life they seemed to have minds precisely alike. Of course there were points of emphatic divergence. For instance, it was plain from Henry's talk that he was a very handsome negro, and he was known to be a light, a weight, and an eminence in the suburb of the town, where lived the larger number of the negroes, and obviously this glory was over Jimmie's horizon; but he vaguely appreciated it and paid deference to Henry for it mainly because Henry appreciated it and deferred to himself. However, on all points of conduct as related to the doctor, who was the moon, they were in complete but unexpressed understanding. Whenever

Jimmie became the victim of an eclipse he went to the stable to solace himself with Henry's crimes. Henry, with the elasticity of his race, could usually provide a sin to place himself on a footing with the disgraced one. Perhaps he would remember that he had forgotten to put the hitching strap in the back of the buggy on some recent occasion, and had been reprimanded by the doctor. Then these two would commune subtly and without words concerning their moon, holding themselves sympathetically as people who had committed similar treasons. On the other hand, Henry would sometimes choose to absolutely repudiate this idea, and when Jimmie appeared in his shame would bully him most virtuously, preaching with assurance the precepts of the doctor's creed, and pointing out to Jimmie all his abominations. Jimmie did not discover that this was odious in his comrade. He accepted it and lived in its shadow with humility, merely trying to conciliate the saintly Henry with acts of deference. Won by this attitude, Henry would sometimes allow the child to enjoy the felicity of squeezing the sponge over a buggy-wheel, even when Jimmie was still gory from unspeakable deeds.

Whenever Henry dwelt for a time in sackcloth, Jimmie did not patronize him at all. This was a justice of his age, his condition. He did not know. Besides, Henry could drive a horse, and Jimmie had a full sense of this sublimity. Henry personally conducted the moon during the splendid journeys through the country roads, where farms spread on all sides, with sheep, cows, and other marvels abounding.

"Hello, Jim!" said Henry, poising his sponge. Water was dripping from the buggy. Sometimes the horses in the stalls stamped thunderingly on the pine floor. There was an atmosphere of hay and of harness.

For a minute Jimmie refused to take an interest in anything. He was very downcast. He could not even feel the wonders of wagon-washing. Henry, while at work, narrowly observed him.

"Your pop done wallop yer, didn't he?" he said at last.

"No," said Jimmie, defensively; "he didn't."

After this casual remark Henry continued his labor, with a scowl of occupation. Presently he said: "I done tol' yer many's th' time not to go a-foolin' an' a-projjeckin' with them flowers. Yer pop don' like it nohow." As a matter of fact, Henry had never mentioned flowers to the boy.

Jimmie preserved a gloomy silence, so Henry began to use seductive wiles in this affair of washing a wagon. It was not until he began to spin a wheel on the tree, and the sprinkling water flew everywhere, that the boy was visibly moved. He had been seated on the sill of the carriage-house door, but at the beginning of this ceremony he arose and circled toward the buggy, with an interest that slowly consumed the rememerance of a late disgrace.

Johnson could then display all the dignity of a man whose duty it was to protect Jimmie from a splashing. "Look out, boy! look out! You done gwi' spile yer pants. I raikon your mommer don't 'low this foolishness, she know it. I ain't gwi' have you round yere spilin' yer pants, an' have Mis' Trescott light on me pressen'ly. 'Deed I ain't."

He spoke with an air of great irritation, but he was not annoyed at all. This tone was merely a part of his importance. In reality he was always delighted to have the child there to witness the business of the stable. For one thing, Jimmie was invariably overcome with reverence when he was told how beautifully a harness was polished or a horse groomed. Henry explained each detail of this kind with unction, procuring great joy from the child's admiration.

III

After Johnson had taken his supper in the kitchen, he went to his loft in the carriage-house and dressed himself with much care. No belle of a court circle could bestow more mind on a toilet than did Johnson. On second thought, he was more like a priest arraying himself for some parade of the church. As he emerged from his room and sauntered down the carriage-drive, no one would have suspected him of ever having washed a buggy.

It was not altogether a matter of the lavender trousers, nor yet the straw hat with its bright silk band. The change was somewhere far in the interior of Henry. But there was no cake-walk hyperbole in it. He was simply a quiet, well-bred gentleman of position, wealth, and other necessary achievements out for an evening stroll, and he had never washed a wagon in his life.

In the morning, when in his working clothes, he had met a friend— "Hello, Pete!" "Hello, Henry!" Now, in his effulgence, he encountered this same friend. His bow was not at all haughty. If it expressed anything, it expressed consummate generosity—"Good-evenin', Misteh Washington." Pete, who was very dirty, being at work in a potato-patch, responded in a mixture of abasement and appreciation—"Good-evenin, Misteh Johnsing."

The shimmering blue of the electric arc-lamps was strong in the main street of the town. At numerous points it was conquered by the orange glare of the outnumbering gaslights in the windows of shops. Through this radiant lane moved a crowd, which culminated in a throng before the post-office, awaiting the distribution of the evening mails. Occasionally there came into it a shrill electric street-car, the motor singing like a cageful of grasshoppers, and possessing a great gong that clanged forth both warnings and simple noise. At the little theatre which was a varnish and red-plush miniature of one of the famous New York theatres, a company of strollers was to play "East Lynne." The young men of the town were mainly gathered at the corners, in distinctive groups which expressed various shades and lines of chumship, and had little to do with any social gradations. There they discussed everything with critical insight, passing the whole town in review as it swarmed in the street. When the gongs of the electric cars ceased for a moment to harry the ears, there could be heard the sound of the feet of the leisurely crowd on the bluestone pavement, and it was like the peaceful evening lashing at the shore of a lake. At the foot of the hill, where two lines of maples sentinelled the way, an electric lamp glowed high among the embowering branches and made most wonderful shadow-etchings on the road below it.

When Johnson appeared amid the throng a member of one of the profane groups at a corner instantly telegraphed news of this extraordinary arrival to his companions. They hailed him. "Hello, Henry! Going to walk for a cake tonight?"

"Ain't he smooth?"

"Why, you've got that cake right in your pocket, Henry!"

"Throw out your chest a little more."

Henry was not ruffled in any way by these quiet admonitions and compliments. In reply he laughed a supremely good-natured, chuckling laugh, which nevertheless expressed an underground complacency of superior mettle.

Young Griscom, the lawyer, was just emerging from Reifsnyder's barber shop, rubbing his chin contentedly. On the steps he dropped his hand and looked with wide eyes into the crowd. Suddenly he bolted back into the shop. "Wow!" he cried to the parliament; "you ought to see the coon that's coming!"

Reifsnyder and his assistant instantly poised their razors high and turned toward the window. Two belathered heads reared from the chairs. The electric shine in the street caused an effect like water to them who looked through the glass from the yellow glamor of Riefsnyder's shop. In fact, the people without resembled the inhabitants of a great aquarium that here had a square pane in it. Presently into this frame swam the graceful form of Henry Johnson.

"Chee!" said Reifsnyder. He and his assistants with one accord threw their obligations to the winds and, leaving their lathered victims helpless, advanced to the window. "Ain't he a taisy?" said Reifsnyder, marvelling.

But the man in the first chair, with a grievance in his mind, had found a weapon. "Why, that's only Henry Johnson, you blamed idiots! Come on now, Reif, and shave me. What do you think I am—a mummy?"

Reifsnyder turned, in a great excitement. "I bait you any money that vas not Henry Johnson! Henry Johnson! Rats!" The scorn put into this last word made it an explosion. "That man was a Pullman-car porter or someding. How could that be Henry Johnson?" he demanded, turbulently. "You vas crazy."

The man in the first chair faced the barber in a storm of indignation. "Didn't I give him those lavender trousers?" he roared.

And young Griscom, who had remained attentively at the window, said: "Yes, I guess that was Henry. It looked like him."

"Oh, vell," said Reifsnyder, returning to his business, "if you think so! Oh, vell!" He implied that he was submitting for the sake of amiability.

Finally the man in the second chair, mumbling from a mouth made timid by adjacent lather, said: "That was Henry Johnson all right. Why, he always dresses like that when he wants to make a front! He's the biggest dude in town—anybody knows that."

"Chinger!" said Reifsnyder.

Henry was not at all oblivious of the wake of wondering ejaculation that streamed out behind him. On other occasions he had reaped this same joy, and he always had an eye for the demonstration. With a face beaming with happiness he turned away from the scene of his victories into a narrow side street, where the electric light still hung high, but only to exhibit a row of tumbledown houses leaning together like paralytics.

The saffron Miss Bella Farragut, in a calico frock, had been crouched on the front stoop, gossiping at long range, but she espied her approaching caller at a distance. She dashed around the corner of the house, galloping like a horse. Henry saw it all, but he preserved the polite demeanor of a guest when a waiter spills claret down his cuff. In this awkward situation he was simply perfect.

The duty of receiving Mr. Johnson fell upon Mrs. Farragut, because Bella, in another room, was scrambling wildly into her best gown. The fat old woman met him with a great ivory smile, sweeping back with the door, and bowing low. "Walk in, Misteh Johnson, walk in. How is you dis ebenin', Misteh Johnson—how is you?"

Henry's face showed like a reflector as he bowed and bowed, bending almost from his head to his ankles. "Good-evenin', Mis' Fa'gut; good-evenin'. How is you dis evenin'? Is all you' folks well, Mis' Fa'gut?"

After a great deal of kowtow, they were planted in two chairs opposite each other in the living-room. Here they exchanged the most tremendous civilities, until Miss Bella swept into the room, when there was more kow-tow on all sides, and a smiling show of teeth that was like an illumination.

The cooking-stove was of course in this drawing-room, and on the fire was some kind of a long-winded stew. Mrs. Farragut was obliged to arise and attend to it from time to time. Also young Sim came in and went to bed on his pallet in the corner. But to all these domesticities the three maintained an absolute dumbness. They bowed and smiled and ig-nored and imitated until a late hour, and if they had been the occupants of the most gorgeous salon in the world they could not have been more like three monkeys.

After Henry had gone, Bella, who encouraged herself in the appropri-ation of phrases, said, "Oh, ma, isn't he divine?"

IV

A Saturday evening was a sign always for a larger crowd to parade the thoroughfare. In summer the band played until ten o'clock in the little park. Most of the young men of the town affected to be superior to this band, even to despise it; but in the still and fragrant evenings they invari-ably turned out in force, because the girls were sure to attend this concert, strolling slowly over the grass, linked closely in pairs, or preferably in threes, in the curious public dependence upon one another which was their inheritance. There was no particular social aspect to this gathering, save that group regarded group with interest, but mainly in silence. Perhaps one girl would nudge another girl and suddenly say, "Look! there goes Gertie Hodgson and her sister!" And they would appear to regard this as an event of importance.

On a particular evening a rather large company of young men were gathered on the sidewalk that edged the park. They remained thus beyond the borders of the festivities because of their dignity, which would not ex-actly allow them to appear in anything which was so much fun for the younger lads. These latter were careering madly through the crowd, pre-cipitating minor accidents from time to time, but usually fleeing like mist swept by the wind before retribution could lay hands upon them.

The band played a waltz which involved a gift of prominence to the bass horn, and one of the young men on the sidewalk said that the music reminded him of the new engines on the hill pumping water into the reservoir. A similarity of this kind was not inconceivable, but the young man did not say it because he disliked the band's playing. He said it because it was fashionable to say that manner of thing concerning the band. However, over in the stand, Billie Harris, who played the snaredrum, was always surrounded by a throng of boys, who adored his every whack.

After the mails from New York and Rochester had been finally distributed, the crowd from the post-office added to the mass already in the park. The wind waved the leaves of the maples, and, high in the air, the blue-burning globes of the arc lamps caused the wonderful traceries of leaf shadows on the ground. When the light fell upon the upturned face of a girl, it caused it to glow with a wonderful pallor. A policeman came suddenly from the darkness and chased a gang of obstreperous little boys. They hooted him from a distance. The leader of the band had some of the mannerisms of the great musicians, and during a period of silence the crowd smiled when they saw him raise his hand to his brow, stroke it sentimentally, and glance upward with a look of poetic anguish. In the shivering light, which gave to the park an effect like a great vaulted hall, the throng swarmed, with a gentle murmur of dresses switching the turf, and with a steady hum of voices.

Suddenly, without preliminary bars, there arose from afar the great hoarse roar of a factory whistle. It raised and swelled to a sinister note, and then it sang on the night wind one long call that held the crowd in the park immovable, speechless. The bandmaster had been about to vehemently let fall his hand to start the band on a thundering career through a popular march, but, smitten by this giant voice from the night, his hand dropped slowly to his knee, and, his mouth agape, he looked at his men in silence. The cry died away to a wail and then to stillness. It released the muscles of the company of young men on the sidewalk, who had been like statues, posed eagerly, lithely, their ears turned. And then they wheeled upon each other simultaneously, and, in a single explosion, they shouted, "One!"

Again the sound swelled in the night and roared its long ominous cry, and as it died away the crowd of young men wheeled upon each other and, in chorus, yelled, "Two!"

There was a moment of breathless waiting. Then they bawled, "Second district!" In a flash the company of indolent and cynical young men had vanished like a snowball disrupted by dynamite.

V

Jake Rogers was the first man to reach the home of Tuscarora Hose Company Number Six. He had wrenched his key from his pocket as he tore down the street, and he jumped at the spring-lock like a demon. As the doors flew back before his hands he leaped and kicked the wedges from a pair of wheels, loosened a tongue from its clasp, and in the glare of the electric light which the town placed before each of its hose-houses the next comers beheld the spectacle of Jake Rogers bent like hickory in the manfulness of his pulling, and the heavy cart was moving slowly toward the doors. Four men joined him at the time, and as they swung with the cart out into the street, dark figures sped toward them from the ponderous shadows in back of the electric lamps. Some set up the inevitable question, "What district?"

"Second," was replied to them in a compact howl. Tuscarora Hose Company Number Six swept on a perilous wheel into Niagara Avenue, and as the men, attached to the cart by the rope which had been paid out from the windlass under the tongue, pulled madly in their fervor and abandon, the gong under the axle clanged incitingly. And sometimes the same cry was heard, "What district?"

"Second."

On a grade Johnnie Thorpe fell and, exercising a singular muscular ability, rolled out in time for the track of the oncoming wheel, and arose, dishevelled and aggrieved, casting a look of mournful disenchantment upon the black crowd that poured after the machine. The cart seemed to be the apex of a dark wave that was whirling as if it had been a broken dam. Behind the lad were stretches of lawn, and in that direction front doors were banged by men who hoarsely shouted out into the clamorous avenue, "What district?"

At one of these houses a woman came to the door bearing a lamp, shielding her face from its rays with her hands. Across the cropped grass the avenue represented to her a kind of black torrent, upon which, nevertheless, fled numerous miraculous figures upon bicycles. She did not know that the towering light at the corner was continuing its nightly whine.

Suddenly a little boy somersaulted around the corner of the house as if he had been projected down a flight of stairs by a catapultian boot. He halted himself in front of the house by dint of a rather extraordinary evolution with his legs. "Oh, ma," he gasped, "can I go? Can I, ma?"

She straightened with the coldness of the exterior mother-judgment, although the hand that held the lamp trembled slightly. "No, Willie; you had better come to bed."

Instantly he began to buck and fume like a mustang. "Oh, ma," he cried, contorting himself—"oh, ma, can't I go? Please, ma, can't I go? Can't I go, ma?"

"It's half-past nine now, Willie."

He ended by wailing out a compromise: "Well, just down to the corner, ma? Just down to the corner?"

From the avenue came the sound of rushing men who wildly shouted. Somebody had grappled the bell-rope in the Methodist church, and now over the town rang this solemn and terrible voice, speaking from the clouds. Moved from its peaceful business, this bell gained a new spirit in the portentous night, and it swung the heart to and fro, up and down, with each peal of it.

"Just down to the corner, ma?"

"Willie, it's half-past nine now."

VI

The outlines of the house of Dr. Trescott had faded quietly into the evening, hiding a shape such as we call Queen Anne against the pall of the blackened sky. The neighborhood was at this time so quiet, and seemed so devoid of obstructions, that Hannigan's dog thought it a good opportunity to prowl in forbidden precincts, and so came and pawed Trescott's lawn, growling, and considering himself a formidable beast. Later, Peter Washington strolled past the house and whistled, but there was no dim light shining from Henry's loft, and presently Peter went his way. The rays from the street, creeping in silvery waves over the grass, caused the row of shrubs along the drive to throw a clear, bold shade.

A wisp of smoke came from one of the windows at the end of the house and drifted quietly into the branches of a cherry tree. Its companions followed it in slowly increasing numbers, and finally there was a current controlled by invisible banks which poured into the fruit-laden boughs of the cherry tree. It was no more to be noted than if a troop of dim and silent gray monkeys had been climbing a grapevine into the clouds.

After a moment the window brightened as if the four panes of it had been stained with blood, and a quick ear might have been led to imagine the fire-imps calling and calling, clan joining clan, gathering to the colors. From the street, however, the house maintained its dark quiet, insisting to a passerby that it was the safe dwelling of people who chose to retire early to tranquil dreams. No one could have heard this low droning of the gathering clans.

Suddenly the panes of the red window tinkled and crashed to the ground, and at other windows there suddenly reared other flames, like bloody spectres at the apertures of a haunted house. This outbreak had been well planned, as if by professional revolutionists.

A man's voice suddenly shouted: "Fire! Fire! Fire!" Hannigan had flung his pipe frenziedly from him because his lungs demanded room. He tumbled down from his perch, swung over the fence, and ran shouting to-

ward the front door of the Trescotts'. Then he hammered on the door, using his fists as if they were mallets. Mrs. Trescott instantly came to one of
the windows on the second floor. Afterward she knew she had been about
to say, "The doctor is not at home, but if you will leave your name, I will
let him know as soon as he comes."

Hannigan's bawling was for a minute incoherent, but she understood
that it was not about croup.

"What?" she said, raising the window swiftly.

"Your house is on fire! You're all ablaze! Move quick if—" His cries
were resounding in the street as if it were a cave of echoes. Many feet pattered swiftly on the stones. There was one man who ran with an almost
fabulous speed. He wore lavender trousers. A straw hat with a bright silk
band was held half crumpled in his hand.

As Henry reached the front door, Hannigan had just broken the lock
with a kick. A thick cloud of smoke poured over them, and Henry, ducking his head, rushed into it. From Hannigan's clamor he knew only one
thing, but it turned him blue with horror. In the hall a lick of flame had
found the cord that supported "Signing the Declaration." The engraving
slumped suddenly down at one end, and then dropped to the floor, where
it burst with the sound of a bomb. The fire was already roaring like a winter wind among the pines.

At the head of the stairs Mrs. Trescott was waving her arms as if they
were two reeds. "Jimmie! Save Jimmie!" she screamed in Henry's face. He
plunged past her and disappeared, taking the long-familiar routes among
these upper chambers, where he had once held office as a sort of second
assistant house-maid.

Hannigan had followed him up the stairs, and grappled the arm of the
maniacal woman there. His face was black with rage. "You must come
down," he bellowed.

She would only scream at him in reply: "Jimmie! Jimmie! Save Jimmie!" But he dragged her forth while she babbled at him.

As they swung out into the open air a man ran across the lawn and,
seizing a shutter, pulled it from its hinges and flung it far out upon the
grass. Then he frantically attacked the other shutters one by one. It was a
kind of temporary insanity.

"Here, you," howled Hannigan, "hold Mrs. Trescott—And stop—"

The news had been telegraphed by a twist of the wrist of a neighbor
who had gone to the fire box at the corner, and the time when Hannigan
and his charge struggled out of the house was the time when the whistle
roared its hoarse night call, smiting the crowd in the park, causing the
leader of the band, who was about to order the first triumphal clang of a
military march, to let his hand drop slowly to his knees.

VII

Henry pawed awkwardly through the smoke in the upper halls. He had attempted to guide himself by the walls, but they were too hot. The paper
was crimpling, and he expected at any moment to have a flame burst under his hands.

"Jimmie!"

He did not call very loud, as if in fear that the humming flames below
would overhear him.

"Jimmie! Oh, Jimmie!"

Stumbling and panting, he speedily reached the entrance to Jimmie's
room and flung open the door. The little chamber had no smoke in it at
all. It was faintly illuminated by a beautiful rosy light reflected circuitously
from the flames that were consuming the house. The boy had apparently
just been aroused by the noise. He sat in his bed, his lips apart, his eyes
wide, while upon his little white-robed figure played caressingly the light
from the fire. As the door flew open he had before him this apparition of
his pal, a terror-stricken negro, all tousled and with wool scorching, who
leaped upon him and bore him up in a blanket as if the whole affair were
a case of kidnapping by a dreadful robber chief. Without waiting to go
through the usual short but complete process of wrinkling up his face,
Jimmie let out a gorgeous bawl, which resembled the expression of a calf's
deepest terror. As Johnson, bearing him, reeled into the smoke of the hall,
he flung his arms about his neck and buried his face in the blanket. He
called twice in muffled tones: "Mam-ma! Mam-ma!"

When Johnson came to the top of the stairs with his burden, he
took a quick step backward. Through the smoke that rolled to him he
could see that the lower hall was all ablaze. He cried out then in a howl
that resembled Jimmie's former achievement. His legs gained a frightful
faculty of bending sideways. Swinging about precariously on these reedy
legs, he made his way back slowly, back along the upper hall. From the
way of him then, he had given up almost all idea of escaping from the
burning house, and with it the desire. He was submitting, submitting
because of his fathers, bending his mind in a most perfect slavery to this
conflagration.

He now clutched Jimmie as unconsciously as when, running toward
the house, he had clutched the hat with the bright silk band.

Suddenly he remembered a little private staircase which led from a
bedroom to an apartment which the doctor had fitted up as a laboratory
and work house, where he used some of his leisure, and also hours when
he might have been sleeping, in devoting himself to experiments which
came in the way of his study and interest.

When Johnson recalled this stairway the submission to the blaze departed instantly. He had been perfectly familiar with it, but his confusion had destroyed the memory of it.

In his sudden momentary apathy there had been little that resembled fear, but now, as a way of safety came to him, the old frantic terror caught him. He was no longer creature to the flames, and he was afraid of the battle with them. It was a singular and swift set of alternations in which he feared twice without submission, and submitted once without fear.

"Jimmie!" he wailed, as he staggered on his way. He wished this little inanimate body at his breast to participate in his tremblings. But the child had lain limp and still during these headlong charges and counter-charges, and no sign came from him.

Johnson passed through two rooms and came to the head of the stairs. As he opened the door great billows of smoke poured out, but, gripping Jimmie closer, he plunged down through them. All manner of odors assailed him during this flight. They seemed to be alive with envy, hatred, and malice. At the entrance to the laboratory he confronted a strange spectacle. The room was like a garden in the region where might be burning flowers. Flames of violet, crimson, green, blue, orange, and purple were blooming everywhere. There was one blaze that was precisely the hue of a delicate coral. In another place was a mass that lay merely in phosphorescent inaction like a pile of emeralds. But all these marvels were to be seen dimly through clouds of heaving, turning, deadly smoke.

Johnson halted for a moment on the threshold. He cried out again in the negro wail that had in it the sadness of the swamps. Then he rushed across the room. An orange-colored flame leaped like a panther at the lavender trousers. This animal bit deeply into Johnson. There was an explosion at one side, and suddenly before him there reared a delicate, trembling sapphire shape like a fairy lady. With a quiet smile she blocked his path and doomed him and Jimmie. Johnson shrieked, and then ducked in the manner of his race in fights. He aimed to pass under the left guard of the sapphire lady. But she was swifter than eagles, and her talons caught in him as he plunged past her. Bowing his head as if his neck had been struck, Johnson lurched forward, twisting this way and that way. He fell on his back. The still form in the blanket flung from his arms, rolled to the edge of the floor and beneath the window.

Johnson had fallen with his head at the base of an old-fashioned desk. There was a row of jars upon the top of this desk. For the most part, they were silent amid this rioting, but there was one which seemed to hold a scintillant and writhing serpent.

Suddenly the glass splintered, and a ruby-red snake-like thing poured its thick length out upon the top of the old desk. It coiled and hesitated, and then began to swim a languorous way down the mahogany slant. At the angle it waved its sizzling molten head to and fro over the closed eyes of the man beneath it. Then, in a moment, with a mystic impulse, it moved again, and the red snake flowed directly down into Johnson's upturned face.

Afterward the trail of this creature seemed to reek, and amid flames and low explosions drops like red-hot jewels pattered softly down it at leisurely intervals.

VIII

Suddenly all roads led to Dr. Trescott's. The whole town flowed toward one point. Chippeway Hose Company Number One toiled desperately up Bridge Street Hill even as the Tuscaroras came in an impetuous sweep down Niagara Avenue. Meanwhile the machine of the hook and ladder experts from across the creek was spinning on its way. The chief of the fire department had been playing poker in the rear room of Whiteley's cigar store, but at the first breath of the alarm he sprang through the door like a man escaping with the kitty.

In Whilomville, on these occasions, there was always a number of people who instantly turned their attention to the bells in the churches and schoolhouses. The bells not only emphasized the alarm, but it was the habit to send these sounds rolling across the sky in a stirring brazen uproar until the flames were practically vanquished. There was also a kind of rivalry as to which bell should be made to produce the greatest din. Even the Valley Church, four miles away among the farms, had heard the voices of its brethren, and immediately added a quaint little yelp.

Dr. Trescott had been driving homeward, slowly smoking a cigar, and feeling glad that this last case was now in complete obedience to him, like a wild animal that he had subdued, when he heard the long whistle, and chirped to his horse under the unlicensed but perfectly distinct impression that a fire had broken out in Oakhurst, a new and rather high-flying suburb of the town which was at least two miles from his own home. But in the second blast and in the ensuing silence he read the designation of his own district. He was then only a few blocks from his house. He took out the whip and laid it lightly on the mare. Surprised and frightened at this extraordinary action, she leaped forward, and as the reins straightened like steel bands, the doctor leaned backward a trifle. When the mare whirled him up to the closed gate he was wondering whose house could be afire. The man who had rung the signal-box yelled something at him, but he already knew. He left the mare to her will.

In front of his door was a maniacal woman in a wrapper. "Ned!" she screamed at sight of him. "Jimmie! Save Jimmie!"

Trescott had grown hard and chill. "Where?" he said. "Where?"

Mrs. Trescott's voice began to bubble. "Up—up—up—" She pointed at the second-story windows.

Hannigan was already shouting: "Don't go in that way! You can't go in that way!"

Trescott ran around the corner of the house and disappeared from them. He knew from the view he had taken of the main hall that it would be impossible to ascend from there. His hopes were fastened now to the stairway which led from the laboratory. The door which opened from this room out upon the lawn was fastened with a bolt and lock, but he kicked close to the lock and then close to the bolt. The door with a loud crash flew back. The doctor recoiled from the roll of smoke, and then bending low, he stepped into the garden of burning flowers. On the floor his stinging eyes could make out a form in a smouldering blanket near the window. Then, as he carried his son toward the door, he saw that the whole lawn seemed now alive with men and boys, the leaders in the great charge that the whole town was making. They seized him and his burden, and over-powered him in wet blankets and water.

But Hannigan was howling: "Johnson is in there yet! Henry Johnson is in there yet! He went in after the kid! Johnson is in there yet!"

These cries penetrated to the sleepy senses of Trescott, and he struggled with his captors, swearing, unknown to him and to them, all the deep blasphemies of his medical-student days. He rose to his feet and went again toward the door of the laboratory. They endeavored to restrain him, although they were much affrighted at him.

But a young man who was a brakeman on the railway, and lived in one of the rear streets near the Trescotts, had gone into the laboratory and brought forth a thing which he laid on the grass.

IX

There were hoarse commands from in front of the house. "Turn on your water, Five!" "Let 'er go, One!" The gathering crowd swayed this way and that way. The flames, towering high, cast a wild red light on their faces. There came the clangor of a gong from along some adjacent street. The crowd exclaimed at it. "Here comes Number Three!" "That's Three a-comin'!" A panting and irregular mob dashed into view, dragging a hose cart. A cry of exultation arose from the little boys. "Here's Three!" The lads welcomed Never-Die Hose Company Number Three as if it was composed of a chariot dragged by a band of gods. The perspiring citizens flung themselves into the fray. The boys danced in impish joy at the displays of prowess. They acclaimed the approach of Number Two. They welcomed Number Four with cheers. They were so deeply moved by this whole affair that they bitterly guyed the late appearance of the hook and ladder company, whose heavy apparatus had almost stalled them on the Bridge Street hill. The lads hated and feared a fire, of course. They did not particularly want to have anybody's house burn, but still it was fine to see the gathering of the companies, and amid a great noise to watch their heroes perform all manner of prodigies.

They were divided into parties over the worth of different companies, and supported their creeds with no small violence. For instance, in that part of the little city where Number Four had its home it would be most daring for a boy to contend the superiority of any other company. Likewise, in another quarter, when a strange boy was asked which fire company was the best in Whilomville, he was expected to answer "Number One." Feuds, which the boys forgot and remembered according to chance or the importance of some recent event, existed all through the town.

They did not care much for John Shipley, the chief of the department. It was true that he went to a fire with the speed of a falling angel, but when there he invariably lapsed into a certain still mood, which was almost a preoccupation, moving leisurely around the burning structure and surveying it, puffing meanwhile at a cigar. This quiet man, who even when life was in danger seldom raised his voice, was not much to their fancy. Now old Sykes Huntington, when he was chief, used to bellow continually like a bull and gesticulate in a sort of delirium. He was much finer as a spectacle than this Shipley, who viewed a fire with the same steadiness that he viewed a raise in a large jack-pot. The greater number of the boys could never understand why the members of these companies persisted in re-electing Shipley, although they often pretended to understand it, because "My father says" was a very formidable phrase in argument, and the fathers seemed almost unanimous in advocating Shipley.

At this time there was considerable discussion as to which company had got the first stream of water on the fire. Most of the boys claimed that Number Five owned that distinction, but there was a determined minority who contended for Number One. Boys who were the blood adherents of other companies were obliged to choose between the two on this occasion, and the talk waxed warm.

But a great rumour went among the crowds. It was told with hushed voices. Afterward a reverent silence fell even upon the boys. Jimmie Trescott and Henry Johnson had been burned to death, and Dr. Trescott

himself had been most savagely hurt. The crowd did not even feel the
police pushing at them. They raised their eyes, shining now with awe,
toward the high flames.

The man who had information was at his best. In low tones he described the whole affair. "That was the kid's room—in the corner there.
He had measles or somethin', and this coon—Johnson—was a-settin' up
with 'im, and Johnson got sleepy or somethin' and upset the lamp, and the
doctor he was down in his office, and he came running up, and they all got
burned together till they dragged 'em out."

Another man, always preserved for the deliverance of the final judgment, was saying: "Oh, they'll die sure. Burned to flinders. No chance.
Hull lot of 'em. Anybody can see." The crowd concentrated its gaze still
more closely upon these flags of fire which waved joyfully against the black
sky. The bells of the town were clashing unceasingly.

A little procession moved across the lawn and toward the street. There
were three cots, borne by twelve of the firemen. The police moved sternly,
but it needed no effort of theirs to open a lane for this slow cortège. The
men who bore the cots were well known to the crowd, but in this solemn
parade during the ringing of the bells and the shouting, and with the red
glare upon the sky, they seemed utterly foreign, and Whilomville paid them
a deep respect. Each man in this stretcher party had gained a reflected
majesty. They were footmen to death, and the crowd made subtle obeisance to this august dignity derived from three prospective graves. One
woman turned away with a shriek at sight of the covered body on the first
stretcher, and people faced her suddenly in silent and mournful indignation. Otherwise there was barely a sound as these twelve important men
with measured tread carried their burdens through the throng.

The little boys no longer discussed the merits of the different fire companies. For the greater part they had been routed. Only the more courageous viewed closely the three figures veiled in yellow blankets.

X

Old Judge Denning Hagenthorpe, who lived nearly opposite the Trescotts,
had thrown his door wide open to receive the afflicted family. When it was
publicly learned that the doctor and his son and the negro were still alive,
it required a specially detailed policeman to prevent people from scaling
the front porch and interviewing these sorely wounded. One old lady appeared with a miraculous poultice, and she quoted most damning Scrip-
ture to the officer when he said that she could not pass him. Throughout
the night some lads old enough to be given privileges or to compel them

from their mothers remained vigilantly upon the curb in anticipation of a death or some such event. The reporter of the *Morning Tribune* rode thither on his bicycle every hour until three o'clock.

Six of the ten doctors in Whilomville attended at Judge Hagenthorpe's house.

Almost at once they were able to know that Trescott's burns were not vitally important. The child would possibly be scarred badly, but his life was undoubtedly safe. As for the negro Henry Johnson, he could not live. His body was frightfully seared, but more than that, he now had no face. His face had simply been burned away.

Trescott was always asking news of the two other patients. In the morning he seemed fresh and strong, so they told him that Johnson was doomed. They then saw him stir on the bed, and sprang quickly to see if the bandages needed readjusting. In the sudden glance he threw from one to another he impressed them as being both leonine and impracticable.

The morning paper announced the death of Henry Johnson. It contained a long interview with Edward J. Hannigan, in which the latter described in full the performance of Johnson at the fire. There was also an editorial built from all the best words in the vocabulary of the staff. The town halted in its accustomed road of thought, and turned a reverent attention to the memory of this hostler. In the breasts of many people was the regret that they had not known enough to give him a hand and a lift when he was alive, and they judged themselves stupid and ungenerous for this failure.

The name of Henry Johnson became suddenly the title of a saint to the little boys. The one who thought of it first could, by quoting it in an argument, at once overthrow his antagonist, whether it applied to the subject or whether it did not.

"Nigger, nigger, never die,
Black face and shiny eye."

Boys who had called this odious couplet in the rear of Johnson's march buried the fact at the bottom of their hearts.

Later in the day Miss Bella Farragut, of No. 7 Watermelon Alley, announced that she had been engaged to marry Mr. Henry Johnson.

XI

The old judge had a cane with an ivory head. He could never think at his best until he was leaning slightly on this stick and smoothing the white top with slow movements of his hands. It was also to him a kind of narcotic. If by any chance he mislaid it, he grew at once very irritable, and was likely to speak sharply to his sister, whose mental incapacity he had patiently endured for thirty years in the old mansion on Ontario Street. She was not at all aware of her brother's opinion of her endowments, and so it might be said that the judge had successfully dissembled for more than a quarter of a century, only risking the truth at the times when his cane was lost.

On a particular day the judge sat in his arm chair on the porch. The sunshine sprinkled through the lilac bushes and poured great coins on the boards. The sparrows disputed in the trees that lined the pavements. The judge mused deeply, while his hands gently caressed the ivory head of his cane.

Finally he arose and entered the house, his brow still furrowed in a thoughtful frown. His stick thumped solemnly in regular beats. On the second floor he entered a room where Dr. Trescott was working about the bedside of Henry Johnson. The bandages on the negro's head allowed only one thing to appear, an eye, which unwinkingly stared at the judge. The latter spoke to Trescott on the condition of the patient. Afterward he evidently had something further to say, but he seemed to be kept from it by the scrutiny of the unwinking eye, at which he furtively glanced from time to time.

When Jimmie Trescott was sufficiently recovered, his mother had taken him to pay a visit to his grandparents in Connecticut. The doctor had remained to take care of his patients, but as a matter of truth he spent most of his time at Judge Hagenthorpe's house, where lay Henry Johnson. Here he slept and ate almost every meal in the long nights and days of his vigil.

At dinner, and away from the magic of the unwinking eye, the judge said, suddenly, "Trescott, do you think it is—" As Trescott paused expectantly, the judge fingered his knife. He said, thoughtfully, "No one wants to advance such ideas, but somehow I think that that poor fellow ought to die."

There was in Trescott's face at once a look of recognition, as if in this tangent of the judge he saw an old problem. He merely sighed and answered, "Who knows?" The words were spoken in a deep tone that gave them an elusive kind of significance.

The judge retreated to the cold manner of the bench. "Perhaps we may not talk with propriety of this kind of action, but I am induced to say that you are performing a questionable charity in preserving this negro's life. As near as I can understand, he will hereafter be a monster, a perfect monster, and probably with an affected brain. No man can observe you as I have observed you and not know that it was a matter of conscience with you, but I am afraid, my friend, that it is one of the blunders of virtue." The judge had delivered his views with his habitual oratory. The last three words he spoke with a particular emphasis, as if the phrase was his discovery.

The doctor made a weary gesture. "He saved my boy's life."

"Yes," said the judge, swiftly—"yes, I know!"

"And what am I to do?" said Trescott, his eyes suddenly lighting like an outburst from smouldering peat. "What am I to do? He gave himself for—for Jimmie. What am I to do for him?"

The judge abased himself completely before these words. He lowered his eyes for a moment. He picked at his cucumbers.

Presently he braced himself straightly in his chair. "He will be your creation, you understand. He is purely your creation. Nature has very evidently given him up. He is dead. You are restoring him to life. You are making him, and he will be a monster, and with no mind."

"He will be what you like, Judge," cried Trescott, in sudden polite fury. "He will be anything, but, by God! he saved my boy."

The judge interrupted in a voice trembling with emotion: "Trescott! Trescott! Don't I know?"

Trescott had subsided to a sullen mood. "Yes, you know," he answered, acidly; "but you don't know all about your own boy being saved from death." This was a perfectly childish allusion to the judge's bachelorhood. Trescott knew that the remark was infantile, but he seemed to take desperate delight in it.

But it passed the judge completely. It was not his spot.

"I am puzzled," said he, in profound thought. "I don't know what to say."

Trescott had become repentant. "Don't think I don't appreciate what you say, Judge. But—"

"Of course!" responded the judge, quickly. "Of course."

"It—" began Trescott.

"Of course," said the judge.

In silence they resumed their dinner.

"Well," said the judge, ultimately, "it is hard for a man to know what to do."

"It is," said the doctor, fervidly.

There was another silence. It was broken by the judge: "Look here, Trescott; I don't want you to think—"

"No, certainly not," answered the doctor, earnestly.

"Well, I don't want you to think I would say anything to—It was only that I thought that I might be able to suggest to you that—perhaps—the affair was a little dubious."

With an appearance of suddenly disclosing his real mental perturbation, the doctor said: "Well, what would you do? Would you kill him?" he asked, abruptly and sternly.

"Trescott, you fool," said the old man, gently.

"Oh, well, I know, Judge, but then—" He turned red, and spoke with new violence: "Say, he saved my boy—do you see? He saved my boy."

"You bet he did," cried the judge, with enthusiasm. "You bet he did." And they remained for a time gazing at each other, their faces illuminated with memories of a certain deed.

After another silence, the judge said, "It is hard for a man to know what to do."

XII

Late one evening Trescott, returning from a professional call, paused his buggy at the Hagenthorpe gate. He tied the mare to the old tin-covered post, and entered the house. Ultimately he appeared with a companion— a man who walked slowly and carefully, as if he were learning. He was wrapped to the heels in an old-fashioned ulster. They entered the buggy and drove away.

After a silence only broken by the swift and musical humming of the wheels on the smooth road, Trescott spoke. "Henry," he said, "I've got you a home here with old Alek Williams. You will have everything you want to eat and a good place to sleep, and I hope you will get along there all right. I will pay all your expenses, and come to see you as often as I can. If you don't get along, I want you to let me know as soon as possible, and then we will do what we can to make it better."

The dark figure at the doctor's side answered with a cheerful laugh. "These buggy wheels don' look like I washed 'em yesterday, docteh," he said.

Trescott hesitated for a moment, and then went on insistently,

"I am taking you to Alek Williams, Henry, and I—"

The figure chuckled again. "No, 'deed! No, seh! Alek Williams don' know a hoss! 'Deed he don'. He don' know a hoss from a pig." The laugh that followed was like the rattle of pebbles.

Trescott turned and looked sternly and coldly at the dim form in the gloom from the buggy-top. "Henry," he said, "I didn't say anything about horses. I was saying—"

"Hoss? Hoss?" said the quavering voice from these near shadows. "Hoss? 'Deed I don' know all erbout a hoss! 'Deed I don't." There was a satirical chuckle.

At the end of three miles the mare slackened and the doctor leaned forward, peering, while holding tight reins. The wheels of the buggy bumped often over outcropping boulders. A window shone forth, a simple square of topaz on a great black hillside. Four dogs charged the buggy with ferocity, and when it did not promptly retreat, they circled courageously around the flanks, baying. A door opened near the window in the hillside, and a man came and stood on a beach of yellow light.

"Yah! yah! You Roveh! You Susie! Come yah! Come yah this minit!"

Trescott called across the dark sea of grass, "Hello, Alek!"

"Hello!"

"Come here and show me where to drive."

The man plunged from the beach into the surf, and Trescott could then only trace his course by the fervid and polite ejaculations of a host who was somewhere approaching. Presently Williams took the mare by the head and, uttering cries of welcome and scolding the swarming dogs, led the equipage toward the lights. When they halted at the door and Trescott was climbing out, Williams cried, "Will she stand, docteh?"

"She'll stand all right, but you better hold her for a minute. Now, Henry." The doctor turned and held both arms to the dark figure. It crawled to him painfully like a man going down a ladder. Williams took the mare away to be tied to a little tree, and when he returned he found them awaiting him in the gloom beyond the rays from the door.

He burst out then like a siphon pressed by a nervous thumb. "Hennery! Hennery, ma ol' frien'. Well, if I ain' glade. If I ain' glade!"

Trescott had taken the silent shape by the arm and led it forward into the full revelation of the light. "Well, now, Alek, you can take Henry and put him to bed, and in the morning I will—"

Near the end of this sentence old Williams had come front to front with Johnson. He gasped for a second, and then yelled the yell of a man stabbed in the heart.

For a fraction of a moment Trescott seemed to be looking for epithets. Then he roared: "You old black chump! You old black—Shut up! Shut up! Do you hear?"

Williams obeyed instantly in the matter of his screams, but he continued in a lowered voice: "Ma Lode a' massy! Who'd ever think? Ma Lode a' massy!"

Trescott spoke again in the manner of a commander of a battalion. "Alek!"

The old negro again surrendered, but to himself he repeated in a whisper, "Ma Lode!" He was aghast and trembling.

As these three points of widening shadows approached the golden doorway a hale old negress appeared there, bowing. "Good-evenin', docteh! Good-evenin'! Come in! come in!" She had evidently just retired from a tempestuous struggle to place the room in order, but she was now bowing rapidly. She made the effort of a person swimming.

"Don't trouble yourself, Mary," said Trescott, entering. "I've brought Henry for you to take care of, and all you've got to do is to carry out what I tell you." Learning that he was not followed, he faced the door, and said, "Come in, Henry."

Johnson entered. "Whee!" shrieked Mrs. Williams. She almost achieved a back somersault. Six young members of the tribe of Williams made a simultaneous plunge for a position behind the stove, and formed a wailing heap.

XIII

"You know very well that you and your family lived usually on less than three dollars a week, and now that Dr. Trescott pays you five dollars a week for Johnson's board, you live like millionaires. You haven't done a stroke of work since Johnson began to board with you—everybody knows that—and so what are you kicking about?"

The judge sat in his chair on the porch, fondling his cane, and gazing down at old Williams, who stood under the lilac bushes. "Yes, I know, Jedge," said the negro, wagging his head in a puzzled manner. "'Tain't like as if I didn't 'preciate what the docteh done, but—but—well, yeh see, Jedge," he added, gaining a new impetus, "it's—it's hard wuk. This ol' man nev' did wuk so hard. Lode, no."

"Don't talk such nonsense, Alek," spoke the judge, sharply. "You have never really worked in your life—anyhow, enough to support a family of sparrows—and now when you are in a more prosperous condition than ever before, you come around talking like an old fool."

The negro began to scratch his head. "Yeh see, Jedge," he said at last, "my ol' 'ooman she cain't 'ceive no lady callahs, nohow."

"Hang lady callers!" said the judge, irascibly. "If you have flour in the barrel and meat in the pot, your wife can get along without receiving lady callers, can't she?"

"But they won't come ainyhow, Jedge," replied Williams, with an air of still deeper stupefaction. "Noner ma wife's frien's ner noner ma frien's 'ill come near ma res'dence."

"Well, let them stay home if they are such silly people."

The old negro seemed to be seeking a way to elude this argument, but, evidently finding none, he was about to shuffle meekly off. He halted, however. "Jedge," said he, "ma ol' 'ooman's near driv' abstracted."

"Your old woman is an idiot," responded the judge.

Williams came very close and peered solemnly through a branch of lilac. "Jedge," he whispered, "the chillens."

"What about them?"

Dropping his voice to funereal depths, Williams said, "They—they cain't eat."

"Can't eat!" scoffed the judge, loudly. "Can't eat! You must think I am as big an old fool as you are. Can't eat—the little rascals! What's to prevent them from eating?"

In answer, Williams said, with mournful emphasis, "Hennery." Moved with a kind of satisfaction at his tragic use of the name, he remained staring at the judge for a sign of its effect.

The judge made a gesture of irritation. "Come, now, you old scoundrel, don't beat around the bush any more. What are you up to? What do you want? Speak out like a man, and don't give me any more of this tiresome rigamarole."

"I ain't er-beatin' round 'bout nuffin, Jedge," replied Williams, indignantly. "No, seh; I say whatter got to say right out. 'Deed I do."

"Well, say it, then."

"Jedge," began the negro, taking off his hat and switching his knee with it, "Lode knows I'd do jes' 'bout as much fer five dollehs er week as ainy cul'd man, but—but this yere business is awful, Jedge. I raikon 'ain't been no sleep in—in my house sence docteh done fetch 'im."

"Well, what do you propose to do about it?"

Williams lifted his eyes from the ground and gazed off through the trees. "Raikon I got good appetite, an' sleep jes' like er dog, but he—he's done broke me all up. 'Tain't no good, nohow. I wake up in the night; I hear 'im, mebbe, er-whimperin' an' er-whimperin', an' I sneak an' I sneak until I try th' do' to see if he locked in. An' he keep me er-puzzlin' an' er-quakin' all night long. Don't know how'll do in th' winter. Can't let 'im out where th' chillen is. He'll done freeze where he is now." Williams spoke these sentences as if he were talking to himself. After a silence of deep reflection he continued: "Folks go round sayin' he ain't Hennery Johnson at all. They say he's er devil!"

"What?" cried the judge.

"Yesseh," repeated Williams, in tones of injury, as if his veracity had been challenged. "Yesseh. I'm er-tellin' it to yeh straight, Jedge. Plenty cul'd people folks up my way say it is a devil."

"Well, you don't think so yourself, do you?"

"No. 'Tain't no devil. It's Hennery Johnson."

"Well, then what is the matter with you? You don't care what a lot of foolish people say. Go on tending to your business, and pay no attention to such idle nonsense."

"'Tis nonsense, Jedge; but he *looks* like er devil."

"What do you care what he looks like?" demanded the judge.

"Ma rent is two dollehs and er half er month," said Williams, slowly.

"It might just as well be ten thousand dollars a month," responded the judge. "You never pay it, anyhow."

"Then, anoth' thing," continued Williams, in his reflective tone. "If he was all right in his haid I could stan' it; but, Jedge, he's crazier 'n er loon. Then when he looks like er devil, an' done skears all ma frien's away, an' ma chillens cain't eat, an' ma ole 'ooman jes' raisin' Cain all the time, an' ma rent two dollehs an' er half er month, an' him not right in his haid, it seems like five dollehs er week—"

The judge's stick came down sharply and suddenly upon the floor of the porch. "There," he said, "I thought that was what you were driving at."

Williams began swinging his head from side to side in the strange racial mannerism. "Now hol' on a minnet, Jedge," he said, defensively. "'Tain't like as if I didn't 'preciate what the docteh done. 'Tain't that. Docteh Trescott is er kind man, an' 'tain't like as if I didn't 'preciate what he done; but—but—"

"But what? You are getting painful, Alek. Now tell me this: did you ever have five dollars a week regularly before in your life?"

Williams at once drew himself up with great dignity, but in the pause after that question he drooped gradually to another attitude. In the end he answered, heroically: "No, Jedge, I ain't. An' 'tain't like as if I was er-sayin' five dollehs wasn't er lot er money for a man like me. But, Jedge, what er man oughter git fer this kinder wuk is er salary. Yesseh, Jedge," he repeated, with a great impressive gesture; "fer this kinder wuk er man oughter git er Salary." He laid a terrible emphasis upon the final word.

The judge laughed. "I know Dr. Trescott's mind concerning this affair, Alek; and if you are dissatisfied with your boarder, he is quite ready to move him to some other place; so, if you care to leave word with me that you are tired of the arrangement and wish it changed, he will come and take Johnson away."

Williams scratched his head again in deep perplexity. "Five dollehs is er big price fer bo'd, but 'tain't no big price fer the bo'd of er crazy man," he said, finally.

"What do you think you ought to get?" asked the judge.

"Well," answered Alek, in the manner of one deep in a balancing of the scales, "he looks like er devil, an' done skears e'rybody, an' ma chillens cain't eat, an' I cain't sleep, an' he ain't right in his haid, an'—"

"You told me all those things."

After scratching his wool, and beating his knee with his hat, and gazing off through the trees and down at the ground, Williams said, as he kicked nervously at the gravel, "Well, Jedge, I think it is wuth—" He stuttered.

"Worth what?"

"Six dollehs," answered Williams, in a desperate outburst.

The judge lay back in his great arm-chair and went through all the motions of a man laughing heartily, but he made no sound save a slight cough. Williams had been watching him with apprehension.

"Well," said the judge, "do you call six dollars a salary?"

"No, seh," promptly responded Williams. "'Tain't a salary. No, 'deed! 'Tain't a salary." He looked with some anger upon the man who questioned his intelligence in this way.

"Well, supposing your children can't eat?"

"I—"

"And supposing he looks like a devil? And supposing all those things continue? Would you be satisfied with six dollars a week?"

Recollections seemed to throng in Williams's mind at these interrogations, and he answered dubiously. "Of co'se a man who ain't right in his haid, an' looks like er devil—But six dollehs—" After these two attempts at a sentence Williams suddenly appeared as an orator, with a great shiny palm waving in the air. "I tell yeh, Jedge, six dollehs is six dollehs, but if I git six dollehs for bo'ding Hennery Johnson, I uhns it! I uhns it!"

"I don't doubt that you earn six dollars for every week's work you do," said the judge.

"Well, if I bo'd Hennery Johnson fer six dollehs er week, I uhns it! I uhns it!" cried Williams, wildly.

XIV

Reifsnyder's assistant had gone to his supper, and the owner of the shop was trying to placate four men who wished to be shaved at once. Reifsnyder was very garrulous—a fact which made him rather remarkable among barbers, who, as a class, are austerely speechless, having been taught silence by the hammering reiteration of a tradition. It is the customers who talk in the ordinary event.

As Reifsnyder waved his razor down the cheek of a man in the chair, he turned often to cool the impatience of the others with pleasant talk, which they did not particularly heed.

"Oh, he should have let him die," said Bainbridge, a railway engineer, finally replying to one of the barber's orations. "Shut up, Reif, and go on with your business!"

Instead, Reifsnyder paused shaving entirely, and turned to front the speaker. "Let him die?" he demanded. "How vas that? How can you let a man die?"

"By letting him die, you chump," said the engineer. The others laughed a little, and Reifsnyder turned at once to his work, sullenly, as a man overwhelmed by the derision of numbers.

"How vas that?" he grumbled later. "How can you let a man die when he has done so much for you?"

"'When he has done so much for you?'" repeated Bainbridge. "You better shave some people. 'How vas that?' Maybe this ain't a barber shop?"

A man hitherto silent now said, "If I had been the doctor, I would have done the same thing."

"Of course," said Reifsnyder. "Any man vould do it. Any man that vas not like you, you—old—flint-hearted—fish." He had sought the final words with painful care, and he delivered the collection triumphantly at Bainbridge. The engineer laughed.

The man in the chair now lifted himself higher, while Reifsnyder began an elaborate ceremony of anointing and combing his hair. Now free to join comfortably in the talk, the man said: "They say he is the most terrible thing in the world. Young Johnnie Bernard—that drives the grocery wagon—saw him up at Alek Williams's shanty, and he says he couldn't eat anything for two days."

"Chee!" said Reifsnyder.

"Well, what makes him so terrible?" asked another.

"Because he hasn't got any face," replied the barber and the engineer in duet.

"Hasn't got any face!" repeated the man. "How can he do without any face?"

"He has no face in the front of his head,
In the place where his face ought to grow."

Bainbridge sang these lines pathetically as he arose and hung his hat on a hook. The man in the chair was about to abdicate in his favor. "Get a gait on you now," he said to Reifsnyder. "I go out at 7.31."

As the barber foamed the lather on the cheeks of the engineer he seemed to be thinking heavily. Then suddenly he burst out. "How would you like to be with no face?" he cried to the assemblage.

"Oh, if I had to have a face like yours—" answered one customer.

Bainbridge's voice came from a sea of lather. "You're kicking because if losing faces became popular, you'd have to go out of business."

"I don't think it will become so much popular," said Reifsnyder.

"Not if it's got to be taken off in the way his was taken off," said another man. "I'd rather keep mine, if you don't mind."

"I guess so!" cried the barber. "Just think!"

The shaving of Bainbridge had arrived at a time of comparative liberty for him. "I wonder what the doctor says to himself?" he observed. "He may be sorry he made him live."

"It was the only thing he could do," replied a man. The others seemed to agree with him.

"Supposing you were in his place," said one, "and Johnson had saved your kid. What would you do?"

"Certainly!"

"Of course! You would do anything on earth for him. You'd take all the trouble in the world for him. And spend your last dollar on him. Well, then?"

"I wonder how it feels to be without any face?" said Reifsnyder, musingly.

The man who had previously spoken, feeling that he had expressed himself well, repeated the whole thing. "You would do anything on earth for him. You'd take all the trouble in the world for him. And spend your last dollar on him. Well, then?"

"No, but look," said Reifsnyder; "supposing you don't got a face!"

XV

As soon as Williams was hidden from the view of the old judge he began to gesture and talk to himself. An elation had evidently penetrated to his vitals, and caused him to dilate as if he had been filled with gas. He snapped his fingers in the air, and whistled fragments of triumphal music. At times, in his progress toward his shanty, he indulged in a shuffling movement that was really a dance. It was to be learned from the intermediate monologue that he had emerged from his trials laurelled and proud. He was the unconquerable Alexander Williams. Nothing could exceed the bold self-reliance of his manner. His kingly stride, his heroic song, the derisive flourish of his hands—all betokened a man who had successfully defied the world.

On his way he saw Zeke Paterson coming to town. They hailed each other at a distance of fifty yards.

"How do, Broth' Paterson?"

"How do, Broth' Williams?"

They were both deacons.

"Is you' folks well, Broth' Paterson?"

"Middlin', middlin'. How's you' folks, Broth' Williams?"

Neither of them had slowed his pace in the smallest degree. They had simply begun this talk when a considerable space separated them, continued it as they passed, and added polite questions as they drifted steadily apart. Williams's mind seemed to be a balloon. He had been so inflated that he had not noticed that Paterson had definitely shied into the dry ditch as they came to the point of ordinary contact.

Afterward, as he went a lonely way, he burst out again in song and pantomimic celebration of his estate. His feet moved in prancing steps.

When he came in sight of his cabin, the fields were bathed in a blue dusk, and the light in the window was pale. Cavorting and gesticulating, he gazed joyfully for some moments upon this light. Then suddenly another idea seemed to attack his mind, and he stopped, with an air of being suddenly dampened. In the end he approached his home as if it were the fortress of an enemy.

Some dogs disputed his advance for a loud moment, and then discovering their lord, slunk away embarrassed. His reproaches were addressed to them in muffled tones.

Arriving at the door, he pushed it open with the timidity of a new thief. He thrust his head cautiously sideways, and his eyes met the eyes of his wife, who sat by the table, the lamplight defining a half of her face. "Sh!" he said, uselessly. His glance travelled swiftly to the inner door which shielded the one bedchamber. The pickaninnies, strewn upon the floor of the living-room, were softly snoring. After a hearty meal they had promptly dispersed themselves about the place and gone to sleep. "Sh!" said Williams again to his motionless and silent wife. He had allowed only his head to appear. His wife, with one hand upon the edge of the table and the other at her knee, was regarding him with wide eyes and parted lips as if he were a spectre. She looked to be one who was living in terror, and even the familiar face at the door had thrilled her because it had come suddenly.

Williams broke the tense silence. "Is he all right?" he whispered, waving his eyes toward the inner door. Following his glance timorously, his wife nodded, and in a low tone answered:

"I raikon he's done gone t' sleep."

Williams then slunk noiselessly across his threshold.

He lifted a chair, and with infinite care placed it so that it faced the dreaded inner door. His wife moved slightly, so as to also squarely face it. A silence came upon them in which they seemed to be waiting for a calamity, pealing and deadly.

Williams finally coughed behind his hand. His wife started, and looked upon him in alarm. "'Pears like he done gwine keep quiet ternight," he breathed. They continually pointed their speech and their looks at the inner door, paying it the homage due to a corpse or a phantom. Another long stillness followed this sentence. Their eyes shone white and wide. A wagon rattled down the distant road. From their chairs they looked at the window, and the effect of the light in the cabin was a presentation of an intensely black and solemn night. The old woman adopted the attitude used always in church at funerals. At times she seemed to be upon the point of breaking out in prayer.

"He mighty quiet ternight," whispered Williams. "Was he good terday?" For answer his wife raised her eyes to the ceiling in the supplication of Job. Williams moved restlessly. Finally he tiptoed to the door. He knelt slowly and without a sound, and placed his ear near the keyhole. Hearing a noise behind him, he turned quickly. His wife was staring at him aghast. She stood in front of the stove, and her arms were spread out in the natural movement to protect all her sleeping ducklings.

But Williams arose without having touched the door. "I raikon he ersleep," he said, fingering his wool. He debated with himself for some time. During this interval his wife remained, a great fat statue of a mother shielding her children.

It was plain that his mind was swept suddenly by a wave of temerity. With a sounding step he moved toward the door. His fingers were almost upon the knob when he swiftly ducked and dodged away, clapping his hands to the back of his head. It was as if the portal had threatened him. There was a little tumult near the stove, where Mrs. Williams's desperate retreat had involved her feet with the prostrate children.

After the panic Williams bore traces of a feeling of shame. He returned to the charge. He firmly grasped the knob with his left hand, and with his other hand turned the key in the lock. He pushed the door, and as it swung portentously open he sprang nimbly to one side like the fearful slave liberating the lion. Near the stove a group had formed, the terror-stricken mother, with her arms stretched, and the aroused children clinging frenziedly to her skirts.

The light streamed after the swinging door, and disclosed a room six feet one way and six feet the other way. It was small enough to enable the radiance to lay it plain. Williams peered warily around the corner made by the doorpost.

Suddenly he advanced, retired, and advanced again with a howl. His palsied family had expected him to spring backward, and at his howl they heaped themselves wondrously. But Williams simply stood in the little room emitting his howls before an open window. "He's gone! He's gone! He's gone!" His eye and his hand had speedily proved the fact. He had even thrown open a little cupboard.

Presently he came flying out. He grabbed his hat and hurled the outer door back upon its hinges. Then he tumbled headlong into the night. He was yelling: "Docteh Trescott! Docteh Trescott!" He ran wildly through the fields and galloped in the direction of town. He continued to call to Trescott, as if the latter was within easy hearing. It was as if Trescott was poised in the contemplative sky over the running negro, and could heed this reaching voice—"Docteh Trescott!"

In the cabin, Mrs. Williams, supported by relays from the battalion of children, stood quaking watch until the truth of daylight came as a reinforcement and made them arrogant, strutting, swashbuckler children and a mother who proclaimed her illimitable courage.

XVI

Theresa Page was giving a party. It was the outcome of a long series of arguments addressed to her mother, which had been overheard in part by her father. He had at last said five words, "Oh, let her have it." The mother had then gladly capitulated.

Theresa had written nineteen invitations, and distributed them at recess to her schoolmates. Later her mother had composed five large cakes, and still later a vast amount of lemonade.

So the nine little girls and the ten little boys sat quite primly in the dining-room, while Theresa and her mother plied them with cake and lemonade, and also with ice-cream. This primness sat now quite strangely upon them. It was owing to the presence of Mrs. Page. Previously in the parlor alone with their games they had overturned a chair; the boys had let more or less of their hoodlum spirit shine forth. But when circumstances could be possibly magnified to warrant it, the girls made the boys victims of an insufferable pride, snubbing them mercilessly. So in the dining-room they resembled a class at Sunday school, if it were not for the subterranean smiles, gestures, rebuffs, and poutings which stamped the affair as a children's party.

Two little girls of this subdued gathering were planted in a settle with their backs to the broad window. They were beaming lovingly upon each other with an effect of scorning the boys.

Hearing a noise behind her at the window, one little girl turned to face it. Instantly she screamed and sprang away, covering her face with her hands. "What was it? What was it?" cried every one in a roar. Some slight movement of the eyes of the weeping and shuddering child informed the company that she had been frightened by an appearance at the window. At once they all faced the imperturbable window, and for a moment there was a silence. An astute lad made an immediate census of the other lads. The prank of slipping out and looming spectrally at a window was too venerable. But the little boys were all present and astonished.

As they recovered their minds they uttered warlike cries, and through a side door sallied rapidly out against the terror. They vied with each other in daring.

None wished particularly to encounter a dragon in the darkness of the garden, but there could be no faltering when the fair ones in the dining-room were present. Calling to each other in stern voices, they went dragooning over the lawn, attacking the shadows with ferocity, but still with the caution of reasonable beings. They found, however, nothing new to the peace of the night. Of course there was a lad who told a great lie. He described a grim figure, bending low and slinking off along the fence. He gave a number of details, rendering his lie more splendid by a repetition of certain forms which he recalled from romances. For instance, he insisted that he had heard the creature emit a hollow laugh.

Inside the house the little girl who had raised the alarm was still shuddering and weeping. With the utmost difficulty was she brought to a state approximating calmness by Mrs. Page. Then she wanted to go home at once.

Page entered the house at this time. He had exiled himself until he concluded that this children's party was finished and gone. He was obliged to escort the little girl home because she screamed again when they opened the door and she saw the night.

She was not coherent even to her mother. Was it a man? She didn't know. It was simply a thing, a dreadful thing.

XVII

In Watermelon Alley the Farraguts were spending their evening as usual on the little rickety porch. Sometimes they howled gossip to other people on other rickety porches. The thin wail of a baby arose from a near house. A man had a terrific altercation with his wife, to which the alley paid no attention at all.

There appeared suddenly before the Farraguts' a monster making a low and sweeping bow. There was an instant's pause, and then occurred something that resembled the effect of an upheaval of the earth's surface. The old woman hurled herself backward with a dreadful cry. Young Sim had been perched gracefully on a railing. At sight of the monster he simply fell over it to the ground. He made no sound, his eyes stuck out, his nerveless hands tried to grapple the rail to prevent a tumble, and then he vanished. Bella, blubbering, and with her hair suddenly and mysteriously dishevelled, was crawling on her hands and knees fearsomely up the steps.

Standing before this wreck of a family gathering, the monster continued to bow. It even raised a deprecatory claw. "Don' make no botheration 'bout me, Miss Fa'gut," it said, politely. "No, 'deed. I jes' drap in ter ax if yer well this evenin', Miss Fa'gut. Don' make no botheration. No, 'deed. I gwine ax you to go to er daince with me, Miss Fa'gut. I ax you if I can have the magnifercent gratitude of you' company on that 'casion, Miss Fa'gut."

The girl cast a miserable glance behind her. She was still crawling away. On the ground beside the porch young Sim raised a strange bleat, which expressed both his fright and his lack of wind. Presently the monster, with a fashionable amble, ascended the steps after the girl.

She grovelled in a corner of the room as the creature took a chair. It seated itself very elegantly on the edge. It held an old cap in both hands. "Don' make no botheration, Miss Fa'gut. Don' make no botheration. No, 'deed. I jes' drap in ter ax you if you won' do me the proud of acceptin' ma humble invitation to er daince, Miss Fa'gut."

She shielded her eyes with her arms and tried to crawl past it, but the genial monster blocked the way. "I jes' drap in ter ax you 'bout er daince, Miss Fa'gut. I ax you if I kin have the magnifercent gratitude of you' company on that 'casion, Miss Fa'gut."

In a last outbreak of despair, the girl, shuddering and wailing, threw herself face downward on the floor, while the monster sat on the edge of the chair gabbling courteous invitations, and holding the old hat daintily to his stomach.

At the back of the house, Mrs. Farragut, who was of enormous weight, and who for eight years had done little more than sit in an armchair and describe her various ailments, had with speed and agility scaled a high board fence.

XVIII

The black mass in the middle of Trescott's property was hardly allowed to cool before the builders were at work on another house. It had sprung upward at a fabulous rate. It was like a magical composition born of the ashes. The doctor's office was the first part to be completed, and he had already moved in his new books and instruments and medicines.

Trescott sat before his desk when the chief of police arrived. "Well, we found him," said the latter.

"Did you?" cried the doctor. "Where?"

"Shambling around the streets at daylight this morning. I'll be blamed if I can figure on where he passed the night."

"Where is he now?"

"Oh, we jugged him. I didn't know what else to do with him. That's what I want you to tell me. Of course we can't keep him. No charge could be made, you know."

"I'll come down and get him."

The official grinned retrospectively. "Must say he had a fine career while he was out. First thing he did was to break up a children's party at Page's. Then he went to Watermelon Alley. Whoo! He stampeded the whole outfit. Men, women, and children running pell-mell, and yelling. They say one old woman broke her leg, or something, shinning over a fence. Then he went right out on the main street, and an Irish girl threw a fit, and there was a sort of a riot. He began to run, and a big crowd chased him, firing rocks. But he gave them the slip somehow down there by the foundry and in the railroad yard. We looked for him all night, but couldn't find him."

"Was he hurt any? Did anybody hit him with a stone?"

"Guess there isn't much of him to hurt anymore, is there? Guess he's been hurt up to the limit. No. They never touched him. Of course nobody really wanted to hit him, but you know how a crowd gets. It's like—it's like—"

"Yes, I know."

For a moment the chief of the police looked reflectively at the floor. Then he spoke hesitatingly. "You know Jake Winter's little girl was the one that he scared at the party. She is pretty sick, they say."

"Is she? Why, they didn't call me. I always attend the Winter family."

"No? Didn't they?" asked the chief, slowly. "Well—you know— Winter is—well, Winter has gone clean crazy over this business. He wanted—he wanted to have you arrested."

"Have me arrested? The idiot! What in the name of wonder could he have me arrested for?"

"Of course. He is a fool. I told him to keep his trap shut. But then you know how he'll go all over town yapping about the thing. I thought I'd better tip you."

"Oh, he is of no consequence; but then, of course, I'm obliged to you, Sam."

"That's all right. Well, you'll be down tonight and take him out, eh? You'll get a good welcome from the jailer. He don't like his job for a cent. He says you can have your man whenever you want him. He's got no use for him."

"But what is this business of Winter's about having me arrested?"

"Oh, it's a lot of chin about your having no right to allow this—this—this man to be at large. But I told him to tend to his own business. Only I thought I'd better let you know. And I might as well say right now, doctor, that there is a good deal of talk about this thing. If I were you, I'd come to the jail pretty late at night, because there is likely to be a crowd around the door, and I'd bring a—er—mask, or some kind of a veil, anyhow."

XIX

Martha Goodwin was single, and well along into the thin years. She lived with her married sister in Whilomville. She performed nearly all the house work in exchange for the privilege of existence. Every one tacitly recognized her labor as a form of penance for the early end of her betrothed, who had died of smallpox, which he had not caught from her.

But despite the strenuous and unceasing workday of her life, she was a woman of great mind. She had adamantine opinions upon the situation in Armenia, the condition of women in China, the flirtation between Mrs. Minster of Niagara Avenue and young Griscom, the conflict in the Bible class of the Baptist Sunday-school, the duty of the United States toward the Cuban insurgents, and many other colossal matters. Her fullest experience of violence was gained on an occasion when she had seen a hound clubbed, but in the plan which she had made for the reform of the world she advocated drastic measures. For instance, she contended that all the Turks should be pushed into the sea and drowned, and that Mrs. Minster and young Griscom should be hanged side by side on twin gallows. In fact, this woman of peace, who had seen only peace, argued constantly for a creed of illimitable ferocity. She was invulnerable on these questions, because eventually she overode all opponents with a sniff. The sniff was an active force. It was to her antagonists like a bang over the head, and none was known to recover from this expression of exalted contempt. It left them

windless and conquered. They never again came forward as candidates for
suppression. And Martha walked her kitchen with a stern brow, an invincible being like Napoleon.

Nevertheless her acquaintances, from the pain of their defeats, had
been long in secret revolt. It was in no wise a conspiracy, because they did
not care to state their open rebellion, but nevertheless it was understood
that any woman who could not coincide with one of Martha's contentions
was entitled to the support of others in the small circle. It amounted to an
arrangement by which all were required to disbelieve any theory for which
Martha fought. This, however, did not prevent them from speaking of her
mind with profound respect.

Two people bore the brunt of her ability. Her sister Kate was visibly
afraid of her, while Carrie Dungen sailed across from her kitchen to sit respectfully at Martha's feet and learn the business of the world. To be sure,
afterward, under another sun, she always laughed at Martha and pretended
to deride her ideas, but in the presence of the sovereign she always remained silent or admiring. Kate, the sister, was of no consequence at all.
Her principal delusion was that she did all the work in the upstairs rooms
of the house, while Martha did it downstairs. The truth was seen only by
the husband, who treated Martha with a kindness that was half banter,
half deference. Martha herself had no suspicion that she was the only pillar of the domestic edifice. The situation was without definitions. Martha
made definitions, but she devoted them entirely to the Armenians and
Griscom and the Chinese and other subjects. Her dreams, which in early
days had been of love, of meadows and the shade of trees, of the face of a
man, were now involved otherwise, and they were companioned in the
kitchen curiously, Cuba, the hot-water kettle, Armenia, the washing of the
dishes, and the whole thing being jumbled. In regard to social misdemean-
ors, she who was simply the mausoleum of a dead passion was probably
the most savage critic in town. This unknown woman, hidden in a kitchen
as in a well, was sure to have a considerable effect of the one kind or the
other in the life of the town. Every time it moved a yard, she had personally
contributed an inch. She could hammer so stoutly upon the door of a proposition that it would break from its hinges and fall upon her, but at any rate
it moved. She was an engine, and the fact that she did not know that she
was an engine contributed largely to the effect. One reason that she was
formidable was that she did not even imagine that she was formidable. She
remained a weak, innocent, and pigheaded creature, who alone would
defy the universe if she thought the universe merited this proceeding.

One day Carrie Dungen came across from her kitchen with speed. She
had a great deal of grist. "Oh," she cried, "Henry Johnson got away from

where they was keeping him, and came to town last night, and scared everybody almost to death."

Martha was shining a dish-pan, polishing madly. No reasonable person could see cause for this operation, because the pan already glistened like silver. "Well!" she ejaculated. She imparted to the word a deep meaning. "This, my prophecy, has come to pass." It was a habit.

The overplus of information was choking Carrie. Before she could go on she was obliged to struggle for a moment. "And, oh, little Sadie Winter is awful sick, and they say Jake Winter was around this morning trying to get Doctor Trescott arrested. And poor old Mrs. Farragut sprained her ankle in trying to climb a fence. And there's a crowd around the jail all the time. They put Henry in jail because they didn't know what else to do with him, I guess. They say he is perfectly terrible."

Martha finally released the dish-pan and confronted the headlong speaker. "Well!" she said again, poising a great brown rag. Kate had heard the excited newcomer, and drifted down from the novel in her room. She was a shivery little woman. Her shoulderblades seemed to be two panes of ice, for she was constantly shrugging and shrugging. "Serves him right if he was to lose all his patients," she said suddenly, in blood-thirsty tones. She snipped her words out as if her lips were scissors.

"Well, he's likely to," shouted Carrie Dungen. "Don't a lot of people say that they won't have him any more? If you're sick and nervous, Doctor Trescott would scare the life out of you, wouldn't he? He would me. I'd keep thinking."

Martha, stalking to and fro, sometimes surveyed the two other women with a contemplative frown.

XX

After the return from Connecticut, little Jimmie was at first much afraid of the monster who lived in the room over the carriage house. He could not identify it in any way. Gradually, however, his fear dwindled under the influence of a weird fascination. He sidled into closer and closer relations with it.

One time the monster was seated on a box behind the stable basking in the rays of the afternoon sun. A heavy crepe veil was swathed about its head.

Little Jimmie and many companions came around the corner of the stable. They were all in what was popularly known as the baby class, and consequently escaped from school a half hour before the other children.

They halted abruptly at sight of the figure on the box. Jimmie waved his hand with the air of a proprietor.

"There he is," he said.

"O-o-o!" murmured all the little boys—"o-o-o!" They shrank back and grouped according to courage or experience, as at the sound the monster slowly turned its head. Jimmie had remained in the van alone. "Don't be afraid! I won't let him hurt you," he said, delighted.

"Huh!" they replied, contemptuously. "We ain't afraid."

Jimmie seemed to reap all the joys of the owner and exhibitor of one of the world's marvels, while his audience remained at a distance—awed and entranced, fearful and envious.

One of them addressed Jimmie gloomily. "Bet you dassent walk right up to him." He was an older boy than Jimmie, and habitually oppressed him to a small degree. This new social elevation of the smaller lad probably seemed revolutionary to him.

"Huh!" said Jimmie, with deep scorn. "Dassent I? Dassent I, hey? Dassent I?"

The group was immensely excited. It turned its eyes upon the boy that Jimmie addressed. "No, you dassent," he said, stolidly, facing a moral defeat. He could see that Jimmie was resolved. "No, you dassent," he repeated, doggedly.

"Ho?" cried Jimmie. "You just watch!—you just watch!"

Amid a silence he turned and marched toward the monster. But possibly the palpable wariness of his companions had an effect upon him that weighed more than his previous experience, for suddenly, when near to the monster, he halted dubiously. But his playmates immediately uttered a derisive shout, and it seemed to force him forward. He went to the monster and laid his hand delicately on its shoulder. "Hello, Henry," he said, in a voice that trembled a trifle. The monster was crooning a weird line of negro melody that was scarcely more than a thread of sound, and it paid no heed to the boy.

Jimmie strutted back to his companions. They acclaimed him and hooted his opponent. Amid this clamor the larger boy with difficulty preserved a dignified attitude.

"I dassent, dassent I?" said Jimmie to him. "Now, you're so smart, let's see you do it!"

This challenge brought forth renewed taunts from the others. The larger boy puffed out his cheeks. "Well, I ain't afraid," he explained, sullenly. He had made a mistake in diplomacy, and now his small enemies were tumbling his prestige all about his ears. They crowed like roosters and bleated like lambs, and made many other noises which were supposed to bury him in ridicule and dishonor. "Well, I ain't afraid," he continued to explain through the din.

Jimmie, the hero of the mob, was pitiless. "You ain't afraid, hey?" he sneered. "If you ain't afraid, go do it, then."

"Well, I would if I wanted to," the other retorted. His eyes wore an expression of profound misery, but he preserved steadily other portions of a pot-valiant air. He suddenly faced one of his persecutors. "If you're so smart, why don't you go do it?" This persecutor sank promptly through the group to the rear. The incident gave the badgered one a breathing-spell, and for a moment even turned the derision in another direction. He took advantage of his interval. "I'll do it if anybody else will," he announced, swaggering to and fro.

Candidates for the adventure did not come forward. To defend themselves from this counter-charge, the other boys again set up their crowing and bleating. For a while they would hear nothing from him. Each time he opened his lips their chorus of noises made oratory impossible. But at last he was able to repeat that he would volunteer to dare as much in the affair as any other boy.

"Well, you go first," they shouted.

But Jimmie intervened to once more lead the populace against the large boy. "You're mighty brave, ain't you?" he said to him. "You dared me to do it, and I did—didn't I? Now who's afraid?" The others cheered this view loudly, and they instantly resumed the baiting of the large boy.

He shamefacedly scratched his left shin with his right foot. "Well, I ain't afraid." He cast an eye at the monster. "Well, I ain't afraid." With a glare of hatred at his squalling tormentors, he finally announced a grim intention. "Well, I'll do it, then, since you're so fresh. Now!"

The mob subsided as with a formidable countenance he turned toward the impassive figure on the box. The advance was also a regular progression from high daring to craven hesitation. At last, when some yards from the monster, the lad came to a full halt, as if he had encountered a stone wall. The observant little boys in the distance promptly hooted. Stung again by these cries, the lad sneaked two yards forward. He was crouched like a young cat ready for a backward spring. The crowd at the rear, beginning to respect this display, uttered some encouraging cries. Suddenly the lad gathered himself together, made a white and desperate rush forward, touched the monster's shoulder with a far-out-stretched finger, and sped away, while his laughter rang out wild, shrill, and exultant.

The crowd of boys reverenced him at once, and began to throng into his camp, and look at him, and be his admirers. Jimmie was discomfited for a moment, but he and the larger boy, without agreement or word of any kind, seemed to recognize a truce, and they swiftly combined and began to parade before the others.

"Why, it's just as easy as nothing," puffed the larger boy. "Ain't it, Jim?"

"Course," blew Jimmie. "Why, it's as e-e-easy."

They were people of another class. If they had been decorated for courage on twelve battle-fields, they could not have made the other boys more ashamed of the situation.

Meanwhile they condescended to explain the emotions of the excursion, expressing unqualified contempt for any one who could hang back. "Why, it ain't nothin'. He won't do nothin' to you," they told the others, in tones of exasperation.

One of the very smallest boys in the party showed signs of a wistful desire to distinguish himself, and they turned their attention to him, pushing at his shoulders while he swung away from them, and hesitated dreamily. He was eventually induced to make furtive expedition, but it was only for a few yards. Then he paused, motionless, gazing with open mouth. The vociferous entreaties of Jimmie and the large boy had no power over him.

Mrs. Hannigan had come out on her back porch with a pail of water. From this coign she had a view of the secluded portion of the Trescott grounds that were behind the stable. She perceived the group of boys, and the monster on the box. She shaded her eyes with her hand to benefit her vision. She screeched then as if she was being murdered. "Eddie! Eddie! You come home this minute!"

Her son querulously demanded, "Aw, what for?"

"You come home this minute. Do you hear?"

The other boys seemed to think this visitation upon one of their number required them to preserve for a time the hang-dog air of a collection of culprits, and they remained in guilty silence until the little Hannigan, wrathfully protesting, was pushed through the door of his home. Mrs. Hannigan cast a piercing glance over the group, stared with a bitter face at the Trescott house, as if this new and handsome edifice was insulting her, and then followed her son.

There was wavering in the party. An inroad by one mother always caused them to carefully sweep the horizon to see if there were more coming. "This is my yard," said Jimmie, proudly. "We don't have to go home."

The monster on the box had turned its black crepe countenance toward the sky, and was waving its arms in time to a religious chant. "Look at him now," cried a little boy. They turned, and were transfixed by the solemnity and mystery of the indefinable gestures. The wail of the melody was mournful and slow. They drew back. It seemed to spellbind them with the power of a funeral. They were so absorbed that they did not hear the doctor's buggy drive up to the stable. Trescott got out, tied his horse, and approached the group. Jimmie saw him first, and at his look of dismay the others wheeled.

"What's all this, Jimmie?" asked Trescott, in surprise.

The lad advanced to the front of his companions, halted, and said nothing. Trescott's face gloomed slightly as he scanned the scene.

"What were you doing, Jimmie?"

"We was playin'," answered Jimmie, huskily.

"Playing at what?"

"Just playin'."

Trescott looked gravely at the other boys, and asked them to please go home. They proceeded to the street much in the manner of frustrated and revealed assassins. The crime of trespass on another boy's place was still a crime when they had only accepted the other boy's cordial invitation, and they were used to being sent out of all manner of gardens upon the sudden appearance of a father or a mother. Jimmie had wretchedly watched the departure of his companions. It involved the loss of his position as a lad who controlled the privileges of his father's grounds, but then he knew that in the beginning he had no right to ask so many boys to be his guests.

Once on the sidewalk, however, they speedily forgot their shame as trespassers, and the large boy launched forth in a description of his success in the late trial of courage. As they went rapidly up the street, the little boy who had made the furtive expedition cried out confidently from the rear, "Yes, and I went almost up to him, didn't I, Willie?"

The large boy crushed him in a few words. "Huh!" he scoffed. "You only went a little way. I went clear up to him."

The pace of the other boys was so manly that the tiny thing had to trot, and he remained at the rear, getting entangled in their legs in his attempts to reach the front rank and become of some importance, dodging this way and that way, and always piping out his little claim to glory.

XXI

"By the way, Grace," said Trescott, looking into the dining-room from his office door, "I wish you would send Jimmie to me before school-time."

When Jimmie came, he advanced so quietly that Trescott did not at first note him. "Oh," he said, wheeling from a cabinet, "here you are, young man."

"Yes, sir."

Trescott dropped into his chair and tapped the desk with a thoughtful finger. "Jimmie, what were you doing in the back garden yesterday—you and the other boys—to Henry?"

"We weren't doing anything, pa."

Trescott looked sternly into the raised eyes of his son. "Are you sure you were not annoying him in any way? Now what were you doing, exactly?"

"Why, we—why, we—now—Willie Dalzel said I dassent go right up to him, and I did; and then he did; and then—the other boys were 'fraid; and then—you comed."

Trescott groaned deeply. His countenance was so clouded in sorrow that the lad, bewildered by the mystery of it, burst suddenly forth in dismal lamentations. "There, there. Don't cry, Jim," said Trescott, going round the desk. "Only—" He sat in a great leather reading-chair, and took the boy on his knee. "Only I want to explain to you—"

After Jimmie had gone to school, and as Trescott was about to start on his round of morning calls, a message arrived from Doctor Moser. It set forth that the latter's sister was dying in the old homestead, twenty miles away up the valley, and asked Trescott to care for his patients for the day at least. There was also in the envelope a little history of each case and of what had already been done. Trescott replied to the messenger that he would gladly assent to the arrangement.

He noted that the first name on Moser's list was Winter, but this did not seem to strike him as an important fact. When its turn came, he rang the Winter bell. "Good morning, Mrs. Winter," he said, cheerfully, as the door was opened. "Doctor Moser has been obliged to leave town to-day, and he has asked me to come in his stead. How is the little girl this morning?"

Mrs. Winter had regarded him in stony surprise. At last she said: "Come in! I'll see my husband." She bolted into the house. Trescott entered the hall, and turned left into the sitting-room.

Presently Winter shuffled through the door. His eyes flashed toward Trescott. He did not betray any desire to advance far into the room. "What do you want?" he said.

"What do I want? What do I want?" repeated Trescott, lifting his head suddenly. He had heard an utterly new challenge in the night of the jungle.

"Yes, that's what I want to know," snapped Winter. "What do you want?"

Trescott was silent for a moment. He consulted Moser's memoranda. "I see that your little girl's case is a trifle serious," he remarked. "I would advise you to call a physician soon. I will leave you a copy of Dr. Moser's record to give to any one you may call." He paused to transcribe the record on a page of his note-book. Tearing out the leaf, he extended it to Winter as he moved toward the door. The latter shrunk against the wall. His head was hanging as he reached for the paper. This caused him to grasp air, and so Trescott simply let the paper flutter to the feet of the other man.

"Good morning," said Trescott from the hall. This placid retreat seemed to suddenly arouse Winter to ferocity. It was as if he had then recalled all the truths which he had formulated to hurl at Trescott. So he followed him into the hall, and down the hall to the door, and through the door to the porch, barking in fiery rage from a respectful distance. As Trescott imperturbably turned the mare's head down the road, Winter stood on the porch, still yelping. He was like a little dog.

XXII

"Have you heard the news?" cried Carrie Dungen, as she sped toward Martha's kitchen. "Have you heard the news?" Her eyes were shining with delight.

"No," answered Martha's sister Kate, bending forward eagerly. "What was it? What was it?"

Carrie appeared triumphantly in the open door. "Oh, there's been an awful scene between Doctor Trescott and Jake Winter. I never thought that Jake Winter had any pluck at all, but this morning he told the doctor just what he thought of him."

"Well, what did he think of him?" asked Martha.

"Oh, he called him everything. Mrs. Howarth heard it through her front blinds. It was terrible, she says. It's all over town now. Everybody knows it."

"Didn't the doctor answer back?"

"No! Mrs. Howarth—she says he never said a word. He just walked down to his buggy and got in, and drove off as co-o-o-l. But Jake gave him jinks, by all accounts."

"But what did he say?" cried Kate, shrill and excited. She was evidently at some kind of a feast.

"Oh, he told him that Sadie had never been well since that night Henry Johnson frightened her at Theresa Page's party, and he held him responsible, and how dared he cross his threshold—and—and—and—"

"And what?" said Martha.

"Did he swear at him?" said Kate, in fearsome glee.

"No—not much. He did swear at him a little, but not more than a man does anyhow when he is real mad, Mrs. Howarth says."

"O-oh!" breathed Kate. "And did he call him any names?"

Martha, at her work, had been for a time in deep thought. She now interrupted the others. "It don't seem as if Sadie Winter had been sick since that time Henry Johnson got loose. She's been to school almost the whole time since then, hasn't she?"

They combined upon her in immediate indignation. "School? School? I should say not. Don't think for a moment. School!"

Martha wheeled from the sink. She held an iron spoon, and it seemed as if she was going to attack them. "Sadie Winter has passed here many a morning since then carrying her school bag. Where was she going? To a wedding?"

The others, long accustomed to a mental tyranny, speedily surrendered.

"Did she?" stammered Kate. "I never saw her."

Carrie Dungen made a weak gesture.

"If I had been Doctor Trescott," exclaimed Martha, loudly, "I'd have knocked that miserable Jake Winter's head off."

Kate and Carrie, exchanging glances, made an alliance in the air. "I don't see why you say that, Martha," replied Carrie, with considerable boldness, gaining support and sympathy from Kate's smile. "I don't see how anybody can be blamed for getting angry when their little girl gets almost scared to death and gets sick from it, and all that. Besides, everybody says—"

"Oh, I don't care what everybody says," said Martha.

"Well, you can't go against the whole town," answered Carrie, in sudden sharp defiance.

"No, Martha, you can't go against the whole town," piped Kate, following her leader rapidly.

"'The whole town,'" cried Martha. "I'd like to know what you call 'the whole town.' Do you call these silly people who are scared of Henry Johnson 'the whole town'?"

"Why, Martha," said Carrie, in a reasoning tone, "you talk as if you wouldn't be scared of him!"

"No more would I," retorted Martha.

"O-oh, Martha, how you talk!" said Kate. "Why, the idea! Everybody's afraid of him."

Carrie was grinning. "You've never seen him, have you?" she asked, seductively.

"No," admitted Martha.

"Well, then, how do you know that you wouldn't be scared?"

Martha confronted her. "Have you ever seen him? No? Well, then, how do you know you *would* be scared?"

The allied forces broke out in chorus: "But, Martha, everybody says so. Everybody says so."

"Everybody says what?"

"Everybody that's seen him say they were frightened almost to death. 'Tisn't only women, but it's men too. It's awful."

Martha wagged her head solemnly. "I'd try not to be afraid of him."

"But supposing you could not help it?" said Kate.

"Yes, and look here," cried Carrie. "I'll tell you another thing. The Hannigans are going to move out of the house next door."

"On account of him?" demanded Martha.

Carrie nodded. "Mrs. Hannigan says so herself."

"Well, of all things!" ejaculated Martha. "Going to move, eh? You don't say so! Where they going to move to?"

"Down on Orchard Avenue."

"Well, of all things! Nice house?"

"I don't know about that. I haven't heard. But there's lots of nice houses on Orchard."

"Yes, but they're all taken," said Kate. "There isn't a vacant house on Orchard Avenue."

"Oh yes, there is," said Martha. "The old Hampstead house is vacant."

"Oh, of course," said Kate. "But then I don't believe Mrs. Hannigan would like it there. I wonder where they can be going to move to?"

"I'm sure I don't know," sighed Martha. "It must be to some place we don't know about."

"Well," said Carrie Dungen, after a general reflective silence, "it's easy enough to find out, anyhow."

"Who knows—around here?" asked Kate.

"Why, Mrs. Smith, and there she is in her garden," said Carrie, jumping to her feet. As she dashed out of the door, Kate and Martha crowded at the window. Carrie's voice rang out from near the steps. "Mrs. Smith! Mrs. Smith! Do you know where the Hannigans are going to move to?"

XXIII

The autumn smote the leaves, and the trees of Whilomville were panoplied in crimson and yellow. The winds grew stronger, and in the melancholy purple of the nights the home shine of a window became a finer thing. The little boys, watching the sear and sorrowful leaves drifting down from the maples, dreamed of the near time when they could heap bushels in the streets and burn them during the abrupt evenings.

Three men walked down Niagara Avenue. As they approached Judge Hagenthorpe's house he came down his walk to meet them in the manner of one who has been waiting.

"Are you ready, Judge?" one said.

"All ready," he answered.

The four then walked to Trescott's house. He received them in his office, where he had been reading. He seemed surprised at this visit of four very active and influential citizens, but he had nothing to say of it.

After they were all seated, Trescott looked expectantly from one face to another. There was a little silence. It was broken by John Twelve, the wholesale grocer, who was worth $400,000, and reported to be worth over a million.

"Well, doctor," he said, with a short laugh, "I suppose we might as well admit at once that we've come to interfere in something which is none of our business."

"Why, what is it?" asked Trescott, again looking from one face to another. He seemed to appeal particularly to Judge Hagenthorpe, but the old man had his chin lowered musingly to his cane, and would not look at him.

"It's about what nobody talks of—much," said Twelve. "It's about Henry Johnson."

Trescott squared himself in his chair. "Yes?" he said.

Having delivered himself of the title, Twelve seemed to become more easy. "Yes," he answered, blandly, "we wanted to talk to you about it."

"Yes?" said Trescott.

Twelve abruptly advanced on the main attack. "Now see here, Trescott, we like you, and we have come to talk right out about this business. It may be none of our affairs and all that, and as for me, I don't mind if you tell me so; but I am not going to keep quiet and see you ruin yourself. And that's how we all feel."

"I am not ruining myself," answered Trescott.

"No, maybe you are not exactly ruining yourself," said Twelve, slowly, "but you are doing yourself a great deal of harm. You have changed from being the leading doctor in town to about the last one. It is mainly because there are always a large number of people who are very thoughtless fools, of course, but then that doesn't change the condition."

A man who had not heretofore spoken said, solemnly, "It's the women."

"Well, what I want to say is this," resumed Twelve: "Even if there are a lot of fools in the world, we can't see any reason why you should ruin yourself by opposing them. You can't teach them anything, you know."

"I am not trying to teach them anything." Trescott smiled wearily. "I—it is a matter of—well—"

"And there are a good many of us that admire you for it immensely," interrupted Twelve; "but that isn't going to change the minds of all those ninnies."

"It's the women," stated the advocate of this view again.

"Well, what I want to say is this," said Twelve. "We want you to get out of this trouble and strike your old gait again. You are simply killing your practice through your infernal pig-headedness. No, this thing is out of the ordinary, but there must be ways to—to beat the game somehow, you see. So we've talked it over—about a dozen of us—and, as I say, if you want to tell us to mind our own business, why, go ahead; but we've talked it over, and we've come to the conclusion that the only way to do is to get Johnson a place somewhere off up the valley, and—"

Trescott wearily gestured. "You don't know, my friend. Everybody is so afraid of him, they can't even give him good care. Nobody can attend to him as I do myself."

"But I have a little no-good farm up beyond Clarence Mountain that I was going to give to Henry," cried Twelve, aggrieved. "And if you—and if you—if you—through your house burning down, or anything—why, all the boys were prepared to take him right off your hands, and—and—"

Trescott arose and went to the window. He turned his back upon them. They sat waiting in silence. When he returned he kept his face in the shadow. "No, John Twelve," he said, "it can't be done."

There was another stillness. Suddenly a man stirred on his chair.

"Well, then, a public institution—" he began.

"No," said Trescott; "public institutions are all very good, but he is not going to one."

In the background of the group old Judge Hagenthorpe was thoughtfully smoothing the polished ivory head of his cane.

XXIV

Trescott loudly stamped the snow from his feet and shook the flakes from his shoulders. When he entered the house he went at once to the dining-room, and then to the sitting-room. Jimmie was there, reading painfully in a large book concerning giraffes and tigers and crocodiles.

"Where is your mother, Jimmie?" asked Trescott.

"I don't know, pa," answered the boy. "I think she is upstairs."

Trescott went to the foot of the stairs and called, but there came no answer. Seeing that the door of the little drawing-room was open, he entered. The room was bathed in the half-light that came from the four dull panes of mica in the front of the great stove. As his eyes grew used to the shadows he saw his wife curled in an arm-chair. He went to her. "Why, Grace," he said, "didn't you hear me calling you?"

She made no answer, and as he bent over the chair he heard her trying to smother a sob in the cushion.

"Grace!" he cried. "You're crying!"

She raised her face. "I've got a headache, a dreadful headache, Ned."

"A headache?" he repeated, in surprise and incredulity.

He pulled a chair close to hers. Later, as he cast his eye over the zone of light shed by the dull red panes, he saw that a low table had been drawn close to the stove, and that it was burdened with many small cups and plates of uncut tea-cake. He remembered that the day was Wednesday, and that his wife received on Wednesdays.

"Who was here today, Gracie?" he asked.

From his shoulder there came a mumble, "Mrs. Twelve."

"Was she—um," he said. "Why—didn't Anna Hagenthorpe come over?"

The mumble from his shoulder continued, "She wasn't well enough."

Glancing down at the cups, Trescott mechanically counted them. There were fifteen of them. "There, there," he said. "Don't cry, Grace. Don't cry."

The wind was whining round the house, and the snow beat aslant upon the windows. Sometimes the coal in the stove settled with a crumbling sound, and the four panes of mica flashed a sudden new crimson. As he sat holding her head on his shoulder, Trescott found himself occasionally trying to count the cups. There were fifteen of them.

"THE UPTURNED FACE"

I

What will we do now?" said the adjutant, troubled and excited.

"Bury him," said Timothy Lean.

The two officers looked down close to their toes where lay the body of their comrade. The face was chalk-blue; gleaming eyes stared at the sky. Over the two upright figures was a windy sound of bullets, and on the top of the hill, Lean's prostrate company of Spitzbergen infantry was firing measured volleys.

"Don't you think it would be better—" began the adjutant. "We might leave him until tomorrow."

Ainslee's Magazine. March 1900.

"No," said Lean, "I can't hold that post an hour longer. I've got to fall back, and we've got to bury old Bill."

"Of course," said the adjutant at once. "Your men got entrenching tools?"

Lean shouted back to his little firing line, and two men came slowly, one with a pick, one with a shovel. They stared in the direction of the Rostina sharpshooters. Bullets cracked near their ears. "Dig here," said Lean gruffly. The men, thus caused to lower their glances to the turf, became hurried and frightened merely because they could not look to see whence the bullets came. The dull beat of the pick striking the earth sounded amid the swift snap of close bullets. Presently the other private began to shovel.

"I suppose," said the adjutant, slowly, "we'd better search his clothes for . . . things."

Lean nodded; together in curious abstraction they looked at the body. Then Lean stirred his shoulders, suddenly arousing himself. "Yes," he said, "we'd better see . . . what he's got." He dropped to his knees and approached his hands to the body of the dead officer. But his hands wavered over the buttons of the tunic. The first button was brick-red with drying blood, and he did not seem to dare to touch it.

"Go on," said the adjutant hoarsely.

Lean stretched his wooden hand, and his fingers fumbled blood-stained buttons. . . . At last he arose with a ghastly face. He had gathered a watch, a whistle, a pipe, a tobacco pouch, a handkerchief, a little case of cards and papers. He looked at the adjutant. There was a silence. The adjutant was feeling that he had been a coward to make Lean do all the grizzly business.

"Well," said Lean, "that's all, I think. You have his sword and revolver."

"Yes," said the adjutant, his face working. And then he burst out in a sudden strange fury at the two privates. "Why don't you hurry up with that grave? What are you doing, anyhow? Hurry, do you hear? I never saw such stupid—"

Even as he cried out in this passion, the two men were laboring for their lives. Ever overhead, the bullets were spitting.

The grave was finished. It was not a masterpiece—poor little shallow thing. Lean and the adjutant again looked at each other in a curious silent communication.

Suddenly the adjutant croaked out a weird laugh. It was a terrible laugh which had its origin in that part of the mind which is first moved by the singing of the nerves. "Well," he said humorously to Lean, "I suppose we had best tumble him in."

"Yes," said Lean. The two privates stood waiting bent over on their implements. "I suppose," said Lean, "it would be better if we laid him in ourselves."

"Yes," said the adjutant. Then apparently remembering that he had made Lean search the body, he stooped with great fortitude and took hold of the dead officer's clothing. Lean joined him. Both were particular that their fingers should not feel the corpse. They tugged away; the corpse lifted, heaved, toppled, flopped into the grave, and the two officers, straightening, looked again at each other—they were always looking at each other. They sighed with relief.

The adjutant said: "I suppose we should . . . we should say something. Do you know the service, Tim?"

"They don't read the service until the grave is filled in," said Lean, pressing his lips to an academic expression.

"Don't they?" said the adjutant, shocked that he had made the mistake. "Oh, well," he cried suddenly, "let us . . . let us say something while . . . while he can hear us."

"All right," said Lean. "Do you know the service?"

"I can't remember a line of it," said the adjutant.

Lean was extremely dubious. "I can repeat two lines but—"

"Well, do it," said the adjutant. "Go as far as you can. That's better than nothing. And . . . the beasts have got our range exactly."

Lean looked at his two men. "Attention!" he barked. The privates came to attention with a click, looking much aggrieved. The adjutant lowered his helmet to his knee. Lean, bare-headed, stood over the grave. The Rostina sharpshooters fired briskly.

"*O, Father, our friend has sunk in the deep waters of death, but his spirit has leaped toward Thee as the bubble arises from the lips of the drowning. Perceive, we beseech, O, Father, the little flying bubble and—*"

Lean, although husky and ashamed, had suffered no hesitation up to this point, but he stopped with a hopeless feeling and looked at the corpse.

The adjutant moved uneasily. "*And from Thy superb heights—*" he began, and then he, too, came to an end.

"*And from Thy superb heights,*" said Lean.

The adjutant suddenly remembered a phrase in the back part of the Spitzbergen burial service, and he exploited it with the triumphant manner of a man who has recalled everything and can go on.

"*O, God, have mercy—*"

"*O, God, have mercy—*" said Lean.

"*'Mercy,'*" repeated the adjutant in a quick failure.

"'*Mercy,*'" said Lean. And then he was moved by some violence of feeling, for he turned suddenly upon his two men and tigerishly said: "Throw the dirt in."

The fire of the Rostina sharpshooters was accurate and continuous.

II

One of the aggrieved privates came forward with his shovel. He lifted his first shovel-load of earth and for a moment of inexplicable hesitation it was held poised above this corpse which from its chalk-blue face looked keenly out from the grave. Then the soldier emptied his shovel on—on the feet.

Timothy Lean felt as if tons had been swiftly lifted from off his forehead. He had felt that perhaps the private might empty the shovel on—on the face. It had been emptied on the feet. There was a great point gained there—ha, ha!—the first shovelful had been emptied on the feet. How satisfactory!

The adjutant began to babble. "Well, of course . . . a man we've messed with all these years . . . impossible . . . you can't, you know, leave your intimate friends rotting on the field. . . . Go on, for God's sake, and shovel, *you.*"

The man with the shovel suddenly ducked, grabbed his left arm with his right hand and looked at his officer for orders. Lean picked the shovel from the ground. "Go to the rear," he said to the wounded man. He also addressed the other private. "You get under cover, too. I'll . . . I'll finish this business."

The wounded man scrambled hastily for the top of the ridge without devoting any glances to the direction from whence the bullets came and the other man followed at an equal pace but he was different in that he looked back anxiously three times. This is merely the way—often—of the hit and the unhit.

Timothy Lean filled the shovel, hesitated, and then in a movement which was like a gesture of abhorrence, he flung the dirt into the grave and as it landed it made a sound—plop. Lean suddenly paused and mopped his brow—a tired laborer.

"Perhaps we have been wrong," said the adjutant. His glance wavered stupidly. "It might have been better if we hadn't buried him just at this time. Of course, if we advance tomorrow, the body would have been—"

"Damn you," said Lean. "Shut your mouth." He was not the senior officer.

He again filled the shovel and flung in the earth. Always the earth made that sound—plop. For a space Lean worked frantically like a man digging himself out of danger.

Soon there was nothing to be seen but the chalk-blue face. Lean filled the shovel. . . . "Good God," he cried to the adjutant. "Why didn't you turn him somehow when you put him in? This—" Then Lean began to stutter.

The adjutant understood. He was pale to the lips. "Go on, man," he cried, beseechingly, almost in a shout. . . . Lean swung back the shovel; it went forward in a pendulum curve. When the earth landed it made a sound—plop.

APPROACHING THE AMERICAN CENTURY

Phyllis Frus and Stanley Corkin, Volume Editors

"The Open Boat" is Crane's best-known and most admired short story. It is regarded as a masterpiece in not only Crane's oeuvre but the entire canon of the American short story. No doubt this is because, despite its basis in fact, the story lends itself to formal analysis and literary historical treatment, as Crane tells of four men in a dinghy pitted against the elements of wind, water, and sharks. It contains no explanation of *why* the men are in the boat, just that they *are* there. They scan the horizon in search of land, oblivious of the beauties of nature. As the famous opening line, "None of them knew the color of the sky," indicates, these are men *in extremis,* not out for a row of pleasure.

As he often did, Crane chose not to develop his characters. They are differentiated only by a generic title—the oiler, the correspondent, the captain, and the cook. Crane's use of universal, or "every man," characteristics gave clues to his readers about how to read the story, and beginning with his friend Joseph Conrad readers have complied. As the older author wrote to Crane in admiration of what he called "the boat thing," "The illusions of life come out of your hand without a flaw. It is not life—which nobody wants—it is art" (Wertheim and Sorrentino, *Correspondence* 315). Crane composed his short story in accordance with an aesthetic common to realists, naturalists, and certain types of modernists, designing it so that the significance of the tale would come from his art in telling it, not from its depiction of specific characters experiencing certain circumstances. He intentionally deleted concrete references so that, unless readers were willing to dig up what Henry James called "the story of the story," they would be prompted to read it for its cosmic significance rather than its local interest.

Despite New Critical principles that led critics to urge readers not to mistake the point-of-view character, the correspondent, for journalist Stephen Crane, the story is based on fact. It refers to events that took place after the sinking of the steamer *Commodore* off the coast of Florida early in 1897. The ship was one of many employed by U.S. interests to smuggle arms to the Cuban insurrectionists to use in their battle for independence from Spain in the last years of the nineteenth century. By the laws of neutrality, U.S. citizens were prohibited from providing arms, but this was a common practice and one winked at by customs officials. Crane had to sign on as a crew member in order to get passage to Cuba, however, for journalists were officially barred from the island. "Stephen Crane's Own Story" is his nationally syndicated first-person report of events that led up to the ship's foundering (the story appeared nationwide on January 6,

1897); in keeping with the chronology, it appears first in this section. Reading the first-person account before reading "The Open Boat" (which appeared in *Scribner's* a few months later) makes "The Open Boat" a bit less mystifying; the reader has a partial answer to the question the correspondent is trying to understand: "why he was there." It becomes apparent that the correspondent in "The Open Boat" was a participant-observer in actions that would culminate in the Spanish-American War little more than a year later.

One of the reasons Crane was there was that he was a famous writer and a well-known, even notorious, journalist. One paragraph in a *New York Press* advance story on January 4, 1897, begins "Stephen Crane has been talked about more in New York than any writer of recent years," a reference not only to the Dora Clark affair but to other press reports of his alleged vices and immorality (Crane, *Stories and Tales* 247). Such star reporters were paid well to get to the scene of revolution (or disaster or worker exploitation) to investigate matters and to report what they saw. Crane finally got to Cuba eighteen months later as a war correspondent for Joseph Pulitzer's *World.* In the meantime he had been to Greece to cover the Greco-Turkish War, sending dispatches to William Randolph Hearst's *New York Journal* and the McClure syndicate.

The primary and secondary materials collected here chronicle, in brief, Crane's role as a correspondent in the events that took place in Cuba and Puerto Rico in 1898. Taken together, they tell a variety of stories that can be linked to show how developments in the mass media contributed to the United States' actively seeking to become a world power.

Some political leaders and most newspaper publishers avidly supported the Spanish-American War as a fitting expression of national character and will. Others felt that it violated the very basis of such definitions. The contextual materials represent voices from both sides, helping to reveal Crane's role in this national debate. Although Crane was no jingoist, neither was he clearly in the antiwar camp. Providing a sense of the debate over the direction of the United States' international behavior may enable readers better to note the subtlety of his writing, to detect his beliefs about U.S. expansionist aims, and to get a more complex sense of this conflict and its ramifications.

Theodore Roosevelt and Henry Cabot Lodge were at the forefront of the political forces clamoring for an assertion of U.S. power on the international stage. They were friends and colleagues who shared many interests and opinions, which is not surprising considering their similar backgrounds: both belonged to families of wealth and social prominence. Roosevelt was of the seventh generation of a prominent New York line with roots dating back to the settlement of New Amsterdam. Lodge was from an even more patrician New England family, for both Cabots and Lodges epitomized high-caste Brahmin blood. Both men had prominent careers in public service, with Lodge serving in the U.S. Senate for more than three decades and Roosevelt eventually becoming vice president, and then president. Both men, as is clear from the previous excerpts from their writings, were convinced that their biology was their destiny, that their blood made leadership their rightful place and their responsibility. This applied to national and international politics. Each in his way played a vital role in bringing the United States to war with Spain. Lodge and Roosevelt were leading architects of U.S. imperial foreign policy, seeking to place the nation at the hub of a burgeoning system of trade. It was this economic centrality that was perhaps the most attractive feature of becoming a world power, yet it is that aspect of their discussion that remains least explicit.

These men were devotees of naval power and used their considerable influence to direct federal dollars to military use (as assistant secretary and, frequently, acting secretary of the navy Roosevelt played a large part in readying the fleet for the war he sought). These writings show their deep belief in the necessity and legitimacy of the United States as an imperial power. Roosevelt and Lodge both wrote of the responsibilities facing the United States, arguing that to lead the world was the destiny of Anglo-Saxons. Even in the opening paragraph of his autobiographical account of his participation in the war, *The Rough Riders,* Roosevelt reported having "preached" for more than a year of "our duty to intervene . . . and to take this opportunity of driving the Spaniard from the Western World" (1).

Although Crane remained skeptical of Roosevelt, who maintained his disdain for Crane after their conflict in New York, their views of battle and reckless behavior under fire seem to have been of a kind. Roosevelt became a national celebrity through the recounting of his July 1, 1898, exploits, when he charged up what became known as San Juan Hill with his Rough Riders, a cavalry regiment made up of an assortment of Southwestern lawmen and cowboys, Ivy League athletes, and upper-class volunteers. Crane's account, headlined "Stephen Crane's Vivid Story of the Battle of San Juan," seems not to have been part of the publicity machine that made Roosevelt a national hero. Yet, it certainly added to the public's sense of the tale.[1] It also added to the larger story about why the United States was fighting in Cuba.

---

[1] *The Rough Riders* was so self-aggrandizing an account that Mr. Dooley, the Irish persona and nom de plume of Finley Peter Dunne, said in a parody-review that Roosevelt should have called it "Alone in Cubia [sic]." If Teddy "done it all he ought to say so an' relieve th' suspinse," he concludes (18).

Figures such as Lodge and Roosevelt, although well connected and politically powerful, were not without opposition. We have also included selections from anti-imperialist writings by Twain and Cuban revolutionary leader José Martí. Twain was one of a number of opponents of this particular U.S. enterprise, particularly when it meant occupying other nations. He served as vice president of the Anti-Imperialist League, which also included Moorfield Storey, who would become the first president of the National Association for the Advancement of Colored People; and three figures whose views are included in Part I: Jane Addams (also founder of the Women's International League for Peace and Freedom), Andrew Carnegie, and Samuel Gompers. Twain's "To the Person Sitting in Darkness" captures both his politics and the bitterly ironic tone that marked so many of the writings of his later life. He explicitly challenges the racist explanation for bringing other peoples under U.S. sovereignty and calls attention to the barbarism involved in doing so. He also attacks Roosevelt, who by the end of 1901 occupied the White House. This polemical essay by Twain probably received more criticism than any of his other short works, and it is appropriate for this collection because, as the editor of a World Wide Web site on anti-imperialism points out, the many responses it provoked were not "scholarly analyses of literary form and style. Instead, it provoked heated debates about U.S. foreign policy, and the propriety of Mark Twain's criticism of it, . . . in editorial pages throughout the country" (Zwick).

In the story "The Upturned Face," which is one of four set in a war between two mythical countries and published in 1899, Crane universalizes the setting of the Spanish-American War to dwell on the general effects of battle. With the story Crane becomes the precursor of writers like John Dos Passos (*Three Soldiers*, 1920) and Hemingway (*In Our Time*, 1925, and *A Farewell to Arms*, 1929), who would debunk the homilies that they felt had created a false sense of the experience of war and its effects, but would do so in a similarly nonspecific way—making their works antiwar in general, not simply against the one they were writing about. The terse style and the sense of anecdote apparent in "The Upturned Face" links Crane's war fiction with that of the young Hemingway, author of the collection *In Our Time*. The story's emphasis on a search for faith in circumstances that mock religious ritual also brings to mind Hemingway's *A Farewell to Arms*, particularly Frederic Henry's lack of respect for the tenets of Catholicism as he serves in Italy and his search for "a separate peace."

Like Howells, José Martí distrusted U.S. intentions in the Caribbean. He was well aware that the nation had a history of being interested in annexing the Caribbean island, an interest in part justified by the Monroe Doctrine. He was also aware of the general rise of jingoism in the period. Martí had taken part in Cuban nationalist insurrections against Spain as early as 1868. He was exiled to Spain in 1871 and came to the United States in 1880. He returned to Cuba to lead the revolution against Spain in 1895. Martí's letter to Manuel Mercado was written just before he was killed in a cavalry skirmish and remained unfinished and unsent. In the letter Martí sees the coming of U.S. domination in the Caribbean. He laments the U.S. "tradition of expansion" and its general lack of respect for other cultures. His suspicions of the United States proved prescient. In 1901 the passage of the Platt Amendment made Cuba, in effect, a U.S. colony. The amendment limited Cuba's rights as a nation and made its neighbor to the north its guarantor of "sovereignty" and its political overseer. Martí reminds us that America defines a region and the United States is but one country within that area. In the late nineteenth century, leaders such as Lodge and Roosevelt sought to minimize the distinction between regional and national senses of the term. This effort to define the United States as the ruling presence in the Western hemisphere has continued to motivate presidents, from William McKinley in 1900 to Bill Clinton in 2000. U.S. troops have been active not only in Cuba and Puerto Rico, but in Haiti and the Dominican Republic, Mexico, Nicaragua, Grenada, and Panama, to mention some of the best-known examples.

Another tale that can be gathered from events surrounding the national experience of the Spanish-American War concerns the new terms and power of American journalism in the late nineteenth century. This "new journalism," or "yellow journalism," of the 1880s and 1890s was introduced to New York by Joseph Pulitzer, who bought the *World* in 1883. William Randolph Hearst, new owner of the *New York Journal*, embraced it in 1895. These publishers openly courted popular approval by mixing news and entertainment, breezy headlines and illustrations, crusades and stunts, exposés and promotions (such as raising money to build a base to support the Statue of Liberty). The two even engaged in a circulation war that included Hearst's hiring away much of Pulitzer's staff.

Most readers probably associate yellow journalism with the public outcry that put pressure on the U.S. government to intervene in the Cuban insurrection against Spain, which led to the Spanish-American War. For various reasons, including increased sales as well as expansionist sentiment, Hearst and Pulitzer did indeed fan these flames, but the new journalism did more than warmonger. Charles Brown reports that "by 1898 almost one-half the daily newspapers in twenty-six major cities were of the blatantly yellow variety," or "at least a primrose hue" (C. H. Brown 19),

which meant that readers all over the country were treated to sensation-
alist stories of scandal and disasters; large-type, sloganeering headlines;
reform efforts of investigative editors; self-advertisements boasting of
circulation increases and subscriber contributions to campaigns; and by-
lined stories by celebrity writers. Other important innovations, all of
which form the context of Crane's career in journalism, were the growth
of newspaper publishing as a business, the increasing professionalism of
journalism, the appeal to what was primarily an urban phenomenon of
mass readership, and the supplanting of big-name editors and publishers
by writers and correspondents, to the point that journalism histories call
the period from 1880–1910 the "age of the reporter" (C. H. Brown 20;
Schudson 68–70).

Prominent among the war reporters was Richard Harding Davis, who
here provides further testimony of Crane's star status, which he broadly
defines, then reinforces with his tale of Crane's exploits in Puerto Rico.
This stature is furthered by Frank Norris's reminiscence. In all these writings the journalist emerges in nearly the same terms as the hero of a battle.
Indeed, in such writings we can see a prototype emerging that would
prevail in the twentieth century. Amy Kaplan believes that Crane's real
achievement in the war dispatches and the stories growing out of the Spanish-American War was to create a "figure who straddles the boundary line
between spectator and actor," and she quotes Martin Green in *The Great
American Adventure,* who claims that Crane "invented the persona of the
war correspondent for the novelist" of the twentieth century (106).[2]

The reporters became well known from their by-lines, but not only for
their writing: in many cases they became actors in the dramas they reported.
Two histories detailing the role of the press in the Spanish-American War
give central place to journalists, as is obvious from their titles: Charles H.
Brown's *The Correspondents' War* and Joyce Milton's *The Yellow Kids;*
Crane is prominent in both. Beginning in 1895, many of the correspondents in Cuba were also participants, serving as scouts (and sometimes
spies) to determine the extent of the insurrection, acting as liaisons to rebel
leaders before the United States went to war, carrying messages on dispatch boats hired by their publishers, even digging trenches and firing on
enemy soldiers (C. H. Brown vii).

Thematically, "The Monster" complements these other selections,
even though it was written in 1898 when Crane was living the life of an

---

[2] Furthermore, Kaplan says that this fence-straddling figure is already present in *The Red
Badge of Courage* and that is why Hemingway wrote in 1942 that Crane's novel "was
the only enduring 'real literature of our Civil War'" ("Spectacle" 106).

English country squire at Brede Place in England. It provides a tantalizing example of some vital issues of Crane's time and the present, though it does so somewhat elusively. It is a tale of a black man, Henry Johnson, who sacrifices himself to save his employer's little boy from a fire and explosions and who is rewarded by being made monstrous, first by the chemicals in Dr. Trescott's home laboratory that, because of the fire, erase his features, then by the townspeople, who project upon his blank face all their racist fantasies and fears. When the doctor saves Johnson's life in turn by insisting on treating him without regard for the consequences, his career is ruined. Thus Trescott puts himself in the category of Victor Frankenstein, using his science to perpetuate an abomination that mocks the order of nature. This late Crane work also serves to illustrate the difference historical knowledge makes in comprehending the complexity of thought and depth of the moral struggle undergone by this ambitious writer who was only twenty-five years old when he wrote it.[3]

The story lends itself to a number of allegorical readings, all emphasizing significant characteristics of Crane's United States. Henry Johnson can be read as the image of the African American brute, a figure we see in the racist popular fiction of writers like Thomas Dixon. We can view him as the failed attempt of science to create or perpetuate life where none does or should exist, a view that takes into account but remains skeptical of late-nineteenth-century science and its potential. When a crowd of townspeople has chased after Johnson at night, throwing rocks at him and necessitating his being jailed for his own safety, the scene is all too similar to a lynching. The police chief as much as admits this to Dr. Trescott, when he says, "Nobody really wanted to hit him, but you know how a crowd gets. It's like—it's like—" The phrase he cannot bring himself to utter is "a lynch mob."

Johnson is constantly belittled. The white men in the barbershop get an inflated sense of their importance as they reduce Johnson to an absurd stereotype. The boys make him a slave in a nonsense rhyme they chant, in which they hope he will "never die," all the while denying him a chance to a full life. In "Twentieth-Century Fiction and the Black Mask of Humanity" Ellison claims that American life "is a drama acted out upon the body of a Negro" (28). That is, the disruptions of American history, ultimately, further compromise the status of African Americans. No wonder he regarded "The Monster" as a meditation on the failure of Reconstruction;

---

[3] For the circumstances of composition and possible influences on this "novelette," as Crane called it, see Wertheim, *Crane Encyclopedia* 234–40.

indeed, it showed the results of an "abandonment" of African Americans amounting to "the continuation of the Civil War by means other than arms" (Ellison 67).[4]

Malcolm Foster cites many historical referents to support his claim that the story is "nothing less than an allegory of the black man in America in the nineteenth century, and an angry condemnation of white America" (87). For example, Foster compares the rumor spreading in the town that Johnson caused the fire rather than being the hero of it to the way that "parts of the North blamed the Negro for precipitating the Civil War, which led to such savage reprisals as the New York Draft Riots of July 1863, when blacks were beaten and murdered in the streets" (88). Similarly, in the aftermath of the Spanish-American War, black soldiers who served the nation that denied them civil rights were chastised by none other than Theodore Roosevelt for their lack of valor in battle (Kaplan, "Black and Blue" 219–36).

"The Monster" cannot be read simply as an indictment of the town of Whilomville (Crane's fictional setting—based on Port Jervis, New York—for a group of stories), despite some critics' use of evidence in a letter from Crane expressing his hope that his former neighbors will not recognize themselves in the townspeople in the story (Wertheim and Sorrentino, *Correspondence* 446). After all, Crane makes no obvious effort to distance himself from the narrator, who clearly shares the dominant view of Negroes derived from minstrel shows. The narrator depicts Henry as dressing for a cakewalk and ridicules his attendance on Bella Farragut and her mother by saying, "[I]f they had been the occupants of the most gorgeous salon in the world they could not have been more like three monkeys."

There are many historical cues crying out to be noticed, yet they seem to defy systemization. The social scientism of Spencer and the scientific racism of Nathaniel Shaler, whose writings are in Part I, allow some significant insight into Crane's way of thinking in this story. Knowing that Crane's brother tried to prevent a lynching of a black man, Robert Lewis, in New York in 1892, bring to mind Ida Wells-Barnett's inclusion of lynchings in Northern states in her reports as well. Crane seems torn between sympathy and revulsion for Henry Johnson, between comprehension and condescension. Certainly Crane sees Johnson as the object of ridicule and horror. But he also sees him in stereotypical fashion, as a man of the min-

---

[4] As part of his introduction to an edition of *The Red Badge of Courage* that also included "The Monster" and other stories ("Stephen Crane and American Fiction"), Ellison cited this long story as evidence of his claim that no other writer between Twain and Faulkner "looked so steadily at the wholeness of American life and discovered such far-reaching symbolic equivalents for its unceasing state of civil war" (75–76).

strel tradition; because Johnson is given no inner life, this role forms the sum of his character. The story also dwells on the proto-Spencerian question of whether man should employ science to save those whom nature has chosen to destroy.

Finally, "The Monster" evokes feelings related to Crane's treatment of the Spanish-American War. That is, a paternalism is present, as the doctor acts out of a sense of responsibility that is akin to the United States' obligation to assist the "backward" people of the world. Though Crane's intentions, as evidenced in his fiction and nonfiction, were humane and liberal, he also emerges as a figure who apprehends the world through the peculiarly slanted lenses bent thus by his times. How could it be otherwise? How could he share the fin de siècle attitudes of today, rather than those abroad in his times?

"THE STRENUOUS LIFE"

Theodore Roosevelt

In speaking to you, men of the greatest city of the West, men of the State which gave to the country Lincoln and Grant, men who preeminently and distinctly embody all that is most American in the American character, I wish to preach, not the doctrine of ignoble ease, but the doctrine of the strenuous life, the life of toil and effort, of labor and strife; to preach that highest form of success which comes, not to the man who desires mere easy peace, but to the man who does not shrink from danger, from hardship, or from bitter toil, and who out of these wins the splendid ultimate triumph.

A life of slothful ease, a life of that peace which springs merely from lack either of desire or of power to strive after great things, is as little worthy of a nation as of an individual. I ask only that what every self-respecting American demands from himself and from his sons shall be demanded of the American nation as a whole. . . . A mere life of ease is not in the end a very satisfactory life, and, above all, it is a life which ultimately unfits those who follow it for serious work in the world. . . .

As it is with the individual, so it is with the nation. It is a base untruth to say that happy is the nation that has no history. Thrice happy is the

Address to the Hamilton Club of Chicago, 10 Apr. 1899.

nation that has a glorious history. Far better it is to dare mighty things, to win glorious triumphs, even though checkered by failure, than to take rank with those poor spirits who neither enjoy much nor suffer much, because they live in the gray twilight that knows not victory nor defeat. If in 1861 the men who loved the Union had believed that peace was the end of all things, and war and strife the worst of all things, and had acted up to their belief, we would have saved hundreds of thousands of lives, we would have saved hundreds of millions of dollars. Moreover, besides saving all the blood and treasure we then lavished, we would have prevented the heartbreak of many women, the dissolution of many homes, and we would have spared the country those months of gloom and shame when it seemed as if our armies marched only to defeat. We could have avoided all this suffering simply by shrinking from strife. And if we had thus avoided it, we would have shown that we were weaklings, and that we were unfit to stand among the great nations of the earth. Thank God for the iron in the blood of our fathers, the men who upheld the wisdom of Lincoln, and bore sword or rifle in the armies of Grant! Let us, the children of the men who proved themselves equal to the mighty days, let us, the children of the men who carried the great Civil War to a triumphant conclusion, praise the God of our fathers that the ignoble counsels of peace were rejected; that the suffering and loss, the blackness of sorrow and despair, were unflinchingly faced, and the years of strife endured; for in the end the slave was freed, the Union restored, and the mighty American republic placed once more as a helmeted queen among nations.

We of this generation do not have to face a task such as that our fathers faced, but we have our tasks, and woe to us if we fail to perform them! We cannot, if we would, play the part of China, and be content to rot by inches in ignoble ease within our borders, taking no interest in what goes on beyond them, sunk in a scrambling commercialism; heedless of the higher life, the life of aspiration, of toil and risk, busying ourselves only with the wants of our bodies for the day, until suddenly we should find, beyond a shadow of question, what China has already found, that in this world the nation that has trained itself to a career of unwarlike and isolated ease is bound, in the end, to go down before other nations which have not lost the manly and adventurous qualities. If we are to be a really great people, we must strive in good faith to play a great part in the world. We cannot avoid meeting great issues. All that we can determine for ourselves is whether we shall meet them well or ill. In 1898 we could not help being brought face to face with the problem of war with Spain. All we could decide was whether we should shrink like cowards from the contest, or enter into it as beseemed a brave and high-spirited people; and, once in, whether failure or success should crown our banners. So it is now. We cannot avoid the responsibilities that confront us in Hawaii, Cuba, Puerto Rico, and the Philippines. All we can decide is whether we shall meet them in a way that will redound to the national credit, or whether we shall make of our dealings with these new problems a dark and shameful page in our history. To refuse to deal with them at all merely amounts to dealing with them badly. We have a given problem to solve. If we undertake the solution, there is, of course, always danger that we may not solve it aright; but to refuse to undertake the solution simply renders it certain that we cannot possibly solve it aright.

We cannot sit huddled within our own borders and avow ourselves merely an assemblage of well-to-do hucksters who care nothing for what happens beyond. Such a policy would defeat even its own end; for as the nations grow to have ever wider and wider interests, and are brought into closer and closer contact, if we are to hold our own in the struggle for naval and commercial supremacy, we must build up our power without our own borders. We must build the isthmian canal, and we must grasp the points of vantage which will enable us to have our say in deciding the destiny of the oceans of the East and the West.

So much for the commercial side. From the standpoint of international honor the argument is even stronger. The guns that thundered off Manila and Santiago left us echoes of glory, but they also left us a legacy of duty. If we drove out a medieval tyranny only to make room for savage anarchy, we had better not have begun the task at all. It is worse than idle to say that we have no duty to perform, and can leave to their fates the islands we have conquered. Such a course would be the course of infamy. It would be followed at once by utter chaos in the wretched islands themselves. Some stronger manlier power would have to step in and do the work, and we would have shown ourselves weaklings, unable to carry to successful completion the labors that great and high-spirited nations are eager to undertake.

The work must be done; we cannot escape our responsibility and if we are worth our salt, we shall be glad of the chance to do the work—glad of the chance to show ourselves equal to one of the great tasks set modern civilization. But let us not deceive ourselves as to the importance of the task. Let us not be misled by vainglory into underestimating the strain it will put on our powers. Above all, let us, as we value our own self-respect, face the responsibilities with proper seriousness, courage, and high resolve.

We must demand the higher order of integrity and ability in our public men who are to grapple with these new problems. We must hold to a rigid accountability those public servants who show unfaithfulness to the interests of the nation or inability to rise to the high level of the new demands upon our strength and our resources.

Now, apply all this to our public men of today. Our army has never been built up as it should be built up. I shall not discuss with an audience like this the puerile suggestion that a nation of seventy millions of freemen is in danger of losing its liberties from the existence of an army of one hundred thousand men, three fourths of whom will be employed in certain foreign islands, in certain coast fortresses, and on Indian reservations. No man of good sense and stout heart can take such a proposition seriously. If we are such weaklings as the proposition implies, then we are unworthy of freedom in any event. To no body of men in the United States is the country so much indebted as to the splendid officers and enlisted men of the regular army and navy. There is no body from which the country has less to fear, and none of which it should be prouder, none which it should be more anxious to upbuild.

Our army needs complete reorganization—not merely enlarging— and the reorganization can only come as the result of legislation. A proper general staff should be established, and the positions of ordnance, commissary, and quartermaster officers should be filled by detail from the line. Above all, the army must be given the chance to exercise in large bodies. Never again should we see, as we saw in the Spanish war, major generals in command of divisions who had never before commanded three companies together in the field. Yet, incredible to relate, Congress has shown a queer inability to learn some of the lessons of the war. There were large bodies of men in both branches who opposed the declaration of war, who opposed the ratification of peace, who opposed the upbuilding of the army, and who even opposed the purchase of armor at a reasonable price for the battle-ships and cruisers, thereby putting an absolute stop to the building of any new fighting-ships for the navy. If, during the years to come, any disaster should befall our arms, afloat or ashore, and thereby any shame come to the United States, remember that the blame will lie upon the men whose names appear upon the roll-calls of Congress on the wrong side of these great questions. On them will lie the burden of any loss of our soldiers and sailors, of any dishonor to the flag; and upon you and the people of this country will lie the blame if you do not repudiate, in no unmistakable way, what these men have done. The blame will not rest upon the untrained commander of untried troops, upon the civil officers of a department the organization of which has been left utterly inadequate, or upon the admiral with an insufficient number of ships; but upon the public men who have so lamentably failed in forethought as to refuse to remedy these evils long in advance, and upon the nation that stands behind those public men.

In the West Indies and the Philippines alike we are confronted by most difficult problems. It is cowardly to shrink from solving them in the proper way; for solved they must be, if not by us, then by some stronger and more manful race. If we are too weak, too selfish, or too foolish to solve them, some bolder and abler people must undertake the solution. Personally, I am far too firm a believer in the greatness of my country and the power of my countrymen to admit for one moment that we shall ever be driven to the ignoble alternative.

The problems are different for the different islands. Puerto Rico is not large enough to stand alone. We must govern it wisely and well, primarily in the interest of its own people. Cuba, is, in my judgment, entitled ultimately to settle for itself whether it shall be an independent state or an integral portion of the mightiest of republics. But until order and stable liberty are secured, we must remain in the island to insure them, and infinite tact, judgment, moderation, and courage must be shown by our military and civil representatives in keeping the island pacified, in relentlessly stamping out brigandage, in protecting all alike, and yet in showing proper recognition to the men who have fought for Cuban liberty. The Philippines offer a yet graver problem. Their population includes half-caste and native Christians, warlike Moslems, and wild pagans. Many of their people are utterly unfit for self-government, and show no signs of becoming fit. Others may in time become fit but at present can only take part in self-government under a wise supervision, at once firm and beneficent. We have driven Spanish tyranny from the islands. If we now let it be replaced by savage anarchy, our work has been for harm and not for good. I have scant patience with those who fear to undertake the task of governing the Philippines, and who openly avow that they do fear to undertake it, or that they shrink from it because of the expense and trouble; but I have even scanter patience with those who make a pretense of humanitarianism to hide and cover their timidity, and who cant about "liberty" and the "consent of the governed," in order to excuse themselves for their unwillingness to play the part of men. Their doctrines, if carried out, would make it incumbent upon us to leave the Apaches of Arizona to work out their own salvation, and to decline to interfere in a single Indian reservation. Their doctrines condemn your forefathers and mine for ever having settled in these United States.

England's rule in India and Egypt has been of great benefit to England, for it has trained up generations of men accustomed to look at the larger and loftier side of public life. It has been of even greater benefit to India and Egypt. And finally, and most of all, it has advanced the cause of civilization. So, if we do our duty aright in the Philippines, we will add to that national renown which is the highest and finest part of national life, will greatly benefit the people of the Philippine Islands, and, above all, we will play our part well in the great work of uplifting mankind. But to do this work, keep ever in mind that we must show in a very high degree the qualities of courage, of honesty, and of good judgment. Resistance must be stamped out. The first and all-important work to be done is to establish the supremacy of our flag. We must put down armed resistance before we can accomplish anything else, and there should be no parleying, no faltering, in dealing with our foe. As for those in our own country who encourage the foe, we can afford contemptuously to disregard them; but it must be remembered that their utterances are not saved from being treasonable merely by the fact that they are despicable.

When once we have put down armed resistance, when once our rule is acknowledged, then an even more difficult task will begin, for then we must see to it that the islands are administered with absolute honesty and with good judgment. If we let the public service of the islands be turned into the prey of the spoils politician, we shall have begun to tread the path which Spain trod to her own destruction. We must send out there only good and able men, chosen for their fitness, and not because of their partisan service, and these men must not only administer impartial justice to the natives and serve their own government with honesty and fidelity, but must show the utmost tact and firmness, remembering that, with such people as those with whom we are to deal, weakness is the greatest of crimes, and that next to weakness comes lack of consideration for their principles and prejudices.

I preach to you, then, my countrymen, that our country calls not for the life of ease but for the life of strenuous endeavor. The twentieth century looms before us big with the fate of many nations. If we stand idly by, if we seek merely swollen, slothful ease and ignoble peace, if we shrink from the hard contests where men must win at hazard of their lives and at the risk of all they hold dear, then the bolder and stronger peoples will pass us by, and will win for themselves the domination of the world. Let us therefore boldly face the life of strife, resolute to do our duty well and manfully; resolute to uphold righteousness by deed and by word; resolute to be both honest and brave, to serve high ideals, yet to use practical methods. Above all, let us shrink from no strife, moral or physical, within or without the nation, provided we are certain that the strife is justified, for it is only through strife, through hard and dangerous endeavor, that we shall ultimately win the goal of true national greatness.

FROM *THE WAR WITH SPAIN*

Henry Cabot Lodge

Much dispute and opposition have arisen among people successful in war in times past, and will rise again, over treaties of peace, but such opposition has always proceeded on the ground that the victor nation received too little. The treaty of the United States with Spain, signed in Paris on December 10, 1898, has the unique distinction of having excited opposition and attack among the victors because it secured too much and was too triumphant. An organization called by the strange name of the Anti-Imperialist League was formed in the Eastern States. Some men who had once been eminent in politics gave their names to its support, and others who felt that they ought to be eminent in politics gave it their services. A vigorous crusade was begun, but the popular response in the way of the easily signed petition was surprisingly small for the good sense of the American people made two points clear to them. One was that a peace treaty ought to be ratified, the other that they had won these new possessions, and had no doubt that they could trust themselves to deal with them honestly, ably, and for their own truest and best interests, as well as for those of the people of all the islands. A failure in the field of popular discussion before the people and in the newspapers, the fight against the treaty was transferred to the Senate of the United States.

The constitutional provision which require a vote of two-thirds of the Senate to ratify a treaty simplifies the work of opposition to ratification. It seemed incredible at first that a treaty of peace could possibly be defeated. Party lines were not drawn on the question, and it was at first supposed that resistance to the ratification of the treaty would be confined to a very few Senators, who had been opposed to the movement in favor of the Cubans, as well as to the entrance into war, and were now consistently opposed to its results. But as time went on the necessities of factions in the Democratic party developed an opposition which included a majority of

New York: Harper, 1899.

the Democratic Senators, and this made the minority formidably large—nearly one-third of the Senate, if not in excess of it. It is not needful to trace in detail the course of the debate, which from the side of opposition proceeded on three line—lack of constitutional power to acquire and hold the Philippines, the violation of the principles of the Declaration of Independence involved in doing so, and sympathy and admiration for the Filipinos, feelings as profound as they were rapid in growth. The friends of ratification took the very simple ground that the treaty committed the United States to no policy, but left them free to do exactly as seemed best with all the islands, that the American people could be safely entrusted with this grave responsibility, and that patriotism and common-sense alike demanded the end of war and the reestablishment of peace, which could only be effected by the adoption of the treaty. The contest was earnest and bitter, the canvass energetic to a degree never seen in the Senate, and the result close. When the Senate went into executive session on Monday, February 6, with the time for the vote fixed for three o'clock, the treaty had only 58 sure votes, 60 being needed for ratification; the opposition had 29 sure votes, and the remaining 3 were doubtful. At half past two one of the doubtful voters was declared to be for the treaty, making 59. Just before three o'clock another vote was promised, and the third doubtful vote was given to the treaty after the roll had been called. The final vote stood 57 to 27—including the pairs, 61 to 29, just two-thirds and one vote to spare. It had been a heated struggle. Opinion as to the outcome had fluctuated, even among those best informed, down to the last moment. Yet as one looks back when all is done, it seems clear that no other result was possible. The responsibility which had come to the American people with the flash of Dewey's guns on May 1 could not be avoided, and the American people were too strong, too high-spirited, too confident, to run away from it. The hand of fate was knocking at the door of the Senate as it had knocked at the door of the American commissioners in Paris. To that knock all doors fly open, and to the stern visitant without but one answer could be given.

Nothing remained after the end of the conflict in the Senate but the exchange of ratifications, which took place on April 11, 1899, and so the war ended. Its causes lie far back in the history and character of nations. Its immediate results were as striking as they were important and full of meaning. What the more distant outcome of these results will be in the future years no man can tell. We can only say with certainty that they will be far reaching and momentous. The war was brief, but it served to let loose forces which had long been gathering strength, and to complete movements which had been going on for centuries. For three hundred years the conflict between the English-speaking people on the one side, and the French and Spanish on the other, for the control of the New World, had been in progress. France went down in 1760, the last vestige of Spanish power was swept away by the war of 1898. The result was inevitable, and the English-speaking people owned at last one-half of the New World, and had shut out Europe from all control in the other half or in the great islands of the West Indies.

Thus were the immediate object and purpose of the war achieved in fulfilment of the irresponsible conflict of centuries between races, systems, and beliefs inherently antagonistic. But war is a fire, and when it begins no one can tell where it will stop or what it will burn away. The only thing we can be quite sure of is that war, once entered upon, cannot be limited, and may produce results of which no man dreamed at the outset. This war, merely as such, was not only short, but was far from being a large or extensive one. Yet it suddenly made clear many things not realized before, and brought forth unimagined results. For thirty years the people of the United States had been binding up the wounds and trying to efface the scars of their great and terrible Civil War. They knew that they had done much, they felt that the old passions had softened and were dying. The war came, and in the twinkling of an eye, in a flash of burning, living light, they suddenly saw that the long task was done, that the land was really one again without rent or seam, and men rejoiced mightily in their hearts with this knowledge, which the new war had brought.

For thirty years the people of the United States had been absorbed in the development of their great heritage. They had been finishing the conquest of their continent, and binding all parts of it together with the tracks and highways of commerce. Once this work was complete, it was certain that the virile, ambitious, enterprising race which had done it would look abroad beyond their boundaries and seek to guard and extend their interests in other parts of the world. The work was done, but they did not realize it. Even the Venezuela intervention, a pure manifestation of the new spirit and the new time, did not make it clear to them. Then the war note rang through the land, and with dazzled eyes at first, and then with ever clearer and steadier gaze, they saw that in the years of isolation and self-absorption they had built up a great world power, that they must return to the ocean which they had temporarily abandoned, and have their share in the trade of every country and the commerce of every sea. Suddenly came the awakening to the great fact that they had founded an empire on their Western coasts, that they held one side of the Pacific, and could no longer be indifferent to the fate of the other side in the remote East. Now they read with instructed vision the prophecy of Seward, which foretold that the future course of trade and empire would lie in the Pacific. They knew at last that the stream of Eastern trade, which for centuries had flowed to the West, building up great cities and enriching nations as it passed from Byzantium to Venice, from Venice to Portugal, and from Portugal to Holland and to London, was now to be divided, and in part, at least, to pour eastward over the Pacific. Now men saw that the long connection, ever growing closer, with the Hawaiian Islands had not been chance; that the culmination of the annexation movement in the very year of the Spanish War was not accident, but that it all came from the instinct of the race, which paused in California only to learn that its course was still westward, and that Americans, and no one else, must be masters of the cross-roads of the Pacific.

But while the United States had moved so slowly for half a century toward Hawaii, the work of one May morning carried them on to the Philippines and made them an Eastern power. Whatever the final disposition of the islands, whether we hold and govern much or little, our flag is there, our footing has been made, and in the East we shall remain, because we are entitled to, and will surely have, our share of the great commerce with the millions of China, from whom we shall refuse to be shut out.

One other great result of the war is, like the last, a world result. We found in the trial of war who were our enemies in Europe, and we saw that they were many. We also found who our friend was, not as a matter of sentiment or community of speech and thought, but on the firm and solid ground of common interests. In the brief crash of the short-lived Spanish war the English-speaking people came together. In the light of those eager, hurrying days we saw that the English fleets made any attack on Dewey, even by combined Europe, impossible; and England saw that so long as the United States was her friend her base on the Atlantic was secure, her food-supply safe, and that all Europe in arms could not harm her. Very plain also did it become to all men that in the East, where England had been so long, and where we had just entered, the interests of both nations were identical in preserving China for equal trade to all.

All these things the war made clear and certain. What these new conditions may come to mean in the future no one now can safely say. But if that future is to bring the struggle which many men peering into the darkness foresee—a conflict between the Slav and so much of Europe as he can drag with him on the one side, and the English-speaking man on the other; between the military socialism of Russia and Germany and the individualism and freedom of the United States and England; between the power of the land and the sea power—then the future historian will date the opening of this new epoch and of this mighty conflict, at once economic and social, military and naval, from the war of 1898, which in three months overthrew the empire of Spain in the Antilles and the Philippines.

FROM "TO THE PERSON SITTING IN DARKNESS"

Mark Twain

At this point in our frank statement of fact to the Person Sitting in Darkness, we should throw in a little trade-taffy about the Blessings of Civilization—for a change, and for the refreshment of his spirit—then go on with our tale:

"We and the patriots having captured Manila, Spain's ownership of the Archipelago and her sovereignty over it were at an end—obliterated—annihilated—not a rag or shred of either remaining behind. It was then that we conceived the divinely humorous idea of *buying* both of these spectres from Spain! [It is quite safe to confess this to the Person Sitting in Darkness, since neither he nor any other sane person will believe it.] In buying those ghosts for twenty millions, we also contracted to take care of the friars and their accumulations. I think we also agreed to propagate leprosy and smallpox, but as to this there is doubt. But it is not important; persons afflicted with the friars do not mind the other diseases.

"With our treaty ratified, Manila subdued, and our Ghosts secured, we had no further use for Aguinaldo and the owners of the Archipelago. We forced a war, and we have been hunting America's guest and ally through the woods and swamps ever since."

At this point in the tale, it will be well to boast a little of our war-work and our heroisms in the field, so as to make our performance look as fine as England's in South Africa; but I believe it will not be best to emphasize this too much. We must be cautious. Of course, we must read the war-telegrams to the Person, in order to keep up our frankness; but we can throw an air of humorousness over them, and that will modify their grim eloquence a little, and their rather indiscreet exhibitions of gory exultation. Before reading to him the following display heads of the dispatches of November 18, 1900, it will be well to practice on them in private first, so as to get the right tang of lightness and gaiety into them:

North American Review, Feb. 1901.

"ADMINISTRATION WEARY OF PROTRACTED HOSTILITIES!"
"REAL WAR AHEAD FOR FILIPINO REBELS!"[1]
"WILL SHOW NO MERCY!"
"KITCHENER'S PLAN ADOPTED!"

Kitchener knows how to handle disagreeable people who are fighting for their homes and their liberties, and we must let on that we are merely imitating Kitchener, and have no national interest in the matter, further than to get ourselves admired by the Great Family of Nations, in which august company our Master of the Game has bought a place for us in the back row.

Of course, we must not venture to ignore our General MacArthur's reports—oh, why do they keep on printing those embarrassing things?— we must drop them trippingly from the tongue and take the chances:

> During the last ten months our losses have been 268 killed and 750 wounded; Filipino loss, *three thousand two hundred and twenty-seven killed,* and 694 wounded.

We must stand ready to grab the Person Sitting in Darkness, for he will swoon away at this confession, saying: "Good God, those 'niggers' spare their wounded, and the Americans massacre theirs!"

We must bring him to, and coax him and coddle him, and assure him that the ways of Providence are best, and that it would not become us to find fault with them; and then, to show him that we are only imitators, not originators, we must read the following passage from the letter of an American soldier-lad in the Philippines to his mother, published in *Public Opinion,* of Decorah, Iowa, describing the finish of a victorious battle:

> We never left one alive. If one was wounded, we would run our bayonets through him.

Having now laid all the historical facts before the Person Sitting in Darkness, we should bring him to again, and explain them to him. We should say to him:

"They look doubtful, but in reality they are not. There have been lies; yes, but they were told in a good cause. We have been treacherous; but that was only in order that real good might come out of apparent evil. True, we have crushed a deceived and confiding people; we have turned against the weak and the friendless who trusted us; we have stamped out

---

[1] "Rebels!" Mumble that funny word—don't let the Person catch it distinctly.

a just and intelligent and well-ordered republic; we have stabbed an ally in the back and slapped the face of a guest; we have bought a Shadow from an enemy that hadn't it to sell; we have robbed a trusting friend of his land and his liberty; we have invited our clean young men to shoulder a discredited musket and do bandit's work under a flag which bandits have been accustomed to fear, not to follow; we have debauched America's honor and blackened her face before the world; but each detail was for the best. We know this. The Head of every State and Sovereignty in Christendom and ninety percent of every legislative body in Christendom, including our Congress and our fifty State Legislatures, are members not only of the church, but also of the Blessings-of-Civilization Trust. This world-girdling accumulation of trained morals, high principles, and justice, cannot do an unright thing, an unfair thing, an ungenerous thing, an unclean thing. It knows what it is about. Give yourself no uneasiness; it is all right."

Now then, that will convince the Person. You will see. It will restore the Business. Also, it will elect the Master of the Game to the vacant place in the Trinity of our national gods; and there on their high thrones the Three will sit, age after age, in the people's sight, each bearing the Emblem of his service: Washington, the Sword of the Liberator; Lincoln, the Slave's Broken Chains; the Master, the Chains Repaired.

It will give the Business a splendid new start. You will see.

Everything is prosperous, now; everything is just as we should wish it. We have got the Archipelago, and we shall never give it up. Also, we have every reason to hope that we shall have an opportunity before very long to slip out of our Congressional contract with Cuba and give her something better in the place of it. It is a rich country, and many of us are already beginning to see that the contract was a sentimental mistake. But now— right now—is the best time to do some profitable rehabilitating work— work that will set us up and make us comfortable, and discourage gossip. We cannot conceal from ourselves that, privately, we are a little troubled about our uniform. It is one of our prides; it is acquainted with honor; it is familiar with great deeds and noble; we love it, we revere it; and so this errand it is on makes us uneasy. And our flag—another pride of ours, our chiefest! We have worshipped it so; and when we have seen it in far lands—glimpsing it unexpectedly in that strange sky, waving its welcome and benediction to us—we have caught our breath and uncovered our heads, and couldn't speak, for a moment, for the thought of what it was to us and the great ideals it stood for. Indeed, we *must* do something about these things; we must not have the flag out there, and the uniform. They are not needed there; we can manage in some other way. England manages, as regards the uniform, and so can we. We have to send soldiers—we can't get out of that—but we can disguise them. It is the way England does in South Africa. Even Mr. Chamberlain himself takes pride in England's honorable uniform, and makes the army down there wear an ugly and odious and appropriate disguise, of yellow stuff such as quarantine flags are made of, and which are hoisted to warn the healthy away from unclean disease and repulsive death. This cloth is called khaki. We could adopt it. It is light, comfortable, grotesque, and deceives the enemy, for he cannot conceive of a soldier being concealed in it.

And as for a flag for the Philippine Province, it is easily managed. We can have a special one—our States do it: we can have just our usual flag, with the white stripes painted black and the stars replaced by the skull and cross-bones.

And we do not need that Civil Commission out there. Having no powers, it has to invent them, and that kind of work cannot be effectively done by just anybody; an expert is required. Mr. Croker can be spared. We do not want the United States represented there, but only the Game.

By help of these suggested amendments, Progress and Civilization in that country can have a boom, and it will take in the Persons who are Sitting in Darkness, and we can resume Business at the old stand.

TO MANUEL MERCADO

José Martí

Dos Ríos, May 18, 1895

My dearest brother:

Now I can write, now I can tell you how tenderly and gratefully and respectfully I love you and that home which I consider my pride and responsibility. I am in daily danger of giving my life for my country and duty, for I understand that duty and have the courage to carry it out—the duty of preventing the United States from spreading through the Antilles as Cuba gains its independence, and from overpowering with that additional strength our lands of America. All I have done so far, and all I will do, is for this purpose. I have had to work quietly and somewhat indirectly, because to achieve certain objectives, they must be kept under cover; to proclaim them for what they are would raise such difficulties that the objectives could not be realized.

From *Our America*. Ed. Philip S. Foner. New York: Monthly Review Press, 1977.

The same general and lesser duties of these nations—nations such as yours and mine that are most vitally concerned with preventing the opening in Cuba (by annexation on the part of the imperialists from there and the Spaniards) of the road that is to be closed, and is being closed with our blood, annexing our American nations to the brutal and turbulent North which despises them—prevented their apparent adherence and obvious assistance to this sacrifice made for their immediate benefit.

I have lived in the monster and I know its entrails; my sling is David's. At this very moment—well, some days ago—amid the cheers of victory with which the Cubans saluted our free departure from the mountains where the six men of our expedition walked for fourteen days, a correspondent from the *Herald,* who tore me out of the hammock in my hut, told me about the annexationist movement. He claimed it was less to be feared because of the unrealistic approach of its aspirants, undisciplined or uncreative men of a legalistic turn of mind, who in the comfortable disguise of their complacency or their submission to Spain, halfheartedly ask it for Cuba's autonomy. They are satisfied merely that there be a master— Yankee or Spanish—to support them or reward their services as gobetweens with positions of power enabling them to scorn the hardworking masses—the country's halfbreeds, skilled and pathetic, the intelligent and creative hordes of Negroes and white men.

And that *Herald* correspondent, Eugene Bryson, told me more: about a Yankee syndicate, endorsed by the customs authorities who are too closely associated with the rapacious Spanish banks to be involved with those of the North, a syndicate fortunately unable, because of its sinewy and complex political structure, to undertake or support the idea as a government project. And Bryson continued talking, although the truth of his reports could be understood only by a person with firsthand knowledge of the determination with which we have mustered the revolution, of the disorganization, indifference, and poor pay of the untried Spanish army, and of Spain's inability to gather, in or out of Cuba, the resources to be used against the war, resources which it had obtained the time before from Cuba alone. Bryson recounted his conversation with Martínez Campos, at the end of which Martínez Campos gave him to understand that at the proper time, Spain would doubtless prefer to come to terms with the United States than hand the island to the Cubans. And Bryson had still more to tell me: about an acquaintance of ours the North is grooming as a candidate from the United States for the presidency of Mexico when the term of the president now in office expires.

I am doing my duty here. The Cuban war, a reality of higher priority than the vague and scattered desires of the Cuban and Spanish annexationists, whose alliance with the Spanish government would only give them relative power, has come to America in time to prevent Cuba's annexation to the United States, even against all those freely used forces. The United States will never accept from a country at war, nor can it incur, the hateful and absurd commitment of discouraging, on its account and with its weapons, an American war of independence, for the war will not accept annexation.

And Mexico, will it not find a wise, effective, and immediate way of helping, in due time, its own defender? It will indeed, or I shall find one for it. This is a life-and-death matter, and there is no room for error. The prudent way is the only way worth considering. I would have found it and proposed it. But I must have more authority placed in me, or know who has it, before acting or advising. I have just arrived. The formation of our utilitarian yet simple government can still take two more months, if it is to be stable and realistic. Our spirit is one, the will of the country, and I know it. But these things are always a matter of communication, influence, and accommodation. In my capacity as representative, I do not want to do anything that may appear to be a capricious extension of it. I arrived in a boat with General Máximo Gómez and four others. I was in charge of the lead oar during a storm, and we landed at an unknown quarry on one of our beaches. For fourteen days I carried my rifle and knapsack, marching through bramble patches and over hills. We gathered people along the way. In the benevolence of men's souls I feel the root of my affection for their suffering, and my just desire to eliminate it. The countryside is unquestionably ours to the extent that in a single month I could hear but one blast of gunfire. And at the gates of the cities we either won a victory, or reviewed 3,000 troops in the face of an enthusiasm resembling religious fervor. We continued on our way to the center of the island where, in the presence of the revolution which I instigated, I laid aside the authority given me by the settlements abroad and acknowledged by the island, and which an assembly of delegates from the Cuban people—revolutionaries in arms—must replace in accord with the new conditions. The revolution desires complete freedom in the army, without the obstacles previously raised by a Chamber without real sanction, without the distrust of its republicanism by a suspicious faction of the young, and without the jealousy and fears, which could become too great a threat in the future, of a punctilious or prophetic leader. But at the same time the revolution is eager for a concise and respectable republican representation—the same decent spirit of humanity, filled with a desire for individual dignity in representing the republic, as that which encourages and maintains the revolutionaries in this war. As for me, I realize that a nation cannot be led counter to or without the spirit that motivates it; I know how human hearts are inspired, and how to make use of a confident and impassioned state of mind to keep enthusiasm at a constant pitch and ready for the attack. But with respect to forms, many ideas are possible, and in matters of men, there are men to carry them out. You know me. In my case I defend only what I consider a guarantee of, or a service to, the revolution. I know how to disappear. But my thoughts will never disappear, nor will my obscurity leave me embittered. The moment we take shape, we will proceed; trust this to me and to others.

And now, having dealt with national interests, I will talk about myself, since only the emotion of this duty could raise from a much-desired death the man who, now that Nájera does not live where you can see him, knows him better and cherishes as his heart's delight that friendship with which you fill him with pride.

I know his silent gestures of annoyance, after my voyage. And however much we told him, from the bottom of our hearts, there was no response! What a fraud he is, and how callous that soul of his, that the honor and tribute of our affection has not moved him to write one more letter on the paper of the maps or newspapers that fill our day!

There are affections of such fragile honesty. . . .

"OUR WAR CORRESPONDENTS IN CUBA AND PUERTO RICO"

Richard Harding Davis

The newspaper correspondents who are allowed to accompany the British army during an active campaign are selected on account of their former experience and reputation, or on account of the importance of the paper they serve. Their number is extremely limited. The two great press associations, Reuter's and the Central News, which furnish the same matter to different papers in all parts of the United Kingdom, are each allowed one or two representatives, and a dozen of the more important London dailies, like the *Times,* the *Daily Telegraph,* and the *Mail,* and one or two of the provincial papers, such as the *Manchester Guardian* and the *Dublin Times,* are each allowed to send one special correspondent to the front.

This plan of selection and limitation is very different from the one pursued during the late war by our own government. With us, nearly every paper in the country that could afford to send a representative was permitted

Harper's Monthly, May 1899.

to do so. Even weekly periodicals of a strictly literary or religious character were represented by men who were anxious to get to Cuba in any capacity, and the big dailies were each given credentials for as many as twenty correspondents, artists, and photographers. As our country, unlike England, is not constantly engaged in military operations, only a few of the men who acted as correspondents during the war with Spain went to the front with any previous experience of the kind of work before them. But they had been trained in a school of journalism which teaches self-reliance and, above all other things, readiness of resource. In consequence they met the new conditions without anxiety, and by using the same methods they had formerly employed in reporting a horse show or a fire, they succeeded in satisfactorily describing the operations of our army.

Before the Santiago campaign had opened, and while our troops were still at Tampa, many of the newspapers promised their readers that when the war really came the "pencil-pushers of Park Row," with no experience of battle or of things military, would develop into great war correspondents, while, on the other hand, the men who had been employed to serve as descriptive writers merely, and who possessed some further experience in campaigning and in roughing it, would show that they were better suited to write fiction in a library than to recognize news when they saw it, or to collect facts.

The war, so far as it concerned itself with the correspondents, proved nothing of the sort. It did not show that the descriptive writer or novelist was capable of gathering news, nor did it prove to the contrary; nor did it prove that the man who had previously reported criminal news and real-estate deals was equally at home when he found himself in a Cuban jungle two thousand miles from the office telephone, and with no friendly policeman to direct his steps. The success of the different men was entirely a question of intelligence and of individual character. Their past experience seemed to count for very little. Some of those who had seen much service with the army and navy in times of peace, who could harness a team to a gun-carriage, or drill a cavalry regiment, or name every part of a battleship, were, when "the real thing" came, lost absolutely from the sight of their fellowmen. All their experience on the plains and in the wardrooms of the White Squadron either failed to get them to the front at all, or did not enable them to take care of themselves once they got there. On the other hand, mere boys, who had been jerked out of the city room of a metropolitan daily and rushed to the front without even a rubber blanket, followed the soldiers from the first to the last, and never left them, except to tramp back to Siboney to file their dispatches on the press-boats. Two of the very best correspondents had served their respective papers, previous to the war, as dramatic critics, and their only knowledge of war had been gathered from performances of *Secret Service* and *Shenandoah*. These were H. James Whigham, of the *Chicago Tribune*, and Acton Davies, of the *New York Evening Sun*. Each of these gentlemen proved most conclusively that serious experience is not necessary to enable either an Englishman or an American to report a war correctly. I have seen the war correspondent whom Kipling describes as the "War Eagle" in his *Light that Failed*. I saw him in Greece, with three horses, three servants, a tent, the British flag flying over his head, cooking-stoves, medicine-chests, writing-desks, and type-writers. He carried letters from prime ministers, and he lunched with the young princes daily. And I have seen a boy, named Sammy, who acted as a courier for the *New York Herald*, eighteen years of age, who had a keener scent for news than the War Eagle ever possessed, who better knew what was going to happen before it happened, and who was in every way more alert, intelligent, and suited to the work in hand.

Whigham, with his two years' residence in America, made, in my opinion at least, a much better war correspondent than the War Eagle with his record of twelve campaigns. And his outfit was limited to a canteen and a bottle of Scotch whiskey. The War Eagle's dispatches are intelligible, and probably of great interest to a drill sergeant; Whigham's letters were equally interesting to the military expert and to the civilian. Whigham came from Oxford to America to lecture in the university extension series, but he is better known in this country as the ex-golf champion of the United States, and as a dramatic critic. He arrived at Key West during the earliest days of the war, and that same night was dropped on the coast of Cuba, where he was promptly made prisoner by the Spaniards, but was later set at liberty in Havana. Immediately on his release he went to Guantanamo, where the marines had landed, and while trying to find their firing-line, walked into a Spanish picket and received a Mauser bullet across the forehead. Later he joined the army at Daiquiri, and was one of the half-dozen correspondents who scaled the San Juan hills immediately after they were charged by the regulars. Later he was invalided home with a fever, which attacked him in a most serious form. His must certainly be considered a full and creditable record, and his only experience of war was gathered on the golf-links of Chicago. It is impossible to designate one correspondent as being better than another, because what is important to one does not seem important to his rival, and their ideas as to their duty differ. One may prefer to stand on the firing-line in order to see what is going forward close at hand, but while he is in greater personal danger, another who watches the battle from an elevation in the rear can obtain a much better view, and a much more correct idea of what is being done in all parts of the field. So the presence of a correspondent on the firing-line, or his absence from it, does not prove that he is not doing his full duty to his paper. The best correspondent is probably the man who by his energy and resource sees more of the war, both afloat and ashore, than do his rivals, and who is able to make the public see what he saw. If that is a good definition, Stephen Crane would seem to have distinctly won the first place among correspondents in the late disturbance. John Fox, Sylvester Scovel, Caspar Whitney, Howard Thompson, and Mr. Millard of the *New York Herald* are close seconds. Of these gentlemen, Mr. Fox and Mr. Whitney were hampered by the fact that they were not writing for a daily paper.

Near the close of the war, a group of correspondents in Puerto Rico made out a list of the events which, in their opinion, were of the greatest news value during the campaign, and a list of the correspondents, with the events each had witnessed credited to his name. Judged from this basis, Mr. Crane easily led all the rest. Of his power to make the public see what he sees it would be impertinent to speak. His story of Nolan, the regular, bleeding to death on the San Juan hills, is, so far as I have read, the most valuable contribution to literature that the war has produced. It is only necessary to imagine how other writers would have handled it, to appreciate that it could not have been better done. His story of the marine at Guantanamo, who stood on the crest of the hill to "wigwag" to the war-ships, and so exposed himself to the fire of the entire Spanish force, is also particularly interesting, as it illustrates that in his devotion to duty, and also in his readiness at the exciting moments of life, Crane is quite as much of a soldier as the man whose courage he described. He tells how the marine stood erect, staring through the dusk with half-closed eyes, and with his lips moving as he counted the answers from the war-ships, while innumerable bullets splashed the sand about him. But it never occurs to Crane that to sit at the man's feet, as he did, close enough to watch his lips move and to be able to make mental notes for a later tribute to the marine's scorn of fear, was equally deserving of praise.

Crane was the coolest man, whether army officer or civilian, that I saw under fire at any time during the war. He was most annoyingly cool, with the assurance of a fatalist. When the San Juan hills were taken, he came up them with James Hare, of *Collier's*. He was walking leisurely, and though the bullets passed continuously, he never once ducked his head. He wore a long rain-coat, and as he stood peering over the edge of the hill, with his hands in his pockets and smoking his pipe, he was as unconcerned as though he were gazing at a cinematograph.

The fire from the enemy was so heavy that only one troop among the entire line of the hills was returning it, and all the rest of our men were lying down. General Wood, who was then colonel of the Rough Riders, and

I were lying on our elbows at Crane's feet, and Wood ordered him also to lie down. Crane pretended not to hear, and moved farther away, still peering over the hill with the same interested expression. Wood told him for the second time that if he did not lie down he would be killed, but Crane paid no attention. So, in order to make him take shelter, I told him he was trying to impress us with his courage, and that if he thought he was making me feel badly by walking about, he might as well sit down. As soon as I told him he was trying to impress us with his courage, he dropped on his knees, as I had hoped he would, and we breathed again.

After that, in Puerto Rico, we agreed to go out together and take a town by surprise and demand its surrender. At that time every town in Puerto Rico surrendered to the first American who entered it, and we thought that to accept the unconditional surrender of a large number of foreigners would be a pleasing and interesting experience. But Crane's business manager, who guarded him with much the same jealousy as that with which an advance-agent guards the prima donna, did not want anyone else to share the glory of the surrender, and sent Crane off by himself. He rode into Juana Diaz, and the town, as a matter of course, surrendered, and made him welcome. He spent the day in establishing an aristocracy among the townspeople, and in distributing largesse to the hungry. He also spent the night there, sleeping peacefully beyond our lines and with no particular interest as to where the Spaniards might happen to be. The next morning, when he was taking his coffee on the sidewalk in front of the only cafe, he was amused to see a "point" of five soldiers advance cautiously along the Ponce road, dodging behind bushes, and reconnoitering with both the daring and skill of the American invader. While still continuing to sip his coffee he observed a skirmish-line following this "point," and finally the regiment itself, marching bravely upon Juana Diaz. It had come to effect its capture. When the commanding officer arrived, his sense of humor deserted him, and he could not see how necessary and proper it was that any town should surrender to the author of *The Red Badge of Courage*.

A week later, Millard of the *New York Herald*, "El" Root of the *New York Sun*, Howard Thompson, and myself, with some slight assistance from four thousand soldiers, captured a much larger city than the one Crane attacked; but as we stumbled into the town first, under the impression that it was filled with American cavalry, the town of Coamo surrendered to us. The question is, whether it is more creditable to take a town of five thousand people with three other correspondents, supported by four thousand soldiers, or to take a town of two thousand soldiers singlehanded. I fear that in the eyes of history Crane's victory will be ranked higher than that of Millard, Root, Thompson, and myself.

One of the most amusing and daring acts of the correspondents was that of Burr W. MacIntosh, of *Frank Leslie's*. When the troops arrived at Daiquiri, a general order was issued forbidding any of the correspondents to accompany soldiers when they made their first landing. The men on the press-boats of course promptly disobeyed this order; but the correspondents on the transports were forced to obey it, or run the risk of losing their credentials. Mr. MacIntosh was the one exception. He was most desirous of obtaining a photograph, taken on the shores of Cuba, which would show the American soldiers making their first hostile landing on that shore. To this end he gave his camera into the hands of a sergeant in one of the shore-boats, and hid his clothes under the cross-seats of another. When these boats started, MacIntosh dived from the stern of the transport, and after swimming a quarter of a mile through a heavy surf, reached the coast of Cuba in time to recover his camera and perpetuate the first landing of our Army of Invasion.

The correspondents might be divided into three classes—the men who gathered the news, the descriptive writers, and those who collected names. Some of them did all of these three things. There was also a fourth class of correspondent, who accompanied a volunteer regiment and told only of what was done by the particular regiment he accompanied, without touching on the war at all, except when the regiment took a part in it. These young gentlemen unconsciously did a very great injury to the men of the regular army, in persuading the public at home that the volunteer is an effective fighting-machine, instead of making it clear that he is an "amateur," and, as such, is a menace and a danger to the safety of the country.

The points of view of these several correspondents were entirely different. Writers like Stephen Crane, John Fox, Caspar Whitney, and Stephen Bosnal were interested in what was most dramatic and picturesque. The fact that the Rough Riders sang "Fair Harvard" in the rifle-pits, within easy ear-shot of the enemy, was of as much value to them as the movements of Sampson's squadron or the terms of the surrender.

But the men in the news-gathering class, although they possessed as quick an eye for what was striking and human as did the magazine-writers, found that their duty led them in another direction. It was their part to treat the whole campaign as a series of events, to describe it as they would a political convention, to ascertain exactly what orders were given and exactly who carried them into effect. The best of these, as a rule, were the representatives of the Associated Press, and they entered into the work in the same impersonal spirit with which they would have handled an annual encampment of the G.A.R., or the first night of a new play. They looked on the thing broadly and from all sides. They wanted the news, all the news, but nothing but the news. The last words of a dying soldier were not important to them. His name, spelled correctly, and the letter of his troop, were to their employers of the highest value. These correspondents were ubiquitous. They were in Jamaica one day, and the next ploughing through heavy seas, and a few hours later back on the firing-line. They were anonymous, and their work, which was at times both brilliant and of historic value, was sunk and lost under the levelling head-line of a press bureau, a machine which would make all men equal, and for which writers sell their birthright of originality and humor and point of view. Howard Thompson, the Washington correspondent of the Associated Press, and E. R. Johnstone, managing editor of the *Minneapolis Times,* are perhaps the two men who, by their individuality, have risen above the anonymity of the bureau they serve. In them the personal element predominates. They are young men who would be conspicuous on a sinking ship or at a dinner table. They are the confidants of presidents and would-be presidents, senators and their "bosses," and they are equally at home in an Indian uprising or at a presidential convention. . . .

"HOW STEPHEN CRANE TOOK JUANA DIAZ"

Richard Harding Davis

At the close of the Spanish-American campaign, the American forces that landed in Puerto Rico were supposed to be invading a hostile territory. Politically, as a colony of the enemy, the inhabitants of the island should have been hostile, but they were not. They received our troops with one hand open and the other presenting either a bouquet, or a bottle. Our troops clasped both hands. There still remained in many of the towns a Spanish garrison, but from the greater number these garrisons had been withdrawn upon San Juana. As a result scouts and officers of our army on reconnaissance were constantly welcomed by the natives as conquering heroes, and at the approach of one of them entire villages would capitulate as readily as though the man had come leading an army corps. One town surrendered to an officer who had lost his way, and stumbled into it by mistake, another fell to the boss of a pack-train, whose only object in approaching it had been to steal some ponies.

From *Many Wars by Many War Correspondents.* Ed. George Lynch and Frederick Palmer. Tokyo: Tokyo Printing, 1904.

In order to make quite sure, some towns surrendered several times. Ponce for instance surrendered four times to as many different American officers. It was not safe for an American wearing anything that resembled a uniform to approach a Puerto Rican stronghold unless he was prepared to have it fall prostrate at his feet.

It struck me that in this surrendering habit of the Puerto Ricans there lay a chance for great entertainment, and much personal glory, especially as one would write the story oneself. It would be a fine thing I thought to accept the surrender of a town. Few war correspondents had ever done so. It was an honor usually reserved for Major Generals in their extreme old age.

Halfway between Ponce and Coamo there is a town called Juana Diaz which, at that time, seemed ripe for surrendering and I accordingly proposed to Stephen Crane, that at sunrise, before the army could advance to attack it we should dodge our own sentries, and take it ourselves. Crane was charmed with the idea, and it was arranged that on the morrow our combined forces should descend upon the unsuspecting village of Juana Diaz. We tossed to see who should wake the other, and I won the toss. But I lost the town. For in an evil moment Crane confided the strategy of our campaign to the manager of his paper, the *New York World*, Charlie Michaelson; and Michaelson saw no reason why in this effort to enlarge our country's boundaries, a man representing a rival newspaper, should take any part. So, no one woke me, and while I slumbered, Crane crept forward between our advance posts and fell upon the doomed garrison. He approached Juana Diaz in a hollow square, smoking a cigarette. His khaki suit, slouched hat, and leggings were all that was needed to drive the first man he saw, or rather, the man who first saw him, back upon the town in disorderly retreat. The man aroused the village and ten minutes later the Alcalde, endeavoring to still maintain a certain pride of manner in the eyes of the townspeople, and yet one not so proud as to displease the American conqueror surrendered to him the keys of the cartel. Crane told me that no General in the moment of victory had ever acted in a more generous manner. He shot no one against a wall, looted no churches, levied no "forced loans." Instead, he lined up the male members of the community in the plaza, and organized a joint celebration of conquerors and conquered. He separated the men into two classes, roughly divided between "good fellows" and "suspects." Anyone of whose appearance Crane did not approve, anyone whose necktie even did not suit his fancy, was listed as a "suspect." The "good fellows" he graciously permitted to act as his hosts and bodyguard. The others he ordered to their homes. From the barred windows they looked out with envy upon the feast of brotherly love that overflowed from the plaza into the by streets, and lashed itself into a frenzied carnival of rejoicing. It was a long night, and it will be long remembered in Juana Diaz. For from that night dates an aristocracy. It is founded on the fact that in the eyes of the conquering American while some were chosen, many were found wanting. To this day in Juana Diaz, the hardest rock you can fling at a man is the word "suspect." But the "good fellows" are still the "first families."

In the cold grey dawn of the morning as Crane sat over his coffee in front of the solitary cafe, surrounded by as many of his bodyguard as were able to be about, he saw approaching along the military road from Ponce a solitary American soldier. The man balanced his rifle alertly at the "ready," and was dodging with the skill of an experienced scout from one side to the other of the long white highway. In a moment he was followed by a "point" of five men, who crept close to the bushes and concealed their advance by the aid of the sheltering palms. Behind them cautiously came the advance guard, and then boldly the Colonel himself on horseback and 800 men of his regiment. For six hours he had been creeping forward stealthily in order to take Juana Diaz by surprise.

His astonishment at the sight of Crane was sincere. His pleasure was no less great. He knew that it did not fall to the lot of every Colonel to have his victories immortalized by the genius who wrote *The Red Badge of Courage.*

"I am glad to see you," he cried eagerly, "have you been marching with my men?"

Crane shook his head.

"I am sorry," said the Colonel, "I should like you to have seen us take this town."

"THIS town!" said Crane in polite embarrassment. "I'm really very sorry, Colonel, but I took this town myself before breakfast yesterday morning."

FROM "NEWS GATHERING AT KEY WEST"

Frank Norris

While we screwed and floundered our way back to Key West the correspondents wrote out their stories. It will be long before I forget the picture which the Young Personage made while at work upon his "stuff." Table there was none and the plunging of the boat made it out of the ques-

The Letter of Frank Norris. Ed. Franklin Walker. San Francisco: Book Club of Calif., 1956.

tion to write while sitting in a chair. The correspondents took themselves off to the cabin and wrote while sitting in their bunks. The Young Personage was wearing a pair of duck trousers grimed and fouled with all manner of pitch and grease and oil. His shirt was guiltless of color or scarf and was unbuttoned at the throat. His hair hung in ragged fringes over his eyes. His dress-suit case was across his lap and answered him for a desk. Between his heels he held a bottle of beer against the rolling of the boat, and when he drank was royally independent of a glass. While he was composing his descriptive dispatches which some ten thousand people would read in the morning from the bulletins in New York I wondered what the fifty thousand who have read his war novel and have held him, no doubt rightly, to be a great genius, would have said and thought could they have seen him at the moment.

Works Cited

Aaron, Daniel. *The Unwritten War: American Writers and the Civil War*. New York: Knopf, 1973.

Adams, Henry. *The Education of Henry Adams: An Autobiography*. Boston: Houghton, 1918.

Anderson, Sherwood. Introduction. *Midnight Sketches and Other Impressions*. Vol. 11 of *The Works of Stephen Crane*. Ed. Wilson Follett. New York: Knopf, 1926. xi–xv.

Angell, Roger. "The Greatest of the Boys." Rev. of *Badge of Courage: The Life of Stephen Crane*, by Linda H. Davis. *New Yorker* 7 Sept. 1998: 85–89.

Benfey, Christopher. *The Double Life of Stephen Crane*. New York: Knopf, 1992.

Binder, Henry. "*The Red Badge of Courage* Nobody Knows." *Studies in the Novel* 10 (1978): 9–47.

Brown, Bill. *The Material Unconscious: American Amusement, Stephen Crane, and the Economies of Play*. Cambridge: Harvard UP, 1996.

Brown, Charles H. *The Correspondents' War: Journalists in the Spanish-American War*. New York: Scribner's, 1967.

Cady, Edwin. *Stephen Crane*. Rev. ed. New York: Twayne, 1980.

Cashman, Sean. *America in the Gilded Age: From the Death of Lincoln to the Rise of Theodore Roosevelt*. 3rd ed. New York: NYU P, 1993.

Cather, Willa. "Stephen Crane's *Wounds in the Rain* and Other Impressions of War." *On Writing: Critical Studies on Writing as an Art*. 1920. Rpt. Lincoln: U of Nebraska P, 1988.

Colvert, James B. "Crane, Hitchcock, and the Binder Edition of *The Red Badge of Courage*." *Critical Essays on Stephen Crane's* The Red Badge of Courage. Ed. Donald Pizer. Boston: Hall, 1990. 238–63.

———. Introduction. *Reports of War*, Vol. 9 of *The University of Virginia Edition of the Works of Stephen Crane*. Ed. Fredson Bowers. Charlottesville: UP of Virginia, 1975.

———. "The Origins of Stephen Crane's Literary Creed." *University of Texas Studies in English* 34 (1955): 179–88. Rpt. in *Stephen Crane's Career: Per-*

spectives and Evaluations. Ed. Thomas A. Gullason. New York: NYU P, 1972. 170–80.

Corkin, Stanley. *Realism and the Birth of the Modern United States: Cinema, Literature, and Culture.* Athens: U of Georgia P, 1996.

Crane, Jonathan Townley. *Popular Amusements.* Cincinnati, 1870. *Making of America.* 22 Apr. 1999. U of Michigan. 18 Aug. 1999. <http://moa.umdl. umich.edu/cgi-bin/moa/sgml/moa-idx?notisid=AGA5086>.

Crane, Stephen. *Maggie: A Girl of the Streets.* Intro. Joseph Katz. Gainesville: Scholars' Facsimiles, 1966.

———. *Poems and Literary Remains.* Vol. 10 of *The University of Virginia Edition of the Works of Stephen Crane.* Ed. Fredson Bowers. Charlottesville: UP of Virginia, 1975.

———. *The Red Badge of Courage: A Facsimile Reproduction of the New York Press Appearance of December 9, 1894.* Gainesville: Scholars' Facsimiles, 1967.

———. *The Red Badge of Courage: An Episode of the American Civil War.* Ed. Henry Binder. New York: Norton, 1982.

———. *The University of Virginia Edition of the Works of Stephen Crane.* Ed. Fredson Bowers. 10 vols. Charlottesville: UP of Virginia, 1969–76.

———. *Stories and Tales.* Ed. Robert Stallman. New York: Vintage, 1955.

Davis, Linda H. *Badge of Courage: The Life of Stephen Crane.* Boston: Houghton, 1998.

Davis, Richard Harding. *Notes of a War Correspondent.* New York: Scribner's, 1910.

DeForest, John William. *A Volunteer's Adventures: A Union Captain's Record of the Civil War.* New Haven: Yale UP, 1946.

Delbanco, Andrew. "The American Stephen Crane: The Context of *The Red Badge of Courage.*" *New Essays on* The Red Badge of Courage. Ed. Lee Clark Mitchell. Cambridge: Cambridge UP, 1986. 49–76.

Dos Passos, John. *The 42nd Parallel.* Boston: Houghton, 1946.

Dunne, Finley Peter. "A Book Review." *Mr. Dooley's Philosophy.* New York: Russell, 1902. 13–18.

Ellison, Ralph. *Shadow and Act.* New York: Random House, 1964.

Foner, Eric. *Reconstruction: America's Unfinished Revolution, 1863–1877.* New York: Harper, 1988.

Foster, Malcolm. "The Black Crepe Veil: The Significance of Stephen Crane's "The Monster." *International Fiction Review* 3 (1976): 87–91.

Frederic, Harold. Rev. of *The Red Badge of Courage,* by Stephen Crane. *New York Times* (1896). Rpt. in *Stephen Crane: The Critical Heritage.* Ed. Richard M. Weatherford. London: Routledge, 1973. 116–20.

Garland, Hamlin. Rev. of *Maggie: A Girl of the Streets,* by Stephen Crane. *Arena* June 1893. Rpt. in *Stephen Crane: The Critical Heritage.* Ed. Richard M. Weatherford, London: Routledge, 1973. 37–38.

Gerwin, David, Vassilios Manolios, and Lia Popodopoulos. "Using Stephen Crane's *Maggie* to Teach the Progressive Era." *Organization of American Historians Magazine of History* 13.2 (1999): 33–35.

Gilkes, Lillian. *Cora Crane: A Biography of Mrs. Stephen Crane.* Bloomington: Indiana UP, 1960.

Gislason, Eric J. *Imaging the Civil War.* 1 Apr. 1997. U of Virginia. 18 Aug. 1999. <http://xroads.virginia.edu/~HYPER/CRANE/reviews/section1. html>.

Gullason, Thomas A., ed. *Stephen Crane's Career: Perspectives and Evaluations.* New York: NYU P, 1972.

Hoffman, Daniel. *The Poetry of Stephen Crane.* New York: Columbia UP, 1957.

Howells, W. D. *My Literary Passions.* New York: Harper, 1895.

Hungerford, Harold. "That Was at Chancellorsville: The Factual Framework of *The Red Badge of Courage.*" *Stephen Crane's Career: Perspectives and Evaluations.* Ed. Thomas Gullason. New York: NYU P, 1972. 205–16.

James, William. *The Principles of Psychology.* Vol. 2. New York: Dover, 1950.

Kaplan, Amy. "The Spectacle of War in Crane's Revision of History." *New Essays on* The Red Badge of Courage. Ed. Lee Clark Mitchell. Cambridge: Cambridge UP, 1986. 77–108.

———. "Black and Blue on San Juan Hill." *Cultures of United States Imperialism.* Ed. Amy Kaplan and Donald E. Pease. Durham: Duke UP, 1993. 219–36.

Katz, Joseph. "The *Maggie* Nobody Knows." *Modern Fiction Studies* 12 (1966): 203–12.

Liebling, A. J. "The Dollars Damned Him." *New Yorker* 5 Aug. 1961: 48–72. Rpt. in *Stephen Crane: A Collection of Critical Essays.* Ed. Maurice Bassan. Twentieth Century Views. Englewood Cliffs: Prentice-Hall, 1967. 18–26.

Loewen, James. *Lies My Teacher Told Me: Everything Your American History Textbook Got Wrong.* New York: New Press, 1995.

Mariani, Giorgio. *Spectacular Narratives: Representations of Class and War in Stephen Crane and the American 1890s.* New York: Lang, 1992.

Marshall, Edward. Rev. of *The Red Badge of Courage,* by Stephen Crane. *New York Press* 13 Oct. 1895: 4. In *Stephen Crane: The Critical Heritage,* Ed. Richard M. Weatherford. London: Routledge, 1973. 85–86.

Mencken, H. L. Introduction. *Major Conflicts.* Vol. 10 of *The Work of Stephen Crane.* Ed. Wilson Follett. New York: Knopf, 1926. ix–xiii.

Milton, Joyce. *The Yellow Kids: Foreign Correspondents in the Heyday of Yellow Journalism.* New York: Harper, 1989.

Mitchell, Lee Clark. "Naturalism and the Language of Determinism." *Columbia Literary History of the United States.* Ed. Emory Elliott. New York: Columbia UP, 1988. 525–45.

Mitchell, Lee Clark, ed. *New Essays on The Red Badge of Courage*. Cambridge: Cambridge UP, 1986.

Nagel, James. *Stephen Crane and Literary Impressionism*. University Park: Pennsylvania State UP, 1980.

New York Draft Riots. Ed. Kevin Eisert. 21 Nov. 1998. BluegrassNet. 18 Aug. 1999. <http://civilwar.bluegrass.net/HomeFront/newyorkdraftriots.html>.

Norris, Frank. "Stephen Crane's Stories of Life in the Slums: *Maggie* and *George's Mother*. *The Wave* 15 (1896): 13. Rpt. in *Maggie: A Girl of the Streets*. Ed. Thomas A. Gullason. Norton Critical Editions. New York: Norton, 1979. 151–52.

O'Donnell, Thomas F. "DeForest, Van Petten, and Stephen Crane." *American Literature* 27 (1956): 578–80.

Parker, Hershel. "*The Red Badge of Courage*: The Private History of a Campaign That—Succeeded?" *Flawed Texts and Verbal Icons: Literary Authority in American Fiction*. Evanston: Northwestern UP, 1984. 147–97.

Pizer, Donald. "*The Red Badge of Courage* Nobody Knows: A Brief Rejoinder." *Studies in the Novel* 11 (1979): 77–81.

———. Rev. of *Maggie*, Vol. 1 of *The Virginia Edition of The Works of Stephen Crane*, ed. Fredson Bowers. *Modern Philology* 58 (1970): 212–14.

Rev. of *Maggie: A Girl of the Streets*, by Stephen Crane. *Port Jervis* [New York] *Union*, 13 Mar. 1893: 3. Rpt. in *Maggie: A Girl of the Streets*. Ed. Thomas A. Gullason. Norton Critical Editions. New York: Norton, 1979. 143–44.

Rev. of *The Red Badge of Courage*. *New York Times*, 19 Oct. 1895: 3. Rpt. in *Stephen Crane: The Critical Heritage*. Ed. Richard M. Weatherford. London: Routledge, 1973. 87–90.

Roosevelt, Theodore. *The Rough Riders*. New York: Scribner's, 1899.

Schaefer, Michael W. *A Reader's Guide to the Short Stories of Stephen Crane*. New York: Hall, 1996.

Schudson, Michael. *Discovering the News*. New York: Basic, 1978.

Selected Civil War Photographs. 19 Oct. 1998. *American Memory*. Prints and Photographs Div., Library of Congress. 26 Apr. 1999. <http://lcweb2.loc.gov/ammem/cwphome.html>.

Shanahan, Daniel. "The Army Motif in *The Red Badge of Courage* as a Response to Industrial Capitalism." *Papers in Language and Literature* 3 (1996): 339–409.

Shulman, Robert. "*The Red Badge of Courage* and Social Violence: Crane's Myth of his America." *Canadian Review of American Studies* 12 (1981): 1–19.

Slotkin, Richard. *The Fatal Environment: The Myth of the Frontier in the Age of Industrialization, 1800-1890*. New York: Atheneum, 1985.

Smith, Allan Gardner. "Stephen Crane, Impressionism, and William James." *Revue Francaise d'Etudes Americaines* 18 (1983): 237–48.

Stallman, R. W. *Stephen Crane: A Biography*. New York: Braziller, 1968.

Stallman, R. W., and E. R. Hagemann, eds. *The New York City Sketches of Stephen Crane*. New York: NYU P, 1966.

Trachtenberg, Alan. *The Incorporation of America: Culture and Society in the Gilded Age*. New York: Hill, 1982.

War Correspondents. Edison Manufacturing Co., 1898. 19 Oct. 1998. *American Memory*. Library of Congress. 18 Aug. 1999. <http://memory.loc.gov/ammem/sawhtml/satitles.html>.

Weatherford, Richard. *Stephen Crane: The Critical Heritage*. London: Routledge, 1973.

Weisberger, Bernard. "*The Red Badge of Courage*." *Twelve Original Essays on Great American Novels*. Ed. Charles Shapiro. Detroit: Wayne State UP, 1958. 96–123.

Wertheim, Stanley. *A Stephen Crane Encyclopedia*. Westport: Greenwood, 1997.

Wertheim, Stanley, and Paul Sorrentino. *The Crane Log: A Documentary Life of Stephen Crane, 1871–1900*. American Authors Log Series. New York: Hall, 1994.

Wertheim, Stanley, and Paul Sorrentino, eds. *The Correspondence of Stephen Crane*. 2 vols. New York: Columbia UP, 1988.

Wilson, Christopher. *A Labor of Words: Literary Professionalism in the Progressive Era*. Athens: U of Georgia P, 1985.

Wilson, Edmund. *Patriotic Gore: Studies in the Literature of the American Civil War*. New York: Oxford UP, 1962.

Zwick, Jim, ed. *Anti-Imperialism in the United States, 1898–1935*. 4 Aug. 1999. Syracuse University. 18 Aug. 1999. <http://www.boondocksnet.com/ail98-35.html>.

For Further Reading

Note: The Works Cited constitutes a thorough bibliography of useful works on the period as well as on Crane's life and career. Below we recommend a few texts not cited in this volume and therefore not listed there.

Biography and Criticism

Beer, Thomas. *Stephen Crane: A Study in American Letters.* New York: Knopf, 1924.

Berryman, John. *Stephen Crane.* London: Methuen, 1950.

Bloom, Harold, ed. *Stephen Crane's* The Red Badge of Courage. New York: Chelsea, 1987.

——, ed. *Stephen Crane.* New York: Chelsea, 1987.

Frus, Phyllis. "Writing after the Fact: Crane, Journalism, and Fiction." *The Politics and Poetics of Journalistic Narrative: The Timely and the Timeless.* Cambridge: Cambridge UP, 1994. 13–52.

Kaplan, Amy, and Donald E. Pease, eds. *Cultures of United States Imperialism.* Durham: Duke UP, 1993.

Pizer, Donald, ed. *Critical Essays on Stephen Crane's* The Red Badge of Courage. New York: Hall, 1990.

Late-Nineteeth-Century
United States History

American Social History Project. *Who Built America? Working People and the Nation's Economy, Politics, Culture, and Society.* New York: Pantheon, 1992.

Beer, Thomas. *The Mauve Decade: American Life at the End of the Nineteenth Century.* New York: Knopf, 1926.

Brands, H. W. *The Reckless Decade: America in the 1890s.* New York: St. Martin's, 1995.

Holt, Hamilton, ed. *The Life Stories of Undistinguished Americans As Told by Themselves.* 2nd ed. New York: Routledge, 1990.

Lears, T. J. Jackson. *No Place of Grace: Antimodernism and the Transformation of American Culture.* New York: Pantheon, 1981.

Maddow, Ben. *A Sunday between Wars: The Course of American Life from 1865 to 1917.* New York: Norton, 1979.

Painter, Nell Irvin. *Standing at Armageddon: The United States, 1877–1919.* New York: Norton, 1987.

Sklar, Martin. *The Corporate Reconstruction of American Capitalism, 1890–1916.* New York: Cambridge UP, 1988.

Teaford, Jon C. *The Unheralded Triumph: City Government in America, 1870–1900.* Baltimore: Johns Hopkins UP, 1984.

Wiebe, Robert. *The Search for Order: 1877–1920.* New York: Hill and Wang, 1967.

Williamson, Joel. *The Crucible of Race.* New York: Oxford UP, 1984.

Recommended Sites on the Internet

The American Civil War Home Page. Ed. George H. Hoemann. 17 Aug. 1999. U of Tennessee. 18 Aug. 1999. <http://sunsite.utk.edu/civil-war/warweb.html>.

Gilded Age and Progressive Era: U.S. History Internet Resources. 16 Aug. 1999. Tennessee Technological University. 18 Aug. 1999. <http://www.tntech.edu/www/acad/hist/gilprog.html>.

The Spanish-American War in Motion Pictures. 22 July 1999. *American Memory.* Library of Congress. 18 Aug. 1999. <http://memory.loc.gov/ammem/sawhtml/sawhome.html>.

Credits